Paul Foot was born in Palestine in 1937. He started as a journalist on the *Scottish Daily Record* in 1961, and worked for the *Daily Herald*, the *Sunday Telegraph*, *Private Eye*, *Socialist Worker* and the *Guardian*, where he was a columnist for many years. For fourteen years from 1979 he had his own page in the *Daily Mirror*. He was named Journalist of the Year by Granada's *What the Papers Say* in 1972 and 1989, and, in 2000, Journalist of the Decade (1990s). He was named Campaigning Journalist of the Year in the British Press Awards in 1981 and with Tim Laxton won the George Orwell prize for journalism in 1994. He was the author of *Immigration and Race in British Politics* (1965), *The Politics of Harold Wilson* (1968), *The Rise of Enoch Powell* (1969), *Who Killed Hanratty?* (1971), *Red Shelley* (1981), *The Helen Smith Story* (1983), *Murder on the Farm: Who Killed Carl Bridgewater?* (1986), *Who Framed Colin Wallace* (1989), *Words as Weapons* (1990) and *Articles of Resistance* (2000). He died in 2004.

PAUL FOOT

The Vote

How It was Won and
How It was Undermined

PENGUIN BOOKS

PENGUIN BOOKS

Published by the Penguin Group
Penguin Books Ltd, 80 Strand, London WC2R ORL, England
Penguin Group (USA) Inc., 375 Hudson Street, New York, New York 10014, USA
Penguin Group (Canada), 90 Eglinton Avenue East, Suite 700, Toronto, Ontario, Canada M4P 2Y3
(a division of Pearson Penguin Canada Inc.)
Penguin Ireland, 25 St Stephen's Green, Dublin 2, Ireland
(a division of Penguin Books Ltd)
Penguin Group (Australia), 250 Camberwell Road,
Camberwell, Victoria 3124, Australia (a division of Pearson Australia Group Pty Ltd)
Penguin Books India Pvt Ltd, 11 Community Centre,
Panchsheel Park, New Delhi – 110 017, India
Penguin Group (NZ), cnr Airborne and Rosedale Roads, Albany,
Auckland 1310, New Zealand (a division of Pearson New Zealand Ltd)
Penguin Books (South Africa) (Pty) Ltd, 24 Sturdee Avenue,
Rosebank, Johannesburg 2196, South Africa

Penguin Books Ltd, Registered Offices: 80 Strand, London WC2R ORL, England

www.penguin.com

First published by Viking 2005
Published in Penguin Books 2006
1

Extract from 'A Cooking Egg' by T. S. Eliot (*Collected Poems 1909–1962*) reproduced
by permission of Faber & Faber Ltd. Every attempt has been made to contact the
copyright holders. The publishers will be happy to make good any errors or omissions
in future editions

Index by Oula Jones

Typeset by Rowland Phototypesetting Ltd, Bury St Edmunds, Suffolk
Printed in England by Clays Ltd, St Ives plc

ISBN-13 978-0-140-17592-9
ISBN-10 0-140-17592-X

Publisher's Note

Paul Foot completed this book very shortly before his death but had only drafted bibliographic notes for the first chapter. Clare Fermont and John Foot have compiled the chapter-by-chapter bibliography at the end of the text. It is based upon Paul's notes and the books that were in his study.

Contents

Introduction

This book was commissioned in 1990, while I was a journalist on the *Daily Mirror*. It is the culmination of a lifetime's political activity, reading and thought. I joined the Labour Party in Glasgow in 1961, and was immediately shocked at the impotence of Parliament. Even the mildest aspirations of local and national Labour politicians seemed beyond their reach when they were elected to office. This irritation intensified when a Labour government was elected in 1964, and continued to intensify over the next 35 years. Ever since, I have been intrigued by the problem of socialists' parliamentary impotence. Why were elected politicians committed to socialist ideas so palpably incapable of putting them into practice? Their legitimacy came from the vote. They were important because they had been elected. The working class was in a majority, and from time to time the workers were likely to elect politicians committed to their interests. Why, when this happened, had elected socialists been so pathetic in office?

Many of my Marxist friends told me that the question was 'basically' irrelevant. 'Bourgeois democracy' was a creature of bourgeois society and therefore could not possibly be expected to buck the market or anything else that was central to that society. This view seemed to me entirely unsatisfactory. It overlooked the fundamental principle of democracy: the consent of the people in whose name their representatives carry out policies. It occurred to me that this rejection of electoral democracy came mainly from people who in varying degrees of certainty supported the tyrannies in Russia, China and Eastern Europe. Yet surely, it seemed to me, democracy, the control of society from below, was the very essence of socialism, and capitalism, the control of industry and finance from above, the very opposite of it.

How to resolve the conflict between a democracy that enfranchises the masses and an economic system that enslaves and exploits them? In an attempt to answer that question, I set out to dig up the roots of representative democracy in Britain. The first half of this book traces the history of universal suffrage, how it was first raised by the Levellers and their supporters in Cromwell's New Model Army in the English Revolution, how it vanished off the political map for more than a century and a half, how it was revived in the wake of the American and French Revolutions, and its slow progress through the nineteenth century culminating in the Representation of the People Acts of 1918 and 1929.

The second half of the book assesses how universal suffrage affected the people who most needed it, the working class. It is therefore almost exclusively a story of British Labour. I anticipated, and found, a deep and lasting clash between the forces of property and the elected representatives of the people who had none. I have tried to trace the rises and falls of those clashes, and the way in which they have shaped the conflicting theories of British Labour. I was struck by the constantly recurring theme in the history of British Labour of the conflict between parliamentary or political democracy and economic democracy, and have emphasized the many occasions when this conflict was recognized by Labour politicians and theorists. The experience and the history convinced me even more decisively than when I started that without economic democracy – at least some form of democratic control of industry, finance and services – then political democracy will always be at the mercy of a greedy and predatory economic hierarchy. Capitalism and democracy, in other words, are hostile to each other, and the continued and continuing failure of British Labour to challenge capitalism has undermined the democracy for which it pretends to stand. Indeed, the net result of a hundred years of compromising with capitalism has ended with New Labour, an allegedly social democratic organization which has surrendered both socialism and democracy.

I have, I hope, been consistently hostile to the view, increasingly fashionable in recent years, that history is made by great men and women, by kings and queens, imperialists and potentates. What matters to me is the response from below, from the people at the bottom of the pile. If they don't respond, history becomes slack and even dull. When they do respond, especially when they revolt, history comes to life. The rise and fall of that response has dictated the structure of the book. It has been drawn by social revolution, what Marx called the 'locomotive of history': the English Revolution of the seventeenth century, the French Revolution of the eighteenth, the Russian Revolution of the twentieth and several since. A theme that emerges is that the potential for anything worthy of the name of democracy grows with the activity and confidence of the workers and their organizations. When they compromise or slumber in apathy, despair or even affluence, democracy recedes. When they organize themselves into some form of revolt, the prospect for democracy increases.

The book took very much longer than expected. Before 1993, my work at the *Mirror* knocked out any real progress. In 1993, I left the *Mirror* in disgust at the new management's anti-union behaviour, and went to work on *Private Eye*. I had more time for the book, which started slowly after that. I thought I had read extensively on the subject, but soon discovered the depths of my ignorance. Five years later, at the start of 1999, I was struggling through the long story of votes for women. On a miserable night in April that year, I was carted off to hospital semi-conscious, with a leaking aorta that was hurriedly repaired. After three weeks in a coma and six months in hospital, I was back at home, disabled with spinal damage, so that I cannot walk without a stick, but with my brain mercifully intact. I started the chapter on women all over again and attempted to weave it in with the struggles of the still largely disenfranchised working class, male and female. The long haul through the twentieth century took me another four years. The themes that emerged most powerfully were the impotence of the elected parliaments to make proper use of their vote and the way in which the franchise was undermined by forces beyond its control.

My own political position has not changed for 40 years. In 1972, I joined the staff of *Socialist Worker* and worked there full-time until 1978. I have been a member of the International Socialists/Socialist Workers Party since 1962, and have campaigned all that time to build that organization. At innumerable meetings I have been surprised by the number of times I have been urged to 'go into politics'. When I protested that I was already in politics, I was told that what was meant was 'real politics', meaning Parliament. In Glasgow, in 1963, a Labour Party agent suggested that I put myself forward as a Labour candidate for Parliament, an offer I politely refused. Then and since, I took the view that the main job of socialists must be outside Parliament, making the case for socialism and for socialist organization where it matters most, in the rank and file. On the few occasions I have stood for elected office, I did so chiefly for propaganda reasons, and was suitably and comprehensively rebuffed.

My main contemporary inspiration through all that time, until he died aged 83 in 2000, was Ygael Gluckstein, who in Britain called himself Tony Cliff. Cliff was a Jew who was brought up in Palestine (ironically he was imprisoned there by the British administration in which my father was a district officer). He gave up his entire life to building an anti-Stalinist, anti-Zionist socialist party founded in working-class militancy. Cliff's intellect was immense, his knowledge of Marxist literature breathtaking and his public speaking laced with tremendous anger, passion and above all humour. Every time we spoke together at meetings – very often – I could not help observing how he subtly corrected me on what suddenly seemed an obvious error of judgement. 'Paul, you are soft,' was his constant jibe, followed usually by the entirely mistaken allegation that my father had put him in prison.

Soft I was and soft I probably still am, especially about Cliff's more extreme positions, notably on the suffragettes or socialist reactions in Britain to the outbreak of the Second World War. But with his overall perspective, especially his respect for the democratic will of the working masses and his contempt for careerist social democratic politicians, I entirely agreed and still agree. Other socialists influenced by Cliff who have helped me with this book, and have read and (with certain reservations) approved it, have been John Rees, Lindsey German, Paul Holborow and my partner and lover of the last sixteen years, Clare Fermont, who has an uncanny understanding of the 'softness' for which Cliff used to rebuke me, and a skilful sub-editor's ability to correct it. Others of my friends and comrades who have helped me in various ways have been John Rose, Margaret Renn, Jim Nichol, Paul O'Brien, John Charlton, Melanie McFadyean (who even looked up stuff for me in New Zealand), Colin Leys and Alistair Hatchett, who let me see his thesis on the *Daily Herald* and the industrial agitations after the First World War, every bit as relevant as when he wrote it 30 years ago. I have learned a lot from many apparently endless conversations with my lifelong friend Richard Ingrams, who had been simultaneously writing a book about our joint hero, William Cobbett.

I was lucky to have an uncle and aunt who knew all about this subject. My aunt Jill Craigie first fired my interest in the suffragette movement, on which she became one of the country's leading authorities. She died soon after I came out of hospital in 1999, and I deeply regret I was not able to show her what I had written on her subject. I know she would have disagreed with me about the differing roles of the Pankhursts. She revered Emmeline and Christabel; I preferred Sylvia. I know from my long conversations with her that she would have tolerated the disagreement and concentrated on correcting the errors I have almost certainly made. My uncle Michael, who as I write this celebrates his ninety-first birthday, has put up for more than 30 years with my long-standing rejection of the parliamentary road to socialism. No one in British public life (except possibly his hero, Aneurin Bevan) walked that road more honourably. I felt all that time that he has never (quite) given me up and has continued to argue with me and feed me books in an attempt to persuade me. His vast personal experience of the main personalities in the second half of the book – William Mellor, Stafford Cripps, Dick Crossman, Barbara Castle, Harold Wilson and countless others – and his understanding of the socialist theorists of the Labour Party – Tawney, Strachey and Laski – have enriched the research and pattern of this book, despite its conclusion. In the summer of 2003, I showed him a draft. The result was a long harangue on two matters. The first was my treatment of Emmeline and Christabel Pankhurst and their reaction to the First World War. 'Jill would have been furious with you if she'd seen this!' he exploded, and demanded I look at the passage again. As I did so, I became even more convinced I am right, but I have, out of deference to my aunt, expanded it and explained it a little. His second objection, not surprisingly, was to my account of the Labour Government in which he played a major part, latterly as Deputy Prime Minister. Well, since I lived through this period and was an active campaigner against the Government, I can't in conscience change the thrust, but again I have (probably wrongly – soft again!) modified the section slightly.

Others who have helped me include Meg Message, who runs the library at Leeds Metropolitan University, Julia Jones, who introduced me to Margaret Thomas, later Lady Rhondda, Brian Harrison, who, when I told him I couldn't find his book on women's suffrage, photocopied the whole thing and sent it to me, Solomon Hughes, whose experience as a librarian, a journalist and a socialist helped me find the report of the Macmillan Committee into the banking system in 1930. Betty Whittome, a veteran socialist and peace campaigner from darkest Sussex, gave me a complete set of Claud Cockburn's 1930s commentary *The Week* and an almost complete set of the monthly journal of the Army Bureau of Current Affairs, which told me more about the shifting political mood during the Second World War than any other publication. Bill (Lord) Wedderburn amiably shepherded me through the Tory anti-union laws of the 1980s and 1990s, in which he is the country's most eloquent expert.

Much of the first section was researched in the glorious heights of the library at University College London. When I became disabled in 1999, I was driven back on my own resources and my own books. I owe special thanks to Nick Spurrier, a second-hand bookseller in Folkestone, whose wonderful lists of books and pamphlets, rescued, I suspect, from the estates of dead socialists and communists, have helped build up for me a mighty library on twentieth-century British Labour.

After the initial discussion about the book at Hamish Hamilton/Penguin in 1990, I was swept off to a Kensington pub by Kate Jones, a senior editor.

Volubly, persuasively and rapidly, she persuaded me to commit the project to her. For almost all the time since, encouraged by Gill Coleridge, my agent, she has harried and cajoled me to get on with it. Even after she left Penguin, she continued to support this project. She has read the book and says it is too long. I expect she is right, and I am deeply grateful to her. My editor at Penguin, Kate Barker, who spent many hours cutting the book into some kind of shape, literally stunned me with her editorial skill.

A last word from Philip Townsend, district nurse at a Stamford Hill doctor's surgery, who came to see me often to patch up my back after another operation in the summer of 2003. When I told him about this book, he reflected: 'Yes, my mother used to tell me it was our duty to vote, out of respect for the people who fought for it. I've always followed her advice, but now I'm not so sure.' I thank him for summing up in a couple of sentences what this book is all about.

PART I

How the Vote was Won

1647: Crows and Eagles at Putney

> *Well, what then?*
> *How shall this bosom multiplied digest*
> *The Senate's courtesy? Let deeds express*
> *What's like to be their words: 'We did request it;*
> *We are the greater poll, and in true fear*
> *They gave us our demands.' Thus we debase*
> *The nature of our seats, and make the rabble*
> *Call our cares fears; which will in time*
> *Break ope the locks o'thSenate and bring in*
> *The crows to peck the eagles.*
>
> William Shakespeare,
> *Coriolanus* (1608)

Edward Sexby was angry. On this morning, 28 October 1647, he had worked himself up into a paroxysm of indignation. He was bound for Putney Church, to attend a meeting of the General Council of the Army. Sexby reckoned it would be a 'make or break' meeting. Oliver Cromwell was the enemy, he reminded himself. He had to keep reminding himself of that, since for many months during the Civil War Cromwell had been his comrade and his hero. Sexby had been one of the first to sign up for the parliamentary army to fight against the King. He fought at Edgehill in 1642, where the parliamentary forces were too badly trained and too timid to press home their numerical advantage. The battle was drawn, as all the other Civil War battles would probably have been drawn, had not Cromwell demanded from a reluctant Parliament the means to build a different army – an army of what he called 'men of spirit', a New Model Army, properly trained and properly paid, which brought the war against the King to a speedy end, smashing the royalist armies at Marston Moor (1644) and Naseby (1645). Sexby, who was transferred from Cromwell's regiment to the troop commanded by the parliamentary commander-in-chief, General Tom Fairfax, was in the thick of the battle at Naseby. Cromwell was describing men like Sexby when he wrote to his colleagues in September 1643: 'I had rather have a plain, russet-coated captain that knows what he fights for, and loves what he knows, than that which you call a gentleman and is nothing else.'

For months, however, Sexby had been asking himself exactly what he had been fighting for. In the early days of the New Model Army, the answer was rather vague. The more committed of the parliamentary troopers were passionately against papists, against all interference with the right to worship and against the King. Was not the King's wife a declared papist? Did not the King support Archbishop Laud and the Earl of Strafford whose religious intolerance and sympathy with the papists had helped to start the war? Through the long marches and campaigns of 1644 and 1645, the passionate opposition of men like Sexby to the King and to papists began to develop into something more positive: a feeling, gathering in certainty, that they were fighting for a better world, a world where 'plain, russet-coated people' without rank or estates, and who collected no tithes, would have a chance to live fuller lives.

In the months immediately after Naseby, political ideas were almost unheard of in the New Model Army. In spite of its victories, the army had been depleted by mass desertions and was only maintained by 'press-ganging' – recruitment of new soldiers against their will. Other recruits came to the New Model Army from the defeated enemy armies. None of these were remotely interested in a new world without kings or lords. On the contrary, in the engagements of late 1645 and early 1646, in which the New Model Army had been involved in 'mopping up' royalist remnants across the whole of the south and west of the country, many soldiers had openly admitted to sympathy for the defeated king. Only gradually, especially after the final victory over the King had been celebrated at Oxford in the spring of 1646, did more and more soldiers, especially in the cavalry, start to inquire with increasing concern and anger what was to become of them and their country after their victory.

To their dismay, the Parliament for which they had fought seemed to be turning against them. Their pay, which had been reasonably regular during the war, was cut off, sometimes for weeks and months on end. Even when the pay arrived, heavy arrears were ignored. So the troops were forced to rely more and more on provisions and accommodation grabbed by force from a reluctant civilian population. Especially where large troops of the army had been based in one place for a long time – Sexby had heard shocking reports from Crediton in Devon early in 1646 – whole areas were devastated and whole towns and villages impoverished to keep the army housed and fed. After the dreadful harvest of 1646, the price of wheat and even its less nourishing derivatives soared beyond the people's worst nightmares.

What was the army's future? It had been obvious for more than a year to Sexby and his fellow soldiers that the majority in Parliament, who called themselves Presbyterians, regarded the army as a menace and wanted it disbanded. Even the parliamentary minority who had campaigned for the New Model Army – the Independents, who included Lieutenant General Cromwell and his son-in-law Commissary-General Henry Ireton, both of whom had fought bravely at Naseby – were lukewarm in their support for the army.

The row with Parliament started as a simple bread-and-butter issue over pay and conditions. When it was first suggested that the army might disband and re-form to fight the papists in Ireland, most of the soldiers (and certainly most of the senior officers, including Fairfax and Cromwell) had no real objection, provided they were paid what they were owed. Only when it emerged that Parliament intended to disband the army without paying the soldiers their arrears did the simmering resentment burst into open revolt.

And what a revolt it had been! The last seven months had flashed past in a ceaseless tumult of activity. Sexby himself collected pamphlets – he boasted that he had 1,000 of the 2,500 pamphlets that circulated in the first year of the war, 1642. Even that figure seemed trivial in 1647. Thanks to the comparatively liberal approach of the authorities to unlicensed printing – an approach which owed a lot to the trenchant pamphlet *Areopagitica* written in 1644 by John Milton – pamphlets of every description poured from the innumerable London presses at so fast a rate that not even the most diligent collector could hope to get hold of them all. Many of the pamphlets were religious – every month new and more radical religious sects seemed to sprout from the London streets. Sexby was a religious man, but he preferred the overtly political pamphlets from the men who were known as Levellers. From the host of Leveller pamphlets, Sexby collected the complete works of the three outstanding Leveller writers, all of whom had become his friends. Whenever he could find the time, he visited the merchant/intellectual William Walwyn, always wise, always sensible, always sceptical – so sceptical, in fact, that Sexby wasn't entirely sure that Walwyn even believed in God. Walwyn knew the Bible as well as anyone, but he had a disconcerting habit of quoting it to cast doubt on it. Walwyn was a marvellous writer, clear, compelling, comprehensible. But he took second place, in Sexby's view at least, to Richard Overton. Overton had the knack of communicating ideas so persuasively that his readers immediately believed they had already heard them. In the early years of the war, his pamphlets under the pseudonym Martin Marpriest had been snapped up by thousands of impoverished, hard-working people who suddenly believed they had a right to more from life than hard work and poverty. Overton identified and fanned a rapidly growing wrath that quickly engulfed a Middle England previously sunk in despair and deference.

Sexby's real hero among his Three Wise Men, however, was the least able writer among them and by far the least attractive personality: John Lilburne. At that moment, in October 1647, Lilburne was, as so often, locked up in the Tower of London by the Parliament for which he had fought so courageously in the war. Lilburne had been taken prisoner after the furious battle of Brentford in 1642, hauled in chains to the King's camp at Oxford and sentenced to death there. He survived, through an exchange of prisoners, and went back to London to carry on the fight he had started as early as 1638 – the fight for the freedom of the people from the ancient tyrannies of king, bishops and, above all, judges. He was first surprised then outraged by the way in which the victorious Parliament greeted his demands for free speech and free assembly. Sexby was lost in wonder at Lilburne's daring and tenacity. The more he was cast in prison, the more urgently he sought the means to keep protesting.

For the past two years, Sexby had done everything in his power to supply Lilburne with the writing materials – and the printers – necessary for the constant stream of gloriously entitled and furious pamphlets that flowed from his prisoner's pen in Newgate, the Fleet or the Tower: *England's Birthright Justified* (October 1645); *A Pearl in a Dunghill* (June 1646); *The Freeman's Freedom Vindicated* (June 1646); *London's Liberty in Chains Discovered* (October 1646); *Regal Tyranny Discovered* (January 1647); *Rash Oaths Unwarrantable* (May 1647); and many more. Lilburne's style was repetitive, turgid, legalistic. But the indomitable fury of the man gave the pamphlets urgency and vitality. The great political explosion of 1647 was set off by the ideas that flowed from these three propagandists, Lilburne, Walwyn and Overton, and their followers.

In fact, Sexby reflected, there was really only one idea from which all the others flowed. It could be summed up in two words: representative government. The idea started slowly to creep into the pamphlets after Naseby, late in 1645. Once expressed, it quickly gathered form and strength. The basic idea was simple. Government of one human being over another was indefensible unless the government was chosen by the governed. Sexby had committed huge slabs of John Lilburne's pamphlets to memory. His favourite was a wonderfully intemperate passage from *The Freeman's Freedom Vindicated* that was repeated word for word several months later in *Regal Tyranny Discovered*:

And unnatural, irrational, sinful, wicked, unjust, devilish, and tyrannical it is, for any man whatsoever – spiritual or temporal, clergyman or layman – to appropriate and assume unto himself a power, authority and jurisdiction to rule, govern, or reign over any sort of men in the world without their free consent . . .

It seemed obvious, but the stinging criticism applied to every government in England as far back as the Norman Conquest 600 years previously. Every single government had been unelected by and therefore unrepresentative of the enormous majority of the people it governed. It was only now, however, that the idea of government by free consent was emerging from the gloom of feudal oligarchies. This was clearly due to the Civil War between King and Parliament which had just been fought for three dreadful years. From a population of about 5 million, 100,000 people had been killed, at least as many maimed for life and thousands more sold as prisoners. The King, the commander of one side in this slaughter, was the most obvious symbol of government without consent. He ruled by 'divine right'.

The most intolerable menace of regal tyranny was the greed and intransigence of individual kings, and King Charles I was greedier and more intransigent than most. His greed had forced him to recall his Parliament in 1640 because he needed legislative authority for his endless taxes, especially on the poor. His intransigence forced open the rift between him and his Parliament, even though the parliamentary majority supported the divine right of kings. In 1642, the King raised his standard at Nottingham and declared war on Parliament. Though the King was beaten, however, the victorious Parliament was not a government by consent. Its House of Lords was composed of 13 landed gentlemen, who owed their position entirely to their estates and titles. None of the lords was elected. All of them were still committed to a rapprochement with the King. Nor was the House of Commons government by consent. To start with, only a small minority of the population could vote for it. For more than 200 years, by an Act of 1429, only copyholders (property owners with an estate worth 40 shillings or more) were allowed to vote in parliamentary elections. No one could tell Sexby why this Act had been passed, but Walwyn, who knew more about these things than anyone else, reckoned it had something to do with Wat Tyler and the Peasants' Revolt of 1381. Inflation had swelled the number of voters. More people voted in 1640 than in any previous election, and more people voted in Sexby's native Suffolk than in any other county. Yet still only 2,000 people in Suffolk had cast their votes, less than 3 per cent of the adult population, and no more than 10 per cent of adult males. No women could vote. In most counties, the figures were very much smaller. In Lilburne's native Durham, for instance, no one could vote because there were no parliamentary seats. There were 50 seats in the Commons from backward, reactionary Cornwall, and 24 from progressive, burgeoning Yorkshire, with twice Cornwall's population. Of the Commons' 492 Members, 265 came from tiny boroughs too small for any meaningful election, many of them nominated by the King. Add to this higgledy-piggledy picture the widespread buying of seats, routine bribery and the power of the rising monopolists of industry and trade, and the representative element of Parliament was next to nothing.

This distance from the people could be measured in the views of most Members of Parliament. The Presbyterian majority had been dragged reluctantly into the war and had prosecuted it feebly. They bowed reluctantly to Cromwell's demands for a powerful fighting force. Even now he had done so much to win the war for Parliament, Cromwell could rely on only a minority of about 100 'Independents' in the House of Commons, and many of them, including Cromwell himself and the 18 relatives he could count upon on the Commons benches, were more worried about their estates than about the future of parliamentary democracy.

The glaring truth about Parliament was that it was an assembly of rich men chosen overwhelmingly by rich men for the purpose of safeguarding and extending the property of rich men. Many of the MPs' daily concerns, therefore, were entirely trivial. As Walwyn pointed out in another passage Sexby could repeat from memory, in his pamphlet *England's Lamentable Slavery* (October 1645):

See how busy they have been about the regulating of petty inferior trades and exercises, about the ordering of hunting, who should keep deer and who should not, who should keep a greyhound and who a pigeon-house, what punishment for deer-stealing, what for every pigeon killed contrary to law, who should wear cloth of such a price, who velvet, gold, and silver, what wages poor labourers should have and the like precious and rare business, being most of it put on of purpose to divert them from the very thoughts of freedom suitable to the representative body of so great a people.

Parliament, the Levellers argued, should not be an assembly of rich men, answerable only to the rich. The poor, too, and the 'middling sort of people', people like Sexby, needed representation as much if not more than the rich. The lives of the poor were every bit as much affected by the decisions of the Government as were those of the rich. The Leveller pamphlets of 1646 seethed with the bluff language of equality. In his answer to the charges originally put against him in July 1645, only a month after the victory at Naseby, Lilburne had proclaimed: 'By virtue of my being a free man, I conceive I have as true a right to all the privileges that do belong to a free man as the greatest man in England . . .' A few weeks later, Richard Overton, who was also in prison for 'writing scandalous things' against the House of Commons, declared in almost the exact words which a century and a half later would be made famous throughout the world: 'All men are equally and alike born to like propriety, liberty and freedom.'

Parliament had to be reformed to make it a representative body. That was the central demand of the Levellers. From it flowed all their other demands, for free speech, for religious tolerance, for prisoners' right to silence so that no one could be imprisoned on testimony bullied or tortured out of them by their jailers. The same applied to unfair taxation, in particular the hated tithes, which kept priests rich and fat at the expense of their parishioners – all these could be reformed only when the government of the country was truly representative, when the oligarchical House of Commons, which had sat since 1640, was changed into a body in which everyone could feel confident and everyone could obey because everyone had taken part in voting for it.

Long before the astonishing events of 1647, John Lilburne had applied his mind to the question: how was Parliament to be reformed? His fullest list of specific reforms had been set out a year previously in *London's Liberty in Chains*:

- annual parliaments (so that MPs could not for more than a few months lose sight of the fact that they owed their position to their electors);
- published proceedings, in place of the entirely secret proceedings behind which Parliament constantly hid. The only way to discover how MPs voted was to go to the House of Commons and listen, if you could get in. Publication of division lists ran the risk of instant prosecution;
- payment of MPs, to ensure against the monopoly of the wealthy; and
- equal constituencies and the complete abolition of 'rotten' boroughs, which sent MPs to Parliament solely through the patronage of a peer or a landowner, sinecure seats and royalist stooges.

These were specific demands. Rather more vague was Lilburne's answer to the question – who should vote? The thrust of all those grand declarations that the poorest had as great a right as the richest to be represented was that everyone should vote. In his diatribe against William Walwyn, the royalist hack Francis Edwards had accused the Levellers of wanting to extend the vote even to women. Such an extension would not have worried the rationalist and libertarian Walwyn. Edward Sexby was an Anabaptist, which sect had a proud record of egalitarian treatment of women, including the encouragement of women preachers. But the woman question, like the servant question, was a difficult one, and those early pamphlets tended to ignore it. They would be satisfied, the Levellers indicated, with a wide extension of an annual male franchise.

The gaps in the argument were trivial compared with the boldness and clarity of the main message. Circulating among the poor in the growing cities, especially in London, the Levellers' simple expressions of the universal right to vote for Parliament had a profound revolutionary impact. Sexby thought back to the innumerable church services, meetings and demonstrations, many of them led by women, to free Freeborn John (Lilburne) and Honest Dick (Overton) from the Tower. The cry went up over and over again that Parliament was 'rotten studs', like a building on insecure and rotting foundations, since the source of its power, the elections, was restricted to a greedy and privileged minority who despised the multitude after the war every bit as much as they did before it.

Yet in those days before March 1647, the rage of the poor in London was stunted by a feeling of impotence. The demonstrators could not vote, so they could not remove the representatives who ignored them. They could collect in crowds to confront and abuse the MPs, and indeed had been doing so since the election of 1640. But in the end the crowds were dispersed, and the ringleaders hauled off to jail. Without any real direction or political power, the crowds had no real hope of reform.

All this had changed seven months ago, in March, and Sexby himself had been crucial to the change. It came with the linking of the ideas of the Levellers to the discontent in the New Model Army. Previously, the army discontent had been confined almost entirely to grumbling about pay or the proposed expedition to Ireland – had they not had enough of this endless killing? Now, the soldiers were impressed by the arguments of another leading Leveller, who was also to become Sexby's close friend and collaborator. This was the dashing MP for Berkshire, Henry Marten, whose speeches and writing became increasingly influenced by the Leveller pamphlets, especially on the subject of the proposed invasion of Ireland, to which he was strongly opposed. Marten's republican arguments were increasingly persuasive among common soldiers like Sexby, and gave their grievances a sense of higher purpose. Above all, the Leveller literature turned the attention of the army rank and file to the treachery of the Parliament for which they had fought. Rather than simply carrying on as before, would it not be better now to use the power of the New Model Army to bring about what John Lilburne and his comrades were calling for – a Parliament worthy of the name, a representative democracy?

These were the ideas which, during the last half of 1646 and the first three months of 1647, Sexby and his growing band of Leveller-soldiers had been carrying into the army from the Tower of London and the illegal printing presses in the hovels of Southwark and Clerkenwell. The mix of civilian and military resentments enthused soldiers and commoners alike. The civilian Levellers were reinforced by the might of a real army, the military discontents by sustaining and emancipating ideas. The combination was exhilarating and combustible. When it came, the explosion had rocked the 'rotten studs' Parliament to its foundations.

It was set off by two peaceful petitions. The first, written by William Walwyn, was gentle and reasonable. It called for satisfaction of the people's grievances chiefly by economic measures such as the ending of trade monopolies, of imprisonment for debt, of unfair criminal trials and above all of tithes. All over the country, in the early part of March, men and women sought signatures to what became known as the Large Petition. At the same time a much smaller petition was circulating in the army. Sexby himself and a few comrades had started this one. It had emerged from soldiers without known name or rank, many of whom were so lacking in literacy and confidence that they consulted their officers about the wording. The army petition seemed to be a mild affair, addressing itself exclusively to its own beloved commander, General Fairfax. It called simply for a full account of all income and expenditure, and a settling of all arrears before disbandment; an end to the 'pressing' of men into service; allowances for widows and orphans of dead soldiers; compensation for sickness; and quarters for the army while it waited to be disbanded. Sexby recalled ruefully that, in the interests of unity and of securing signatures, he and his supporters had conceded all sorts of demands. There was not even a hint in either petition of a connection between the two – no hint from the Levellers that they had supporters like Sexby in the army and no mention from the army that they had supporters like Lilburne and Marten in the Levellers.

How did the petitions go down in the House of Commons? The Leveller petition was seized by Government agents while it was being taken round for signature. A copy had been swiped by an informer and leaked to the

House of Commons, where it was greeted with tremendous indignation by the most forceful of the Presbyterians, Denzil Holles.

The very name was enough to make Sexby shiver with anger. Denzil Holles, son of John Holles, the First Earl of Clare. How had his father got that ancient title? By buying it, of course. The peerage cost him £5,000, a bribe squeezed from his impoverished tenants in Nottinghamshire, on top of the £5,000 he had already paid to secure his baronetcy. He'd chosen for his title the name of an Irish county – no wonder his son supported a military expedition to put down the revolt in Ireland. Denzil Holles had all the arrogance, though none of the wit, of his father. He was an irascible tyrant, who had sided with Parliament against the King only because he was irritated by the King's taxes. Holles was the first MP to jump to his feet when the Leveller petition was presented, demanding that the people responsible for it be brought before the House. The MPs concurred at once, and sent their officers out into the lobbies to search for anyone who had promoted the petition. They seized three men, young John Tew, who had merely read the petition to a crowd; an army major, Alexander Tulidah; and a Baptist minister. The three were hauled to the bar of the House of Commons and accused by Holles and his henchman Sir Philip Stapleton of sedition. In an act of typically impetuous cowardice, both noblemen drew their swords on the unarmed Tulidah and threatened to run him through. The three were imprisoned without trial. Two months later, the Commons passed a motion that the petition should be burned by the hangman.

What was it that caused such fury in Members of a Parliament whose supporters had just fought and won a war against the King? They had been frightened of the King all right. He had for a short period imprisoned Holles, and he threatened the noblemen's purse with his endless taxes. But the fear of men like Holles and Stapleton of the King was as nothing compared with their fear of a new spirit of confidence that was inspiring the common people to action. Everywhere stalked the spectre of equality. Holles wrote later:

The wisest of men saw it to be a great evil that servants should ride upon horses and princes walk as servants on the earth . . . The meanest of men, the basest and vilest of the nation, the lowest of the people have got the power into their hands, trampled upon the crown, baffled and misused the Parliament, violated the laws, destroyed or suppressed the nobility and gentry of the kingdom . . . and now lord it over the persons and estates of all sorts of ranks of men from the king on his throne to the beggar in his cottage.

This was nonsense. The nobility and gentry rode as high as ever. But the fear of popular unrest, the spectre of Wat Tyler and the 1381 Peasants' Revolt, had been unsettling the minds of men like Denzil Holles for a decade and more. Now it was coming to the surface, and driving him to draw his sword on an unarmed petitioner plucked at random from the lobbies of the Commons.

If Holles and his gang were angered by the Leveller petition, their fury grew uncontrollable when they heard about the petition in the army. Insubordination from the unruly poor was a common problem on the great estates, but insubordination in the armed forces was treason. On 29 March, less than two weeks after he drew his sword on Tulidah, Holles was in action again, ranting and raving against the army petitioners. Leaving the chamber, he sat down and scribbled on his knee a Commons motion denouncing the army petitioners as 'enemies of the state'. The words were received with outrage and disbelief in the army. Sexby himself had been in constant demand as more and more printing presses were sought out for more pamphlets denouncing Parliament and its arrogance. 'Enemies of the state'! The New Model Army had just fought for the state and preserved it against the King! How dare these landed gentry abuse and threaten their protectors? In a trice, the fear and deference which came naturally to so many soldiers was replaced by anger. What had been a moderate and divided force was suddenly united by its enemies. The hysteria in March of the Presbyterian noblemen who ran the House of Commons majority had set the scene for the astonishing developments of the past few months. Holles and the Presbyterians had imagined that what they declared to be mutiny in the army would be quickly stifled. The usual carrot and stick would be applied. On the one hand the army petitioners would be arrested and punished, preferably executed. On the other, the faithful who signed on for another campaign in Ireland would be rewarded with new and generous terms of service. Parliament sent its commissioners to the army with these proposals. They were astonished and terrified by the response. The more the commissioners ranted and bribed, the more the army resisted. Somehow this armed body of common men, who only a few months previously had been inspired by nothing but the desire for an easy life, and, if they were political at all, had been heavily infiltrated with royalist ideas, had been transformed into a powerful and united political force for parliamentary reform.

How had that happened? Sexby knew the answer at once. It connected with the Leveller ideas that had been running through his head ever since the end of the war – and to the meeting he was about to join at Putney.

The amazing solidarity of the army rank and file over the last few months had been held together by a representative democracy of its own. This representative democracy had grown up spontaneously. No one, not even Sexby who had been at the centre of it, could put an exact time or place on its origin. Sometime in April, he and the others who thought like him had realized that if they left the decisions about what to do about Parliament to their senior officers, they were all, officers included, doomed. The immediate response of General Fairfax and the senior officers (Cromwell had been ill in bed for a couple of months since February so no one had heard from him) was to submit to the Parliament for which they had fought, to stifle the petitioning and to prepare for Ireland. What changed all this was the election of army spokesmen from its rank and file.

Before the end of April, eight regiments from the New Model Army cavalry had each elected two representatives to speak on their behalf in an army council. The representatives were first called agents or (a word which has come to mean something slightly, though not entirely, different) agitators.

It was a simple idea and it spread like wildfire. Fifteen days later, the council spoke for sixteen regiments, all of which had balloted for their representatives. The process of choosing representatives was always cumbrous, usually inefficient. The posts were not, in the main, bitterly contested. What mattered to start with was not who did the representing but the exciting fact that the rank and file were represented at all and that they had chosen their own representatives. The officers were at first uneasy at what seemed like a deliberate affront to their authority, but the convenience and mobility of the new representative council soon convinced them as well. By the end of June, every regiment had elected agitators from both the officers and the rank and file. In July, the whole process was completed with the formation of a General Council of the Army. The New Model Army had become a representative democracy of the type that had been demanded for all England by Lilburne and the Levellers since the middle of 1646. No wonder that the Levellers so quickly made common cause with the New Model Army. In early June, a Leveller pamphlet called *The Poor Wise Man's Admonition Unto All the Plain People of London and the Neighbour-Places* (probably written by William Walwyn) called on its readers to 'look therefore with a clear eye upon the Army ... and see if they be not the truest promoters of just freedom'.

Sexby had been elected as agitator for Fairfax's regiment. He had always been more confident in his ideas than those around him, but his election gave him new strength: a feeling that he spoke not just for himself, nor even for the Levellers whose ideas he treasured, but also for his mates, his fellow-fighters. At once, he teamed up with two other agitators to write an angry letter to Parliament. They rode to London one spring morning to deliver it. They expected trouble from the splenetic Holles – their letter, The Apology of the Common Soldiers of Sir Thomas Fairfax's Army, was far more vitriolic than anything in the Large Petition or anything ever said by Tew or Tulidah. It openly denounced the proposed expedition to Ireland as a 'design to ruin and break this army into pieces'. Far from the petitioning soldiers being enemies of the state, they argued, the state's real enemies were the parliamentary majority who 'seek to become masters and degenerate into tyrants'. This was treasonable language and Sexby knew it. But he and his two companions, William Allen and Thomas Shepherd, were not frightened. As they told the astounded Parliament, the letter had been written at an army rendezvous, read aloud and approved by the entire army. Any action against them would be action against 12,000 armed men.

Holles's sword stayed in its scabbard, and even Stapleton managed to control his temper. The men were asked if they were Cavaliers – supporters of the King. All three replied with their experiences in the parliamentary army. All three had fought for the Parliament. William Allen, indeed, had fought in Holles's regiment, had been taken prisoner (as had Shepherd), had escaped to fight again, had been horribly injured and hauled almost dead from the battlefield.

The Commons compromised, and this time sent Oliver Cromwell, recovered from his illness, to negotiate with the army. The negotiations, to Cromwell's obvious distaste, ended in further stalemate. On his return to London, Cromwell promised Parliament, in response to Holles's demand, that the army would disband – but it refused. Although Generals Fairfax and Cromwell were still held in high regard by the soldiers, they were no longer in control. The army had been 'taken over' by the new representatives, and their energy and enthusiasm was phenomenal. United not by discipline from above but by discipline from below, by its own representatives, by its own discussions and decisions, the army moved from audacity to open rebellion.

On 3 May 1647, Sexby published A Second Apology of all the Private Soldiers to Their Officers – a defiant refusal to disband until the grievances of the army and the people were met. As yet, the demands were vague, echoing Lilburne's general principle that 'the meanest subject should enjoy his right, liberty and properties in all things'. The very next day, after a meeting of the agitators at Saffron Waldon, Sexby wrote a programme to urge the people to support the army's cause. On 19 May, the agitators met again, this time at Bury St Edmunds, and issued to the army a stirring call to 'stand one with another – if you divide you destroy all'. On 25 May, in the House of Commons, Holles once more issued a call for the army to be disbanded. Once more he was answered by a declaration by the council that the army had no intention of disbanding. On the contrary, the council declared, if Parliament continued to be led by enemies of the army such as Denzil Holles, then the whole army would march on London.

June 1647 was an amazing month. On 3 June, the King himself had been moved by order of the agitators, from Holmby Hall in Leicestershire to Newmarket. When the King nervously asked Cornet Joyce, the leader of a troop of horses, what 'commission' he had to move His Royal Highness against his will, Joyce waved his hand at his armed men and declared: 'Sir, there is my commission.' The next day, at a huge rendezvous at Newmarket, the army acclaimed a Solemn Engagement drawn up by its agitators. The Engagement pledged the soldiers not to disband until their grievances were fully met – and, effectively, until Holles and the other MPs who had called the army 'enemies of the state' had been removed. The rendezvous also decided to move towards London. Five days later, on 9 June, the army, as it rolled menacingly towards the capital, met again in rendezvous at Triploe Heath, south of Cambridge. They heard Parliament's new proposals for a compromise – including payment of most of the arrears. These were referred to the agitators, who rejected them, and the army moved south again – Royston, 12 June; St Albans, 13 June. In a state of near panic, the Parliament that had called so recently and so haughtily for the disbandment of the New Model Army now sent a delegation desperately seeking to discover what the army wanted.

What the army wanted, however, was changing with every day of its exhilarating democracy. Whereas a few days earlier it had listed its grievances as 'bread and butter' matters, now, as London grew closer and the news from the city became more frequent, the demands rapidly became political. A rumour ran through the army that the 'trained bands' of the City of London – the militia upon which the rich and the Government could normally depend at time of disorder – were getting ready for a fight. This raised the possibility of another war, this time against Parliament. There was a call to move quickly to snuff out the new military forces of reaction. But even that was no longer enough. The Levellers' political demands raised at all those agitators' meetings had to be satisfied as well. On 14 June, from St Albans, General Fairfax sent Parliament a declaration of demands entirely different from anything he had previously suggested.

His language was Leveller language, flowing direct from the new representative democracy – the Council of the Army:

> We are not a mere mercenary army, hired to serve any arbitrary power of a state, but called forth and conjured, by the several Declarations of Parliament, to the defence of our own and our people's just rights, and liberties. And so we took up arms in judgement and conscience to those ends.

The balance of power had changed and Holles and Co. could do nothing but grovel. The invincible New Model Army was within 20 miles of London and still striding south. All Parliament wanted to know was the precise nature of the army's demands so that they could accede to them. What exactly were the 'people's just rights, and liberties', and how were they to be established and safeguarded? To discuss these questions, the army set up camp at Reading. A meeting of the new General Council of the Army, headed and chaired by the senior officers but open to the agitators, was called for 16 July.

It seemed for one glorious moment that the agitators and the generals were at one, determined to purge the Long Parliament and set up in its place a new representative government that would satisfy the army and the people. Cromwell presided, with his bookish son-in-law Henry Ireton by his side. Both generals seemed keen for instant action – and agreed at once a list of five demands which would take the sting out of any further opposition from London:

- the London militia were to be restored to their former leaders – most of them sympathetic to the London Levellers;
- the armed forces of the country were to be placed under the total and overall control of General Fairfax;
- the arrears were to be paid at once, and regular pay ensured for the future;
- the eleven Members who had supported Holles's 'enemies of the state' declaration were to be impeached and barred from sitting in the House; and
- Richard Overton and John Lilburne were to be released from prison.

The generals agreed that these demands should be packed off straight away to Parliament and no one would tolerate a moment's delay in putting any of them into effect. The first four demands went off – and were at once acceded to. The fifth demand – for the release of Lilburne and Overton – was subtly changed in transit: 'immediate release' became 'fair trial'. So Overton and Lilburne stayed in jail. This backsliding, however, was not immediately clear. In an atmosphere of self-congratulation, the Levellers among the soldiers agreed with the generals not to march at once on London but to wait and see how quickly their demands were met. The political issues seemed clear. Everyone wanted a new type of Parliament, and a committee was set up to discuss the practical proposals. After the discussions, which the agitators won hands down, General Henry Ireton, whom nobody liked but whose qualities as a lawyer nobody could deny, was commissioned to submit a draft of conclusions. He called his draft the Heads of the Proposals, and at first the agitators, including Sexby, were delighted with it. The Long Parliament was to go before the end of the year, to be replaced by elections for a new Parliament that would be re-elected every two years. The rotten boroughs were to be abolished, and religious toleration enshrined in a new constitution. Monopolies and imprisonment for debt were to be heavily restricted, and the rights of petition and the right of prisoners not to incriminate themselves were to be enshrined in law. The Heads of the Proposals sounded at first hearing like a Lilburne Charter – yet almost at once, in the minds of Sexby and the other agitators, doubts began to grow.

These doubts were fed by two furious pamphlets from the Leveller leaders who had been left to rot in prison. From stinking Newgate on 17 July, the same day as the publication of the Heads of the Proposals, came Richard Overton's magnificent *Appeal from the Degenerate Representative Body, the Commons of England, to the Body Represented, the Free People in General and especially to Sir Thomas Fairfax and All the Soldiers at His Command.*

The bulk of the *Appeal* was a call for a thoroughgoing political democracy, a government by consent. It was also a call to arms: 'We must take leave to make use of our hands and swords for the defence and redemption of our lives, our laws and our liberties.' Above all, Overton warned the agitators not to allow the initiative they had seized to pass back into the hands of their generals. The representatives of the common people must, he insisted, keep tight hold of the army, 'for I am confident that it must be the poor, the simple and the mean things of this earth that must confound the mighty and the strong'.

He had not had time to absorb the detail of the Heads of the Proposals, so he did not challenge them directly. His call for political democracy is more general than specific. Lilburne, however, had read the Heads of the Proposals when he sent his *Jonah's Cry out of the Whale's Belly* (July 1647) to the printer. In one sentence he put his finger on the weakness of Ireton's Proposals – their failure specifically to include 'the poor, the simple and the mean things of the earth' in the new electorate for a new Parliament. Yes, there was to be a more even distribution of constituencies and seats. Yes, the rotten boroughs and nominated burgesses were to be abolished. Yes, the Parliament would sit for only two years. But who was to choose that Parliament? As far as the army was concerned, Lilburne was quite specific: 'Every individual private soldier, either horse or foot, ought freely to have the vote, to choose the transactors of their affairs, or else in the sight of God and all rational men, are discharged from obeying, stooping, or submitting to what is done by them.' If the argument applied to the soldier, it applied just as powerfully to the citizen. Moreover, it exposed the yawning gap in the Heads of the Proposals: its failure to define the electorate and therefore its assumption that the electorate would be the same propertied minority as had elected the Long Parliament in 1640.

The real argument about the vote started after Reading. Unleashed, as so often, by Overton and Lilburne, it continued in the streets and coffee houses, in shops and workplaces and taverns all over London – and especially in the army. Almost at once, it seemed, the Heads of the Proposals, which they had all agreed, was exposed as a deliberate attempt by the generals to divert the influence of the agitators and to stifle their longing for a new democratic political constitution. These doubts rankled with the agitators as, quite suddenly, the political balance in London shifted sharply against them. The King at once rejected the Heads of the Proposals and made it clear to his followers that he preferred another war to any weakening of his divine right or his hereditary power. His stubbornness for a moment rallied his supporters in the capital. Many reckoned that the old royal taxes were not as high as the new ones they were forced to pay to keep the army. Mass demonstrations called for the return of the King. By the end of July, the Presbyterians in Parliament had regained their confidence, reorganized the arming of the London militia and welcomed back Holles's Eleven to their seats. They were feverishly preparing for an armed conflict against the New Model Army, which they thought they could win. This time, there was no prevarication. If Cromwell and Ireton dithered about the political solution, they were decisive about the military one.

On 3 August, the New Model Army paraded at Hounslow Heath, 15,000 strong, in front of a hundred Independent MPs. As the MPs passed, each trooper's hat was flung in the air as the cry went up: 'Lords and Commons and a Free Parliament!' The 'free Parliament' was now the army's battle cry, and it was immediately echoed throughout the city. On 4 August, the army slipped into London with the help of the Levellers at Southwark. In a few hours all resistance was at an end. On 7 August, Cromwell led his troops on a huge march through the city. It was cheered like a liberating force by what a royalist observer described contemptuously as 'the common people through the whole City'. The Lord Mayor was rounded up, and his three most reactionary aldermen thrown into the Tower. The Holles Eleven tactfully dismissed themselves once more. All the decrees since 26 July were annulled, and the army was in complete command. Instead of finally purging the Parliament, however, and putting its own proposals for a new one into immediate effect, the New Model Army once more drew back from the brink of a complete victory, retired rather lamely and set up camp five miles outside the City, at Putney.

At the very height of its power, at the moment when the New Model Army could have done what it had ostensibly decided to do, its leaders started to dither and backslide. Cromwell, the beloved general who had won the hearts and minds of every one of his soldiers in the field, started to negotiate with the King. How could he possibly justify such negotiations? The King had openly rejected the Heads of the Proposals. It was obvious that as long as he clung to his office, he would not concede a single one of his powers or privileges. Yet Cromwell, Ireton, Fairfax and the others, instead of pressing on with the purging of the old Parliament and fresh democratic elections for a new one, grovelled to the Court. Had not Cromwell's wife and daughters been 'presented' to the King and Court, and kissed his hand? Henry Marten MP, the Levellers' and the agitators' best friend in Parliament, had asked about the rapprochement with royalty in a debate he initiated in Parliament on 22 September. He moved that 'no further addresses' should be made to the King and that all contact between him and Parliament should be cut off. Only 34 MPs supported him – 84 voted against. The longest and most crucial speech against Marten's motion came from Cromwell, who pretended to put the arguments for and against the King but somehow always ended up in favour. The agitators realized too late that Cromwell and Ireton were negotiating a return to the monarchy. They watched aghast as their generals made appointments and promotions in the army that were designed to weaken the agitators' influence. Colonel Thomas Rainsborough, one of the bravest generals of the war, who was sympathetic to Leveller ideas, was by far the best-qualified parliamentary officer to become Admiral of the Fleet. Yet for an uneasy moment, Cromwell, Rainsborough's old friend and comrade, flirted with the idea of annulling the appointment, and only finally agreed to it when Rainsborough challenged him to a duel.

Why were the generals behaving in this ludicrous and obsequious fashion? Sexby had heard Cromwell describe the King as the 'uprightest man in the three kingdoms'. Someone else had heard Cromwell in an unguarded moment say something even more sinister – that 'no man can enjoy his estates quietly without the King has his rights'. Perhaps that was it. If the King lost his property 'rights' and his Crown, who could guarantee the estates of other important people, like Generals Oliver Cromwell, Henry Ireton and Tom Fairfax?

In the days following Cromwell's royalist speech in the House, the anger and distrust among the agitators grew to boiling point. It grew out of the consternation of the ordinary soldiers who could not understand why their triumphant march on London had not been put to better effect. Why, when they were winning, did their generals behave as though they were losing? The change in the mood of the rank and file was so swift, so effectively fanned by the constant flow of propaganda from Lilburne, Marten and Overton, that many of the agitators who had been elected the previous spring found themselves falling foul of their electorate in the autumn. In the first few weeks after the election of the first agitators, they had been treated with respect, often reverence, by the soldiers who elected them. Now, the great explosion of indignation against the generals was drowning out many of the agitators' cries for caution. Why, they were asked, had they so meekly supported Ireton's Heads of the Proposals at Reading when, as everyone now knew from Overton's *Appeal* and another powerful pamphlet, *A Call to All the Soldiers of the Army by the Free People of England*, by the young Leveller law-graduate John Wildman, the Heads had been specifically designed to keep the common people away from the Government?

There was another explosion of democracy in the army. In the weeks after Cromwell's servile approach to the King in his Commons speech of 20 September, 'old' agitators (those who had been in office for a few months) were summarily dismissed and replaced by young men who had never spoken up before, and whose names were not even known to their commanders. William Allen, for instance, who had accompanied Sexby to the Commons in April as one of the three agitator-representatives of the army, was now sacked and replaced. Each week, another set of agitators' meetings produced new evidence of the swirling democracy which was daily invigorating the army and encouraging its rank and file to more militant demands.

These demands had been summarized only a couple of weeks previously in an amazing document, *The Case of the Army Truly Stated*. It started with a shout of anger: Nothing had been done for the army or the people and nothing would be done without 'MORE SPEEDY AND VIGOROUS

ACTIONS'. Words, it continued, there had been a-plenty: narratives, representations, petitions, engagements, remonstrances – all demanding more democracy and more equality. None had been acted upon. None of the 'public burdens' or 'oppressions, injustices in the law, tithes, monopolies, and restraint of free trade, burdensome oaths, inequality of assessments, excise . . . are removed or lightened'. The army was constantly being divided, and its case seemed even less likely to be put into effect than when it was first stated at Newmarket six months previously.

Back came the pamphlet to the central issue: representative government. The House of Commons had in no way been purged. It was still the same rotten old collection of nepotists, monopolists and landowners. Yet 'the people have a right to new successive elections for Parliament at certain periods of time, and it ought not to be denied them, being so essential to their freedom that without it they are no better than slaves'. Who should have the vote? 'All the freeborn at the age of 21 years and upwards must be the electors, excepting those that have or shall deprive themselves of that freedom either for some years or wholly by delinquency, and that the Parliament so elected shall have a certain time set, wherein they shall of course determine and that before the same period they may not be adjournable and dissolvable by the King, or any other except themselves.' The Commons would then be all-powerful, able to pass laws and repeal them in the full knowledge that the people affected by those laws had voted that Parliament in and would in a short time have the chance to replace it with a new one.

'The power of Commons in Parliament is the thing against which the King had contended, and the people have defended with their lives, and therefore ought now to be demanded as the price of their blood.' Never before had an army document expressed itself so clearly on the subject of votes for all. Indeed, the *Case of the Army* did not even specify that the voters should be male. The only exceptions to the idea of votes for all were 'delinquents': that is, those who had fought openly, and still fought, for the King. Everyone else should vote for an entirely new Parliament, whose laws the people and the army, having voted for it, would then unhesitatingly obey. The Heads of the Proposals had called for a more equitably elected Parliament. The *Case of the Army* called for something entirely different: a Parliament elected by all the people.

The *Case of the Army* was printed and ready for circulation on 15 October. The following fortnight had been crammed with feverish activity as Sexby and the new agitators sought to spread the *Case* throughout the army, and to reinforce it with their own propaganda. Sexby himself wrote a 'letter from the agitators of five regiments', which warned the soldiers not to be frightened by allegations of anarchy and insubordination. The letter restated that the 'chief foundation of all our rights and freedom . . . is a certainty of a constant Parliament every two years', which would consist of representatives chosen by the people and which would therefore be democratically entitled to pass laws. The letter was being rushed out to the regiments the very morning that Sexby crossed the Thames to Putney, 28 October. It was followed closely by a Leveller pamphlet entitled *A Call to All the Soldiers of the Army by the Free People of England*. The *Call* concentrated on the meeting of the General Council of the Army that was about to start at Putney. It was a tirade of controlled anger and agitation, urging the soldiers to 'take heed of crafty politicians and subtle Machiavellis' who 'make fair, long and eloquent speeches' arguing technicalities among themselves but who 'nevertheless in the end agree in evil'. Before long, the pamphlet named the two men whose deceit and trickery the soldiers should most beware: Cromwell and Ireton. Both had already, in private and in public, attacked the *Case of the Army*. Both men, the pamphlet alleged, 'earnestly and palpably carry on the King's design that your best friends in the House of Commons are amazed thereat, and even ready to weep for grief to see such a sudden and dangerous alteration'.

This message had whipped all the agitators, Sexby included, into deep hostility to their Lieutenant General and his son-in-law. Complementary to it, though of very different tone, was a short document entitled *The Agreement of the People* that the Leveller leaders had discussed in draft but had not yet printed. A few copies had been made available for that day's General Council meeting. The *Agreement* was the main question on the agenda. Sexby did not know who had actually written the document. Its quiet and moderate tone, which belied the toughness of its proposals, and the simplicity of its style smacked of William Walwyn – though no doubt Freeborn John and Honest Dick had had something to do with it. The *Agreement* started with the demand for a new representative democracy: 'That the people of England, being at this day very unequally distributed by counties, cities and boroughs for the election of their deputies in Parliament, ought to be more indifferently proportioned according to the number of the inhabitants . . .' To this end, the *Agreement* suggested, the Long Parliament should be disbanded within a year, and a new biennial Parliament be elected. Precise proposals for universal franchise as outlined in the *Case of the Army* were not repeated in the *Agreement*, but the whole tone of the document, including its demands for an end to all religious intolerance and for egalitarian laws, plainly envisaged a democratic Parliament far beyond the imagination of any of the army generals.

Here was Edward Sexby then, with his supporters, waiting for the start of the most important meeting of their lives, inspired on the one hand by the ideas so vehemently expressed in the *Call*, and on the other hand promoting a comparatively moderate *Agreement* for instant action by their generals. Who else was coming to the meeting at Putney? At the General Council meeting the previous week, the senior officers had agreed that the debate on 28 October could be attended by civilians, including representatives of the Levellers who had produced the *Case of the Army*. Lilburne and Overton, who were still, scandalously, in prison, could not come. William Walwyn, with typical modesty, declined. The chief Leveller representative at the meeting, therefore, was the young Cambridge law-graduate John Wildman, whom Sexby had hardly met. Wildman was said to be the author of the *Case of the Army* (though its passionate verbosity was reminiscent of the style of John Lilburne). But Wildman had certainly written the *Call*, and if he could achieve half as much conviction in the flesh as with the pen, he would certainly be a worthy representative of the Levellers. Wildman was supported at the Putney meeting by another civilian Leveller, Maximilian Petty, who had helped to organize and educate the new agitators.

These were represented by Robert Everard, from Cromwell's own regiment, who had argued for immediate military action to force the Long Parliament to dissolve and arrange the election of a democratic one. Sexby's close friend Nicholas Lockyer, from Sir Hardress Waller's regiment, would be there too; as would William Allen, whose ardour had cooled somewhat since he had been replaced as agitator but who still held his place on the General Council. There were at least two other agitators expected, one of whom was Hugh Peter, the fiery preacher and chaplain to the army, who could be relied on to support the Levellers, in spite of his legendary adulation of Cromwell. Peter had warned Cromwell after the latter's September Commons speech that his beloved general was becoming 'too much a courtier' to the King.

Apart from these eight, every other person at the meeting was an officer – there were at least sixteen of them. Most of these officers, some of them officer-agitators, were likely to support *The Agreement of the People*. Foremost among them was Thomas Rainsborough, Admiral of the Fleet, who had fought so bravely through the Civil War and in recent weeks had swung passionately to the side of the Levellers and against Cromwell. Technically, as a naval officer, Rainsborough was not eligible for membership of the General Council. But he had played such a crucial role in the debates at Reading and in the invasion of London that it hardly seemed possible that he would be excluded from the meeting. None of the other officers was as convinced as Rainsborough, but on the whole they supported drastic measures against the Long Parliament. The degree of their commitment was in inverse order to their seniority of rank: Colonels Rich and Rolfe and Waller had commanded regiments; Colonel Tichborne the Tower of London; Commissary Nicholas Cowling had been in charge of provisions and quarter for the New Model Army on its march on London. All these were influenced by Leveller ideas but were also loyal army officers who baulked at challenging their generals. Less loyal were the more junior officers, Captain Lewis Audley, Lieutenant Edmund Chillenden and Captain John Merriman.

These officer-agitators and Levellers made a slightly nervous assembly as they gathered round the great table in the vestry of the church. Cromwell, by rank and by common consent, took the chair. Pride of place also went to William Clarke, the army secretary, who sat with his little pile of pens and an enormous sheaf of parchment, scribbling furiously through the day in his own version of what later became known as shorthand, and whose notes miraculously survived.

Cromwell opened the meeting with two sentences, saying simply that anyone 'that had anything to say concerning the public business . . . might have liberty to speak'. Sexby duly introduced himself, Allen, Lockyer, the other agitators, and Wildman and Petty from the Levellers. Ireton complained at once that he had not had a copy of *The Agreement of the People* that was, he gathered, to be the subject of the meeting. He had thought the meeting had also been called to discuss *The Case of the Army Truly Stated*. All the frustrations and indignations of the past few months poured out of Sexby in a furious flood. He spoke without even a nod of respect for the two generals. 'The kingdom's cause,' he said, 'requires expedition, and truly our miseries . . . cry out for present help.' Yet the chief response of the army leaders was to pander to King and Parliament. 'I think, except we go about to cut all our throats, we shall not please him; and we [shall] have gone to support a house which will prove rotten studs – I mean the Parliament, which consists of a company of rotten Members.' He denounced Cromwell and Ireton to their faces. 'Your credits and reputation have been much blasted,' he told them.

As far as Cromwell was concerned, the meeting could not have started out more disconcertingly. His long reply was nervous and defensive. His lame excuse for his royalist speech in the Commons was that he was representing not the army in Parliament but his own views. He was there-fore, he claimed, not answerable at the General Council of the army for what he said in Parliament.

Before he or Ireton could defend themselves on their record, however, they were brought up short by Robert Everard, the new agitator, who made it clear that he had come with one purpose only: to discuss the *Agreement* and its implementation. Cromwell replied uneasily that the agitators' demands and the *Agreement* 'are new to us'. He was deeply disturbed by the idea that constitutional proposals could be dreamed up by any rank-and-file soldier and put forward for implementation as the permanent law of the kingdom. 'How do we know if . . . another company of men shall not gather together, and put out a paper as plausible perhaps as this?' he asked. He reached out for the remedy of all great men who feel they may not get their own way: delegation to a committee. He proposed that they should all meet the following day at the Quartermaster General's quarters to discuss the *Agreement* and to appoint a committee to discuss it further.

This was widely agreed, and for a moment it looked as if the debate would be called off and adjourned then and there. Instead, it was sidetracked into long and legalistic arguments between the two lawyers – Wildman and Ireton. The Commissary-General, who loved a legal argument, pounced on what he saw as a logical flaw in the way in which the Levellers were proceeding. The army, he said, had 'engaged' to obey their officers and to obey Parliament. They could not legally break that engagement by turning against their officers or Parliament. The suggestion that they, as men engaged to the army, could purge the Parliament that had engaged the army, was a flagrant breach of the law.

Interrupted by an exasperated Wildman and several agitators, he stuck relentlessly to his theme. 'We must be bound to active obedience,' he said. 'For a man to infer that upon any particular issue you may dispute that authority by what is commanded, whether it is just or unjust, this would be the end of all government.' This amounted to the remarkable view that because the army had engaged to obey officers and Parliament, any act of disobedience or even expression of disagreement with either was fundamen-tally a breach of contract, and therefore illegal. 'I am afraid,' he said, 'and do tremble at the boundless and endless consequences of it.'

This was greeted with some scorn by Colonel Rainsborough, who pointed out that the only genuine engagements of the army had been for the liberties of the people. Ireton's argument – that the soldiers were indissolubly engaged to obey Parliament and treat the King – would mean simply that 'we have got the better of them in the field, but they shall be masters of our houses'. But Cromwell returned to the argument in a different form, a form that went to the root of the argument about representative democracy. What worried him about the rise of the agitators and the very existence of the General Council was its power not just to make decisions but also to carry them out. He appreciated that the grievances among the soldiery were intense, and that the rank and file were entitled to a sounding board, a talking shop. That, as far as he was concerned, was the sole purpose of the General Council.

In recent weeks, however, there had been disturbing signs that the agitators were treating the General Council as though it were an executive arm: as though decisions democratically arrived at by the rag, tag and bobtail of rank-and-file representatives, Leveller ideologues and disaffected officers could actually tell the army what to do, and therefore (because the army was omnipotent) tell Parliament what to do as well. If this sort of thing was tolerated, this incendiary talking shop might become an executive committee of government! Moreover, the executive committee was controlled not just by the members of the executive but by groups of people outside the committee who had chosen representatives.

This new notion of representation had, for Cromwell and Ireton, the most appalling consequences. It meant that their ability to speak to and persuade the council was confounded by a mandate by which the represented had bound their representatives. However impressive Cromwell's presence and military record, however silken Ireton's tongue, the elected members of the council, the agitators, owed their allegiance to the rank and file who had sent them to the meeting. The same went for the Leveller civilians. They too had been chosen and mandated. 'These gentlemen,' Cromwell complained, 'who have chosen Mr Wildman, and that other gentleman (Maximilian Petty), to be their mouth at this meeting to deliver their minds, they are, upon the matter, engaged by what they have resolved upon, and they come as engaged men upon their own resolution. If that be so, I think there needs no consideration . . .' Cromwell called therefore for 'an honest and single debate, how we may all agree in one common way for public good', and implored his opponents not to accept any mandate which would render them immune to the persuasive powers and discipline of their generals. Their reply was equivocal. William Allen, the most accommodating of the agitators, suggested that Wildman, Petty and the others should go back to those who had sent them and seek permission to debate freely, unbound by any previous resolution or mandate. Cromwell enthusiastically agreed and begged Wildman to bring along any 'friends' of a 'loving spirit' to the debate so that the meeting could uphold 'our own resolutions and opinions' free from the unwelcome influence of the common people outside. That way, he concluded, as always identifying himself with his Almighty, 'we shall lay down ourselves to be ruled by God'. But he did not have the last word. That was grabbed by Rainsborough, who was not against the mandate in itself. He expressed the idea that the Leveller representatives would come with their mandate but also with permission, if they were so persuaded, to break it. They required only the 'full power to debate. I think there needs no more.' The sparring over, both sides prepared to debate the real issues on the morrow.

There was yet more delay, however, even after the council reassembled in the Quartermaster General's quarters on 29 October. Cromwell, sensing uneasily that support was slipping away from him, pleaded for yet another adjournment before *The Agreement of the People* was discussed, and for yet more legal argument on the nature of the army's engagements. This time he was contemptuously rebuffed. After only an hour or so of fruitless wrangling, the first clause of the *Agreement* – calling for equal constituencies and voting according to the number of inhabitants – was read out for debate. At once, Ireton pounced. The words, he said (quite rightly), were unclear. Did they mean that everyone would have the vote, or simply that the people who now had the right to vote would be more equally represented by fairly drawn constituency boundaries? He was against the former, in favour of the latter. Maximilian Petty answered him immediately. 'We judge,' he said, 'that all inhabitants that have not lost their birthright should have an equal voice in elections.' Rainsborough then explained why – in majestic language which was to become famous, and which at the time most eloquently summarized what Lilburne, Overton, Marten and Walwyn had been saying for months:

For really I think that the poorest he that is in England hath a life to live, as the greatest he; and therefore truly, Sir, I think it's clear, that every man that is to live under a government ought first by his own consent to put himself under that government; and I do think that the poorest man in England is not at all bound in a strict sense to that government that he hath not had a voice to put himself under . . .

In two glorious sentences, Rainsborough summed up the argument for universal suffrage. It was at once fair and democratic. Fair because the vote was extended to everyone regardless of their wealth and background, democratic because it made government legitimate by allowing every person governed to have a say in how they should be governed.

In the murmurs of agreement that greeted Rainsborough, Ireton steeled himself for what turned out to be a whole day's interminable but relentless argument against the most dangerous proposition he had ever heard. Throughout that argument, from first to last, the Commissary-General ignored the thrust of Rainsborough's proposition – that consent from the governed was a necessary condition of fair government. Instead, Ireton propounded a principle of his own:

I think that no person has a right to an interest or share in the disposing of the affairs of the kingdom, and in determining or choosing those that shall determine what laws we shall be ruled by here – no person has a right to this, that has not a permanent fixed interest in the kingdom . . .

This 'permanent fixed interest' could be measured only by property. Choosing a government that could decide about property, he argued, could obviously only be the job of those who had property. The only people who could possibly vote, therefore, were 'the persons in whom all land lies, and those in corporations in whom all trading lies'. He emphasized that he was not arguing for unfair representation for the rich against those with middling incomes. The franchise was at present restricted to people who owned property worth 40 shillings a year. The 40-shilling man would have one vote, as would someone with property worth £10,000. But the vote had to be restricted to people with some property, for a very simple reason. The moment 'we shall go to take away this, we shall plainly go to take away all property and interest that any man hath either in land by inheritance, or in estate by possession, or anything else . . .'

There followed at least an hour of the most intense and passionate argument dominated entirely by Rainsborough and Ireton. This was one of the most extraordinary arguments in British political history. It was charged with passion on both sides, and yet reached the highest intellectual level. Ireton's decision to rest his case on the permanence and sanctity of property had not been anticipated by his opponents. Rainsborough started to answer it by falling back on his original proposition. The foundation of all law, he said, is the people. If the people have no say in the making of that law, its foundation collapses. As for the law of God, cited by Ireton, 'I do not find anything in the law of God, that a lord should choose twenty burgesses, and a gentleman but two, or a poor man shall choose none.' The whole proposition that votes should be linked to property, he mused aloud, was absurd. What about a man who has an estate and a vote, but then loses his estate? Should he then lose his vote? Moreover, he argued, if you restrict the vote to men of property, was that not ceding enormous powers to the King, who had the right to patent corporations and therefore could patent as many corporations as he liked? Since corporations had the right to vote, did this not establish for him a bridgehead of power in Parliament that he could always increase?

Ireton countered that he did not support votes for corporations, and would abolish them. He was entirely in favour of equal distribution of votes and equal constituencies. The present electoral system plainly had to be revised from top to bottom. But, and here he came directly to the point in uncharacteristically blunt language: 'All the main thing that I speak for, is because I would have an eye to property . . . For here is the cause of the most fundamental part of the constitution of the kingdom which if you take away you take away all by that.' Ireton then set up a straw argument and knocked it down most effectively. What was the basis of the argument for universal voting, he asked. Was it 'natural right'? No one except him had used the words 'natural right', but he proceeded to deal with the argument as if it had been at the centre of the opposition case. If all men could vote by natural right, if 'one man must have as much voice as another', why should it not also be 'natural right' that one man should have as much property as another? 'Show me what step or difference there is, why I may not by the same right take your property.' And if any man could take anyone else's property, that was anarchy. Rainsborough retorted that Ireton's argument was dishonest. Those who argued for votes for all men were not 'anarchs'. On the contrary, the rule of the rich, unchecked even by the votes of the poor, was far more anarchic than any threat to property from votes for the poor.

Cromwell intervened to calm things down. 'We should not be so hot one with another,' he cautioned. The advice was useless. The two protagonists were at each other's throats. Ireton insisted, convincingly, that he meant nothing personal against Rainsborough – he was speaking 'to the paper', the *Agreement*. And the *Agreement*, as he now understood it, intended to take away 'the most fundamental civil constitution of this kingdom, and which is, above all, that constitution by which I have any property'. He was repeating himself, apparently endlessly, and so was Rainsborough. And now for the first time, a speaker from the uncommitted joined the argument. Colonel Nathaniel Rich confessed that Ireton had a point. He guessed that there were 'five to one in this kingdom' who had no property at all. Clearly, he said, those who have no property will choose as representatives others who have no property. 'It may happen, that the majority may by law, not in confusion, destroy property; there may be a law enacted, that there shall be equality of goods and estate.'

Colonel Rich, who had inherited a huge estate and a manor in Essex before he came of age, had every reason to dread such a law. He searched for a compromise – a voice for the poor that would not give every poor person an automatic right to vote. Rainsborough was shocked at this backsliding. He denounced it as 'a fine gilded pill'. It was better, he thought, to stick to the issue in front of them; better that the poor should have the vote and the right to choose, even if the result turned out to be against their interests. There was no getting away from the argument – why should some Englishmen have more political rights than others?

John Wildman listened to all this in a state of high alarm. The intervention of Rich, an officer on whom the Levellers originally felt they could rely, suggested that Ireton's scare-talk about the threat to property was making considerable headway. During the discussions among the Leveller leaders before the debates, Wildman had in part anticipated the problem. The richer officers in particular might shy away from the idea of universal suffrage. He therefore agreed to modify the demand for votes for all men. *The Agreement of the People*, as a result, made no specific reference to the extent of the suffrage. But now Ireton had forced the issue, and had wrested from many of the Leveller supporters at the meeting the assurance that the *Agreement* did in fact mean that every man should have the vote. Wildman had not wanted the argument to focus on that issue. He was prepared to compromise on the extent of the franchise in exchange for an assurance that fresh elections on a wider and fairer basis would immediately be arranged. But now the issue had been brought to the front, there was nothing for it but to face it head on. 'We are,' he insisted, 'very much deviated from the first question.' Instead of arguing the principle – what is just – 'I conceive we look to prophecies, and look to what may be the event and judge of the justness of the thing by the consequence'.

The point was not what will happen if all men got the vote. The point was the inherent justice in the granting of that vote. 'We have been under slavery. That's acknowledged by all. Our very laws were made by our conquerors', and everything chronicled was on the side of the conquerors because 'they would suffer nothing else to be chronicled'. However, 'we are now engaged for our freedom. That's the end of parliaments: not to constitute what is already established, but to act according to the just rules of government . . . I conceive that's the undeniable maxim of government: that all government is in the free consent of the people.' That was the central issue, and it should be decided on at once. The question for the council, and Wildman moved it as a resolution, was 'whether any person can be justly bound by law, who doth not give his consent that such persons shall make laws for him'.

Just as Ireton had bent the argument round to frighten those with property, so Wildman brought it back again to the central issue of principle: who could legitimately make laws which bound people, unless all the people bound by them had given their consent by voting?

Forced back to this central argument, Ireton was much less confident. In a stumbling reply, he started by saying that if poor people who had no vote didn't want to live in the country, they could go and live in another one. Confronted at once with the absurdity of that argument – the poor could not afford to leave the country, for a start – he conceded the point of principle. 'I do acknowledge that which you take to be so general a maxim ... that the original power of making laws ... does lie in the people', but then he asked, who were 'the people'? Surely they were the people 'possessed of the permanent interest in the land'. As for the rest, they 'ought to give respect to the property of men that live in the land'. This feeble response put the Levellers and their allies back on the offensive. Major William Rainsborough, Tom's brother, declared that people were more important than property, that the 'chief end' of government 'is to preserve persons as well as estates'. Ireton repeated yet again that he could not agree with anything that might destroy property. With sudden frankness, he abandoned his legalistic arguments and for the first time gave the real reason why he felt so strongly on the subject. 'I have a property,' he said, 'and this I shall enjoy.' Not to be allowed to enjoy it was 'a thing evil in itself and scandalous to the world'.

At this point, more than halfway through the day's long argument, Edward Sexby could control himself no longer. He exploded: 'It seems now, except a man has a fixed estate in this kingdom, he has no right in this kingdom. I wonder we were so much deceived. If we had not a right to the kingdom we were mere mercenary soldiers.' As to the view that the enfranchised poor would destroy the kingdom, he thought exactly the opposite. It was the poor who had saved Parliament from the King. 'I do think the poor and meaner of this kingdom ... have been the means of preservation of this kingdom.' The time had come to make a decision. 'We must be plain. When men come to understand these things, they will not lose that which they have contended for.'

He wanted a vote taken and a decision made. But still Ireton filibustered. He insisted he could not vote for the *Agreement*, and repeated three times that they must all stick by the existing Constitution, because 'at least it is a constitution'. To which Rainsborough could not resist retorting, sarcastically, that he now understood that it was impossible to have liberty but all property be taken away. He went on to wonder 'what the soldier has fought for all this while. He has fought to enslave himself, to give power to men of riches, men of estates to make him a perpetual slave.'

Ireton was delighted he had stung Rainsborough into the argument once more, and thus delayed a decision. His long speech that followed dealt very effectively with the argument that the soldiers had fought for the right of all men to vote. He doubted whether any such idea had even occurred to most of the parliamentary soldiers. If these men had fought for a principle at all, he said, they had fought against omnipotent royalty: 'that one man's will must be a law'. Ireton was technically right. The idea of universal male suffrage was hardly raised even by Lilburne, Overton or Walwyn – and certainly not in the army – before the end of 1646, long after the last battle had been fought. On the other hand, the idea that the real cause of the Civil War was the people's freedom had certainly prevailed in the army during the last few months. The argument that the war was a waste of time unless it resulted in popular liberty for the poor was no less forceful because it was recent.

The argument was once more becalmed in irrelevancies. When the preacher Hugh Peter again called for a decision, it was Cromwell's turn to filibuster. He rebuked Sexby for speaking 'so much of will'. He wanted compromise. Everyone was agreed that Parliament was not representative enough. It should be made more representative. More people, maybe, for instance, copyholders by inheritance, should have the vote. But Cromwell insisted that he didn't agree with votes for all men. If the matter was pushed, he warned, he would withdraw from the debate and allow it to run its course. This was a dangerous gamble. But everyone in the room knew their Lieutenant General was indispensable. Rainsborough replied at once that if the matter went to committee and the committee refused to endorse the vote for all men, he too would withdraw from both council and committee in order to campaign for what he believed to be right. The debate proved what Sexby had long suspected: that Ireton and Cromwell were more interested in their estates than they were in the people's liberties. He shouted: 'I think there are many that have not estates that in honesty have as much right in the freedom of their choice as any that have great estates.'

Yet more legalistic nibbling at the argument was cut short at once by a long and impressive speech from the new agitator Robert Everard. Everard's tone was simple, matter of fact. He had at his disposal none of Rainsborough's eloquence, nor even Sexby's anger. He had come recently into high politics, and the basic issues seemed to him plain. 'The main business is first how we should find [our liberties], and then how we should come by them.' Everard called for plain talk and plain action. 'For my part I shall expect to see nothing but plainness and uprightness of heart made manifest unto you. I will not judge, nor draw any long discourse upon, our disputes this day. We may differ in one thing: that you conceive this debating and disputation will do the work; while we conceive we must without delay put ourselves into the former privileges which we want.' Everard was polite and respectful to his adversaries, especially to the Lieutenant General. But his politeness did not mask the sting of his rebuke: namely that the purpose of the long argument about the *Agreement* was to forestall any action on it. Cromwell and Ireton both realized that in Everard, and the regiment he represented, they had a more powerful opponent than Rainsborough, Wildman and Petty rolled into one. Both answered cautiously, Cromwell appealing, as ever whenever he was losing the argument, to God, Ireton against a rash and hasty decision about such a momentous matter. Waller then demanded some resolution to the argument, and Rainsborough suddenly moved, as a formal motion, that the army be called to rendezvous, and things settled there.

This was the first call for a mass meeting of the entire army to decide the issue. The prospect of such a rendezvous terrified the generals. They knew that a meeting of all the regiments would be likely to uphold the *Agreement* and insist, at the point of their muskets, that new elections be arranged in which the poorest he had as much right to vote as the greatest he. Ireton at once postponed any further discussion of Rainsborough's resolution with another long and discursive speech starting with his old argument that the soldiers could not break their engagements by making such political demands, and going on to pick holes in the *Case of the Army* in the most irrelevant detail. The long day's debate trickled away in another even more tedious legal dispute about the right of the King to veto legislation. Rainsborough's resolution for a rendezvous seemed to have been forgotten as the meeting finally broke up.

Was there a vote? Clarke did not record one. But a letter to the soldiers from the agitators a few days later suggested that there had in fact been a vote on the central issue of votes for all men – and the Leveller/agitators had won with only three against – no doubt Cromwell, Ireton and Lieutenant Colonel William Goffe. If there was indeed such a large majority, it accurately reflected the balance of opinion in the debates themselves. The agitators would certainly have voted unanimously for the *Agreement*, on which they had been mandated. The officers were less sure. Most of them probably voted for the *Agreement*, if only to get things moving.

The vote was won by the Levellers and their sympathizers, but did they win the argument? Certainly Ireton and Cromwell could provide no answer to Rainsborough's basic point: that no government is legitimate or can command the loyalty of the governed unless it has been freely elected by all the governed. The generals were reluctant even to refer to this awkward argument. But the argument was a general one, from principle. On the specific question of whether universal male suffrage should have been introduced there and then, and come into force the following year in 1648, the Levellers and their supporters were not so sure. Despite their name, the Levellers were not drawn from the ranks of the very poor. They were mainly the 'middling sort of people' who had a little property of their own. They stood up for the rights of the poor, and often belaboured the rich; but that was not the same thing as expropriating the rich.

Rainsborough's 'right to live', which he claimed for the 'poorest he' as much as the 'greatest he', referred to political rights, not to economic rights. The Levellers were very much for liberty and fraternity. But they were not at all sure about equality. They shrank from the conclusions of their contemporary Gerald Winstanley, who campaigned for a world in which property was held in common. The earth, predicted Winstanley in a 1649 pamphlet called *The True Levellers' Standard Advanced*, would one day become a 'common treasury'. Winstanley, by far the most advanced political thinker of the English Revolution, developed his communistic theories into a full-blown political philosophy. He argued that true liberty was impossible while property was unequally distributed, and called on the common people to take action to create a new egalitarian world. These calls inspired a handful of like-minded idealists to set up a 'common treasury' on St George's Hill in Surrey, where they became known as the Diggers. The Digger movement was tiny and was quickly put down by force – by the parliamentary army. To most of the Levellers, Winstanley's ideas seemed idealistic and irrelevant. Instead, the Levellers searched for political liberty that threatened no one's property. Ireton's insistence on the gloomy prospects for property if all men got the vote disconcerted the Levellers and their supporters, and to some extent split the hardliners from their support among the officers of the New Model Army. The vote during the Putney Debates shows that those officers sided in the end with the Levellers. But the argument suggests that they were not so confident about the enforcement of *The Agreement of the People* as they were when the debates started.

Now that the vote was won, what would be done to put it into effect? The passion, frankness and clarity of the argument about the vote concealed another, related dispute which worried the generals even more. This concerned the status of the Army Council itself. Was it, as Cromwell and Ireton always intended, a talking shop, a safety valve where these upstart agitators could let off steam? Or was it, as Everard had suggested in his powerful intervention, a mandated executive backed by the armed might of the most powerful force in the country, which could not only decide what to do but also ensure that it was done? The general rendezvous that Rainsborough had moved would have one purpose only: to carry the same resolution that had been carried at the General Council, and to write *The Agreement of the People* into the law of the land. This issue above all others preoccupied the General Council in that first fateful week of November.

Unhappily, William Clarke did not transcribe his notes of these meetings. The best record of them is a long letter from Sexby and his fellow agitators to the people they represented in the army. Despite its tone of foreboding, the letter establishes that in the committee on the weekend following the big debates (30 and 31 October) and in all the meetings for the following week (1–7 November), the Levellers and their supporters had their way. Parliament, the committees agreed, should be dissolved the following September and its replacement would be elected every two years with representatives from equal constituencies. The old burgesses were to be abolished, as were most of the legislative and judicial powers of the House of Lords and the King.

Who was to vote for this new Parliament? The question does not seem to have been put directly. But the consensus seems quite clear – there would no longer be any property qualification for the vote. When someone moved a mere £20 qualification, Rainsborough angrily denounced it and it was voted down. The vote among men was to be free and universal, with the exception of beggars and servants. All this was carried despite verbose arguments in favour of property. Towards the end of the week, when the committee censored Cromwell's obsequious attitude to the King, he stormed out in protest. Meanwhile, the committees agreed that these demands should be submitted to Parliament, and that Parliament should dissolve itself at the very latest by 1 September 1648. The submission to Parliament was of course a technicality, a fiction. The army had proved in the summer that with a flick of its wrist it could bring Parliament to heel.

A central question remained. How was the army to enforce its own resolutions? How could the *Agreement*, as defined by the council's committees that first week in November, be transposed into reality, into a future English constitution? The Rainsborough–Sexby–Wildman answer to this question was clear: a general rendezvous, a mass meeting of all the regiments of the whole army, to which the *Agreement* and the programme agreed by the council and its committee would be put to a vote, and, if agreed, carried out, if necessary once more by force of arms.

At least once in the committee debates Rainsborough moved again, as he had done on the last day of the big debate, for a general rendezvous, and his motion was carried. On the one occasion when the debate came back to the General Council (1 November), Cromwell violently denounced this proposal on the slightly specious grounds that the only person who could call a rendezvous was General Fairfax, who was ill and so was not at the meetings. When Fairfax was at last able to attend a full council meeting (on 9 November), he indicated his support for a rendezvous, though he made it clear that a general rendezvous of an army which was still engaged in many parts of the kingdom was awkward to arrange and anyway unnecessary. What was more appropriate, he suggested, was a series of smaller, local meetings. This shift irritated the Levellers, who saw it as backsliding from the council's resolutions and from promises freely given by the generals. The prevailing mood of resentment among the agitators and Leveller sympathizers in the army at the end of that momentous week shines out clearly from the angry letter Sexby and his fellow agitator-delegates wrote to their regiments:

They [Cromwell and Ireton] declared they would divide the army into three parts, to rendezvous severally [separately]. And all this appears to be only to draw off the army from joining together to settle these clear foundations of freedom propounded to you, and to procure your rights as you are soldiers, effectually. Thus you may observe the strange inconstancy of those that would obstruct our way, and the great matter wherein the difference lies, and the candidness of our actings. But we hope it will be no discouragement to you, though your officers, yea your greatest officers, should oppose you. It is well known that the great officers who now oppose us did as much oppose secretly when we refused to disband according to the Parliament's order. And yet now they would affright you from such actings by telling you it is disobedience to the General's command, and distempers and mutinies. These were the words of that faction in Parliament which opposed you before. And you may consider that you had done as much service for the people by disobedience as ever you did by obedience.

The letter ended with a clear demand for a 'general rendezvous' of the whole army to settle these problems once and for all.

The tone of this letter (which was probably sent out on 11 November) responded to a much angrier tone set by the generals. At some stage in all these tempestuous events, Cromwell, Ireton and Fairfax met to determine entirely new tactics. Increasingly, as the days went by, men like Edward

Sexby had proved that they were too determined and too clear about what they wanted to be patronized. If they ever got that control, there would be nothing to stop them imposing their will on Parliament and on the whole nation. As they surveyed the political and military situation that weekend of 6–7 November, the generals concluded that there was no future in further debates with the Levellers. What was at stake was their position in society, and their right as landed noblemen to instruct and command their countrymen and their army. The English Revolution, as it later came to be known, had reached a crisis point. The army was the power in the land. Its regiments were on fire with discussion and dissent. Just as the agitators' letter had encouraged the army to disobey Parliament, so the agitators were forever encouraging the rank and file to challenge their officers and disobey them. Already one regiment, led by John Lilburne's cousin Henry, was in open mutiny against orders sending it to the North; and was refusing to move far from the site of any future rendezvous. As the incendiary letter from the agitators proved, the debates at the General Council were being relayed daily to the rank and file, and the Levellers' arguments were capturing the minds of soldiers and commoners alike.

The only action available to the generals was to appeal to the military discipline which had won the war against the King, stop the debating and put the whole issue to a final test. This strategy was carried out with great firmness of purpose in the last two meetings of the General Council on 8 and 9 November. The meetings were presided over by Fairfax. Fairfax's reputation in the army was higher even than Cromwell's and was not tainted by Cromwell's open hostility to the agitators in the previous arguments. In a mood quite different from the uneasy, patronizing, argumentative approach they had adopted previously, the generals opened both meetings with angry denunciations of the divisive behaviour of the agitators and dire warnings of the dangers of allowing the disputes to continue. No longer tolerant of debate, they effectively ordered the disbanding of the General Council, an end to the debates, the submerging of all outstanding matters in yet another committee, and, most crucially, the immediate return of the agitators to their regiments.

The more militant agitators resisted these proposals, but the generals won the vote. They did so chiefly because of their promise, incorporated prominently in their motion, that the issues would be put to the rank and file. They promised a series of rendezvous very soon, whose decision would be final. Most of the agitators realized that carrying a vote in a committee was not the same as establishing a new constitution. That could only be done with the active agreement of the army rank and file. Recalling the huge power and pressure of the enormous rendezvous at Triploe Heath, which had started the army on its victorious political campaign, they reckoned they would be better employed with their regiments, organizing and agitating to win the day at the rendezvous. Thus the most powerful and democratically representative body in English history up to that time – the General Council of the New Model Army – meekly disbanded itself, never to be reconstituted. As they soon realized, the agitators had made a dreadful mistake. Their power derived from their ability to keep together, to maintain collective discussion and debate with one another about the mood and aspirations of the soldiers they represented. Their representative strength was weakened beyond repair by their separation from one another. The tactical initiative passed to the generals who never for a moment lost touch with one another, and who for the next vital week concentrated all their effort and genius on the forthcoming rendezvous.

This meeting was held on 15 November in a field (Corkbush) near Ware, Herts. Only seven regiments – four cavalry, three infantry – were called to it. Both sides prepared for the meeting carefully and apprehensively. The Levellers tried without success to stage a coincidental mass demonstration of weavers from the London area. The agitators did what they could to alert the soldiers to the importance of the meeting. Papers declaring 'England's Freedom! Soldiers' Rights!' were printed for insertion in the soldiers' hats. John Lilburne secured a day off from prison and rode to Ware to wait in an inn for the outcome. But these preparations were puny compared to those of the generals. Fairfax and Cromwell hammered away at a reluctant Parliament to secure at least a promise that the matter of the army's arrears of pay would be urgently addressed in the coming month. Officers were organized to parade round the generals at the rendezvous to ensure the customary good order and military discipline.

The generals got their best break when, during the weekend before the rendezvous, King Charles escaped from his captivity at Hampton Court and fled to the Isle of Wight. The danger of the King making new alliances with armies in Scotland or France and declaring war once more on Parliament was suddenly real. On the day of the rendezvous itself, Fairfax surpassed himself. Speaking in front of the seven regiments separately, he won over the rank and file at once with his customary modesty and sense of purpose. The important issue, he said, was the unity of the army, a unity that depended above all on discipline and loyalty. He promised that the outrageous arrears of pay would be met. He dwelt on the escape of the King and the dangers that loomed ahead, and asked, in effect, whether all that had been achieved by the combined force of the united New Model Army should now be thrown away in ideological splits. Fairfax also indicated that if he did not get a vote of confidence from the rendezvous, he would give up his command. The Remonstrance he proposed made it clear that Parliament would be reformed, without any specific promise about the range of the vote.

The other side of the argument was frozen out. Rainsborough was refused permission to put his own resolution to the regiments. One by one the regiments acclaimed Fairfax and his Remonstrance. Serious trouble for the generals came from only two regiments who had disobeyed orders by coming to the rendezvous uninvited. Colonel Thomas Harrison's and Colonel Robert Lilburne's regiments had decided to attend the rendezvous even though they were expressly ordered not to go to it. As the rebel troops arrived at the field, many of them with Levellers' papers in their hats, they chanted slogans hailing *The Agreement of the People*. Well-rehearsed platoons of officers rode into both regiments, tearing the papers from the soldiers' hats and urging the men to listen to their beloved general and obey him. When the more courageous dissenters in Lilburne's regiment continued to shout for freedom and the people's rights, their ringleaders were plucked from the throng. Three men were singled out as leading mutineers, summarily charged and convicted. They were forced to throw dice for their lives. The loser, Richard Arnold, was shot at the head of the regiment by the other two.

For many months to come, the generals and their allies were called to account for what many saw as the murder of Richard Arnold. But on that fateful day on Corkbush Field, the shots that killed Arnold were a reminder to the rebels of the power that still resided in the hands of the generals. As a direct result, the two other army rendezvous later that month – at St Albans and at Kingston – heard not a whisper of dissent to Fairfax's Remonstrance. The mutiny, if it deserved such a name, was over. The ideas which gave rise to the rendezvous were not, of course, destroyed with it. In the streets of London, in particular, arguments and petitions for universal male suffrage continued apace. But the majority on the Army Council had lost its executive arm: the armed might of the army. And the army had lost its General Council. In the months that followed, Fairfax, Cromwell and Ireton made quite sure that they never again placed the fate of their army at the whim of the awesome new democracy that had been so suddenly unleashed on them.

There was soon to be very little time for democracy. All through March 1648, the King sought new allies in Scotland and at the end of April the

Civil War started up again. It was five months before Cromwell's decisive victory over the Scots at Preston, and the war lingered on in a series of bloody sieges, notably at Pontefract, where Colonel Rainsborough was killed in highly suspicious circumstances by royalist conspirators. The demonstrable treachery of the King, the new battles and all their casualties, Rainsborough's death and the movement of the army towards London once more fanned the flames of popular resentment and agitation in the army rank and file. An enormous Leveller petition calling for a new constitutional settlement was circulated in September 1648. John Lilburne and his Leveller allies, who by now had their own newspaper, entitled the *Moderate*, set to work on a new *Agreement of the People*, which was discussed at length at what became known as the Whitehall Debates, in London in December 1648 and January 1649.

Though many of the same protagonists were involved, these debates had none of the intellectual passion that emerges so strongly from Clarke's record of the argument at Putney. The first difference is immediately obvious. There is no longer any argument about the King. While at Putney Cromwell and Ireton were still hoping for settlement with the King, at Whitehall they were both determined to execute him. The second difference, however, was more fundamental. Perhaps because of their doubts and second thoughts at Putney, the Leveller leaders dropped their demands for universal male suffrage. They still argued for regular parliaments, elected by roughly equal constituencies. But once they had conceded the fundamental argument that the poorest he had as much right to vote as the greatest he, they abandoned the constitutional and legal field to Ireton, who occupied it gleefully. The second *Agreement* was presented to Parliament on 20 January 1649. The remaining MPs – Parliament had been purged of all but the most fervent Cromwell supporters – had other things on their minds, and deferred discussion of any action on the second *Agreement*. Ten days later, the King lost his head.

The second *Agreement* stood no chance. The rich and powerful, shorn of their king, now looked to Cromwell and Ireton to protect them from revolution. They knew what the Levellers and the agitators had been demanding in 1647. They knew that whatever the text of the new *Agreement*, its substance still held out the possibility of a popular vote which would remove Parliament from their clutches. Throughout 1649, they bent all their efforts to smashing the popular movement for reform. In February and March, Lilburne and Overton, who had been released from prison, caught the mood of popular resentment with two devastating pamphlets. They were different in style and content but very similar in purpose: to demand democratic concessions from the army and its Parliament. The pamphlets – *England's New Chains Discovered*, in two parts (Lilburne), and *The Hunting of the Foxes* (Overton) – were denounced by Parliament as seditious. Cromwell moved swiftly to cut the head off the Leveller movement. On 30 March 1649, in dawn raids on their homes, Lilburne, Overton, Walwyn and Thomas Prince were arrested and thrown into different prisons. The arrests led to mutinies in the army. Angry troops sacked their officers and set off on long marches to join up with one another. But before they could do so, Cromwell's cavalry and dragoons caught up with the main force of about 300 mutineers at Burford Church on 14 May, surprised them by night and executed three arbitrarily selected leaders in front of the others. Other mutinous detachments were quickly smashed. The Leveller influence in the army was broken for good. At last assured that the threat of revolution was over, Parliament consecrated 7 June as a Thanksgiving Day and the country's upper classes united to hail the conquering heroes. Most rich and comfortable families in England had taken sides against Cromwell and Ireton when they fought the King. Now the once-hated regicides were fêted and feasted throughout the land.

The four political prisoners, Lilburne, Overton, Walwyn and Prince, were shocked by the news from Burford but by no means bowed. On 1 May, from the Tower of London, they proclaimed a third *Agreement of the People*. As though in apology for extemporizing the previous autumn, they called for a new Parliament elected by 'all men of the age of 21 years and upwards' excepting only servants, those receiving alms and those who had served the King in the Civil War. A new Parliament like this should, they demanded, be elected every year. The parliaments would be bound only by a few rules, chief among which was an absolute ban on continuing with the hated tithes. Yet the argument of Ireton at Putney that votes for all could mean property for all haunted the Levellers. At the end of their third *Agreement*, the four prisoners included a proposed binding condition on all future parliaments: 'We therefore agree and declare, that it shall not be in the power of any representative, in any wise, to render up, or give, or take away any part of this agreement, nor level men's estates, destroy propriety, or make all things common.' Moreover if any Member of Parliament sought to do such a thing (or even if any MP failed to register his dissent), he would be tried for high treason and hanged. If proof were needed of the Levellers' belief in existing property rights, it could not have been more emphatically proclaimed. But it made little impact on the generals, who were already preparing imperialist adventures in Ireland and the West Indies. Cromwell was in Ireland when, in

October 1649, news reached him of Lilburne's acquittal on all charges, his triumphant journey through the streets of London and the release of all four prisoners. When he heard the news, Cromwell is said to have offered to trade at least one of his blood-spattered Irish victories for a different verdict.

The release of the four leaders was the Levellers' last gasp. Cromwell's Rump Parliament had proceeded with dispatch to squeeze the Levellers out of the political life of the capital. They did so first with a frontal assault on the unlicensed press. The flow of pamphlets dried up. By the autumn of 1649, the *Moderate*, after 63 issues, was finally censored. Bitterness in the poorer sections of Britain simmered on, but its means of organization and expression were cut off. By the time Cromwell returned victorious from Ireland and had won two more battles, over the Scots at Dunbar (1650) and over King Charles's pretender son at Worcester (1651), to establish military supremacy over all three kingdoms, he was free to choose his own parliaments and his own method of electing them. In April 1653, the Rump was finally dissolved. Three Cromwellian parliaments succeeded it. The first, the short Barebones Parliament of 1653, was not elected at all. The second, for 1654 and 1655, was elected on a franchise limited to people with £200 worth of property. This reduced the number of people voting even from the Register from which the Long Parliament was elected in 1640. The decline in the county vote was especially severe. As for the MPs elected, they came from almost exactly the same backgrounds, and were almost exactly the same people, as in the previous parliaments under the King. More than 100 of the old boroughs were abolished in the 1653 Parliament, but they were revived again either under Cromwell or under his son Richard, who succeeded him as 'Lord Protector' in 1658. In the third Parliament, which was elected in 1657, the old 40-shilling franchise was reintroduced, as was the House of Lords. By the time King Charles II came to the throne in 1660, almost all the marginal reforms introduced by Cromwell to the old, corrupt Parliament had been eased out of existence. The new King at once restored the old voting system and the old Parliament down to the very last rotten borough. The great rebellion had taught him never again to interfere with Parliament, but he quickly ensured that the Parliament he would leave alone would be as unrepresentative and undemocratic as ever it had been in the reign of his father.

The democratic spasm had been very short. The ideas which led to that historic debate at Putney flourished in people's minds for, at most, three years, from 1646 to 1649. By the Restoration of 1660, almost every major participant in the debates was dead. Rainsborough had been killed in mysterious circumstances in 1648. Ireton died near Limerick in Ireland in 1651, soon after his fortieth birthday – a victim of his conquering army's fever. Lilburne, still pouring out invective against the apostate Protector Cromwell, died in 1657 while he was serving a sentence in the Tower. Cromwell himself died of an illness in 1658. Richard Overton was last heard of when he was arrested for printing an anti-royalist tract in 1663. After 30 years of republican agitation, John Wildman changed political horses and died a rich knight in 1693.

As for Sexby, he spent the last decade of his life intensely disillusioned. He tried briefly, and with some success, to export the revolution to Bordeaux in France and then returned to Britain, where he distributed a pamphlet, *Killing No Murder* (1657), calling for Cromwell's assassination. The theme of the pamphlet is fury at the betrayal of the parliamentary democracy for which Sexby and his supporters had argued with such passion at the height of the revolution. The arguments at Putney continued to haunt Sexby until he too, like Lilburne, died in the Tower in 1658.

Those arguments, however, so meticulously preserved by the army secretary, William Clark, threw up two vital issues for representative democracy. The first was about the nature of that democracy – the contrast between representatives who owe their status to property or rank, or even to periodic elections, and representatives like the agitators in the army constantly subject to the people they represent, and liable at any time to be recalled and replaced. The second is about electoral democracy itself. Does it – can it – threaten private property and what happens if the aspirations of people without property, expressed through elections, clash with those of a propertied minority? Neither of these questions was resolved at Putney nor during the whole period of the English Revolution – nor at any time in the three and half centuries since.

1790–1832: The Not-So-Great Reform Act

> *Lord Henry was a great electioneerer,*
> * Burrowing for boroughs like a rat or rabbit.*
> *But county contests cost him rather dearer,*
> * Because the neighbouring Scotch Earl of Giftgabbit*
> *Had English influence in the self-same sphere here.*
> * His son, the Honourable Dick Dicedrabbit,*
> *Was member for the 'other interest' (meaning*
> *The same self-interest with a different leaning).*
>
> Lord Byron, *Don Juan* (1823)

On 1 November 1790, 143 years after those debates at Putney, Thomas Paine stepped out from his lodgings at the Angel Inn, Islington, to buy a new book that promised to be the rage of fashionable London. Paine was 53 years old. If he had died 16 years earlier, when he was desperately ill on a ship bound for America, no one would ever have heard of him.

He was born in 1737, the son of a staymaker in Thetford, Norfolk, and spent his first 37 years wandering round the south of England scraping a living. The best decision he made in his life was to sail for America in 1774. After recovering from the ship fever, he quickly became involved in the agitation among the American colonists for independence from Britain. He discovered his greatest talent: a clear, agitational writing style. Before and during the five-year War of Independence – the American Revolution – he wrote pamphlets that inspired the revolutionaries and achieved a circulation far higher than any other political writing up to that time. The theme of these pamphlets – *Common Sense* (1776) and the *American Crisis* papers (1776–83) – was simple. Government by kings was indefensible. Government by kings from a foreign country was worse. Both had to be overthrown and replaced by representative parliaments.

Through the long years of the fluctuating War of Independence, Paine marched with the rank and file of George Washington's army and argued with the elected committees that started to govern Pennsylvania. Whenever there was political argument, he was with that rank and file against anyone who sought to deprive them of political influence. He played a large part in the ideas which inspired the American Declaration of Independence, whose famous opening words flowed directly down the years from the pamphlets of the London Levellers more than a hundred years earlier: 'We hold these truths to be self-evident, that all men are created equal . . .'

Paine was close to George Washington, Thomas Jefferson and the other leaders of the fight for independence. After the war, though they gave him a house and tried to tie his talents to the routine business of government, the new leaders of the United States soon became as embarrassed by him as he was bored by them. He came back to Britain in 1787, where he fraternized with the political opponents of King George III. He was struck by the undemocratic nature of the British Parliament. The accountability of that Parliament and the franchise on which it was elected had not changed since Rainsborough and Sexby had demanded universal male suffrage at Putney. Parliament was almost exactly the same old corrupt oligarchy. There were a few constituencies where perhaps 10 per cent of the male electorate could vote, but these were easily outnumbered by the 'rotten boroughs', where the Member was effectively nominated by his patron, a lord or a landowner or both. The quarter of the population which lived in urban areas was entirely unrepresented – the franchise was still based on voting in counties and in rural areas. No more than 4 per cent of the male population was entitled to vote, and most of those either didn't vote, or voted according to how much they were bribed or patronized.

If the voting system was very much the same as that encountered by the Levellers in the 1640s, the condition of the British people had changed dramatically. There were many more of them, for a start. In the long reign of George III, the population of England had grown from 7 million to 13 million. The gross division of the people between rich and poor was also of much the same dimension, but the nature of that division had changed in one crucial respect: what E. P. Thompson called 'the pattern of exploitation'. The exploited people were no longer predominantly agricultural labourers and domestic servants. There were still plenty of both, but side by side with them were growing battalions of workers employed in groups, sometimes large groups, which were rapidly becoming the core of burgeoning cities outside London, cities such as Birmingham and Manchester. These groups of workers were discovering new forms of action to protect themselves from the excesses of exploitation, in particular trade unions, which were expanding fast. The notion of collective action instead of individual or violent protest inspired these new unions, which, in spite of the huge pool of unemployed unskilled workers, were already causing dismay among employers. The employers had very quickly established solidarity with each other. They were shocked when workers started to do the same.

The new trade unionists were increasingly remote from the political game at Westminster, played out between Whigs and Tories, two rich men's parties indistinguishable in their contempt for the voteless majority. In the first 50 years of the eighteenth century, there had been occasional, muted demands for reform of this greedy and ramshackle junta. This was a period of unrelieved cruelty and repression by the property-owning minority. A series of game laws prevented the food the rich couldn't get round to eating from getting into the mouths of the starving millions. Hanging was the standard punishment for stealing game. Over every unrepresented village and town stood the shadow of the gibbet. This apparently perpetual repression started to break up under the pressure of the revolt of the American colonies. After the surrender of the English army in America in 1781, a handful of nervous reformers in the House of Commons gingerly dipped their toes into the waters of franchise reform.

In 1782, a young Tory barrister called William Pitt, who came into Parliament for a rotten borough nominated by a peer, moved a motion for a committee to examine the state of representation in Parliament. This was lost by 161 to 141 and was the closest the unreformed Parliament came to reforming itself for the next fifty years. The following year, another motion from Pitt calling for certain marginal reforms in the representation of the cities, especially London, was lost by 293 votes to 149. In 1785, Pitt, who was then Prime Minister, again brought forward a Bill that would have marginally extended the vote – to people with estates in the counties worth 40 shillings or more. This Bill proposed to knock out 36 rotten boroughs and create new seats for London. Leave to introduce it was refused by 248 to 174. Even the Prime Minister could not persuade a Parliament packed with sinecurists, placemen and pensioners to consider the mildest reform to the corruption that secured their seats.

Thomas Paine observed all this with astonishment and disgust. He planned a book to alert the British people to the twin-headed menace of monarchy and oligarchy. Before he could settle down to write it, he was swept off his feet by the storming of the Bastille in Paris in the summer of 1789 and the French Revolution that followed. 'A share in two revolutions is living to some purpose,' he wrote excitedly to George Washington, and before long he was in France, throwing all his formidable energies into support for the Revolution. He argued with his old friend the Marquis de Lafayette for a wide franchise for the people of the new revolutionary France. Lafayette did not agree. The vote for the new revolutionary Assembly was restricted to those who paid taxes worth more than three days' labour – a minority of the population, though a large one. From France, Paine wrote enthusiastically to the Whig MP Edmund Burke about the Revolution, and urged Burke to join the argument for a wider franchise in France.

Burke's ominous silence on this subject puzzled Paine. He had admired Burke as the most eloquent supporter of the American colonists. Had not Burke demanded reforms in the dispensation of sinecures and pensions? Had he not relentlessly exposed corruption in India under the Governor General, Warren Hastings, who had been successfully impeached as a result? Of all the Whig leaders in Parliament, Paine reckoned Burke the most amenable to reform. But Paine had not followed Burke's career closely enough. At every attempt to get Parliament to reform itself, Burke had expressed his adamant, even hysterical opposition. 'Popular election is a mighty evil,' he had declared in a debate in 1780 on the need for more frequent parliaments. In the debate on Pitt's reform motion in 1785, Burke supported the reactionary majority. 'Universal representation,' he said, 'is a mere delusion.' No wonder he didn't respond to Paine's enthusiastic letters from France. Indeed, Burke had always kept a safe distance from Paine, if only because of Paine's rough dress and rather rustic table manners.

Paine expected to be disappointed by Burke's new book, *Reflections on the Revolution in France*, but he had not expected the fury that engulfed him as he voraciously gobbled up its 200 pages. What struck him again and again was the transparency of Burke's class instincts, his snobbery, his fear, hatred and contempt for the common people. Burke's attack on the new French Assembly was not so much on what it had done but on the sort of people who had been elected to it. In the French Assembly, for instance, there were no 'great lawyers', not a sign of 'everything illustrious' which, Burke claimed, could be seen on all sides in the House of Commons. Instead, the new legislators of France were 'a handful of country clowns' or 'mere country curates' or 'tailors and carpenters' from Paris. He cited biblical authority from Ecclesiasticus: 'The wisdom of a learned man cometh by opportunity of leisure; and he that hath little business shall become wise – how can he get wisdom that holdeth the plough, and that glorieth in the goad; and is occupied in their labours; and whose talk is of bullocks?' In a typically eloquent passage, Burke summed up his approach in a prediction of terrible doom: 'Learning will be cast into the mire, and trodden down under the hoofs of the swinish multitude.'

Did Burke suffer from paranoia about the poor? In several passages, he went out of his way to argue that part of the case for the existing order of things is that the poor benefit from it. 'The order of civil life,' he wrote, 'establishes as much for the benefit of those whom it must leave in a humble state as those whom it is able to exalt to a condition more splendid'; and the 'poorest man finds his own importance and dignity' in the unequal distribution of wealth. Burke was opposed to the poor and the humble only when they asked for a share in their government or in their nation's wealth. Government and wealth, he insisted, were matters solely for people with property.

Though more verbose and ornate, Burke's basic argument against the French Revolution was very much the same as Ireton's at Putney more than a century earlier. Ireton had insisted that only those with a 'fixed interest' in the kingdom should have any say over the government of it. Burke noticed with horror that in the new French Assembly there was not a sign of the 'natural landed interest of the country'. Property was the key. 'We entertain a high opinion of our legislative authority,' he wrote, 'but we have never dreamt that parliaments had any right whatever to violate property.'

His conclusion was: 'This [French] legislative assembly of a free nation sits, not for the security, but for the destruction, of property, and not of property only, but of every rule and maxim which can give it stability.' It was as though Ireton's worst nightmare had come true. The vote was more widely distributed, and as a result stable men of property were seeing their fixed interest in the kingdom expropriated.

So offensive was this violation that Burke felt himself obliged to remind his readers of the fundamental rights of the propertied few. Near the end of his book he identified the 'surplus', which was created by the labour of everyone in society, but seized for their own advantage by the rich minority: 'In every prosperous community something more is produced than goes to the immediate support of the producer. This surplus forms the income of the landed capitalist. It will be spent by the proprietor who does not labour.' This 'surplus' was the source of pleasure for the idle rich, but it also inspired the labour which produced it. 'This idleness is itself the spring of labour; this repose the spur to industry.' It followed that anyone who dared to redistribute the surplus was endangering the very future of mankind. For Burke, the real menace of the French Revolution was that it placed some political power in the hands of people without property, who might be persuaded in their new confidence and office to lay their hands on what belonged to others. For that reason, the 'swinish multitude' were simply not fit to rule:

The occupation of an hairdresser or of a working tallow-chandler cannot be a matter of honour to any person – to say nothing of a number of other more servile employments. Such descriptions of men ought not to suffer oppression by the state, but the state suffers oppression if such as they, either individually or collectively, are permitted to rule.

Burke was implacably opposed to all electoral reform on the grounds that any change in the existing arrangements threatened the security of the propertied few. What mattered most, therefore, was the obedience and passivity of the people.

Good order is the foundation of all good things . . . The body of the people must not find the principles of natural subordination by art rooted out of their minds. They must respect that property of which they cannot partake. They must labour to obtain what by labour can be obtained; and when they find, as they commonly do, the success disproportioned to the endeavour, they must be taught their consolation in the final proportions of eternal justice.

For the destitute majority, there was no real hope on earth, so they must wait their chance in heaven. In the meantime, they had no real choice but to bequeath their government to an 'inheritable crown, an inheritable peerage, and a House of Commons and a people inheriting privileges, franchises, and liberties from a long line of ancestors'.

Paine seethed with indignation. He grabbed his quill and wrote solidly for ten weeks. The 40,000 words which were published, after some delay, in February 1791 made up the first part of perhaps the most famous political pamphlet in all British history: *The Rights of Man*. It opened with a burst of indignation against Burke, whom Paine had originally regarded as a 'friend to mankind'. Now he was nothing of the sort. He was 'darkness attempting to illuminate light'. He was full of fine phrases but had no point to make about the real state of society either in Britain or in France. He was hypnotized by the gaudy old-world courtesy of the French Queen, but had no eye for the 'Augean stables of parasites and plunderers' who presided beneath her. He was 'music in the ears, and nothing in the heart'; 'he pities the plumage, but forgets the dying bird.' In place of the young democracy in France, Burke held out the corrupt old Parliament at Westminster. In place of the French Declaration of Rights, he held out the Bill of Rights of 1688, which had specifically rejected any extension of democracy.

Paine's initial blast of rage exhausted, he calmed down to detailed and rational argument. He listed eight points about the new French Assembly and asked each time what Burke would put in its place. Almost all the points concerned the system of government. In France, anyone who paid 50 sous in tax could be an elector. That was not as extensive as Paine would have liked, but it meant that the Assembly had been elected by the 'greatest body of men exercising the right of election the European world ever saw'. The members of the French Assembly, about whom Burke had written so snobbishly, had been elected from roughly equal constituencies. In Britain, the constituencies were hopelessly uneven. The French were committed to triennial parliaments – the British Parliament could sit for seven years without an election. Burke complained about executions in France, but what had he done to stop the interminable hangings of impoverished British people for trivial thefts, mostly inspired by hunger? The French Assembly had no room for the placemen and pensioners who used the House of Commons to cloak themselves in secrecy and then to vote themselves supplies and money – a 'Comedy of Errors' and a 'Pantomime of Hush'. The French Assembly had removed from the King the right to declare war, had abolished titles, and excluded the church and the aristocracy from direct political influence. 'The greatest characters the world has known have arisen on the democratic floor,' wrote Paine. Yet in England the democratic floor had been shut off from the entire system of government. The right of electing their government was 'inherent in the people', yet Burke would deny it to the vast majority of British citizens in perpetuity. Paine's conclusion was plain. There were two possible systems of government – by hereditary succession or by representation and election. The first flowed from ignorance, the second from reason. No compromise between them was possible. The choice was stark, and the American and French Revolutions had placed it firmly on the British agenda.

The Rights of Man was expensive at three shillings, but at once it was a bestseller. Burke's *Reflections* had done well by the standards of bookselling at the time, but Paine's little book outpaced it immediately and comprehensively. By May 1791, *The Rights of Man* was in its sixth edition and had sold an astonishing 50,000 copies, making it by far the bestselling original book ever sold. Whole regiments and fleets ordered it in bulk. In Ireland, the sales per head of the population were even higher.

It was followed by the second part of *The Rights of Man*, published exactly a year later in February 1792. The theme of Part Two is very much the same and the language even stronger:

All hereditary government is in its nature tyranny. An heritable crown or an heritable throne have no other significant explanation than that mankind are heritable property. To inherit a government is to inherit a people, as if they were flocks and herds . . . Kings succeed each other, not as rationals, but as animals.

To His Majesty and His oligarchical Ministry this was even more offensive than Part One. Part Two goaded the authorities into action. The first was Paine's open exultation in revolutions and in their liberating of human potential. In an extraordinary passage, which must have come directly from his experiences in Washington's army, he wrote:

It appears to general observation, that revolutions create genius and talents; but that those events do no more than bring them forward. There is existing in man, a mass of sense lying in a dormant state, and which, unless something excites to action, will descend with him, in that condition, to the grave . . . the construction of government ought to be such as to bring forward, by a quiet and regular operation, all that extent of capacity which never fails to appear in revolutions.

The notion that deep down all human beings had aspirations and abilities, which were held in check by hereditary powers and which, when unleashed, could create an infinitely better and more just society, was received by Pitt's Tory ministers with horror and fear. The French Revolution had moved several huge steps forward from the cosy idealism of 1791. Now came an attack from below not only on the methods by which the old regime had governed, nor even only on their right to govern at all, but also on the 'fraud and force' with which they had acquired their power in the first place. Part Two of *The Rights of Man* concentrated far more than Part One on inequality, exploitation and the relationship between property and reform:

What is called the splendour of the throne is no other than the corruption of the state. It is made up of a band of parasites, living in luxurious indolence, out of the public taxes . . . The man who is in the receipt of a million a year is the last person to promote a spirit of reform, lest, in the event, it should reach to himself.

This is the nearest Paine ever got to describing a class of people – 'a band of parasites' – whose common interest in rejecting all reforms sprang from their joint ownership of excessive property. Unlike Part One, Part Two argued specifically for taxation of the rich to provide welfare for the poor and security for all in old age. In early 1792, when the enraged and hungry sans culottes of Paris were forcing the food manufacturers to lower prices, *The Rights of Man*, Part Two, sounded much more dangerous and explosive than Part One had in the previous year. Paine's 'representative democracy' seemed a cloak for a new revolutionary egalitarianism.

Pitt's ministers decided that this new book could not be tolerated. A law 'against seditious writings' was rushed through Parliament, and the first book to be prosecuted under it was Part Two of *The Rights of Man*. A propaganda campaign against Paine and all his works was orchestrated by the Government. But nothing could stop the book's success. Very soon it was selling more copies than its predecessor. The essayist William Hazlitt remarked that Paine had become so hated that the Government was prepared to go to war, not simply to defeat the revolutionary menace in France but principally to annihilate the revolutionary menace in Britain that Thomas Paine had helped unleash.

The impact of Paine's *Rights of Man* need not blind us, more than 200 years later, to its failings. Paine's impatient and rumbustious style often bounded over obstacles that required more careful circumvention. Paine had only a very sparse knowledge of his country's history. Astonishingly, he never mentions the Levellers. If, like his fellow Radical John Horne Tooke, he had studied the arguments of Richard Overton or John Lilburne, he would have found even simpler and more direct arguments for his representative democracy. His naivety about the class rule that he had started to expose is sometimes breathtaking. For instance, he contends that the open, public, 'simple' democracy of Athens could not be sustained as population and territory expanded, and so became 'unwieldy and impracticable'. 'Had the system of representation been then understood, as it now is, there is no reason to believe that those forms of government now called monarchical or aristocratical would ever have taken place.' Monarchy and aristocracy, on this theory, simply arose by chance because no one had ever thought of the idea of representative democracy. (Much more accurate is Paine's suggestion in Part One that such governments arose purely 'by force of fraud'.) Worse, he never set out how a representative system would work. He did not even argue for universal suffrage. A novelist who visited him quoted him saying 'the minority must in all cases govern' – a statement that sounded odd from a man who championed 'the democratic floor'.

These contradictions were hardly noticed by the masses who absorbed *The Rights of Man* or by the Government that banned it. For the masses, Tom Paine had articulated the unfairness and absurdity of a system of government that denied them any part in choosing it. Burke had put the case for unelected and unaccountable government. Paine had expressed the hatred and contempt in which such a government would always be held by people who could not vote for it. The argument between them was, in essence, a repeat of the argument at Putney in 1647, and it persevered in British public life for more than a century.

The tempo and force of the argument were dictated not by the small handful of reform supporters in Parliament but by the extent of agitation outside. Immediately, *The Rights of Man* was part of a great wave of agitation for reform throughout the country. The cause of franchise reform was inextricably bound up with the cause of economic reform, and with support for the French Revolution. At first, the Government seemed stunned by the agitation. As ministers recovered their breath, they moved not towards the reform which some of them, including Prime Minister Pitt, had supported a decade earlier – but to the most savage repression of all who organized for it.

The declaration of war by France in February 1793 – a declaration plainly provoked by Pitt's Tory ministry – made arrests of dissidents far easier, and gave legal credence to the charge that anyone who defended the French Revolution was a traitor. This was the argument used in a series of trials in which the leaders of the reformers were brought to court on the most solemn indictments. On 30 August 1793, Thomas Muir, a prominent Scottish reformer, was tried in Edinburgh for making seditious speeches and for circulating *The Rights of Man*. The presiding judge, Lord Justice Braxfield, was in no doubt that advocacy of parliamentary reform was in itself seditious. 'There was a spirit of sedition in this country last winter, which made every good man uneasy,' he reminded the jury.

Yet Mr Muir had at that time gone about among ignorant country people and among the lower classes making them leave off their work, and inducing them to believe that a reform was absolutely necessary for preserving their liberty, which, had it not been for him, they would never have suspected was in danger. Judge whether this appears to you, as to me, sedition.

Braxfield's legendary bad temper developed into belligerent fury as he bellowed:

Government in this country is made up of the landed interest, which alone has a right to be represented; as for the rabble, who have nothing but personal property, what hold has the nation of them? What security for the payment of their taxes? They may pack up all their property on their backs and leave the country in the twinkling of an eye . . .

Muir, who had been cheered to the echo by the vast crowd in the courtroom and outside, was found guilty and sentenced to 14 years' transportation to Australia. He escaped and, after a series of extraordinary adventures, finished up in France, where he died in 1799 plotting an invasion of Britain. He was more fortunate than other Scottish reformers who were charged with similar offences. Joseph Gerrald, William Skirving, Rev. Thomas Palmer and Maurice Margarot, all devoted, passionate, non-violent advocates of reform, were similarly convicted and transported. Gerrald, Skirving and Palmer died of illness in Australia, and Margarot returned in 1809, broken in mind and body.

In May 1794, four English reformers – Thomas Hardy, who two years previously had formed the London Corresponding Society (LCS) 'with members unlimited' to campaign for reform; Thomas Holcroft; John Horne Tooke and John Thelwall – stood trial for treason. The prosecution case amounted to the charge that to campaign for parliamentary reform was equivalent to a campaign to assassinate the King. This fantastic charge might have been successful, had it not been destroyed by the publication shortly before the trial of an anonymous pamphlet (almost certainly written by William Godwin, political philosopher and author of the influential *Enquiries concerning Political Justice and Its Influence on Morals and Happiness* (1793)), which proved beyond all doubt that the charge of treason had no foundation in law. The four were acquitted.

Undeterred by this acquittal, and unimpressed even by the fall of Robespierre in France, the Government piled on the repression. In October 1794, habeas corpus was suspended, and the authorities were given carte blanche to arrest and hold dissidents at will. Pitt, who less than ten years previously had been advocating a wide extension of the franchise, now denounced any such advocacy as tantamount to treason. There were, he told a terrified House, 'thirty divisions of the London Corresponding Society' in London alone, all plotting revolution by proposing parliamentary reform. He read out long extracts of LCS resolutions demanding that the House of Commons should consist of 'representatives of the whole body of the people of England' who would 'wrest from the Parliament that power which the people and the Constitution had put in their hands'. Pitt did not explain how he and his MPs could possibly have got their power either from the people, who had no votes, or from a constitution that didn't exist.

Still, the Painite 'rabble' and 'swinish multitude' refused to lie down. Mass meetings in all the urban areas continued to demand a fair system of representation. After two enormous meetings in London in October 1795, the Home Secretary, a barnacled Whig called William Windham, introduced still more repressive legislation: the Seditious Meetings Act made it a criminal offence to take part in a meeting of more than 50 people without prior notice, and gave magistrates the right and duty to disperse any meeting they thought looked dangerous. The Treasonable Practices Act made it an offence, punishable by seven years' transportation, for anyone to say more than once anything that might 'bring into contempt, King, Government or Constitution'. The fear and apprehension which inspired both Bills was admirably summed up by Windham in a private letter:

Suppose someone should take it into their head to write a work addressed to the labouring people exposing to them the iniquity of that system which condemns half the world to labour for the other, and pleading for such a partition of goods as may give to every one a competence and leave none to superfluity?

The very idea that there should be enough for all and that no one should have too much was seditious. The words 'parliamentary reform', Windham had told the Commons on 16 May 1794,

were used by the seditious societies for no other purpose than as a mark of their real intention of a total annihilation of all property, constitution and religion . . . Where there is society there must of course be property, and where there is property there must also be a necessary distinction of ranks. But as the people of no property must ever constitute the majority and the physical strength of a state, all principles which tended to induce that majority to plunder and oppress the minority must be equally dangerous to all governments.

Windham's Bills and their ruthless enforcement drove the reform movement back from the streets and parks into silent and sullen resentment. In Parliament, the flame of reform was quickly doused. In 1797, the Whig peer Charles Grey tried again to bring in a Bill for modest reform of some of the more absurd features of the Commons representation. Grey's supporters were engulfed in the prevailing anxiety that even the gentlest move in his direction would summon up the menace of popular revolt. 'It was in the nature of things,' said Sir William Young, who 'represented' a handful of bribed electors in the village of St Mawes, Cornwall, 'that concessions being made to the multitude, they would take advantage and turn it to their most extravagant designs . . .' Grey's motion was flung out by 256 to 91.

By the end of the century, the movement for reform seemed well and truly scotched, and the wealthy gentlemen who made up the House of Commons could rejoice in the final conversion of their Prime Minister. Pitt the former reformer was now in no doubt that the 'slightest change in the Constitution' would be 'evil, even if the times were proper for experiments'. When he said this, Pitt was engaged in a monumental change in the Constitution – swallowing the whole of the Irish Parliament in order more easily to forestall and crush any future Irish rebellion like that of 1798. What he meant by 'the Constitution' was not the form of government but 'the system of society as we know it' – a system which was not remotely affected by the merging of the Irish Parliament with the British one but which would, he feared, have been very deeply affected by extending the franchise.

Though habeas corpus was restored in 1800, the repression continued. To the long list of repressive laws, the Government added the Combination Acts. They forbade the annoying habit of workers in the new mines, mills and factories combining into trade unions to improve wages and conditions. In the first few years of the new century, there was so little outside agitation for reform that ministers convinced themselves that they had put an end to the unwelcome subject once and for all. There were plenty of petitions to Parliament protesting about corrupt elections, but none of those irritating motions calling for reform of the representation. Burke died in 1797, and Paine in America in 1808, and most of the ruling politicians from both parties comforted themselves that the ferocious argument that had so shaken the country in the 1790s had gone for ever.

All the time, however, pressed by the laws and the standing army stationed in every populous area to enforce them, the yearning for reform was bubbling beneath the surface. It exploded sporadically, often for the most unpredictable reasons. In January 1809, another wave of agitation was set off by the sexual appetite of the Duke of York. The Radical MP Charles Wardle stunned the House of Commons with allegations that a mistress of the Duke, Mrs Clarke, had sold commissions in the army. The allegations led to a public investigation of the scandal on the floor of the House of Commons, a source of endless enjoyment to the Duke's loyal subjects. The investigation opened up a sewer of corruption at the Court and led to another round of angry meetings and petitions demanding parliamentary reform. As soon as the investigation was over, the moderate Whig MP John Curwen moved the mildest possible motion calling on every MP who took his seat to sign a declaration that no money had passed hands. 'Corruption,' said Curwen, 'has destroyed all public confidence . . . by this timely reform you will turn the tide of popular feeling and convert it into increased affection and attachment to the Constitution.'

This theme – that mild reform brings people back to a proper and healthy respect for their government – was to become increasingly popular with moderate Whigs for the next 20 years. Most MPs were prepared to take Curwen's Bill seriously, and set about amending it until it was weak enough to be passed. Even then, the majority was only 12. Burke might be dead but his old friend and supporter William Windham, who was still in the

House, detected even in this mild measure against bribery at election times a dangerous new precedent. 'The Bill it appears,' he scoffed, 'went to do away with boroughmongering and corruption. Would it do away with property? . . . If once we begun on the path to reform, we could never stop; and if once we made a change to please the people, they would go on; they would never know when they had had enough.' The small group of Radical MPs also opposed the Bill. When their leader, Sir Francis Burdett, moved a motion for genuine reform, he was supported by only 15 MPs. The agitation continued however, and in 1810 the Whig MP for Hertfordshire, Thomas Brand, took up the running. He moved another mild reform motion extending the franchise to county copyholders, abolishing some rotten boroughs and transferring their seats to the unrepresented cities. The motion got a respectable 115 votes – against 234. But when Brand tried the same motion the following year (1812), he got only 88 votes, and the matter was dropped. Brand's second motion was opposed by another Whig MP, J. L. Ward, who couldn't understand why anyone should want to change anything, let alone the voting system, at a time like 1812, 'when we enjoy a measure of tranquillity and happiness unknown to any other country in this stormy and disastrous age'.

This tranquillity and happiness was demonstrated at once by the assassination of Spencer Perceval, the Prime Minister, and the uprisings of the impoverished Luddite machine-breakers in Nottinghamshire and Yorkshire. With such disturbing events taking place in the country, and with the war against France at a crucial stage, Tories, Whigs and Radicals agreed by common consent that this was not a time for any responsible citizen to engage in further prattle about connecting the mass of the people to their government.

They were assisted by the splits in the reform movement outside Parliament. The imprisonment of the Hunt brothers, John and Leigh, for publishing an attack on the Prince Regent, summed up the approach of most reformers from the upper reaches of society: they were all for reform, so long as it could be contained. The central issue, even for most reformers, was property. The Hampden Clubs, founded by Major John Cartwright, split between those who wanted votes for those with property at a rateable value of more than £300 – effectively excluding all but a tiny minority of wealthy people – and Major Cartwright, who consistently urged universal male suffrage by secret ballot and annual parliaments. Cartwright sought tirelessly to bring the warring factions together, but every dinner or meeting he arranged ended in interminable squabbles on the central issue of how much property people should have before they should get the vote.

The extreme position was stated, hesitatingly and from the sidelines, by supporters of the Newcastle-born bookseller and schoolteacher Thomas Spence. Spence was outraged by the unspeakable poverty of the people he lived and moved amongst and the contrast between that poverty and the riches of the people who ruled. He argued that this division of property was at the root of all the ills of society, which would not be cured without 'the overthrow of all Establishments'. In the brief period he was allowed out of prison and to publish, he brought out *Pig's Meat* whose title derived from Burke's 'swinish multitude'. 'You see, Citizen,' wrote Spence, 'we are arrived at a very serious crisis ... The question is no longer about what form of government is most favourable to liberty ... but which system of society is most ... capable of delivering us from the deadly mischief of great accumulations of wealth which enable a few unfeeling monsters to starve whole nations in spite of the fruitful seasons God Almighty can send.' All the reformers, including Tom Paine, had missed the next point. 'Who pray among all the revolutionists of either America, France or England or anywhere else ever disputed or attempted to invalidate the rights of the landed interest?'

Isolated and persecuted all his life, Spence was inclined to seek refuge in isolation from the various reform movements. He died, as poor as he had lived, in 1814. But his ideas and his calls for mass action to achieve them had a strong appeal among what he called 'the meagre and beggarly working people'.

The splits and bickerings of the reformers, the defeat and execution of the Luddite leaders in 1813, and a brief respite from slump buried the reform movement until the end of the Napoleonic Wars in 1815. Throughout the wars, ministers had argued that reform was a luxury at a time when all the energies of the nation had to be united in the national effort to defeat Napoleon. The force of the argument disappeared as soon as Napoleon was beaten and banished, the French humiliated at the Congress of Vienna, and peace restored to England. With peace came even greater economic crisis, poverty and starvation – and a new movement for parliamentary reform.

When employers cut wages to 'deal with' the post-war crisis, strikes in defiance of the Combination Acts broke out all over the country. In Wolverhampton in November 1815, in Newcastle in May 1816 and in Radstock, Somerset, in March 1817, coal miners refused to work. A gang of angry Radstock miners shouting 'Bread or Blood!' were faced down by a troop of cavalry led by Sir John Hippisley, chairman of the local magistrates. 'What do you want?' shouted Sir John. Back came the reply: 'Full wages, we are starving.' Sir John replied with all the sophistication of his Tory colleagues in the Government: 'Your minds have been inflamed by parodies on the liturgy and the church, seducing you not only from your King but from your God.' The cavalry charged on the defenceless miners and four men were arrested. There were disturbing signs all over the country that the demands of the strikers and demonstrators were being taken further than the 'full wages' and 'bread' cries of the Radstock miners.

In 1816, the miners of Bilston, Staffordshire, every one of whom had lost their jobs in the post-war depression, decided spontaneously to march to London to present a meek petition to the Prince Regent. Their pathetic procession was suddenly swelled by huge numbers of sympathizers – who were promptly turned back by magistrates supported by armed yeomanry and soldiers. A few months later, starving 'Blanketeers' – marchers armed only with a blanket – set off in groups of 20 from Manchester. Their purpose too was to present a petition to the Prince, and they too were broken up with great force and turned back. At Pentridge, Nottingham-shire, in June 1817, an organized rising of angry and impoverished rural workers was broken up, and their three leaders, all working men, hanged, drawn and quartered. The spies who had infiltrated their movement reported to the authorities that the Pentridge rising, like the miners' and the Blanketeers' marches, was potentially revolutionary. They also re-ported, more accurately, the growing conviction among genuine reform-ers that the unreformed, increasingly corrupt and reactionary Parliament was never going to grant reform, and the only path to a representative government was through mass action.

During the years after the war, this new strategy was adopted with great passion and energy by perhaps the most remarkable reform leader of the time: a county landowner and swashbuckling entrepreneur called Henry Hunt. Hunt started his political career in support of the 'radical' Whigs in Parliament. But he soon cast them aside in favour of an open campaign to mobilize the unrepresented and voteless majority. In 1816 and 1817, he spoke at three monster meetings at Spa Fields in London. His huge voice, indomitable conceit and unshaken belief that the people who did the work had the right and the ability to have a say in how their country was run won him a popular respect to which no other politician of the time could aspire. In all his life he never for a moment trimmed his fundamental belief in universal suffrage backed by secret ballot and annual parliaments. He had no time for any compromise on these demands. He spurned, for instance, Sir Francis Burdett's plan to restrict the vote to the minority who paid direct taxes. Why should 'property only' be represented, he asked, 'whereas labour makes property and therefore in the name of common sense ought to be represented'?

Burdett had introduced his plan to Parliament in a debate in the Commons on 1 July 1819. The debate was overshadowed by the feverish agitation in the country outside. The young Lord John Russell, a Whig by party and a mild reformer by instinct, was terrified. Russell apologized to the House for not supporting Burdett's motion, which was 'calculated to throw a slur upon the representation of the country and to fill the minds of the people with vague and indefinite alarms'. Burdett himself echoed this apprehension by quoting Blackstone on 'the true reason' for property qualifications for voting, 'to exclude such persons as are so mean in situation that they are esteemed to have no will of their own'. After such interventions from Russell and Burdett, there was hardly any need for the Tories to weigh in with even more anxious warnings. Pascoe Grenfell, MP for Great Marlow, who had made his fortune on the backs of Cornish tin miners, said that the 'present system of representation' was 'a better security for property' than any other system ever devised. Another Tory, John Wilmot, warned that parliamentary reform was 'a lever by which the whole force of the lower and more turbulent classes of the community could be applied to the overthrow of all that was stable and salutary in the state'. The whole debate was dominated by apprehension at what was happening before and after mass reform demonstrations all over the country.

Manchester, a city divided by a huge spinners' strike in 1818, was the centre of that agitation. A series of mass meetings in other northern cities culminated in a mighty reform celebration and picnic on 16 August 1819 at St Peter's Fields, Manchester, from where the Blanketeers had set off two years earlier. The propertied minority were so apprehensive about the meeting that they dragooned a large consignment of armed 'yeomen' to police it. The yeomen were infuriated by the sight of Henry Hunt arriving in his carriage to speak to an orderly and peaceful meeting of some 60,000 people on the sole subject of parliamentary reform. Before Hunt could utter a sentence, the yeomanry spurred their horses on to the crowd, flashing their sabres. They killed 11 and injured at least 140.

The shockwaves from what rapidly became known as the 'Peterloo Massacre' spread quickly all over the country. The sense of outrage was most eloquently expressed by the young poet Shelley, then in self-imposed exile in Italy. Shelley read the reports of Peterloo and vanished into his attic where, in five days, he wrote the 92 verses of his poem *The Mask of Anarchy*. Two years earlier, Shelley had written a reasoned pamphlet, *A Proposal for Putting Reform to the Vote*. He had stopped short of advocating universal suffrage, and proposed instead a referendum on the question, in which everyone could take part. It was an attempt to achieve universal suffrage by the back door. When he read the news from Peterloo, Shelley instantly abandoned this cautious approach. *The Mask of Anarchy*, a nightmare, starts with a grim cavalcade led by the three leading political figures of the time, all rich Tories – Lord Castlereagh, the Foreign Secretary; Lord Eldon, the Lord Chancellor; and Lord Sidmouth, the Home Secretary – and ends with a call to make the Peterloo Massacre a beacon of revolt:

> Shake your chains to earth like dew
> Which in sleep had fallen on you –
> Ye are many – they are few.

Henry Hunt had called on the great gathering at St Peters Fields to stand firm against the yeomanry with the assurance 'we are many, they are few'. That philosophy had inspired all his great meetings, but as soon as it met with armed resistance, it faltered. Hunt imagined that the popular anguish and fury that followed Peterloo would lead to a measure of reform. As he basked in the adoration of enormous meetings and processions – 200,000 people greeted him as he rode into London a few weeks after Peterloo – he initiated a series of legal actions against the Government seeking damages and compensation for their illegal actions at Peterloo. This strategy was disastrous. The Government congratulated the yeomanry for their 'forth-right' behaviour, and closed ranks. They were intensely vulnerable to more action of the type Shelley recommended. As long as the resistance was confined to the law courts, they could back off and regroup. The pause gave ministers time to prepare yet another batch of repressive laws, chief among which was the Prevention of Seditious Meetings Act, rushed through the Commons in December. Henry Hunt was imprisoned not long after-wards. So was the indomitable Radical Richard Carlile – for publishing the works of Thomas Paine. So was Dr James Watson, leader of the London militants. Six Acts followed, effectively banning what was left of the right to oppose the Government by speech or by publication. By the end of 1819, the chance to protest by mounting bigger and stronger demonstrations than at Peterloo was gone. As in the 1790s after the publication of *The Rights of Man*, the British people were held down by force.

The fate of Shelley's poem cruelly reflected the fate of the reform move-ment. In September 1819, Shelley sent it to Leigh Hunt, begging him to publish it. He tried again and again, but Hunt tactfully refused to respond. Unlike Shelley, who had escaped any possible prosecution for his levelling views, Leigh Hunt was living and publishing in England and he had read the Six Acts carefully. *The Mask of Anarchy* was, by any definition of the Acts, seditious in the extreme, criminally libellous, blasphemous and treasonable. The poem was not published for another decade, by which time the political atmosphere was more conducive.

With the help of even more repressive measures than those of their predecessors in the 1790s, the Tory Government survived the crises of 1819 and the conspiracies and plots of 1820. Most of their supporters among the boroughmongers and sinecurists in the House of Commons started to believe, as they had done after the initial fright caused by *The Rights of Man*, that the revolt had died away and that everything would return to normal. There were some among the more perspicacious Whigs, however, who understood the real menace of Peterloo. A month after the massacre, the ennobled liberal lawyer Henry Brougham wrote to the Whig leader, Lord Grey: 'Really the tendency of things at present – to end in a total separation of the upper and middling from the lower classes, the property from the population – is sufficiently apparent and rather alarming.' Something had to be done to convince more people that they had a stake in the society, and at least a vote.

Gradually the Whig leaders, reluctant at first to associate with the wild men of Peterloo, began to protest about the repression and to place themselves at the head of those upper- and middle-class people who would rather reform Parliament than lose their property. Though the Tory Government continued, the repression slackened. Henry Hunt came out of prison in 1821. The Combination Acts were repealed in 1824. The stubborn defiance of Richard Carlile won him the right to publish the works of Paine with impunity. The reactionary troika which had effectively governed the country from the end of the war to Peterloo retired. Castlereagh committed suicide in 1822. Sidmouth retired in 1824 and Eldon was out of office in 1827. In those relatively peaceful years what happened to the movement for parliamentary reform?

In 1822, Lord John Russell – the same young blue-blood who in the summer of Peterloo had opposed a reform motion because of the 'vague and indefinite alarms' it might signal to the disaffected masses – took courage and dipped his toe once more in the water of reform. In 1822 and 1823, he moved motions to get rid of 100 rotten boroughs. Both were lost by huge majorities. Outside Parliament the demand for reform seemed to have died out. In 1823, there were 29 petitions calling for reform. In the next six years there were none at all. The Tory ministers who were in office for most of that time congratulated themselves on the firm action they had taken after Peterloo, and convinced themselves that they had by that action stamped out for ever the very notion that there was anything wrong with the system of representation in Parliament. As ever, they were quite unprepared for the third wave of agitation which, like the first two, blew up without warning.

The first shock was in Ireland. In 1828, as a result of the faction fight in the Tory Party between the diehard right led by the Prime Minister, the Duke of Wellington, and the more pragmatic supporters of the former Prime Minister George Canning, the Canningites were thrown out of the Cabinet. Charles Grant, the President of the Board of Trade, was replaced by a Wellingtonian nonentity called William Vesey Fitzgerald. As was the custom, Fitzgerald, before taking office, offered himself for re-election. This was a formality, since in most places there were very few electors, and even fewer who could not be bullied or bribed to support the candidate of the local bigwig. Fitzgerald's seat was County Clare in Ireland, where the all-Protestant electorate could normally be relied on to support any Protestant Tory who entered the lists. But this time there was a hitch. For years, a campaign had been waged for the right of Catholics, the enormous majority of the Irish population, to vote. The leader of the campaign was a powerful orator from Kerry called Daniel O'Connell. O'Connell's most effective tactic was the mass public meeting. He spoke at hundreds of them throughout the 1820s. In 1828, he put himself down as a candidate in the Clare by-election. The candidature was greeted with official derision. After all, O'Connell was a Catholic. Only propertied Protestants could vote. So O'Connell could not vote for himself and neither could any of the Catholic peasantry amongst whom he had worked to such effect. When O'Connell was declared overwhelming victor on the first ballot, the shockwaves spread at once to London.

In 1798, the Irish had staged a rebellion that was supported by a small invasion of French troops. For an exhilarating moment, the rebellion threatened the whole future of British rule in Ireland. The huge British army of occupation was twice defeated and stretched to the very limit. Almost immediately after the 1798 rebellion was crushed, the Irish Parliament was 'absorbed' into the British Parliament at Westminster, and the most savage repression instituted to wipe out further resistance. The 1798 rebellion had shaken the more realistic of the British military leaders, including Wellington, who was always on the alert for any sign of trouble in Ireland. The enormous meetings convened by O'Connell in the run-up to the 1828 Clare by-election worried the British generals. This was no clandestine conspiracy, like the rising led by Robert Emmett in 1803, easily spied upon and easily crushed, or routine political opposition, easily contained. The rising tide of anger and distress in Ireland, it seemed, could develop quickly into full-scale revolt. The Clare by-election was a catalyst. It showed beyond dispute that O'Connell's demand for Catholic emancipation had deep roots not just in the Catholic community but also, crucially, among the poorer Protestant voters.

Catholic emancipation, a Whig demand since 1807, had always been bitterly resisted by Tory ministers, who saw a breach in the privileges of the Church of England as a breach in the dyke of upper-class hegemony. Suddenly, under the threat of another rebellion, which they knew they might not contain, the most unlikely Tories became converts to Catholic emancipation. Wellington himself, the most intransigent of Tories, persuaded a reluctant King, his reluctant lieutenant Robert Peel and a reluctant Tory Party to pass a law allowing richer Catholics to vote. For that backbench support the Tory ministry had to pay a heavy price. In exchange for enfranchising the richer Catholics, they disenfranchised thousands of poorer Protestants. The old 40-shilling property qualification was raised to £10, though only in the counties. The boroughs were left untouched: 'though spectacularly corrupt, they were corrupt in the Protestant interest'. The results were catastrophic to the entire system of Irish representation, especially in the north. In the largely Protestant county of Antrim, 6,246 voters were reduced to 700, in Tyrone, 6,600 to 364. In all Ireland, the county electoral register was reduced from 216,000 to 37,000 voters, removing 34,000 in Galway and 10,000 in Dublin. What was called an emancipation was in fact a disenfranchisement of enormous proportions. The richer Catholics got the vote while poorer Protestant voters summarily lost it. This measure rankled deep in the Protestant communities and helped to fan sectarian hatred and violence for the next century and a half.

In Britain, however, the effect of the Catholic Emancipation Act was to stoke up the fires of the reform movement. The measure, for all its reactionary consequences for the poorer Protestant Irish voters, showed that the unreformed Parliament could extend the franchise to people who previously had not got it – but only under threat of insurrection. Those MPs – the large majority – who had previously argued that any change in the voting system was a concession to revolution, and that revolution would undoubtedly follow any such concession, were suddenly confounded by their own vote in favour of emancipating Catholics.

Many Tories had forecast, mainly as a rhetorical flourish, that Catholic emancipation would 'open the floodgates' to more revolutionary demands for reform, and were horrified as their prediction started to come true. The change in public mood brought on by the Emancipation Act was swiftly compounded by the 1829 harvest, which was one of the worst ever. All through the winter months of 1829 and 1830, the rural poor in England and Ireland, already destitute, were plunged into a famine the like of which they had not seen since the years following the military triumphs of 1815. Supplies of food for the manufacturing districts dried up. At first the workers responded with sabotage. Over a series of nights early in 1830, 45 of the 107 furnaces in Staffordshire and Worcestershire were mysteriously blown up. Very quickly, as the remarkable year drew on, sporadic acts of violence and riot turned into a nationwide demand for parliamentary reform. The people who suffered most from economic distress automatically linked their distress to the fact that they had no control of their government. They were, they believed, victims of a corrupt electoral system that sent people to Parliament with the single intention of preserving the wealth and power of an irresponsible hierarchy.

This view was given new impetus by a series of dramatic events. In July, the regime of Charles X in France was overthrown by a revolution that seemed at first to be just as mighty as its predecessor in 1789. There followed, swiftly, a revolution in Belgium. In Britain, a new breed of agitators among the lowest of the low started to flourish once again. Publications were launched that openly defied the bans imposed by the Six Acts of 1819. William Carpenter published fourpenny *Political Letters*, and Henry Hetherington followed with penny papers. The penny papers were apparently unconnected with each other, and thus technically avoided the definition of newspaper, which would have incurred the hated 'stamp' tax. The first one, on 2 November 1830, spoke up for the poor and dispossessed in a rebellious tone that surpassed even Paine's:

It is the cause of the rabble we advocate, the poor, the suffering, the industrious, the productive classes! And rail at them as ye please, ye learned scribblers and ye well-fed puffed-up scribes and pharisees – yea the rabble are the only beneficial class in the community.

The springboard for such subversive sentiments was the National Union of the Working Classes, which brought together the disparate protest groups under one Radical umbrella. The union's first goal was root-and-branch parliamentary reform which would give every man the vote, regardless of his property, would ensure the regular re-election of Parliament, preferably every year, and would safeguard the secrecy of the ballot.

In 1829, there had been no petitions to Parliament calling for reform. In 1830, there were 645. The number of people signing these petitions was never officially counted, but many of them, like the one from unrepresented

Birmingham in May 1830, signed by at least 25,000 people, were enormous. Many of them called vaguely for reform without being specific about the nature of it. But a large number specifically demanded universal suffrage. To the horror of almost every MP, 280 of the petitions specifically insisted on the secret ballot to protect voters from victimization by their landlords and masters. Even more than the spreading of the franchise, the ballot threatened the control over elections that had been up to that time wielded exclusively by the rich. The frenetic, drunken farce whereby results of elections were publicly 'declared' was wide open to bribery. Secret ballot votes were unpredictable and much more difficult to bribe.

The centre of this Radical agitation was London, where Henry Hunt, who never wavered in his demand for universal suffrage and a secret ballot, joined forces with his old rival William Cobbett, a brilliant pamphleteer whose stream of publications such as *Register* and *Twopenny Trash* poured out relentless invective against what Cobbett called 'The Thing' – the untrammelled rule by the rich through a corrupt Parliament. From the early autumn, inspired by the two revolutions on the continent, Hunt and Cobbett spoke every night to vast meetings in the Rotunda in London's Blackfriars, calling for root-and-branch reform which would give the people the vote. Simultaneously, in Kent and the other Home Counties, an organized movement among farm labourers started to break frames and burn down hayricks. This movement, led by the mysterious 'Captain Swing', awoke in stately homes anxious memories of the equally mysterious Ned Ludd, whose campaign of frame-breaking had, for a few months in 1812 and 1813, so inconsiderately interfered with the smooth process of exploitation in the mills of Yorkshire and Lancashire. In December 1830, as though to consummate a year of unrelieved agitation, sabotage, strikes, and rick-burning, Henry Hunt was at last elected at a by-election in Preston. Preston had a relatively large electorate, but Hunt had tried there twice before and had ended up at the bottom of the poll. His triumph was a measure of the rapidly growing wrath at a system of representation that the vast majority of the population regarded as no longer tolerable.

What was happening in the cloistered seclusion of the House of Commons as these tumultuous events shook the country? The crazy year started crazily even there – with a motion for reform from the Marquis of Blandford, who up to that time had not expressed a single thought on the subject. He called for a committee to 'investigate the state of representation' with a view to extending the vote to all copyholders. Though Blandford's motion echoed the anger outside Parliament, it was jeered out, by 160 votes to 57. A few weeks later, Lord John Russell, who had spoken so urgently against reform during the last agitation, moved a standard motion to enfranchise the big cities of Manchester, Birmingham and Leeds. A sign of the shifting political mood was the small majority against him: his motion went down by 188 to 140. In May, the Radical MP Edward Davenport presented the enormous Birmingham petition for reform. The 'industrious classes', he said, were 'suffering greatly'. The key to their distress, he opined, was that 'property at present has a very unjust and improper influence' on Parliament and that that influence 'might be corrected by the ballot'. He called on his colleagues to attend to the state of affairs in the countryside 'before Parliament loses the confidence of the people and before they take the means of reform into their own hands'. Once again, this was laughed down. Mocker-in-chief was none other than the honourable baronet Sir Robert Peel, the Tory grandee, who told the House there was 'no distress' in the country because there was increased consumption of goods subject to excise duties. Moreover, he concluded with a flourish, the production of 'four-wheel drive carriages' had actually increased during the months of mass starvation and therefore he could confidently assert that 'there has never been less distress in Britain than at the present moment'.

No vote was taken on that occasion, but the House was roused from its slumber once again a few days later when, on 28 May, Daniel O'Connell, now the elected MP for Clare, showed his most radical face yet. O'Connell demanded universal suffrage and, before his motion was defeated by one of the biggest margins ever, he set out the bald figures of corrupt representation: only 134 MPs out of more than 600 were elected in any proper meaning of the word; 240 were under the direct influence of peers, and 159 had taken their seats after interference from the Commons in the way they were elected. The ballot, he said, would protect the poor voter from dependence on the rich, and 'every man of proper age and proper capacity should have the right of voting'. O'Connell's demands were not typical of him. He changed his view according to the political wind. The political wind at that time was blowing into a hurricane, and O'Connell swayed before it. But the enormous majority against his motion showed how sheltered from the hurricane were most MPs. While petitions signed by hundreds of thousands poured into the Commons demanding universal suffrage, only 13 Honourable Members could bring themselves to support the idea. The chief argument against it came from Robert Dundas, who scoffed at O'Connell that he might as well 'legislate against the accumulation of wealth and propose to alter the law of intelligence'. Dundas summed up the central argument against universal suffrage in a passage which would have been cheered by Cromwell and Ireton:

As long as aristocracy is essential to the Constitution and Crown; as long as that class of individuals has a large proportion of the land and wealth of the country, property will have its due weight in returning Members to Parliament, whether the right of voting is placed in the most popular and uniform basis, or is varied or restricted as at present.

Dundas argued that even the most radical proposal for electoral reform should stick to the iron law that the property-owning minority should have its 'due weight' in representation. The House overwhelmingly agreed with him. Later that day, Lord John Russell called for an extension of the basis of representation. He lost too – by 213 to 117. It seemed, even as late as May in that extraordinary year (1830), that the unreformed Parliament could never reform itself and that all demands for reform would be blocked by the boroughmongers and peers' placemen who seemed able at any time to muster a majority against any kind of reform.

As long as the movement for reform was confined to polite petitioning and staged Commons debates, it seemed doomed. Very quickly, however, it emerged that the Commons would reform itself as soon as MPs became infected with the same sort of fear that had stampeded them into granting votes to Catholics in Ireland.

In the general election that followed the death of George IV in August, it was clear that public opinion was running against the Tories. Only 83 constituencies were contested and only 175 new Members returned (out of a total of more than 600). But the Tories suffered some serious losses in seats where their opponents declared openly for reform. Fifteen of the seventeen new Members returned for the English counties were for reform. Yet the same Government took office under the same Prime Minister (Wellington) as though nothing had happened. Almost imperceptibly, however, the revolutions in France and Belgium and the 'Captain Swing' upheavals in the English countryside began to impress themselves on MPs. If any of them broke with custom and returned to their constituencies, they were as likely as not to be hooted at and abused by an angry crowd of potential rick-burners, and to be burdened with a reform petition to present to the Commons. On 16 November, much to their surprise, the Tory ministers were defeated by 29 votes on what was effectively a vote of confidence.

Very suddenly, after what seemed like an aeon, the Tories were out, to be replaced by a Whig Government under the inveterate champion of modest reform, the second Earl Grey. If he and his colleagues were in any doubt about the urgent need for reform, they had only to visit their estates, many of which were on fire by order of Captain Swing. The rick-burners seemed to come from nowhere and to have no regard for the views on reform of the gentry whose fields they were burning.

The newly appointed Whig Home Secretary, Lord Melbourne, reacted ruthlessly in the tradition laid down in 1819 by his predecessor Sidmouth. He set up a special commission with powers to convict anyone remotely suspected of rick-burning. Nearly 500 of the convicts were transported to Australia. But this time, in stark contrast to 1819, rising popular rage was not cowed. The aristocracy's genuine fear was summed up by the Duke of Rutland in a frantic letter on 31 October:

It is my firm belief that we are nearer to a tremendous explosion than we have ever been. It is hard to say how the poison has been so deeply and widely circulated in the minds of the people ... What do you say to a meeting held at Leicester when one of the speakers predicted that, ere long, not a vestige of nobility would be left in England; to which the whole meeting responded: 'The sooner it is done away with the better.'

The danger of insurrection was just as great as it had been the previous year in Ireland, if not greater, and the reaction in the new Whig Government was the same: to appear to concede the reform which the mass of people demanded while ensuring that the Government stayed out of reach for the mass of the people. The urgent need for people with property was to detach from the great body of the reform movement those middle-class elements that were supporting and in some cases leading it. So Lord Grey, the new Prime Minister, and his colleagues went into a prolonged huddle to prepare a parliamentary reform Bill that would concede enough votes to stop the rebellion but not enough to threaten their own power or wealth.

From this huddle of Whig ministers, the new Bill quickly took shape. The most scandalous of the rotten boroughs were to be completely disenfranchised, the slightly less scandalous deprived of one of their two MPs. In all, 168 seats were to be redistributed. Voting would continue to be by property qualification. The original preference was to limit the vote to those with property rated at £20 a year – but this would have reduced the electorate still further – in St Germans in Cornwall there was only one elector who would qualify, and he would elect one MP! So the Cabinet compromised on a £10 franchise – which would limit voting to about 8 per cent of the male population.

To start with, the Bill included the secret ballot but, on Prime Minister Grey's insistence, this was quickly dropped. No mention was made of how often Parliament should sit. The Bill was finally published on 1 March

1831, and the House of Commons debated its first and second readings for nine days.

The debate was opened by Lord John Russell. He announced at the outset: 'The whole people call loudly for reform', and then set out his plans for a reform which would restrict the franchise to a tiny minority of that whole people. He assured the House that the Bill would not 'destroy the power and privileges of the aristocracy'. On the contrary, the aristocracy was far more likely to be secure if the Bill was passed. 'It has now become a question,' he explained, 'of whether or not the Constitution would now perish if reform was defeated.' This theme was taken up three days later in a powerful speech in support of the Bill by Francis Jeffrey, the former editor of the *Edinburgh Review*, who had recently been appointed Lord Advocate in the Whig Government. Jeffrey defined 'the first and foremost of our duties: to detach the discontented and disenfranchised middle classes from the multitude'. The whole point of the property qualification in voting was that it acted 'as a pledge of the voters' interest and disposition to maintain that respect for property in general which all thinking men must feel to be at the bottom of their civil institutions'.

This apparent paradox was most brilliantly expressed in by far the most compelling speech over the whole nine days of debate, given by a young Member elected a few months earlier for the rotten borough of Calne. The prodigious genius of Thomas Babington Macaulay had gone before him to Parliament. The House had eagerly awaited a big speech from the young man, barely 30, who, legend had it, was writing critical essays at the age of four. Macaulay's speech on the first day of the debate on Reform surpassed even the most extravagant expectations. He opened with a blistering attack on the English aristocracy. He explained,

This is not government by property. It is government by certain detached portions and fragments of property, selected from the rest, and preferred to the rest, on no rational principle whatever.

[This is] an aristocracy the principle of which is to invest a hundred drunken potwallopers in one place, or the owner of a ruined hovel in another, with powers which are withheld from cities renowned in the furthest ends of the earth, for the marvels of their wealth and their industry.

'We are legislators,' he mocked, 'not antiquaries.' It was futile and absurd to attack the Bill because it disposed of ancient rights and privileges. The task facing the Commons was to defend something far more important: the very security of property. The object of the Bill was to unite all men of property in a rational system of representation which would then, in a coherent and disciplined manner, be able to deal with the 'terrible cala-mities' threatened by a people in revolt. Revolution was indeed in the air. 'I support this plan because I am sure that it is our best security against a revolution.' How, he asked, was the ramshackle and intellectually shocking representative system of the present Parliament going to defend itself against the social chaos that was emerging in both town and countryside? Were they to indulge in yet another bout of repression? Were they to bring forward yet another Six Acts, ban freedom of expression, censor the press, cut down public meetings? Such a course, Macaulay warned, would be far more dangerous even than it had been in 1794 or 1819. The distress in the countryside was greater than previously, and the revolt against it was increasingly supported by frustrated men of property who were inclined to throw their intelligence and even some of their means behind a movement that could sweep all property away.

The axis of Macaulay's speech was class. He referred to it over and over again. He spoke with pride and self-confidence of the middle class from which he came. In an extraordinary passage, so similar to the words which Marx and Engels used to open *The Communist Manifesto* 16 years later that it is hard to believe that at least one of them had not read it, Macaulay urged on his class to rid itself of the baggage of feudalism and medievalism from which the ludicrous representative system had emerged:

All history is full of revolutions, produced by causes similar to those which are now operating in England. A portion of the community which had been of no account expands and becomes strong. It demands a place in the system, suited, not to its former weakness, but to its present power. If this is granted, all is well. If this is refused, then comes the struggle between the young energy of one class and the ancient privileges of another. Such was the struggle between the Plebeians and the Patricians of Rome. Such was the struggle of the Italian allies for admission to the full rights of Roman citizens. Such was the struggle of our North American colonies against the mother country. Such was the struggle which the Third Estate of France maintained against the aristocracy by birth. Such is the struggle which the free people of colour in Jamaica are now maintaining against the aristocracy of skin. Such, finally, is the struggle which the middle classes in England are maintaining against an aristocracy of mere locality . . .

'The danger is terrible,' he said. 'The time is short.' Only the Bill could protect property 'divided against itself'. While the aristocrats Lord Russell and Viscount Althorp, the Chancellor of the Exchequer, implored the aristocratic MPs to come into line, Macaulay mocked and insulted them. If they wanted to safeguard their wealth, he threatened, they must spread the political control evenly among all people who had property, not confine it to the landed gentry.

Reading this extraordinary speech, it is hard to understand how it did not immediately triumph. The first day of the debate was indeed a walkover for the Bill's supporters. But as the debate wound on through March, the pendulum of MPs' opinion started to swing back to reaction. Despite the overwhelming arguments for some form of rational representation, the Tory Opposition stood firm and even began to make inroads into what had seemed like an impregnable majority for reform. Loyal Whigs started to join the Tories and speak up against the Bill. The arguments deployed by most of them seem pitiful today. They were responding to the adamantine obstinacy of the revered Duke of Wellington, who confided in his letters that the people, in his view, were 'rotten to the core'. To allow any change whatever in the representative system, he believed, would be to open the floodgates of rebellion. In April 1831, he wrote:

I see in thirty Members of rotten boroughs, thirty men, I don't care of what party, who would preserve the state of property as it is, who would maintain by their votes the Church of England, its possessions, its churches and universities; all our great institutions and corporations; the union with Scotland and Ireland; the dominion of the country over its foreign colonies and possessions; the national honour abroad and its good faith with the King's subjects at home.

In similar vein, the Bill's most ardent and persistent opponent in the House of Commons, the deeply reactionary Tory John Wilson Croker, praised the existing representative system. 'No human inequity,' he ventured, 'could have conceived so admirable a system, promoting in such nice and just degrees, the wealth, happiness and liberties of the community at large.' Such arguments, repeated ad nauseam, seemed on the face of it too ridiculous for serious argument. But behind all the bluster there was a serious point to persuade many uncertain MPs. The actual reform measures proposed were minimal. The number of people able to vote after the Bill, compared with the total male population, was marginal. Was it worth breaching the dykes so fiercely manned by the old Parliament for so little advantage? To reinforce this argument came gallons of rhetoric about the 'revolutionary' potential in the Bill.

At the centre of all the arguments was the old adage that if you give the people an inch, they will take a mile. Again and again the Opposition quoted from the petitions which were still pouring into the Commons. They asked for universal manhood suffrage, for the secret ballot, for triennial, even annual parliaments. None of these things were in the Bill, and its sponsors had declared themselves implacably opposed to all of them. But where was the guarantee that one concession to a call for reform might not lead to more and more of them? 'In a year or two,' warned Lord North, 'the Government might be embarrassed by the failure of the harvests, by some sudden panic or by some continental troubles: and at such a time it might be again asserted that all the grievances, real and imaginary, which could be enumerated, were owing to the defects of the representative system.' This fear that a concession to reform would not dampen down the agitation but stoke it up was the most forceful argument against the Bill. Sir Robert Peel summed up the general Tory apprehension when he said that ministers 'have sent through the land the firebrand of agitation and no one can now recall it'.

There was of course a principled argument against all this reaction: an argument for truly wholesale reform which would, by enacting universal suffrage, the ballot and annual parliaments, scotch for ever the protest that further measures would inevitably follow. Yet in Parliament there was only one MP who had the courage to express it. This was Henry Hunt, the new Member for Preston. Hunt was in a bit of a dilemma. He could not vote against the Bill and ally himself inextricably with the Tories who shared Lord Wellington's view of elections as 'evil'. On the other hand, he was contemptuous of the Bill, which he called 'a mere extension of the suffrage to the tenantry of the rich and powerful', without even a ballot. 'The tendency of such arguments,' he said, 'was that because the working classes were poor and because they were suffering, they were to be deprived of their rights.' The central principle of the Bill, he concluded, was the protection of property. Hunt voted for the Bill, but he reserved for it a special salvo of his rhetoric. He claimed that the lower people found themselves in the social scale, the more they needed votes.

So the arguments wound their way to their conclusion on 22 March 1831 – the crucial vote on the Bill's second reading. Sensing that the mood – in the Commons, not in the country – was drifting away from the Bill, Russell made a last despairing speech, first scaring the MPs that unless they brought in reform, the people would bypass them and 'introduce a representative system in which the higher classes would be but little considered'. He reassured them once more: 'I deny altogether that the measure would have the effect of rendering the House a democratic assembly – what I propose will not one jot advance democracy.' His favourite word was 'final'. This, he insisted, was, absolutely and beyond dispute, the 'final' measure of reform that the House of Commons would ever have to pass. These promises later earned Russell the nickname Finality Jack.

The vote on the second reading was held amid scenes of great excitement. The count was so close that it was repeated, twice – 304 MPs voted for the Bill, 303 against: a Government majority of one. The English MPs were against the Bill by 241 to 238; the Scots against by 26 to 13 and the vote was carried only with the help of the Irish, who were for it by 53 to 36.

The celebrations of the Whigs were short-lived. With such a tiny majority, how could they hope to get the Bill over the towering obstacles confronting them – the committee stage where half the committee were preparing destructive amendments and, above all, the House of Lords where even prominent Whig peers recoiled at the slightest whiff of reform? The reformers were boosted a little by further elections in April, in which the Tories were reduced to a Commons rump almost exclusively 'elected' from the rotten boroughs. In July 1831, the new Commons supported a new Reform Bill indistinguishable from the old one and shovelled it through 40 exhausting days in committee. But the House of Lords loomed large, and the Tories were organizing there. On 15 July, eight days after the new Bill got its second reading in the Commons, the Duke of Wellington wrote to his brother Henry, the newly ennobled Lord Cowley, who was Britain's Ambassador in Vienna:

I don't believe that there is a man in England who does not think that this Reform must lead to the total extinction of the power and the property of this country ... the mob, the Radicals, the dissenters from the Church of all religious persuasions hail the Bill as the commencement of a new era of destruction and plunder.

Naturally, in such a crisis, the Duke 'earnestly' urged his brother to start his journey back to England to use his vote in the House of Lords against the Bill. The debate in the Lords went on for six days, from 3 to 8 October 1831. The arguments were a much more reactionary version of the March debates in the Commons. Grey and the Whigs desperately rehearsed the Whig pleas that the Bill was intended to stop a revolution. An almost incoherent Wellington and the Tories, including almost all the bishops, argued on the contrary that the Bill was intended to create a revolution by due process of law. This 'argument' won the day – the Bill was thrown out by 41 votes. It was, for the moment, dead. On their own, despite their original and substantial Commons majority, the parliamentary reformers seemed frustrated by their own undemocratic procedures.

The path to reform was cleared, however, by a new effort from the voteless multitude who flooded once more on to the political stage. All through 1831, the sleeping giant of popular protest had stirred in fits and starts to frighten Whigs and Tories alike. The most serious outbreak was in the mining town of Merthyr Tydfil, South Wales. The trigger for the rising in Merthyr was pulled by the Court of Requests, a state pawnbroker that had the power to seize the furniture and other property of the poor and hold it in exchange for unpaid taxes. On 2 June, after a mass rally in the hills above the town, bands of workers, plainly organized and acting with great determination and self-control, went from house to house writing down how much property was held by the Court of Requests. The bands then stormed the Court's warehouses, seized the confiscated property and returned it to its owners. To their horror, Merthyr's magistrates quickly appreciated that this was no isolated riot but an organized insurrection. The thousands of workers in the town's huge ironworks came out on indefinite strike and an 'army of redressers' set out from the town to call out the people of the surrounding villages. When a detachment of Argyll and Sutherland Highlanders marched in to restore order, the soldiers were repulsed, and for four days the working people held the town against all comers. Twice more, troops and yeomanry were put to flight. Whig 'order' was restored only when the Home Secretary, Lord Melbourne, in high panic, sent to Merthyr a troop of 450 soldiers with levelled muskets. Even then, the thousands of massed townspeople could easily have overwhelmed the troops. But at the crucial moment of confrontation there was a sudden and inexplicable failure of will and determined leadership. The soldiers, sensing victory, opened fire. At least two dozen of the rebels were killed, and 70 of them seriously wounded.

The magistrate who reported on the scene two weeks later opined that such a thing had 'never, I believe, happened in England before'. Mrs Harriet Arbuthnot, a strong supporter of the Duke of Wellington, whose voluble diary gives a revealing picture of ruling-class reactions at the time, wrote:

There has been a great riot in Wales and the soldiers have killed 24 people. When two or three were killed at Manchester, it was called the Peterloo massacre and the newspapers for weeks wrote it up as the most outrageous and wicked proceedings ever heard of. But that was in Tory times. Now this Welsh riot is scarcely mentioned.

Mrs Arbuthnot was never the most reliable chronicler. In fact, 11 people were killed at Peterloo, and most of the newspapers reported the massacre as a brave and courageous intervention by the yeomanry to defend Crown and Constitution. But in another sense her point had some force. The Merthyr rising was a far greater threat to authority than Peterloo had been. Many times during the rising there had been serious talk of spreading the action all over Wales and the industrial Midlands. Melbourne and the Cabinet knew perfectly well that all their troops and spies were impotent to deal with such an insurrection. They concluded that the fewer people who understood the nature of the rising, and the authorities' vulnerability to it, the better. Both Government and press ignored or patronized the rising, which remained effectively hidden from history until 1978, when Gwyn Williams published his book about it.

Central to the rising was the demand for reform. Insurgents had moved around the town under big white banners carrying the single word REFORM. The reform they were calling for was completely different from that proclaimed by the Whig ministers. In the debates in the Commons in March, John Wilson Croker had singled out the petitions from Merthyr to demonstrate to the House that the people there wanted much more than the disqualification of a few rotten boroughs. They wanted the right to vote in secret for the government of their choice. The people of Merthyr, Croker had reported, demanded annual or biennial parliaments, a secret ballot and universal suffrage. At the top of their list was the demand to dismiss all placemen and pensioners. What the people of Merthyr wanted was something quite unrecognizable compared to what was being proposed by Lord John Russell, Viscount Althorp, Lord Advocate Jeffrey or even Thomas Babington Macaulay. There was not the slightest sign of what was later alleged – that the popular agitation was inspired and provoked from above, by the Whig grandees, to frighten Tories into supporting the Bill. The Whigs were every bit as terrified as the Tories by what happened at Merthyr.

That summer of 1831, the broadsheets and penny papers which reflected the demands of the working people were consolidated and strengthened by the publication on 9 July of the first issue of Henry Hetherington's *Poor Man's Guardian*. The new paper was an expression of an entirely different view on reform from anything (or almost anything) said in either House of Parliament. The very first issue made absolutely clear where the paper stood on the Reform Bill: 'We are so fully convinced that the Reform Bill is nothing to you, friends and fellow countrymen, that we will not occupy our columns at the expense of more valuable matter.' Week after week, the *Poor Man's Guardian* denounced the Bill's property qualifications for voting. William Carpenter's *Political Letters* spelt out the same message. One contributor put it better than most:

Of the utter insincerity of the Whigs what further proof do we want than that they have always had the power of compelling a reform of the House of Commons to any extent they wished? Yet they never till now made the slightest effort to do so; and now (if I am not completely deceived) their policy is to effect a sham reform which will have little else but the name: a miserable something which will have the semblance without reality – a something to stop the people's mouths for a season.

The author of this prophetic analysis was a young journalist just over from Ireland, James 'Bronterre' O'Brien. O'Brien was soon to become the most eloquent writer of his time on behalf of the voteless millions. At exactly the same time that Macaulay was hailing the Reform Bill as a wonderful measure to help emancipate a new class, the capitalists, O'Brien was denouncing the Bill because it froze out a newer class still – a class exploited by the capitalists, the working class. In a pamphlet distributed in February 1831, O'Brien wrote:

Look then at the monstrous injustice done to the wealth-producing or labouring people. It may be thus stated in a simplified way: they are compelled by laws, in the framing of which they have no voice directly or indirectly, to raise property to the amount of £150m annually to be distributed, under innumerable names and pretences, among men who give them nothing valuable in exchange . . .

Here, as clear as ever, was the basic argument of the Levellers, which had been so conspicuously missing from the long and tedious debates in the House of Commons: that no Parliament had the right to make laws to direct people's behaviour unless all those people had a free say in choosing that Parliament. To those who replied, as Ireton did in 1647 and the whole Whig Government did in 1831, that the choice of government should be available only to those with property, O'Brien, Hunt and their newspapers argued that those without property needed and deserved the vote even more than those with property. Hunt summed the whole argument up in a glorious passage in the middle of a speech at Leeds at the end of his triumphant autumn tour:

I am not for disfranchising any man, but if any, it should be the rich man. I say to the rich man: 'You have got money, you have got influence, you have friends to protect you; but the poor man has nothing on earth to protect him except his political rights.'

Here was the three-sided background to the decision by the House of Lords to vote down the Reform Bill in the second week of October 1831. On one hand, the aristocracy and the Tory Party resisted, in the interests of old property, any measure of reform; on the second, the capitalists, merchants and at least some of the Whigs proclaimed a measure of reform which would restrict the vote to their close periphery; and on the third, the most articulate tribunes of an increasingly angry multitude refused to cooperate with any reform measure which excluded the majority who had no property at all.

The reaction of all three to the defeat of the Bill in the Lords was predictable: the Tories and the aristocracy were relieved, the Government and the new bourgeoisie depressed and apprehensive, and the militant representatives of the working class indifferent. All were entirely unprepared for the great outburst of popular indignation that followed the Lords vote. Within weeks, several English cities were engulfed in flames. At Nottingham, the huge castle of the Duke of Newcastle, a prominent House of Lords opponent of the Bill, was burned to the ground. At Derby, gangs of angry men roamed the streets at will for four days. They sacked the jail and released all the prisoners. They broke the windows of anyone who was thought to oppose reform. On 9 October, Mrs Harriot Mundy, who lived in a stately home at Markeaton near Derby, wrote to her mother: 'Last night, just as we were nearly all in bed, a large mob came from Derby (having just heard of the Lords vote on reform) and surrounded the house, shouting and halloaing, and smashed all our windows and broke in many doors and frames of windows . . . luckily we were very strong in point of man-servants.' Three days later she wrote again: 'the worst of being so near the town is that one hears shouting and halloaing of the people and any guns that are fired, which is very disagreeable . . .'

The Derby riots scared the wits out of the local gentry, who did not recover from their terror until the entire town was occupied and patrolled by troops. Even more disturbing were the riots at Bristol following the opening of state trials at the Assizes by the Bristol Recorder, Sir Charles Wetherell MP. Wetherell had been a bitter and uncompromising opponent of the Reform Bill. He had endeared himself to the people of Bristol by hurling insults at all those who were mean and stupid enough to live in property rated at only £10. These people, he exclaimed in horror, would now get the vote, and he would have to canvass them! He would not do so, he announced, because it was, he said, beneath his dignity as a Member of Parliament to 'solicit votes in the lazaretto'. He was, in short, a pompous ass, roundly detested by the disenfranchised majority.

The news, much publicized, that he was coming with an armed guard to celebrate the defeat of the Reform Bill by opening the Bristol Assizes was greeted with something close to an insurrection. For seven days, the city was held by unnamed and unknown young men, many armed with muskets. Their chief target was the hotel where Sir Charles was staying. So menacing was the crowd that besieged the hotel that Sir Charles, who had made much of his 'determination to uphold the King's peace' by going to Bristol against Government advice, had to flee over the rooftops in his underclothes in the middle of the night. The four prisons in Bristol were burned to the ground. So were fashionable Queens Square, the Mansion House, the Custom House and the Bishop's Palace. Seventy people, including several soldiers, lost their lives before the large military force dispatched to the city by Home Secretary Melbourne prevailed. Upper-class panic in Derby and Bristol quickly spread to London, where Lord Fitzroy Somerset, who later became Lord Raglan and presided over the disastrous Charge of the Light Brigade in the Crimean War, engaged in earnest discussions with his former general in the Peninsular War, the Duke of Wellington, about the military movements necessary for the protection of London.

The likelihood was, Somerset predicted, that there would be 'a riot with a view to the attack of obnoxious persons, the destruction of property, and the subsequent overthrow of the King's Government'. Somerset then set out his proposals for the deployment of three battalions of guards, the 9th Lancers, the 7th Dragoon Guards, a squadron of Greys, twelve big guns, four battalions of foot guards and 500 marines. 'This,' he wrote apologetically, 'is all the force we can at present muster.' The whole armed might available was to be deployed in response to the calling by the reformers of a single public meeting at White Conduit Fields. 'Your preparations go too far,' the Duke replied to Somerset. 'If you are to take up positions with your troops as often as the turbulent adherents of the Government assemble a mob, you will soon wear them out.' He recommended a more sober, though still substantial, deployment of troops in London. There was more bad news for the Duke three days later, on 5 November, when Guy Fawkes was replaced on the bonfires by effigies of himself and the Tory Opposition in the Lords. His friend the Bishop of Exeter wrote nervously to him:

There are strong indications . . . of insurrection against property among the lowest orders. This detestable Reform Bill has raised their hopes to the utmost . . . almost all the artisans are in full hopes of an equalization of property . . . the principal manufacturer in the city [Exeter] told me today that all his men, 100 in number, refused to be signed in as special constables – they told him that they could not lose by a change.

In those few weeks in November, there was real fear among rich men and women that their property was in peril from popular insurrection. Tory diehards and the aristocracy blamed the Government. Wellington's caricature of a 'mob-ridden government' was taken up and proclaimed far and wide by the *ancien régime*. A giant conspiracy was afoot, so the diehards alleged, between ministers and incendiaries to throw out the whole social order. Thus the Earl of Ellenborough, formerly President of the Board of Trade in Wellington's ministry, recorded in his diary:

The ministers are willing to receive the assistance of the revolutionists in order to produce terror and thus carry the Bill by which they are to stand or fall. The revolutionists take the assistance of the ministers, using them as tools, to effect an object which, once gained, gives them in its results all they want . . . they are creating a power over which they will have no control.

The view that milords Russell, Althorp and Grey were actively conspiring with revolutionists was, of course, ridiculous. The whole point of their Bill was to stave off insurrection by absorbing people of property into parliamentary politics. But there was a small grain of truth in Ellenborough's wild allegations. The Whig ministry was, temporarily at least, paralysed by the Lords vote against their Bill. Parliamentary procedure dictated that the Bill must fall, and a new one had to be presented, its future every bit as uncertain as its predecessor's. The ministry was split. Some ministers recommended caution, others threatened resignation, others urged more militant progress. In the vacuum created by their splits and uncertainties, ministers were reluctant to react too sharply to the riots. The London *Times*, on the day after the Lords vote, summed up what most Government supporters were thinking. An editorial on 10 October hailed 'the just indignation which is felt by the British people on the rejection of their Reform Bill. Everywhere they are in movement . . .' The suggestion was that this 'movement' was justified retribution against those responsible for the defeat of the Bill. Of course, the Whig leaders, led by Home Secretary Melbourne, and the editor of *The Times* were horrified by the violence that followed. The riots were eventually put down by routine repression (four unknown men were hanged at Bristol). But there was nevertheless a pause in the reaction, a moment when the anger of the people was not cut down with the usual determined savagery, a nod and wink across the floor of the House of Commons that if the Reform Bill was junked for ever, nothing could contain the forces of violent revolution which were seething everywhere.

This faint sense of a conspiracy between the Government and the rioters helps to explain the most unpredictable reaction of all – that of the spokesmen for the masses who gained nothing from the Reform Bill. A leading article in the *Poor Man's Guardian* of 5 November complained:

We regret that it is our duty to report the outrageous conduct of some of your fellow-countrymen . . . we have at all times decried the wilful destruction of what much labour has produced, and more especially we do so now, when it was induced, not by any public spirit to serve a public end, but by a private hope of gain or a brutal love of destruction.

The editorial went on to blame the real instigators of the riots as the Government and its 'priests and Lords' who treated the people like beasts and then complained when they behaved accordingly. But the chief purpose and effect of the editorial was to distance the reformers from the riots. Henry Hunt, who had always advocated peaceful protest by mass demonstrations and strikes, was equally critical of the riots at Bristol and Derby. His speeches and those of his trade-union followers may explain why the riots were confined to cities where the influence of the organized reformers was weakest – and why riots did not break out with the same ferocity in the bigger cities like Birmingham or Manchester. Hunt's activities hovered forever on the margins of the law. He had already spent two dreadful years in Ilchester prison for his political activities. The *Poor Man's Guardian* was by definition, and by bold proclamation by its editor on its masthead, an illegal newspaper. None of these people wanted to risk prosecution for association with rioters with whom they had no connection and over whom they had no control – and whose riots had, they believed, disturbed their preparations for organized strikes and protests against both Government and Opposition.

Yet the riots were undoubtedly much more crucial than the *Poor Man's Guardian* and its supporters were prepared to admit. The voting down of the Reform Bill by the House of Lords was not seen at the time as a last-ditch stand by the ultras. After all, as several of their lordships argued, the Bill had been carried in the Commons by one vote. Against such a puny margin, even in spite of the election results, the Lords felt they were entitled to take a stand. In hindsight, the opponents of the Bill appear absurd reactionaries, but the commitment against the Bill of the Duke of Wellington, Peel, Croker, Lord Lyndhurst and many others was founded on the strongest rock of all: anxiety for their property. They genuinely believed that the small increase in the electorate and the abolition of a few rotten boroughs would strike at the very root of their livelihoods: their inherited wealth. After the Lords debate in November, there was not even a sign of surrender. These Tories meant to use every ounce of their constitutional strength to defeat the Bill and save their estates.

They knew, if they held fast, that they controlled the parliamentary timetable. They knew that the Whig Government was split all ends up, and that the large body of waverers in both Houses of Parliament would, at the slightest sign of a shift in the balance of the argument, come out in favour of the reactionaries and dispense with their lukewarm support for reform. If there had been no popular revolt against their lordships, if the people had appeared as quiescent over reform as their Tory patronizers pretended, even if the argument outside had been confined to petitions, meetings and peaceful protests, there was hardly a parliamentary observer who would have predicted that November that the Bill would be law within seven months.

The sharp change in the political atmosphere, and the surge in the confidence of the Government to confront the Lords and fight for 'the Bill and nothing but the Bill' can only be explained in terms of the tumultuous disturbances and the rise in insurrectionary violence after the Lords vote. The uneasy feeling in the stomachs of all men of property, Whigs, Tories and Radicals alike, that their castles and estates were in peril concentrated their minds wonderfully. However determined were Wellington's Tories to defeat the Bill, they could not banish from their minds the vision of Sir Charles Wetherell in his underclothes grappling his precarious way over the roofs of Bristol at dead of night. They might bluster that the agitations led by Hunt and the *Poor Man's Guardian* were all got up by the Whigs, but they knew in their hearts that no Whig conspiracy could possibly have been responsible for the burning of the Mansion House in Bristol or the liberation of the Derby prisoners. Government ministers knew even more directly that these riots could and almost certainly would continue to an extent where they could not be suppressed. So they bent themselves with even greater determination than previously to putting a new, very similar Reform Bill on the order papers and to driving it through Parliament with the greatest possible dispatch. The new Bill, which was presented by Lord John Russell on 12 December 1831, made several quite unnecessary concessions to the reactionaries, and was passed on second reading by 324 votes to 162. It sailed through the Commons and, on 13 April 1832, passed its second reading in the Lords by nine votes.

As it went to committee in the Lords on 7 May, the reactionaries made a final push to emasculate the already emasculated Bill to a state where it could no longer be described as a Reform Bill at all. Lord Lyndhurst moved to postpone any further discussion on enfranchisement until all the Tory amendments to restore rotten boroughs had been debated. This was too much even for the Government, which refused to accept the amendment. The waverers switched sides once again, and voted for Lyndhurst. The

Government was defeated by 151 to 116, and once again the whole Bill was in peril.

The crisis of 'the days of May' which followed is often described as if it were solely a contest between the 'great men' of the time: Grey, Brougham, Althorp and Russell for the Whig ministry on the one hand and the Grand Old Duke of Wellington on the other. The issue for all these gentlemen was simple. Should the Government create enough new peers to ensure the Bill's further progress in the House of Lords? On 8 May Prime Minister Grey and Lord Brougham, his Lord Chancellor, went to Windsor to ask the King for permission to create 60 new peers; and to offer their resignations if he refused that permission. The King refused permission for the new peers and accepted the ministers' resignations. The Duke of Wellington then scratched around the meagre and demoralized talent on the Tory benches to try to form a new Tory Government committed to getting the Bill through Parliament. He tried a repeat of his performance with the Catholic Emancipation Bill, which he had forced through Parliament three years earlier against his own and his colleagues' better judgement. This time, he met with stiffer resistance. Robert Peel, on whom the Duke based most of his hopes, refused point blank to have anything to do with such blatant hypocrisy. So did Croker and several other anti-reform Tories. The Duke had to confess to the King that he could not cobble together another Tory Government. The King sourly agreed to make the necessary new peers, the Whig ministers took up their offices once again and the Bill sailed through committee and the House of Lords third reading by 106 votes to 22. On 7 June 1832, the Bill finally got reluctant royal assent.

The Whig ministers' success in the days of May is usually ascribed to their own steadfastness, although steadfastness was never a Whig characteristic. On the contrary, the ministers were at constant loggerheads for most of the early months of 1832. Once again, the fate of the Bill was decided not so much by the characteristics of the ministers or by the numbers game in the House of Commons as by the movement in the country at large. There was, in those few days of May, no time to organize the kind of protest which had greeted the Lords blockage of the Bill the previous November, but there were all sorts of signs that the November protests would be doubled and redoubled if the Bill was once again ditched by the Lords. Mass meetings materialized as if from nothing – in London and Liverpool reformers' meetings shouted the new slogan: 'More Lords – or none!' The worst news for Government and Opposition came from Birmingham, where the reformer Thomas Attwood had used his mighty voice to bellow to a monster meeting of 200,000 at Newhall Hill that no one should pay a penny of their taxes until the Bill was passed. He reminded the vast throng, which constantly interrupted him with cheers, that the Government had no right to levy taxes on people who could not vote. He then reminded the people of their constitutional right to carry arms.

The rumour ran round the meeting – and Attwood did nothing to dispel it – that the Birmingham Political Union was sponsoring a mass march to London that very night (10 May). The rumour caused great anxiety among the officers of the Scots Greys, the regiment sent to Birmingham to police the growing reform movement there. One of them wrote:

We had been readily and nightly booted and saddled, with ball cartridge in each man's possession, for three days ready to mount and turn out on a moment's notice. On that day we were marched to the riding school, no prayers, and were employed all day in sharpening our swords on the grindstone . . . the purpose of so roughening the edges was to leave a jagged wound . . . On this memorable day we sharpened our swords to prevent these new boroughs from obtaining any representatives.

The non-commissioned officer who wrote that passage, Alexander Somerville, was himself an enthusiastic reformer. As the new Reform Bill progressed through the Commons he and his colleagues predicted that they were likely to be 'pressed' into armed action against their own countrymen, and made prodigious efforts to avoid such a conflict. In a series of letters and proclamations to Wellington and the War Office, they made it clear that they would 'not draw swords or triggers upon a deliberative public meeting or kill the people of Birmingham for attempting to leave their town with a petition to London'. This open defiance shook the War Office to its foundations. Not only was there every likelihood of enormous marches on London but the normally reliable Scots Greys were openly threatening mutiny if they were called upon to 'do a Peterloo' on the proposed reformers' march. The mood in Parliament in response to the threatened uprising in Birmingham and elsewhere was well described by Denis Le Marchant, who had been made secretary to his old Etonian school chum the Lord Chancellor, Lord Brougham, and who kept a lively diary. On 15 May, he wrote: 'Tuesday was an exciting day . . . The accounts from the country now poured in, and were of the most alarming description.'

He reported a visit to the Commons by Joseph Parkes, a Birmingham solicitor, who supplied the Government with information and had managed to keep aloof from the Birmingham Political Union until 10 May, when he declared: 'I and two others would have made the revolution on our own if necessary.' 'Parkes came on a deputation from Birmingham,' wrote Le

Marchant. 'He told me that it was with extreme difficulty that the people would be kept from coming to extremities.' An even more graphic account of the state of Birmingham was given to Le Marchant by the ageing General Rowland Hill, close friend and ally of Wellington. Hill described the state of public feeling there very forcibly:

The people are so excited that anything at all unusual throws them into confusion. A man blowing a horn is immediately taken for an express, and the arrival of a coach from London at an unusual hour emptied the workshops in an instant. Very little work is done. The workmen walk about talking of nothing but the Bill.

Le Marchant went on:

The account of the vote in the Lords was received as a public calamity. The churches and dissenting chapels tolled their bells the whole night. Well might the general in command be alarmed. He wrote to Lord Hill that he was wholly incapable of resistance in case of an insurrection . . . Strickland [George Strickland, MP for Saddleworth] showed me a letter from some of his leading constituents. They told him the people were tired of signing petitions and addresses. They wished to fight it out at once and the sooner the better. The fight was believed to be so near at hand that a manufacturer offered to supply the Birmingham Political Union with 10,000 muskets at 15s a piece. Bob Smith [a junior minister] told me that in his part of Bucks, the respectable classes came to the resolution of not acting as special constables.

Here was the ultimate nightmare for the ministry – not just the soldiers but also the 'respectable classes', the very gentlemen who had waded into the crowd at Peterloo, were refusing to take the oath as special constables. Whole sections of the 'respectable classes', who could in the past be relied on to protect property from the people, were now wondering whether they should instead protect the people from property. No more persuasive proof was needed that the respectable classes must be enfranchised immediately.

All this stiffened the resolve and confidence of the Grey ministry and at the same time knocked the stuffing out of the Lords ditherers. There really was a danger of insurrection, and the time had come to stop prevaricating, face down the idiot King, expose the iron Duke as a man of straw and ram the Bill through Parliament.

One question remains. The agitation which so scared the Whig ministers was not confined to respectable people. On the contrary, its thrust came from people who would gain nothing from the Bill. Why, then, were so many prepared to strike and march and protest for so few? It was a question that puzzled even Henry Hunt. At a huge meeting at St Peter's Fields,

Manchester, in 1831, he ridiculed the Bill: 'to give what they call the middle classes, which amount to about a million people, a share in the representation, in order that they might join the higher classes to keep seven millions of the lower classes down'. As the roars of 'hear hear' and 'shame' echoed across the field, Hunt bellowed: 'Do they propose to lessen our taxes?' ('NO' came the roared reply.) 'Do they propose to keep their hands out of our pockets? ('NO!') 'To give us cheaper bread, cheaper meat, cheaper clothing, to work us fewer hours, or give us better wages?' To the deafening crescendo 'NO, NO, NO!' Hunt asked: 'Then how the devil are you interested, pray?'

How the devil were they so interested? There are two answers, which partly contradict each other. The first was that the Reform Bill seemed to most people to be some sort of progress. It was true that the extension of the franchise was minimal but surely, people argued, there was likely to be some change, some advance on hundreds of years of hereditary hierarchy. After such an eternity of darkness, would there not be some break in the gloom, a tiny change at least which might, just might, lead to a better life for the majority? This response was based almost entirely and, as it turned out, futilely on hope. But there was much more than hope in the tumultuous popular agitation that forced the Reform Bill through. There was the unusual and as yet undeveloped feeling of the people's own power: a sense that by agitation, by striking, by defying the law about what they should read and when and where they should meet, by secretly storing arms and talking about them, they, the lowest of the low, had appropriated a fragment of the political power which had been held exclusively by the rich and powerful. This power could, it now appeared, change the political agenda. Again and again the masses had intervened to change the parliamentary timetable of the Reform Bill. Voteless men and women everywhere were suffused with the intoxicating feeling that they could, even in minor ways, seize the political initiative from their ancestral rulers. A new sense of political power was for the first time experienced by the politically powerless.

As the Reform Bill became an Act, as scores of the old rotten-boroughmongers left the House of Commons never to return, the Whig ministers congratulated themselves on the peace and calm in which they had passed their new measure. According to 'Finality Jack' Russell, the battle to extend the franchise had been won and need never be fought again. The matter of reform had been 'finally' dealt with. Now, with the help of their new middle-class voters, the Whigs could prepare themselves for a long period of peaceful exploitation. They reckoned without the rising expectations and rising confidence of the unenfranchised masses. The expectations would soon be smashed, but in the process the confidence would grow apace. This combustible mixture of popular political ambition and popular political power was not even noticed by Whigs or Tories. Neither party imagined that the mixture would blow up, or even started to imagine the extent of the resulting explosion.

Revolt of the Chartists

The Spirit that lifts the slave before his lord
Stalks through the capitals of armed kings,
And spreads his ensign in the wilderness . . .
Percy Bysshe Shelley, *Hellas* (1822)

As he gazed proudly at the vast crowd pouring in from every direction, huddling together for warmth on a freezing January afternoon, George Julian Harney, 21 years old, remembered the last time he had been in Derby. Three years previously, in February 1836, he had celebrated his nineteenth birthday skipping around the Derby streets avoiding the persistent stamp officer who had been specially sent from London to catch him. Harney had been asked to go to Derby by the Radical London bookseller B. D. Cousins, whose unstamped and illegal *Political Register* had been selling well there – until its seller had been arrested and sent to prison.

Harney knew exactly what he was doing and the risks he was running. He had already been in prison three times – for selling the *Poor Man's Guardian*. Before long, the stamp officer, who sent out spies to buy the newspapers so as to trap the sellers, caught up with him and he was up in front of the Derby magistrates once again. He made his usual defiant speech against the stamp laws, which, he reminded the magistrates, were not made by him or by his ancestors but by the iniquitous post-war Tory Government under the hated Lord Castlereagh. He got the usual six months. Serving the sentence in an especially nasty jail – the same Derby jail that had been burst open in the 1831 riots – had nearly finished him off.

When he was finally turfed out of the prison gates, he had no money, nothing to eat and did not know anyone in Derby. He set off for London and collapsed on the road from hunger and illness. Derby in 1836 was a cold and friendless place, especially for a determined campaigner for free speech, and he swore that he would never return there.

But now here he was again – in January 1839 and Derby was quite different. The local organizer for the new Chartist movement had begged him to be the star speaker at the first big Chartist rally in the town. Harney was delighted at the invitation. Derby had a reputation for caution and moderation, but there was nothing remotely cautious or moderate about the young Harney. Because so little had been organized by the Chartists in the town up to that time, he arrived a week early. For six days, he and the small band of local Chartists traversed the city speaking to small groups on street corners and knocking on doors. 'Are you fed up with the Government?' 'Do you want the vote?' 'What can we do about the new Poor Law?' they asked every citizen they came across. Almost everyone answered 'yes' to the final question: 'Are you coming to the meeting?' In the end, many thousands turned up. The local paper contemptuously put the figure at 1,200, but anyone could see that there were many more than that. For Harney this was a comparatively small turn-out.

The previous November, he had started out on a round of enormous rallies. In Norwich that month, in the company of the legendary orator Rev. J. R. Stephens, who with his fiery speeches and calls to arms did for Chartism what Rev. Hugh Peter had done for Puritanism 200 years previously, he spoke to a rally of more than 30,000. From Norwich, Harney went back, briefly, to his native London, but before long he was on the road again, this time to Newcastle upon Tyne, for two and a half freezing days on top of a coach, with no blankets and very little to eat. Arriving on Christmas Day, he spoke to a mighty outdoor meeting of 60,000 people. In the week after Christmas, he spoke every day at hastily summoned but packed rallies in the rural villages of Cumberland and Northumberland. On New Year's Day, he spoke to half the population of Carlisle. From there he plunged into Lancashire, where the reception was even warmer. He spoke at Preston, Bury, Ashton-Under-Lyne, Stalybridge and Leigh before crossing the Pennines for a huge meeting in Bradford. It was after the meeting in Bradford that he was invited to Derby, and here he was, on 21 January, looking down on one of the biggest public gatherings that that normally passive city had ever encountered.

Harney went over again in his mind what he wanted to say and how. They were looking for tough argument and solid guidance. People's livelihoods were at stake and they would give short shrift to any tub-thumper who came to town to toy with their distress. So Harney started where the Chartist movement started, with the argument for universal suffrage. He had been a founder member of the London Working Men's Association

(LWMA), which had launched itself in 1836 with a pamphlet entitled *The Rotten House of Commons*, a furious assault on what became for Harney a favourite phrase, 'mock reforms'. The Whig Reform Act of 1832 had proved itself to be more of a mockery of the poor and the voteless than even Henry Hunt or William Cobbett had ever imagined. Both those campaigners had died within a few months of each other in 1835, but neither, in their most doom-laden forecasts, had conceived how grotesque the image of reform would become in the hands of the rich, proud, smug Whigs who still sat in government.

In 1832, of the 13 million adults in England, Wales and Scotland, 720,784 had the vote. By 1839, after seven years of 'reform', the figure had crept up to 858,270. Of the total number of MPs, a third (219) were elected by fewer than 1,400 votes. Half the MPs were closely related to or descended from peers. Perhaps 12 per cent of adult males were entitled to vote before the 1832 Reform Act, and about 18 per cent after it. From the point of view of the vast, unenfranchised, majority of the population, the House of Commons was as rotten as it had ever been.

The LWMA pamphlet was followed by a meeting in February 1837 at the Crown and Anchor public house in London. A petition drawn up by the Cornish carpenter William Lovett was approved unanimously. The petition started with arguments that flowed almost word for word either from the American Declaration of Independence, which most people at the meeting had heard of, or from the arguments of Rainsborough and Sexby at Putney, which no one could have known about. 'Obedience to laws,' it began, 'can only be justly enforced on the certainty that those who are called upon to obey them have had, either personally or by their representatives, a power to enact, amend or repeal them.' Any laws made by a Parliament that did not give the people any power over them were merely 'despotic enactments'. Moreover: 'The universal political right of every human being is superior to and stands apart from all customs, forms or ancient usage; a fundamental right not in the power of man to confer or justly to deprive him of.' The petition then directed itself to the specific argument set out by wealthy men through the ages from Henry Ireton to the Home Secretary of the time, Lord John Russell. 'To take away this sacred right from the person and to vest it in property is wilful perversion of justice and common sense, as the creation and security of property are the consequences of society – the great object of which is human happiness.'

The petition set out six demands:

- equal representation – the division of the country into equal constituencies so that there should be no favour for any district;
- universal male suffrage – 'every male person over the age of 21 shall be entitled to have his name registered as a voter';
- annual parliaments, so that the people's mandate should be regularly and frequently renewed;
- no property qualifications for Members of Parliament;
- vote by secret ballot, to avoid bullying or bribing from masters and landlords; and
- regular sittings of Parliament during the year and payment of Members who attended.

These six points were incorporated in the People's Charter, which was published in May 1838 and which unleashed tremendous agitation throughout Britain's big cities.

The easy part of the speech was always this one, the demand for the vote. Yet Harney knew that the vast crowds were looking and hoping for something more. They approved the Six Points, and saw the People's Charter as a rallying standard which united the vast majority of the voteless. But they had come to this meeting hoping for more than the vote. They had come because of their distress, their hunger, their joblessness, their poverty. So Harney wound into his assault on the central policies of the Whigs since securing their so-called reforms. 'What about 1834?' he asked the crowd. How had the Whig Government and its haughty leader Lord Melbourne responded to the desperate cries of the common people in 1834? They had imprisoned and then deported six farm labourers from Tolpuddle in Dorset, whose only crime had been the secret swearing of a trade-union oath. This barbaric punishment coincided with the collective effort of the employers, especially in Derby, to smash what was left of the trade unions.

As the formidable alliance of Government and employers broke the workers' organizations, they also passed the new Poor Law Amendment Act. The Act had one purpose: to cut the relief paid to the poor. That relief amounted to about a fifth of the national budget. Under the old system, poor-relief money was allocated by local parish worthies, most of whom got the money back in rent or in their shops. The new Whig system abolished all such relief and provided only workhouses, where poor people of all ages and in all states of health mingled in scenes of unutterable degradation. The workhouses were prisons for the poor. Control over them passed from the parishes to a bureaucracy of commissioners who paid themselves huge salaries and concentrated on forcing the budget down.

The rationale for the new law came from Thomas Malthus, who argued that there were too many people in the world and followed his logic through to its inevitable conclusion: that poor, old and sick people who could not fend for themselves should be left alone to die. The architect of the new Act was Lord Brougham, a Whig grandee who had keenly supported the 1832 electoral reforms. Malthus, Brougham and the Secretary of the Poor Law Commission, Ewan Chadwick, were a detested trinity on whom the early Chartist orators, especially Stephens, poured a river of abuse and mockery. Harney called on his audiences to put the Malthus doctrine to the test. 'Let those who do not labour leave the land, let those who work not leave the country, and when the aristocracy betake themselves to Van Diemen's Land and the moneymongers to the devil, take my word for it, there will be enough for you and me.' Nothing went down better with his half-starved audiences than this mockery of the rich 'reformers'.

Every year since 1834, Harney went on, the miseries of the poor had increased. Not a single one of the confident predictions of the free-market Malthusians had come true. Wages had not gone up – they had come down. Employment had not gone up – it had come down. In Carlisle, he had only to gaze at the anxious and emaciated faces in front of him to appreciate the appalling fact that a quarter of the population were starving. Labour had not become more mobile. It had become more static, trapped in hopeless deprivation. Yet this abominable Poor Law Amendment Act, which he called the Poor People's Destruction Act, had sailed through the House of Commons with only 50 votes against.

The Whigs' two-pronged attack on the unions and on the poor had doubled and redoubled in ferocity through the desperate economic crisis of 1836 and the strikes it provoked. Harney singled out the trial of the leaders of the Glasgow spinners' strike, acquitted of the murder of a blackleg for which they had been arrested but found guilty of being part of an 'illegal association' and deported for seven years. Here were the two political parties in typical alliance, claimed Harney – the Tory Sheriff of Glasgow, Archibald Alison, who had opposed the Reform Act, and the Whig Judge Henry Thomas Cockburn who had supported it. When the working class struck against reductions in their wages, the Whig and the Tory united as prosecutor and judge in combined cruelty and repression.

The case of the Glasgow spinners led Harney on to another arch-enemy: Daniel O'Connell, the former emancipator of Irish Catholics, who had flirted with the Chartists when they were formed but who disassociated himself from the spinners' strike and all such actions. O'Connell divided protest into 'political' and 'industrial'. He was in favour of political action but against industrial action. Harney mocked the distinction. In his attacks on the Glasgow spinners, O'Connell had proved himself as bitter an enemy of the working people as Brougham or Cockburn or Alison. His mockery of O'Connell took his speech on to its central message. He was only 21, Harney observed, and had learned nothing from the authorities. Everything he'd learned came from the speakers and papers of the poor. His main mentor was 'the schoolmaster of Chartism', James 'Bronterre' O'Brien, who had been writing almost continually in the papers of the workers and the poor, especially in the *Poor Man's Guardian*, from 1831 to 1835, and wrote now in the new and astonishingly successful *Northern Star*. Harney had been prepared to go to prison three times for selling these papers because of his passionate determination to spread the message so brilliantly and succinctly spelled out by 'Bronterre'. O'Brien had taken the nickname 'Bronterre' to link himself, his politics and his papers to the French Revolution. He had come to England from his native Ireland with a respectable education and a degree, and had flung himself wholesale into the Radical movement. He discovered almost at once that he had a plain and infectious writing style combining mocking invective with meticulous reporting.

Bronterre had taken part in the agitation before the Reform Act and had warned against its consequences. He was a strong supporter of universal suffrage, but contemptuous of those who argued for it as an abstract 'right'. There was, he argued, only one point of universal suffrage – to set right the system of society in which the few exploited the many. Though he spoke on many platforms with men like J. R. Stephens who regarded the plight of the poor as an insult to God and the fundamental rights of human beings, O'Brien was not interested in God or fundamental rights. He was concerned with economic exploitation. The characteristic of the world he lived in that seemed to him incomparably more prominent than any other was its division by class. This division had always existed, he explained. There was no golden age in the past when the common people were treated decently:

The history of mankind shows that from the beginning of the world, the rich of all countries have been in a permanent state of conspiracy to keep down the poor of all countries, and for this plain reason: because the poverty of the poor man is essential to the riches of the rich man. No matter by what means they may disguise their operations, the rich are everlastingly plundering, debasing and brutalizing the poor.

The centre of this exploitation was the workplace. The 'idlers' at the top of society through their 'usury', 'profit-hunting' and 'moneymongering' gorged themselves on the 'fruits of another's labour'. They seized the surplus from the vast and limitless wealth created by workers in the factories, mines and mills.

This system of exploitation, O'Brien went on, was wholly undemocratic. The few ran the world so that they could plunder the many. The structures they set up were by their very nature undemocratic. In October 1834, he wrote in the *Poor Man's Guardian*:

Take a factory for instance – and is not the proprietor a sort of petty monarch? Has he not a sort of absolute control over all the wealth produced in it, though he has not added one single particle to that wealth? ... Is it right that one man should thus hold the lives of hundreds at his pleasure, or that he should be able to say to one man – 'stay and accumulate for me upon my terms', and to another 'go and starve for I do not want your services'?

And in another article that month he wrote:

The factory is governed by an autocrat, who is self-elected, and responsible to no one for the proceeds of the establishment. These proceeds are the sole result of the labour and skill of the hands employed – to those hands should the wealth therefore belong. But here the autocrat steps in and says: 'No, I am the master of this concern. I was appointed by you to organize and direct your industry; but you were commanded by me, under a penalty of starvation, to slave for me as you have slaved and to take as much as I gave you and no more' ... and so it runs throughout society – the monarchic principle prevails in all, and, as a consequence, all are slaves except a few great capitalists. The wealth which the people produce, instead of being a source of enjoyment to them, becomes an instrument for oppression in the hands of their task-masters.

No wonder, then, he went on to argue, that the capitalists and their sup-porters opposed any extension of democracy. Popular choice of government might lead to popular choice in the factories and mines. Indeed, Bronterre argued, the whole point of a political democracy was to install an economic and industrial democracy as well. There was, he argued in a key passage, which he emphasized, 'only one way' to stop the exploitation which plunged so many people in misery – 'to establish democracy not only in the Govern-ment but throughout every industrial department of society'. Directors and managers of factory policy should, for instance, each be elected and their remuneration subjected to the will of the majority.

In a stream of articles, Bronterre O'Brien returned again and again to this theme. He turned the old argument against democracy on its head. Henry Ireton, Edmund Burke and the Whigs of 1830–32 had all argued that only people with property should have the vote. O'Brien argued that the whole and only point in getting the vote was to redistribute the property of the few and to reorganize economic power in a democratic fashion. Whereas the Levellers and even Tom Paine had shrunk from the argument that political democracy must lead to economic democracy, O'Brien took the argument head on. Yes, he agreed with relish, once the majority had political power in Parliament they would use it to end their economic misery – and would do so at the expense of the rich.

Though he constantly attacked the rich, O'Brien reserved special venom for the middle classes, who had since 1832 snuggled under the wing of the rich. The middle classes, he argued, had designed and administered the new Poor Law and cheered on the persecution of trade unionists from Dorchester to Glasgow. Bronterre taught Harney a word both men used frequently to convey their detestation of the new middle classes: shopocracy – the monstrous army of shopkeepers with their sanctimonious Sunday suits and their precious privileges. The most important lesson of 1832 was that working men and women neither could nor should any longer rely on middle-class leaders to represent them. If they were to achieve anything, they had to represent themselves. 'Fellow countrymen!' O'Brien called out in the *Poor Man's Guardian* in the middle of the dreadful year of 1834. 'Be not deceived . . . What concerns us is that we ourselves be represented in the legislative body and that we employ our own power to emancipate ourselves from the middle class . . . Become your own governors in the workshop as well as out of it.' The conclusion was obvious: 'Universal suffrage can be of little use if applied only to political purposes. In fact it is only as an auxiliary to social reform, or as a means of protecting the multitude in the establishment of new institutions for the production and distribution of wealth, that universal suffrage will develop its virtues.'

This bold analysis had a profound effect on the new Chartist movement. The last part of Harney's Derby speech dealt with the strategy for the movement – what was to be done and how? The London Working Men's Association, which had first established the principles of the Charter, had been run by men who hoped to win the vote for the masses by rational persuasion. These made up what later became known as the 'moral force' wing of the movement, and were well represented by William Lovett in London and Thomas Attwood in Birmingham. In the first few months of the Chartist revolt, these 'moral force' men easily held sway. But as the agitation grew, and the petition started to gain mass support, the 'moral force' arguments ran into the sand. What was the use of rational persuasion when the people in power were wholly insensitive to reason? Did anyone really believe that the Whigs who drew up the Reform Act and the Poor Law Amendment Act would extend the franchise just because they were rationally convinced of the logical case for that extension? The contrary seemed to be true. The greater the argument for the franchise, the more impervious the authorities became to it. Since the whole point of franchise reform was to remove the people now in Parliament, why should Parliament approve it unless it was forced to do so?

So it was that as the Charter started to circulate, and as vast meetings gathered to hail it and sign it, so the argument shifted from political demands to economic demands, from passivity to activity, from 'moral force' to 'physical force'. Lovett and Attwood were replaced in popularity by Feargus O'Connor, another Irishman, an orator of alternating charm, humour and passion who could hold the attention of vast crowds for hours on end. In 1837, O'Connor launched the *Northern Star*, which was edited by Bronterre O'Brien. This was the first mass-circulation paper written for and sold to working people. O'Connor argued that the concessions the Chartists demanded would not be conceded without a fight, so there had to be a fight. Suddenly all the talk was of fighting. Harry Vincent, a charismatic young Chartist firebrand, swept through the West Country in a series of enormous meetings. 'Perish the privileged orders!' was his cry, which was taken up with vigour by two doctors from Wigtownshire in Scotland – Peter McDouall and John Taylor. McDouall and Taylor, in constant demand at mass meetings all over the North, argued that the days for prevaricating and petitioning were over and that it was time for a showdown.

George Julian Harney played a crucial role in this argument. He attended the original meetings of the LWMA but quickly grew angry and frustrated at the cautious tone adopted by its leaders. He wanted action. When he was voted down at the LWMA, he formed the East London Democratic Association which, as it quickly grew, changed its name to the London Democratic Association. Harney's youth, his good looks, his flowing hair and his infectious oratory brought him quickly to the attention of the Chartist organizers outside London. At his Norwich meeting the previous November, Harney was amazed at the near-fanatical enthusiasm with which 'physical force' arguments were greeted. When J. R. Stephens urged the huge crowds to 'fight with your swords, fight with pistols', he was cheered to the echo. On the platform with Stephens and Harney was the 'moral force' man John Cleave, whose speech calling for moderation and urging people not to provoke the authorities to violence, traditionally a popular theme, was heard almost in silence. Harney's triumphant tour of the North over Christmas and the New Year proved to him beyond any doubt that the 'physical force' men were in the ascendancy. All those arguments so patiently rehearsed by Bronterre O'Brien in the *Poor Man's Guardian* had suddenly exploded into popular consciousness. The end of Harney's speech at Derby that January afternoon left no one in any doubt what he was doing. He was calling the people to arms:

Our country may be compared to a bedstead full of nasty, filthy, crawling aristocratic and shopocratic bugs. In answer to our calumniators who say we wish to destroy property, I answer that we will not destroy the bedstead but we will annihilate the bugs!

My friends, we demand universal suffrage because it is our right, and not only because it is our right but because we believe it will bring freedom to our country, and happiness to our homesteads; we believe it will give us bread and beef and beer . . . We will make our country one vast howling wilderness of desolation and destruction rather than the tyrants shall carry out their infernal system. I have given you to understand that the men of the North are armed. I invite you to follow their example . . . Believe me there is no argument like the sword, and the musket is unanswerable.

The men of the North certainly were arming themselves. In his *Odd Book of the Nineteenth Century* (1882), T. A. Devyr reported in great detail the strenuous popular arming in the Newcastle area. Guns were disguised in wooden casings. The most popular weapon and the easiest to make was the pike. 'We computed,' wrote Devyr, '60,000 pikes made and shafted on the Tyne and Wear between August and November 1838.' In the huge torchlight meetings held at night so that workers could come straight from the factories and foundries, their faces still black with grime, the slogans, placards and speeches were all of violent vengeance against the rulers. R. G. Gammage, a historian of the Chartist revolt in which he took part, described a meeting at Hyde in Lancashire. No fewer than 15,000 torches lit up the posters: 'FOR CHILDREN AND WIFE, WE WAR TO THE KNIFE', 'HE THAT HATH NO SWORD LET HIM SELL HIS GARMENT AND BUY ONE', 'ASHTON DEMANDS UNIVERSAL SUFFRAGE OR UNIVERSAL VENGEANCE'. J. R. Stephens was the main speaker. At the end of his speech, in which he described the men who ruled the country as a gang of murderers who deserved the ultimate penalty, he reported on the rolling pageant of mass meetings he had addressed throughout the North. He had noticed, he said, that even the burial clubs, into which workers put small sums each week to pay for their funerals, were now diverting their funds to buy arms. Bellowing at full throttle,

Stephens asked the crowd: 'Are you ready – are you armed?' For answer there came from the crowd a single gun shot, then another. 'Is that all?' he asked. His answer was a mighty volley of shots. Still not satisfied, he urged the crowd to pledge themselves by a show of hands to buy arms. When a forest of hands went up, he said at last: 'I see it is all right, and I wish you goodnight.'

The ostensible purpose of most of these meetings was to elect delegates to the General Convention of the Industrious Classes. The idea of the Convention, which was conceived in the early discussions of the LWMA, was to elect through meetings of the disenfranchised an alternative parliament, a representative convention that would by example and through its debates challenge the unrepresentative Parliament at Westminster. The precise role of the Convention had not been properly worked out. Its only executive function was to organize mass signatures for the Charter. But undoubtedly in the minds of some of the people who set it up, its aim was to subvert the 'moneymongers' Parliament' by showing what a real workers' parliament would do. A minority of the delegates who attended the opening of the Convention a few weeks after Harney's speech at Derby half-hoped to establish a system of dual power. They wanted the Convention to usurp the functions of Parliament and establish itself as a genuinely democratic representative power base. As the Convention assembled, it quickly became clear that such notions were fanciful.

The Convention met at the British Coffee House in Cockburn Street near the Strand in London. There were 49 delegates, all men, most of them respectable and middle class. At once the delegates were plunged into days of argument about what they were there for. One group, the most respectable, insisted on declaring by resolution that the only purpose of the Convention was to organize the petition for the Charter. When this resolution was voted down, the group resigned. The remaining delegates discussed tactics if the petition to Parliament was refused. Some thought they should continue the 'moral force' campaign of persuasion. The others, growing in influence under pressure from the people they represented, called for preparations for war. The argument was still going on when the Convention, in an effort to get closer to the seething masses it was trying to represent, moved to Birmingham in May. After a week's discussion, the Convention adjourned until 1 July. Its members dispersed all over the country to fill the insatiable demand for speakers at endless and enormous meetings.

In the spring and summer of 1839, Britain came closer to an armed revolution than ever since. Every speaker noticed the astonishing change in the mood of their supporters. In Lancashire, Yorkshire and especially in the North-East, there was regular drilling and instruction in the use of pikes and guns. Everywhere the armed and starving workers wondered out loud when and where 'the thing' would happen. Hundreds of thousands of people were looking for a lead. So rapid was the rise in revolutionary preparations that the authorities were taken by surprise. The idea of a national police force had only just taken root, and the recruitment among the middle classes of special constables was hindered by a mixture of fear of the Chartist forces and sympathy with their plight. Even the magistrates were infected with distaste for the Poor Law and the condition of the people who flooded into their courtrooms.

The forces of law and order came to rely almost exclusively on the army, whose northern battalions were in the charge of General Sir Charles Napier. Napier was as sympathetic to the Charter as he was determined to stamp out any popular rebellion to enforce it. His letters and dispatches reveal a permanent nervousness about the volatility of the mutinous masses and the inadequacy of his forces to deal with them. Perhaps his greatest fortune was the strange fact that in 1839 there was little or no response in Ireland to the mass agitation in England. Six regiments – three each of infantry and cavalry – were brought over from Ireland in the first six months of 1839 and placed at Napier's disposal. Without these, Napier would have been sorely stretched. His comments during that time waver between self-confidence and nervous uncertainty. He understood better than many of the Chartist leaders that the North of England was a tinderbox that could be set alight by a single spark. He concentrated his troops in five areas and insisted that they kept together in large detachments. He was anxious about the prospect of a single random military victory by Chartists over even a small or isolated military unit. 'Should one detachment be destroyed,' he wrote, 'the soldiers would lose confidence; they would be shaken while the rebels would be exalted beyond measure.' The confidence of each side was, Napier reckoned, the determining factor in a struggle he was determined to avoid. This caution informed all his tactics. In May, when the revolutionary mood was at its most ferocious, he laid detailed plans to isolate the areas of agitation that seemed to him most dangerous. Some Chartist leaders, notably Harney, were pressing for a mass Charter march on London – a demonstration that in Napier's view would set off a huge number of unpredictable and uncontrollable sympathy meetings and marches. Napier had also been talking to workers in Manchester. If the workers of that city could confine the demands in their strikes to local wage increases, Napier felt safe. The moment they started to link up with one another and act together – as he feared they would on 25 May – the game was up for the military. Fortunately for him, the march to London never started and the huge meetings in Manchester at the end of May dispersed peacefully.

If their general in the North was worried, there were few signs that the Government had any conception of the mounting danger. The parliamentary debates for 1839 show little or no concern by ministers or backbenchers at the seething discontent of the people they pretended to represent. In February, Tom Duncombe, the Radical MP for Finsbury in London and one of the very few in the House of Commons who even noticed the plight of the people who could not vote, moved an extension of the franchise. He referred in passing to 'a Chartist parliament assembled within a stone's throw of this House'. This was the only parliamentary reference to the Convention during all the time it was sitting down the road in Cockburn Street. On 9 April, Lord Sibthorp asked the Home Secretary about the rumour he'd heard from his friends in the North that thousands of people in Manchester were making pikes. Lord John Russell replied breezily that he was 'looking into it'. In answer to another question, on 30 April, Russell conceded that 'there had been reports for some considerable time with respect to arming in parts of the country and especially in Lancashire' and that he had been 'in correspondence' with the army authorities about it. So deeply concerned was he by the cataclysmic events of May that he adjourned the House for most of the month. This complacency continued through June. It was inspired partly by the traditional arrogance of Whig ministers who believed that they, the enlightened aristocracy, governed on behalf of the people and that therefore any sustained hostility from the people was impossible. More importantly, Russell was anxious to keep his general's plans away from the public gaze. For all his smugness in the Commons, he knew direct from Napier's dispatches how serious the situation was. His instinct was to keep Parliament in the dark. He did not even boast about the considerable steps he had already sanctioned to curb the Chartist threat – a total ban on torchlight demonstrations; an order to magistrates to arrest speakers after Chartist meetings when the crowd was dispersing; and the arrest in May of two of the most effective and popular of the Chartist agitators, Harry Vincent and Peter McDouall.

On 12 July, the Chartists' great day, the climax of all their activities for a year or more, the national petition was brought by carriage to the House of Commons carrying a million and a half signatures. Much was made by the petition's enemies of double-signing and false entries. But even if all these mostly bogus allegations were taken into account, the genuine signatures represented more than twice the entire electorate for the House of Commons. The mildest possible motion – to debate the petition in a Commons committee – was moved by Thomas Attwood, the veteran banker who had been associated for years with the leadership of the campaign for universal male suffrage in Birmingham. Attwood referred sarcastically to the 'fruits of the Reform Bill' – the repressive Coercion Bill in Ireland and the Poor Law Amendment Act – 'more odious than any other new Bill since the Conquest'. He stressed the patience of the people in demanding their right to vote – their constant petitioning met with constant rebuffs. He repeated many times and in several different ways what Rainsborough had said at Putney: that the poor had as much right to vote for their government as the rich. He urged MPs to consider 'the thought that the Commons of England ought to be the Commons of England'.

On the demand for payment of Members, Attwood urged 'that the commons should send into their House men accustomed to the calamities of the people'. Foxes, he pointed out, made poor representatives for geese. In other words, 'the man whose bread and the bread of whose children depends on his labour has as great a stake in the country as the Duke of Northumberland'. He ended by reminding the House what had happened to Louis XVI and Charles X of France, who had 'been out hunting when the Crown fell from his head', and directed their attention to the 'social volcano opening under their feet . . . we cannot tell when it will burst'. Attwood was seconded by the only other genuine Chartist supporter in the House, John Fielden, and supported with lukewarm rhetoric by four or five Radical Members. The best speech in support of the Chartists came from the novelist and young Tory MP for Maidstone, Benjamin Disraeli. Disraeli mocked his colleagues' suggestion that the Chartists were motivated solely by a desire for sedition. He referred to Chartism as 'this great movement' and to the Poor Law Amendment Act as 'a very great blunder'. He ridiculed the traditional Tory argument, much favoured by the Tory leader Sir Robert Peel, that the disturbances were all the fault of the Reform Bill that had let into office a class of people who took the power without the duties. He sympathized with the Chartists, he said, and asked sarcastically whether 'the noble Lord [Prime Minister Melbourne] had his colonies in a condition so satisfactory . . . and his monetary system was in so healthy a state that he could afford to treat with such nonchalance a social insurrection at his very threshold'. He concluded with a warning that 'seeds were sown, which would grow up to the trouble and dishonour of the realm'.

A few years later, Benjamin Disraeli wrote a novel about the Chartists. It was called *Sybil, or the Two Nations* (1845), a deeply sympathetic and beautifully written account of the rise of Chartism and of its appeal to the suffering masses. The central theme of the novel is the distinction between 'moral force' Chartism, espoused by the unblemished heroine, Sybil, and 'physical force' Chartism, described with obvious distaste. The theme of the novel was that the conflict between the good on the 'moral force' side and the evil on the 'physical force' side became so bitter that it could not be solved by mere working people. The solution had to come from outside, from on high, from a brilliant, sensitive and eloquent Tory MP, Charles Egremont. Sybil's disillusionment with her rougher supporters, who include her beloved father, begins when she reads an account of an emotional speech in Parliament by Egremont, who then conveniently arrives in the midst of 'physical force' chaos to carry off his beloved and make a lady of her. The inspiration for this banal ending to what starts as a furious polemic is only too obvious. In the end, however intractable the social problems, they can best be solved by the Good Tory arriving in the nick of time on his charger. As we shall see, Disraeli returned to this theme later – as Chancellor of the Exchequer and later as Prime Minister. In July 1839, he spoke up persuasively for the arguments in the Chartist petition – and then voted to reject it.

The debate was ended, inevitably and as usual at insufferable length, by Lord John 'Finality Jack' Russell. Cut out the repetitive bombast which passed for parliamentary eloquence, and Russell was saying that to concede a demand made by the threat of force would imperil the whole future of authority. The real argument against the Chartists was that the established order, military authority, colonial authority, fiscal authority, the very essence of law and order itself was threatened by their revolt. Worst of all, these new revolutionaries threatened to strike at the root of all those authorities: the inalienable right of the rich minority periodically to plunge the majority into penury.

Even Lord John Russell might have been embarrassed in ordinary peace-time conditions to commit himself to such a crude version of the old rulers' motto: 'The poor are always with us, so let us thank God we are rich.' What forced this out of him was the concentration, even by wealthy MPs like Attwood and Fielden, on the economic arguments for the vote. The Six Points of the Chartist petition seemed mild enough. On their own, they might well have gone on to a Commons committee for further deliberation. But coming as they did from enraged and poverty-stricken masses whose representatives were calling for an armed uprising, the proposals could not even be contemplated. Russell did not need any more support. When the vote was taken, only 46 MPs voted to consider the petition further; 235, including Disraeli, voted against.

The news of the vote was passed on to an already inflamed mass movement. Since the Chartist Convention had adjourned at the beginning of May, the delegates had been engaged in a ceaseless array of public meetings in every town and city in the country, all of them demanding the vote and all of them threatening dire consequences if it was denied. The meetings were bigger than ever before. Even in small, relatively comfortable towns like Bath, thousands of people turned out to cheer the speakers and swear vengeance on the authorities. The meetings were combined with disturbances and riots, the most prolonged and serious of which were in Birmingham. The authorities had plainly decided to teach the Chartists a lesson even before the petition came to Parliament. In the week before the Commons vote, a gang of newly recruited Metropolitan policemen – called 'Peelers' after their founder, Sir Robert Peel – tried out their new equipment and powers on an unarmed and peaceful demonstration in Birmingham's Bull Ring, a traditional place for public meetings. Declaring the demonstration illegal and seditious, the police charged into the crowd batoning anyone in range. The crowd showed none of the meekness that had cowed the demonstrators at Peterloo 20 years previously. They fled the batons, regrouped in the narrow streets around the Bull Ring and charged the astonished police with tremendous ferocity, wounding many of them with railings torn from the side of the streets. The police were pursued to their quarters, battered, abused and humiliated. The riots went on at Birmingham throughout 12 July 1839 – the day of the Commons vote – and afterwards. Young people everywhere started to respond. The youth of working-class England, and Scotland too, was on fire.

A small group of the Chartist Convention met on the following day to decide the next move. Their initial reaction was to fall back on a series of previous resolutions committing them, if the petition was rejected, to a 'national holiday'. (This euphemism for a general strike was first coined by the veteran suffrage campaigner William Benbow, who was still active.) They voted to call for a month-long general strike starting on 12 August. This call split the Chartist leadership. The first word of caution came from Bronterre O'Brien, who had spoken at 90 meetings in a third as many days. He insisted that the reaction of the public at the meetings was not uniform, and certainly did not indicate mass support for a mass strike. O'Brien drew up a long motion for the Convention to discuss. The motion marks the beginning of the end of O'Brien's formerly steadfast commitment to 'physical force'. The nine paragraphs of the motion restated the commitment to the strike, but were cautious about calling for a date: 'We cannot take upon ourselves the responsibility of dictating the time or circumstances of such a strike.' Seven reasons were given, chief among which were the diversity of opinions on the subject in the population at large, the doubt whether a call for a strike would be obeyed, the danger into which the Convention would be plunging its supporters and the belief 'that the people themselves are the only fit judges of their right and readiness to strike work, as also of their own resources and capabilities of meeting the emergencies which such an event would entail'. The resolution then called for a committee to prepare an address on which 'the people' would themselves decide whether or not to stop work on the 12th. After a long and fractious debate on 24 July the Convention voted for this compromise by twelve to six with seven abstentions. Fergus O'Connor voted for the motion, though he spoke eloquently both for and against it.

As at Putney in 1647, the vote for a committee was a fig leaf to cover the leaders' indecision. As soon as they failed to name the date for the strike, the Chartist leaders shrank from their responsibilities. Effective leaders in such circumstances promote a course of action, argue for it and then call for a vote of support. The apparently democratic course of leaving any decision to the people effectively removes from them the option of acting on what the leaders propose. It is to propose nothing and therefore to do nothing. The committee of three duly 'took soundings' and recommended that the strike should be called off and replaced by a three-day agitation. This was moved by O'Brien, seconded by O'Connor and finally adopted unanimously by the Convention on 6 August. The resolution declared that the month-long strike, if it took place, would lead to a 'revolution in blood' which 'will terminate in the utter subjection of the working people to the monied murderers of society'. The resolution was bitterly denounced by the militants among the Chartist leaders, especially by McDouall and Harney, who sarcastically called on the Convention to 'go to sleep for a year'. Both men believed that the strike would be a catalyst for revolutionary activity. Even if their views were not shared by the majority of the people, they argued, the Chartist Convention should play the role of Jacobins urging and leading their supporters into the kind of action which would secure their just demands.

Historians have argued ever since about this Convention decision. Most agree with R. G. Gammage's first full *History of the Chartist Movement*, originally published in 1854. Gammage, who was an active 'moral force' Chartist, strongly supported the decision to hold back from the national holiday in 1839. He cited the dreadful consequences that would surely have followed. In the same way, the biographer of Bronterre O'Brien, Alfred Plummer, congratulates him for 'narrowly' avoiding the 'plunge over the precipice'. Later historians have not been so sure. Dorothy Thompson agrees that the response to a call for a strike would have been different in different parts of the country and in different trades, and that the likeliest outcome would have been a series of localized and sporadic outbreaks of violence. 'Popular revolutions,' she observes, 'do not as a rule begin by disciplined armed attacks on the centres of authority', but rather by 'the mass movement of poorly armed crowds' helped by the 'unwillingness of troops to treat their fellow-countrymen in the same way as an enemy army'.

In the summer of 1839, the existence almost everywhere of precisely such 'poorly armed crowds' thirsting for action, and the doubts and worries of the leaders of the armed forces ranged against them, are beyond dispute. There was a hugely powerful argument for the Chartist leaders to take the lead, to call the strike and to offer it every support, especially where troops replied by violence. That way, there was at least a chance of success. In the event, the calling-off of the strike was greeted with tremendous relief by the authorities, who, as though acting on a signal, at once went on the attack. Harry Vincent, the Chartist leader in the West, and three of his colleagues had already been arrested. So had Peter McDouall. Now began a systematic rounding up of prominent Chartists all over the country. All through the summer and autumn, a newly formed and invigorated police force, informed by spies and backed by magistrates' warrants, burst into the homes of suspected Chartists and charged them under the formidable array of laws which banned seditious meetings, speeches and journals.

The persecution made no distinction between 'physical force' and 'moral force' Chartists. The leaders and rank and file of the right were swept into the prisons with their former opponents on the left. J. R. Stephens, the fiery preacher, in a sad speech from the dock, denounced the Chartists and effectively apologized for his association with them. He got 18 months. William Lovett, leader of the 'moral force' faction, bitterly contested the charge that he had whipped up his Chartist audiences to violence. The evidence was all on his side but he was convicted and sent to prison for 12 months. The most stalwart and consistent of all the Chartist leaders, Peter McDouall, followed Stephens into the dock at Chester Assizes. His four-hour speech from the dock was never forgotten by anyone who heard it – including several soldiers from the barracks, who were sent to guard him but who toasted his eloquence and his passionate support for the poor. McDouall went down for 12 months. Like all the Chartist leaders (except Stephens, who was given special privileges and never again spoke from a Chartist platform), McDouall was shockingly treated in prison. Perhaps because he had fallen in love with the daughter of a prison officer, he soon recovered and continued to campaign for Chartism until his mysterious death in 1854. Most of the hundreds of other Chartists who were imprisoned or deported were broken by the experience.

In Wales, where Chartism had developed a mighty following and at least two riots had bordered on insurrection, the repression was particularly savage. In the same month that Stephens and McDouall were tried at Chester, Harry Vincent, the young, popular 'Chartist Demosthenes' who had enraptured huge crowds throughout the area, stood trial with three other local Chartist leaders on charges of conspiracy and attending illegal meetings. The courtroom at Monmouth Assizes was packed with local landed gentry and their wives, who hissed the speeches of defence barrister J. A. Roebuck, Radical MP for Bath. The prosecution evidence was systematically destroyed – witness after witness at the 'illegal meetings' Vincent addressed confirmed that he repeatedly called for order and warned against sporadic and unnecessary violence. But the loyal jury took a token quarter of an hour to find Vincent guilty, and the judge sent him to prison for a year. Indignation at the sentence and the manifest injustice of the trial swept through the Welsh valleys. A protest meeting was held at Dukestown, at which at least 100,000 people demanded Vincent's immediate release. John Frost, a magistrate and a member of the Chartist Convention, appealed for calm and reason, urging every possible constitutional effort to free Vincent. Frost himself organized that effort, travelling again and again to London to appeal to Home Office ministers and civil servants for compassion and a stay of the sentence. These appeals were contemptuously rejected.

Though the Chartist movement lost its momentum throughout the autumn of 1839, the fury in Wales at the fate of Harry Vincent continued to smoulder. The Convention had disbanded in August, so there was no national leadership. The initiative in South Wales was seized by new, anonymous leaders, who called for action to free Vincent and encouraged the secret arming of the Chartist rank and file. This agitation culminated in the march of thousands of Chartists on Newport on the night of 3–4 November 1839. The crowd was armed with guns and pikes, and the attack had been planned for several weeks. John Frost himself was reluctant to take part, but was convinced by the obstinacy of the authorities that drastic action had to be taken. The insurrectionary crowd, exhausted from a night's marching and soaked by a series of thunderstorms, converged on Newport's Westgate Hotel, where a troop of soldiers was waiting for them. A volley of fire from the soldiers killed or wounded at least 20 of the crowd, which promptly fled or dispersed.

The events at Newport that November have been either ignored or patronized by official historians. Yet even the most sceptical cannot deny the enormous numbers of people who took part in what was plainly intended to be an armed uprising. It was precisely the sort of encounter that General Napier had warned about in his dispatches about the balance of forces. If it had occurred earlier in the year, when most of the Chartist leaders were out of prison, when the Convention was sitting and when the mood in other parts of the country was more favourable to armed revolt, if the leaders of the uprising had been more determined, if the Westgate Hotel detachment could have been overwhelmed and their weapons seized, the insurrectionary mood could well have been revived, with shattering consequences for the authorities. These are some of the great 'ifs' of British history. But the rebellion was quickly contained. The ringleaders, John Frost, Zephaniah Williams and William Jones, were tried and convicted of high treason. The Lord Chief Justice decreed that each of them should be hanged, drawn and quartered. As the three men left the court under the shock of this awful sentence, Jones turned to the enormous crowd and called for three cheers for the Charter. After a powerful campaign, and to the fury of the Whig Prime Minister, Lord Melbourne, the sentences were commuted to transportation for life and the three men were hastily bundled out of the country. Frost survived the appalling journey and unspeakable deprivation in Tasmania. After 17 years, he came home to a rapturous reception and lived until 1877, when he died aged 93.

The defeat of the Newport uprising was celebrated by the Whig Government with another round of repression. By the middle of 1840 almost all the known leaders and many lesser-known followers were rotting in jail or on their way to join John Frost in Van Diemen's Land. Very few of them returned to politics. Stephens vanished from the Chartist scene. O'Brien, though he continued to write and speak for the Charter, forsook his former militancy. The Whigs and their judges had two aims – to cut the head off Chartism and to expunge for ever the chilling memory of the revolutionary year of 1839. In the first they were entirely successful, in the second not so. Twice again, in 1842 and 1848, the Chartist revolt smashed its way into the heart of bourgeois England. These two other waves of revolt, which were progressively less mountainous and less threatening, had the same basic features as in 1839. There was, first, the same economic background – a trade depression that plunged the working class into unimaginable distress. The distress contrasted grotesquely with the growing luxuries of the rich that derived from unchecked exploitation, in which the governments of both parties (Whig in 1839 and 1848, Tory in 1842) excelled.

Unemployment, unabated by any system of public welfare, was rife. A Factory Inspectors' Report in the spring of 1842 showed that half the working population of most industrial towns in Lancashire, the West of Scotland and the West Midlands were out of work, and the wretchedness of those in work was constantly being increased by systematic wage cuts against which there was no appeal and no recourse. Many new Chartists were made that year out of fathers and mothers who had to starve so that their children could eat. Workhouses and prisons were regularly raided for bread by gangs of starving workers. Another trade depression at the end of 1847 plunged the country back into conditions almost as bad as in 1842.

In Ireland, they were much worse. In the six years from 1845 to 1851, more than a million Irish people died from starvation. The Government's experts as usual blamed famine on the weather or, more typically, on the starving people themselves. The real cause was exactly the same in both years as in 1839: exploitation, encouraged and subsidized by Whigs and Tories and their shared enthusiasm for the 'free market'.

The chief response from the impoverished masses in both years was constitutional and passive. As in 1839, their main political activity was the collection of signatures for a petition to Parliament to enact the Six Points of the Charter. In 1842, the petition, presented to Parliament on 3 May, dwarfed its 1839 predecessor, with 3.5 million signatures. In 1848, though enthusiasm for a third petition had waned, the lowest estimate for genuine signatures was 1.5 million.

In both years, the petitions were summarily and insultingly rejected by the House of Commons. In 1842, the vote against even hearing the petitioners was 236 to 49, and in 1848, the petition was packed off to a committee, where it was denounced as a fake, and never even debated. The arguments against the petition from Whigs and Tories were the usual mixture of bombast and prejudice. By far the most illuminating speech in 1842 came from Thomas Babington Macaulay, whose comprehensive demolition of the reactionaries in the debates on the 1831 Reform Bill had made such an impression on the House. Soon after the 1832 Act became law, he went to India as a member of the Supreme Imperial Council, and returned to England in time to be elected unopposed for Edinburgh. In 1831, he had spoken for reform of the suffrage – in the interests of the middle class. Now, in the interests of the middle class, he spoke vehemently against the central reform proposed in the Charter – universal suffrage. The great reformer of 1831 had become the great reactionary of 1842. Yet Macaulay's basic views, like his eloquent language and his devotion to logical argument, had not changed at all. He started by asserting his belief that 'universal suffrage is incompatible . . . with all forms of govern-ment, and with everything for the sake of which forms of government exist . . . it is incompatible with property, and . . . consequently incompatible with civilization'. For this view, Macaulay had only one argument – the preservation of property:

On the security of property civilization depends . . . Where property is insecure, no climate however delicious, no soil however fertile, no conveniences for trade and navigation, no natural endowments of body or mind, can prevent a nation from sinking into barbarism; . . . where, on the other hand, men are protected in the enjoyment of what has been created by their industry and laid up by their self-denial, society will advance in arts and in wealth, notwithstanding the sterility of the earth and the inclemency of the air, notwithstanding heavy taxes and destructive wars.

This was, he explained, an argument about class:

If it be admitted that on the institution of property the well-being of society depends, it follows surely that it would be madness to give supreme power in the state to a class which would not be likely to respect that institution.

There seemed to Macaulay no doubt at all that universal suffrage would lead automatically to such disrespect for property. In other words, any government elected by the mass of the people who had no wealth was certain to start by expropriating the wealth of the rich. Macaulay had hard and fast proof for his argument to hand – the very petition the House was debating. For the Chartist petition, though its demands restricted themselves to changes in the vote and the reorganization of Parliament, ranged much wider. Macaulay quoted a passage denouncing the exorbit-ant luxuries of the landed rich, and stated: 'I believe it to be impossible to make any distinction between the right of a fundholder to his dividends and the right of a landholder to his rents.' The Chartist petition, he mocked, called for an end to monopolies 'arising from class legislation' and asked whether that meant that landed property should cease to exist or that the railways should be confiscated. Such confiscations, he warned, would lead not just to the ruin of the rich. It would also make the poor poorer. Draw-ing on his experience in India, he likened the petitioners to Indians outside a granary. Opening it turns 'a scarcity into a famine'. The petition, he argued, meant inevitably that 'in every constituent body throughout the empire' capital and accumulated property would be 'placed at the feet of labour'.

Macaulay was not by comparison with his colleagues in the House of

Commons a rich man. He had gone to India on a comfortable salary partly to recoup his family's debts. He did not directly represent the landed aristocracy or the industrial capitalists. But he spoke against reform with the same militant class solidarity with which he had spoken for it in 1831. He spoke with the same passion that had inspired Henry Ireton nearly 200 years previously. His plea was the same: do not allow the impoverished masses to vote for government since they will, as sure as night follows day, proceed with the authority of government to take away our property. As in 1647, this argument, once frankly put, was too much for its opponents. The officers and Levellers who sat round the table in the church at Putney had no more desire to do away with people's property than had even the most radical of the few parliamentary reformers scattered around the Whig benches at Westminster in 1842. Macaulay won the vote and he also won the argument. For in the rising chaos and clamour of 1842, as the Chartists recalled their Convention and prepared for another round of agitation, it was impossible for anyone on either side of the parliamentary argument to distinguish between the demand for the vote and the demand for the confiscation of rich people's property.

Outside Parliament, the balance of the argument was quite different. In 1842 and 1848, as the trade depressions turned into mass sackings and vicious wage cuts, the parliamentary opposition to the Charter was seen for what it was: the rich clinging to their luxuries, oblivious of the wretchedness of the masses outside. The *Northern Star* concluded: 'The same class is to be a slave class still. The mark and brand of inferiority is not to be removed ... The people are not to be free.' As in 1839, the contemptuous rejection of enormous petitions by these smug MPs led to a working-class revolt far more powerful than the passive, and demonstrably useless, petitioning of the past. In 1842, the revolt took the form of the first general strike in British history. This time the strike was not ordered by any national leadership. It started spontaneously in May as a protest against wage cuts by miners in the Black Country to the north and west of Birmingham. The strike quickly spread through the Potteries, up into Lancashire and on over the Pennines into Yorkshire. The trade-union branches merged with those of the National Charter Association, which had brought all Chartist groups together in Manchester in July 1840, and new leaders emerged from new forms of activity. Workers marched from town to town, from factory to factory, pulling the plugs on the furnaces and calling on their fellow workers to join the strike. They did so in increasing numbers, throwing up delegate conferences and locally elected committees until, by the second week in August, there were half a million people on strike from Cornwall to North

Yorkshire. In 1848, after the dispersal of a mass Chartist meeting in April, there was a month of intense activity – marches, demonstrations and, in London, sporadic riots. Though the areas that had been so active in 1842 were relatively quiet, the biggest Chartist meeting ever was reported to have been held in Bradford.

As in 1839, the Chartist leadership backed away from both these confrontations. Bronterre O'Brien was openly hostile to the 1842 strike, and the National Charter Association refused to support it. George Julian Harney, who had so contemptuously assailed the Chartist leaders for their backsliding in 1839, was an ardent opponent of the strike three years later. He was by then a Chartist organizer in Sheffield, and his opposition may explain why that traditionally militant city did not respond to the strike wave. In 1848, the newly assembled Chartist Convention called a mass meeting for 10 April on London's Kennington Common, vaguely expecting or hoping that a mighty assembly, as it delivered the new petition, would somehow scare the authorities into submission. The authorities responded by deploying thousands of troops on the London bridges and enrolling at least 100,000 special constables to face down the demonstration. O'Connor successfully called on the meeting to disperse, and, despite the heroic efforts of Peter McDouall to sustain the agitation in Bradford, the Chartist leaders played little or no part in the upheavals in May and June.

And as in 1839, the strikes and demonstrations of 1842 and 1848 were followed by mass arrests and charges. In 1843, O'Connor and 58 others stood trial at Lancaster, accused of supporting the mass strike. Many of the defendants, notably Harney, accurately protested that they had done their best to stop the strike. After eight days of speeches and ruthless cross-examination of the Government informers by the defendants, the jury found 23 of the defendants not guilty and others guilty only on minor charges that were not followed up. Eventually, the cases against all the defendants were dropped on a technicality about the style of the indictment. R. G. Gammage described the whole trial as 'a farce', and concluded that 'the Government never intended to imprison the defendants'. But the show trial of the 58 has obscured the systematic repression with which the more militant rank-and-file strike leaders were persecuted. Thomas Cooper, for instance, went down for two years for seditious speeches to strikers in the Potteries. Peter McDouall, the strike leader the Government most wanted to imprison, was hunted high and low. 'Wanted' posters with his picture were displayed all over the country. After a series of narrow escapes and exciting adventures, he fled to France, but as soon as another Chartist revolt broke out in 1848, he was back in the thick of it. Less well known are the names of rank-and-file strike leaders imprisoned and deported by magistrates and 'Special Commissions' (carefully picked from the most vengeful of the wealthy). At Stafford, where the magistrates and commissioners were especially concerned about the threat the strike posed to their dividends, 49 strikers were transported and a further 116 imprisoned for up to 2 years. In Cheshire, 4 were transported and 12 sent to prison for 18 months or more. The Liverpool Special Commission transported 11 and imprisoned 115. The rulers' revenge spread all over the North and the Midlands. In 1848, when yet another, though a weaker head had grown on the Chartist hydra, the authorities made a supreme and special effort to chop it off for ever. They added to their already monstrous repertoire of 'offences' against free speech and free assembly a new charge of 'treason-felony'. This enabled them to deport people to Australia for daring to insult or even criticize the Government. The judges, all from the same background and the same universities, carefully coordinated the forces of their newly renovated police force. Their aim was simple: to knock the stuffing out of the Chartist leadership all over the country, especially in London, where the dangers of insurrection had been most pronounced. In two sets of trials throughout the summer, which depended almost entirely on the dubious and suborned 'evidence' of spies and informers, nearly 300 Chartist leaders were sent to prison or deported. The usual sentence was two years in prison, but in the 'more serious' cases, a further five-year sentence was tacked on.

Such was the fate of the London Chartist leader Joseph Fussell, whose lawyers utterly destroyed the pathetic, perjured 'evidence' against him but who was found guilty nonetheless. William Cuffay, a black Chartist tailor who had protested about his leaders' decision to disperse the great demonstration on 10 April, got two years for 'sedition'. So did the most articulate and persuasive of the 1848 Chartist leaders, Ernest Jones. In prison, Jones was treated with special savagery. He spent many months picking oakum (unravelling old ropes to get the hemp) in solitary confinement and, though he kept up his commitment to Chartist principles, his spirit never fully recovered. 'The English political trials of 1848,' wrote the historian John Saville, in his comprehensive survey of that tumultuous year, 'were exercises in the miscarriage of justice: the obliteration of reason by prejudice and the subversion of legal principles by partisanship of a virulent order.'

As so often before and since, the claim of lawyers and judges that they preside over a legal system objectively and dispassionately was proved to be the exact opposite of the reality. Lord Abinger, the chief judge of the tyrannous Liverpool Special Commission in 1842, summed up all the objectivity of his ilk. 'The doctrines promulgated by the Chartists,' he observed, 'were doctrines of perfect insanity, and no man but a fool or a knave could promulgate them. The executive committee of the National Charter Association wanted to carry the principle of the Charter, that is to say that the labouring classes who have no property are to make laws for those who have property.' Repeating consciously or not the prejudice of General Ireton, Abinger went on: 'A popular assembly devoted to democratic principles and elected by persons, a vast majority of whom have no property and depend on manual labour . . . the first thing such an assembly would do would be to aim at the destruction of property and the putting down of the monarchy.'

Baron Alderson, who had been on the bench at Chester and Liverpool for the 1848 Chartist trials, wrote to his sister that 'trade is steadily improving'. This improvement, he wrote, 'will put an end to Chartism more effectively than any trials. Both together will for some time annihilate it – the leaders all in gaol – the people at work again.' The Baron could have had little idea how long that precious 'some time' of class peace would last. Though there were several attempts in the 1850s and 1860s to revive the Chartist agitation, they were quickly submerged. The improvement in trade and the economy was, as the Baron observed, the main reason. But another, no less important, as he realized, was the naked oppression for which he and his fellow judges were so proudly responsible.

The three waves of the great Chartist revolt broke on these judges and their class with successively diminishing force. The fright they got in 1839 stiffened their resolve and forced them to replenish their judicial, military and police powers. Yet in 1842, once again, they were stunned by the strength and solidarity of the general strike, and in 1848 further terrified by emerging signs of what worried them most, a linking of the hands of the oppressed across the Irish Sea. In 1848, the massed ranks of troops and spies at the behest of the Government were much more preoccupied with the suppression of revolt in Ireland – whose climax was the trial and hurried deportation of the Young Ireland revolutionary John Mitchel – than in 1839 or 1842. Yet on all three occasions the forces of the British state, so anxiously marshalled against its most deadly enemy, its own people, emerged victorious.

'Did Chartism fail?' is a common question in history examinations. The quick answer, of course, is yes. Chartism failed to wring from Parliament a single one of the Six Points which, with the solitary exception of annual parliaments, seem so mundane today. The 1832 franchise remained intact for 20 years after the defeat of Chartism. Yet in another sense the revolt was not a failure. It branded on to the history of the century an indelible memory as frightening to the rulers as it was exciting to the ruled. Like a rude noise in church, this memory was blithely ignored by official historians.

For the rest of the century, they wrote as diligently as ever about their kings and queens, their admirals and their generals, without noticing the near-insurrection which had occurred in their own lifetimes, on their doorsteps. Even when the Labour historians of the twentieth century came to grips with the Chartists, they tended to describe the events of 1839 to 1848 in standard historical terms, chiefly by singling out the Chartist leaders and discussing their attributes and shortcomings. *Chartist Portraits* (1941), by the earnest and prolific Oxford professor G. D. H. Cole, brought to the reading public a series of mini-biographies of William Lovett, Rev. J. R. Stephens, Richard Oastler, Thomas Attwood, John Frost, Thomas Cooper, Bronterre O'Brien, George Julian Harney, Feargus O'Connor and Ernest Jones.

Many of the more militant Chartist leaders were left out of the book – most notably Peter McDouall, who took part in all three waves of the revolt, regularly secured the highest vote for the executive of the Charter Association and alone among the Chartist leaders urged them to turn themselves into a disciplined and coherent leadership with a strategy for national insurrection.

But any discussion as to who were the most able or important of the Chartist leaders is entirely to miss the point: that the Chartist revolt was a mass movement which for long periods over nine years attracted hundreds of thousands of people to day-to-day political activity, the like of which they had never previously contemplated. This mass rank-and-file activity united the working people of the British towns and cities in a joint endeavour and burst through their prejudices and discriminations. The bitter hostility of English and Scottish workers to immigrants from Ireland, which paralysed the trade unions for so long throughout the nineteenth century, was laid to rest during the high peaks of the Chartist revolt.

This was not merely because so many of the national Chartist leaders, like O'Connor and O'Brien, were Irish but also because the plight of the Irish masses was seen as an integral part of the plight of the British masses. During the Chartist years, both pursued a common aim: to rid themselves of their common enemy. And, just as the Irish Chartist leaders symbolized a new unity between British and Irish workers, so other leaders symbolized an end to even deeper prejudices. Robert Lowery, a tailor, who bitterly opposed the compromise in 1842, was physically disabled. William Cuffay, who bitterly opposed the compromise of 1848, was black. Chartism proclaimed itself an international movement that provided platforms for oppressed people anywhere – for Hungarian or French workers in revolution, or for black American slaves fighting for emancipation. Even older prejudices fell by the wayside. Locked up in Lancaster gaol awaiting trial in 1840, the Chartist leader R. J. Richardson wrote a pamphlet entitled *Rights for Women*. 'I have now shown you,' he concluded, 'that woman bears her share in the burdens of the state, and contributes more than her fair proportion to the wealth of the country. I ask you, is there a man, knowing these things, who can lay his hand upon his heart, and say, "woman ought not to interfere in political affairs"? No, I hope there is none.'

The Chartist revolt was sustained and invigorated by the active support of new female unions, whose gaudy banners lit up the demonstrations. It was no silly romantic notion of Benjamin Disraeli to make the central character of his novel about the Chartists a woman, and to make the political conversation of her women supporters a central theme. Women flocked in huge numbers to the great Chartist rallies, especially if George Julian Harney or Harry Vincent was a speaker. Every speech of theirs in 1839 paid tribute to the indomitability of the women Chartists. When, early in 1841, a Mrs King of Manchester brought her son to be christened Feargus O'Connor King, the registrar scolded her, and advised her to take the child away and come back with a better name. When the woman furiously refused, he asked her: 'Is your husband a Chartist?' 'I don't know,' was the instant reply, 'but his wife is.'

In 1839, at the height of the highest peak of the Chartist revolt, the female political union of Newcastle issued an address to their fellow countrywomen:

We are a despised caste; our oppressors are not content with despising our feelings, but demand the control of our thoughts and wants! Want's bitter bondage binds us to their feet – we are oppressed because we are poor. The joys of life, the gladness of plenty and the sympathies of nature are not for us. The solace of our homes, the endearments of our children and the sympathies of our kindred are denied us, and even in our graves our ashes are laid with disrespect.

The demand in the address was a simple one: 'to pass the People's Charter into law and emancipate the white slaves of England. This is what the working men of England, Ireland and Scotland are struggling for and we have banded ourselves together in union to assist them and we call on our fellow countrywomen to join us.'

The address was headed with a quotation from Shelley's *Revolt of Islam*:

> ... well ye know
> What Woman is, for none of Woman born
> Can choose but drain the bitter dregs of woe,
> Which ever from the oppressed to the oppressors flow.

Shelley had died, aged 29, in 1822. Almost all his revolutionary political poetry and prose had been censored or ignored during his lifetime. It was revived and read on a massive scale during the Chartist years. What was going on in those years was something he had celebrated in his dreams and in his most vivid poetry, something even more exciting than the bursting of the discriminations and prejudices he loathed. Shelley's poetry, all of it written in defiance of the reaction which followed the French Revolution, is full of erupting volcanoes, flowering seeds, bursting clouds – all of it symbolic of the dramatic fulfilment of human potential which revolution stirs up in the very dregs of society. The majority of human beings, he believed, were not destined to spend their lives in drudgery and ignorance.

Shelley would have been 46 in May 1839, if he had lived. How his poetry, which suffers so much from the vagueness of its hopes, would have been transformed by what really happened in the Chartist years. The real achievement of the Chartists was the glimpse they afforded of human emancipation. In every city, town and village, people who would otherwise never have been known to anyone except their family and closest neighbours became organizers, administrators, public speakers, secretaries of hardship or strike committees, delegates to other places where the same infectious revolution was taking place.

The poet Arthur Hugh Clough took on some of Shelley's mantle. He was 20 in 1839, and by 1842 was so committed to the Chartist cause that he resigned his comfortable fellowship at Oxford and condemned himself to a life of difficulty and constraint. His favourite image was the sudden transformation of darkness into light. In his great poem about Liverpool at the height of the Chartist revolt, he starts with Shelleyan references to the Atlantic ocean, and goes on:

> So in my soul of souls, through its cells and secret recesses,
> Comes back, swelling and spreading, the old democratic fervour.
>   But as the light of day enters some populous city,
> Shaming away, ere it come, by the chilly day-streak signal,

High and low, the misusers of night, shaming out the gas-lamps –
All the great empty streets are flooded with broadening clearness,
Which, withal, by inscrutable simultaneous access
Permeates far and pierces to the very cellars lying in
Narrow high back-lane, and court, and alley of alleys . . .

The 'broadening clearness', the 'old democratic fervour' permeated down to the poorest of the poor and lit them up with the real chance that they might have some say in the world in which they lived. The story of this rank-and-file involvement has been buried deeper than any other feature of the Chartist revolt. With the single exception of R. G. Gammage's book, the whole revolt was systematically obscured in all the encyclopaedias and standard histories of the remainder of the nineteenth century. The cautious *Chartist Portraits* of G. D. H. Cole or *Chartist Studies* (1959), edited by Asa Briggs, though they could not ignore the movement from below, concentrated on the top. The first historian to introduce us properly to the Chartist rank and file was Dorothy Thompson, whose seminal book *The Chartists*, published in the year of the great miners' strike of 1984, ripped the veil of historical condescension off the rank-and-file Chartists, and provided her readers with the names and enthusiasms of the 'common' men and women who for nearly a decade stirred up a nation.

It was the strength, confidence and self-activity of the rank and file which persuaded the Government and its allies in the military and judiciary that the revolt must be crushed with the utmost dispatch and the utmost cruelty – and hidden from history for at least half a century afterwards.

Powerful testimony to the revolutionary essence of Chartism came from a young German intellectual who made friends with Harney and other Chartist leaders in 1845, and wrote extensively on Chartism in the German Radical press. Frederick Engels's famous horror story, *The Condition of the Working Class in England*, was published in 1845, at a time when the Chartists were at a low ebb and most of the leaders of the 1842 strike were still in prison or just out of it. Engels at once identified the real significance of the Charter:

The Six Points, which for the radical bourgeoisie are the beginning and end of the matter, which are meant, at the utmost, to call forth certain reforms of the Constitution, are for the proletarian a mere means to further ends. 'Political power our means, social happiness our ends' is now the clearly formulated war-cry of the Chartists. The knife-and-fork (bread and cheese) question of the preacher Stephens was a truth for a part of the Chartists only in 1838. It is a truth for all of them in 1845.

Engels's view was shared by Karl Marx, his friend and co-author of *The Communist Manifesto*, which was first published in English in 1850. Marx, in exile in London for most of his life, scraped together a miserable income from writing, chiefly for the *New York Herald Tribune*. In August 1852, Marx wrote in the *Tribune*:

We now come to the Chartists, the politically active portion of the British working class. The Six Points of the Charter which they contend for contain nothing but the demand of universal suffrage, and of the conditions without which universal suffrage would be illusory for the working class ... But universal suffrage is the equivalent of political power for the working class of England ... where, in a long, though underground civil war, it has gained a clear consciousness of its position as a class, and where even the rural districts know no longer any peasants, but only landlords, industrial capitalists (farmers) and labourers. The carrying of universal suffrage in England would, therefore, be a far more socialistic measure than anything which has been honoured with that name on the Continent.

Its inevitable result, here, is the political supremacy of the working class.

This passage has been used for a century and a half to scoff at Marx. After all, runs the argument, we have had universal suffrage in Britain for 80 years or so and the political supremacy of the working class is still a dream. But the inspiration for Marx's and Engels's conclusion was not the bare demand for universal suffrage. It was rooted in the mass meetings, strikes, demonstrations and uprisings which demanded not just the vote but also, once the vote was granted, a redistribution of wealth. For the rulers to grant the main Chartist demand in the heat of their struggle would indeed have been the equivalent of surrendering political power to the working class. Everyone who took part in the debates of the time, Macaulay and Marx, Tories and Whigs, republicans and royalists, all conceded that the granting of the Charter meant the granting of much more than a right to vote – far too much at any rate for the rulers even to contemplate.

If it was true in 1852 that the 'inevitable result' of universal suffrage in Britain in the wake of the Chartist revolt was equivalent to political power for the working class, was it likely to be true for ever? Was it, in Marx's word, 'inevitable' that the granting of the Six Points would result at any time in a surrender of the property of the rich? Was it even true at the time in countries other than Britain? These questions arose in a number of different guises even before the Chartist revolt was over.

In the summer of 1837, as William Lovett and his disciples prepared their 'moral' campaign to engage working men in the political process, they were confronted by an immediate problem. What was happening in the

United States of America? For more than half a century, the government there had been elected by something approaching universal male suffrage. Yet the condition of the American working class seemed to be very much the same as in England. Indeed, for large numbers of black people, especially in the South, their condition was far worse – they were bought and sold into a life of permanent slavery. How could it be that universal suffrage and the institutions that flowed from it – seen by Lovett as the panacea for British workers – had not corrected these excesses in America?

This burning question was the theme of an eloquent address in 1837 by Lovett's Working Men's Association to the Citizens of the American Republic. The *Address* started off by defending the democracy of America against Whig and Tory sniping. But very quickly it hurried on to the worrying conundrum:

You have climbed heights of political liberty yet to be attained by all the nations of Europe; and if you have not realized all the social and political advantages of your position – nay, if you possess not the power to assist in the emancipation of others – it is high time to ask yourself the reason and investigate the cause. Why, when your institutions are so excellently founded, when your noble race of philosophic statesmen legislated, fought and bled to invest you with political power and left you as their choicest legacy the best advice to use it – why, after sixty years of freedom have you not progressed further? Why are you to so great an extent ruled by men who speculate on your credulity and thrive by your prejudice? Why have lawyers a preponderating influence in your country – men whose interests lie in your corruptions and dissensions and in making intricate the plainest questions affecting your welfare? Why has so much of your fertile country been parcelled out between swindling bankers and grinding capitalists, who seek to establish (as in our country) a monopoly in that land which nature bestowed in common to all her children? Why have so many of your cities, towns, railroads, canals and manufactories become the monopolized property of those who 'toil not neither do they spin'?

The most urgent issue was slavery:

Why, when your country afforded a home and an asylum for the destitute and oppressed among all nations, should oppression be legalized and bondage tolerated? Did nature, when she cast her sunshine over the earth, and adapted her children to its influence, intend that her varied tints of skin should be the criterion of liberty?

The question persisted unanswered – how could swindling bankers and grinding capitalists be just as powerful and oppressive where most men voted for their government?

In February 1848, a revolution in France toppled the despotic Government. Monarchy was replaced by a new Parliament elected in May by universal suffrage. There was no property qualification for voting. Yet there were now even more big landowning and wealthy MPs than in any of the previous parliaments elected by restricted franchise. How could so many swindling bankers and grinding capitalists have been voted in by the masses, even three months after a revolution? One early answer came from Karl Marx himself, who identified universal suffrage in France as something very different from what universal suffrage would have been if it had been introduced in England at the point of a Chartist pike:

Universal suffrage in France did not possess the magical power attributed to it by republicans of the old school. They saw throughout France *citoyens* with the same interests, views, etc. This was their cult of the people. Instead of these imaginary people, the electors revealed the real people, that is the representatives of the different classes which comprised the people.

This was written in the same year (1852) as his article on the Chartists that equated universal suffrage in England with political power for the working class. Yet here he was attacking the anti-working-class nature of a French government elected by universal suffrage. The French Government of May 1848 and its subsequent repressions quickly proved that it was possible for a government elected by universal suffrage to be just as oppressive as its predecessor, which wasn't.

That such distinctions were beginning to intrigue the more sophisticated political thinkers in Britain was clear even before the Chartist revolt. In 1835, a Commission on Municipal Corporations recommended substantial changes to the structure of local government. Before 1835, the big towns and cities had been run by self-appointing corporations, bastions of Tory hierarchy. After their triumph of 1832, the more liberal Whigs and the capitalists they represented resolved to 'clean up' local government as well. The Commission proposed the replacement of the old closed corporations with new, elected councils. This was agreed – but how were the new councils to be elected? The Commission proposed a regular ballot based on universal suffrage. Thus, two years before the People's Charter was published, universal suffrage was proposed for local government by a Commission consisting entirely of important people – there was not a worker or a Chartist on it. The proposal was too much for the House of Lords, which watered it down so that the local franchise was restricted by property qualifications very similar to those which neutered the parliamentary franchise. But the mere fact that a high-powered Commission representing the rich could even contemplate handing the vote in their precious cities to the swinish multitude was highly significant. It showed that even in 1835, at the height of the agitation over the Tolpuddle martyrs and the Poor Law Amendment Act, rich burghers were flirting with the idea that the franchise could be extended without any serious damage to their wealth.

For a few months, this idea infiltrated the Chartist movement itself. Perhaps the most puzzling entry in G. D. H. Cole's *Chartist Portraits* is that of Joseph Sturge. Sturge was never a Chartist. He was a Quaker who believed that human problems could be solved best 'from within', by self-contemplation, self-analysis and prayer. But he was also driven by that sense of public duty that inspired so many worthy English liberal gentlemen before and since. Enormously rich from his business as a corn-dealer and a director of the London and Birmingham Railway, Sturge believed passionately in the sanctity of private property. But he was also genuinely shocked by inhuman or unfair treatment. He spent a lot of his life campaigning against the slave trade and then against slavery itself. When the Charter was first published, Sturge did not support it. He was appalled by the revolutionary upheaval of 1839 and angrily distanced himself from it. But its chief effect on him was to increase his uneasiness about the lack of democratic representation for the masses. In 1841, when he came back from an anti-slavery tour in the United States, the full force of the revolutionary activity of the Chartists compelled him to apply his mind to the plight of the white wage slaves of his native country. He started to campaign for a solution to what he called 'the enormous evil of class legislation', while seeking above all to separate that campaign from the social upheaval created by the Chartists. He founded the Complete Suffrage Union (CSU) dedicated to universal manhood suffrage (he was always a bitter enemy of female suffrage, or indeed women's involvement in politics of any kind). He and his supporters set out at once to recruit from the ranks of 'moral force' Chartists and from the growing Anti-Corn Law League, a free-trade propaganda organization heavily subsidized by the wealthy few who would exclusively benefit from it.

What was Sturge doing? Proud, strong and independent, he did not accept the old aristocratic maxim that the common people, if allowed the vote, would seize the wealth of the rich and put a stop to their power and influence. Like many deeply religious rich people, he believed not only in the divine right of his class to rule but also that the people over whom they ruled looked up to their betters with proper respect. The human race was all of one blood, he would preach, and each member of it was entitled to choose its government. If the vote was granted, he believed, he and people like him would be chosen to govern just as before, and would as a result govern with even more authority. His aim was therefore very simple: to split the Chartist movement and to isolate the demand for universal suffrage from the 'something extra', the 'knife-and-fork question', Engels's 'social democracy' with which it was inextricably entwined and which gave it its revolutionary flavour.

In April 1842, as the second wave of Chartism broke, the CSU held a conference in Birmingham. Several Chartists attended, including the once tempestuous Harry Vincent, who had recently joined the 'moral force' men. William Lovett was there too, though he made clear at once that he was not going to take part in a split in the Chartist movement. Indeed, Lovett moved that the conference accept every one of the Six Points of the Charter. To Sturge's dismay, this resolution was passed. But Sturge still insisted that his movement was essentially different from the Chartists, and proposed successfully that its petition for franchise reform should be organized completely separately from the petition for the Charter. Thus in the spring and early summer of 1842, two separate petitions were separately circulated and canvassed – with exactly the same demands.

Most of the Chartist leaders greeted Sturge's initiative with unmitigated fury. The *Northern Star* denounced his CSU as a stalking horse that would split the movement and leave the working class 'prostrate to the capitalists'. O'Connor called the Sturgeites 'scabby sheep' who were inspired by the 'Malthusian starve-beggar faction'. At a distance of 150 years, this furious dispute seems unreal. Both groups, after all, were making exactly the same demands. But the outrage of the *Northern Star* and, at least at the outset, of Feargus O'Connor dated back to what they saw as the middle-class treachery of 1831 and 1832. Working-class people had been encouraged to agitate for franchise reform – only to find that the reform, when achieved, was used further to impoverish and oppress them. The 'something extra' was not just tacked on to the Charter for the 'physical force' Chartists. It was essential both to winning the Charter and to what happened after it was won. Sturge's initiative was eventually eclipsed by the great strike of 1842, and the Complete Suffrage Union disintegrated. But for a brief moment it opened up the possibility that real and substantial franchise reform might be possible without seriously tipping the balance between rich and poor.

Moreover, it made one highly influential convert among the Chartist leaders – Bronterre O'Brien. O'Brien's attendance and many interventions in the CSU conference in April 1842 infuriated O'Connor and led to a violent row between the two Irishmen which lasted for several months. O'Brien's meetings were regularly boycotted or invaded by angry O'Connor supporters. This was not just a sectarian argument between two men who always suspected and disliked each other. Bronterre's tone had changed a great deal since his excoriating articles in the *Poor Man's Guardian*. In 1842 and in 1848 he was no longer the revolutionary of 1839. He wrote to his readers in his new paper, the *British Statesman*, in 1842 that in the old days, 'it was necessary to rouse you as with a rattling peal of thunder. The case is different now.' The truth was, however, that 'the case' was no different. The case for the rattling peal of thunder, for forcing concessions from the bigots in the House of Commons was even stronger in 1842 (and stronger still in 1848) than in 1839. What had changed was not the argument nor the external circumstances but Bronterre.

Though Joseph Sturge played only a small role in the saga of the Chartist revolt, he was among the very first of his class to disagree with the received notion of Whigs and Tories alike – that universal suffrage spelled the end of civilized society. He argued with his rich friends that their hold on the country's wealth was much more likely to be loosened if they persisted in their resistance to universal suffrage than if they conceded it. In the end, he warned, it would be impossible to resist the argument that any unelected government is illegitimate. Sooner or later, if the masses remained unrepresented, they would overthrow their government in a manner more ruthless than that of the Chartists. The Chartists showed how deep, passionate and even violent was the movement for electoral reform. The question was: could a means be found to introduce representative government without either the violence of the 'physical force' Chartists or the social democracy and equality which the best of them demanded as a necessary condition of the Charter? Could the vote be conceded and the property of the rich safeguarded? These were the questions to which, after squashing the Chartists in the most relentless repression, the more rational elements in the British ruling class now began, reluctantly and gingerly, to turn their minds.

The Leap in the Dark

'Well, they say – you've got the Reform Bill; what more can you want? . . . But I say, the Reform Bill is a trick – it's nothing but swearing-in special constables to keep the aristocrats safe in their monopoly; it's bribing some of the people with votes to make them hold their tongues about giving votes to the rest. I say, if a man doesn't beg or steal, but works for his bread, the poorer and the more miserable he is, the more he'd need have a vote to send an inspector to parliament – else the man who is worst off is likely to be forgotten; and I say, he's the man who ought to be first remembered.' A political speaker in George Eliot's novel
Felix Holt, The Radical (1866)

St James's Hall was the largest indoor meeting place in London, and on 28 March 1863 it was full to capacity. There was a marked difference in class between the audience and the platform. The main speakers were politicians: John Bright, the Liberal MP for Birmingham, who combined a passion for most forms of emancipation with a deep hostility to the emancipation of labour, especially the labour in the profitable factories which he owned. He was flanked by two powerful lieutenants who would soon join him on the Liberal benches in the Commons, John Stuart Mill and Henry Fawcett. The subject of the meeting was the war between the South and the North in the United States. The vast majority of MPs on both sides of the House and almost the entire House of Lords supported the South. They felt an instinctive solidarity with the slaveholders, and argued with some force that British economic interests would be far better served by a victory for the South. Sensing this mood among the men of his class, the ageing Prime Minister Lord Palmerston reached instinctively for his gunboats. He believed, and publicly indicated more than once, that the way to end the war quickly was to send in the Royal Navy to break the North's marine blockade of the South.

Saner Liberals like Bright, Mill and Fawcett strongly opposed this policy, and were delighted to speak at the meeting, though the Liberal Party had not organized it. The meeting had been called by the newly formed London Trades Council, which brought together the trade unions in the city. The Council's committee had been harangued some weeks earlier by Edward Beesly, a history professor at London University. Beesly played such a vital and selfless part in the growth and influence of trade union-ism in the third quarter of the nineteenth century that he does not merit a single line in *The Dictionary of National Biography*. His argument to the Trades Council was simple. The Government was going to war, and only a mass demonstration of British workers' opinion would stop it. The Coun-cil was impressed, and the meeting was widely advertised. The enormous crowd that collected at the hall long before the scheduled time was a tribute to the strong anti-war sentiment among British workers. The tide of British support for the North had been rising ever since January 1862, when President Abraham Lincoln committed his armies to the emancipation of the slaves.

Mill and Fawcett were well received, Bright rapturously so. All three concentrated on the case for the American North against the South. When Beesly rose to speak last, the hall was echoing with flowery Liberal oratory, and several sceptical campaigners, including Karl Marx, had gone home. Those who stayed heard a speech more remarkable by far than anything heard previously that evening or in Parliament during the whole of the last decade.

Beesly applied himself to only one sentence in the resolution before the meeting: 'The cause of labour is the same all over the world.' 'I am far from impugning to our upper classes the design or desire to buy or sell you like cattle,' he declared, to mocking laughter, 'but I think the greater part of them, even of those calling themselves Liberals, are of the opinion that you have got a great deal more independence and freedom of action than is good for you.' If the upper classes could have their way without hindrance, then 'at length you would differ from negro slaves in nothing except the colour of your skin [prolonged cheers]'.

As his speech went on, Beesly made it plain that he was not talking only about the American Civil War but also about British class war, not only about the emancipation of American slaves but also about the emancipation of British workers:

Our governing classes may refuse to enfranchise you. They may shut the door of the House of Commons in your face and value themselves on their cleverness. But when there is need, you know how to make your voice heard . . . We are met here tonight, we say it openly, not merely as friends of emancipation but as friends of reform [loud cheers].

They may call themselves Whigs and Tories, but they have borrowed the motto of your societies – 'Union is Strength'. For they have found one cardinal principle on which they can agree. It is the key to the whole political situation . . . Shall I tell you what this all-absorbing sentiment is? It is the fear of you [applause]. Over and over again I have heard it as a proof of the danger of entrusting you with the franchise. Now, fellow citizens, when you are seriously bent on having the franchise and tell them so plainly, of course they will have to give way . . . This is the first time, I believe, that the trade unionists of London have met together to pronounce on a political question, but I am sure it will not be the last.

The speech was greeted with cheering of the type only the old Chartists there could remember. Unlike the other speakers, Beesly had made the connection between the agitation against British involvement in the American war and agitation for franchise reform, of which there had been almost none since the Chartist demonstration at Kennington Common 15 years earlier. At a rally in Manchester, a month before the St James's Hall meeting, an unnamed orator had hailed the American people of the North for 'not merely contending for themselves, but for the rights of the unenfranchised of this and every other country. If the North succeed, liberty will be stimulated and encouraged in every country on the face of the earth; if they fail, despotism like a great pall will envelop all our political and social institutions.' Reading the reports of these meetings, and musing on the enthusiasm at St James's Hall, Karl Marx predicted that a victory for the North would 'sound the tocsin' to the disenfranchised workers of Europe just as the winning of American Independence in the 1770s had heralded the French Revolution.

In 1863, Marx was absorbed in research for his most ambitious and prodigious work, *Capital* (1867). Disappointed at the collapse of the Communist League, which he had helped to found, and irritated by the sectarian squabbles of the post-Chartist left, he had committed himself to concentrate on *Capital* and not to engage in British politics. The internationalism of the American Civil War meetings and their success in stopping Palmerston going to war for the South jolted him into renewed activity. The following year, 1864, he was invited to attend another big London meeting – this time at St Martin's Hall – called on 28 September by two of the city's most prominent trade-union leaders, George Odger, shoemaker president of the council of all-London trade unions, and William Cremer, a leading member of the carpenters' and joiners' union. Both men had spoken at the American Civil War meeting in St James's Hall and had been inspired by the mood of that meeting to set up an international workers' organization. Marx realized that at last something was happening in the British labour movement involving 'people who really count'. He had accepted the invitation to St Martin's Hall grudgingly, and sat silent on the platform. He went home bubbling with pleasure at the quality of the speeches and the unanimous vote to establish an International Working Men's Association. He had been elected on to a sub-committee to write a manifesto of the aims of the International but could not get to the first two meetings because of illness. When he finally made it, he was appalled at the vagueness and drift of the proposed aims, and persuaded his colleagues to hand the drafts over to him for editing. The result was an entirely rewritten version, the *Inaugural Address to the International Working Men's Association*, which gives us a clearer picture than any official document at the time of the state of society in Britain in the 1860s.

The *Address* starts by contrasting the staggering growth in production and productive capacity with the desperate poverty of the workers who had achieved it. Drawing on his feverish research in the Government's statistical 'blue books', Marx revealed that British export and import trade had grown by 300 per cent in 20 years but in the same period the condition of the workers and the poor had not improved at all. A recent survey, set up when an outbreak of mugging in London sent the middle classes into blind panic, showed that deported criminals in Australia and New Zealand were living fuller lives than agricultural labourers in Britain. When the American Civil War plunged thousands of workers in the cotton trade, especially in the North-West, into sudden and prolonged unemployment, a Government doctor had been sent to Lancashire to calculate the minimum carbon and nitrogen intake necessary to 'avert starvation diseases'. No one in authority was remotely embarrassed when the same doctor discovered that the 'silk-weavers, needlewomen, kid-glovers, stocking-weavers' were consuming even less than the minimum he had recommended to avoid starvation – and that the Lancashire operatives thrown out of work 'were actually improving in health, because of their temporary exclusion by the cotton famine from the cotton factory', and that the mortality of the children was decreasing, 'because their mothers were now at last allowed to give them, instead of Godfrey's cordial, their own breasts'. Marx observed that 'death by starvation rose almost to the rank of an institution during this intoxicating epoch of economical progress in the metropolis of the British Empire'.

None of this was exaggerated. Palmerston's Chancellor of the Exchequer, William Ewart Gladstone, observed in strikingly similar terms that the 'intoxicating augmentation of wealth and power is entirely confined to classes of property'. A minority of workers had increased their wages, but by 1864 the index of real wages had hardly risen at all since 1848.

If the rate of exploitation had increased, therefore, why had the workers not reacted more fiercely? If the basic economic reasons for the Chartist revolt were as relevant as ever, what had happened to the revolt? 'The short-lived dreams of emancipation,' Marx noticed, 'vanished before an epoch of industrial fever, moral marasm, and political reaction.' The workers' movement in all the European countries had been 'crushed' by the English Government in concert with Russian tyranny. Most of the workers' leaders, including the Chartists, had fled to America. The workers' newspapers had folded. What was later described as a workers' aristocracy had been 'caught by the temporary bribe of greater work and wages', and there was throughout the workers' movements in Europe a 'solidarity in defeat'.

The effect on Marx of this long period of defeat was clear from his tone. The *Address* was the first polemical work for mass consumption he had written since *The Communist Manifesto* in the year of the 1848 Revolutions. Both works railed against the effects of the capitalist system. The *Manifesto* had proposed an alternative system, that of communism. In the *Address* there is not even a hint of socialism or indeed any alternative to capitalism. Marx had not changed his own ideas one iota. He was just as committed to communism as he had been in 1848. But the effect of the defeats since then had been to change the mood of his working-class audience. In the revolutionary mood of 1848, his prescription was revolutionary. In 1864, his aim was much more limited: to build an international workers' organization committed to solidarity between workers fighting capitalism in different countries. He therefore left out of his *Address* any reference to socialism, which might alienate anarchists, militant freedom-fighters or trade unionists who had no interest or commitment to any form of politics. He was irritated by the degree of self-censorship he had to impose on himself to make the necessary compromises. 'It was,' he wrote to Frederick Engels, 'very difficult to frame the thing so that our views should appear in a form acceptable from the present standpoint of the workers' movement ... It will take time before the awakened movement allows the old boldness of speech.'

As if to prove that point, he sought to raise the low spirits of the workers by welcoming two reforms which had been accomplished in spite of 'solidarity in defeat': the Ten Hours Bill (limiting the working day to ten hours) and the cooperative movement, which flourished in Lancashire. The cooperatives had shown, he wrote, that 'production on a large scale . . . may be carried on without the existence of a class of masters'. On the other hand, he predicted with uncanny accuracy, 'if kept within the narrow circle of the casual efforts of private workmen', consumer cooperation 'will never be able to arrest the growth in geometrical progression of monopoly, to free the masses nor even to perceptibly lighten the burden of their miseries'. The 'lords of the land and the lords of capital' would always combine to safeguard their monopolies. Anyone who needed proof of that had only to study the speeches of Prime Minister Palmerston. He had proudly described the House of Commons as 'the house of the landed proprietors'. Marx concluded: 'To conquer political power has therefore become the great duty of the working classes.' There was some hope of this, moreover, since in England, Germany, Italy and France there had been 'simultaneous efforts' at political reorganization by the formation of a working-class political party.

What did Marx mean by that vague phrase – 'to conquer political power'? Since it came so soon after the quotation from Palmerston about the Commons, and so soon after the equation between the victory of the American North and the demand for the working-class franchise, the reader might conclude that 'to conquer political power' meant to win the vote for the workers and to gain control of Parliament. Yet the demand for the vote nowhere appears in Marx's *Address* or in the Rules of the International appended to it. There are plenty of references to 'emancipation', but the word defines a general, all-pervasive freedom from exploitation, something much more powerful and larger than simply the right to vote.

As we have seen, in 1852, at the sunset of Chartism, Marx had predicted that the granting of universal suffrage in Britain would lead automatically to the transfer of political power to the working class. If the Chartists had won the vote, the secret ballot and the annual parliaments they demanded, their victories would have led automatically to the control of society by their class, which had marched so far down the road to social revolution that they could not possibly have been fobbed off with anything less than economic emancipation. Twelve years of defeat later, Marx was not so sure. The Rules attached to his *Address* say nothing about the fight for the vote or for enfranchisement. There is no hint of a prediction that an extension in the suffrage would lead inevitably to an extension in working-class power. The very first paragraph of the Rules declared: 'That the emancipation of the working class must be conquered by the working class themselves.' The use of the word 'conquered' echoes the passage in the *Address* that calls on the working class 'to conquer political power'. The language suggests something more than a peaceful transition to working-class power by voting for parliamentary candidates. It was as though the long decade and a half of defeats had changed Marx's approach to the franchise, and obliged him to switch his attention from the fight for the suffrage to working-class self-activity and international solidarity.

The trade unionists who had been elected by acclamation on to the General Council of the Working Men's International were delighted with Marx's version of their aims and rules. With a few minor changes, which only mildly irritated the author, the text was adopted wholesale and with great enthusiasm. An attempt by Italian nationalists under the influence of Giuseppe Mazzini to gut the address by removing its core – its references to class and exploitation – was abruptly rejected, and the *Address* was published and circulated throughout Europe and the United States. In its early months at least, Marx triumphantly if prematurely reported the rapid growth of the new International. Within weeks of its circulation, Marx heard news from his friends at the International of arrangements for yet another great meeting, again in St Martin's Hall, the third in a trilogy of huge working-class London meetings in successive years. The subject this time was a familiar one – though for years it seemed to have vanished from popular consciousness: parliamentary reform.

In the 17 years since the defeat of the Chartists, there had been no mass agitation for any change to the 1832 franchise. Almost all the pressure for change came from above, from a Parliament dominated by two parties: the Tories, led for most of the time by Lord Derby, who were instinctively hostile to reform, and the Liberal Party, as it came increasingly to be known, which spread from old Whigs to new Radicals. In this calm period, parliamentary politics reached its nadir. It was almost entirely cut off from the people it pretended to represent and most of its arguments were confined to intrigue and gossip. There was no discernible ideological gap between the parties and the great issues, including reform, were played out between them with all the sincerity of a sporting tournament. Charles Dickens, who began his career as a parliamentary reporter, developed a healthy contempt for these politicians. His novel *Bleak House*, which he started in 1851, caught the cut and thrust of parliamentary debate precisely. Lord Coodle on one side and Sir Thomas Doodle on the other discussed when next they would swap places on the Treasury bench: 'England has been in a dreadful state for some weeks. Lord Coodle would go out, Sir Thomas Doodle wouldn't come in, and there being nobody in Great Britain (to speak of) except Coodle and Doodle, there has been no Government.'

This was the atmosphere in which the old opportunist Lord John 'Finality Jack' Russell, who dithered at the top of the Liberal Party for more than a quarter of a century, three times introduced Bills to replace his 'final' Reform Act of 1832. The Bills sought to lower the property qualification for the franchise by a pound or two, mainly in the towns and cities, thus enfranchising a few hundred thousand more people. These Bills were hedged around with conditions holding the proposed enfranchisement firmly in check. They were dogged by the inherent contradiction of Russell's aims – the desire to 'bring more people within the pale of the constitution' without threatening the interests of the gentry. The first Bill, in 1852, was withdrawn almost as soon as it was introduced. The second, in 1854, was littered with what became known as 'fancy franchises', allotting extra votes to people with inherited property or large bank balances. This Bill didn't last much longer. Russell withdrew it and, to sympathetic cheers from Coodle and Doodle, burst into tears in the chamber. His very similar effort in 1860 abandoned the fancy franchises and proposed a straightforward reduction of the voting qualification in the towns from £10 to £6 (and from £14 to £10 in the counties). This was introduced in what one observer called 'profound indifference', passed its second reading without being opposed and was eventually 'postponed' when it got bogged down in committee.

In 1858, the Tories took their turn at the same game. Lord Derby had come to office at the head of a minority Government. Though he instinctively hated reform, he was persuaded by his influential colleague Benjamin Disraeli that he could upset the Opposition by proposing a Tory Reform Bill. The 1859 Bill copied out the 'fancy franchises' from Russell's Bill of 1854 and left the electorate in towns and cities almost unchanged. The major change was to enfranchise about 200,000 people in the counties and to bring the rural qualifications into line with the boroughs. The Liberals, partly by promising wider reforms in the future, managed to defeat the measure and turn the Tories out.

The arguments against all these measures were very much the same as in 1832. The House of Commons represented people with property, most of whom were terrified of any surrender of power that could possibly lead to the surrender of any of that property. Speaking on the 1860 Bill, Sir Edward Bulwer-Lytton, MP for Hertfordshire (unopposed), explained that 'reducing the franchise to allow manual labour must end by giving manual labour the political power over the capital that employs it and the mind that should direct it . . .' The House, he concluded, 'must not admit poverty and passion'. The Hon. Sir John Packington, Tory MP for Droitwich (394 voters), regarded the measure 'as making but one proposal – which is simply hereafter to overwhelm the property and intelligence of the country by force of numbers . . . a more grave and serious consequence it is impossible to contemplate'. This was not just rant from the backbenches. The cultured and articulate Benjamin Disraeli, MP for Buckinghamshire (unopposed), objected to the 1860 Bill because it enfranchised 203,000 people in the boroughs and these would cast their votes 'all of one class, bound together by the same entitlements and habits – we must recollect that half the boroughs are already under the influence of the new class . . . we are conferring power on a class'. Such arguments were not confined to Tories. M. H. Marsh, Liberal MP for Salisbury, had just come back from Australia where he was able to sample a wider franchise at first hand. 'Magistrates,' he told a shocked house, 'were being appointed from the lowest classes, persons wholly unfit for such a situation, and thus the habitual reverence Englishmen had for the law was weakened.' The ultimate outrage had been achieved, he said, when the workers, through their new votes, had 'forced public spending on railways'. These notions went right to the top of the Liberal Party, whose most distinguished grandee, Lord Palmerston, continually frustrated his own party's efforts for reform. When he was shown the figures for the consequences of his party's extremely mild 1860 reforms, he was appalled. 'The returns we have got,' he wrote to Russell, 'show up an awful increase in voters in the large towns, whatever standard of franchise we adopt.' The noble imperialist septuagenarian devoted much of the rest of his life to protecting the House of Commons from that 'awful increase'.

A consistent theme of the opponents of reform all these years was apprehension about the growing influence of trade unions and strikes. The lockout of 20,000 cotton workers by employers at Preston, who refused even to negotiate with the spinners' and weavers' union committees, lasted from October 1853 to May 1854 before the workers were finally starved back to work. The employers were shocked by the nationwide solidarity of the trade unions, which contributed £105,000 – an enormous sum – to the Preston hardship fund. In a haughty letter to Russell about the Liberal 1854 Reform Bill, Palmerston drew attention to the 'excitement in the working class' over the Preston strike, and warned that the new Bill would be 'giving great power to the agitating but secret leaders' of the unions, who wielded 'the most absolute despotism over the rest'. He went on: 'The direct consequence would be an increased and plausible cry for the ballot and the introduction of men into the House of Commons who would be following impulses not congenial to our institutions . . . Your intended

course is openly disapproved of by all the intelligent and respectable classes.'
The Tory Reform Bill of 1859 was introduced at the beginning of the long
London builders' strike for the nine-hour day. This stubborn and partly
successful strike was made possible only by regular contributions from
other unions and other cities. The strike profoundly influenced the debates
on the Reform Bill through 1859 and 1860. On 26 April 1860, Mr A.
Black, the Liberal Member for Edinburgh (unopposed), warned MPs of the
dangers of handing the vote to 'great masses of half-educated men'. He told
of his recent encounter with a group of 'noisy agitators' for the Ten Hours
Bill. 'I was asked – would I reduce the day to eight hours. I told them to
their face that the putting of such a question only showed the danger of
giving them the franchise.' In his great speech on the American Civil War
with which this chapter started, Professor Beesly argued:

It was the builders' strike in 1859 that settled the fate of the Reform Bill. They
[the Tories and the Whigs] were thrown into a state of crazy terror by the glimpses
they then caught of your unanimity and organization. Over and over again I have
heard it alleged as proof of the danger of entrusting you with the franchise.

The Radicals and Russellite Liberals argued that it was high time that
'the valuable body of artisans', as described in the Lords by the old Whig
Lord Brougham, should be 'admitted within the pale of the Constitution'.
Some, like Bright, argued for one household, one vote. Others argued for
a lower limit for the borough franchise than the £6 usually demanded by
Liberal Bills. But all were united in opposing universal suffrage. In all the
parliamentary debates there was not a whisper of the argument used by the
Levellers that the poorest he had as much right to vote as the richest he, or
that no one could legitimately be governed unless they had a chance to vote
for their government. Nor was a single voice raised in the House of Commons to echo the six demands of the Chartists. No MP called for universal
suffrage, or for ballots, or for equal constituencies, or for payment for MPs
or for annual parliaments. Coodle came and Doodle went, and neither paid
the remotest attention to the fact that, whichever of their Reform Bills was
passed or defeated, the enormous majority of the people over whom they
governed had no say in choosing their government.

Until 1865, the parliamentary cynicism and torpor on the question of
reform was matched by cynicism and torpor outside. Though there were
plenty of old Chartists who stayed true to their principles, there was none
of the mass agitation of the Chartist years. In the Commons, Whigs and
Tories taunted the reformers with the lack of popular demand for it. There
was, they argued, no sign among the people that they wanted the miserable

reforms proposed by Russell or by Derby. In a sense, this mockery was justified. The fact that there was no mass agitation for reform was partly due to the paucity of the reforms proposed. Admitting in 1859 to a group of northern clergymen that the reform campaign had failed, the free-trader Richard Cobden mourned the absence of 'some multitudinous demonstrations by the unenfranchised in favour of Parliamentary reform – something as earnest as in the days of Henry Hunt, but without the disorder of the time'. He attributed the lack of demonstrations to the fact that 'you are too prosperous and the people too well fed'. This was true of clergymen but, as Marx had so strikingly revealed in his *Address*, not remotely true of the working people. At least part of the reason for the lack of multitudinous demonstrations was that most of the multitude had nothing to gain even from the reforms Cobden was advocating. Why should the impoverished masses rise up or even demonstrate in favour of reforms that would not touch them? The defeat of the Chartists was seen as a defeat for the idea of universal suffrage. In the atmosphere of the 'solidarity of defeat', there was no incentive even to notice the silly reform games of Coodle and Doodle. If reform meant enfranchising the few, why should the many show the slightest interest?

Marx detected a possible shift in this despondent tone when, early in 1865, he heard of a move among the founders of the International Working Men's Association to form a new workers' movement for parliamentary reform. The move turned into that third great meeting, at St Martin's Hall on 23 February 1865. It was addressed by the same speakers as at the International meeting a few months earlier. This meeting voted to establish a Reform League to campaign for one man, one vote. This aim contrasted sharply with that of the Reform Union, set up by rich Liberals the previous year, to campaign for one household, one vote. There was a huge gap both politically and numerically between the two reforms. Both excluded all women. But household suffrage also excluded what later became known as 'the residuum', a large minority of working-class men. Marx was not on the committee to organize the formation and programme of the new Reform League, but the elected committee was almost exactly the same as that which had founded the International: the trade-union leaders George Odger and William Cremer, the building-union organizer George Howell, William Dell, William Stainsby, Robert Hartwell, Benjamin Lucraft. When Marx heard the names on the committee, he wrote excitedly to Engels: 'The International Association has managed so to constitute the majority on the committee to set up the new Reform League that the whole leadership is in our hands.' This delight continued through most of 1865. On May Day, he wrote again to Engels: 'The great achievement of the International Association is this: The Reform League is OUR WORK.' On 13 May, he was rejoicing to Engels again: 'Without us this Reform League would never have come into existence . . .' And when, in December, the League organized one of the biggest meetings of the decade, Marx went right over the top: 'The Reform League, one of the organizations we founded, has had a triumphant success at the St Martin's Hall meeting, the largest and most purely working-class meeting that has taken place since I have been living in London. The people from our committee were at the head of it and put forward our ideas.'

Like all political enthusiasts, Marx was keen to accentuate the positive, to see a silver lining in the political gloom. His claim that the Reform League was 'our work', and therefore could be expected to respond and deliver according to Marx's priorities, or even those of the International, was hopelessly optimistic. To start with, as Marx admitted, the League was controlled by a committee of twelve, only six of whom were working class. The others were lawyers, businessmen and financiers who could just as well have been on the committee of the Reform Union. The chairman was Edmund Beales, a likeable old Etonian barrister from Middlesex who was active in almost all the London Radical associations. Marx had no illusions about Beales. When the barrister was moved for membership of the Council of the International, Marx hurried to block him. He wrote:

I could, of course, have prevented the matter by force as all the Continentals would have voted with me. But I did not like any such division. So, by means of private letters . . . I have managed to persuade Beales's proposer not to bring forward his motion again. The official reason given was: 1. that Beales will stand for Marylebone at the next parliamentary elections and that our Association must by all means avoid appearing to serve the interests of any parliamentary ambition; 2. that Beales and we ourselves can be of greater assistance to each other if we sail our separate ships.

Tactfully, perhaps, Marx made no reference to the fact that this ambitious parliamentarian was chairman of the Reform League that was 'our work' and supposedly fielded only working-class speakers. Nor did he refer to the tensions and arguments, often bitter, between the trade unionists and the wealthy League committee members. The very fact that six rich men had been sought out by the trade unionists and asked to sit on their committee was an indication of how far they had sunk from the purity of their Chartist predecessors. There were other clues to the real situation. At another big meeting at St Martin's Hall in May to launch the League, Beales explained that the granting of the vote to working men would 'put an end to animosities ... amongst the different classes ... and weld all classes together by unity of interest into one harmonious whole'. In June 1865, a few weeks before the general election, the new secretary of the League, the builders' trade-union leader George Howell, wrote and circulated an address by the Reform League: 'To the trade unionists of the United Kingdom: "Let us once be able to maintain by the force of intellect our rights as workmen in that House [of Commons], and, depend upon it, we shall rise in the social scale."' What Marx thought of these blatant calls to class collaboration is unfortunately not on record. In his marvellous book on this period, *Before the Socialists* (1965), Royden Harrison could not help comparing the egalitarian demands of the Chartists with Howell's aim 'to rise in the social scale'. As Marx was soon angrily to recognize, both the ends and the means of the Reform League were crucially different from those of the Chartists.

The general election that summer of 1865, fought out with great bitterness and at enormous expense between Coodle and Doodle, returned a Liberal Government with a majority of 80. Lord Palmerston continued in his dotage as Prime Minister, and in October he died. He was replaced, inevitably, by 'Finality Jack' Russell. Palmerston's death tilted the balance in the Liberal Party away from the old landed Whigs towards the reformers, led by the Chancellor of the Exchequer, the 'phrasemaker' William Ewart Gladstone, who was to dominate Liberal politics for more than 20 years. Gladstone and Russell at once got to work on a new Reform Bill, which they assumed, with their big majority, they could at last push through the Commons.

They commissioned a mountain of research about the wealth of the existing electorate and how the electorate would change if they brought down the property qualification. Gladstone, who never for a moment drifted beyond what he called 'middle-class enfranchisement', was amazed to discover how many of the 1832 electors came from what he described as 'the working classes'. Slightly more than a fifth (21 per cent) of the existing voters were working class, he calculated. This scared him into raising the lower property limit enabling people in the boroughs to vote – from £6 (the figure originally moved by Russell) to £7. Gladstone also proposed a new fancy franchise, allowing a second vote to anyone who had £50 or more in the bank.

It was clear by early February 1866 that the new Liberal Government was in earnest about bringing in a mild Reform Bill of the type that had been brought forward many times since 1848. What was the effect on the Reform League? The League had grown steadily, though not hugely, in the year since its formation. The delegates who collected for its first annual conference – again at St Martin's Hall – were rather different from the small committed group who had set the League up. The delegation from the League's Central Council, still controlled by supporters of the International, came forward with a standard resolution committing the League to universal suffrage and nothing less. This resolution was hotly debated throughout the conference, which opened on 28 February and went on to 1 March. To the old campaigners' amazement, the bulk of the new delegates were inclined to support the Liberal Government's Bill, whatever it said. They made it clear that they would back, for instance, a Bill proposing household suffrage – the central demand of their rival organization, the Reform Union, and its éminence grise, John Bright. Above all, they insisted on a full meeting of the Council as soon as the Bill was published. On 12 March, Gladstone brought his new Bill to the House of Commons with its £7 limit and its £50 fancy franchise. It was much worse than even the most abject Government supporter in the League had imagined. The League's Council met again on 16 and 20 March. The debate was furious. A handful of the International men furiously denounced the miserable proposals of the Government and insisted that the League must oppose the measure root and branch. They found, again to their horror, that they were completely out of touch with the mood of the delegates. There was a strong and irresistible undertow pulling the delegates towards Gladstone and his ministers. Better some votes than no votes, argued the majority. Better to remain friends and allies of the Government over a difficult period than to join the Tories in opposition. The union leaders Odger and Cremer were most ardent in this view. The meeting, by a large majority, though it reaffirmed the League's commitment to universal suffrage, wished the new Bill well.

The decision led to predictable hostility from Marx and his followers. The former Chartist leader Ernest Jones, who had spent two years in prison after 1848 and was now trying to scrape a living as a lawyer in Manchester, was furious with the compromisers. On 2 April, Karl Marx, who had so enthusiastically supported the formation of the League and even claimed it as 'all our own work', wrote to Engels:

The accursed traditional nature of all English movements is manifesting itself again in the REFORM MOVEMENT. The same 'INSTALMENTS' which but a few weeks ago were rejected with the utmost indignation by the people's party – they had even refused Bright's ultimatum of household suffrage – are now treated as a prize worthy to be fought for. And why? Because the Tories are screaming blue murder. These fellows lack the mettle of the old Chartists.

'These fellows' did indeed 'lack the mettle of the old Chartists'. As Marx himself had grudgingly admitted when he came to write his *Address* and mourned his sacrifice of 'the old boldness of speech', the times were very different from those of the Chartists. The aristocracy of labour, and the trade-union leaders, were not even interested in the transformation of class society championed by the Chartists. They were happy with piecemeal reform, and if the Liberal Government could procure votes for the new Labour aristocrats, that was fine. They could worry about the rest later.

So, with both reform organizations dormant, and any threat of mass agitation consequently ruled out, the whole scene and argument shifted to Parliament. The interminable debate on reform that Gladstone had started on 12 March 1866 followed exactly the same unflurried and predictable course as had all the other debates on the subject. Lord Derby, the Tory leader, got it just about right when he wrote in his diary: 'Bill discussed everywhere. There is great excitement in the upper classes, not shared by the people.' A great gulf was fixed between the House of Commons and the people, which all the developments since 1832 had failed to close. More than a third of MPs (225 of them) were either peers or the sons or grandsons of peers or baronets, represented almost equally in both parties (175 Tories, 150 Liberals). More than a fifth (110) of the total came from 31 noble families. No wonder Gladstone's Commons audience was apathetic. Their scepticism was enhanced by Gladstone's ponderous and repetitive speaking style. He seldom used one word where two or, usually, three would do. 'Such were the doubts, such were the misgivings, such was the scepticism . . .' he began his historical survey of reform, and went on like that for nearly two hours. The Radicals squirmed as Gladstone devoted more and more of his speech to an attack on the concept of democracy. His whole Bill, he explained, had been devised to ensure the smallest possible impact on the relatively few new working-class voters on the House. In the counties, the reduction of the franchise qualification from £50 to £14 would let in so few workers 'as not to be worth taking into consideration'. The savings-bank franchise was introduced 'to diminish' the relative share of working-class votes. Altogether, the Bill would produce 232,000 new voters in the towns, an increase of 82 per cent, but the population of the towns had increased by 71 per cent since 1831. So the overall effect of the Bill would be to ensure that the working classes were a 'dwindling and diminishing proportion of the whole number of the new constituency'. If there was ever any doubt, his peroration confirmed on which side of the class barrier he and his Government stood: 'The Bill does not give the absolute majority to the working classes ... it is a tribute to the working classes' admirable performance at least of their duties towards their superiors.' Above all it promised the Liberals' old friend finality, or nearly so. It was 'a settlement for a considerable period'.

The debate went on for eight nights, by far the longest debate on reform since 1831. The main theme of the loyal Liberals who supported the Government followed Gladstone in insisting that the Bill would not disturb the balance of power between the classes. The Government depended on the support of the Radicals, especially those who had just been elected to Parliament. Supreme among these was the new MP for Westminster, John Stuart Mill, widely acclaimed as the outstanding Liberal intellectual of his time. His book *Considerations on Representative Government* had been published in 1861, and a special People's Edition was published at the end of 1865, just in time for the 1866 debates. The book's arguments were directed more to the educated academic than to the disenfranchised worker. The opening chapters make the case for representative institutions in preference to oligarchy or benevolent dictatorship. This argument came close to Rainsborough's – that no government can claim legitimately to rule over anyone who does not have a chance to choose it. 'In this country, for example,' wrote Mill, 'what are called the working classes may be considered as excluded from all direct participation in the government.' As a direct result, 'when a subject arises in which the labourers as such have an interest, is it regarded from any point of view but that of the employers of labour? ... On the question of strikes, for instance, it is doubtful if there is so much as one among the leading Members of either House who is not firmly convinced that the reason of the matter is unqualifiedly on the side of the masters, and that the men's view of it is simply absurd.'

For these reasons, Mill argued, in a formidable chapter entitled 'On the Extension of the Suffrage':

There ought to be no pariahs in a full-grown and civilized nation; no persons disqualified, except through their own default ... No arrangement of the suffrage, therefore, can be permanently satisfactory in which any person or class is peremptorily excluded; in which the electoral privilege is not open to all persons of full age who desire to attain it.

The thread of this argument seemed to flow directly from Rainsborough at Putney through Paine, Shelley and Hunt, and even through the Chartists but then, suddenly, the thread was cut. Mill went on to list 'certain exclusions' from his general rule. For instance, 'I regard it as wholly inadmissible that any person should participate in the suffrage without being able to read, write, and, I will add, perform the common operations of arithmetic'. People should be tested in these matters before they voted. 'It would be easy,' he mused, 'to require from everyone who presented himself for registry that he should, in the presence of the registrar, copy a sentence from an English book, and perform a sum in the rule of three . . .' Illiterate and innumerate people, in short, probably still the majority of the British people, would be denied the vote. Moreover, 'I regard it as required by first principles, that the receipt of parish relief should be a peremptory disqualification for the franchise'. Indeed anyone who had received any parish relief at any time in the five years before the election should be denied the right to vote.

Mill went on ostensibly to argue against the principle that people's right to vote should be determined by their property. This criterion, he complained, 'is so imperfect'. People were rich often by accident and to afford them electoral privileges because of their wealth 'is always, and will continue to be, supremely odious'. On the other hand, there was a case, he argued, for giving electoral privileges to people of 'mental superiority'. For example, he observed, an 'employer of labour is on the average more intelligent than a labourer; for he must labour with his head, and not solely with his hands'. Moreover, a 'foreman is generally more intelligent than an ordinary labourer, and a labourer in the skilled trades than in the unskilled'. As proof of their superior intelligence, therefore, employers, foremen, perhaps even skilled workers, should get two votes to one for the unintelligent masses. Nor did Mill's process stop there. 'All graduates of universities, all persons who have passed creditably through the higher schools, all members of the liberal professions, and perhaps some others' should be specially registered so that they could cast extra votes because of these qualifications. The point of all these fancy franchises, Mill explained, was 'to assign to education, as such, the degree of superior influence due to it, and sufficient as a counterpoise to the numerical weight of the least educated class'. Mill's own prodigious education – he is said to have been fluent in Greek at the age of four – his liberal values and his mastery of logic and philosophy did not equip him to avoid the glaring contradictions of his argument. He started from the position that no one could be compelled or taxed by a government in which they had no choosing and that therefore it was 'odious' that the voting system should be influenced by property. He then proposed a system of voting which placed huge powers and privileges in the hands of the educated minority, who, necessarily, were the people with more property. The more he insisted that his voting system was not based on property, the more his argument led him to the opposite, and drove him to the view that reform of the suffrage must somehow provide an 'equipoise' to the swinish multitude.

In this leap against the stream of his original and principled argument, Mill was flying in precisely the opposite direction of the Levellers and the suffrage campaigners of 1819, 1839, 1842 and 1848. They all argued, like the radical speaker in the novel *Felix Holt*, that the poor and uneducated needed the vote precisely because they were poor and uneducated; that their numerical majority would, once universal suffrage was granted, swing the balance of economic power away from the minority to the majority and that that was the whole point of it. Mill argued the precise opposite, that universal suffrage was a grand idea provided it was not universal. Mill's speech on the second reading of the Bill was dogged throughout by the same contradictions. He scoffed at the Tories for 'recoiling in terror from the abyss into which they have not fallen', complained that 'working men's aspirations are not represented here', but stuck close to his party leaders' view that there was in the Reform Bill 'no question about making the working classes predominant'.

Similarly, John Bright, who spoke twice in the debate, curbed his irritation with what he called the 'feebleness' of Gladstone's Bill. The thrust of his argument was that, although there was no sign of mass agitation, there soon would be unless some form of reform was granted. In a speech reminiscent of Macaulay's in 1831 (though not half as well argued or powerfully expressed), Bright reminded the Commons of how 'most of you were running for your lives' from the social 'conflagration' in 1832, which had been set off by 'an accident' – the French Revolution of 1830. There was an urgent need to act immediately to prevent any such accident in the future. He prophesied: 'If you reject the Bill, you will find some accident happening when you will have something more to do than you are asked to do tonight under threats – it may be under the infliction of violence.' Bright's case for reform was based on the importance of the workers' quiescence rather than their participation. Only the previous year, he had spoken just as passionately against the application of the Ten Hours Bill to the trades in Birmingham, in which his own factories played such a vital part. 'A bourgeois of that kind really is INCORRIGIBLE,' Marx wrote to Engels, comparing Bright's opposition to economic reform with his support for electoral reform. 'The fellow does that [opposes the Ten Hours Bill] at a moment when he wants to make use of the workers to beat the oligarchs.'

Assorted Liberal employers applied Bright's line. J. T. Hibbert, another 'radical' Liberal MP (1,102 votes), was a partner in Platt & Sons of Oldham, where trade unions were ruthlessly suppressed. Hibbert said that one advantage of enfranchising the workers was that it would enable them to let off steam on political questions and so divert them from their obsession with trade unions. He confidently predicted that new MPs from working-class areas would never bother the House of Commons with the arguments between employers and workers. These were 'private questions subject to the laws of political economy' and 'must be fought outside the House, between capital and labour, and not by political discussion'. The laws of England had to be passed by a more representative assembly partly in order to ensure that the laws of political economy could be decided by crude class conflict on the factory floor.

Such were the arguments supporting the Government, which were immediately set upon by the Tories. The Tory attack was led by Robert Cecil, Viscount Cranborne, heir to the earldom of Salisbury, who at the age of 36 was beginning to think of himself as an elder statesman fighting in the last ditch for the values of a glorious but bygone age. Cranborne reacted to proposals to extend the franchise exactly as Henry Ireton had done. 'What are we to say to the owners of property if such a Bill is passed into law?' he asked anxiously, for his family were the owners of huge swathes of land all over England. 'What about the case of wealth? We have a right to ask for some consideration for a class not much thought of now . . . You would think that a man who contributed £10,000 a year in taxes should have rather more voice than the man who contributed, say, £10 a year.' Cranborne set the tone for a series of Tory speeches by quoting at length from the trade-union leader George Odger at a Reform League meeting in St Martin's Hall. Odger had declared that 'nothing short of manhood suffrage would satisfy the working people'; he had said, 'Give us votes and we will see that the poor man's daughter, who has worked 12, 14 and 16 hours a day should have time to go abroad and view the face of nature'; he had said that the vote would 'prevent the labourer working for eight shillings a week'; he had said that 'all men willing to work should have work provided for them'. Was it possible, asked the noble viscount, even to countenance such horrors? Odger was no loony extremist. He was a personal friend of William Ewart Gladstone. Cranborne continued:

The very fact that the men whom they trust as their speakers and delegates at political meetings urge such subjects on the notice of their hearers ought to be sufficient to warn you of the danger of the course upon which you are about to enter when you propose to give the working classes entire and undisputed control over the policy of Parliament.

If the Tories had had to rely on their own numbers in the Commons, such arguments would never have prevailed. But the threat to property from even partial electoral reform seduced to the Tory side a band of Whigs, supporters of Lord Palmerston, who saw in the very word reform a serious threat to their own landed estates or those of their patrons. These men had stood in the 1865 election as Liberals, and made up the Liberal majority. Their opposition to the Bill threatened the Government from the outset. The Government was prepared for some splits, but they could not have envisaged the flow of angry rhetoric that now spilled from the Liberal benches. In the debate on the first reading, the Rt. Hon. Edward Horsman, a former Liberal Cabinet minister and MP for Stroud (687 votes), broke ranks at once with a furious assault on 'projected changes which are not suited to the wants and trumpets of the times'. His central point, which recurred throughout the debates, was that there was no mass agitation for reform and that the whole idea was a notion dreamed up by the villainous John Bright. As a result, mourned Horsman, 'the old tree of English liberty will be transformed into a brazen image of ignorance and intolerance which the worshippers of transatlantic equality want to set up'. Turning to Bright, he whined: 'You are unsettling everything,' especially 'the old principle of the representation of property'. 'Democracy is upon us!' he concluded, reminding the House that 'there is an irreconcilable enmity between democracy and freedom' and that 'the first law of political life is that we in Parliament should rule by the voice of the educated minority'.

It seemed impossible that any speech in the debate could be as long and sententious as Horsman's, but a new record was at once established in both respects by Horsman's former colleague in Palmerston's Government Robert Lowe. Lowe, Liberal MP for Calne (174 votes), unleashed the first in a series of huge tirades against the whole notion of electoral reform. He was worried above all else by the rising power of the working class and the trade unions. The working classes, he warned, 'will say: we have the machinery; we have our trade unions, we have our leaders all ready, we have the power of combination – when we have a prize to fight for we will bring our new voting power to bear with tenfold more force than ever before'. He beseeched the House to consider 'the system of terrorism that lurks behind these trade unions, and then look at this tremendous machinery if you only arm it with the one thing it wants – the parliamentary vote. Surely the heroic work of so many centuries, the matchless achievements of so many wise heads and strong hands, deserve a nobler consummation than to be sacrificed at the shrine of revolutionary passion.' In a passage widely quoted in later months, Lowe gave vent to his contempt, fear and even hatred for what he called the 'swarming millions'. 'If you want venality, if you want ignorance; if you want drunkenness and facility for being intimidated; or if you want impulsive, unreflecting and violent people, where do you look for them in the constituencies? Do you go to the top, or do you go to the bottom?' The question was left unanswered. Most objective observers hunting for venality and violence might have gone to the top, to the people responsible for the Crimean War, for child labour, for the starvation of the working masses or for widespread banishment and capital punishment of offenders. Robert Lowe was looking in the opposite direction, to the victims of exploitation rather than to its perpetrators.

John Bright, rising to speak on the Bill's first reading after Horsman and Lowe, blamed the two men on one another and derided Horsman for retiring 'into what may be called the political cave of Adullam'. This was a reference to the Book of Samuel, which tells the story of David retreating in terror from various vengeful kings and escaping 'to the cave of Adullam', where he was joined 'by every one that was in distress and every one that was in debt and every one that was discontented'. The jibe stuck, and the dissident Palmerstonians led by Horsman and Lowe at once became known as Adullamites or Caveites. For all the satire at their expense, these Adullamites were a continuing menace to the Liberals' majority, and the Cabinet members who spoke in the debates devoted more and more time to the extremist oligarchical arguments from their own benches. Every effort was made to buy them off. The Caveite Member for County Galway, W. H. Gregory, was even offered a post in the Liberal Cabinet, which he tactfully refused. It was Gregory, on the fourth night of the debate (19 April), who first noticed that the argument was 'going against the Government'. The two main reasons for the drift were very much the same as in all the other parliamentary attempts at reform since the Chartists.

The first was the marginal nature of the proposed reform. In an unguarded moment in 1865, Gladstone had allowed himself to declare that anyone 'made of flesh and blood' had a basic right to vote. Throughout the debates this quotation was used against him to prove, first, that he was really in favour of universal suffrage, which he wasn't, and secondly that his calls for a partial enfranchisement of a few workers made nonsense of any argument based on 'flesh and blood'. Sir Edward Bulwer-Lytton asked whether Gladstone's message to the masses was that 'a £7 voter is real flesh and blood, but the rest of you are only gradual flesh and blood'. Giving the vote to so few people could hardly be expected to engage the masses, and the few who were going to get it were by definition 'more responsible' and therefore less likely to engage in agitation. Gladstone spent half his final speech before the vote praising the 'heroism of the mass' during the American Civil War, and the other half reassuring everyone that only a tiny fraction of the same heroic mass would get the right to vote from his Bill.

This contradictory, partial, step-by-step approach led to the second great weakness of the Bill: its isolation from people outside Parliament. The Tories and the Adullamites sensed quite quickly that there was no popular clamour for Gladstone's proposals because very few of the people would benefit from them. Why then move at all? Why 'unsettle everything' for a marginal reform which no one seemed to want very much? These questions gave the reactionaries confidence to make a stand to defeat the Bill as they had defeated so many similar ones in the past. Their growing confidence was handsomely illustrated by the final speech for the Tories of Benjamin Disraeli. He started by saying he was voting against the Bill because he could not foretell its consequences, and ended it by foretelling its consequences in language which, even by the bloated rhetorical standards of the age, must have stuck in his elegant throat. If the Bill passed, he predicted, there would be left in the House:

no charm of tradition; no families of historic lineage; none of those great estates around which men rally when liberty is assailed; no statesmanship, no eloquence, no learning, no genius. Instead of these, you will have a horde of selfish and obscure mediocrities incapable of anything but mischief, and that mischief devised and regulated by the raging demagogue of the hour.

The most raging demagogue of that particular hour was none other than Benjamin Disraeli.

The vote on the second reading, on 27 April, was almost as close as on the first Reform Bill 35 years previously. Then the Bill was carried by one vote, now it was carried by five (318 to 313). The chief difference between 1831 and 1866 was the situation outside. In 1831, it soon became clear that any further stalling of the Reform Bill, or its demise, would be met with popular violence. The one-vote victory on second reading had to be consolidated. In 1866, there seemed to be peace and good order outside. The Bill could be dispensed with. It staggered through more and more contested divisions until 18 June, when it finally expired in a Government defeat on an obscure amendment by 315 to 304. Disraeli and Lord Stanley, Lord Derby's son, went to the Carlton Club to drink champagne. The Russell–Gladstone Government sulked and resigned in high bad temper. No one except the politicians seemed to care. Four days before the vote on the second reading, Marx had written to Engels: 'In England, the Tories and Palmerstonian Whigs really deserve thanks for frustrating Russell's quiet settlement.' He despised the Liberal Bill because it was based on popular quietism. Would the people remain quiet? Marx hoped not. His letter went on: 'At one of the latest sittings, Mr Gladstone himself expressed his "melancholy" conviction that now, quite contrary to his benevolent expectation, a "long series of struggles" was imminent.' Neither he nor Gladstone could possibly have realized how soon or how dramatically those struggles would break out.

Those Tories who had scoffed at the lack of agitation in the country had typically misjudged the popular mood. People were not interested in Gladstone's Reform Bill because it enfranchised so few of them. The 'demise' of the Reform League lasted only as long as the prospect of some reform from the Liberal Party in Parliament. As soon as that prospect died, and the Liberal Government died with it, the moderate Reform leaders lost the argument for restraint. The case for compromise vanished. The demand for full universal manhood suffrage and the secret ballot were back on the agenda, and almost overnight the Reform League became a fighting force once more. The shift of the balance of influence inside the League was already becoming clear as the Reform Bill stumbled to parliamentary defeat. On 21 May, a huge demonstration assembled on Primrose Hill to declare support for the dying Bill. The tone of most of the League speakers was subdued – the Bill they were supporting was obviously finished and they could not bring themselves to admit it. The early speeches were boring, the huge crowd restless. They were cheered up by a furious speech from Charles Bradlaugh, who had shocked comfortable Britain by declaring himself an atheist. Bradlaugh warmed the crowd by reminding them that though they were on this occasion supporting a Government measure, their 'normal condition' was 'one of opposition to all government'. It would not be long, he predicted, before the Government would be banning meetings such as this one and 'I might have to call upon you then to meet under the walls of the sham Parliament in Westminster, when the whole strength of the Government would be put forth to prevent the meeting, and when the English people would rise in their might'.

It was a brilliant prediction. As the Bill and the Government fell, the splits in the Reform League between the cautious reformers and the dwindling band of militants who took their lead from Karl Marx were healed. On 2 July, an enormous demonstration in Trafalgar Square protested against the fall of the Government and the return of the Tories. The sneers and insults against the workers and their ability to govern themselves which had featured so prominently in the speeches of Tories and Adullamites were published, circulated and angrily recited from the plinth. Who were these shifty and venal plutocrats Derby, Cranborne, Horsman, Lowe, who denounced the workers for their venality and their shiftiness? They had toppled the reforming Government and were now, most of them, ministers of the Crown.

The protest meetings seemed to go on almost continually as a new minority Tory administration took office at Westminster. The infuriated crowds demanded daily gatherings in Trafalgar Square. The call went out for a vast national demonstration in Hyde Park on 22 July. The call sent 'Feargus O'Connor shivers' down the backs of the authorities. Even the suggestion of a national demonstration in London provoked in their fertile minds memories of the showdown on Kennington Common in 1848. Hyde Park, moreover, was closer to the nerve centre of political power than Kennington Common. There was no river to act as a barrier between Parliament and the people it purported to represent. Hyde Park had been specially redesigned to make it an agreeable place for the gentry in their carriages. There had been some trouble there for the riders in 1855, caused by demonstrators against the new rules banning Sunday trading. The knee-jerk reaction of the authorities to all these fears and complaints was predictable. The chief of the London police, Sir Richard Mayne, issued a proclamation banning the demonstration. The Home Secretary, an indecisive Tory called Spencer Walpole, told the Commons he was 'bound to exclude any meeting for political demonstration – so entirely opposed to the purpose for which the parks are open to the public'. In this endeavour he was wholeheartedly supported by the Liberal leaders.

The executive of the Reform League met on 20 July to discuss their reaction to the proclamation. Chairman Beales and the trade-union leaders, especially Cremer, were worried about the consequences of breaking the law, and recommended reluctant acceptance of the ban. Bradlaugh moved outright defiance. Though the majority supported Bradlaugh, the outcome of the meeting was a compromise. The demonstration would gather at Marble Arch and attempt to get into the park. If their way was barred by police, they would proceed peacefully to Trafalgar Square.

On the day, the size of the demonstration exceeded the most extravagant predictions. Procession after procession marched from different starting points to Marble Arch. There, in front of the huge closed gates, they faced lines of police with truncheons drawn. After demanding entry, Beales, supported by Bradlaugh and the others, quickly agreed to take the march off to Trafalgar Square. But the continuing charges of the police and their indiscriminate use of batons on unarmed demonstrators' heads provoked the more militant sections of the crowd. Though the majority followed the

League leaders to more speechifying in Trafalgar Square, a sizeable minority tore up the railings of the park, swarmed into it and engaged in a long and furious battle with the police. The battle (described by some reporters as 'skirmishes', by others as 'riots') went on for three days. Home Secretary Walpole grew increasingly nervous, and agreed to meet a deputation of League leaders. Beales offered to hold a meeting in the park at which he would call on his supporters to stop the violence.

This offer was reported by some of the deputation to have moved the secretary of state to tears. George Holyoake, a well-known Chartist and atheist, who was always quick to rush to the aid of his Tory adversaries, denied this publicly. But the story took hold. League supporters manufactured little packets of 'Walpole's tears', whose wide sale boosted the League funds. Noble families were outraged that one of their very own, the man responsible for law and order, should so demean himself in the company of the class enemy. The weeping Home Secretary symbolized the shifting balance of confidence between the reformers and their opponents. In a letter to Engels, five days after the demonstration, Karl Marx described the whole episode with a mixture of glee at the rising popular defiance and irritation at those who were holding it back: 'The Government has almost caused a mutiny here.'

As the summer months wore on, the people described by chief London magistrate Knox as 'the scum and refuse of the town', and many other towns, took to the streets demanding votes. John Bright told a huge Reform League banquet in September that the League was organizing a series of demonstrations and meetings on reform which would dwarf anything of the kind since the Chartists. If anything, he underestimated the size of these meetings. In October and November, he led 300,000 people through Birmingham, a quarter of a million in Manchester and what he later called 'an incredible number' in Glasgow. These meetings, all peaceful, were complemented by thousands of smaller gatherings in every village and town in the country. The leaders of the Reform League were in constant demand. Crowds gathered as if from nowhere to hear them speak, even when they were not scheduled or advertised. Charles Bradlaugh described Luton as 'a small town in a small country' which on a bleak rainy day on 23 November gave him 'a great welcome'. His daughter/biographer wrote:

It had been arranged that a conference of delegates (amongst whom were Mr Beales and Mr Bradlaugh, representing London) should be held previous to the Town Hall meeting at Messrs Willis and Co.'s factory, but, much to the amazement of the delegates, when they reached the factory gates they found a meeting of several thousand persons collected there without call or summons; the gathering was such as, according to the local newspaper, 'no living person had ever seen in that town'.

The delegate conference was quickly abandoned and a public meeting held instead in Park Square. The speeches, especially Bradlaugh's, 'were interrupted again and again by the cheering of the audience'. By 9 October, Marx wrote to a German friend: 'The reform movement here, which was called into being by our Central Council (in which I played an important part), has now assumed enormous and irresistible dimensions.'

These dimensions were made even more enormous and irresistible by other political developments not directly associated with reform but which, as so often at times of mass political awareness and activity, seemed to merge with the central issue. The London Jamaica Committee, a group of reformers shocked by the savage suppression of a revolt of former black slaves in Morant Bay, Jamaica, held vast meetings all of which demanded that the then Governor of Jamaica, Edward Eyre, should be prosecuted for supervising the oppression. The Jamaica agitation coincided exactly with the mass movement for reform. In the same letter, Marx referred to the cholera which is 'paying Londoners its respects with the utmost gravity', adding wryly that a recent report on the housing of the poor 'is presumably intended to serve Madam Cholera as a directory of addresses calling for preferential visitation'. Such poor households were further plagued by the first major economic recession since the Chartists.

The tide of working-class discontent kept on rising, threatening as it did so to cross the Irish Sea. Men and women who had never been seen before in the Reform League, including Gustave-Paul Cluseret who, four years later, was to be elected chief of staff of the Paris Commune, appeared at meetings with leaders of the Fenian rebels in Ireland, urging formal links between the League and the struggle for Irish independence. Even more ghastly ghosts haunted the propertied class. On 12 October, the General Council of the League discussed – and rejected after a fierce debate – a proposal to arrange elections on the basis of manhood suffrage for a People's Parliament, and a full delegate meeting of the League on 27 February 1867 warned that unless universal suffrage was granted by Parliament, 'it will be necessary to consider the propriety of these classes adopting a universal cessation of labour until their political rights are conceded'. This was backed by the builders' union leader George Potter, the name of whose London Working Men's Association was borrowed from the Chartists. In a speech in Trafalgar Square in March 1867, Potter threatened a full week's general strike if the vote was not at once granted to every household and every lodger.

Despite this mobilization for reform, however, the popular mood was still very different from that of the Chartists. The demand was still for political concession rather than economic egalitarianism. The Reform League leaders, right and left, called on their supporters to avoid any reference to the 'physical force' slogans of O'Connor, Harney and O'Brien in the early years of the Chartists. But the mood was changing so swiftly that no one could guarantee that the movement for reform might not, in the event of one of those accidents Bright had warned about, change into a movement for revolution.

This was the atmosphere in which Benjamin Disraeli, Chancellor of the Exchequer in the new minority Tory administration, wrestled with his colleagues in the new Cabinet about a new Reform Bill. He had no difficulty in persuading the majority that the Tories should sponsor a much milder Bill than Gladstone's the previous year. Such a measure, he argued, would steal Liberal clothes that were likely to stay in the cupboard again for a generation. Gladstone would be paralysed with embarrassment and, most importantly, the leaders of the Reform League would be split, as they had been last year, between the hotheads and the moderates. As a result, the stormy meetings and demonstrations would cease. Most of the Cabinet agreed. The chief exception was Lord Cranborne, whose hostility to all reform was ideological. He regarded any extension of the working-class vote as treachery to his class, and he was supported in that view by two other Neanderthal members of the Cabinet, Lord Caernarvon and General Jonathan Peel.

These arguments went on all through the winter months of 1866–7. Every time Disraeli reckoned he had a package he could commend to the House, the tumultuous events outside altered his course. His original plan, hatched by Prime Minister Derby, was not to bring a Reform Bill to the House at all but to proceed by way of 'resolutions', which could be put to the House in general terms and passed on to a prestigious commission. This procedure would certainly have delayed any change in the voting system for a year and might even be stretched out so that the next election could be fought on the old register. Disraeli was at first delighted with this 'compromise', but the rising agitation in January and February made many of his colleagues nervous. More and more Tories began to shed their ideological hostility to reform and to look for a compromise which would wrap the matter up and get the multitudes off the streets. Almost as soon as he introduced his 'resolutions', Disraeli was forced to shelve them and

produce yet another Reform Bill. He thought for a moment that the complicated measure he brought to the Cabinet in early March might be agreed
even by the diehards. At Cabinet, Cranborne appeared to agree. He took
the Bill home and studied it over a weekend. He concluded that it would
give far more votes to the workers than his aristocratic stomach could
endure. He spoke to his allies and eventually all three – Cranborne,
Caernarvon and Peel – resigned from the Cabinet.

Disraeli persevered, and on 18 March brought his Bill to the House. It
was the usual hotchpotch of checks and balances, whose purpose, much
like Gladstone's the previous year, was to give the vote to a few more
'responsible' workers while keeping the control of the House of Commons
firmly in the grip of the great estates. Thus his proposals for 'one ratepayer,
one vote' in the boroughs, he reckoned, would enfranchise another 237,000
people – but there would be 305,000 more votes in 'fancy franchises' for
people with property or money or both. Similarly, his proposed reduction
of the county qualification from £50 to £15 would enfranchise another
170,000 poorer men in the counties, but this would be 'balanced' by
another 139,000 votes in extra fancy franchises for the rich. All in all,
the Bill as originally proposed enfranchised no more workers than had
Gladstone's the previous year. It was seen by Disraeli, as the previous year's
Bill had been seen by Gladstone, as a 'bulwark against democracy'. As
Disraeli warned in his speech on the second reading on 18 March, he did
not confuse 'popular rights with democratic rights'. He ended with the firm
assurance: 'We do not live – and I trust it will never be the fate of this
country to live – under a democracy.'

Furious that the man who had led the attack on the previous year's
complicated and restrictive Reform Bill was now proposing something just
as complicated and just as restrictive, Gladstone rose to the bait and savaged
the Bill. He picked endless holes in its inconsistencies and hypocrisies. The
stage was set for yet another pointless and interminable parliamentary game
in which the leading antagonists would joust furiously across the floor of
the House, Coodle denouncing Doodle for the same inconsistencies for
which Doodle had denounced Coodle the previous year. If the same conditions had applied in early 1867 as in early 1866, there would have been
no reason why the parliamentary orators could not all have had their say
again at the same inordinate length, the same instructions be laid and the
same amendments put, with the same inevitable result that absolutely
nothing would change.

The same conditions, however, did not apply. The atmosphere outside
the House of Commons was entirely different. The passivity and indiffer-

ence with which the masses greeted Gladstone's measure were replaced by popular outrage. The Reform League, whose leaders did nothing at all during the 1866 debates except hope that Gladstone would win, was now campaigning all over the country for universal suffrage. Though it differed only marginally from the Bill the League had supported in 1866, Disraeli's Bill was furiously denounced by League campaigners. On a hot April Fool's Day, a huge delegation, some 300 strong, went to see Disraeli and Stanley at the House of Commons. Stanley recorded: 'Beales made a long pompous speech with very little in it. I thought him a charlatan. Two of the other notabilities, a Mr Cremer and one Odger, spoke fairly well, though rather vague about their use of Hs. The only one of the party who seemed to have any oratorical power was one Mantle.' Lord Stanley, who knew how to pronounce his Hs, had no idea that George Mantle was an old Chartist, whose memory of the great years of Chartism was becoming more and more relevant to the fight outside the Commons for Reform.

As the Bill limped on into April, the League meetings intensified and the calls on the executive for more drastic action grew more shrill. Gladstone's instinct was to lead his Party in overt hostility to Disraeli's Bill, and use his Commons majority to defeat it. But many Liberal Members were worried about what was going on in their constituencies, and began openly to demand that this wretched reform business should be settled as soon as possible. They were worried about the effect of another smashed Reform Bill. What would replace it? Would the tide gathering outside the House sweep away all the safeguards protecting the House of Commons from the people? At a meeting in the Commons tearoom on 8 April, about 50 Liberal MPs debated the matter. Two influential backbenchers spelled out what most of the others were thinking. John Locke, MP for Southwark (unopposed), said it was 'dangerous' to tamper with the Bill 'and so risk toppling into manhood suffrage'. Charles Seely, MP for Lincoln (878 votes), put the point more graphically. He would support the Bill he said, 'because it is better to have these matters settled by Disraeli and Derby than by Beales and Potter'.

The tearoom meeting pushed Gladstone and the Liberal Party into luke-warm support for the Tory Bill. But the crucial question still lurked at the back of all their minds: was Disraeli's timid measure, so constantly derided at all those meetings and demonstrations, even remotely likely to achieve Disraeli's stated ambition, to 'extinguish the agitation'? The answer came almost at once. On 16 April, the League held another vast rally in Birming-ham. It was addressed by a Radical, George Nuttall, whose angry speech was reported at length in the *Morning Star*, the paper associated with John Bright (though he never owned or edited it):

Not the Tories only but the House of Commons hated reform and would never grant it until they could not withhold it. The landlords, army lords, navy lords and law lords, who looked eagerly for a share of taxes for themselves and their dependants, would never let the people's nose from the grindstone if they could help it. But the people had the power in their hands if only they knew how to use it. Let them set their backs up, and show their bristles, and they would get the Reform Bill they wanted [cries of 'We'll do it!']. They must show they are prepared to burst open the doors of the House of Commons should they be kept persistently closed against them [cheers]. He hoped they were not coming to an end of a peaceful agitation . . . but when an aristocracy declared that the people should not be heard in the councils of the nation . . . that was a very dangerous and criminal thing ['Hear hear']. The people should rise in their might and majesty. If like the raging sea they should sweep on in their righteous indignation, every barrier set up against them – the aristocracy itself – might be swept into oblivion for ever.

This impatience and eagerness for direct action seeped upwards into the leadership of the Reform League. Two days later, the League's executive council met in London, unanimously condemned Disraeli's Bill as 'partial and oppressive' and reaffirmed their commitment to 'a vote for a man because he is a man'. What to do about it? It was probably the irrepressible Charles Bradlaugh who first mentioned the magic words 'Hyde Park'. He moved for another national demonstration there. Beales whined about the dangers of breaking the law, but Bradlaugh insisted on putting his motion. It was carried by five votes to three. At once placards started to go up all over the country, backed up by 36,000 leaflets announcing a mass demonstration for universal manhood suffrage on 6 May.

The plans for yet another demonstration in their favourite park caught ministers on the hop. Partly to maintain the fiction that the park was open to all members of the public, the Government had not proceeded with their proposed Park Bill that would have made all political meetings in Hyde Park illegal. The state of the law was therefore unclear. The only way the Government could stop the demonstration was by issuing a proclamation. On 1 May, the Home Secretary, 'weeping Walpole', ordered to be circulated and posted up in official places in London the following historic document:

Whereas it has been publicly announced that a meeting will be held in Hyde Park on Monday the sixth day of May next for the purpose of political discussion: and whereas the use of the Park for the purpose aforesaid is illegal, and interferes with the enjoyment of the Park by the people, and is calculated to endanger the public peace, now all persons are hereby warned and admonished that they will attend any such meeting at their peril, and all her Majesty's loyal and faithful subjects are required to abstain from attending, aiding or taking part in any such meeting, or from entering the Park with a view to attend, aid or take part in any such meeting.

On the same day, the Reform League staged another big demonstration in Trafalgar Square. The police rightly identified Charles Bradlaugh as the danger man on the League executive, and tactfully chose to serve him with the prohibition proclamation while he was speaking at the rally. Bradlaugh was overjoyed. He read the proclamation to the crowd, mocking it mercilessly and moving then and there that it should be defied. The crowd roared their approval. Any hope of overturning this acclamation by nervous members of the League executive that evening was abandoned. Indeed, as soon as he knew he was committed beyond doubt to defying the law which gave him a living, Edmund Beales seemed to warm to his task.

The Government and the police grew more and more nervous as 6 May approached. Their proclamations were torn down as soon as they were posted up or, more frequently, pasted over with the Reform League's announcements of the meeting. There were plainly large numbers of people intent on defying the law, and the Government responded at first as though they were facing another Kennington Common crisis or even another Peterloo. Troops of Hussars were summoned up and held in waiting round the Park. Thousands of special constables were sworn in, and Woolwich Arsenal worked overtime making staves and even pikes. A mighty confrontation seemed inevitable. Yet, long before the Clerkenwell Branch banner of the Reform League arrived at the head of an enormous procession at the Marble Arch gate of Hyde Park at 6p.m. on 6 May, Walpole and his advisers backed away. There were so many demonstrators, so many gates to the park, so many separate meetings planned there. The troops, the police and the special constables kept their distance. Vast crowds flocked into the park through all the entrances. As always with such demonstrations, versions of the numbers varied hugely – from 20,000 in some Tory papers to 500,000 in the League accounts. Some proof that the latter figure was closer to the reality came from the 14 separate platforms from which even the most accomplished speakers could not make themselves heard. The most popular meeting was that of Bradlaugh, who declared that the reformers who had been killed at Peterloo and beaten at Kennington Common were now at last victorious.

This was the first time that any political organization representing the working class had openly and successfully defied the law of their masters, and the effect on the masters was catastrophic. Government newspapers shrieked abuse at the Reform League leaders and at Walpole. They demanded the arrest of the former and the resignation of the latter. As so often, they had completely misunderstood the relation of forces and the sombre consequences for the Government of their humiliation. There were no arrests. On 13 May, exactly a week after the demonstration, Spencer Walpole resigned as Home Secretary, his career finished. Prime Minister Derby made a graceful little speech regretting the loss of a valued and trusted colleague, going on a little too long about how the resignation had been planned for a long time and had nothing to do with the events in Hyde Park. No one believed him.

A week later still, on 20 May, by a stroke of the pen which had not even been discussed let alone agreed by the Cabinet, Disraeli transformed his Reform Bill. The architect of the transformation was Grosvenor Hodgkinson, an obscure solicitor who represented 710 voters at Newark and had until that day played very little part in the debates on the Bill, or in any others for that matter. Hodgkinson proposed an apparently innocuous amendment obliging all householders to be registered as ratepayers. At a stroke, this made new voters out of the hundreds of thousands of householders whose rates were 'compounded' in rents they paid to their landlords. They had been specifically excluded from the register by both Gladstone's and Disraeli's Bills. When Hodgkinson's amendment was posted, MPs were amused at his gall. How could a dull Liberal backbencher seek to change the very nature of the Bill? Everyone assumed that ministers and even the Liberal front bench would oppose it. Then, suddenly, on a sultry afternoon in a poorly attended House, Disraeli announced that he was accepting the amendment. As the news sped round the Westminster dinner tables, it was met first by disbelief, then by horror. The amendment would quadruple the number of enfranchised workers! It would give votes to a million more people, most of whom had no wealth but their wages! Lord Cranborne hurried down to the Chamber to denounce the amendment as 'entirely an abnegation of all the principles of our party'. Robert Lowe shot out of the Cave of Adullam to express his horror at what the amendment would do to his ancient pocket borough at Calne. 'You will give us some Wiltshire labourers with eight shillings a week wages!' he exclaimed. 'What will their politics be? With every disposition to speak favourably of them, their politics must take one form or another of socialism . . . we are going to make a revolution.'

But it was all to no avail. The Cabinet, when they were finally allowed to discuss the amendment, reluctantly but unanimously conceded it. Disraeli's

conclusive argument was that nothing less than such a dramatic enfranchisement could hope to halt the rolling tide of revolt. From then on, it was all
downhill for the reactionaries. Clauses in the Bill which had been introduced
to balance the new working-class voters and restrictive conditions denying
the vote to workers were systematically dropped. Out went the 'dual vote'
which allowed people with property to vote in town and country. Out went
the fancy franchises giving extra votes to people with savings or education.
Out went the requirement that ratepayers would need to show two years'
residence – the condition was reduced to one year. When the Bill was finally
read a third time on 15 July, a furious Cranborne declared that 'all the
precautions, guarantees, and securities in the Bill' had disappeared. There
had, he said, never been a Bill that had been treated in this way, and he
identified the cause. 'You are afraid of the pot boiling over,' he scoffed. 'At
the first threat of battle you throw your standard in the mud.' But he and
Lowe had lost the argument. Disraeli summed up with a speech which
downgraded the emphasis on property that he himself had introduced into
the debate a year previously: 'England is safe in the race of men who inhabit
her, safe in something much more precious than her accumulated capital –
her accumulated experience. She is safe in her national character, in her
fame and in that glorious future which I believe awaits her.' Gladstone
sulked in impotent abstention – and the Bill passed without a division.

The transformation of the Bill by the Hodgkinson amendment was seen
for many years as a bit of a mystery. Charles Seymour, author of what is
still a standard text, *Electoral Reform in England and Wales: The Development and Operation of the Parliamentary Franchise, 1832–1885*, first
published in 1915, wrote:

the explanation . . . if hidden explanation there be, remains yet to be discovered . . .
Why the Chancellor of the Exchequer was willing to accept so easily Hodgkinson's
alteration in the law of rating cannot be clearly demonstrated. It was only a few
weeks before that he had dubbed the proposal of such a measure 'rash counsel'.
The Cabinet itself was surprised . . .

The mystery with which Seymour wrestled arises only for those historians
and commentators who start from the certainty that politicians and other
important people determine what happens according to their deliberations.
No doubt, the essentially reforming disposition of Disraeli, and his effective
leadership of a minority Government in 1866 and 1867, played an important part in the passing of the Reform Bill. 'The capital thing about Disraeli,'
wrote Marx later that year, 'is that his hatred for the country gentlemen in
his own party and his hatred of the Whigs have set things going on a course

which can no longer be halted.' But, as Seymour himself concedes, the transformation of the Bill through the Hodgkinson amendment cannot possibly be explained by Disraeli's leadership qualities. The explanation lies outside Parliament, in the great wave of agitation that arose quite suddenly after the defeat of the Liberal Bill in 1866, and in the blatant defiance of attempts by the Government to suppress the agitation by force. Even the parliamentary debates themselves bear witness to the sense of panic that was shattering the solidarity and confidence of an unrepresentative assembly.

Yet the limited aims of that agitation, and its essential difference from Chartism, explain also how quickly it subsided. Just as the Reform League had effectively wound itself up as it waited for the Liberal Government of 1866 to produce a small part of what the League demanded, so, after the 1867 Bill, the League effectively dissolved itself into the Liberal Party. George Howell, the former builders' union leader who was Secretary to the League, kept his organization going through the rest of 1867 and most of 1868 by begging for donations from Liberal grandees. The donations were only forthcoming as long as Howell and his colleagues acted as glorified election agents for the Liberal Party in the 1868 general election. Once elected with another majority in that year, and having established that the only real political alternative for the working man was to vote Liberal, the Party leaders had no more use for the scruff of the League, and dropped it. Without the subsidies and without any independent working-class political orientation, the League collapsed.

The most striking result of the 1867 reform was that all the terrified predictions by the Tories and the Adullamites about its revolutionary consequences were comprehensively disproved. The new electorate, still a minority, quickly and submissively merged with the minority it replaced. The 'great estates', the end of which Lowe had mourned, were not only secure – they actually increased their influence in Parliament. There were more nobles and sons of nobles in Gladstone's Liberal administration of 1868 than there had been in 1865. The working-class reformers who had demanded more labour representation in Parliament were so delighted with what they got in 1867 that they immediately, and unsuccessfully, started to seek office within it. The trade-union leaders who had unconditionally supported the Chartists and had sat with Marx on the General Council of the First International preferred, after 1867, to concentrate their attention on the Liberal Party. The notion of 'Lib-Lab' MPs, Labour by origin but Liberal by party, began to take hold. In the 1874 election the Scottish miners' leader Alexander MacDonald was elected to Parliament for

Stafford, and his colleague Tom Burt, also a miners' leader, for Morpeth. Both were Lib-Labs. So was Henry Broadhurst, who was Secretary of the Parliamentary Committee set up by the newly formed Trades Union Congress (TUC) in 1867 and was elected to Parliament in 1880. The demands of the TUC's Parliamentary Committee were almost laughably mild. They were drawn up by the small band of lawyers who supported the unions, and concentrated almost entirely on marginal changes in the criminal law. The TUC seemed content with the enfranchisement of skilled workers in the towns, and showed little interest in further electoral reform. Throughout the 1870s, for instance, there was not a single TUC resolution even for manhood suffrage. Even the extension of the 1867 vote to the rural areas was not endorsed by the TUC until the Liberal Government introduced it after its re-election in 1880. All the emphasis by the newly enfranchised workers and their representatives was on moderation, responsibility and 'realism'.

In this atmosphere, Gladstone's new Liberal Government moved to legislate over a traditional and central demand of suffrage reformers ever since the beginning of the century: the secret ballot. This was, after universal suffrage, the most cherished demand of the Chartists, who poured their most vitriolic scorn on the bribery, violence and farce of 'open' elections. Unless people voted by secret ballot, they argued, their votes could be bought or scared out of them by employers and landlords. On 3 April 1871, the Commons gave a formal second reading to a Bill to provide for voting by secret ballot. The formal reason for postponing debate on the issue was to avoid 'sitting through Passion Week'. The real reason was more probably the tempestuous events in Paris where, two weeks earlier, the people had risen against their government and installed a democracy far richer and deeper than anything previously experienced anywhere in the world. The Paris Commune lasted from 16 March to 29 May, when it was crushed with the most brutal force. Some 20,000 Communards were slaughtered, their leaders arrested, publicly humiliated, stoned, tortured and executed. On 30 May, Karl Marx read his furious pamphlet on the Commune, *The Civil War in France*, to the General Council of the International Working Men's Association in London – on which still sat several trade-union leaders:

The Commune was formed of the municipal councillors, chosen by universal suffrage in various wards of the town, responsible and revocable at short terms. The majority of its members were naturally working men, or acknowledged representatives of the working class. The Commune was to be a working, not a parliamentary, body, executive and legislative at the same time. Instead of continuing to be the agent of the central government, the police was at once stripped of its political attributes, and turned into the responsible and at all times revocable agent of the Commune. So were the officials of all other branches of the administration ... The vested interests and the representation allowances of the high dignitaries of state disappeared along with the high dignitaries themselves. Public functions ceased to be the private property of the tools of the central government. Not only municipal administration, but the whole initiative hitherto exercised by the state was laid into the hands of the Commune.

Here was a democracy unrecognizable from that at Westminster with which the trade-union leaders of the International were rapidly associating. The hallmarks of the Commune were responsibility and revocability. The representatives were closely controlled by the represented. They were paid average wages, and if they reneged on commitments given when elected, they could be instantly removed and replaced. In every respect, this democracy differed decisively from anything even contemplated by the wealthy and irresponsible MPs in the British House of Commons.

The events in Paris that spring became a beacon for working-class democrats for more than a century. At the time, perhaps not surprisingly, the British House of Commons refused even to notice it. The first overt reference was on 29 June, a full month after Marx's oration to the International. John Locke, MP for Southwark, asked the Foreign Secretary whether 'the insurgents are still being shot without trial'. 'Have you made representations to the French authorities?' he asked mildly. Viscount Enfield mumbled in reply that he had 'no further information'.

In fact, however, the noble gentlemen from both parties in the House of Commons had followed the Revolution in Paris closely and nervously. One result was that the Tory Party under Benjamin Disraeli opposed the Government's mild proposals for holding the next election by secret ballot. His main argument (though he could not bring himself to mention the dreaded words 'Paris' or 'Commune') was that in the wake of the Revolution in France nothing should be done to rock the boat.

On the Continent, he reminded the House on 29 June (in what is a fine example of the 'polished' oratory fashionable at the time),

new systems of government, new principles of property, every subject that can agitate the minds of nations have been promulgated and patronized with more effect by sections of the people, especially during the last six months, than hitherto; and it is at this very time when the principles of government, the principles of property, all those things on which liberty and order alike depend, are called in question that the Prime Minister of England seizes the opportunity of intimating to the Parliament of this country that there are questions that must occupy their attention which must greatly affect the distribution of power, which must affect even the distribution of property . . . This arrangement about the ballot is part of the same system, a system which would dislocate all the machinery of the state, and disturb and agitate the public mind . . .

The secret ballot was passed by the Commons, postponed and then flung out by the Lords, no doubt to allow time to see how far the public mind had been agitated by the Paris events. As the memory of the Commune and its hideous suppression faded away, so the British Parliament's confidence was restored and the secret ballot became law in 1872. At once, the hooliganism, drunkenness and blatant bribery which had marred all previous elections vanished. Employers' and landlords' influence was still brought to bear on elections, but politely, lawfully, beneath the surface. At the 1874 general election, the first by secret ballot, none of Disraeli's terrible prophecies came true. The distribution of power and property was not affected, the machinery of the state was not dislocated, the public mind was not agitated. Instead, in 1874, as though to prove that anything reactionary could happen with the reformed franchise and the secret ballot, the Tories were returned to office with Disraeli as Prime Minister. In 'middle England', the whole area south of the Trent, excluding Cornwall, only four Liberals were returned to Parliament.

The new Tory Government was not disposed to risk its new power by dabbling any further in franchise reform. But the tide was running strongly for the reformers. The point was not just that the same political parties and the same politicians were carrying out the same policies without hindrance. More important was the legitimacy which the new electorate gave the politicians. Even Tories like Disraeli could claim that their legislation represented at least to some extent the will of millions of people. The fear of the 'leap in the dark' in 1867 – the fear that the property of the wealthy would in some way be threatened – had almost entirely vanished by the time Disraeli took office in 1874. Moreover, the reforms of 1867 on their own were anomalous. If people with a small amount of property in the towns could vote, why should not the people with the same amount of property in the countryside vote as well? The distinction lost all semblance of logic as the towns and cities spread into the countryside – or down industrial rivers like the Clyde and the Tyne. In 1878, the blue-blooded Liberal frontbencher George Trevelyan, seconded by the up-and-coming young Liberal barrister Sir Charles Dilke, moved in the Commons that the urban franchise should be extended to the countryside. They were defeated, but only just: 275 votes to 222. The debate and even the vote underlined the weakness of the Tory case. Though Robert Lowe was still there, fulminating about doom to come for the landed gentry, his arguments sounded thin and shrill even to his supporters. Dilke did some calculations from the division lists. The 275 had been elected by 1,083,758 electors, the 222 by 1,126,151. The discrepancy arose from the enduring unevenness of parliamentary elections – from the plural voting, pocket boroughs, universities and other anachronistic constituencies which still existed and whose MPs voted almost unanimously against reform.

These imbalances continued into the general election of 1880, in which both parties increased their vote: the Tories from 978,000 to 1,022,000; the Liberals from 934,000 to 1,199,000. As in 1874, the small majority for one party, in this case the Liberals, resulted in an absurdly large majority of seats. Just as Disraeli's Tories in 1874 had a disproportionate majority over the Liberals of 82, so Gladstone's Liberals in 1880 had a disproportionate majority over the Tories of 115. This time, however, the new Government was firmly committed to franchise reform.

There was nothing remotely democratic or proletarian in the new Parliament or the new Liberal Government. Only one other working man, the trade-union leader Henry Broadhurst, was elected under the Liberal banner, and swiftly joined the Government as a junior minister for trade. In the Cabinet of fourteen members (as at 1 January 1884), there were six earls (Selborne, Granville, Derby, Kimberley, Northbrook and Spencer), a marquis (Hartington), a baron (Carlingford), two baronets (Harcourt and Dilke) and only four commoners (Gladstone, Childers, Dodson and Joseph Chamberlain). This Cabinet was not overcome with enthusiasm for any extension of democracy, but the commitment at the election and the absurd anomaly which denied householders in the country a right conceded more than a decade earlier to their exact equivalents in the towns were far too obvious to be avoided. Moreover, for Gladstone and his advisers, the prospect of another big Commons battle over electoral reform was not altogether unwelcome. The issue was likely to unify the Party's uneasy coalition between old Whigs, who still predominated, and new Radicals. The intractable differences on Ireland, which were soon to drive Joseph Chamberlain out of the Cabinet and cast the Liberal Party into almost uninterrupted opposition for two decades, could for a time be disguised by uniting against the Tories and the House of Lords on franchise reform.

As ever, Gladstone started cautiously, proposing in 1882 a complicated

Bill to outlaw corrupt practices, most of which was eventually passed in 1883. The new law laid down strict rules on every aspect of electioneering, defining the maximum which could be spent by the candidates and their agents and setting out severe punishments for bribery or impersonation or using undue influence to secure votes. The Act was easy to circumvent – it did not, for instance, prevent the hiring of election workers or the provision of 'picnics' for whole workforces and even communities – but it did stamp out the more monstrous bribery and corruption that polluted elections up to that time.

As soon as the Corrupt Practices Act became law, the Liberal Party started to organize a countrywide campaign in favour of electoral reform. The campaign was launched with a furious letter to the Battersea Radical Association from the most popular Cabinet speaker at subsequent meetings all over the country: the Radical MP for Birmingham and President of the Board of Trade, Joseph Chamberlain. The campaign called in the aid of the numerous franchise reform associations that had been formed around the country, especially by the trade unions. The Durham Franchise Association was formed in 1872. Its Secretary from 1875 was John Wilson of Durham, a victimized miner and a popular figure among the North-East miners he represented. Meetings throughout the North-East, culminating in a monster meeting of more than 50,000 people in Newcastle, demanded the vote for miners, most of whom lived outside the urban boundaries. On 17 October 1883, a vast conference was convened in Leeds, at which delegates from 500 Liberal constituency parties voted unanimously for household franchise for the counties. In January 1884, a deputation representing a quarter of a million trade unionists packed into the biggest meeting hall in the Commons to confront the Prime Minister with their demands. Gladstone was delighted by the moderate and grovelling tone adopted by John Wilson and the other deputation leaders. Gracefully absorbing their flattery, he noted with relief that their demands stuck firmly at equalizing the franchise in town and country. He reflected contentedly that there had been no unpleasantness during the agitation that had been scrupulously controlled by the increasingly influential Liberal Party caucuses.

On 28 February, he brought his Bill to the House of Commons. He was as cautious as he had been in 1866. The sole purpose of the Bill was to extend the franchise that the Tories had given to occupiers in the towns to the countryside. He insisted that there was nothing remotely revolutionary or dangerous in the Bill. Its purpose was 'to strengthen the state', for he had discovered in the last 18 years that 'the strength of the modern state lies in its representative system'. The legitimacy of government depended on the degree to which it represented the people, and parliamentary representation lay at the very centre of 'this happy country and this happy Constitution'. On the other hand there was no question of ceding power to the majority or to the working class.

The Tories, under the nominal leadership of Sir Stafford Northcote, were hopelessly split on the issue. Most of them were instinctively opposed to any extension of the franchise. On the other hand, their own Government and their own hero Disraeli had been responsible for the 1867 reform. How could they oppose granting the franchise to people just because they did not live in towns or cities? They solved their dilemma in different ways. Most complained that the Bill applied equally to Ireland and would therefore enormously strengthen the Irish Home Rule Party under Charles Parnell, which already had more than 60 seats in the Commons. Others objected to introducing such a controversial measure at a time when British forces were engaged against the Mahdi of Sudan. Others refused to support the Bill without a reform of the distribution of votes and the constituency boundaries. They were nervous, they said, of 'swamping' the existing voters in a new wave. Their arguments were not assisted, as they had been in 1866, by the Whigs on the Liberal benches. Robert Lowe had 'gone upstairs' as Lord Sherbrooke. The only substantial 'Adullamite' to take part in the debates was G. J. Goschen, a wealthy merchant who had been elected for Ripon with 591 votes and had refused a Cabinet place because of his nervousness of electoral reform. But Goschen started his speech on second reading on 3 March 1884 by demolishing the central argument of the Bill's opponents:

The argument against the enfranchisement of the working class was this – and no doubt it is a very strong argument – the power they would have in any election if they combined together on questions of class interest. We are bound not to put that risk out of sight. Well, at the last election, I carefully watched the various contests that were taking place and I am bound to admit that I saw no tendency on the part of the working classes to combine on any special question where their pecuniary interests were concerned. On the contrary, they seemed to me to take a genuine political interest in public questions . . . The working classes have given proofs that they are deeply desirous to do what is right.

The Radical parliamentarians of the 1860s, Cobden, Bright, etc. had all been proved right. The evidence was that the workers who got the vote did not use it to further their class interest. As John Wilson, the Durham miners' leader, had written in one of many obsequious letters to his hero Gladstone:

Some have seen in the future the working classes misusing the freedom given them and rolling like a mighty human avalanche filled with the vilest passions overturning and destroying the institutions of the nation ... but you, Sir, have an opinion more creditable to the people ... I believe those persons whom we ask you to enfranchise ought rather to be welcomed as you would welcome recruits to your army or children to your family.

Wilson, Broadhurst, Burt and the other trade-union leaders of the time insisted they did not want the vote to further the interests of their class. They were not Levellers. They wanted only a level playing field for voting, and indeed not even that. They were not seeking universal suffrage, not even for men. Goschen and his wealthy friends recognized these pacific intentions in the workers' leaders and welcomed them. If he still opposed the Bill, he explained, it was because he had also noticed in the representative assembly he loved a disturbing tendency to represent the voters. 'The powers of resistance to any popular demand had notably decreased,' he mourned. There was a dangerous inclination among MPs to listen to people 'out of doors'. Goschen's arguments were demonstrably weak, as were those of the other opponents of the Bill during six long nights of debate. The second reading was eventually carried by 340 to 210. The majority contrasted sharply with the single vote and the five votes with which numerically smaller reforms had been carried on second reading in 1832 and 1867. Indeed, as the weeks went on, the Tories dropped their opposition altogether and on 26 June the third reading was carried without a vote against, not even Goschen's.

There remained a formidable obstacle: the House of Lords. On 7 July, by a majority of 59, and without once even mentioning the real reason for their opposition – the extension of the franchise – the Lords voted against the Bill because it was not accompanied by another measure to redistribute constituencies. Another, consistent argument was that there had not been any genuine popular agitation for further franchise reform and that the big meetings the previous autumn had all been artificially got up by the Liberal Party. Their lordships got their answer now in a manifestation of popular outrage. What roused people to protest was not so much the loss of the county franchise as the effrontery of the Lords in overturning the Commons. The London Trades Council speedily organized a mass demonstration in Hyde Park. On 21 July, an estimated 30,000 people marched through the city to merge with at least that many already assembled in the park. It was the spring of 1867 all over again, with seven separate mass meetings being held in different sections of the park. 'Down with the Lords – Give us the

Bill' was the universal slogan. The Radical MP for Southwark, Professor Thorold Rogers, likened the House of Lords to 'Sodom and Gomorrah and the abominations of the Egyptian temple'. Joseph Chamberlain told the biggest of the seven crowds: 'We will never, never, never be the only race in the civilized world subservient to the insolent pretensions of a hereditary caste.' His speech produced a furious response from Her Majesty the Queen. Queen Victoria was opposed to the extension of the franchise – no one, after all, had elected her – but she was much more concerned that the rising temperature of popular fury would sweep away her beloved House of Lords. In August, Chamberlain held a series of enormous meetings in Birmingham at which he denounced the Lords with renewed fervour. The Queen protested again – and again: on 6, 8 and 10 August. In the pathetic belief that as many of her people supported the Lords as opposed them, she encouraged the Tory leaders to whip up counter-demonstrations in favour of the Lords and against the extension of the suffrage. Lord Randolph Churchill obliged at once and urged Midlands Tories to organize a huge ticket-only Queen, Country and Lords meeting at Aston Park for 13 October. Birmingham Radicals organized a mass purchase of tickets. When the meeting opened, it was immediately clear that the Tories were in a minority. A near-riot ensued. Seats were ripped up and hurled at the platform. 'At last – a proper distribution of seats!' was the triumphant shout of the demonstrators.

When Parliament reconvened, on 6 November, Gladstone brought a new, very similar franchise Bill to the Commons once again, and the Tories moved the same amendment. The speeches bore witness to the mood of the country. Thorold Rogers persisted in his contemptuous assault on the House of Lords. For this blatant defiance of the rules of the House, Rogers was not even reprimanded. The moderate Liberal MP for Liverpool, Samuel Smith, warned: 'In the country, the agitation has reached a point which might be described as alarming. I have no desire to see the agitation assume a revolutionary character which it would certainly assume if it continued much longer.' He said he felt 'afraid that there would emerge from out of the strife a new party like the social democrats of Germany and that the guidance of parties would pass from the hands of wise statesmen into that of extreme and violent men'.

Wise statesmen everywhere took note. The Bill passed in the Commons by 372 to 232. What had threatened to be a nasty confrontation between Lords and Commons dissolved in a hasty compromise. Gladstone met the Tory leaders secretly and agreed to introduce a Redistribution Bill to rearrange constituency boundaries. The Tories called off their allies in the

Lords and the Bill proceeded to a (grudging) Royal Assent. The Redistribution Act of 1885 fixed new boundaries according to population. There were still gross anomalies – even after the redistribution. For instance, the boroughs in the South-West had one Member for a population of 28,000, while in the industrial North-West the ratio was one to 58,000. Tenants had to be resident for a full year before they could register to vote. The university seats and some plural voting persisted, and the single-Member constituency system, a favourite of Lord Salisbury, protected Tory voters in the towns and cities. But in general the new Parliament was substantially more representative than its predecessor. Gladstone was happy. He had got his franchise Bill through 'without destroying the ancient traditions of the country'. The Tories too were satisfied, and no wonder. Thanks mainly to Liberal divisions over Ireland, they won the 1886 election on the new register by a huge majority – and stayed in office almost continuously for 20 years.

The 1884 Act added 1,762,441 voters to the register, compared to 217,000 in 1832 and 938,000 in 1867. The result was an all-male electorate of nearly 4 million. A few of these (35,066) were qualified to vote by 'ancient rights'. Some (508,554) had more than one vote through ownership of extra property in the counties. The vast majority were entitled to vote because, as owners or tenants, they occupied property worth £10 a year or more. The percentage of men allowed to vote varied hugely from place to place. In some urban constituencies, Wimbledon or Pudsey for instance, one in four men could vote. In rural areas, such as Basingstoke or Carmarthen, the ratio of voters to the male population was one in eight. On average, about one in six, about 17 per cent, of the population were entitled to vote. Given that half the population, women, could not vote at all, about 58 per cent of men had won the vote.

The story of the 1885 franchise reform and the emancipation of the agricultural labourers, as with each new increase in the franchise, is inextricably entwined with the struggle of the agricultural labourers for better conditions and higher pay. More than a century later, it is easy to forget that in the 1880s agriculture was still by far the biggest employer. Though the numbers were falling fast, there were in Britain nearly a million agricultural labourers, shepherds and farm servants, and a tenth of them were under the age of 15. Most of them were employed in conditions of desperate insecurity and poverty not much improved since the dark days of the Tolpuddle martyrs in the 1830s. In 1871, they were still paid less than half the wretched wages in industry. Added to this poverty was the deference and obedience demanded of the labourers by the farmers. In 1864, for instance, two labourers in Cornwall were sent to prison for refusing to obey their master's 'lawful command' to go to church. Building a union among these isolated and impoverished rural workers, most of whom lived in 'tied cottages' under threat of instant eviction, was a grim business, but the greed and insensitivity of the farmers drove the organizers on. On 7 February 1872, two worried farm labourers in rural Warwickshire called at the cottage of a local hedge-cutter, carpenter and lay Methodist preacher called Joseph Arch. They asked him if he would help them form a union. Arch agreed, and before long he was addressing a historic meeting of 2,000 labourers in the small village of Wellestone. The movement for the union spread like wildfire through the Warwickshire countryside. Against all odds, Arch organized a series of successful strikes. In a few months, on the back of the successful strikes and the increase in wages prised out of the farmers, the national union grew rapidly to 80,000 members. The growth stimulated great interest in the Liberal Party and its press, and Joseph Arch rapidly became a prized speaker on Liberal platforms. But the farmers, stung to fury by the new movement, rapidly regrouped and by the start of the trade recession of 1874 began to counter-attack. In many of the areas where the union had flourished, its leaders were sacked and evicted. As the movement he had done so much to create was reduced to a quarter of its former strength by 1875, Joseph Arch turned away from the defeated labourers and towards the Liberal Party. He spoke up for the extension of the franchise in 1884 and benefited from it. He was elected to Parliament in 1885, 1892 and 1895. But he did and said little or nothing there, and finally died, passive and self-satisfied, at the ripe old age of 93.

How far, then, by the time the Tories took office in 1886, had the British Parliament met the six demands set out by the Chartists more than 40 years previously? The only principle conceded in full was voting by secret ballot. Universal male suffrage? Some two-thirds of men – the more prosperous two-thirds – had the vote. No more property qualifications? In a sense, all voters needed property qualifications, but they were quite small. Only about half a million had an extra vote because of their large property holdings. Equal Member constituencies? They hadn't been achieved either, or anything like it, but at least the more ridiculous anomalies in the constituencies had been ironed out. Payment of Members? None were paid, but several, led by John Wilson, Joseph Arch and the ten other working men who were elected as Liberals to the Commons on the new 1884 franchise (most of them, including Arch and Wilson, lost their seats again in 1886), started earnestly to demand payment. Finally, the demand for annual parliaments was the only one not even mentioned let alone conceded then, or ever since.

The most common interpretation of this partial achievement is that the British Parliament in its steady and dependable British way gradually and peacefully conceded what in other countries might only have been won in civil strife. The real history, however, suggests something rather different.

From early on, the old rulers were disposed to spread the franchise. Though they never intended voters to represent any more than their own class interests and their own bigoted views, they were excited by the idea that they were representing something more democratic. On the other hand, they were terrified that by allowing people without property into the process they endangered their own property. From 1852 to 1867 they dithered on the brink of franchise extension without plucking up the courage to take the plunge, and were finally pushed by forces outside Parliament. There was never any major concession on franchise reform without some sign that people would fight for it. The concessions were not voluntary. They were not inspired by the ingenuity, generosity or democratic spirit of the politicians. Each one of them in 1867 and in 1884 was wrung out of Commons and Lords by mass agitation and mass action. Though the Liberal Party organized some of that agitation, the two most decisive concessions – the Hodgkinson amendment in 1867 and the submission of the Lords in 1884 – were secured when it became obvious, as it had done in 1831, that even the most radical representatives in Parliament had lost control of the action outside and that what John Wilson disparagingly called an 'avalanche' of political activity had been set off against the politicians' will.

That agitation, though crucial, was different from that of the Chartists. The Chartists proudly proclaimed their working-class orientation and demanded the vote as part of a campaign for economic democracy as well as political democracy. The vote, for them, meant a redistribution of property, and therefore a change in the control of property. Chartism was in essence a revolutionary movement that demanded the vote to push through their revolution. In those circumstances, even those like Disraeli, whose basic intellectual and emotional instinct was to support the demand for increased representation, realized that to concede the vote to the Chartists would threaten their own control of property. This was the fear which produced those lucid arguments from Henry Ireton in 1647, and which still haunted the wealthy. Political power, they insisted, should only be conceded if and when property was safe from the people who might seize it. This explains the obsessive hatred of so many MPs of strikes and trade-union action. Did the agitators for the vote come from the same stable as strikers and trade unionists? Would they make common cause with the strikers and trade unionists and pool their new-found power in Parliament with their detested inclination to go on strike or raise funds in solidarity with them? It was only when the answer to these questions was plainly No; only when franchise agitators like John Bright reassured the House again and again that there were safe walls between political activity and industrial action; only when Liberal employers could positively assure them that the Liberal activists among the trade unionists were often the most docile workers on the shop floor; only when continuity of the old House of Commons and the old political parties with their old political policies were guaranteed; only when it became perfectly clear that economic oligarchy could exist side by side with growing parliamentary democracy, that the concessions were granted. Proof positive that these were the conditions of the extended franchise is the remarkable fact that throughout all those hundreds of hours of parliamentary debate and all the resolutions and aspirations of the franchise associations and trade union congresses, not a single voice even suggested that a vote for the poor and exploited would start to put an end to the poverty and exploitation which remained throughout the Victorian age the dominating features of society.

The other crucial question at Putney – could a government legitimately govern anyone who could not vote for it? – still required an answer. For all the gains made in 1867 and 1884, at least two-thirds of the population – all the women and more than a third of the men – still had no votes, and would not get them without another stupendous agitation.

Women

At the end of 1884, when the new Reform Bill became an Act, some 60 per cent of all adult men were entitled to vote for their government but not a single woman could do so. That remained the state of British democracy for the next 34 years. Looking back more than a century later, the contrast seems preposterous. How could it possibly have come about? What bizarre contortion of reason or justice could deprive all women of the right to choose their government when that right had been conceded to a majority of men? How could such a huge gap yawn between the political rights of human beings living side by side with one another, speaking the same language, conceiving and sustaining children and keeping house together?

Between March and May 1884, while the Third Reform Bill was going through the House of Commons, Frederick Engels was working feverishly on an answer. The result was a little book published at the end of the year the new Reform Bill became an Act. It was called *The Origin of the Family, Private Property and the State*. Engels explained that the book was a 'bequest' to his friend and mentor Karl Marx, with whom he had collaborated all his adult life and who had died in March 1883. The book was a wide-ranging historical survey based largely on the work of the American anthropologist Lewis Morgan. Its central purpose was to find practical and scientific explanations for the problems arising from the relations between men, women and their families – problems that were usually explained away by priests and reactionaries as immutable laws of God. Engels had come across Marx's copious notes on the work of Morgan, who had studied primitive societies. Morgan showed that there had been very long periods in human history where men (and a single male God) had not been in the ascendancy, and some indeed where women (and goddesses) ranked higher

than men in the social and religious scale. Engels concluded that the shift
from primitive equality and even female dominance to male supremacy
came about over many thousands of years not through divine order but
because of biological differences between men and women connected with
the production of wealth.

As productive techniques improved, a surplus was created and increasingly controlled by a minority. Human society was cut into classes. Increasing the surplus demanded more and more people in production. Because of
women's role in rearing children, they became less able to take part in
producing the surplus and therefore in controlling it. Though they still
worked, women were systematically marginalized, exploited and patronized. The hierarchies of the emerging class society reproduced themselves
in increasingly uneven relationships between men and women. Just as there
were masters in the productive process, so there were masters in the home.
For reasons to do with human physical strength and child-bearing, Engels
explained:

man's position in the family became superior to that of woman, and the desire
arose to use this fortified position for the purpose of overthrowing the traditional
law of inheritance in favour of his children. But this was not feasible as long as
maternal law was valid. This law had to be abolished, and so it was.

Engels described the abolition of the old maternal laws of inheritance as
'the historic defeat of the female sex'. This was compounded in the growth
of 'the monogamous family founded on the open or disguised domestic
slavery of women'. Monogamy was not pre-ordained let alone idyllic. It
was, in essence, the 'victory of private property over primitive and natural
collectivism'. In a striking metaphor, Engels explained:

In the great majority of cases the man had to earn a living and support his family.
He thereby obtains a superior position . . . in the family, he is the bourgeois, the
woman represents the proletariat.

More than a hundred years of research since Engels wrote his book have
hugely improved the material on which it was based. In many cases, his
conclusions have been damaged and even discredited. But his three fundamental messages are unshaken. First, that men and women were not always
unequal. Secondly, that there were discernible secular and economic reasons
for that inequality. And thirdly, that there is no reason why that inequality
should persevere. If the economics of production had at different times in
the past promoted women and then men to supremacy, those economics
could change again. Indeed, there were many signs, Engels reflected, that

the development of capitalism with its ever-changing methods of mass production would remove the economic conditions for the historic defeat of the female sex. Chief among these conditions, which he stressed at least three times, was the increasing involvement of women in social production: 'The emancipation of women is primarily dependent on the reintroduction of the whole female sex into the public industries.' And again, a hundred pages later:

The emancipation of women and their equality with men are impossible and remain so as long as women are excluded from social production and restricted to domestic labour. The emancipation of women becomes feasible only when women are enabled to take part extensively in social production.

Loud and almost unanimous was the indignation that greeted Engels's little book, and followed it into its translations into almost every European language. Few of the British critics noticed even in passing that much of Engels's theory was gradually being vindicated right there in Britain – in the attempts to break down the most obvious of all the discriminations against women: the obstinate refusal to allow any of them to vote.

The Chartists, as we have seen, stood for universal *male* suffrage. The suggestion that their demands for the working-class vote should extend to working-class women was made only fleetingly. In 1851, however, only three years after the rout on Kennington Common, a long anonymous article appeared in the *Westminster Review* entitled 'Enfranchisement of Women'. The article was prompted by a series of meetings in the United States of America – culminating in a Woman's Rights Convention in 1850 in Worcester, Massachusetts. The central principle of the resolution adopted by the Convention could have been borrowed directly from the Putney Debates 200 years earlier: 'That every human being, of full age, and resident for a proper length of time on the soil of the nation, who is required to obey the law, is entitled to a voice in its enactment.' The Massachusetts resolution went on: 'Women are entitled to the right of suffrage, and ... every party which claims to represent the humanity, the civilization, and the progress of the age, is bound to inscribe on its banners equality before the law, without distinction of sex or colour.' The *Westminster Review* author continued majestically:

With what truth or rationality could the suffrage be termed universal while half the human species remained excluded from it? To declare that a voice in the government is the right of all, and demand it only for a part – the part, namely, to which the claimant himself belongs – is to renounce even the appearance of principle. The Chartist who denies the suffrage to women is a Chartist only because he is not a lord; he is one of those levellers who would level only down to themselves.

The author of 'Enfranchisement of Women' was Harriet Taylor, wife of John Stuart Mill, whose treatise *Considerations on Representative Government* we have already encountered. Harriet Taylor demanded the vote for all women, regardless of class. During Harriet Taylor's long love affair with Mill, she shifted him to more radical politics than those into which he had been bred and to which he had become accustomed. After Harriet died, in 1858, he slipped back again. In the general election of 1865, Mill was elected MP for Westminster. On 10 May 1867, as Disraeli's Reform Bill wound its way through the Commons, Mill moved an amendment to supplant the word 'man' with the word 'person'. When the ideas in his speech were later published in his famous essay, *The Subjection of Women* (1869), Mill's distrust of the masses, which we saw in his earlier essay, was paraded once again. He was at least consistent. He was opposed to universal suffrage for men and for women. His demand for votes for women was restricted only to those women who would qualify to vote on the property criteria laid down for men.

Mill's amendment to Disraeli's Bill was crushed – by 196 votes to 73. But it blasted away an obstacle that had until then prevented the political rights of half the British people being raised in the British Parliament. Mill was defeated in the 1868 election but others took up his torch. In the 40 years after 1867, there were no fewer than 22 Commons debates on the question of women's votes, all of them on proposals to allow women to vote on the same terms as men.

This proposal was greeted again and again with the most ferocious hostility. It is impossible to study the speeches of its opponents without returning with Frederick Engels to the very dawn of time. Primeval prejudices were plucked from the depths of prehistory and unashamedly declaimed as certain truth. The simplest and most direct argument was that the condition of women, including their right to vote, had long ago been determined by the Almighty. Answering Mill's amendment in May 1867, Earl Percy, whose ancestors had come across the Channel with William the Conqueror and had enriched themselves with dubious land deals ever since, put the point plainly: 'The real fact is that man in the beginning was ordained to rule over woman and this is an eternal decree which we have no right or power to alter.' This should have put an end to the matter – if there was no right or power to alter a state of affairs, why even discuss it?

Other opponents of women's votes fell back on their knowledge of human character. In that same debate in 1867, Samuel Laing, Liberal Member for Wick, led the way: 'In all that requires rough, rude, practical force, stability of character and intellect, man is superior; whereas in all those situations of life that demand mildness, softness of character and amiability, women far exceed. I hope the day is far distant when our women should become masculine and our men effeminate.' Mr Laing told MPs that the Latin maxim '*propria quae maribus*' had 'remained fixed in my mind ever since it had been installed into it under the influence of the birch'. Variations on the view, expressed by the Tory MP for Maidstone, Beresford Hope, in 1870 – that 'the male intellect is logical and judicial, the female instinctive and emotional' – filled up whole columns of the reports of the debates. In 1892, the Liberal Home Secretary, H. H. Asquith, opposed the vote for women on the grounds of 'those indelible differences of faculty and function by which Nature herself has given diversity and richness to human society'. In similar vein, Sir William Brampton Gordon, Hon. Member for Norfolk North, explained as late as March 1907 that the granting of the vote would undo thousands of years in which men had elevated women: 'The more civilized man became, the more he elevated woman until he himself did all the hard work and left her only the lighter duties and the pleasures of life.' Expressions like this seemed to vindicate (from the opposite point of view) the central thesis of Engels's *Origin of the Family*, though it is unlikely that Sir William read it. Nor, certainly, had the MP for Hereford, C. W. Radcliffe Cooke, who expanded on the importance of the physical differences between men and women in his own colourful style: 'All the material framework of society, all that enabled this country to be a social and civilized community was made and executed by men, so they should govern it. Until women are *bigger* than men, I will oppose their right to vote.' The essential tool for measuring people's rights to choose their government, therefore, was the tape measure.

The same point was made ad nauseam in relation to wars and the Empire. How, it was asked, could decisions on such matters be taken by women, who did not have the physical strength to do the necessary fighting? Other opponents of women's suffrage, like the Liberal former Cabinet minister Sir William Harcourt, had done their calculations and found out that there were a million more adult women than men in Britain. 'This is a Bill,' declared Sir William in February 1897, 'for the ultimate enfranchisement of a popular womanhood majority.' Women, in short, would vote not as citizens but as women and would therefore, in a phrase that was used by Sir J. S. B. Simeon, Liberal Unionist MP for Southampton, and by scores of others, 'swamp men with their votes'. In the same breath, the same MPs, without apparently even noticing the contradiction, protested that women – the potential swampers – didn't want the vote anyway, so why give it to them?

Another chilling fear in the minds of the opponents of the women's vote was the prospect of losing control over their wives' property. In that very first debate in 1867, the Tory MP for Colchester, E. K. Karslake, who had been elected with 685 male votes, urged John Stuart Mill to show a little common sense:

A woman in marriage should give over all she has, including herself, to her husband for better, for worse. The wife should be absolutely and entirely under the control of her husband not only in respect of her property but of her personal movements. She may not 'gad about', and if she does, her husband is entitled to lock her up. Some hold that he might beat her. I have my doubts about that and if my advice were asked as a lawyer, I would say 'do not do it'. But undoubtedly the husband has entire dominion over the person and property of his wife.

Just as Henry Ireton had argued that if everyone had the vote, the poor majority would resolve to confiscate rich people's property, now Mr Karslake was protesting that if women got the vote, they might resolve to swipe their property from their husbands. Worse, they might even insist on developing their own point of view. 'What if the wife disagrees with her husband?' asked Mr Karslake. 'What, even worse, if she yearned to vote in a different way?' Women would thus be debased and degraded by the franchise, and were in danger of losing their gentleness, affection and domesticity. Anyway, he concluded triumphantly, 'not a lady in Essex had asked him to support the amendment'.

Karslake's speech was spiced with the facetious banter that kept the House of Commons amused in those early debates. Few Members could resist a jocular jibe at the male supporters of women's franchise who had obviously been seduced into their point of view. Radcliffe Cooke in 1897 scoffed at the men on the Liberal benches who were 'under the influence of women', and in 1867 the Earl of Onslow, Liberal MP for Guildford (with 333 male votes), told the House that he had been 'talking to two young ladies who said they would vote for the man who would give them the best pair of diamond earrings'. Such jibes were played out to the full by the most consistent of all the House's opponents of the suffrage Bills. Henry Labouchere was, on the face of it, the most unlikely politician to lead the ranks of the anti-suffragists. For 22 years he was Radical Liberal MP for Northampton, and he was a strong supporter of the long struggle of his fellow Northampton MP Charles Bradlaugh to sit in the House of Commons as an atheist. Enormously rich, and educated at Eton, Labouchere had no fear of or respect for authority and spent much of his political career denouncing British imperialist ventures in Egypt, South Africa and, most potently, in Ireland. Queen Victoria detested him and barred him from holding ministerial office. Yet he seldom missed a chance to denounce any attempt to extend the franchise to women. Though he voted for John Stuart Mill's amendment in 1867, he did so merely out of respect for Mill's intellect. As soon as Mill died, Labouchere renounced his 1867 vote and, in a string of extraordinary speeches, plumbed the full depths of discrimination, patronage and prejudice. 'As a man,' he told the House in February 1897, 'I have always objected to petticoat government. I have always observed that ladies, for whom I have the highest respect and admiration, are incapable of argument.'

As Tories and Whigs (whom on every other issue he detested) roared with laughter and cheered him on, Labouchere delivered a terrible warning to his colleagues. 'If women ever went into the House of Commons, this august assembly will become an epicene club . . . I take it that the Whips will be ladies,' he observed, to howls of masculine mirth. Conjuring up the most appalling vista imaginable, he concluded: 'I really believe that the Speaker's seat will not be sacred and that it is probable that we will have a Speakeress.' Cries of 'Shame!' and 'Outrage!' echoed round the Tory benches.

In March 1904, he returned, like a dog to its vomit, to his most earnest message – as sincere a piece of advice as any old Etonian millionaire has ever offered to his inferiors: 'The mission of a working man's wife is to look after the home, to mind the baby, to cook the dinner and do the washing. She has no time for electioneering. The business of the husband is to take an hour off, go to public meetings and, if he is a wise man, adopt the radical principles addressed to him.' Among those radical principles, no doubt, was the comforting certainty that the working man's wife was condemned to a lifetime of drudgery and servitude.

As the years went on, the balance of the argument shifted away from the reactionaries. Mill's defeat in 1867 was followed quickly by two striking advances for the women's cause. In 1869, the year Mill's *Subjection of Women* was published, propertied women won the right to vote in local elections and, in the Education Act of 1870, propertied women won not just the right to vote but also to stand for election to the new school boards. The antis tried to use these advances to bolster their arguments against women's parliamentary franchise. They argued that local government and schools might well be appropriate areas for women to vote and even serve; and that their successes at that level should keep them even further away from central government. But the inclusion of women's names on the local electoral registers dispensed with yet another taboo. Women did not vote as women but according to their judgement. Very quickly they proved that they were just as capable and conscientious representatives on the school boards as were any of their male colleagues, if not more so.

The onward march of the women's suffrage movement in other parts of the world continually caught the leading opponents in Britain on the hop. James, later Viscount Bryce, who served in three Liberal Cabinets and whose opposition to the suffrage clashed oddly with his lifelong work to extend women's education, asked mockingly in 1892 'why our great democratic colonies had not tried women's suffrage'. Almost at once, in 1893, New Zealand became the first country in the world where women won the vote. The confident prediction that women, once they had the vote, would not bother to use it, was comprehensively exposed at the New Zealand polls that year, where 90,290 women of the 109,461 on the register cast their vote: an 81 per cent turn-out, which compared very favourably with the 66 per cent turn-out of New Zealand males. In 1894, women got the vote in South Australia.

The weaknesses in the antis' arguments were shown up clearly by the voting figures in the House of Commons. In the 17 years between Mill's amendment in 1867 and November 1884, all 12 Commons motions to extend voting rights to women were lost. The majorities against hovered between 69.8 per cent in 1870 and 53.2 per cent in June 1883. After 1884, the picture changed dramatically. In February 1886, the antis lost, with only 39.1 per cent of the Commons vote. The biggest debate in the 1890s was in 1897, under a Tory Government. The Tory MP for Glasgow, St Rollox, Faithful Begg, made much of women's advances in Australasia and the United States and ridiculed the anomaly whereby women could vote for county councils, town councils and school boards but not for Parliament. Begg's motion to extend the vote to women on the same terms as men was carried by 230 to 159, a majority of 71.

One reason for such a large majority was the resignation in 1894 of the veteran Liberal leader William Ewart Gladstone after a lifetime's implacable opposition to female suffrage. On 4 May 1870, only three years after the defeat of Mill's amendment, Jacob Bright, brother of John but unlike his brother a strong supporter of votes for women, moved the second reading of a Bill to grant votes for women on the same terms as men. To the horror of Prime Minister Gladstone, the second reading question was 'put' (carried) by 124 votes to 33. In three years, the mood of the Commons on this issue had changed dramatically in women's favour. The Grand Old Reformer decided that he himself must intervene to prevent so grand a reform. On 12 May, he took part in a debate to stop Bright's Bill. 'The question,' he thundered (that ponderous repetitive rhetoric came to his aid once more), 'is whether there is a necessity, nay even whether there is a desire or demand for this measure . . . I cannot recognize either the one or the other which would justify such an unsettling, not to say uprooting of the old landmarks of society which are far deeper than any of the political distinctions which separate honourable gentlemen on these benches from those on the other.' Liberals and Tories might have their differences, in other words, but were united in defending the 'old landmarks of society' such as the banning of half the human race from any choice of or control over their government. The intervention of the Grand Old Man was enough to send scores of Liberal MPs who had voted for reform scuttling back to their landmarks. Jacob Bright's motion was annihilated by 220 votes to 94.

For a fleeting moment in a debate on women's suffrage the following year (1871), the Prime Minister seemed to lose sight of his landmarks. In a passage obscure even by Gladstonian standards, he admitted 'so far as I am able to form an opinion' that 'the law does less than justice to women'. He declared that any man who was able to 'arrange a well-adjusted alteration of the law as to political power' would be 'a real benefactor to his country'. This was similar to Gladstone's brief flirtation in the 1860s with universal suffrage. It was a rhetorical mirage soon to be blown away by 'practical politics'. Never again did Gladstone offer the slightest support for women's suffrage. When the Tories lost the 1880 election and a Liberal Government under Gladstone committed to franchise reform took office, the women campaigners' hopes rose. Surely now, especially after their Prime Minister's equivocation in 1871, the new Government would give a fair hearing to the case for women's suffrage?

When Gladstone's Reform Bill was published in 1884, however, there was no mention of women. The proposal was to allow an extra 2 million men to vote, but to continue to withhold the franchise from all women. Furious protests to ministers were greeted with an odd metaphor. The Bill, it was argued, was like an overloaded ship. There were far too many extra votes crowded into it. To throw any more in would be to make the ship top-heavy. The cargo, ran the argument, was so heavy that the women had to be thrown overboard. In her concise little history, *Women's Suffrage*

(1912), Millicent Fawcett reflected wryly on the difference between the old chivalry on board a sinking ship – 'Women and children first!' – and the new chivalry: 'Throw the women overboard!'

Gladstone was now absolutely clear where he stood on the subject. On 10 June 1884, when the Liberal MP for Hanley, W. Woodall, put down the standard amendment to the Reform Bill to give women the vote on the same terms as men, the Prime Minister declared: 'I offer it the strongest opposition in my power.' The Liberal Party in the Commons was whipped into line. The vote was overwhelming: 135 for votes for women, 271 against. The majority included 104 Liberals who had promised their constituents to support women's suffrage but had put party before promise or principle. In 1892, as he prepared for a general election after which he would take hold of the reins of government for the last time, the Grand Old Man made a final effort in the interests of gender discrimination. A Tory MP, Sir Albert Rollit, had secured time to promote yet another Bill to give the vote to propertied 'widows and spinsters'. Both front benches issued a 'whip' urging Members to be in their places to vote against it. Gladstone wrote a letter to his friend and neighbour, the Liverpool businessman Samuel Smith, who had indicated that he would support Rollit's Bill. The Bill, wrote Gladstone, would be bad for women. 'It would trespass upon their delicacy, their purity, their refinement, the elevation of their whole nature.' With such a dedicated discriminator at the helm, it was obvious that no more moves to give votes for women would be contemplated or even tolerated by Gladstone's last administration.

Gladstone's looming influence over the Liberal Party, and especially over those Liberals who called themselves radicals, just managed to hold the line against women's suffrage during the prolonged attempts to change electoral law after 1867. Even with the leader of the Liberal Party on their side, however, the antis seemed to be fighting a losing battle. This was partly due to the weakness of their arguments. It was also partly due to the indefatigable campaign of the leading women suffragists. Mill's 1867 amendment had been prompted by a petition presented in June 1866 and signed by 1,499 influential women, among them Florence Nightingale, Harriet Martineau, Frances Power Cobbe and Josephine Butler. The petition was organized and circulated by a handful of women reformers: Elizabeth Garrett, Emily Davies, Millicent Fawcett, Lydia Becker and Flora Stevenson. Undeterred by the defeat of Mill's amendment in 1867, they went to law seeking to establish that the word 'male' in a statute applied to the entire human race (as it did in plenty of other statutes). When that failed, the reformers set up women's suffrage societies all over the country. These societies worked tirelessly to lobby Parliament for a limited women's suffrage, and it was largely their work that brought about the reforms of 1869 and 1870 introducing women into local government. They were quick to make use of the reforms they won. In the very first school board elections in which women could take part, in November 1870, Elizabeth Garrett, Emily Davies, Flora Stevenson and Lydia Becker were elected.

The women in these societies were almost exclusively upper class. Their methods were strictly limited to holding public meetings, circulating petitions and lobbying MPs. Their readiness to water down even the principle of equality between propertied men and propertied women soon plunged the new women's movement into disarray.

In 1874, a Tory Government was elected and held office until 1880. Jacob Bright, who had come so close in 1870 to getting a limited women's suffrage Bill through the Commons, lost his seat, and the job of bringing forward a Bill to grant votes to women on the same terms as men fell to the Tory MP for Marylebone, W. Forsyth QC. Forsyth insisted that his Bill should withhold the vote from married women. As a distinguished lawyer, he took the view that in spite of minor reforms to the law on married women's property in an Act of 1870, the law of the land still insisted that the property and person of a married woman belonged to her husband. Lydia Becker, a driving force in the suffrage movement of the time, was prepared to accept a new clause excluding all married women from the vote – and every Bill until 1892 included such a clause. Becker's concession infuriated many of the original supporters of the Bill. To limit the vote to spinsters and widows was, they argued, grossly to betray the principle of equality for women at the heart of the campaign for women's suffrage. To exclude married women reduced the number of women proposed for the electoral register to a rump – tiny compared to the ranks of voting men.

These concessions held the movement up but by no means extinguished it. Between 1877 and 1879, for instance, there were 1,400 public meetings on the subject, and 9,563 petitions for women's votes were signed by nearly 3 million people. But after the exclusion of married women, a lot of the passion and thrust went out of the campaign. In her history published more than half a century later, *The Suffragette Movement: An Intimate Account of Persons and Ideals* (1931), Sylvia Pankhurst observed:

The suffrage movement was honeycombed with people – women as well as men – who themselves were prepared to go only a small part of the way towards complete social equality for women. Though thus half-hearted in their views, many of these persons came to occupy official positions in the movement because they possessed means and leisure . . . The women's movement, in short, passed from timidity to timidity.

Much the same could be said of the leaders of the trade unions, most of whom shared the view of the Secretary of the Trades Union Congress Parliamentary Committee, Henry Broadhurst, that a woman's proper place was not at work but in the home. The view conveniently ignored the plight of millions of women workers who were not organized. Their case was championed by a handful of courageous pioneer women trade unionists who refused to be browbeaten by the sarcasm and patronage of their male colleagues. Emma Paterson, the daughter of a London schoolteacher, founded the Women's Protective and Provident League in 1874. Its central aim was to promote trade unionism among women workers. From 1872, moreover, she was simultaneously Secretary of the Association for the Promotion of Women's Suffrage. She lost a baby in childbirth in 1880 and, when her husband died in 1882, she was reduced to working as a proof-reader for sixpence a day, but she attended almost every Trades Union Congress from 1879 to 1886, and never missed an opportunity to draw the reluctant delegates' attention to the plight of women workers in the grim recession of the period. In 1885, the year after the passing of the Reform Act and the granting of the vote to 2 million men, Emma Paterson was invited to a prestigious 'remuneration conference' organized by Sir Charles Dilke, the Liberal Government's Minister for Local Government. The chief object of the conference was to discuss the conditions of the British working people. It was the biggest such conference ever called, and the fact that its sponsor was a prominent minister showed that even the Gladstone Government was still worried about the effects of the 'great (post-1879) depression' on workers' pay and conditions. The wounds caused by the depression were beginning to heal – though its impact was not easily forgotten. Trade-union membership had only just climbed back to what it had been 10 years previously, and the violent fluctuations in trade, especially in shipbuilding and engineering, had thrown huge sections of the working population into abject misery. Some comfort was afforded to ministers by the main paper drawn up for discussion at the conference. It was entitled 'Progress of the Working Classes', and its author was the wealthy Scottish accountant Robert Giffen. Giffen was a fanatical crusader for private enterprise, and was anxious to prove that the system he loved showered its benefits on everyone.

His paper at Dilke's remuneration conference was vigorously contested by Emma Paterson. Giffen's statistics, she pointed out, completely ignored all women workers except those occupied in weaving, who were by far the best paid. Where in all Giffen's thesis, she asked, were the 3,800,000 other working women, including 1,300,000 domestic servants? If the miserable pay of this huge section of workers was taken into account, she said, Giffen's case collapsed. The figures about these women workers, at the very bottom of the pile, not only dragged the average pay of British workers far below Giffen's optimistic averages but also revealed a sharp decline in the six years since the start of the great depression in 1879. No wonder, she mocked, that Giffen had consigned all these workers to the contemptuous category of 'residuum still unimproved'.

The word 'residuum' soon entered the language of franchise reform. It described the 42 per cent of men who were so poor that they did not get a vote even after the 1884 franchise extension. Also in that residuum, Emma Paterson reminded the conference, were 100 per cent of women, who had no vote. The hideous exploitation of so many working women, she said, was the other side of the coin to their exclusion from the franchise. Because they had no vote, women workers were treated by ministers and politicians with utter contempt. Her own pleas even for a hearing on two vital issues – the appointment of women factory inspectors and changes in the Factory Acts to improve women's working conditions – had been arrogantly rejected in recent years by Home Secretaries from both parties, Sir Richard Cross for the Tories and more recently Sir William Harcourt for the Liberals. Women workers, she went on, had no power industrially – only a tiny fraction of women outside weaving were organized in trade unions. The employers paid no attention to them because they were not organized, and they had been entirely left out of the previous year's franchise reform. Women's impotence at the ballot box, she said, complemented their impotence at work. The movement she represented could proceed only by walking on two legs. Suffrage reform should include votes for women to help free them from the shackles of a male-dominated society; and many more women should at the same time be organized in trade unions to help free them from industrial tyranny.

Both arguments were regarded by the trade-union leaders of the time as close to heresy. Indeed, Henry Broadhurst and his colleagues were not sure that women should be allowed at trade-union conferences at all. In 1874, the first affiliated all-women union, the National Union of Working Women from Bristol, was represented at the TUC by a man, who only managed to take his seat after an outburst of opposition from the floor. One delegate explained: 'The next thing they'll be wanting is to represent themselves.' This warning was vindicated the following year, 1875, when for the first time women delegates were admitted to the TUC annual conference. If they dared to speak, as Emma Paterson almost always did, they were subjected to the usual catcalls and advised to 'go and get married'. They were horrified to discover that the leaders of the male trade unions spent a lot of time and effort on laws that made it more difficult for women to hold on to what few jobs were available to them. For instance, the thousands of 'pit-brow' women, who worked on the surface of coal mines, were shocked to hear of proposed laws to ban them from employment – and even more shocked when they learned that the proponents of the new laws included the two stalwarts of the TUC Parliamentary Committee, Henry Broadhurst and Thomas Burt, both of whom had been elected to Parliament through pacts with the Liberal Party. The discriminatory amendments (to the Mines Regulation Bill, 1886) were eventually defeated by Liberal and Radical MPs, but Burt, Broadhurst and the rest of the TUC's Parliamentary Committee continued to argue that women should stay at home and keep out of jobs that should be exclusively available for men. As for women's suffrage, the Parliamentary Committee could not even bring itself to allow the TUC to discuss the issue. Even the demand for votes for all men was regarded as extreme. Twice before 1880, by huge majorities, the TUC, on the advice of its influential Parliamentary Committee, rejected motions for manhood suffrage. Very few of the delegates represented anyone from the despised 'residuum' and even fewer could see the point of giving the vote to a lot of roughs who could not even be relied upon to join a trade union. It followed quite logically that granting votes to women was intolerable.

Racked by diabetes and exhaustion, Emma Paterson died in 1886, aged 38. Her loyal ally Jeanette Wilkinson died in the same year. Though both women had earned the grudging respect of most male trade unionists for their refusal to be intimidated by continuous condescension, their deaths in the same year must have come as some relief to the Parliamentary Committee, especially to Henry Broadhurst, who had taken time off his union duties to become an under-secretary in the Home Office in the brief Liberal Government of 1885–6. The truth was that during the recession of 1879 to 1885, the Trades Union Congress, led by its Parliamentary Committee, degenerated into a rabble. In their monumental *History of British Trade Unionism*, Sidney and Beatrice Webb described the TUC of that time as a glorified 'sick and burial club' which shied away from any industrial confrontation and dared to ask for political reforms 'only in so far as they happened to coincide with the proposals of the Liberal Party'. Union membership slumped from over a million in 1874 to fewer than 400,000 ten years later, and the leaders lost all contact with the growing army of impoverished workers which sullenly multiplied in British cities, especially in the capital.

Almost as soon as the long recession drew to a close, the TUC leaders were subjected to the most ferocious assault from new agitators. In 1886, Tom Mann, a member of the engineers' union, fulminated: 'The truest union-ist policy of aggression seems entirely lost sight of: in fact the average unionist of today is a man with a fossilized intellect either hopelessly apathetic or supporting a policy that plays directly into the hands of the capitalist exploiter.' Tom Mann and his ally John Burns had just been converted to a new creed, socialism, which provided for the dispossessed some answers to the questions posed by the slumps and booms of capital and offered a way out of the workers' plight by strengthening their own class organiza-tions and, through revolution, winning industrial and financial power.

Such protests coincided powerfully with the end of the trade depression and the growing fury and desperation of the poor. In the summer of 1888, what Emma Paterson had identified as the twin goals of women's trade unionism and women's suffrage got an enormous boost from a most unexpected quarter – hundreds of mainly Irish, mainly teenage women workers at the Bryant and May match factory at Bow, East London. The workers were approached by a socialist journalist Annie Besant, editor of a small agitational paper called the *Link*. She had heard of their conditions at a meeting of the Fabian Society. The young workers poured out the full horrific details of their exploitation by Bryant and May. Their problem was not just low pay but the fact that they hardly ever received it. Their working lives were plagued by fines and threats of fines. There was no limit to the interference of Bryant and May directors in the workers' right to a living wage. When Bryant and May denied that recent sackings had anything to do with the *Link*'s allegations, Annie Besant returned to the charge with a glorious open letter to the 40 Bryant and May shareholders who, she discovered, were clergymen:

Country clergymen with shares in Bryant and May. Draw down on your knee your 15-year-old daughter; pass your hand tenderly over the silky clustering curls, rejoicing in the dainty beauty of the thick shining tresses. Then, like a ghastly vision, let there rise up before you the pale worn face of another man's daughter, with wistful pathetic patient eyes and see her as she pulls off her battered hat and shows a head robbed of its hair by the constant rubbing of the carried boxes, robbed thereof that your dividends might be larger, Sir Cleric . . . I hold you up to the public opprobrium you deserve and brand you with the shame that is your rightful doom.

Annie Besant and her colleagues spread the match girls' case all over London. Radical and even Liberal newspapers took up her charges. The Bryant and May directors, who originally threatened to sue for libel and denied all the charges, were closely questioned by factory inspectors and independent investigators who found the workers' case largely proven. Mass meetings were staged on Mile End Green and protest marches headed by the match girls poured into the West End. The strikers were out for three weeks, after which the directors promised never again to levy the fines and penalties whose existence they had so angrily denied – and the women were allowed for the first time to form a union.

The victory of these impertinent teenagers launched a huge strike movement, especially in London. The gas stokers of Beckton, who had been trying for years, under the energetic leadership of Will Thorne, to form a strong union, reacted to further demands for a rate of speed-up that made their work almost impossible. A mass meeting shouted for a union and the Amalgamated Union of Gas Workers was formed on the spot, with Will Thorne as paid Secretary. Without even going on strike, the new union forced the management to concede an eight-hour day. Suddenly the propaganda of these new socialist trade-union leaders seemed to make sense and to connect with the workers' yearning for proper representation. Within a year, the clamour for a fully fledged trade union set alight the unorganized and casualized London docks. Against the combined and furious opposition of the employers, the great dock strike of 1889, involving tens of thousands of impoverished dock workers, won a new wage deal based on sixpence a day, and the right to organize in a union. That victory in turn set in motion a wave of trade unionism quite different from the staid societies organized by the official trade-union leaders. Other strikes broke out all over the country, notably among London garment workers. A new breed of delegate, without top hat or watch chain, started to appear at the Trades Union Congress. The new union leaders who had organized the dockers were socialists. Men like John Burns, Tom Mann, Will Thorne and Ben Tillett resolved to break with the passive 'sick and burial club' traditions of the old trade unions and to form new unions whose first priority was to improve the conditions of the vast unorganized army of poor workers. As means to that end, they proclaimed the twin virtues of militancy and solidarity. The new mood of confidence showed itself in a great May Day demonstration in London – the first such celebration in Britain of this historic day for Labour. An enthusiastic observer at the 1890 demonstration in Hyde Park was Frederick Engels:

Around the seven platforms of the central committee, thick crowds, in countless numbers, approaching with music and flags, more than 100,000 in a column swelled by almost as many who had come on their own ... On 4 May 1890 the English working class joined up in the great international army. Its long winter sleep is broken at last. The grandchildren of the old Chartists are entering the line of battle.

Most of the workers awaking from their long winter sleep had no votes. And a curious feature of the new mood and the new unionism was the absence of any serious agitation for universal suffrage. As far as the 40 per cent of men who were still denied the vote were concerned, there was nothing more than token agitation for enfranchisement during the entire period from 1884 to 1918. There was an Adult Suffrage Society, chaired by the radical Liberal frontbencher Sir Charles Dilke. Dilke's second wife, Emilia, led the Women's Trade Union and Provident League, which campaigned for the rights of women trade unionists. Though the WTUPL had some successes, and though its membership grew after the match girls' triumph, there was a marked reluctance to campaign for women's votes. The Adult Suffrage Society and the main women's trade union organization were effectively fiefdoms of Sir Charles and Lady Dilke, and the agitation for votes for some 70 per cent of the population was almost non-existent.

Why? Perhaps the chief reason was the swift reversal of the new union victories. While the dockers were celebrating their victory in late 1889, the employers launched a ferocious counter-offensive that continued all through 1890 and 1891. This counter-offensive reached its climax in Bradford, where 30,000 people demonstrated in support of workers resisting a crude 30 per cent wage cut in the vast and sprawling Manningham mills. The employers faced down the strikers with savage determination and shrewd use of the local police. The workers were forced back with hardly a penny to show for their long effort and mass support. In a repeat of the experience of Joseph Arch and the agricultural workers in the 1870s, defeat in open class struggle was followed by renewed parliamentary activity. The formation of the Independent Labour Party (ILP) in Bradford in 1892 flowed directly from the defeat of the strike at Manningham. In the view of many delegates at the founding conference, the formation of the new party was the best way to counter the industrial catastrophe at Manningham. For years afterwards, most leading thinkers of the ILP drew a sharp distinction between political action (which they defined as getting votes for Parliament, and supported) and industrial action, which seemed to them at best disastrous and at worst undemocratic and which, with some honourable exceptions, they were inclined to oppose.

One sign of their lack of confidence in the workers' rank and file was the ILP leaders' failure to campaign for the disenfranchised multitude. Though 'adult suffrage' was always part of the official ILP programme, meaningful ILP campaigns for votes for the majority who had not got them were notable by their absence. Another, contradictory, strain of fashionable thought among the ILP leaders worked against any mass campaign for votes for the majority. The best of those who relished the success of industrial action in London in 1889 tended to dismiss any campaign for the vote as an irrelevant delaying tactic. If conditions could be improved by strikes and unions, they argued, why bother with parliaments? This view, soon to be known as syndicalism, was already forming in the minds of the best of the new union leaders such as Tom Mann and Ben Tillett. They were far more at ease building unions and fomenting strikes than pressing for an extension of the franchise. At another level, several influential socialists were infected with a belief in masculine superiority that bordered on misogyny. The worst offender in this regard was a prominent leader of the Social Democratic Federation (SDF), the first socialist party in Britain, founded in 1884. (Ernest) Belfort Bax was described by Frederick Engels in 1886 as a 'thoroughly good sort'. But one aspect of Bax's politics that must have driven Engels to despair, though he seems never to have noticed it, was Bax's remorseless opposition to female suffrage and indeed to the entire female sex. In 1907, in a special edition of his work *Essays in Socialism, New and Old*, Bax argued that women were inferior, and therefore should be denied the franchise. 'Not merely is the female brain absolutely smaller but relatively smaller,' he revealed. Bax was utterly opposed to any reform that would usher women into the political arena. Nor was he alone in the small world of early British socialists. Though they were less inclined to express such plainly reactionary views in public, and though the official manifesto of the Social Democratic Federation called for universal suffrage, there were other SDF leaders, notably H. M. Hyndman and Harry Quelch, who were sympathetic to Bax's reactionary views on women.

To some extent, this abstinence on the left from any agitation for extending the franchise left the parliamentary field clear for the TUC. For years, the Congress had resisted any public effort on behalf of the voteless majority. It endorsed the formation, in 1869, of the Labour Representation League 'to organize fully the strength of the operative classes as an electoral power', but did nothing to help the League financially or administratively. Proceeding on its own, with limited resources, the League organized the nomination of a founding member of the International Working Men's

Association, Cornish-born shoemaker George Odger, in a by-election at Southwark in 1870. Odger stood at least partly in protest at the way he had been treated in the 1868 general election, when he had been forced to withdraw in favour of a Liberal. At the by-election, Odger, who stood as a 'Radical Working Man', polled extremely well, with 4,382 votes – only 304 fewer than the victorious Tory's 4,686. The Liberal was far behind in third place, with 2,966 votes. Here was proof that in a working-class area independent Labour could smash the Liberals and come within a whisper of winning the seat. At the general election of 1874, however, the Labour Representation League could muster only 12 candidates. Two of these, Thomas Burt and Alexander MacDonald, were elected for mining seats – but only after pacts with the Liberals. The passivity of the TUC and the League gave new confidence to the Liberal Party, which had been greatly shocked by Odger's big vote at Southwark. In the years that followed, as the Liberal Party effectively adopted the few working-class representatives whom it allowed to stand, the Labour Representation League disappeared. The mood at the Trades Union Congress was tested as late as 1882 with a motion demanding a special fund to help working-class candidates in future elections. By 63 votes to 43 the motion was replaced by a demand that election expenses – and payment of MPs – should be met by the returning officers and by the state. The approach of the leading trade unionists of the 1870s and 1880s was that there was little point in spending TUC money on parliamentary candidates when the organizing work and most of the cost could be left to the wealthy Liberal Party, and when few if any trade unionists could afford to take their seats in a Parliament in which the elections cost the candidates a lot of money and the state paid no salaries.

The TUC's next move to secure some political representation for the workers had to wait until 1886, 20 years after the first Congress. A committee was set up to be elected annually by Congress and 'to act in conjunction' with the Parliamentary Committee and sympathetic MPs. Perhaps because of the vagueness of its terms of reference, this committee soon broke away from the Congress and became an independent body called the Labour Electoral Association, which was succeeded later by the rather grander-sounding Labour Electoral Congress. Meeting for the first time in Sheffield in October, the Association revealed its 'platform of the Labour Party'. Top of the list of its demands was payment of MPs and election expenses, followed by land nationalization, adult suffrage, triennial parliaments, free education and separate national parliaments for England, Ireland, Scotland and Wales. That first meeting ambitiously promised the formation of associations all over the country. None such were formed, however. Instead, the

Labour Electoral Association/Congress went on meeting in some pomp each year – at Liverpool in 1889, Hanley in 1890, London in 1891, Leicester in 1892 and Hull in 1893. At Hanley, a leaflet was circulated to expose the state of representation in the House of Commons. There were 209 MPs representing land and property owners; 136 from executives of trading, commercial and manufacturing firms; 136 lawyers; 128 from the military; 33 from finance; 62 from railway company boardrooms; 24 from the liquor trade – and 9 from the entire working class. To rub the point in, the leaflet observed that 655,000 miners were represented by 5 MPs who were miners while 20 MPs were coal-owners. The remedy to all this, the leaflet proclaimed, was obvious: payment of MPs and returning officers' expenses.

The last Labour Electoral Congress met in Hull in June 1893. On this occasion the Congress openly called itself 'the Labour Party', and extended its platform. At the top of the list of aims were the old favourites, payment of MPs and returning officers' expenses. Added to these were 'the second ballot' (a form of proportional representation), adult suffrage, free education, triennial parliaments, income tax (at a rate unspecified), land nationalization and municipalization (take-over by local councils) of gasworks, waterworks, allotments and electric light. The President gave an account of the general election of 1892. There had been 37 'workmen candidates', of whom 25 had been accepted by the local Liberal association and only 12 had been elected. Only one working-class candidate (Joseph Havelock Wilson at Middlesbrough) had been elected against opposition from Liberals and Tories. The Congress showed almost universal distaste for the ILP and its candidate for West Ham, Keir Hardie. Hardie was forever on the move, putting the case for the newly formed ILP in Scotland and in Ireland, and even, to the anguish of many of his ILP colleagues, supporting strikes. Somehow, in all its reported proceedings, the Labour Electoral Association and Congress, though it formally stood for adult suffrage, did not pass a single resolution which even mentioned the great mass of the British workers who could not vote for its government, let alone discuss how that glaring democratic discrepancy could be remedied.

In 1899, the Trades Union Congress at last passed a resolution to convene a special conference to set up a political party based on labour, a resolution that led to a historic (though at the time almost unreported) meeting in the Memorial Hall, Farringdon, London, on 27 February 1900. Represented at that meeting were the TUC, the ILP, the SDF, the Fabian Society and a handful of other socialist societies. Arguments raged between the trade unionists and the socialists as to the purpose of the new party. A compromise resolution emerged, committing the new organization to represent labour in the House of Commons without a declared political line. The suggested rules for the new Labour Party did not even insist that Labour MPs when elected should submit to the political discipline of the Party. The attitude of the trade unionists was summarized much later by John Hodge, then leader of the steel smelters' trade union – the first successfully to ballot its members on the formation and financing of a Labour Party. Grilled by ILP members, he told them that in his view socialism was 'unobtainable', and the best labour representatives could hope to achieve was the municipalization of gas and water. So important a role did the founding meeting of the Labour Party in 1900 play in the life of John Hodge that in his autobiography – proudly entitled *Workman's Cottage to Windsor Castle* (an improvement, no doubt, on the title of the 1909 'life story' of Will Crooks MP, *From Workhouse to Westminster*, or for that matter the title of the 1924 autobiography of George Barnes, *From Workshop to War Cabinet*) – he did not mention it. Despite this rather unenthusiastic approach, however, the new Labour Party was an almost instant electoral success, winning by-elections and returning 29 MPs in the general election of 1906. The executive report to the 1906 Labour Party conference, which was also held in the Memorial Hall, Farringdon, crowed with delight. 'Organized labour as a political force is already a menace to the easy-going gentlemen of the old school who have slumbered so long on the green benches of St Stephen's . . . organized labour has at last realized its power and learned how to use it.' Less emphasis was given to the disturbing fact that 16 out of those 29 seats had been won without Liberal opposition, that only three had been won against both a Liberal and a Tory candidate, and that the Liberal majority after the 1906 election was impregnable. Before too long it seemed clear that, with one or two honourable exceptions, the easy-going gentlemen among the new Labour MPs were preparing to take part in the time-honoured practice of slumbering on those green benches. There seemed little point in organizing too hard against such a huge majority, especially when the hated Tories were in opposition and so much of Liberal policy overlapped with that of Labour. It followed, moreover, that adult suffrage, though it still occupied a proud place in the list of Labour policies, was hardly worth talking about when the existing franchise seemed to be doing so well for Labour. Immediately before and after the 1906 election, however, much to the irritation of most of the 29 Labour MPs, the suffrage issue engulfed them in a long controversy of neither their making nor their choosing.

The issue was votes for women – which we left, at the end of the century, vegetating in apparently hopeless apathy and compromise. During the first six years of the new century, the issue was wrenched into the open not so much by conventional reformers from the upper classes as by working-class women in Cheshire and Lancashire, the one area where women were in the majority in the trade unions. Of the 200,000 women cotton workers in the area, 90,000 were organized in trade unions – five-sixths of all women trade unionists in Britain.

If Frederick Engels had been even half right to predict that effective agitation to reverse the historic defeat of the female sex must come from women in social production, the thrust for any new movement for votes for women had to start with the textile workers of Lancashire and Cheshire. And so it did. On 1 May 1900, in Blackburn, the centre of the weaving trade, the North of England Society for Women's Suffrage launched a petition confined exclusively in its own words 'to the undersigned women workers in the cotton factories of Lancashire'. The petition went on to claim

that in the opinion of your petitioners the continued denial of the franchise to women is unjust and inexpedient. In the home, their position is lowered by such an exclusion from the responsibilities of national life. In the factory, their unrepresented condition places the regulation of their work in the hands of men who are often their rivals as well as their fellow workers.

There followed a year of sustained agitation as the petition was taken round the Lancashire cotton towns. All the organization and speaking was carried out by women. Some, like Eva Gore-Booth and Esther Roper, came from the middle or upper class; others like Helen Silcock, Sarah Reddish and Selina Cooper were working-class women attracted to the campaign by the arguments promoted so courageously by Emma Paterson a generation earlier. The petition drew into activity all sorts of working women who had never before been engaged in anything of the kind. The agitation took the form of mass meetings to greet the petition when it was brought into towns and villages via the local railway stations. The meetings would then break up into deputations, handfuls of women who would take the petition on to doorsteps of friends, neighbours or acquaintances. As early as November, Esther Roper could report to the North of England Society that there was 'no difficulty in getting signatures'. She added the 'encouraging fact' that a lot of men met by the petitioners have 'shown themselves in sympathy'. In the spring of 1901, 15 cotton workers took the petition, signed by nearly 30,000 women wage-earners, to the House of Commons, where it was hauled to the table by the friendly MP for Radcliffe, who said he had seen many large petitions delivered there but never one larger.

The working-class springboard of the radical suffragists led them naturally to the TUC, whose record on women's suffrage was, as we have seen, not very inspiring. In 1901, Helen Silcock, President of the Wigan Weavers, went to the TUC to move a resolution for women's suffrage. The radical suffragists were not clear how far the vote should be extended to women. They coined a new phrase, 'womanhood suffrage', which left open the awkward question – how many women should be enfranchised? Before Helen Silcock could get to the rostrum at the 1901 Congress, her male colleagues on the Franchise Committee cobbled together a resolution calling for universal suffrage, which was to be moved in opposition to her. Silcock's resolution introduced a familiar phrase – 'on the same terms as men' – later to become controversial in the suffrage movement: 'That in view of the unsatisfactory state of legislation for women, especially those employed in our mills and workshops, the parliamentary franchise should be extended to women on the same terms as men.' Her speech was warmly applauded, but her resolution was rejected in favour of the universal suffrage resolution moved by her colleagues.

The success of the 1901 petition led to similar agitations among working-class women. Petitions continued to circulate in the same way in Yorkshire, the Potteries, Leicestershire and Scotland. In the summer of 1903, a new organization was formed cumbrously called the Lancashire and Cheshire Women Textile and Other Workers Representation Committee. They took the name 'representation committee' from the Labour Representation Committee, which had been formed in February 1900 and was the predecessor of the Labour Party. The following year the committee issued a trenchant appeal for a campaign 'to send their own representative to the House of Commons pledged to secure the enfranchisement of the women workers of the country'. This committee, and several others that sprang up beside it, carried out a determined programme of public meetings and propaganda. It supported Thorley Smith as a suffrage candidate for Wigan in the 1906 general election. Though he lost the seat, Smith's 2,000 (male) votes greatly cheered his supporters among the working women.

Well before the general election of 1906, however, the radical suffragists had run out of steam. The chief reason was the isolation of women in production, and of women in trade unions, in one part of the country – Lancashire and Cheshire. The suffrage petitions had been based on this area, and had exhausted it. There were very few women trade unionists in either county who had not been approached by the petitioners for a signature for a suffrage resolution. And working-class organization based on patient petitioning was no longer bringing in results, as the successful petition of 1900 and 1901 had done. The slowing of the momentum led to

sharper arguments among the radical suffragists. Some insisted on continuing the same patient petitioning. Others yearned for more direct, dramatic
and militant action, which required organization of a quite different character from that favoured by the radical suffragists. On 10 October 1903, a
group of such women met in the Manchester home of Emmeline Pankhurst,
a widow, whose husband Richard had been a popular lawyer in the city
and a supporter of the ILP. Like all the other women on similar committees
at the time, Mrs Pankhurst assumed that the movement for women's suffrage would grow in influence in the same way as the labour and socialist
movement had grown; and that just as there had been a Labour Representation Committee, so the new women's organizations should be called
'representation committees'. Her eldest daughter, Christabel, didn't agree.
Christabel, then a law student who soon developed into a forceful public
speaker, had been involved in the women's representation committees with
Eva Gore-Booth and Esther Roper. She argued that any new organization
should distinguish itself by dropping the phrase 'representation committee'. Instead she proposed the name: Women's Social and Political Union,
which her devoted mother instantly accepted. So, that autumn afternoon
in Manchester, the WSPU was founded.

As its name suggested, the new organization did not intend to sever its
links with the Labour movement. But the women who met that afternoon
in Manchester were determined to speed things up. Women's emancipation
could not be left to other people in society: it was primarily an aim for
women, to be fought for by women. The WSPU argued that the withholding
of the vote from women was an act of government, and the granting of the
vote to women would also be an act of government. All the effort of the
WSPU therefore had to be directed against the Government. Nor was it
enough to demonstrate and petition. From early on, the WSPU founders,
led by Christabel, insisted that the tactics employed by the WSPU should
be single-minded. All other issues were submerged in favour of the demand
for the vote. No other party should be supported but the WSPU, no
allegiance or alliance tolerated unless it placed votes for women at the top
of, and throughout, the agenda. It followed that the method of organization
favoured by the radical suffragists – patient, persuasive and democratic –
had to be replaced by something much more dramatic and immediate.

In the dying years of the Tory Government, this split in the suffrage
movement was submerged. As the prospect loomed of a change of government, and of a majority for the Liberal Party, the WSPU concentrated on
demanding from the Liberal Opposition an unequivocal commitment to
votes for women. The first practical test of their 'militant tactics' came

almost exactly two years after the organization was formed. So strong was
the tide against the Tories that when the Shadow Foreign Secretary, Sir
Edward Grey, was scheduled to speak at a Liberal rally at Manchester's
Free Trade Hall on 13 October 1905, everyone expected a Liberal Government to be formed after the general election. The WSPU wrote to Sir
Edward in advance, asking for his commitment to votes for women. There
was no reply. In the middle of his portentous speech to a packed meeting,
Sir Edward was startled by a small white banner shooting up in the middle
of his audience. Almost at once, a young woman with a strong Lancashire
accent announced that she came from a trade-union committee of textile
workers and asked, simply: 'Will the Liberal Government give women the
vote?' She was hauled back down into her seat by the man sitting next to
her, her protesting voice muffled by a hat held in front of her face by
another indignant male Liberal. Suddenly, another young woman in a seat
in the same row repeated the question: 'Will the Liberal Government give
women the vote?' The hall erupted in pandemonium. Some of the audience
cried out for free speech – 'let the lady speak'. Most, however, wanted the
impertinent ladies shut up and somehow got out of the hall. William
Peacock, Chief Constable of Manchester, agreed to take the question in
writing to the platform. Up it went, and round the various speakers, many
of whom, like Sir Edward Grey, were supporters of at least a limited female
suffrage. Not one platform speaker would answer yes or no. It was not,
they claimed, a fair question since the franchise issue was 'not a party
matter'. Once again, the two young women shouted their protest, and were
dragged from the hall. Outside, they met some supporters and tried to hold
a meeting. Both were arrested, and charged with breach of the peace
offences. Annie Kenney, the textile worker, was fined five shillings or, in
default of payment, sent to prison for three days. Her supporter, the insti-
gator of the demonstration, was Christabel Pankhurst, who got a fine of
ten shillings or seven days. Both women refused to pay the fine and went
to prison. Before long, the *Daily Mail* nickname for these protesting women
was taken up by the entire press: the suffragettes.

The arrests and imprisonments set off an explosion of agitation around
a single issue the like of which had not been seen before in British politics.
The WSPU's militant tactics gathered pace, and quickly excited the imagination and enthusiasm of large numbers of British women. In the summer
of 1906, the Pankhursts moved with their fledgling organization from
Manchester to London. In October 1906, there was a small nucleus of half
a dozen WSPU branches, and the organization was still running from day
to day on a few voluntary donations. A year later, there were 58 branches

and income at the WSPU's headquarters had risen to £100 a week. The subsequent growth of the new movement was astonishing. In 1906, suffragette literature sales brought in £60, in 1910, £9,000. The cramped premises at Clement's Inn became too small for the regular meetings organized for the faithful by the Pankhursts, so the copious Queen's Hall was booked for regular meetings. In October 1907, Frederick and Emmeline Pethick-Lawrence took control of WSPU literature sales and started a money-spinning weekly paper called *Votes for Women*. A series of stunts and demonstrations kept the Cabinet constantly on the defensive. No minister was safe from repeated outbursts and interruptions. The memoirs of Jack Pease, Liberal Chief Whip from 1908 to 1910, are full of such incidents, which shocked him and his beloved Prime Minister Asquith. On 18 October 1908, Pease reported that the Prime Minister 'was more nettled than I had previously seen him'. The problem was demonstrating women: 'It was not the fact that suffragettes had chained themselves to the grille and made an undignified scene or the uproar in the strangers' gallery which really upset him but the action of 13 women who had broken into his serious address at a religious bazaar in Islington.' The enthusiasm of the new movement swept through the country. Charlotte Despard, already a convinced socialist and republican, mused about the effect the new movement had on women of her time:

I had found comradeship of some sort with men. I had marched with great processions of the unemployed. I had stood on platforms with Labour men and socialists ... I had listened with sympathy to furious denunciations of the Government and the capitalistic system to which they belong. Amongst all these experiences I had not found what I met on the threshold of this young, vigorous union of hearts.

Margaret Thomas, whose father, a Liberal coal-owner, became Viscount Rhondda, could hardly contain her enthusiasm when she came in contact with the WSPU. 'For me and many other young women like me, militant suffrage was the very salt of life,' she wrote in her autobiography, *This was My World*, published in 1933. She continued:

The knowledge of it had come like a draught of fresh air into our padded, stifled lives. It gave us release of energy, it gave us that sense of being some use in the scheme of things, without which no human being can live in peace. It made us feel that we were part of life, not just watching it ... It gave us hope of freedom and power and opportunity ... the things people expected one to mind, speaking at rowdy street corner meetings, selling papers in the gutter, walking clad in sandwich boards in processions, I for my part thoroughly enjoyed, and I expect that most of my contemporaries did the same. Nothing can stop this movement.

Nor were these feelings and enthusiasms confined to upper-class women. Half a century later, the popular musical *Mary Poppins* created a caricature of the upper-class suffragette leader, abandoning her children to the maids while she rushed off 'to lead our courageous women prisoners in song'. No doubt there were such women to titillate the prejudices of their opponents. But certainly in the early years of the movement, from 1906 at least until 1910, the infectious spirit of militant defiance which had been unleashed by the Pankhursts and the WSPU spread deep into the consciousness of women of all classes. Everywhere, women's confidence grew. For the first time in known history, women took the political stage, speaking repeatedly in public at meetings at which they were ridiculed, cat-called and abused. The suffragette speakers developed a fine line in irony, turning the banter back on the hecklers and using sardonic humour to ridicule the ridiculers.

For a moment, it looked as though the Liberal Government, with its landslide majority, would crack in face of the protest. Henry Campbell-Bannerman, Prime Minister in 1906, confessed that he was in sympathy with the suffragettes, and called on them to keep pestering the Government. The pests responded with vigour but in April 1908, Campbell-Bannerman died, to be replaced as Prime Minister by H. H. Asquith, a bitter opponent of women's enfranchisement. From the outset, Asquith, described by novelist and journalist Rebecca West as 'the least remarkable Yorkshireman who ever lived', behaved as if he set some personal store on depriving women of the vote and deceiving them with false hopes in the process. The more militant, forceful and implacable the protesters, the more undeniable the evidence that votes for women was a popular demand in Parliament and in the country, the more determined was the Prime Minister to resist them. Almost at once came dramatic proof of the size and popularity of the women's campaign. The WSPU called a Votes for Women rally in Hyde Park for Midsummer Day – 21 June 1908. Sylvia Pankhurst, Christabel's sister, later described it as 'the greatest meeting ever known'.

Thirty special trains were commissioned to carry demonstrators to London from 70 provincial towns. Frederick Pethick-Lawrence had prescribed new colours for the movement – purple, white and green. Encouraged by the huge increase in subscriptions and donations to the WSPU, he ordered massive spending on preparations for Hyde Park. Huge new wall posters and endless banners were specially commissioned.

Sylvia's Chelsea procession into the park consisted of 7,000 women in white, with at least double that number of men and women swarming alongside it. When they got to the park, the crowd already there was so immense that they could hardly find their way to their allocated platform – there were 20 of these, all with nominated speakers. Sylvia and the other organizers were perhaps inclined to exaggerate the size of the demonstration. Such a charge, however, could not be laid against the newspapers, all of whose reporters, however hostile they were to the cause, were swept away by the size and style of what they saw and heard. The organizers, reported *The Times*, by no means a champion of women's suffrage, had counted on an audience of 250,000. 'That expectation was certainly fulfilled, and probably it was doubled, and it would be difficult to contradict anyone who asserted that it was trebled. Like the distances and number of the stars, the facts were beyond the threshold of perception.'

Emmeline Pankhurst's speeches in those early years reflected her socialist origins. On 14 March 1908 – a few weeks before the great Hyde Park demonstration – she spoke at the Portman rooms in London. Her speech started with some observations about democracy that could have come straight from the Levellers debates at Putney: 'Government without the vote is more or less a form of tyranny. Government with the vote is more or less representative according to the extent to which the vote is given.' She was at her most scornful when she dealt with the proposal of the new minister at the Local Government Board – the former militant organizer of the dock strike John Burns – that the right of married women to go to work independently to earn a wage should be curtailed.

Everyone who ever heard Emmeline and Christabel Pankhurst speak in public testified to the astonishing power of both to hold not just sympathetic female audiences but hostile male audiences as well, to force them to listen and to convert at least a minority. In this sense, as in so many others, the WSPU campaign transcended anything of the kind that had gone before. Margaret Thomas tells the story of two such hostile meetings in South Wales. The first was organized for her by the local Liberal Party out of deference to her father, the local Liberal MP. It was packed with young roughs who came with strong voices and musical instruments and entirely drowned out everything Margaret and her fellow speaker had to say. They left after the hour (the minimum allowed by the WSPU) after not a word had been heard, much less appreciated. The other WSPU meeting she described was in Newport and the speaker was Emmeline Pankhurst.

The young roughs were there again, but this time the outcome was rather different:

When a youth interrupted, she turned and dealt with him, silenced him, and, without faltering in the thread of her speech, used him as an illustration of an argument. The audience was so intent to hear every word that even when one little group of youths let out that aforementioned evil-smelling gas, it did no more than cause a faint stir in one small corner of the hall. As Mrs Pankhurst continued, the interruptions got fewer and fewer, and at last ceased altogether. Even when at the end came question-time, members of the audience were uncommonly chary of delivering themselves into her hands. That meeting was a revelation of the power of a great speaker.

This sort of thing was going on in halls all over the country. The Pankhursts and their allies had developed a high standard of public speaking; but the WSPU also automatically accepted, nationally and locally, any invitation to speak not just to cheering crowds in the big cities but also to small, fractious and sometimes impossible meetings in small town and village halls.

Long before the WSPU there were campaigns for women's votes. The difference between the WSPU and these other suffrage organizations was militancy. The WSPU leaders believed that the time had come for action in defiance of the law. Ever since Annie Kenney's and Christabel's stand at the Manchester Free Trade Hall during the 1905 general election campaign, women flocked to take up the challenge and broke the law to publicize their point of view. The figures were astonishing. In the year from the spring of 1907, suffragette demonstrators were sent to prison for a total of 191 weeks. In the following year, to the spring of 1909, suffragette imprisonments rose to 350 weeks. In the same period, membership and funds of the WSPU doubled, and at the same time the constitutional activity of the WSPU increased at a rate that defies belief. In the first six years of its existence, the Union held more than 100,000 meetings. The biggest meeting halls in London, Manchester, Liverpool, Bristol, Scotland and Wales were booked to overflowing. In the same period, the Albert Hall, the biggest in the country, was filled no fewer than 13 times by the WSPU, whose public meetings exceeded sometimes by three or four times the total number of meetings sponsored by all other political organizations. The growth in the Union's influence was directly connected to the imprisonment of so many of its activists. Women who were passively outraged by the injustice of their electoral qualifications now felt that there was something they could do about it. They could demonstrate, or publicly protest, and when they were arrested (as they invariably were), they would refuse to be bound over and were sent to prison. The momentum of the great Hyde

Park demonstration in the summer of 1908 was maintained four months later when the three suffragette leaders – Emmeline and Christabel and their faithful warrior Flora Drummond – were accused of breach of the peace after a demonstration outside the House of Commons. To the fury of the magistrate who heard the case, the defendants issued writs demanding the appearance in court as witnesses of two Cabinet ministers, David Lloyd George and Herbert Gladstone. Gladstone, who was Home Secretary, was the victim of a brilliant cross-examination by Christabel. He had, she revealed, justified the violence of men seeking the vote, but now he was punishing women for the same sort of violence.

These exchanges were publicized alongside historic photographs of the three defendants in the dock. The spectacle of the tenacious and articulate young woman mocking the secretary of state was not lost on the tens of thousands of women who flocked to join or subscribe to the WSPU. The magistrate refused to state his case, and paid no attention to the arguments or the evidence. He observed that between 5,000 and 6,000 police had been required to keep order in response to the WSPU handbill publicizing the demonstration, and concluded therefore that a breach of the peace had plainly been incited. He fined each of the two older women £100, or three months in prison. Christabel was fined £50, or ten weeks in prison. The three refused to pay the fines or to give any assurances of good behaviour, and were banged up in Holloway. On her release, just before Christmas 1908, Christabel went straight to the Queen's Hall, where she made another defiant appeal for direct action to win the vote.

The high-water mark of the WSPU and its influence can be etched in here – at the end of this year of great demonstrations and throughout the following year, 1909. Most of the militant activity in that period took the form of protest demonstrations and interruptions of public meetings. So astonishing was the rise of the WSPU, so striking its early successes, that most of its leaders and supporters assumed that victory was at hand. The Liberal Government, it was assumed, could not go on ignoring this vast protest and the views of the majority of its own MPs for ever. Sooner rather than later a Votes for Women Bill was surely bound to pass through the Commons and become law.

There were, however, already signs of looming political problems which threatened the WSPU advance. The first stemmed from the insistence of the Pankhursts and the Pethick-Lawrences that they control the Union without recourse to even the most rudimentary democratic checks and balances. This issue came to a head over the pledge by the leaders to hold an annual conference of the WSPU with powers to decide on tactics and on policy. The first such conference was due to take place in October 1907. According to the constitution of the WSPU, which was modelled on the constitution of the ILP, the annual conference would bring delegates together to discuss and comment on national perspectives and initiatives. It quickly became obvious at headquarters that nothing could stop the conference turning into a hot debate, especially on the attitude of the Union to other political parties at by-elections. In Scotland, one of the most energetic of the Union's new organizers, Teresa Billington-Greig, had set up more than 70 branches of the Union and was campaigning among them for a highly critical line at the conference, especially on the WSPU's neutrality towards Labour and the ILP. Emmeline Pethick-Lawrence voiced the concern at headquarters, complaining that many of the prospective critics were 'quite ill informed as far as the realities of the political situation were concerned'. In this, she said, they were in sharp contrast to Christabel Pankhurst who had 'conceived the militant campaign as a whole ... and could not trust her mental offspring to the mercies of politically untrained minds'. The Pankhursts and the Pethick-Lawrences acted promptly to ward off the proposed rebellion by tearing up their constitution, cancelling the October conference, setting up a new, smaller and more powerful committee, and demanding from its proposed members an oath of loyalty to the Pankhursts and a pledge not to support any political party in any circumstances until women had achieved the vote. One of the Pankhursts' nominees for their new committee was perhaps the most prestigious of the new recruits to the WSPU, and certainly one of its most trained political minds. Charlotte Despard, a socialist, was, we have seen, bowled over by early enthusiasm for the WSPU. She had not lost her critical faculties, however, or her independence. In spite of her continuing admiration for the Pankhursts, she observed with alarm the growth of their control over the new movement. There was no way in which she could possibly sign the loyalty document placed in front of her. Instead, she and the other critics went ahead with the conference that had been so arbitrarily cancelled. The result was the Women's Freedom League, which campaigned not just for the vote but on women's issues generally until its dissolution more than half a century later. The League sponsored and supported large numbers of meetings and demonstrations. Many of its champions, including Charlotte Despard, went to prison alongside WSPU members. In the short term, the foundation of the League did nothing to stop the momentum of the WSPU, but the imperious behaviour of the Pankhursts and Pethick-Lawrences lost the Union many of its keenest supporters and cut it off from all future internal criticism and debate.

The second main issue of concern was the attitude of the Pankhursts and the WSPU to the other political parties. From the outset, Christabel and her mother made it clear that the single purpose of the new Union was to campaign against the Liberal Government. Governments made policy, ran the argument, and the government of the hour was the only possible origin of a law to give the vote to women. It followed that the new militant organization should direct all its fire exclusively on the Government. This argument was bolstered by the result of the 1906 election, and the huge Liberal majority. At least part of the force behind the WSPU argument was the fact that the Liberal Party, so many of whose members were committed to female suffrage, were now in power and should proceed at once to deliver the vote to women on the same terms as those on which their predecessors in 1884 had delivered it to men.

One immediate result of the WSPU policy was the rejection of all claims for suffragette support from other parties, notably the new Labour Party, which was from the outset ostensibly committed to universal suffrage, male and female. The rift with Labour was all the more dramatic since the Pankhursts had started their political careers in the ILP. Indeed, in the early debates in the ILP on this issue, the Pankhursts played a prominent part. Emmeline was a strong supporter of the 'on the same terms as men' (OSTAM) resolution on women at the 1904 Cardiff conference of the ILP, as follows:

In order to improve the industrial and social position of women, it is necessary to extend to women the parliamentary franchise on the same terms as it is, or may be, granted to men, Conference instructs the executive to propose and introduce into Parliament a Bill to amend the Representation of the People Act so that words importing the masculine gender should include women.

The resolution was passed, and Emmeline Pankhurst was duly elected on to the executive of the ILP. As we have seen, she had formed the WSPU a year earlier, so in the months after the Cardiff conference she was a founder member of an organization devoted to militant tactics to get women the vote and at the same time a member of the executive of the ILP, which shared her policy. The following year, 1905, the ILP conference was held in Manchester, the home of the Pankhursts, and Christabel was the delegate from Manchester East. The resolution on female suffrage was moved by H. S. Wishart, the delegate from Woolwich – a traditionally Tory constituency which, in a by-election in 1903, described at the time as 'the greatest by-election victory of modern times', had elected the Labour candidate, Will Crooks, to Parliament. Wishart strongly supported the declared policy of the ILP that female suffrage should be granted 'on the same terms as men'. That OSTAM phrase was to become the core of a long and bitter controversy in and out of the Labour Party. Wishart started his speech by referring to the Women's Enfranchisement Bill, to be brought to the Commons later that year by Keir Hardie, the country's only ILP MP. He came at once to the issue which was troubling the conference as it continued to trouble the Labour movement at large: would the new Bill, and ILP policy, result in votes for purely middle-class women, and thus possibly postpone still further the day when workers and poor people would be able to elect a majority in the House of Commons? Wishart observed:

It doesn't matter very much whether the Bill would enfranchise middle- or working-class women. Until the sex disability is removed, the organization of women on class-conscious lines would be hindered by the cross-current of women's interests, which were not confined to a class but were common to the whole sex. What we have to do is cultivate class-consciousness among the workers, and for that purpose we want every man and woman alike to have as clear a view as possible of the grievances from which they suffered. When you have that clear view, I ask you not to think of males or females but of a party of workers and of the one great class to which we belong.

Wishart's speech anticipated and dreaded the argument that was about to split the Labour Party. He could see the dangers inherent in support for OSTAM. He argued nevertheless that the real issue was a simple one of discrimination, and that as long as that issue was not resolved, all the other issues would be diverted by or absorbed in it. There was no hope, he thought, of any meaningful suffrage policy on class issues unless the discrimination issue was first cleared up. It was no use whatever passing motions about Government policies when at least half the human race, including half the working class, were, because of their sex, denied the right to vote.

His motion was seconded by Christabel Pankhurst:

The alternative to the Women's Enfranchisement Bill is not adult suffrage – it is manhood suffrage. To put women on the same footing was to remove a barrier. We claim all the rights men have – nothing more, nothing less. We claim simple equality. This is a socialist question, and the Labour Party cannot afford to neglect their sisters in their hour of need.

An amendment was moved to replace support for the Women's Enfranchisement Bill with support for adult suffrage. The Bill, some delegates argued, would give the votes to the 'well-to-do' and widows, and that would hardly improve democracy or working-class representation. This argument was countered in a stormy speech from a new ILP recruit – Teresa Billington-Greig. She poured scorn on the objection that the Bill would produce only a 'nasty property vote'. She mocked 'those who throw up their hands in horror at the Bill, yet often in the streets exhort the workers to use their votes'. 'What votes should they use?' she inquired. 'Their nasty property votes?' To mounting applause she went on: 'We have been twitted that the Bill is opposed to the adult suffrage movement. It is nothing of the kind. It is a step towards it – a practical achievable step.' Only 29 delegates voted for the amendment, 126 against. The Bill was thus endorsed by the ILP, whose leader Keir Hardie duly tried to get it through the Commons, only to see it 'talked out' like its predecessors.

The argument then shifted on to a bigger stage – the Labour Party. In the 1906 general election, as we have seen, 29 candidates nominated by the Labour Party were elected to Parliament. In the general euphoria of the 1906 Labour Party conference, little attention was paid to the debate on women's suffrage, led off by Ben Turner, the General Secretary of the National Union of Weavers. Turner – whose wife later joined the WSPU and took part in several of their demonstrations – habitually moved an OSTAM motion at conferences of the ILP, of which he was a founder member. In his home town of Batley (where he later became Mayor), he said, nine-tenths of the women likely to be enfranchised by an OSTAM Bill were working class, and anyway the argument for the immediate granting of votes to women was based on a detestation of sex discrimination. Turner's motion was opposed by Harry Quelch of the London Trades Council. Quelch was a member of the SDF, a party that had always been 100 per cent opposed to what its leaders helped to make known as 'the limited Bill'. Quelch argued that the extension of the franchise to women on the same terms as men was 'a retrograde step, and should be opposed'. Granting the propertied franchise for women, he said, would mean that 'the overwhelm-ing number of women electors would not belong to the working classes' and that therefore 'the tendency would be to increase the power of the propertied classes'. The vote was called for in a hurry – the delegates were keen to get on with the celebrations of the great Labour triumphs at the polls. No one was called to answer Quelch's arguments. No one pointed out, for instance, that neither he nor anyone of his persuasion had argued against the extension of the limited franchise to men in 1884, still less denounced it as a 'retrograde step'. On the contrary, the SDF, including Quelch himself, had consistently put themselves up for election to a male electorate whose votes to some extent depended on their property. The result of the vote was very close. Quelch's amendment to Turner's motion was carried by 435,000 to 432,000. The Labour Party, by this slender majority, was committed against extending the vote to women on the same terms as men.

The issue would not go away. At the 1907 Labour Party conference in Belfast, held over three days in January, H. S. Wishart was there once more to move the 'immediate extension of the vote to women' and Harry Quelch was there again to denounce the proposal as 'a retrograde step'. Though the limited Bill was powerfully supported by Selina Cooper, a working-woman delegate from Nelson, Lancashire, it was lost this time by a much larger majority than the year before – 605,000 to 268,000. The process was repeated the following year (1908, the year of the huge demonstration in Hyde Park) when Quelch again put forward an amendment to a Ben Turner motion for OSTAM. Quelch asked:

What has changed since the previous year? Surely it could not be the Merry Andrew antics of those ladies who think the best way to advance a cause is to suppress the right of public meeting or of those others who played the part of modern Andromeda in the prosaic surroundings of Downing Street. Surely these are not the tactics which would commend themselves to the moderate respectable Labour Party?

Harry Quelch was a master of irony, and it was not lost on many delegates that his own support for the respectable Labour Party had always been equivocal. Nine times out of ten, he would find himself speaking against the platform and denouncing the moderate tone of the Labour leadership. When the issue was women's suffrage, however, and discrimination against women at the polls, Quelch lined up unequivocally with Labour's most right-wing and respectable faction. He was put promptly in his place by a delegate whose very presence at the conference was resented by the platform. In July 1907, a young orator called Victor Grayson had stood on his own initiative and expense in a by-election in Lancashire's Colne Valley, a Liberal stronghold. He was not endorsed by the national ILP, who thought him reckless and his cause hopeless. He stood as Independent Labour, and won. In the House of Commons, he continued to infuriate his new colleagues by supporting causes they held unsafe. He vigorously supported the suffragettes and opposed the repressive measures taken against them. Speaking at the Hull 1908 Labour Party conference immediately after Quelch, he mocked the old sectarian:

Harry Quelch raised his hands in holy horror because the ladies who had been fighting for the franchise had not been pretty, limp, submissive little things who asked beautifully for the vote. When we meet a hungry man who is so hungry that he cannot be adequately attended to without a 7-course dinner, we say: 'As we cannot give you that, it would not be fair to give you bread and cheese.'

The conference did not agree. Quelch's majority grew again – to over half a million. Worse, when Eva Gore-Booth moved to extend the franchise to women workers, 'the poorest of your own class', she too was rebuffed – by 791,000 to 224,000.

What was it that persuaded the Labour delegates to vote so heavily for the Quelch amendments? Their central argument – that they were in favour of adult suffrage, and that the 'limited' OSTAM proposals were a reactionary distraction – would have carried greater weight if there was the slightest sign that any of the Labour or SDF leaders were involved at any time in any mass campaign for adult suffrage. As Keir Hardie consistently pointed out, there was no meaningful agitation for full adult suffrage in all the years before the formation of the WSPU. In her autobiography, *The Hard Way Up* (1956), Hannah Mitchell, a working-class convert to the ILP, wrote of her disillusionment with the socialists on the issue of the vote:

When we began to approach Labour candidates for support we were often snubbed. When I went myself with a deputation to interview a candidate, who later held high office in a Labour Government, he listened with ill-concealed impatience while we stated our case; then he said very grandly: 'I am an adult suffragist' and so dismissed us from his presence. We heard a lot about adult suffrage at this time from men who never seemed to have thought about it before.

The issue of the extension of the franchise was raised in the most dramatic form by the suffragettes, and the response to their main demand, for the vote on the same terms as men, was the real test of opinion at the time. The sophisticated ducking of the argument – 'adult suffrage or nothing' – blended conveniently with the masculine prejudice that infected so many Labour MPs and delegates. Sylvia Pankhurst recorded her and her colleagues' disgust at a speech by Sir William Cremer in a House of Commons debate on the issue of enfranchising women on the same terms as men. Cremer had served on the council of the International Working Men's Association when it was founded by Marx, but had gone down the drain ever since. In 1885, he was elected to Parliament as a Lib-Lab Member for Haggerston in East London – and was later honoured with a knighthood. He could be relied upon to beg MPs never to open the door to women electors 'since it would be practically impossible ever to close it'. Cremer was terrified of being 'swamped' by the female majority. Sylvia admitted that although she was angry with him 'he was an object of pity as he stood there, undersized and poorly made, obviously in bad health and with that narrow grovelling and unimaginative point of view, flaunting his masculine superiority'. But the flaunting was by no means confined to clapped-out reactionaries like Cremer. The misogynist shadow of Hyndman and Bax still influenced a large proportion of delegates to Labour conferences. Nor was Labour opposition to OSTAM confined to men. Many pioneer women trade unionists of the time took their stand against the suffragettes. Margaret Bondfield, who at the age of 24 (in 1897) had become an executive member of the National Union of Shop Assistants, and her more fiery Scottish colleague Mary Macarthur clung tenaciously to the notion that organization of women in unions was more important than campaigning for the vote and that the women's suffrage campaigners were distracting attention from the main aims of the Labour movement, including adult suffrage. These ideas inspired both women to argue and vote for the Quelch amendments, though both were uneasy about Quelch's language and style.

The arguments in the Labour Party over the immediate demand of the suffragettes – votes for women now, on the same terms as men – has perplexed and harassed sympathetic authors ever since. As late as 1996, Logie Barrow and Ian Bullock, the authors of *Democratic Ideas and the British Labour Movement, 1880–1914*, sympathized with the socialist feminist of the time torn 'between loyalty to her class and loyalty to her sex'. They bemoaned 'the unanswerable nature of that question'. Yet the chief reason why the question was not answered at the time was not that it was unanswerable but that both sides dug deep into extreme positions, neither of which, with the admitted advantage of hindsight, seems tenable. To establish their working-class credentials, many socialists opposed OSTAM, and in doing so appeared to many campaigning women as supporters of discrimination who did not want any truck with women's enfranchisement. However unfair such a charge may have been at the time – and there is enough on record to prove it against many of the more formidable Labour leaders – the effect of their opposition was to drive a wedge between Labour and the greatest agitation against discrimination ever known in Britain.

Looking back on these arguments over nearly a century, a solution emerges quite plainly. It was, at best, sectarian folly for any Labour supporter at the time to oppose a mass movement for franchise reform, however small the effect of such a reform. Without a clear alternative strategy, or an alternative mass movement with alternative demands, opposition to OSTAM meant nothing more or less than the status quo, with no more votes for anyone. To do nothing, or to demand nothing in the light of the mass campaign, was to ignore hundreds of thousands of people campaigning for progress. On the other hand, to accept as final the limits of the suffragette demand was to concede that nothing could be achieved except a vote for propertied women. This was plainly an unsatisfactory conclusion for any socialist, male or female, for whom the most stringent divisions in society were founded not on sex but on class. In such circumstances, the obvious course was to join the mass agitation for votes for women with enthusiasm and vigour, and, within it, to press for votes for everyone. Very few voices were raised for this position. Robert Blatchford was editor of the socialist weekly *Clarion* – the only Labour paper since the time of the Chartists to pay its way. In those early years of the suffrage movement, *Clarion*'s articles on the suffrage question had been critical of the WSPU and their 'limited Bill'. In a simple sentence, Blatchford argued for a position that, if it had been seriously adopted and campaigned for even in his own newspaper, would have gone a long way to healing the rift between the growing Labour movement and the popular challenge of the suffragette campaign. 'I am,' said Blatchford, 'for universal adult suffrage, but I am not against the limited Bill.'

The debate over OSTAM and its failure to win the support of the Labour Party infuriated the WSPU leaders. Emmeline Pankhurst resigned from the executive of the ILP, and Christabel became increasingly hostile to Labour. Thus they set out their policy for the Union: absolute independence from all other parties. It was a policy that many supporters of votes for women found very hard to accept. At a by-election at Cockermouth in Cumberland in August 1906, the Labour candidate was the miners' leader Robert Smillie. He supported women's suffrage, but the WSPU, in one of its first electoral appearances, instructed its supporters to campaign only for a vote against the Liberal candidate. This instruction disturbed many Labour women who went to help Smillie at Cockermouth, including Charlotte Despard, and went on disturbing them all the way to the outbreak of war in 1914. During all that time, Christabel moved further and further away from her socialist origins, dragging her mother with her. Even as early as 22 December 1908, when Christabel spoke at the Queen's Hall, her pitch to her followers lost all sight of the 'socialist question' she had raised four years earlier at the 1904 ILP conference. Her speech should be compared with that of her mother at the beginning of the same year, 1908. Emmeline had appealed to her audience on behalf of the exploited women in sweated trades. No such issue bothered Christabel, whose speech concentrated exclusively on the wrongs done to her sex, and occasionally strayed into matters ethereal: 'We know what we ought to strive for and I believe that nothing is impossible to the human will and the human spirit because, you see, after all, we, every one of us, believe that it partakes of the divine and in so far as it does that, it can bend our circumstances.' The speech marked a further step by Christabel away from the Labour movement. Based in London, she was increasingly patronized and fêted by wealthy women who had no contact or sympathy with her socialist origins.

Even at the height of the movement, in 1908 and 1909, these three developments – the tendency to authoritarianism in the WSPU, the insensitivity and misogyny of Labour participants in the OSTAM debate and the resulting split with Labour – weakened the Union and held up its advance.

In January 1910, Asquith and the Liberal leaders, worn out by their long constitutional battle with the House of Lords, whose powers the Government had not the guts to abolish, appealed to the electorate for a new mandate. There were two general elections that year, in January and in December. Both produced the same stalemate. The Liberal majority over the Tories was two in January, one in December. Effectively, the Liberals stayed in office with the help of the Labour Party, which won 42 seats in December, and the Irish Nationalist Party, which won 74. Despite this, there was no doubting the fact that Liberal influence had been drastically cut since the 1906 landslide. The policy of the WSPU, which had concentrated all their militant energies on humbling the Liberal Government, appeared for a moment to have succeeded. But before the women could press home any advantage, the militancy was suddenly called off – by the WSPU leaders themselves. The reason was a truce organized early in 1910 by the newly formed Conciliation Committee of MPs.

The driving force behind the Committee was Henry Noel Brailsford, a journalist who had made his name as a leader writer on the Liberal *Daily News*. In October 1909, Brailsford and his equally brilliant colleague H. M. Nevinson resigned as leader writers in protest against the refusal of the *Daily News* editor to oppose the forcible feeding of suffragette prisoners. The idea of forcibly feeding prisoners who went on hunger strike had been patented by officers at Winson Green prison, Birmingham, the previous month. Eight women had been arrested while protesting against the Prime Minister at the Bingley Hall, and were sent to Winson Green where they promptly went on hunger strike. On 24 September 1909, reports appeared in the press that the prisoners had been fed by force, either by stomach pump or by tubes through the mouth or nose. The majority on both sides of the House of Commons regarded this news with great hilarity, but as the days went by more and more medical experts drew attention to the dangers with which such treatment threatened the prisoners. 'We cannot denounce torture in Russia and support it in England,' declared Brailsford and Nevinson in the letters column of their own Liberal newspaper. 'Nor can we advocate democratic principles in the name of a party which confines them to a single sex.' Brailsford disapproved of the militant tactics of the WSPU, to which his wife, Jane, had recently been converted, but he was more angrily opposed to the violent reaction of the authorities. In October 1909, Jane Brailsford was arrested and imprisoned with Lady Constance Lytton and others for smashing windows in Newcastle as part of a WSPU protest demonstration against the Chancellor of the Exchequer, David Lloyd George. At once, Brailsford set about trying to find a compromise.

He started from the undeniable fact that the vast majority of Members of Parliament, even after the 1910 elections, favoured votes for women in some measure. Surely, he reflected, a deal could be arranged so that majority could be converted into enfranchising legislation. Tirelessly, he put together what became known as the Conciliation Committee, composed of 36 MPs all in favour of some sort of women's enfranchisement. The Committee cobbled together a Conciliation Bill that would grant the vote to some women. Emmeline and Christabel Pankhurst and the Pethick-Lawrences were suspicious of the new Bill but did not oppose it. Reluctantly, they agreed a temporary truce in which all militant activities, including by-election campaigning against Liberal candidates, would cease until the fate of the Conciliation Bill was clear.

The Pankhursts' suspicions were firmly based. The Bill was infected by the rotten compromises that had dogged so many similar measures in the past. Under its provisions, married women were barred from voting in the same constituency as their husbands. Lodgers, too, had no vote – a restriction that especially shocked Emmeline Pankhurst. Far too many concessions, she complained, were made to the Tories on the Committee, all of whom were terrified by the spectre of universal suffrage. Nevertheless, the truce held. After a two-day debate in July 1910, the Bill was carried by 109 votes, and immediately sent to a committee of the whole House, thus ensuring that at least until the second general election of 1910 it was doomed. Studying the division lists, Brailsford and his colleagues were surprised to see the name of Rt. Hon. Winston Churchill, Home Secretary, as an opponent. Churchill had given an assurance to the Conciliation Committee that he would support the Bill, and had even allowed his name to be published as a supporter. Brailsford had the first clear sign of the duplicity of the Liberal politicians with whom he was dealing.

In November 1910, in protest at the failure of the first Conciliation Bill, Emmeline Pankhurst convened a huge meeting and enjoined the audience to 'come with me to the House of Commons'. Hundreds of women followed her. It looked as though the truce was at an end, but the brutality of the police that evening was disgusting enough to swing the pendulum of public opinion towards the protesters. Brailsford himself took charge of the collection of evidence from the demonstrators. His report contained enough irrefutable testimony not just of brutality by the police but also of indecent assault – now becoming a common practice among police officers – to shock many newspaper editors, and the report was published widely. Its impact went way beyond the bounds of the Woman's Press, which had commissioned it. The report, and the new Liberal Government that took office after the election of December 1910, also bought more time for the WSPU truce on militancy. The truce held while a new Conciliation Bill was published without the £10 property qualification for voting that had been in the first Bill, and without an express ban on husbands and wives voting together. In a sudden surge of public and parliamentary enthusiasm, the second reading of this Bill passed the Commons on 5 May 1911 with a majority of 167, and for a brief moment it seemed to Brailsford, Nevinson and Co. that their prodigious negotiations had been worthwhile.

They were reckoning without top Liberal politicians, in particular the Chancellor of the Exchequer, David Lloyd George. Lloyd George loved high office. He was not remotely interested in votes for women, and he regarded the campaigners, especially the militant ones, as an infernal nuisance. On the other hand, he understood that the Conciliation Committee posed a problem for the Government. A Commons majority of 167 could hardly be ignored, especially when the Bill had been passed two years running. But Lloyd George was convinced that the chief effect of the Bill, if it became law, would be to hand more votes to the Tory Party. The problem called for what Lloyd George would have described as diplomacy, but quickly turned out to be duplicity. After stalling the WSPU all through the summer, Lloyd George started secret discussions with Brailsford and the Conciliation Committee. On 7 November 1911, he told the Committee he would support the Conciliation Bill if another Bill to introduce manhood suffrage failed. No such Bill had even been suggested, but, as if by magic, the following day Prime Minister Asquith announced that in the next session of Parliament he would introduce a Bill to enfranchise most men – a Bill that, he promised, could be amended to include women.

When Emmeline and Christabel Pankhurst heard of these 'diplomacies' they could hardly contain their fury. For well over a year they had called a halt to a powerful mass movement that had built up an almost unstoppable momentum. Their truce had been inspired by a genuine belief that the Government would act to provide women with a compromise. Now all they were left with was a promise of a dubious 'Franchise Bill', aimed only at men, which could be amended to include women. Such an amendment would be highly vulnerable to the House of Lords. At a stroke, the announcement of this new Bill smashed the fragile alliance between pro-suffrage Liberals and Tories that had been built on the Conciliation Committee. All the Tories were against universal suffrage, and their opposition to the Government's new franchise Bill was certain. In the atmosphere of the Commons at the time, the chances of the new Bill being amended to include votes for women were negligible. Asquith's new Bill was seen at once for what it was – a ruse to 'torpedo' (Lloyd George's sensitive word) the Conciliation Bill and to postpone women's suffrage indefinitely. No wonder the WSPU took once more to the streets.

In a demonstration on 21 November 1911, shop windows were smashed all over London's West End. The truce was over. When Brailsford went to see the Pankhursts to ask them once again to control their troops he met an explosion of rage. 'I wish I had never heard of that abominable Conciliation Bill!' snapped Emmeline. She and Christabel promptly called for more militant demonstrations. Brailsford clung to the hope that there was still some prospect of success for the Conciliation Bill, which came up again in the Commons on 28 March 1912. After all, the Bill had passed by 109 votes in 1910 and 167 in 1911. In March 1912, however, it was lost by 14 votes, with the Irish Party, desperate not to upset the Liberals, voting against. The chief argument against the Bill was the Government's commitment to a full franchise reform Bill, amendable to include women. That Bill never came. When, in 1913, the Speaker announced that the amendment to include women was out of order, Asquith dropped the entire Bill. The Prime Minister had, in the wry conclusion of George Dangerfield, author of the glorious *The Strange Death of Liberal England* (1936), 'dishonestly broken a promise which he honestly believed should not be kept'.

While the Pankhursts kept their indignant army in check through most of 1910 and 1911, something else was stirring in the political forest, something so dramatic as to threaten the very foundations of the state. In the 20 years since the victorious dock strike of 1889, the trade unions had slumbered. Though trade-union membership, especially among women, increased during the period, the horizons of the trade-union leaders were firmly limited by the Liberal Party, which most of them still supported, and the new but supine Labour Party. Ever since the defeat of the strikers at Bradford in 1891, and the consequent formation first of the ILP and then of the Labour Party, the advice passed on by trade-union leaders to militant demands from below was to 'hold your fire'. Pretty well everyone in the new Labour leadership agreed that strikes were a waste of time and effort, and that time and effort should be devoted instead to Labour's advance in Parliament.

In May 1910, Tom Mann, the fiery trade-union leader and hero of the dock strike, returned from Australia. He believed as passionately as ever in the power of strikes, and was one of the greatest platform speakers in British Labour history. In the months after his return, he developed a winning pastiche, in which he flung himself on his knees in front of his audiences and reduced them to tears of laughter as he prayed to Parliament for the workers' salvation. In the same week, another sea passenger arrived at London docks: Prime Minister Asquith. Asquith had taken himself off on a cruise of the Mediterranean to settle his jangled nerves after the disappointment of the first 1910 general election. When he heard of the death of King Edward, the Prime Minister ordered his ship back home. Within a few months of the New Year – 1911 – he and Tom Mann were to take up positions on opposite sides of the greatest class confrontation in Britain since the Chartists.

The causes of the Great Unrest, as it came to be called, are easy to identify. Trade-union membership had trebled since the dock strike, but wages fell by 10 per cent between 1900 and 1912. Everyone in society seemed to have gained in the glittering Edwardian era – except the workers. In *The Strange Death of Liberal England*, George Dangerfield explained:

To interfere in the question of pensions, health, strikes, education, conditions of labour – ah yes, this could be done; to destroy the absolute power of the Lords, to cripple the vast landed estates – such actions were highly desirable: but to insist that employers should pay a living wage? That was a frightful impairment of freedom.

The strike started at Southampton on June 1911, where sailors refused to unload the SS *Olympic*. Their union's General Secretary, Havelock Wilson, appealed to the newly formed Transport Workers' Federation for sympathy action. A claim was formulated – for 8d an hour plus a shilling an hour overtime – which quickly became a chant throughout the vast Port of London. The employers begged for negotiations, and agreed to compulsory arbitration. When the arbitrator decided that the claim should be met in full on both counts, the decision was cheered by the strikers – who promptly decided to stay on strike until similar claims were paid to every section of the union, however lowly. Suddenly, to the terror and fury of the employers, the spirit of 1889 swept once more through the Port of London. In a fever of militancy, workers started rejecting offers greater than their claims. The spirit spread through Southampton, Goole, Hull, Liverpool and into other industries. Flour-millers in Hull and cake-workers in Liverpool joined in. Old sectarian differences between workers, soured by centuries of prejudice, were swept aside. In Liverpool and Dublin, Orange and Green banners joined in the strikers' demonstrations. In South Wales, the police went on strike. So did schoolchildren – in 1911 alone there were 62 school strikes, most of them in South Wales. The number of workers involved in strikes in 1911 was 961,800 – 300,000 more than in any previous year. More than 10 million days were 'lost' (or won) in strikes, about a day for every member of the industrial population. Trade-union membership in that single year grew by 600,000. The unions themselves were transformed. The old 'moderate' leaders had no stomach for these new battles. Where there were elections, as in the South Wales miners' federation, the veterans were replaced by eager young militants, hungry for action. The famous 1912 pamphlet *The Miners' Next Step*, which positively yearned for strike action, was the work of these tempestuous young leaders.

Most commentators assumed that the storm would soon pass. After all, the great dock strike had lasted only a few weeks, and was soon forgotten as other big disputes ended in defeat. But, to the horror of the Government and the employers, the Great Unrest of 1911 went on and on. Even the defeat of another transport strike in 1912 failed to stop the growing mood of working-class resentment. So desperate was the situation in May 1912 that the celebrated novelist and journalist H. G. Wells was commissioned to write a five-part series for the *Daily Mail*, entitled 'The Labour Unrest'. The country is, he wrote, 'in a dangerous state of social disturbance . . . the opening phase of a real and irreparable class war'. His cry was 'Wake up, gentlemen! . . . we have to "pull ourselves together" . . . Our class has to set to work and make those other classes more interested and comfortable and contented.' If something was not done to make the condition of the working class more amenable, he warned, there would be a revolution that everyone would regret. Such was the mood nearly a year after the outbreak of the Great Unrest – and so it continued, through 1912, 1913 and 1914 right up to the start of the First World War. All the signs of mass popular protest which had accompanied the revolt of the Levellers in the 1640s and the revolt of the Chartists 200 years later could be seen in abundance. There was the same popular hunger for radical and revolutionary literature. Tom Mann's new *Transport Worker* built up a regular circulation of 20,000; the newly published *Daily Herald* (founded in the middle of a printing strike in 1911) was an instant success; even the old papers of the established socialist parties were suddenly in high demand. *Justice* reported as early as December 1910, from the Marxian Club at Blaenclydach in South Wales, 'We failed to bring a single copy to the Club from the railway station, the whole 500 copies you sent being sold in half an hour.'

The Great Unrest was not confined to men. Hundreds of thousands of women workers were involved. In August 1911, in Bermondsey, South London, only weeks after the start of the transport strike, hundreds of women workers at a sweet factory decided to walk out. They were joined instantly by women workers who had never before even been counted in a trade-union statistic, since none of them were members of trade unions. Mary Macarthur, President of the National Federation of Women Workers, set up a strike headquarters at the Bermondsey Institute. The Institute was packed with women workers on strike from local factories – at one stage 15,000 striking women cheered the transport-strike leaders at an enormous meeting in Southwark Park. They had been the lowest of the low in outcast London, but now suddenly they were the highest of the high. They demanded a huge wage increase, and it was quite plain to anyone who tried to deal with them that they would not return to work without one. In 20 tumultuous days, the employers surrendered in 18 of the strikes in which the Federation was negotiating and 4,000 women joined the Federation. Throughout, in the boiling streets and the stinking Institute, the women were laughing, joking, singing. George Dangerfield reported: 'Many of them, dressed in all their finery, defied the phenomenal temperature with feather boas and fur tippets, as though the strike was some holiday of the soul, long overdue.' At the centre of it all, feverishly collecting money and food for her thousands of new members, was the tall, redoubtable Scots woman Mary Macarthur.

Through all this, the Asquith Government lay low, intervening only occasionally, further irritating the strikers. Shocked into torpor, the Government and the employers surrendered control of the unrest to the Board of Trade and its chief arbitrator, George Askwith. Askwith went everywhere, endlessly rebounding like a rubber ball from what seemed like hopeless defeat to yet another negotiation, yet another mass meeting of angry workers, yet another settlement. By the onset of war in August

1914, however, even Askwith was forecasting disaster. However many negotiating fingers he shoved into the dyke, it would not hold.

Yet in all this turbulence, all this proof positive that the workers and the poor were no longer prepared to lie down and be exploited as in the past, hardly a single voice was raised to demand for the majority of strikers and their families a say in the electing of their representatives in Parliament. At the Labour Party conference in 1912, Mary Macarthur, inspired no doubt by her thrilling experiences at Bermondsey, finally abandoned her long insistence that the demand for votes for women on the same terms as men was reactionary. She was persuaded by the duplicity of the Government over its illusory franchise Bill and its double-dealing over the Conciliation Bill. If the Government's new franchise Bill did not include women, she argued, then Labour should finally take its stand on the women's side and refuse to countenance any extension of the franchise that did not include women.

Robert Smillie, the miners' leader, pointed out that Mary Macarthur's line was inconsistent. In every year since 1906 she and her supporters, including Margaret Bondfield, had argued on what they claimed were class lines. A vote for workers, they argued, was to be welcomed but votes for 'bourgeois women' on the same terms as men was 'retrograde'. Here, said Smillie, was a proposal from the Liberal Government to enfranchise more men. The vast majority of those newly enfranchised by such a measure would be working class or poor. How, in the light of her past arguments, could Mary Macarthur possibly oppose that? In a passionate speech Mary replied that any franchise Bill that did not include women pandered to the misogynists. Such a Bill was worthless and reactionary and could not be supported. The miners' amendment was defeated by 919,000 votes to 686,000.

In her 1984 biography of Selina Cooper, *A Respectable Rebel*, Jill Liddington shows how the 1912 vote at the Labour Party conference led to a new alliance between Labour and the constitutional suffragists, many of whom, including Selina Cooper, became full-time organizers for the National Union of Women's Suffrage Societies (NUWSS), and worked closely with the Labour Party at by-elections. Yet this new unity between Labour and the women's movement did little to connect the massive industrial agitation with the demand for the suffrage.

What was the attitude of the militant suffragettes to the Great Unrest? At the outset they were as bemused by it as everyone else. On 18 August, a leading article in *Votes for Women* on the issue of the strikes concluded:

[Women's] part in the strike has been mainly this – they have paid the greater part of the price and have endured the greater part of the suffering. For the men on strike, the interest and the joy of conflict. For their wives, the troubles which visit the housewife when the cupboard is bare and the children cry to be fed and when the present lack of the weekly income brings a burden of debt to landlord and pawnbroker . . .

In the middle of this sad litany, the leader-writer suddenly recalled that many of the strikers were women. 'Thousands of women and girls in South London have struck against their miserably low wages,' the editorial conceded. 'One of the most urgent necessities of the time is the raising of the starvation wages earned by women, whereon whole families have to exist.' The remedy, moreover, was a simple one: 'and the means to this end is the parliamentary vote.'

A slightly different tone was adopted by the reporter on *Votes for Women* who attended the great rally in Southwark Park for the Bermondsey strikers. 'The meeting,' she reported, 'was one of triumph to celebrate the astonishing success of the women who have won – a success that has surprised even those who fought for it.' The consistent theme of this enthusiastic account of the meeting was solidarity between men and women workers. Mary Macarthur was quoted praising the women workers for standing by the men workers, and vice versa. In many cases, she pointed out, male workers had refused to return to work until the women's demands were met. Charlotte Despard, 67, who had devoted herself to the strike from the moment it started, was greeted with rapturous cries of 'Good Old Suffragette!' Perhaps the loudest reception of all greeted the newly elected MP for Bow and Bromley, George Lansbury. The women's strikes, he emphasized, were part of the 'greater struggle of labour which has yet to be settled'. All this was accurately and enthusiastically reported, but the tone of the editorial in *Votes for Women* that day (25 August 1911) was overtly hostile to the strikers. The theme was: If they have votes, why do they strike? Not all women campaigning for the vote shared this hostility. Sylvia Pankhurst pointed out that there were many suffragettes who not only sympathized with the strikers, but actively supported them. Charlotte Despard's involvement in the Bermondsey strike was just one example. Another emerged in a line from Rebecca West's moving account in the *Clarion* of the funeral of Emily Davison, who died after seizing the reins of the King's horse during the Derby in 1913. Rebecca West recalled meeting Emily Davison in the street in 1912, 'when she was collecting money for the dockers and their families'. Again and again, the most pugnacious spirits among the suffragettes were inspired by the fury, confidence and self-sacrifice of the strikers. Their enthusiasm conflicted with the official line of the WSPU leadership. When Tom Mann was sent to prison in 1912 for inciting troops to mutiny by urging them not to shoot on their fellow workers, *Votes for Women* noted grumpily that the sentence for such a shocking crime was lower than many of those handed down to militant suffragettes. When, on 1 March 1912, Emmeline Pankhurst was arrested for throwing stones at No. 10 Downing Street, she made a long statement at the police station comparing her actions with those of the miners who had just come out on strike:

What we have done, Sir, is a fleabite as compared with what the miners in this country are doing today. They are paralysing the whole of the life of the community. They have votes, they have a constitutional means of redressing their grievance, but they are not content to rely on the constitutional means. If we had the vote, we would be constitutional . . .

No one could read or hear that passage without concluding that the suffragette leaders were not neutral on the strikes. They were against them. The workers who had the vote, they insisted, should use their vote to try and redress their grievances. That vote was a 'guarantee' of decent working conditions, and it was as disgraceful for the male workers (or at any rate those male workers who had the vote) to turn their backs on constitutional protest as it was futile for the suffragettes to rely on such protest. There was throughout this whole line of argument an enduring faith in the power of the vote to transform the lives of human beings – and a distaste for industrial action by workers. If the Pethick-Lawrences and even Emmeline Pankhurst were reluctant to push this argument to its logical conclusion, no such reluctance deterred Christabel, who was most firmly antagonistic to the strike wave. When the Pethick-Lawrences and Mrs Pankhurst were arrested and put on trial for conspiracy in May 1912, editorial responsibility for *Votes for Women* passed exclusively to her. 'We would ask the Government,' she thundered, 'if they propose to make the organization of strikes punishable by law.' In theory, this was mainly an argument to demonstrate the hypocrisy of the Government in criminalizing suffragette activity while leaving the miners and other strikers free of the criminal law. In practice, many active trade unionists, male and female, saw the demand for what it was: yet another attack on the right of organized workers to strike.

The drift away from the workers' action was identified clearly by the young Rebecca West, who wrote a front-page column in Robert Blatchford's *Clarion*. She devoted it again and again to defence of the suffragette cause. Yet she was often critical of the WSPU leadership. In her column on 15 November 1912, she complained that the 'movement grows more and more specialized'. She observed the difference between what Emmeline Pankhurst was saying as late as 1908 and what Christabel was saying in 1912:

In its early days it dealt boldly with the wrongs done women by the industrial system and spoke out plainly on subjects such as the dismissal of married women teachers. Now it is concerned chiefly with the dreary tactical struggle for the vote ... It is because there is just as much courage and genius in the suffrage movement as there ever was that one wishes that it would keep in closer touch with the only movement which could make feminism possible.

The 'only movement' was the industrial movement. In her column on 18 October 1912, she concluded:

Every woman who has risen from the floral stage of political activity (that is, the Primrose League) or the vegetable stage (that is, the Women's Liberal Association) must admire the suffragettes. Yet we may wish that they had spared a little of their dear irreverence and blessed pluck to stir the industrial women to revolt.

For most of 1912, however, the hostility of the WSPU leaders to the strikers did not dampen the enthusiasm for the suffragette cause across a wide spectrum of workers and socialists enthused by the Great Unrest. The imprisonment of the three suffragette leaders in the conspiracy trial of May 1912 shocked many Labour MPs sympathetic to the strikers. Foremost among these was George Lansbury, ILP MP for Bow and Bromley. A confirmed Christian and pacifist, Lansbury was a passionate and courageous socialist who was sustained all his life by a horror of exploitation and cruelty. In 1889, when still in the Liberal Party, he became election agent to Jane Cobden, daughter of the famous Liberal Richard Cobden, who was elected as a Progressive candidate in the London County Council elections. After a series of court actions coordinated by the Tory Party, Jane Cobden and the two women who were elected with her were either removed from their posts as ineligible or told that they could take their seats as councillors provided they played no active part in the council. (It was not until 1907 that women were allowed to become full county councillors.) These impudent judicial decisions infuriated Lansbury, who at one stage advised Jane Cobden to go to prison rather than relinquish her seat. Soon afterwards, Lansbury became a socialist. He left the Liberals and joined the Social Democratic Federation and later the ILP. As a new Labour MP elected in 1910 he revelled in the Great Unrest and played a key role in persuading striking printers in Fleet Street to start the *Daily Herald* as a socialist daily newspaper. He called the *Herald* 'the miracle of Fleet Street', and was associated with it as columnist and editor for many years afterwards. He was outraged by the conspiracy trial of Emmeline Pankhurst and the Pethick-Lawrences and the monstrous six-month prison sentences imposed on them on 22 May 1912.

As the suffragette campaign responded to their leaders' call for more and more militancy, and the abuse and forcible feeding of prisoners in Holloway became harsher, Lansbury was overwhelmed with indignation. This indignation burst to the surface on 25 June. Three days earlier, Emily Davison, a suffragette of extraordinary determination, had hurled herself from a window in Holloway, falling by chance on a wire netting that saved her from serious injury or death. Labour MP Keir Hardie asked the Home Office for information about the incident and whether Emily Davison had been and was still being forcibly fed. The reply came from the parliamentary under-secretary of state, Ellis Griffiths. He confirmed that Emily Davison 'threw herself onto wire netting on the landing below, and then threw herself again another three feet onto an iron stairway'. Hardie asked the Minister if he was aware that the 'object of this lady in attempting to commit suicide was to call attention to the cruel barbarities which are being inflicted on these ladies in the hope that by the sacrifice of her life they might be brought to a stop'. Griffiths replied peremptorily that he had 'no means of gauging what was in the mind of this lady at the time. In regard to the attempt to commit suicide, the distance was only eight feet, and if that was her intention she must have known that it could not have been gratified in that particular instance.' This sensitive riposte was regarded as hilarious on Government and Tory benches, and greeted with cheers and guffaws. They could not have known that Emily Davison would in fact be killed the following year, when she interrupted the Derby to seize hold of the King's horse. In the resulting din, Tim Healy, the Irish barrister who so often represented suffragette prisoners in court, called on the Prime Minister to intervene to prove that he at least 'will not lightly treat a matter of this kind'. A number of these prisoners, he said, were to be discharged at the weekend. Could the Prime Minister 'see his way to make a slight concession and have them discharged at once? Why keep up this needless torture?' Asquith then rose, as if determined to justify Rebecca West's description of him as the 'chief of all flunkeys'. No, he replied, it was not for him to interfere with the action of a colleague. This was a matter not for the Prime Minister but for the Home Secretary. In his accustomed patrician tone, which mixed condescension with obstinacy, he went on: 'I must point out that there is not a single one of those women but could come out of prison this afternoon if they gave the undertaking which has been asked for' (i.e. to renounce all further militancy). The remark drove George Lansbury to fury. 'You know they cannot,' he shouted. 'It is perfectly disgraceful that the Prime Minister of England should make such a statement.'

This was already a breach of Commons etiquette and the Tory and Liberal benches exploded. 'Order! Order!' shouted scores of MPs, but Lansbury was not listening. In an unusually detailed account of what happened next, the Official Report disclosed:

Mr Lansbury left his seat below the Gangway and walked to the end of the Ministerial Bench above the Gangway. Speaking directly to Asquith, he shouted once more: 'You are beneath contempt!' (Further cries of 'Order! Order!') 'You call yourselves gentlemen and you forcibly feed and murder women in this fashion! You ought to be driven out of office.'

Consumed in fury, Lansbury walked back to his seat where he was ordered by the Speaker to leave the House as a result of his 'grossly disorderly conduct'. Lansbury refused. 'I am not going out,' he replied. Turning to the massed ranks of Tory MPs, who were now, suddenly, quiet, he told them: 'You ought to be ashamed of yourselves.' He sat down firmly in his seat once more and would no doubt have stayed there all day and night if the Labour leaders Ramsay MacDonald and Philip Snowden had not scurried across and begged him to leave. Still shouting at Asquith, he did so.

But Lansbury was not finished with the issue. Before the summer was over he resigned his Commons seat, announcing that he would stand again for Bow and Bromley as an independent candidate for women's suffrage. The by-election took place the following October. Sensing victory, the supporters of the Tory candidate, whose name was Blair, poured resources into the East End. Lansbury's supporters, including the WSPU, responded energetically, and almost every meeting hall in the constituency was booked and filled for every day of the campaign. Lansbury was sure he had won, but for all his enthusiasm and his forthright platform style he failed to build a big enough bridge between the militant women's suffrage campaigners and the Labour support that had elected him in 1910. On polling day, it rained heavily, and the carriages made available to Lansbury's campaign by the wealthy WSPU supporters were for several crucial hours withheld from the election agent by suffragettes who declared that the Pankhursts would never allow the campaign to be run by men. This nonsense was stopped in the end by Emmeline Pankhurst, but not before many crucial votes were lost. Charlie Banks, Lansbury's election agent, never approved

Lansbury's decision to resign his seat and could hardly contain his irritation with his new allies in the WSPU. Similarly, the constitutional suffragists, the NUWSS, refused to take part in the campaign. The result was that the Tories won the seat by 751 votes. Lansbury got 3,291 votes to Blair's 4,042.

Even after his defeat, George Lansbury never regretted his decision to force the by-election or wilted in his support for the victims of forcible feeding. Another speech for the suffragettes in April 1913 had him convicted of incitement, imprisoned and released after only three days. From the day of his release he became increasingly uncertain about the line of the WSPU leadership. He disagreed strongly with Christabel's lurch into what Rebecca West called 'sex antagonism', culminating in her series of articles about venereal disease in the new paper founded by the Pankhursts, edited by Christabel, *The Suffragette*. She seemed to be saying that all men were evil, and want nothing but sexual gratification. Quietly, without rocking the WSPU boat, Lansbury preferred to support Sylvia Pankhurst's breakaway East London Federation of Suffragettes and the Herald Leagues. We shall come across this extraordinary man in prison for his principles once again soon enough. But his stand for the suffragettes in 1912 proved the essential truth about him. 'The only way to get anything is to fight for it,' he once declared.

After the ordeal of the conspiracy trial in May 1912, the leadership of the WSPU, which had already split in 1907 over the question of democratic control, split once again. This time, the split was caused by an appeal by Emmeline and Christabel Pankhurst for a new burst of militancy, qualitatively different from anything that had gone before. This approach was bitterly opposed by the Pethick-Lawrences, and by Sylvia Pankhurst, who believed that there was plenty of fight left in the traditional approach of the WSPU, and that the new militancy demanded by Emmeline and Christabel would isolate the determined minority of suffragettes from most of their supporters. The argument was a crucial one, with strong points to be made on both sides. Unfortunately there was no democratic structure in the WSPU and nowhere therefore where the argument could be conducted. The issue was decided by force of personality. When, on release from prison in the autumn of 1912, the Pethick-Lawrences voiced their disagreements, Emmeline Pankhurst replied: 'We will smash you.' The Pethick-Lawrences did not wait around to be smashed. They were determined not to bring into disrepute the movement they had sustained for five years. So they meekly withdrew from the public arena.

When she rose, alone, to delirious applause at the Albert Hall on

17 October 1912, Mrs Pankhurst devoted the first few minutes of her speech to the rift with her former colleagues. 'In an army, you need unity of purpose,' she began. 'In an army you also need unity of policy. When unity of policy is no longer there, then I say tonight what I have always said, it is better that those who cannot agree, who cannot see eye to eye as to policy, should set themselves free, should part.' No explanation was given as to why two WSPU leaders should feel obliged to 'set themselves free' and 'part' from the two others.

Mrs Pankhurst went on to explain the WSPU's new turn to militancy. First, she insisted on intractable opposition to all three political parties that made up what she called the Coalition Government. The Labour Party, which was cooperating everywhere with constitutional suffragists and, as we have seen, was committed from that year to opposing any measure for increasing the franchise if it did not include women's suffrage, was singled out for special attack. 'We have summoned the Labour Party to go into opposition to the Government on every question until the Government do justice to women.' This was effectively a demand that Labour oppose everything proposed by the Liberal Government – Home Rule for Ireland, for instance, or the payment of pensions through a national insurance scheme – until votes for women were conceded. This represented a sharp shift from the WSPU's previous position, which was neutral towards the Labour Party except on franchise questions. Then Mrs Pankhurst turned to the real meaning of the new WSPU policy: a new interpretation of militancy. 'There is something,' she said, 'that governments care for far more than they care for human life, and that is the security of property. Property to them is far dearer and tenderer than is human life and so it is through property that we shall strike the enemy.' Mrs Pankhurst quickly pointed out that she herself was 'no enemy to property'. The attack on property she was advocating was 'only an instrument of warfare in this revolution of ours'. Owners of property attacked by the WSPU should, she argued, go to the Government and insist on the removal of the causes of the attack on property and grant the suffrage to women. She ended with a furious appeal that brought the audience to their feet, cheering:

Those of you who can break windows, do so. Those of you who can still further attack the sacred idol of property so as to make the Government realize that property is as greatly endangered by women as it was by the Chartists of the old days, do so . . . I incite this meeting to rebellion.

This speech ushered in the final stage of the suffragette movement, which lasted for almost two years until the outbreak of the First World War. As the suffragettes grew more militant, the Prime Minister and the Cabinet hardened in their implacable opposition to women's suffrage. Their so-called Reform Bill – always a trick – was formally dropped. Any amendment to it to extend male suffrage to females was ruled out of order. The sly double-dealing with which leading ministers like Lloyd George and Churchill pretended to support the women's cause, and even befriended the friends of the suffragette leaders, vanished. In its place came repression and cruelty against the women who continued the campaign. Forcible feeding continued apace. Reginald McKenna had become Home Secretary in October 1911. He brought from the Admiralty a reputation for orthodoxy and militarism, which he carried with him through his long Cabinet career – and his subsequent stint as chairman of the Midland Bank. McKenna resolved at the outset that he would not preside over any further martyrdom by the suffragettes. Yet he did not stop the forcible feeding. Physical and verbal abuse of the most disgusting kind was tolerated and even inspired by the prison authorities. McKenna's most heroic legislation was the Temporary Discharge of Prisoners Act (1913), whereby forcibly fed prisoners who showed signs of physical weakness could be released – but only for as long as it took them to get better, when they could be arrested and imprisoned once again.

This peculiarly loathsome law became known as the Cat and Mouse Act, under which scores of desperately ill hunger strikers were released, rearrested, released and rearrested all over again. The passing of the Act, which was supported by the majority of MPs in all parties, including the Labour Party, itself became a cause for further demonstrations and further hunger strikes. Mary Richardson, a 'mouse', was sentenced on 18 July 1913, for throwing an inkpot through a window of a police station in protest against the Cat and Mouse Act. She was sentenced to a month's hard labour, went on immediate hunger strike and was released five days later. Five days later she was arrested again, and shortly afterwards released. The process of arrest and release went on for nearly a year until finally, a few days before war broke out, Mary Richardson was released with acute appendicitis, her mouth and body torn to shreds by the fingernails of prison officers. The persistence of the hundreds of women bruised and battered in this way was matched blow for blow by the savagery of the authorities. When anyone sings the praises of the great reforming Liberal administration from 1906 to 1914, the roles of Harcourt, Asquith and Lloyd George in deceiving the campaigning women and of Churchill and McKenna in torturing them should never be forgotten. No one could have put the case better than Rebecca West:

Twenty-five years ago London was sick with fear because a maniac crept through the dark alleys of Whitechapel mutilating and murdering unfortunate women. In those days people cursed him. They tried to hunt him out of his black hiding place and make him pay for his crime. But today Jack the Ripper works free-handed from the honourable places of government: he sits on the front bench at St Stephen's or in those vast public sepulchres of conscience in Whitehall, and works not in secret but through Home Office orders and scarlet-robed judges. Scotland Yard is at his service. The medical profession, up to the President of the Royal College of Surgeons, places its skill at his disposal so that his mutilations may be the more ingenious. And for his victims he no longer seeks the shameful women of mean streets. To him before the dull eyes of the unprotesting world fall the finest women in the land, the women of the most militant honour and the wisest courage. How times have changed in a quarter of a century.

The heroism of the suffragette hunger strikers never dimmed throughout the period. The movement continued, and the huge funds which had sustained it from its formation actually increased in 1913 and the first half of 1914. Yet for the first time since the formation of the WSPU ten years previously, there were signs of deep unease about the new ultra-militant strategy. This division was greater than the traditional split between the constitutional suffragists and the militant suffragettes, though by 1912, encouraged at least in part by the shift in the official Labour Party line on votes for women, many of the former militants – Ada Nield Chew, for instance, and Selina Cooper – had joined the constitutional suffragists, and some were working full-time for them. Rebecca West's support for the suffragettes never wavered, but her *Clarion* articles in 1913 were more critical of the WSPU. The clearest sign of the division was in the Pankhurst family itself. Sylvia, an ardent supporter of the WSPU from its origins, was bitterly hostile to the new turn to militancy and, after the split with the Pethick-Lawrences, set up a new organization, the East London Federation of Suffragettes. The Federation concentrated on winning the support of working-class women. It was strongly influenced by Sylvia's commitment to socialist ideas. This initiative horrified her mother and her sister, who expelled Sylvia from the WSPU. The division among many WSPU supporters can be exaggerated. In many cases, support for the WSPU overlapped with a growing conversion to socialist organization. In her little autobiography, *Molly Murphy: Suffragette and Socialist*, published by the University of Salford in 1998, Molly Murphy described her conversion to the WSPU, and her appointment at the age of 22 as full-time WSPU organizer in Sheffield. While in that job, she became increasingly attracted to socialist argument and a regular and devoted reader of *Clarion*, but she never lost her admiration for all the Pankhursts and the Pethick-Lawrences. Yet the fact remains that after 1912 the enthusiasm of all but the hard core of the suffragettes was dimmed.

The mixed reaction of many women to Emmeline Pankhurst's incitement to rebellion in 1912 was based on the uneasy feeling that there was a central flaw in her approach. The flaw can be found in the definition of militancy and in the obsession of both Emmeline and Christabel with historical precedent. Their argument went like this. Men won the vote only after militancy, and militancy took the form of random attacks on property. Thus, for instance, (ran the argument) the burning down of Nottingham Castle and the riots in Bristol were harbingers of the franchise concessions in the early 1830s, and the riots in Hyde Park led to the concessions of 1867. The way for women to win the vote was therefore to follow the lead of the Bristol rioters, the 'Chartists of old' and the people who ripped up the Hyde Park railings in 1866. 'Militancy' could be defined by the degree of defiance and by the random destruction of property.

The type of violence in which the WSPU engaged in 1913 and 1914 – stone-throwing at Government window panes, setting fire to postboxes, restaurants, railway stations, etc., false fire alarms (there were 425 in 1912 and even more in 1913), desecration of paintings and historical relics and interruption of sporting events like the Derby – was of a different order from that of the 1830s. But the real difference was not in the type of violence but in the nature of its support. The violence of the 1830s represented the fury of the masses. It symbolized much more than support for a single demand about the franchise. It was the expression of a revolutionary ferment that threatened not just the property of the rich but also their ability to hold on to that property. Men like Macaulay recognized that violence for what it was – a revolutionary warning. Moreover, the violence was spontaneous and sporadic. It was impossible to tell where it would strike next. It came from below. The suffragette violence of 1912 and 1913 by contrast came on orders from above. It had wide support among women but it had none of the class character that so terrified the Whigs and their class in 1830 and 1831.

Ironically, simultaneously with the suffragette militancy but increasingly isolated from it, the working masses of Britain were in revolt. From 1911 right up to 1914, huge sections of British workers, male and female, were so disaffected with their employers that they were prepared to go on strike and endure the most terrible deprivations in a display of mass resistance. Many if not most of these strikes led to violence, but there was about this violence and this agitation a unique element that was not matched by any other form of disorder. The strikes struck at the root of exploitation. They threatened the core of class power in society, not just because they exposed the hideous poverty of the poor and the workers but also because they exposed the cause of that poverty: the control of society by a class of people who owed their wealth to a surplus ground out of the workers' labour. Every strike was a threat to minority ownership of the means of production by a small class of wealthy people who were not subject to democratic control. It was not just the wealth of the wealthy that was put at risk by the strikes – but the continuing access of the wealthy to the source of their wealth.

This was the key to the success of the agitation in 1830 and, to a lesser extent, in 1867. Even more crucially it was the key to the challenge of the Chartists. When Emmeline Pankhurst urged her followers to behave as the 'Chartists of old', she was calling up old slogans from her socialist youth whose real meaning she had forgotten. She did not emphasize, indeed probably did not even remember, that the hallmark of the Chartist revolt was its class character. The symbols of the three great peaks of Chartist agitation were general strikes and 'national holidays', and the whole purpose of the vote for the Chartists was to put an end to the exploitation of labour. The irony of the story of the pre-war suffrage movement is that in its later years it ran side by side with a mighty workers' movement that held out far more hope of toppling the Government and establishing a truly democratic society than did sporadic outbursts of arson against pillar boxes or breaking shop-window panes. And the tragedy of both movements is that they ran side by side without appearing even to notice one another. The strike leaders too often regarded the women's movement as a bourgeois sideshow, a distraction. And the WSPU leaders mentioned the strikers usually only to denounce them.

Nevertheless, in spite of their isolation from and their suspicion of each other, there was some evidence that by the start of the Great War the two movements were moving inexorably to success. The fact that the industrial militancy continued without slackening through the first seven months of 1914 confused both Government and employers and even depressed that indefatigable negotiator, the Board of Trade's George Askwith. Between January and July 1914 there were no fewer than 9,037 strikes. Summarizing Askwith's reaction to them, George Dangerfield wrote:

Something was stirring which – try as they would – his reason could not elucidate nor his imagination apprehend. It was not simply a desire for shorter hours, better wages, and improved conditions of labour which threatened once again to convulse the country's industry; it was a fever, an effervescence; and the causes of it were hidden from him.

What was going on in Dangerfield's view was the growth of a revolt among the workers that was far greater than a yearning for decent wages and conditions. This was a revolutionary consciousness that yearned for 'the birth of a new world', and there was nothing that either Askwith, the civil servant spelled with a 'kw', or Asquith, the Prime Minister spelled with a 'qu', could do about it.

Then suddenly and tragically both movements shuddered to a halt. Workers' militancy and suffragette militancy were stopped in their tracks by the guns of August. The strikes stopped instantly, as, in a great wave of militarism, workers signed up for the colours. The women's movement was split as it had never been split before. The WSPU had always insisted that the question of the vote should predominate over every other political issue. Now the question of the vote was tossed aside. Emmeline and Christabel Pankhurst declared that the supreme priority was the need to win the war. Both women went round the country using all their oratorical skills to shovel young men into the charnel house. By contrast, Sylvia Pankhurst and her sister Adela campaigned against the war. So did Charlotte Despard. So did a handful of other women suffragists. Labour split in almost exactly the same way. Ramsay MacDonald resigned as Parliamentary Labour Party Secretary because of his half-hearted opposition to the war. Also opposed, more whole-heartedly, was Keir Hardie, who died in 1915. Otherwise, almost all the Labour leaders supported the war. Arthur Henderson, the new Labour leader, joined the War Cabinet as Education Secretary in 1915. A year later, John Hodge became Minister of Labour, and set about systematically breaking strikes. Mary Macarthur, who had played such a crucial role in the strikes of 1911 and in shifting the masculine prejudice of the Labour Party in 1912, refused to join the anti-war movement.

In April 1915, the periodical *The Suffragette* changed its name again: to *Britannia*. All the passion and zeal that Emmeline and Christabel Pankhurst had devoted to the 'cause' was now junked in favour of jingoism. When a revolution broke out in Russia in February 1917, Emmeline led a delegation to Moscow to seek to keep Russia in the war. Their jingoism won them new friends. In 1916, Prime Minister Asquith finally declared that he had changed his mind on women's suffrage, and was now in favour. Far from rejoicing at this conversion, Emmeline Pankhurst called a meeting at the Queen's Hall to announce her suspicion of it. The important issue, she declared, was votes for fighting men. Women, she insisted, were not to be used as an excuse to duck that commitment. Asquith, she claimed, had previously used the men to 'dish the women' but was now using the women 'to dish the men'. Small wonder that the most vociferous opponents of women's suffrage – the newspaper proprietor Lord Northcliffe was the most ridiculous example – now hailed Christabel and Emmeline as modern Boadiceas; or that Government ministers, especially after the departure of Asquith as Prime Minister and his succession by David Lloyd George in December 1916, came to see their old adversaries as allies.

Historians have differed about the chauvinism (or 'patriotism' as it is more pleasantly described) of Emmeline and Christabel during the 1914–18 War. Feminists with anti-war instincts have been inclined to write it off as an aberration, a departure from their role as leaders of the WSPU. More contemporary defenders argue that both women saw the German threat as far more dangerous than that of the British ministers. This was certainly the view not only of Emmeline and Christabel Pankhurst but also of many of their previous supporters – including socialists like H. G. Wells, Rebecca West, H. M. Hyndman and Robert Blatchford. All these people argued that the overwhelming political priority was patriotic inspiration of the people. Their approach would certainly have horrified Richard Pankhurst, who had campaigned against all wars, including the Boer War.

Yet in many ways the approach of Emmeline and Christabel was consistent with their more recent past. We have seen how their hostility to the strikers of 1911–14 grew in intensity and how their single-minded concentration on the vote pushed every other issue out of their heads. In the process, both women lost the allegiance not just of Sylvia and Adela Pankhurst but also of many of their more devoted supporters. Their ingrained suspicion of democracy in their own movement plumbed new depths. When their attempts to divert the energies and funds of the WSPU met with some opposition, they denounced the dissidents as pro-German. And when sections of the labour movement began to recover their confidence and when workers in Scotland or South Wales even dared to go on strike, they were denounced as traitors assisting the enemy. Against all the arguments deployed by the two women and their increasingly respectable and reactionary supporters, were piled millions of corpses on both sides of the conflict that in the end decided nothing. The arguments of the courageous minority who opposed the war were that the senseless slaughter could only damage the movement of reform on both sides of the conflict, that the war aims of both sides had nothing to do with democracy but were governed on both sides by imperialist ambitions which would benefit no one but imperialists. One immediate result of the war was a low priority for votes for women. As they both confessed – even boasted – Emmeline and Christabel and what was left of the WSPU played little part in the few moves that were made to maintain the pre-war momentum for votes for women. It was left to the constitutional suffragists, led by Millicent Fawcett, who was also hypnotized and obstructed by an over-riding commitment to the war, and chiefly to the anti-war minority of women, represented by Sylvia and many of the more militant suffragettes, to raise the old slogans.

The decision of Emmeline and Christabel Pankhurst to postpone any further agitation for an extension of the franchise, however, coincided with preparations for a huge change in people's ability to vote. In the Parliament Act of 1911, the instrument used by the Liberal Government to weaken the powers of the House of Lords, ministers had taken the opportunity to enact two major reforms. The first was payment of MPs, the central demand of aspiring Labour politicians for at least two decades. The second was the repeal of the old Septennial Act, which required the House of Commons to be re-elected every seven years, and its replacement by a new law limiting the life of each elected Commons to five years. The last election was in December 1910, so a new House of Commons had to be elected by December 1915. This meant in turn that a new electoral register would have to be drawn up. As early as the spring of 1915, MPs on all sides grew increasingly uneasy about qualifications for the register. Two questions to the Home Secretary from widely differing political quarters were early signs of that unease. On 27 April 1915, the Tory jingo Colonel Claude Lawther stumped the Prime Minister with an awkward question:

In view of the fact that the country may be involved in a general election at any moment, will he introduce legislation extending the franchise to every man who is at present serving his country in a naval, military or industrial capacity and to provide means for those on active service to register their votes?

Asquith stammered that the Government would 'take all relevant circumstances into account' but did not answer the question. Nor did he or any of his colleagues have an answer to another question from the new MP for Sheffield, Attercliffe, W. C. Anderson, a former chairman of the ILP, who had been opposed to the war from the moment it had been declared. He asked Asquith:

whether, in view of the removals of workmen caused by the pressure of munitions and other work, the social and domestic changes involved by millions of men joining the colours, the service and sacrifice of the womanhood of the country, the toll of suffering now and in the future, and the problems of reconstruction, the Government will consider the desirability of establishing a fully enfranchised democracy based on manhood and womanhood suffrage?

Once again the Prime Minister was stumped. This time he handed the question over to his Secretary of State for the Colonies, the future Tory leader Bonar Law, who replied unsurprisingly that the Government was 'considering every aspect' of the matter.

To keep within the terms of their own Parliament Act, Asquith and his ministers pushed through a Bill to postpone the creation of a new register, on the grounds that there was a war on. This delaying tactic lasted for a few months, but by the summer of 1916 the Government was under fire again, from an even more formidable source: Sir Edward Carson MP, leader of the Orange rebellion in the North of Ireland. Sir Edward had been handsomely rewarded for his subversion. In May 1915, Asquith, whose Government Sir Edward had so violently defied, formed a Coalition Government, and called into his Cabinet leading Tories and Unionists. There was an obvious post for Sir Edward, who had spent at least four years defying the forces of British law and order. He was made Attorney General, in charge of British law and order. The appointment did not last long. In October, Carson resigned from the Coalition Government out of a deranged loyalty to Serbia. He became overnight the unofficial leader of the Opposition. One of the many issues he raised in that capacity was the absence of a proper electoral register, and any extension of the franchise involved in the creation of a new one. In July 1916, he asked for a statement from the Prime Minister on these matters. Asquith replied lamely, if truthfully, that his Government just could not find a 'practical or uncontroversial' solution. He hesitantly proposed a select committee of the House to deal with the problem, only for the delay to be denounced by Carson as 'a public scandal'. The Government dithered under fire for another week, until the Home Secretary, Herbert Samuel, proposed a select committee of 15 MPs to investigate the new franchise. 'Men who fought must be included on the register and must vote,' promised Samuel, and he was prepared to sweep away the property qualifications in the existing laws preventing that reform. But there was a problem, a familiar one. 'If you make special provision for the soldiers, the sailors and the munition workers,' he explained, 'the committee will no doubt consider whether it is possible or desirable to avoid embarking Parliament on the great controversy of women's suffrage.'

Carson was on his feet at once. The setting up of this committee was, he said, 'a shelving programme'. He went on: 'I believe in giving the franchise to the soldiers and sailors who are fighting our battles. That is the real property qualification – for what property would any man have in this country if it were not for the soldiers and sailors who are fighting our battles?'

Another Tory knight, Sir Courtney Warner, told the Government not to set up a select committee but to do something at once. Asquith nervously withdrew the motion for the select committee. A month later, on 14 August 1916, he came back with a motion to extend the existing Parliament until 31 May 1917, and to compile in the interim a fresh electoral register based on the voting rights of fighting men. ('If they are fit to fight, they are fit to vote,' intervened the veteran Labour MP, and leader of the 1888 gas workers' strike, Will Thorne.) Asquith could not resist a mention of what he called 'another formidable proposition – what are you to do with the women? I have no special disposition to bring women under the pall of the franchise, but I have received a great many representations from those who are authorized to speak for them. I am bound to say that they presented to me not only a reasonable but I think from their point of view an unanswerable case.'

This case, so suddenly unanswerable to a man who had answered it with such bigoted obstinacy for at least two decades, was based on what Frederick Engels had written 32 years previously: the joining of women in the great army of labour. Asquith conceded:

The women fill our munition factories. They are doing the work which the men who are fighting had to perform before. They have taken their places. They are the servants of the state and they have aided in the most effective way the prosecution of the war . . . I say quite frankly that I cannot deny that claim.

He could not deny it but, in the true tradition of his long stay at No. 10 Downing Street, he could do his best to postpone it. Four days later, the Government brought forward a Special Register Bill to include men in the armed forces. It was not until November that Asquith, his time as Prime Minister almost exhausted, assured the House that 'we shall not proceed with the Bill until after the discussion of the larger questions'. This discussion was shuffled off on to another device dreamed up by the Coalition Government in general and by the Local Government Board Minister, the Tory Walter Long, in particular. In August, Long had proposed a 'representative conference of earnest men holding strong views, bitterly opposed to each other' which could thrash out a 'lasting settlement' for the future of the franchise. This became known as the Speaker's Conference. The Speaker took the chair, and the membership of the committee included a string of lords, knights and dignitaries from the great and good in the Commons. The original list included such bitter opponents of franchise extension as the Marquis of Salisbury and Sir Frederick Banbury – though these two resigned (presumably in protest at the pro-suffrage balance in the committee) on the day of its first meeting, 12 October 1916. The Conference sat 26 times until 26 January 1917, and debated 37 resolutions of which 34 were passed unanimously. Not unanimous was a decision to extend the vote to women – though not to all women: for some reason young women were deemed a greater threat to the established order than older women. The Conference was undecided as to the age at which the vote should be extended to women – some thought 30, some thought 35, but no one argued against votes for women in principle.

The recommendations of the Speakers' Conference were incorporated in a new Representation of the People Bill, which was brought to the House by the Home Secretary, Sir George Cave, in May 1917. 'In the old days,' Cave observed, 'this measure would have been described as a leap in the dark. Now it excites no emotion whatever.' He saw the new Bill as a triumphant vindication of the new spirit of classlessness that had swept the country during the war. 'It is impossible to contemplate the revival of the old class feeling which was responsible for the exclusion of so many from the class of electors.' As for women, he asked, 'is it possible for us having called upon women for so large a contribution to the work of carrying on the war, and having received so splendid a response to that call, to refuse to women a voice in moulding the future of the country?' No, it was not possible, and in spite of a dreary rehearsal of the old arguments against women's suffrage, the Bill got its second reading by a massive majority – 341 to 62. The antis kept up their whining through a long debate in a committee of the whole House, but they had lost the support of most MPs. The Bill rolled through the House of Lords with the grudging support of the Government spokesman there, Lord Curzon, formerly chairman of the Anti-Suffrage League, and on to its royal assent in February 1918. Two million more men and 6 million women, 5 million of them married, were on the electoral register in time for the post-war election in December. Seventeen women stood for Parliament for the first time. Only one – Countess Markievicz, for Sinn Fein in Ireland – was elected, but she did not take her seat. Christabel Pankhurst fought the Midlands seat of Smethwick for the short-lived Women's Party, newly founded by her mother. The Tories bowed out of the seat to give her a free run against Labour, and Lloyd George, the Prime Minister, her old adversary in the halcyon days of the suffragettes, wrote her a warm message of Government support. She lost the seat to the Labour candidate, J. E. Davison, by a majority of 775. Mary Macarthur stood as the Labour candidate at Stourbridge in Worcestershire. The returning officer refused to allow her to stand in the name by which everyone knew her, so she stood as Mary Anderson (her husband was the anti-war MP for Sheffield Attercliffe, W. C. Anderson) and lost to the Liberal by 1,333 votes (8,920 to 7,587). She did better than her husband, who paid a heavy price for his opposition to the war and was defeated in Sheffield after a particularly nasty smear campaign against him. Charlotte Despard was soundly defeated as the Labour candidate for Battersea, and Ray Strachey, whose history of the women's movement, *The Cause*, was published ten years later, lost as an Independent at Chiswick.

In the debate on the Representation of the Bill in May 1917, Ramsay MacDonald, the Labour leader who had taken a back seat during the war, announced that he was in favour of adult suffrage. 'Why,' he asked with some force, 'didn't these arguments about women getting the vote apply in 1911 and 1912', when the Government had been so hostile to women's suffrage? No one answered his question then, and different answers came from feminists and historians all the way through the twentieth century.

One common answer is that in 1916 and 1917, the people who ruled Britain were confronted with the real possibility of a social revolution and were pushed by the revolutionary tide towards enfranchising almost the entire adult population. Certainly everyone in high places was keenly aware of what was happening in Russia. The February Revolution there, although it did not lead to elections, threw out the Tsarist dictatorship and replaced it with a regime based on parliamentary leaders at the top and workers' councils or soviets at the bottom. Nor had the revolutionary tide stopped at the shores of Russia. In Ireland, the Easter Rising in 1916, and the repression that followed, promoted precisely the revolutionary atmosphere, W. B. Yeats's 'terrible beauty', of which the insurrectionists dreamed. The Tory Walter Long told the Commons that 'excluding the masses would bring us very near to rebellion'. Brian Harrison, when researching his book on the opponents of women's suffrage, came across a letter from Lord Islington to Lord Curzon warning against defeat of the Bill in the Lords. 'In a great crisis,' one reactionary hereditary peer warned the other, 'the greater issues should override the less.' In a revolutionary period, he implied, it was folly, not to say class suicide, to persist in denying the vote to the masses, even the female masses.

All these arguments no doubt played their part in convincing the Government and most of its supporters (including many Tories) to promote the extension of the franchise and to shepherd it through both Houses of

Parliament. But they were probably not decisive. To start with, the Russian Revolutions in February and October 1917 took place several months after the British parliamentary discussions about extending the franchise, and although the Revolutions increased the nervousness and apprehension of the British rulers, they did not directly inspire the move to franchise extension. Nor could they explain the quite extraordinary conversion of so many important people in Government, business and the press to the case for votes for women. Much more significant was the miraculous vindication in every town, city and workplace of what Engels had argued in 1884. On a scale quite unprecedented, and in numbers unimagined and unimaginable by him or anyone else, women suddenly joined in collective production.

The figures are stupendous. Between 1914 and 1918, the number of women in jobs rose by 1,345,000. In 1914, there were 357,956 women in unions affiliated to the TUC, in 1918, there were 1,086,000. Three-quarters of a million women worked in munitions factories, 594,000 in engineering, 170,000 in machine shops. In 1914, Woolwich Arsenal, the largest munitions factory in the world, employed 14,000 men and no women. By 1918, the place was bursting at the seams with more than 100,000 workers, 50,000 of them women. A third of workers in the fledgling aircraft industry were women. These vast increases led naturally to demands for pay rises, sometimes on equal terms with men. Often the new women trade unionists were confronted with male-dominated trade unions that refused to accept the principle of equal pay. Just as often, however, there were stirring examples of solidarity. When a pay rise at Glasgow's enormous munitions works at Parkhead Forge was held up by the Government, the rank-and-file leader of the shop stewards, David Kirkwood, teamed up with the leader of the National Federation of Working Women to threaten a strike throughout the works. The rise was immediately conceded. When Kirkwood was arrested for sedition and deported to Edinburgh in 1916, the women's Federation called at once for his release. In August 1918, as the war was drawing to its bloody finale, there was a strike among male transport workers in defence of women who had struck to support their male colleagues.

These examples of trade-union activity and solidarity with male colleagues had precisely the effect Engels had foreseen. Though women were by no means liberated from hundreds of years of patronizing subservience, many of their shackles were weakened or smashed. A quarter of the hundreds of thousands of women in domestic service left it. A third of the women who had surrendered to domestic tyranny in the home became workers with independent lives. For the first time in centuries, there were clear signs that what Engels described as the historic defeat of the female sex was halted and even reversed. These dramatic changes in the economic conditions of women and the economic circumstances in which they found themselves was a crucial cause of the sharp shift in high society which resulted in all the main demands of the suffrage movement being so suddenly and noiselessly granted.

Can we conclude, then, by writing off the women's suffrage movement? Can we say that the whole effort, both constitutional and militant, was a waste of time, and probably premature? Can we say that votes for women would have been granted anyway, as soon as women's economic conditions changed? Can the whole long story, the years of argument, the awful sacrifices of the militant suffragettes, the anguish and the passion, be written off as irrelevant to the relentless march of economic determinism? Frederick Engels would have been the first to reject such an approach. Like his friend Karl Marx, he made himself an expert in discovering and explaining the forces of history, and identifying the precise moments when a revolution or substantial change in the condition of the oppressed might be accomplished. Both men were quite clear that changes against the interests of the rulers could not be achieved without some direct action by the ruled. If no one disturbed the rule of the class in power, then that class would continue to rule without concession. The greatest ally of such rule was the passivity of the ruled. No matter how plainly the 'objective circumstances' pointed to change, there was little prospect of any change until the oppressed did something about it, and, by their actions, wrenched their own minds and aspirations away from the prejudices of their oppressors. The victory of 1918 would not have been achieved without the long years of struggle that preceded it. The militant activities of the suffragettes loosened the ideological hold of men over women. They gave women a real sense of their equality, and a determination to put it into practice. By their actions as much as by their thought and argument, the militant women from 1906 to 1914 liberated themselves and hundreds of thousands of their sex from the condescension of past ages. By their actions, they erased for ever from the political record the monstrous prejudices of male ministers. Just as the vote for most men was won when large quantities of men stepped outside their routine lives and fought for political representation, so, even more certainly, votes for women would never have been surrendered had it not been for the arguments of the Millicent Fawcetts and Lydia Beckers, the tireless propaganda of the Ada Nield Chews, the Eva Gore-Booths and Esther Ropers, the Selina Coopers and Helen Silcocks, the formidable, single-minded courage of all the Pankhursts, of Annie Kenney, of Emily Davison and of the hundreds of thousands of women who fought for their cause more relentlessly than had any of their male predecessors, and won it.

PART 2

How the Vote was Undermined

1918–28: Mond's Manacles

I shall not want Capital in Heaven
For I shall meet Sir Alfred Mond.
We two shall lie together, lapt
In a five per cent Exchequer Bond.

T. S. Eliot,
'A Cooking Egg' (1920)

David Lloyd George, Prime Minister from 1916 to 1922, had many admirers, but he cannot possibly have expected or appreciated a dedication from Lenin, the leader of the second Russian Revolution of 1917. The original version of Lenin's 1920 pamphlet, *Left-Wing Communism, an Infantile Disorder*, was dedicated to 'The Right Honourable Mr Lloyd George as a mark of appreciation of the speech he delivered on March 18, 1920, which was almost Marxian in character and at all events very useful for Communists and Bolsheviks all over the world'. Lloyd George's speech was made to a meeting of Liberals and others to whom the Welsh wizard was anxious to explain his decision to split the Liberal Party and lead a Coalition Government made up mostly of Tories. In his speech he explained that he had joined up with the Tories to forestall a victory of the Labour Party, which he described as a socialist party 'which strives for the collective ownership of the means of production'. Liberalism, he declared, stood above all else for private property. Such was the size and preponderance of the British working class that 'this country is more top-heavy than any country in the world and if it begins to rock, the crash here . . . will be greater than in any land'. Lenin concluded therefore: 'The reader will see that Lloyd George is not only a clever man, but that he has learned a great deal from the Marxists.'

There were many reasons for leading Liberals to form a coalition with the Tories after the war – Lloyd George could hang on to his job as Prime

Minister, for one – but by far the most urgent was the threat to private property and therefore to all civilized society posed by the combination of the new almost universal franchise and the Labour Party. The ghost of Thomas Rainsborough haunted Lloyd George, his old allies in the Liberal Party and his new allies in the Tory Party. Now that the workers and the people without property, male and female, were entitled to vote, what was to stop them voting for a party which would take power by parliamentary means and then by parliamentary legislation redistribute the property of the rich? To avoid such a ghastly outcome, a conservative coalition was necessary, even if it spelled doom for the Liberal Party that had nurtured Lloyd George and provided the springboard for his insatiable political ambition.

The post-war election was held in great haste within a few weeks of the Armistice, and before the votes of the armed forces could properly be canvassed or even registered. This was the first election in which most British people could vote. Candidates of any party who favoured coalition under Lloyd George were allocated a 'coupon'. On the face of it, the most extraordinary feature of the election under so much wider a franchise was not the number of people who voted but the number who didn't. Just 57 per cent of those entitled to do so cast their vote. Lloyd George's 'coupon' dominated the whole process. The Liberals were split literally down the middle. Those who regrouped under Asquith and fought under the Liberal banner got as many votes as their colleagues who took the 'coupon', but only 36 proper Liberals were elected (nine of them promptly scuttled into the Coalition Government), while 127 Liberals who took the coupon were elected. They joined 332 elected Coalition Tories in the new Parliament. No fewer than 473 pro-Coalition MPs were elected. They formed an apparently impregnable anti-Labour majority of the type Lloyd George had intended.

The Labour Party took 20 per cent of the votes, an enormous increase on the 6 per cent it won in December 1910, but only 57 Labour MPs were elected (compared to 42 in 1910). Considering the rise in the electorate, Labour's performance was disappointing. The Party in Parliament lost its undistinguished leader, Arthur Henderson, who had resigned from the War Cabinet in 1917 at least partly because of his short-lived enthusiasm for the first Russian Revolution. The leadership passed to even more dreary and chauvinistic figures – William Adamson and J. R. Clynes. They concentrated not on policy – there really was no distinctive Labour policy throughout the war – but on building up Party organization. Those ILP leaders who had the guts, however half-heartedly, to oppose the war – men like Ramsay MacDonald at Leicester, Philip Snowden at Blackburn and W. C.

Anderson at Sheffield – were all annihilated at the polls and Henderson, savaged by Lloyd George for his alleged treachery over Russia, lost his seat in East London.

In spite of its poor showing at the polls, however, the fortunes of the Labour Party soon improved. The loose Labour Representation Committee was junked in favour of a single organization with proper local parties and even a constitution. The latter was drafted jointly by Arthur Henderson and the Fabian Sidney Webb in 1918. They came up with a clear formula describing Labour's main objective: 'to secure for the workers by hand or by brain the full fruits of their industry and the most equitable distribution thereof that may be possible upon the basis of the common ownership of the means of production, distribution and exchange . . .' This aspiration – Clause IV of the Constitution (originally known as Clause III, and without the words 'distribution and exchange', which were added in 1928) – was printed on every Labour Party card for the next 78 years. The other clauses, indicating among other things the pledge that this aim was to be achieved in Parliament through the parliamentary process, were not given the same wide distribution.

In the tumultuous three years after the war, the Parliamentary Labour Party, dwarfed by the massive Coalition majority, played little part. Indeed for a short time the wider franchise seemed almost irrelevant. The political stage switched dramatically back to the Great Unrest that had dominated British politics before the war.

The deafening jingoism that accompanied the outbreak of war for a time drowned out the militancy and the confidence of the Great Unrest. The strikes stopped dead. But almost at once, starting on the Clyde in the winter of 1914–15, new grievances arose that led to new forms of workers' organizations. Lloyd George recalled in his *War Memoirs* (1933–6) that 'industrial unrest spelt a graver menace to our endurance and ultimate victory even than the military strength of Germany'. Two factors, closely interlinked, combined to inflame that 'menace'. First was what Thomas Jones, Deputy Secretary to the Cabinet, described in a memorandum to the Prime Minister as 'the mutiny of the rank and file against the old established [trade-union] leaders'. This gave rise to shop stewards' committees led by unsalaried elected rank-and-file leaders with nothing to gain by their position. These stewards were active not only in the early strikes and disputes on the Clyde but also in the massive strikes mainly in munitions factories that paralysed Barrow and Rochdale in 1917. These stewards, as Jones warned, were much more difficult to placate than the old trade-union leaders, most of whom were bound hand and foot to the Labour Party.

The second factor was the Russian Revolution in February 1917, described by Lloyd George in his *Memoirs* as 'a new infection'. The germ that brought this new infection was the democratic force that sprang up spontaneously in the Russian Revolution – the soviet or workers' council. The idea behind these councils appealed at once to the growing army of British shop stewards. Lloyd George and his ministers were profoundly irritated by this new infection and didn't really know how to deal with it. Testily, Lloyd George described what was happening in the minds of shop stewards and other working people after that Revolution:

In Russia, they pointed out, the workmen formed a separate authority, co-ordinated with the Government. There, they were more powerful than their peers in England. Their veto was effective in the administration as well as in the legislative sphere. They dominated the military activities of the nation. Why not in Britain? That was the question asked in every workshop and on every street corner.

The immediate result was a huge increase in the number of strikes, many of them led by shop stewards who felt no loyalty to the war or to the Government. Indeed, many of them were infuriated by the Government's introduction, in the spring of 1916, of conscription – a move that enabled many employers, in league with the Government, to isolate militant stewards and victimize them. In this new manifestation of what Lloyd George himself called 'a great unrest', a new version arose of the syndicalism that had flourished in the pre-war industrial agitation. This was 'guild socialism', pioneered by such early socialist thinkers as William Mellor, industrial editor of the new *Daily Herald*, which had been started in 1911 as a strike sheet, and G. D. H. Cole, an adviser to the engineers' union, the ASE. The two men combined to write *The Meaning of Industrial Freedom*, a pamphlet published early in 1918. 'Political liberty by itself,' they claimed, 'is in fact always illusory. A man who lives in economic subjection six days if not seven a week does not become free merely by making a cross on the ballot paper once in five years. If freedom is to mean anything it must include industrial freedom.' The pamphlet then outlined a rather complicated system of the control of industry by guilds formed by rank-and-file workers, with officials elected and permanently subject to recall. Combined with the Russian Revolution where 'guilds' seemed to have been put into practice, these ideas had an enormous impact on workers during the First World War.

The consummation of the Russian Revolution in October 1917 and the ending of the war in November 1918 followed by further revolutions in Germany and Hungary inspired yet more hope for a new and genuine democracy, hopes which ran far beyond the relatively mundane right to vote in the general election of December 1918. Victorious troops, buoyed no doubt by Lloyd George's election promise to provide them with a 'land fit for heroes', were shocked by delays in their demobilization and in some cases by their further call-up for service overseas. A spate of mutinies shook the Prime Minister and his High Command. Soldiers and sailors boycotted new postings and in many cases refused to carry out quite ordinary duties. Tens of thousands of soldiers and sailors were involved in these mutinies all over the country. Common to most of them was an enduring suspicion of the officer class and hostility to church parades. Most disturbing of all to the authorities was the spontaneous way in which mutinous troops formed themselves into councils, modelled on the Russian soviets and the workers' councils formed in Germany after the mutiny of the German Fleet at Kiel in 1918, a mutiny which led to revolution throughout Germany. All the British social upheavals of 1919 have to be seen against the background of the revolutions in Russia, Germany and Hungary and the spontaneously democratic development in all three countries.

Despite the British generals' horror at such mutinous behaviour among soldiers of the Crown, the mutineers' demands were swiftly conceded. None of the mutinies was smashed by force and very few mutineers were tried or punished. No new British troops were sent to Russia, and even in Ireland the occupying British army had to rely mainly on reckless and savage volunteers, the hated Black and Tans.

No sooner had the mutinies been put down, however, than the unrest started up again in more conventional ways. There was a huge wave of strikes of every variety, including a police strike that seriously affected the forces of law and order in many towns and cities. The number of working days 'lost' in strikes in 1919 was six times the figure for 1918. There was almost exactly the same atmosphere in these disputes as there had been in the heady days before the war. All the sacrifices, bitterness and privations of war exploded in an endless cascade of strikes and demonstrations.

The greatest threat to the Government and the social order came from the Triple Alliance, formed during the war by the Miners' Federation, the National Union of Railwaymen (NUR) and the organized transport workers. The alliance was formed to counteract the fragmentation of workers' actions in the pre-war period. The idea behind it was simple: if one of the three sections came under attack, the other two would come to its assistance. The prospect of millions of organized workers united in action against their employers when the latter were weakened by the war and when, because of the war, state action had curbed at least some of the rampant and wasteful private enterprise, was precisely what terrified Lloyd George and drove him into the arms of the Tories.

Twice in that revolutionary year of 1919 great armies of organized labour steeled themselves for a fight with the Lloyd George Government. The first threat was by far the most potent. In a ballot whose result was announced in February, the miners voted by 615,164 to 105,082 to strike in order to restore the miners to something like their pre-war standard of living. The demands were for an immediate 30 per cent wage rise and a six-hour day. Another demand was for the nationalization of the coal industry. Lloyd George, thrown on to the defensive, played for time. If the miners would drop their action, he proposed a Royal Commission headed by one of the very few judges believed to harbour Labour sympathies, Mr Justice Sankey. He proposed that the Miners' Federation and supporters among Labour intellectuals, led by Sidney Webb and the historian R. H. Tawney, should sit on the commission. Despite a howl of protest from the miners' rank and file (and from *Workers' Dreadnought*, a socialist paper edited by Sylvia Pankhurst), the miners' executive agreed to postpone the strike. The hearings of the Sankey Commission were a devastating indictment of private ownership in general and of the coal-owners in particular. The greed and incompetence of the owners were contrasted daily to the sickness, injuries and poverty of the miners. In its interim report, the Commission concluded: 'Even upon the evidence already given, the present system of ownership and working in the coal industry stand condemned, and some other system must be substituted for it, either nationalization or a method of unification by national purchase and/or by joint control.' In a Labour Party pamphlet published in 1919 recommending the nationalization of the coal industry, R. H. Tawney, already a dedicated Labour propagandist, recorded that 'one by one the defences of the present system were reconnoitred and overthrown'.

The miners were delighted. They voted by a huge majority in another ballot not to take any further action but to wait until the Sankey proposals became law. For a short time, the prospect looked good. Bonar Law, the Tory leader who deputized as Prime Minister when Lloyd George was out of the country, told the Commons that the Government accepted the Sankey report 'in the spirit and in the letter'. But Lloyd George, Bonar Law and the Tories didn't want coal nationalization. So they prevaricated. During the months that followed, the coal-owners and the Tories filled up their newspapers with hysterical propaganda against nationalization. The Sankey Commission was still sitting, preparing its final report, and the miners waited passively for the Government to come to a final decision. In

August, Lloyd George announced that the coal industry would not be nationalized. Both the spirit and the letter of the Sankey report were consigned to the rubbish heap.

Their hopes dashed and their energies drained, the miners voted against a strike at a special congress in March 1920. Lloyd George's tactics, enthusiastically backed by the Tories – pretending to offer something in a moment of crisis, and then withdrawing from any such commitment when the moment passed – paid off handsomely. No wonder Lenin hailed him as a student of Marxism. Always a devoted enemy of working-class action and of socialism, the Prime Minister had a Marxist's instinct for timing. He knew that when workers vote overwhelmingly to strike, and the strike cannot be resisted by brute force, the most powerful weapon in the hands of an employer and an employer's Government is delay.

He also knew that even if his cleverest tricks of timing failed, the trade-union leaders were far more interested in preserving a society in which they could remain as trade-union leaders than in a revolution which they might not be able to control. He saw and understood the tremendous power of the Triple Alliance. He spent an enormous amount of his time in the tumultuous years of 1919, 1920 and 1921 sidestepping the union leaders, greeting them with charm and good cheer when they were winning and stamping on them as soon as it was clear that they had lost. Thirty years later, in 1952, Aneurin Bevan, a South Wales miner who had been Minister of Health in the post-war Labour Government, published his political testament, *In Place of Fear*. He included in it a story from 1919 passed on to him by his former union president Bob Smillie. The story recounted how, at the peak of the influence of the Triple Alliance, Lloyd George sent for the key union leaders. Prepared for a furious argument about the strength of the workers' case, the union leaders hardly expected the wily Prime Minister to concede it. This he did at once, before coming to the point. Were the union leaders, he asked, really prepared to triumph in open struggle over the elected Government and the state?

Gentlemen, you have fashioned in the Triple Alliance . . . a most powerful instrument. I feel bound to tell you that in our opinion we are at your mercy. The army is disaffected and cannot be relied on. Trouble has occurred already in a number of camps. We have just emerged from a great war and the people are eager for a reward for their sacrifices, and we are in no position to satisfy them. In these circumstances if you carry out your threat and strike, then you will defeat us. But if you do so, have you weighed the consequences? The strike will be in defiance of the Government of the country and by its very success will precipitate a constitutional crisis of the first importance. For if a force arises in the state which is stronger than the state itself, then it must be ready to take on the functions of the state or withdraw and accept the authority of the state. Gentlemen, have you considered, and, if you have, are you ready?

From that moment on, Robert Smillie told Aneurin Bevan, 'we were beaten and we knew we were'.

Beaten the miners certainly were, and there was no strike by the Triple Alliance all through the storms of 1919. The '40-hours strike' by shipbuilding and engineering workers in Glasgow at the beginning of 1919 was defeated in scenes of appalling state violence, at the end of which one of the strike leaders, Emmanuel Shinwell, was sent to prison. The railwaymen came out in a solid strike in September, but went back after ten days with no substantial gains. Workers did win victories in smaller strikes all over the country. Nevertheless the constitutional challenge thrown down to the Triple Alliance leaders by Lloyd George gave the Government and the employers the breathing space they needed to survive.

The Great Unrest that had started in 1911 paused in the early war years, and continued through 1917, 1918, 1919 and into 1920. During those years it was obvious to everyone that the short-lived boom in the economy, together with the 'land fit for heroes' and all the rest of the Lloyd George gobbledegook, was a mirage. The slump of 1920 devastated the employed population. By the end of that year there were over a million out of work. The second phase of the Great Unrest was at an end. At last Lloyd George saw the opportunity for a counter-attack to put the unions in their place. He appointed as Minister of Labour, and later as President of the Board of Trade, the Tory MP for Glasgow Hillhead, Sir Robert Horne. Horne was an accomplished and dedicated class warrior. In his memoirs, published in 1924, the retired miners' leader Robert Smillie wrote that Horne was both terrified and pugnacious at the thought that the revolution was at hand. 'He tells us,' wrote Smillie of Horne, 'that he never walked along Whitehall without paying very close attention to the lamp-posts. He even found himself wondering which of them would be selected for the honour of supporting his body when the revolution took place.' Small wonder then that Sir Robert stood shoulder to shoulder with the corrupt and greedy coal-owners. He did not even recognize the desperate condition of the miners. He was just the man for the planned offensive of 1921. In February, Sir Robert summoned the miners' leaders and told them he intended to remove all wartime controls on the mining industry. This single measure would, he boasted, wipe out the 'war wage' and the 'Sankey wage', the little bonuses the miners had won over the years. Horne and any other Government minister who deigned to take part in the farce of the ensuing negotiations made their intentions quite plain. They wanted to clear out of the mining industry, to wash their hands of any responsibility for miners' wages and conditions. They agreed that decontrol would wreck the lives of thousands of miners and their families, but insisted that that was a necessary consequence of the free market they supported. Faced with the indivisible unity of employers and Government, the miners' leaders resigned themselves to confrontation. They called up the Triple Alliance, which responded enthusiastically. Most rail and transport workers could tell at once that decontrol of the coal industry would mean desperate conditions in the pits, and that those conditions would soon spread to the railways and the ships. In reply, the coal-owners, true to form, locked out a million miners and refused to take them back to work unless they agreed to the employers' and the Government's terms.

Friday 15 April 1921 was the historic date set down for a combined strike by the Triple Alliance, a strike that would have brought all industry to a halt. The day held out real hope to organized labour that the workers would finally stamp their democratic authority on the industrial process: that coal mines, railways and transport undertakings could and should be run in the joint interests of workers and consumers.

There was no doubting the enthusiasm among the workers' rank and file. A yearning for a battle that the unions could win spread rapidly beyond the Triple Alliance. Unions representing electrical workers, post-office workers and engine drivers got ready for action to support the miners. Even the National Council of Labour, representing the Parliamentary Labour Party and the Trades Union Congress, met to declare their support for the miners. Then on 14 April, the eve of the climax, the Triple Alliance started to fall apart, not from the bottom, where it was still strong, but from the top.

Frank Hodges, the miners' General Secretary, went down to the House of Commons for an eve-of-strike discussion with MPs. What Hodges said that night no one knows, but certain employers' representatives understood that the miners' federation would contemplate a settlement of the dispute on a district basis. As soon as he heard this rumour, Lloyd George fired off a letter to Hodges demanding a Downing Street meeting. The miners replied that a meeting was pointless. Whatever Hodges had said that evening, the miners took their stand on a national wages board and a national pool of wages, to make sure that the miners in less profitable pits earned the same as their colleagues elsewhere. This proposal was non-negotiable, said the miners' union committee. Hodges offered to resign but the offer was not accepted.

That should have been the end of the matter had it not been for the intervention of a trade-union leader who spent his life snatching defeat from the prospect of industrial victory. Jimmy Thomas MP was General Secretary of the National Union of Railwaymen. As soon as he heard of Hodges's gaffe in the House of Commons and of Lloyd George's letter offering more negotiations, Thomas dashed round to the miners' offices and demanded that they accept the Prime Minister's invitation. The miners angrily refused, and insisted that the Triple Alliance should strike as promised the following day. Back at NUR headquarters, Thomas addressed his union conference specially convened to prepare for the strike, and persuaded the delegates to call it off.

Black Friday was the name angry trade unionists gave to 15 April 1921. The miners were left to battle on alone and their protest ended in June when the Government threatened to withdraw even the miserable £10 million they had offered to tide the mines over decontrol. The miners' two main demands for a national pool of coal profits and nationally negotiated wages had been lost, and the miners were cast adrift into the recession, abandoned by their industrial allies.

From the Armistice in November 1918 to Black Friday in 1921 was a period of almost continuous militant activity by the unions. The political pendulum on the left swung further to the syndicalism that had been so popular before the war and had been developed during it. Two books published in 1920 testified to this mood. *Direct Action* by William Mellor challenged the view expressed the previous year by Lloyd George that 'the threat of direct action is a complete subversion of every democratic doctrine' and that such a threat, whatever its merits, 'has no justification now, after the great extension of the franchise witnessed over the last couple of years'. Not so, Mellor argued. Such a view was ridiculous in a society split into classes where a small class of people owned the wealth. Unless the principle of democracy 'runs in the workshops it is useless to expect it to exist elsewhere for the whole of a man's life depends ultimately upon the sort of existence he leads while at work'.

Work, moreover, was utterly removed from democracy. The power structure there was 'sheer autocracy, tempered by the power of trade unionism'. He concluded his argument like this: 'In a sense it is true that any extension of the franchise represents an advance by the workers in their struggle for freedom, for such an extension does mark the fact that the owners of property have been compelled to meet their enemy at the gate. The fly in the ointment however is that they hold the gate.'

The second book was *Chaos and Order in Industry* by G. D. H. Cole, who was to become one of the foremost intellectuals in the Labour movement. He wrote:

One strike epidemic after another may pass without achieving any big result, but that does not make them any the less serious; for they are manifestations of a general sense of insecurity and dissatisfaction that is everywhere and every day growing stronger and more insistent. It is out of economic movements that under present conditions political movements are almost bound to proceed.

Cole then identified the profit system as the cause of strikes and set out, in much greater detail than in his earlier pamphlet, alternative methods of industrial organization by guilds. Industrial workers, he argued, should be organized in guilds and power over the nation's affairs shared between directly elected representatives of the industrial guilds and a geographically elected Parliament.

Another book published soon after Black Friday, R. H. Tawney's *The Acquisitive Society*, went into several editions and affected the thinking and practice of Labour supporters for the next three decades. This was due partly to Tawney's majestic prose style, partly to the obvious passion that inspired his socialist faith. All his long life Tawney was a committed Christian who believed that socialism was the true political manifestation of Christianity. He argued in his book that most human beings in society had rights and functions, but that the class of people who made money out of other people's work had plenty of rights but no functions attached to them: 'In all societies which have accepted industrialism there is an upper layer which claims the enjoyment of social life while it repudiates its responsibilities.'

The curious aspect of all three books was their failure to answer the question, how was the change they advocated to be achieved? There is, for instance, not a single reference to the most important political development of the age: the enormous increase in the number of people who could vote for their government.

The essentially syndicalist ideas in all three books, though powerful at the time, did not last very long. Their influence vanished as the strikes and demonstrations of 1917–21 disintegrated. Almost immediately after Black Friday, the political axis on the left swung away from industrial action back to Parliament. Black Friday, it was assumed, had proved that industrial action was doomed to failure. The truth about Black Friday, however, was not that industrial action had failed but that it had never been properly tested. The show of strength had been rejected at the last moment not by the workers who were prepared to go on strike but by their leaders, in particular Jimmy Thomas, the railway-union leader.

Oblivious to the anguish and fury he had inspired among the rank and file, Thomas turned away from the industrial battlefield to the Labour Party, for which he had been the MP for Derby South since January 1910. In 1920, he wrote a little book entitled *When Labour Rules*. He dedicated the book to 'the people who, persuaded at last of the seriousness and strength of the Labour Movement, realize that before long Labour will rule, but fail to understand what it portends'. So what did Labour portend? In almost unreadable prose Thomas set out a vision of a land of milk and honey. When Labour rules, he predicted, 'there will be no profiteers, no unemployment, no slums, no hungry children'. Moreover, 'the lives of the people will without exception be far happier than they have ever been before'. Housing was a priority, but would present few problems. 'The people, or the workers, call them what you please, will all, without exception, live under decent conditions: their homes will be decently built, will be sanitary and will be so constructed that they will involve a minimum, rather than a maximum, amount of labour for those who have to live in them.'

Such utopianism became increasingly popular as the Labour Party and its trade-union affiliates backed away from confrontation, the avoidance of which had brought them defeat on Black Friday, and applied themselves with renewed vigour to winning more votes. Thomas and the other Labour leaders argued successfully that the grand ideas of industrial democracy that had inspired the syndicalist leaders during and after the war should be jettisoned and replaced by more prosaic electoral democracy. These efforts were rewarded almost at once. On 19 October 1922, Tory MPs meeting at the Carlton Club voted overwhelmingly to dispense with Lloyd George, to abandon the Coalition and to face the electorate as pure Tories. The next day, Lloyd George resigned as Prime Minister and a general election under the old party labels was fought in November.

The Tories won handsomely, with 344 MPs. The Liberals were still split – the National Liberals, including Lloyd George, who was elected unopposed, won 53 seats, the 'pure' Liberals 62. But the real winner was the Labour Party, whose vote nearly doubled – from 2,245,777 to 4,237,349 – and whose representatives in Parliament rose from 57 to 142. Labour was now by far the biggest opposition party and for the first time Lloyd George's nightmare of a Labour Government seemed a possibility. At last the votes of working men and women looked as though they might have an impact on Parliament and on political power.

The key question now for Labour was not 'can we achieve high office?' but rather 'what do we do with it when we get it?'

The question had already been asked in the most dramatic form in an argument between two new Labour mayors in London who were later to achieve high office in the Party. Both were elected in the council elections of November 1919, less than a year after the landslide national victory of Lloyd George and the Tories. In those council elections, Labour made huge gains all over the country. In London, they took 12 borough councils, including Poplar, where their first mayor was the former MP for Bow George Lansbury, and in Hackney, where the mayor was an ambitious and energetic local politician called Herbert Morrison. Like so many Labour leaders of the time, both men had been reared in the Marxist school of the Social Democratic Federation. The argument between the two men about what to do with their newly won municipal office after 1919 went on running through the Labour Party in different forms all the way through the twentieth century.

Morrison believed that the best course for Labour was to prove that it could govern as efficiently as the Tories or the Liberals. His view was that working men and women could run things every bit as well as the toffs from the other two parties. In order to establish their capacity for efficient government, it followed that Labour mayors and councillors had to play the game according to the rules, in particular to raise rates and keep council spending within the limits of what was collected. Morrison's challenge to Tories and Liberals was rooted not so much in the policies Labour pursued as in Labour's ability to administer its councils efficiently, and to balance the books.

Lansbury took a different view. He started from the condition of the people who elected him. In the months following the collapse of the post-war boom in April 1920, hundreds of thousands of Labour voters were thrown out of work through no fault of their own. The employers resorted to their time-honoured method of making the workers who were lucky to keep their jobs work harder at them. As for the unemployed, they depended for their only income on the elected Board of Guardians, who distributed 'relief'. As soon as the new recession started to bite the people who voted Labour, Labour councillors were confronted with a grim choice. If they were to pay the pittance in relief paid before the slump, they had no alternative but to raise the rates. The money for the Guardians came directly from locally raised rates. Other services throughout London were paid for by rates raised throughout the city, which spread the load much more evenly between rich and poor. But crucial local services, including relief for the unemployed, had to be paid for directly by the Poplar ratepayers, the poorest in London. The product of a penny on the rates in Poplar was £3,643. At the same time a penny on the rates in London's richest borough, Westminster, produced nearly nine times as much, £31,719.

As unemployment soared, as dockworkers hired by the day were turned away from the dock gates in droves, so George Lansbury and his colleagues on the council were faced with an intractable problem. The only way to pay the poor was to raise money from the poor. It was no use simply blaming the capitalist system, as Herbert Morrison did, or to protest, as Morrison did, that poverty and unemployment would be features of the political landscape until the socialist commonwealth was proclaimed. The point for the Poplar councillors was that they had been elected by the working people of Poplar so that they could improve the lives of the working people of Poplar. How could they remain councillors and do their duty by the people who elected them? Certainly not by raising the rates by enough to pay proper relief to the unemployed and in so doing squeezing beyond endurance the Poplar poor who were lucky enough to be employed.

The conundrum dominated the anxious council meetings of 1920 and 1921. Everyone agreed that the system of finance in London local government was unfair. Everyone agreed that if relief for the unemployed was paid for by raising a rate right across London, the burden on the poorer ratepayers would be far lighter; and that at least some of the cost of that relief would be met by London's more prosperous ratepayers. But to change the system of local government finance by law might take decades. While Lloyd George, the Tories and the Liberals were in office, any such measure was unthinkable. How should the councillors proceed? Should they penalize the people who voted Labour or simply hand back their elected office to the Tories and Liberals who had always had it before?

During the first few months of 1921 an idea started to gain favour among the Labour councillors. This was to raise a lower rate than previously, and to refuse to pay the London County Council for the police, the water boards and the asylum boards. The money raised could go instead to the Poor Law Guardians so that they could pay more to the unemployed. After the proposal had been discussed at great length at Labour Party gatherings throughout the borough, it was endorsed with only one vote against by the full council on 22 March 1921, just a fortnight before Black Friday. The rate levied by the council for the following three months was 4 shillings and 4 pence compared to 6 shillings and 10 pence, which the council would have raised if they collected the London County Council precepts for police, water and asylums. The bold decision to defy the law on council finance was taken in a mood of self-confidence at least in part inspired by the tumultuous developments in the mines and on the railways. Many of the transport trade unionists involved in the discussions before Black Friday were dockers from Poplar.

The response of the London County Council, on which Labour councillors were a small minority, to this blatant but entirely unexpected defiance was to call in their lawyers. To their irritation, the London county councillors discovered that the laws on such matters had been drawn up mainly to punish people who did not pay their rates because of their individual poverty. There was no obvious remedy for collective defiance by those poor people's elected representatives. After a few weeks of anxious discussion, the LCC lawyers applied to the High Court for a writ of mandamus ordering the councillors to deliver the precepts they had withheld. The judge who delivered the judgement on 7 July was none other than Mr Justice Sankey, the man who presided over the Royal Commission into the future of the coal mines and whose conclusion – for some form of public ownership – had been so blandly rejected by the Government. On the Poplar issue, any sympathy Sankey may have had for the impoverished masses was swept away by the majesty of the law. The law had to be obeyed, whatever the cost to the elected representatives' ideals and to the people who elected them. The irritation of the judges was succinctly illustrated by an exchange between Henry Slessor, barrister for the councillors, and Lord Chief Justice Trevethin:

TREVETHIN: I cannot imagine the reasons for the Poplar councillors' action unless it be popularity.
SLESSOR: No, my Lord, I am afraid it is poverty.

The thrust from below, the determination to alleviate the grinding poverty of the people they represented, drove the councillors on. On 4 August 1921, they unanimously reaffirmed their decision not to levy rates for the LCC precepts. They were all sublimely aware of the fate that awaited them – they would face proceedings for contempt of court and almost certainly be sent to prison. They faced this prospect with courage and solidarity.

George Lansbury was a respected, towering figure. Even more determined and persuasive was his son Edgar and his niece Minnie, one of four women councillors in Poplar who were among the first women to be elected as councillors anywhere thanks to the changes in the franchise in 1918. The

Lansburys' determination to resist the law was shared by all 30 Labour councillors, many of whom had been groomed in the SDF and brought up in the spirit of trade-union militancy before, during and after the war. In the first week of September, the 30 began to be arrested for contempt, and were carried off to Brixton prison or, in the case of the four women, to Holloway. They had prepared their electorate for this crisis and had secured their support. Sales and fairs had been arranged to raise money for the councillors' legal costs and for maintaining their children in the event of their imprisonment. Their final march to the courts was accompanied by thousands of Poplar citizens and brass bands from all over the borough. By the end of the first week of September 1921, all 30 councillors had been arrested, had insisted on regular meetings in prison and had started to raise the demand, taken up by the mass pickets outside the prison gates, for special treatment as political prisoners and for the right, eventually conceded, to hold councillors' meetings in prison. There were 32 such meetings, all carefully recorded in minutes.

From the moment they went into prison, the Poplar councillors held the whip hand over the authorities, judicial and political. As luck would have it, their imprisonment coincided with a Trades Union Congress resolution unanimously supporting the Poplar councillors, who had 'rendered a real national service'. Though most other Labour London boroughs limited their support to platitudes (except in Hackney, where the Labour councillors voted to disassociate themselves from Poplar), two other London boroughs with large Labour majorities followed the lead of Poplar. In neighbouring Stepney, the motion to withhold the LCC precepts was moved by a young councillor called Clement Attlee.

The rising tide of working-class support for the Poplar councillors was illustrated day by day by pickets and demonstrations outside the prison, in the streets and even outside Parliament. The Home Secretary, Edward Shortt, made his position absolutely clear. He had, he said, 'no power' to release the prisoners. The courts, not he, had put the councillors in prison, and the courts, not he, must release them. This obduracy quickly shifted. Among the imprisoned councillors was Nellie Cressall, who was expecting a baby in October. The protests on her behalf from her electorate and from women's organizations all over the country grew so shrill that an unheard-of creature suddenly appeared in the courts on her behalf. This was the Official Solicitor who managed to persuade the judges that Nellie Cressall should be released on humanitarian grounds. At first she refused to be released until it was made quite clear that she had made no concessions to the Government on the question of the rates or the precepts, and that she supported her imprisoned colleagues 100 per cent. The extraordinary power of the Official Solicitor to release prisoners whom Home Secretaries swore they had no power to release had never before been understood by anyone. Half a century later it was to be used again.

Buoyed by surging support throughout the Labour movement, and continuing concessions on their prison conditions, the remaining 29 imprisoned councillors stuck it out. On 12 October, they were released by the High Court without any of them making or even suggesting a single concession on the raising of the precepts. The Health Secretary, Sir Alfred Mond, who was also in charge of local government, indicated that he would call a conference on the equalization of the rates. He was told that no Labour councillor, not even Herbert Morrison, would take part in the conference, unless the Poplar councillors were there too. Hesitant and uncertain of the majesty of their own law, the Lord Chief Justice and his two colleagues (including Sankey) agreed that a mere declaration that the councillors would try to sort matters out in the interests of their electorate was enough to secure their release. They emerged from jail into scenes of unprecedented enthusiasm and triumph.

The story of Poplar and the rates rebellion of 1921 irritates traditional historians and Labour constitutionalists. Jimmy Thomas, the hero of Black Friday, dismissed the whole effort as 'a threat to the constitution'. Herbert Morrison poured scorn on the Poplar councillors who, he insisted, by breaking the law had set back Labour's magisterial progress to respectability. In his book *Consensus And Disunity* (1979), perhaps the most comprehensive history of the Lloyd George post-war coalition, Kenneth O. Morgan wrote of the Poplar episode: 'It was magnificent but it was not politics, even if George Lansbury acquired the mantle of martyrdom. Nor was it electorally popular. Poplarism cost Labour dear. The Party won 143 seats on London Boards of Guardians in 1919, only 112 in 1922.'

This analysis conveniently ignored the real effect of the Poplar revolt – the equalization of the Poor Law rates. Under a compromise rapidly hammered out after the councillors were released from prison, it was agreed that the costs of Poor Law relief should be shared across London. This had been the main demand of the councillors when they refused to collect the precepts. The effect on the people of Poplar was instantaneous and dramatic. In 1920–21, Poplar ratepayers had paid 22 shillings and 10 pence. In 1921–2, if the LCC precepts had been collected, the Poplar rates would have gone up to 27 shillings and 3 pence – a huge and intolerable increase. In fact, thanks to the actions of the councillors and the Local Authorities (Financial Provisions) Act that followed, the rate in Poplar in 1921–2 was

18 shillings and 3 pence – nearly 30 per cent less than the previous year. Even the following year, despite the continuing recession and mass unemployment, the Poplar rate was 22 shillings and 8 pence – less than the rate two years previously. This was the immediate impact of the 'cost' to Labour deplored by Kenneth O. Morgan.

At the time, moreover, no one in any political party had any doubt that the reason for the lower rates was the defiance of the imprisoned councillors. Reginald Blair, Tory MP for Bromley and Bow, who, as we have seen, first won the constituency when George Lansbury resigned so dramatically on the women's issue in 1912, spoke angrily in the debate on the Local Authorities (Financial Provisions) Act. 'I am sorry,' he lamented, 'that this Bill owes its inception to the policy of direct action carried out by the Poplar Borough Council . . . This is a great discouragement to those who believe in constitutional action.' Nor was the equalization of the rates a transitory measure. The principle that the burden on the poorer boroughs should be shared throughout London, with a levelling effect imposing higher rating costs on the richer areas, lasted through several administrations of different party persuasions for more than 60 years. It was not until a Tory Government under Margaret Thatcher abolished the Greater London Council in 1986 and the Inner London Education Authority in 1988 that the ancient and entirely undemocratic principle of abandoning the government of the London poor areas to the miserable rate revenues of the London poor was once again re-established.

What, then, was the effect of the relief in Poplar and the other poorer boroughs on the fortunes of the Labour Party? Here too Kenneth O. Morgan's statistics are highly selective. In her comprehensive book *Poplarism*, also published in 1979, Noreen Branson showed that in Poplar in 1921 the turnout for the Guardians' poll rose by an extraordinary 43 per cent from the figures for the 1919 elections. In 1919, there were 16 Labour men and women elected to the Poplar Board of Guardians. In 1922, this figure jumped to 21.

The same pattern emerged from the LCC elections in the same year. Labour increased its representation there by only one – a disappointing result, which was immediately blamed by expert psephologists such as Jimmy Thomas and Herbert Morrison on the reckless behaviour of subversives on Poplar Council. In fact, the Labour vote in Poplar increased hugely in all four of the Poplar wards and in other areas where the Labour candidates identified themselves with the defiance of the Poplar councillors.

In the borough elections held a fortnight before the general election in November 1922, Labour succumbed to the joint offensive of the Conservatives and their allies, who joined forces to challenge what they called the recklessness of council spending especially in Poplar. Labour lost 300 seats across the country, but once again the results in Poplar showed a much higher turnout (51.5 per cent) than the average in London (36.4 per cent). Only three of Labour's 39 seats were lost, and in most wards the Labour vote increased substantially. The argument of Herbert Morrison, Jimmy Thomas and the like that the voters would respond to cautious, efficient Labour stewardship was not vindicated by the results in the elections after Poplar. In Morrison's Hackney, for instance, every single Labour candidate was defeated.

Proof that Labour had not been annihilated or even substantially set back was immediately available in the results of the general election later that November. Among the new Labour MPs was George Lansbury, who sailed in for the constituency he had so courageously sacrificed in 1912 (and which he had lost by a whisker in 1918). He remained the MP for Poplar until his death in 1940. Sam March, another of the imprisoned Poplar councillors, was also elected to Parliament, kicking out the Liberal in South Poplar. Clement Attlee, who, as Labour leader in Stepney had supported the Poplar councillors, was elected MP for Limehouse. In exact contrast to the mythology promoted by historians such as Kenneth O. Morgan, the evidence from the polls was that illegal defiance at Poplar, Stepney and Whitechapel had garnered more votes than legal respectability in Hackney or anywhere else.

The word 'Poplarism' found its way into the *Concise Oxford Dictionary*. Its definition was given as the 'policy of giving extravagant out-relief (as practised by the Poplar Board of Guardians, *c.* 1920); any similar policy tending to raise the rates'. The definition was completely inaccurate. The whole purpose of the policy pursued by the Poplar Board of Guardians (not in 1920, as the dictionary guessed, but in 1921) was not to raise the rates but to lower them.

Another definition of 'Poplarism' became common usage in the language of the Labour movement for long after 1921. Its real meaning was expressed again and again by anguished Labour councillors who found that they could not use their powers as elected councillors to alleviate the plight of the people who voted for them. 'The workers,' said George Lansbury, 'must be given tangible proof that Labour administration means something different from capitalist administration.' Charles Key, another imprisoned Labour councillor, made the same point in a different way. 'We have come to make a change,' he said. They understood that if an elected Labour council carried on its business in exactly the same way as its Tory predecessor, the electorate would in due course become bored or cynical or both. The eventual beneficiaries would be the Tories or the Liberals, the people responsible for the dreadful conditions working people had to endure.

The Poplar councillors quickly discovered that they were hemmed in on all sides by an economic system over which they had no control. More infuriating still were the regulations and the unelected accountants who, in the clear interests of the rich minority, prevented the elected councillors from carrying out policies to benefit the poor. On all sides, it seemed, the elected councillors were frustrated by the economic 'realism' of the capitalist world and the host of district auditors and other unelected 'regulators' with draconian powers over the councillors.

The Poplar councillors chose to break out of this seemingly rigid circle. 'We have got nothing by being passive and quiet,' said Lansbury, 'and we are going to be passive and quiet no longer.' So in one sense Poplarism meant the 'direct action' that persuaded Sir Reginald Blair, the Tory MP for the area, to denounce the councillors for their 'revolutionary methods'.

Very few, if any, Poplar councillors of 1921 were revolutionaries, however. They wanted to change their world by the means provided for them by the 1918 Representation of the People Act, through the ballot box. But they were not prepared to sit passively by while their power as elected councillors was whittled away by the economic system and the judges and regulators imposed not by ballot but by ancient prejudices and reactionary laws.

The real meaning of Poplarism is the use by elected representatives of their democratic power to challenge laws and customs that restrict democracy. The Poplar councillors not only used that power. They used it at least to some extent successfully, and for that they could never be forgiven, least of all by the compilers of the *Concise Oxford Dictionary*.

All through 1921 and most of 1922 another argument persuaded many Labour supporters that the Poplar councillors had acted too hastily. Laws were made not by councillors but by MPs in Parliament. The real test of the future for the reactionary laws that still weighed down the statute book in 1922 was not a change in this or that council but a change of Government. Not until Labour formed a Government could the laws and economy be shifted in a socialist direction. The results of the election in November 1922, from which Labour emerged as the second strongest party with 142 seats, held out a real prospect that a Labour Government would soon be elected.

Who should lead the new Party? Moderate opinion favoured the dull and inoffensive John Clynes. But there was a clamour, especially from the new MPs from Scotland, most of them members of the ILP, for someone else. Clynes's main rival was the new Labour MP for Aberavon, James Ramsay MacDonald. MacDonald had been Secretary of the old Labour Representation Committee and an influential member of the Parliamentary Party since 1906. His opposition to the war was always cautious, but he had been publicly hounded nevertheless as a treacherous pacifist. Both the wartime abuse and the fury in the Labour Party that he incurred much later on obscure the crucial role MacDonald played in the Labour Party before and after the First World War.

His mother was a Scottish domestic servant who was unmarried when Ramsay was born in 1866. From this humblest of origins, MacDonald travelled south and was soon caught up in Labour politics. He was elected to Parliament for Leicester in 1906, and kept his seat for 12 years until he was swept out in the chauvinist tide of 1918.

Between 1906 and 1922, MacDonald wrote a series of political books and pamphlets, almost all about socialism. Of these the main titles were *Socialism and Society* (1905) and *Socialism and Government* (1909), published by the Socialist Library; *The Socialist Movement* (1911); and *Parliament and Revolution* (1919). The result was a consistent body of socialist theory that far surpassed anything written by any of the other Labour leaders, including Keir Hardie, who died in 1915.

The first aim of the books was to present to an ever-expanding audience the case for socialism. These arguments were, in the words of David Marquand, MacDonald's biographer, 'starkly collectivist'. The whole point about socialism, MacDonald argued, was to replace capitalist individualism with collective cooperation. 'Society,' he wrote in *Socialism and Government*, 'becomes more efficiently organized by the extension of communal property.' Everyone wanted more individual liberty, but such liberty 'becomes effective only when social ownership in the necessary means of production protects the individual against the chaos which follows upon the private ownership of those social requirements'. There was no absolute freedom to own property. On the contrary: 'Individual freedom to own property becomes possible only when it is conditioned by social ownership in those kinds of property which, if owned privately, produce poverty.' Two years later, when MacDonald wrote *The Socialist Movement* in the middle of the Great Unrest in 1911, his 'constructive programme' had become more radical. He demanded 'municipalization and nationalization in every shape and form, from milk supplies to telephones'.

How were these drastic measures to be carried through? The ends were easy to describe, if a trifle vague. In all these books and innumerable speeches, MacDonald did for the Labour Party what Eduard Bernstein had done for the German Social Democratic Party. Back in 1899, Bernstein published *Evolutionary Socialism*, a book published later in Britain in the Socialist Library and which greatly influenced MacDonald.

Bernstein argued against what was then the received view in the German Social Democratic Party – that socialism could only come by revolution. That view had, according to Bernstein, been transformed by the progress of the suffrage and the election of substantial numbers of socialists to the German Parliament. This offered a more credible and less violent course for socialists, he argued. Instead of the vagaries and unpleasantness of revolution, socialists could now concentrate on getting votes to Parliament. If they got enough votes for a majority – and why shouldn't they as the workers were the majority in society? – they could legislate for socialism, and eventually bring about public ownership by constitutional, parliamentary methods.

Bernstein's pamphlet provoked a furious response from the revolutionary Rosa Luxemburg, who argued in a scorching pamphlet that those who sought to change the system by parliamentary methods were not really seeking the same aims as the revolutionaries, 'but a different goal'. Luxemburg's argument soon lost ground on the German left. The long German Revolution of 1918 to 1923 eventually petered out and the Social Democratic Party held on to office by parliamentary means. One of its leaders' early democratic initiatives was to arrange the murder of Rosa Luxemburg.

No such cataclysmic events disturbed the British Labour movement. MacDonald's arguments directed themselves almost exclusively to proclaiming Bernstein's arguments for gradual and peaceful change. MacDonald hailed Karl Marx for his insistence that private capital should be brought under democratic control, but did not agree with Marx's conclusion that such democratic control could only be established by revolution. On the contrary, he wrote in *Socialism and Society*, Marx had misunderstood Darwin. Darwin had put the case for gradual changes in species, and it was such 'organic' but essentially gradual change that would eventually transform capitalism into socialism.

Almost all MacDonald's early works were devoted to arguing for the parliamentary road to socialism. Before universal suffrage in 1918, MacDonald's arguments were hypothetical. He agreed that capital and capitalists wielded enormous and undemocratic power over the process of elections and even flirted with the idea that the 'parasites', as he described

capitalists, should be banned from voting to create a more level playing field for the votes of the masses. But he dismissed such a course as unworkable and unfair. Allowing the rich to vote was a small price to pay
for the enfranchisement of the masses. 'Enfranchisement of the common
folk', he wrote, would bring about a 'fundamental change in the political
intelligence'. The state would become the ally of the poor, not their rival.

One advantage of this approach was that it allowed the socialist propagandist the most extreme licence in explaining the precise methods by which
socialism would be brought about. All the books MacDonald wrote before
1918 are as vague about specific socialist politics as they are precise about
the importance of gradualism and the parliamentary road. The vagueness
and the precision were aided by MacDonald's prose style, as flamboyant
in its metaphors as it was vague about its policies. For instance (from *The
Socialist Movement*):

Like cordite burning in the open, old conditions will be harmlessly transformed;
they will not, like cordite burning in a confined place, become explosive.

But when MacDonald moved on to practical policies, all remained obscure:

The approach to socialism is by the parliamentary method. Step by step we shall
go, experiencing every incident on the way and deciding stage by stage where the
next day's journey leads and whether the inducement and expectations point our
way. The problems will be solved as they arise.

The luxury of such vagueness soon vanished. The 1918 Representation
of the People Act spread the vote so widely that a Labour Government was
no longer just a dream. The Act followed one Revolution in Russia and
preceded another one in Germany. Both Revolutions threw down fierce
challenges to gradualism in general and parliamentary methods in particular. In a series of ferocious pamphlets during and after the Russian Revolution, Lenin poured his most vitriolic scorn on parliamentary democracy.
Far from being the 'ally' of the workers and the poor, as MacDonald had
argued, the state, whether nominally under the control of Parliament or
not, would continue as an engine of exploitation, always taking the side of
property against poverty, of the rich against the poor. In a pamphlet in
October 1918, Lenin exclaimed:

Bourgeois democracy, although a great historical advance in comparison with
medievalism, always remains, and under capitalism is bound to remain, restricted,
truncated, false and hypocritical, a paradise for the rich and a snare and deception for the exploited, for the poor ... deceit, violence, corruption, mendacity,

hypocrisy and oppression of the poor [are] hidden beneath the civilized, polished and perfumed exterior of modern bourgeois democracy.

Lenin's Bolshevik Party took part in the parliamentary elections prepared by the old social democratic regime and got 10 million votes. But side by side with the parliamentary institutions was a new form of democracy based on the soviet. The soviet, founded on elections in the workplace, elected delegates to a higher authority and so on up to the Supreme Soviet, which ran the country. Lenin argued that soviet democracy was infinitely superior to parliamentary democracy. It was much less cumbrous, less corrupt and more sensitive to shifts in the public mood. The enormous shift towards his Bolshevik Party in the elections to the soviets during 1917 persuaded Lenin and his colleagues to unleash the October Revolution.

Back in Britain, workers could not help but notice the difference in the democratic sensitivity of the soviets and the entrenched and reactionary parliamentary democracy that had by such a huge majority elected the Tories under Lloyd George in December 1918. There was a strong pro-Russian mood among British workers. It was assisted by a small book published in 1919 by Arthur Ransome, who later became famous for his children's stories. His book, *Six Weeks in Russia*, converted a lot of people to the case for the infant workers' democracy in Russia. For a time during the tumultuous events of 1919 and early 1920, Ramsay MacDonald and the other Labour leaders knew that their anxious pleas to their supporters to keep their heads and aspirations down and focus on the vote for Labour at election times were under severe challenge.

So it was that Ramsay MacDonald put his mind in 1919 to yet another small book, entitled *Parliament and Revolution*. Much of it defends the Russian Revolution and repudiates the right of the wealthy to criticize it. But its chief aim was to castigate the institutions thrown up by the Revolution and to distance the Labour Party and the ILP from them. Soviet democracy is described as a 'pyramid of local governing authorities'. Because there was no overall popular vote for the controlling institution, its 'representative value is nil' and it 'has only a very remote contact with the mass of the people ... instead of making the people responsible for policy it makes the people's representatives responsible'.

Moreover, the system of election led inevitably to bureaucracy and the suppression of the free press. Quite why the soviet voting system should lead automatically to bureaucracy and suppression of the press was never explained. The parliamentary system on the other hand, he wrote, was 'directly based upon national opinion', and should therefore provide the basis for transforming society in a socialist direction. But MacDonald did not conclude that the parliamentary system was perfect. The greatest of the many weaknesses of parliamentary government, he argued, was the predominance of the rich:

Parliament, though elected by citizens, is drawn in its personnel far too exclusively from one class of interest, one tradition and one section of the community. It is moved by class interests and class assumptions just as much as if it was elected by a stockbrokers' guild, a guild of city merchants, a guild of landowners, a guild of lawyers. The actual working of the territorial system of constituencies does lend itself to the dominance of rich men.

Nowhere in his book does MacDonald explain why the rich should predominate in a democratic system based on one vote for every citizen. Nowhere does he even ask the question whether one vote for a millionaire is genuinely equal to one vote for a pauper. But he does concede, no doubt under the pressure of the tumultuous times, that 'a reform in the governing machine is urgently needed by which the industrial life of the country may be brought into more direct and certain contact with political life'.

His conclusion to the nagging contradiction – between an apparently fair democratic system and the bias it demonstrates in practice to the rich – is arresting: 'Let us then have a second chamber on a soviet franchise . . . guilds or unions, professions and trades, classes and sections, could elect to the second chamber their representatives.' Thus Ramsay MacDonald's solution to what he regarded as the undemocratic bias of the parliamentary system was to balance it with a second chamber elected on the soviet system he so firmly rejected. This startling conclusion was short-lived. It never appeared again in anything MacDonald wrote or spoke.

Parliament and Revolution showed that its author, while utterly committed to gradual and parliamentary means of change, was nevertheless sensitive to the prevailing mood in the Labour movement, and was prepared to argue with revolutionaries. This sensitivity no doubt won him vital support of the huge band of 144 Labour MPs who met to elect a new leader in November 1922.

In the election for Party leader in late November, MacDonald beat Clynes by five votes – 61 to 56. Almost at once, the rejuvenated Parliamentary Labour Party put down a historic motion on the House of Commons order paper. It was debated over two days in 1923 – 20 March and 16 July. The motion, entitled Capitalist System, encapsulated the hostility to capitalism and the commitment to gradualism that had dominated most of the new Labour leader's thinking over the past two decades:

That, in view of the failure of the capitalist system to adequately utilize and organize natural resources and productive power, or to provide the necessary standard of life for vast numbers of the population, and believing that the cause of this failure lies in the private ownership and control of the means of production and distribution, this House declares that legislative effort should be directed to the gradual supersession of the capitalist system by an industrial and social order based on the public ownership and democratic control of production and distribution.

The debate was opened by the veteran ILP campaigner Philip Snowden, whose long stints on socialist platforms in Yorkshire and Lancashire had been hampered by lameness caused by a bicycle accident in his youth, which forced him to move about on sticks. Snowden was irritated by the way in which Ramsay MacDonald had snatched the Party leadership. But his views had not changed at all. The cause of the disease in society he identified as 'the private ownership and monopoly by certain individuals of land and the instruments of production'. 'What is your remedy?' shouted a Tory heckler, and Snowden answered: 'We propose no revolution and I certainly will always resist any proposal of confiscation.' Instead, 'hitherto the Government's attempts to supersede capitalism and private enterprise have been made hesitantly and reluctantly. What we ask is that it should be the conscious policy of Government and that the Government's energies should be directed by legislative and administrative acts, to bring about that result.' The motion was opposed by the Liberal MP and successful capitalist Sir Alfred Mond. He argued that 'it is quite impossible for human beings to control any industry beyond a certain magnitude' – though he himself had not found it at all impossible to control one of the biggest industries (chemicals) in the country. The movers of the motion, he said, had not found another system better than capitalism, and the one they suggested, socialism, would require 'Hon. Members' wives to take the state pattern and dress after the state fashion'. The sophisticated baronet drowned interruptions by shouting: 'You cannot get away from that, and we shall have to dress as the state tailor or the state dressmaker directs.'

The debate was wound up by Ramsay MacDonald. A student of MacDonald's career could discern in his long speech that summer evening a slackening in the commitments he had made in all those books about socialism. He ridiculed capitalism, but was much less clear about its dependence on private enterprise. Nor was he as emphatic as were some of his colleagues, even Snowden, that the essence of socialism was public ownership. There was not even a whisper of a commitment that any future

Labour Government would do anything at all to challenge capitalism. Snowden's motion was beaten by Mond's amendment, substituting capitalism for socialism, by 368 Tory and Liberal votes to 121, all Labour, a majority for capitalism of 247.

The Tories had little time to enjoy their 1922 victory before their leader, Stanley Baldwin, plunged them recklessly into another general election, explaining that he wanted a mandate for protectionist policies. The election was held on 6 December 1923. It turned out, in terms of the popular vote, very much the same as the election the year before. But in terms of seats the result was very different. The Tory vote went up slightly, from 5,502,298 to 5,514,541. Labour's rose less slightly – from 4,237,349 to 4,439,780. The Liberals, if all brands of Liberal were taken together, had also gained a few votes – up from 4,113,012 to 4,299,121. These small changes led to a very different House of Commons – 258 Tories (down from 344), 159 Liberals (up from 115) and 191 Labour (up from 142). Baldwin's protectionist gamble had flopped, and it was now seriously suggested that Labour should become the Government and Ramsay MacDonald should become the Prime Minister. Among the enthusiasts for this idea was H. H. Asquith, the newly re-elected leader of the Liberal Party, who wanted the Tories out but was incapable of forming a Government. He was not in the least worried or scared by the prospect of a Labour Government. 'It is we, who really understand our business, who really control the situation,' he explained modestly.

Robert Smillie, the former miners' leader, who was returned as Labour MP for Morpeth, wrote in his memoirs that he 'was very doubtful indeed as to the wisdom' of Labour forming a minority Government against such a vast array of Tory and Liberal MPs. David Kirkwood, the militant shop steward from the Clyde, who a year earlier had been triumphantly sent off with his newly elected Labour colleagues by a quarter of a million people at St Enoch's station, Glasgow, disclosed that 'at our Party meetings, most of us on the left wing were against assuming the responsibilities of office'. Others argued that Labour should take office for a single dynamic purpose – perhaps to initiate public works for the unemployed – and challenge the Opposition to defeat the measure.

The huge anti-Labour majority seemed an insuperable burden for any Labour Government. But gradually at first and then with increasing speed the Party's sceptics could not resist the fascinating scenario of Labour men and women becoming Cabinet ministers. Resolutions from every quarter of the Labour movement urged MacDonald to accept the seals of office, and MacDonald revelled in the prospect. His speech at a vast victory rally in the Albert Hall on 8 January 1924 rang with the utopian clichés in which he excelled. 'We are a party,' he declaimed, 'that away in the dreamland of imagination dwells in a social organization fairer and more perfect than any organization that mankind has ever known.' Silenced for a moment by deafening cheers, he went on cautiously: 'That is true, but we are not going to jump there. We are going to walk there. "One step enough for me" [laughter]. One step! Yes, my friends, but on one condition, that it leads to the next step.' Even in the full flight of fatuous oratory, the Labour leader was careful to stress his belief in gradualism.

By the time the first Labour Cabinet was announced, it was clear that the new Government intended no threat at all to the status quo. There was one representative of the Labour left – John Wheatley, Minister of Health, which included housing. He was balanced by two declared Tories, Lord Parmoor, who agreed to become Lord President of the Council, and Viscount Chelmsford, the former Tory Secretary of State for Air as First Lord of the Admiralty. The Lord Chancellor, second in rank to the Prime Minister, was the Liberal Lord Haldane. Thus the two opposition parties could claim the allegiance of three Cabinet ministers in the first Labour Government. Others on the list were scarcely likely to breathe confidence into the Labour rank and file. The new Secretary of State for Air, Lord Thomson, was MacDonald's golfing friend at Lossiemouth. The new Secretary of State for War, Stephen Walsh, was so overcome by the top military brass over which he now had nominal control that he told them: 'I know my place. You have commanded armies in the field when I was nothing but a private in the ranks.' Even more penitent was Jimmy Thomas, the new Secretary of State for the Colonies. He was a proud speaker at the Chamber of Trade in his native Newport, to which he admitted: 'I once wrote a book, *When Labour Rules*. It was a foolish thing to do. It was in the days when I bothered about material things and wanted money. Although in the book I set out very clearly how to govern the Empire, when on Monday morning my principal private secretary comes to me, I cannot very well say to him, "Yes that is a very serious problem, and the answer is found on page 28 of the book. I cannot get out of it like that . . . It is only cowards that fail to face facts. It is only cowards that pretend that consistency is a virtue.'

As so often, Thomas's approach to his ministry, which he entered with the solemn promise that he was not going to put up with any 'mucking about with the Empire', was an extreme example of the instinctive passivity of Labour Party members when they achieved the high office to which their political lives had been devoted. Again and again Thomas revelled in the fact that a former engine cleaner could gain access to the corridors of power and hobnob with senior civil servants and even, in Thomas's case, the men who ran the British Empire. To do anything which might threaten the security of that high office was to imperil the whole process. Therefore the best course was to listen to people with experience of government, the generals in the case of Stephen Walsh, the imperialists in the case of Thomas, and to do their bidding without ever even considering what promises were made to that part of the electorate which voted Labour. All his life, Thomas was ensnared in what became known as the 'aristocratic embrace'. One of his most strenuous interventions at Cabinet was to urge his colleagues to hire the court dress traditionally necessary for the acceptance from the King of the seals of office. A photograph of himself dressed in just such a uniform was proudly printed at the start of his almost unbelievably self-serving autobiography.

Passivity was the watchword of almost all the new ministers for the eleven months they clung to their offices. Philip Snowden's budget did not deviate an inch from what was ordered by Treasury mandarins and could well have been introduced by a Tory or Liberal Chancellor. The only minister who dared to rock the boat was John Wheatley, the red Clydesider, whose housing Bill for the first time gave powers to local authorities to build substantial numbers of houses at rents working people could afford. Wheatley's most challenging decision, however, was to remove the threat of surcharge to the Poplar councillors who had dared to challenge the law by not collecting rates for precepts. So confident was Wheatley of support from the Prime Minister that he did not even tell Downing Street before announcing the wiping out of the Poplar surcharge. MacDonald was furious, but there was nothing he could do about it. When the Tories, backed almost hysterically by the Liberals, denounced Wheatley's contempt for the rule of law, Wheatley replied, calmly and powerfully, that no one had dared surcharge the Poplar councillors in the past for fear of another Lansbury revolt. His reply silenced the Opposition and no more was heard of the matter. In this, the only occasion of genuine defiance by a Labour minister, the Tory and Liberal Opposition shrank from a confrontation that might lead to a general election on an issue that might provoke the votes of masses of working people.

Wheatley was the exception to prove the rule. In every other department of state, the Labour ministers carried on in the style and policies of their Tory or Liberal predecessors. No one heeded precedent more ardently than the Prime Minister, who resolved to do something at once about the state of his own finances. He was delighted by an offer from Alexander Grant, a friend from the Highlands who had become chairman of the biscuit manufacturer McVitie's and Price. In February 1924, Grant offered the Prime Minister £40,000 in shares and the use of a Daimler car. MacDonald snapped up the offer, banked the shares and took possession of the car. What did Grant get out of it? In April 1924, he got a baronetcy in recognition of his philanthropy.

The sale of honours had already become a public scandal under Lloyd George. MacDonald, who was, even more firmly than Thomas, clasped in the aristocratic embrace, continued the tradition in the most blatant style. Thus infected by personal corruption, dazzled by high office and even a little bemused by their political impotence, the Labour ministers stumbled on until the end of the year when they were tipped out of office in yet another election – the third in three years. The chief talking point in the election was a letter allegedly written by Gregory Zinoviev, Russian revolutionary and Politburo Minister, urging MacDonald and Co. to victory. Many decades later, the letter was exposed as a complete fabrication, concocted by MI5 and assiduously promulgated in the *Daily Mail*. It is usually regarded as the reason for the Tory victory at the polls, but in truth the Labour ministers had sealed their own fate. Their supporters voted for them in the hope that they would, in Charles Key's words at Poplar, 'make a change'. When they did not make a change, the enthusiasm for a Labour Government faded.

Nevertheless, the Labour vote actually increased (by 1,130,882), though Labour lost 40 seats. The chief reason for their defeat and the huge increase in Tory seats – to 412 – was the final demise of the Liberal Party, which lost 118 seats leaving it with a rump of 40 seats – an irrelevance the Liberal Party managed to sustain for at least the rest of the century.

Any pleasure gained in Labour ranks by the increase in their vote and the fact that Labour and the Tories were unquestionably the two parties battling for supremacy at Westminster was lost in the size of the Tory majority and the certainty that Prime Minister Stanley Baldwin was not going to waste his time in office as Labour had done.

Two familiar developments followed Labour's defeat at the polls. The first was a substantial swing to the left inside the Labour Party. The second was another shift in the political battle away from Parliament and into industry. In the Labour Party, the ILP and the movement at large, including the trade unions, there was a groundswell of revolt not only against Mac-Donald but also against the idea that society could be substantially changed through Parliament. In 1925, *Lansbury's Labour Weekly*, a new publication, proclaimed the foundation of the Socialist Club. The Club expressed indignation at the failure of the Labour Government, and then set out a programme for the next one. 'A Labour Government,' it stated, 'would be pledged to establish a socialist state.' Once elected, it would not be subject to the vicissitudes of the electorate. 'There would be no more Ins and Outs, no more of the swing of the pendulum. It [the Labour Government] must be determined to carry through the proposals and stay until it has become impossible to stop them.'

One way it could stay in office would be to create enough peers to ensure a majority in the House of Lords for its abolition. It would also be committed to a series of revolutionary proposals such as 'no court dress', 'no slums cheek by jowl with mansions', 'abolish race slavery', 'disarmament by agreement' and 'granting full trade-union rights to the armed forces'. The most remarkable feature of this incoherent document was the wide support it received.

Among the Club's subscribers were George Lansbury, his private secretary, Ernest Thurtle, and two other stalwarts of the Poplar campaign, John Scurr and Susan Lawrence. A surprising addition was Marion Phillips, women's organizer for the Labour Party, who had been regarded by the leadership as one of their most reliable officials. The tone of the document highlighted the feelings of frustration with the first Labour Government, in particular with the way it had been shoved out of office so quickly. The rather bizarre remedy to this, it was assumed, was not to increase the Party's dependence on democracy but to suspend regular elections, thus giving it time to carry out its programme.

Long before this opposition could regroup and form coherent proposals for the next Labour Government, politics on the left were plunged in yet another industrial confrontation originating as ever in a crisis in the mining industry.

The coal-owners had celebrated their escape from nationalization in 1919 by introducing low investment and low wages. The crisis of 1925 was precipitated by the resumption of coal production in the occupied Ruhr, and the resulting collapse of British coal exports. Unemployment in the pits, the lowest in any industry in 1923, soared to 300,000. The coal-owners' profits slumped and they announced that the wages agreement with the union would come to an end in July 1925. Everyone concerned realized what this meant: swingeing wage cuts, and an attempt to curb the power of the union.

There had, meanwhile, been a dramatic change in the leadership of the miners' union. In 1923, Frank Hodges, whose vacillation had been at least partly responsible for Black Friday in 1921, was elected Labour MP for

Lichfield, and, under the rules of the union, was obliged to resign as General Secretary of the Federation. Much hung on the election of his successor. When the result was announced in June 1924, the General Secretary of the TUC, Fred Bramley, was so horrified that he charged down the passage to convey his outrage to his Assistant General Secretary, Walter Citrine. 'Have you seen who's been elected Secretary of the Miners' Federation?' he bawled. 'Cook! A raving, tearing communist! Now the miners are in for a bad time!'

Arthur James Cook was born at Wookey, Somerset, in 1883, and had worked for most of his life in the pits of South Wales. He had risen to high office in the union in South Wales on the strength of a reputation for blunt honesty. His oratory, as all who heard him testified, derived from single-minded determination to the cause of the men around him and an entrenched hatred of the employers and their exploitative system.

In his youth, he had joined the church and the ILP but rapidly forsook both for revolutionary politics. His politics were founded in the syndicalism of the Great Unrest of 1911 and the South Wales miners' pamphlet that gave expression to that unrest, *The Miners' Next Step*. He was sceptical and dismissive of the Labour Party and its leadership, believing that any real hope for the workers lay in the union and its ability to halt production and, by strikes, to bring the employers to heel.

Immediately after his election, Cook forsook the relative comforts of his office in Russell Square in London and set off on a ceaseless campaign round the mining areas urging his members on to a struggle with the employers that he believed would be decisive. He embarrassed conventional Labour speakers not only by his style (he took his jacket off) but also by his refusal of a single penny in fees. Long before the confrontation he predicted, he became a legend on the platform, drawing people from every section of the working class and enthusing them with his straightforward ideas of class struggle delivered in rough-and-ready language that everyone understood.

So profound was the effect of Cook's campaign and so desperate the crisis affecting the mining industry that when, in the summer of 1925, the owners locked out the miners and made clear their intention to cut miners' wages, the new Tory Government, unprepared for the furious union resistance that followed, including a ban on coal movements organized by the revived Triple Alliance, hurried forward with a subsidy to tide the owners over for the next nine months. In the enthusiasm over what became known as Red Friday, many trade-union leaders assumed that the subsidy would continue indefinitely.

That was never the intention of the Tory ministers or of their Prime Minister, Stanley Baldwin. Their oft-proclaimed independence from the coal-owners was symbolized by Baldwin's appointment as his Minister of Labour of Sir Arthur Steel-Maitland, a coal-owner. Any hesitation in the ranks of the Cabinet was swiftly dispelled by hardened class warriors such as their new convert from Liberalism, Winston Churchill, and the veteran reactionary barrister Lord Birkenhead. Such men were kept awake at nights by the awful humiliation they suffered as a result of a Government subsidy for the miners. The central purpose of Government, in their view, was to protect employers from the menace of subversives like A. J. Cook. They accepted the subsidy with grudging reluctance, and only on the unconditional assurance that it would end the following May and that the entire machinery of the state would be organized on the employers' side for the confrontation that would follow.

In the nine months from the summer of 1925 to the spring of 1926, every sinew of the state was applied to the single objective of defeating the miners in open conflict. The police were trained to deal with riots and demonstrations; the press lords got special briefings from Cabinet ministers, their reporters showered with ripe gifts of information about the private lives and communist sympathies of TUC leaders such as George Hicks and Alonzo Swales. A new strike-breaking force called the Organization for the Maintenance of Supplies (OMS), entirely free of trade unions, was set up for the distribution of vital food and raw materials. The Government then annexed into their class army their prosecutors and judiciary. In the same month as the birth of the OMS, the entire executive of the Communist Party was arrested, charged and convicted on the slenderest evidence of seditious libel, an offence almost unheard of since the repressive Tory Government of 1817, and incitement to mutiny under an Act dating back to the naval mutinies of 1797. Some Communist leaders, including their General Secretary Harry Pollitt, were sent to prison for a year, a sentence that kept them out of action the following spring. Other trials and convictions of miners' union militants took place in South Wales.

During those anxious and hectic months, the free press, the objective police force and the independent judiciary were all thrown into the organized battle against the unions. Government ministers proclaimed that their main argument for their activities was the elected Parliament which most of them and their predecessors had opposed for so long. In August, the Home Secretary, William Joynson-Hicks, warned: 'sooner or later this question has got to be fought out by the people of the land. Is England to be governed by Parliament and the Cabinet or by a handful of trade unionists?' Winston Churchill asked whether 'the country is to be ruled by Parliament or by some other organization not responsible to our elective processes'. And Stanley Baldwin sealed the argument by insisting 'no minority in a free country has ever yet coerced the entire community'. In the excitement of the time, and as the pressure grew for some form of democratic argument to counter the growing threat from the country's millions of organized workers, Baldwin and his colleagues conveniently forgot that for centuries before universal franchise in 1918, their social and political ancestors, a tiny minority, had, to coin a phrase, coerced the entire community by exploitation and force.

While one side prepared for a ruthless struggle, the other side did not prepare at all. Indeed the trade-union leaders seemed paralysed by their own passivity. Nothing was done to block the movement and stockpiling of coal. Nothing was done to use trade-union strength to stop the victimization of the Communist Party. Nothing was done to prepare a workers' press to resist the plans for a press assault on any strike. The trade-union leaders hovered between desperately hoping that somehow the expected confrontation would never happen and seeking yet more negotiations to settle the miners' dispute. The more the Tories made it clear that they would not negotiate 'under pressure' and would not even talk about the coal industry until the unions abandoned all plans for a strike, the more the trade-union leaders begged for more talks. As the biggest industrial confrontation in all British history became more and more inevitable, the trade-union leaders became more and more terrified. Clynes summed up their mood: 'The only class I fear,' he said, 'is our own'.

There was little sign of this apprehension, however, when the trade-union executives met in the Memorial Hall, Farringdon, to respond to the Government's announcement that the coal subsidy would end on 1 May and the coal-owners' ultimatum that unless the miners negotiated substantial wage cuts, they would be locked out of work. The conference rose to applaud the transport-union leader Ernest Bevin, as he indicated that as far as he was concerned the whole axis of political power had shifted from Parliament to the unions. 'You are to be our Parliament,' he told the delegates, 'you are to be our assembly, our constituent assembly, an assembly where we will . . . at the end take your instructions.'

His speech addressed what he considered to be a new Parliament, based on a quite different form of democracy from that which sustained the debating chamber at Westminster. Here were the elected delegates of millions of working people, who in the period of struggle that lay ahead would act as the workers' Parliament. In the prolonged enthusiasm that greeted

Bevin's call to arms, no one noticed the routine exchanges in the House of Commons not more than two miles away.

On Saturday 1 May, the executives met again in the Memorial Hall to hear their leaders' report, much more in sorrow than in anger, that the Government was utterly determined to challenge the movement to open warfare. There would be no subsidy, no solution save cuts in the miners' wages and an increase in the hours they had to work for them. One by one, and with only one exception, the unions signified support for a general strike to defend the miners. Bevin said:

We look upon your 'yes' as meaning that you have placed your all upon the altar for the great movement and, having placed it there, even if every penny goes, if every asset goes, history will ultimately write up that it was a magnificent generation that was prepared to do it rather than see the miners driven down like slaves.

The cheers rolled on and on, rising to a crescendo as the miners' President, Herbert Smith, mounted the platform. The call to a general strike was approved by acclamation and the only people in the hall who seemed demoralized were the Labour Party leaders, Ramsay MacDonald and Arthur Henderson, and, of course, their parliamentary colleague, the General Secretary of the National Union of Railwaymen, Jimmy Thomas.

No one on either side of the conflict was prepared for the astonishing solidarity of the workers in the affiliated unions the following Monday, 3 May. Transport, targeted by the General Council, was brought completely to a halt. In spite of Government press reports that railwaymen were drifting back to work, 99 per cent of them were on strike for all the nine days that followed. Workers from every union called out by the General Council of the TUC responded with alacrity and enthusiasm. By Tuesday 4 May, transport workers, dockers, building workers, power workers, steel workers, chemical workers and printers were all out on strike. The carefully laid plans for volunteers from the 'patriotic and the prosperous' proved utterly useless and in some cases an actual hindrance to production and services. In every area, in spite of the considerable restrictions placed upon them by the General Council, elected councils of action from the strikers took initiatives to demonstrate their overwhelming support for the strike. The circulation of the unimaginative *British Worker*, the organ of the General Council, soared. Wherever the local strike committees assumed complete control, they prospered. In the North-East, a joint strike committee in Durham and Northumberland directed the movement of food supplies, and, with the help of hundreds of couriers on bicycles, took control of production and distribution in the entire area. The strike-committee bulletin reported: 'The success of the strike is completely assured. It is clear to everyone that the OMS organization is completely unable to cope with the task imposed on it. There is no change from the ordinary except for the quietness of the streets and the absence of traffic.'

Not all the councils of action were as effective or as confident as in Northumberland and Durham, but by the end of that first tempestuous week there was no doubt that a new system of power was being established. Parliament had in effect lost control of the situation. On the Government side, there were the unorganized and ineffective OMS, backed by the military, a censored BBC and a biased press edited by the most militant of Cabinet ministers, Winston Churchill. On the workers' side, in most areas there was increasing confidence that the strike could be won, and the miners' wages protected. The burgeoning examples of self-help and popular organization by local elected committees heralded a new form of democracy far more vibrant than Parliament. The threat of violence, though constantly reiterated by liberal commentators then and now, was only sporadic.

The General Council had several more plans of action. There were plenty more affiliated unions yet to call out their members, and every possibility that they would respond to the call as effectively as the strikers already out. By the beginning of the second week of the strike, it looked as if it must succeed. Succeed in what, however? Much was made at the time and since of the prospect of the strike turning into a revolution. By far the most graphic and detailed account of the strike, Christopher Farman's *The General Strike*, published in 1974, carried the sub-heading: *Britain's Aborted Revolution*. At the time, however, even in the newspapers of the Communist Party, there was hardly a reference to revolution.

The truth was that the General Strike was in furtherance of a trade-union demand – the protection of the miners' standard of living – and the deployment in support of that demand of the maximum power of the organized labour movement. It was, in modern terms, a sympathy strike in which workers not immediately affected by the dispute stopped working solely in the economic interests of other workers. The overwhelming majority of workers who responded to their General Council's call did so in the hope and belief that the Government would concede the miners' case and either take over the mines themselves and deal decently with the miners, or at least continue the subsidy which they themselves had granted the previous year. These concessions were easily within the grasp of ministers. They had already 'afforded' the subsidy for nine months and there was no reason, economic or otherwise, why they should not continue to do so.

The Tory Cabinet, however, had a different view. Urged on by Birkenhead, Churchill, Steel-Maitland and other class warriors, they regarded the General Strike as a threat to the very fabric of the social order: namely their own class power. To them, the General Strike harked back over the centuries to the argument at Putney between the Levellers and the generals. If we give them the vote, argued Cromwell and Ireton, the people will seize our property. In 1926, Churchill and Birkenhead repeated the argument in slightly different form: If the strikers can tell us what wages we should pay the miners, they are seizing from us the control of society. Will they not then begin to tell us how else we are to run the society? The two arguments seemed on the face of it a long way apart, but there was some substance in the alarm of Churchill, Birkenhead and the others. For if the strike turned out to be successful, the organized workers would indeed have staked their claim to run society. A truly democratic power would have been established that went far beyond the power of Parliament. The General Councillors of the TUC would have shown that they could successfully challenge the employers even in circumstances where the elected Government ranged itself unconditionally on the employers' side.

This was the significance of the tug of war between the classes fought out in May 1926. By the start of the second week of the strike, the issue was very much in doubt, with the balance shifting towards the workers. There was no sign of a drift back to work. The machinery of society was seizing up. It was decided not by the people on strike, nor by the employers nor by the Cabinet, all of whose members remained obdurate. The issue was decided by the TUC General Council, whose leaders, terrified of victory, opted for surrender. On Wednesday 12 May, the General Council trooped into Downing Street to tell the Prime Minister that the strike had been called off without any concessions to the miners. The slogan had been 'not a minute on the day, not a penny off the pay', but the settlement accepted by the General Council meant substantial wage cuts with increases in working hours. There was no guarantee from the employers to lift the lock-out notices, indeed no guarantee by the owners to do anything at all. There was not even an assurance that there would be no victimization of strikers. The General Council that had gone into the battle assuring their affiliated unions that they were to be 'their Parliament' had not even recalled the executives to debate the surrender. In the name of their members, they abandoned the struggle so unconditionally and on such humiliating terms that even Lord Birkenhead was embarrassed by it. The surrender of the trade-union leaders in Downing Street, he wrote to his colleague Lord Halifax, was 'so humiliating that some instinctive breeding made one unwilling even to look at them'.

What lay behind this astonishing surrender? Partly, it was the hard work put in by the members of the General Council who were implacably opposed to the strike in the first place. Chief among these was Jimmy Thomas, the railway union's leader. In 1921, Margot Asquith, wife of the former Prime Minister, wrote to him exulting in his presence at a society dinner, and urging him 'to keep tight hold of your men'. As we have seen, he followed this instruction with almost religious fervour during the great strikes of 1921, and, in the atmosphere of industrial peace and good will that he had helped to create, settled down in relief to a career in parliamentary cretinism.

Much to his irritation, that career was threatened by the General Strike. Never in a lifetime of heavy petting was he so overwhelmed by the aristocratic embrace as he was in those nine days of the General Strike. The settlement 'formula', or, more accurately, the terms for the surrender, was devised at the luncheon table of the grand imperialist Lord Wimborne on the Saturday evening at the end of the strike's first week. To consult with Thomas, Wimborne brought to his table the coal-owners Lord Londonderry and Lord Gainford and Ethel Snowden, the social-climbing wife of the Shadow Chancellor of the Exchequer. Also present was Lord Reading, former Viceroy of India. Thomas delighted this august company with the wholly false news that the miners were ready to accept wage cuts. This was rapidly conveyed to the Prime Minister, and, despite the continued and vehement denial by the miners' leaders that they would even contemplate such cuts, the fabrication quickly became the basis for the final sell-out by the General Council. At the anxious discussions on the General Council, when someone asked Thomas whether the Government would accept the surrender terms, Thomas, puffing himself up to the full stature of his self-importance, said that his information came from the highest conceivable source. 'You may not trust my word,' he blustered, 'but will you accept the word of a British gentleman who has been Governor of Palestine?'

Thomas's view of the General Strike was almost exactly the same as that of Baldwin, Churchill and Birkenhead. It was, he said, a tussle 'between the workers and the Constitution and heaven help us unless the Constitution won'. The chief difficulty with this statement was that Britain had no Constitution. What Thomas and the Tories meant by Constitution was the rule of Parliament. Their argument was that the rule of Parliament dated back for centuries, and should not be challenged, even (or perhaps particularly) by trade unions led by Jimmy Thomas. The basis of this theory was not connected in Thomas's language or even probably in his mind with universal suffrage. Even as late as 1926, the suffrage was not universal.

Women under 30, many of them workers, still could not vote. But in all his life Jimmy Thomas never addressed the question of the relative rights and powers of trade unions defending the interests of their members on the one hand and of an elected Parliament on the other. He appealed instead to a constitution that did not exist.

Thomas's approach won the day for the employers and the Government not only because of his own prejudices but because all the trade-union leaders, right and left, shared his terror of victory. All were apprehensive about winning the dispute they had started. Even the trade-union leaders of the left Alonzo Swales and George Hicks, both of whom had travelled to Russia and voiced support for the revolutionary government there, feared the prospect of a victory, as it would threaten what the union leaders regarded as the very core of their existence: the delicate equilibrium between employers and workers negotiating with one another. During the strike, the story gained momentum of a trade-union official negotiating with employers and reporting back to his workers. 'I can get you rises of £10 a week,' he exulted. 'Not enough,' was the reply. 'Well, at a pinch, £20 a week?' implored the official. 'Not enough,' was the reply. 'Well, what is it you want then?' shouted the exasperated official. 'We want the social revolution!' replied a loud voice. 'Oh no,' replied the official. 'Management will never agree to that.'

Although there were few voices calling for social revolution in those tumultuous nine days in 1926, the possibility of a workers' victory, and the consequent shift in the balance of power towards the workers and their representatives, was enough to confuse and disorientate the trade-union leaders and usher them into Downing Street for their complete (and voluntary) humiliation.

Most of the workers who had responded with such enthusiasm and solidarity did not believe the news of the surrender. On the day after the strike was called off, 100,000 more workers were on strike than on the day the surrender was announced. As the news filtered through to the rank and file that the strike had been called off and that the miners had been abandoned to a long, lone struggle and inevitable defeat, there was an outburst of fury and resentment. Many strikers joined the Communist Party. But fury and resentment are poor substitutes for collective action. Almost at once the anger and confidence in the rank and file dissipated and the union leaders settled down to a long surrender.

The surrender was defined as conciliation and cooperation. The trade-union leaders, headed by the TUC President, Ben Turner, began a series of talks with industrialists led by the Liberal capitalist Sir Alfred Mond. The essence of the talks was that industrial problems could best be solved by joint action between employers and workers. The talks and the philosophy behind them were bitterly opposed by the miners' leader A. J. Cook, who denounced them as blatant surrender to the employers. Cook wrote a stream of pamphlets (*Mond Moonshine*, *Mond's Manacles*) and articles in the *Sunday Worker* against what became known as the Mond–Turner talks.

The preface to *Mond's Manacles* took the form of a parable by an ILP veteran, Joseph Southall, entitled 'How the Wolves Made Peace with The Shepherds and What Happened to The Sheep':

Mundus the Wolf said to the shepherds: 'Why should there not be peace between you and us, seeing that both depend on the sheep for a living so that our interests are the same?' Then Bender, Digger and Lemon, three of the shepherds, said: 'Let there be peace and cooperation', and with this most of the shepherds agreed, for they thought: 'Why should we have the danger and trouble of fighting the wolves who speak so pleasantly?' But Cocus, sturdy shepherd, who had fought hard for the sheep when other shepherds fled, did not trust the wolves, and especially old Mundus, whose origin was doubtful. And Cocus answered: 'Are not the jaws of the wolves red even now with the blood of the sheep?' To which Lemon replied loftily: 'Cocus speaks only for himself – the council of shepherds will deal with him.' And Bender, who had charge of the shearing and was naturally woolly in consequence, said to the wolves: 'Let us get round a table and explore every avenue, without prejudice, to hammer out ways and means to get out of the present chaos on to the highway of comfort and prosperity like that of Rome which was not built in a day.' Now what he meant by this nobody knows, but while he was speaking the wolves made off with a number of lambs and many valuable fleeces. Then did the wolves rejoice for they knew the value of sheep's clothing.

The parable perfectly explained what had happened. Mundus was Mond, Bender was Ben Turner, Diggit was Ben Tillett, the former leader of the dock strike of 1889 and syndicalist scourge of the Labour Party in its early years. Like that other former militant trade-union leader Will Thorne MP, Tillett was now a supine supporter of the right-wing leaders of Labour and the TUC. Lemon was Walter Citrine, the Assistant General Secretary of the TUC, who wrote at the time that the end of the General Strike was a time 'to put the dogs back in their cages'. Cocus was Cook, who was hated by the other TUC leaders for his tireless opposition to Mondism. In Glasgow in July 1928, Cook combined with the left-wing ILP MP James Maxton to launch a socialist campaign in the Labour movement. A pamphlet, *Our Case*, summarized their argument for a more socialist Labour Party and a more militant TUC. Though it called for the Labour Party to adopt 'root-and-branch' socialist policies designed to transform capitalist society into a socialist one, there was very little space devoted to how such a momentous change was to be achieved. Apart from a brief reference to the need to get rid of the House of Lords, there was hardly any mention of other 'barriers' set up by capitalist society to protect it from such a transformation. In fact, the pamphlet relied almost entirely on rhetoric.

Huge meetings followed in Sheffield, Nottingham and London. Though their pamphlet denounced the tendency of Labour leaders to tolerate joint activities with Tories and businessmen, while witch-hunting anyone who spoke with Communists or Communist-front organizations, Maxton strove in all the meetings to avoid antagonizing the leaders of the Labour Party, and Cook's normally irrepressible oratory was replaced by a prepared text. Rapturous though the meetings were, the Cook–Maxton campaign failed to shift the TUC or the Labour Party from the drift to the right in which both were earnestly engaged.

That drift to the right following the defeat of the General Strike permeated every area of the labour and trade-union movement, including the miners' union, whose President, Herbert Smith, an angry militant during the 1926 strike, now swung far over to the right and grappled in constant, and sometimes even physical controversy with his General Secretary. The miners' union publicly disassociated itself from its General Secretary's denunciations of 'Mond moonshine'. Cook remained popular in the union at the time (he was re-elected to the TUC General Council in 1928) and was a legend for many years afterwards (when a son was born to Mr and Mrs Scargill of Barnsley in 1938, they called him Arthur after A. J. Cook, not realizing how closely the youngster would follow in the footsteps of his namesake). But ever since the defeat of the strike in 1926, though he tried to stick to his principles, Cook became less and less influential. As he was forced to veer to the right he was attacked and abused by his former allies in the Communist Party. He became lame from a wound he had picked up in a brawl during the strike, contracted cancer and, in 1931, died in the trade-union hospital in North London, aged 47. His decline in his later years, like the defeat of his policies in the union, was inextricably linked to the defeat of the miners and the whole trade-union movement in 1926.

As in 1921, defeat on the industrial front led to a revival of parliamentary politics and the growing excitement at the possibility of the election of another Labour Government. To this end, the Labour leadership carefully honed its policy statements to fit the conciliatory policies of the TUC. Just as trade-union leaders could sit down and discuss industrial politics with Sir Alfred Mond, so Ramsay MacDonald, Jimmy Thomas and the others, glorying in their freedom from strikes or any other bumptious behaviour among their rank and file, sat down to discuss parliamentary politics with the most important people in the land. The atmosphere of industrial peace led to an atmosphere of political peace, and a confident feeling among Britain's employers that Labour leaders could be relied on to behave properly.

The Grey Decade

The general election of 1929 was the first fought in Britain under universal suffrage – and the first election in which Labour won more seats than any other party. The Tories had a small majority in votes – 8,656,228 to Labour's 8,370,417. But Labour had more seats, 287 to the Tories' 260. One reason for the narrow Labour lead in seats was the slight revival of the Liberal Party, which got 5,308,738 votes and 59 seats. There was plainly a swing by the voters against the Tory Government, and before long Ramsay MacDonald was back in Buckingham Palace being sworn in as Prime Minister.

The Labour victory was greeted with jubilation throughout the labour and working-class movement. George Lansbury declared that England had arisen, and that the long, long night was over. The triumphant Labour leaders lost no time in pointing out that they were only a few votes away from an overall majority, and that winning votes was much easier and more democratic than winning strikes.

'Labour and the Nation', the programme on which the election had been won, had been specific on this point. The Labour Party's socialism, it declared, was 'a conscious, systematic and unflagging effort to use the weapons forged in the victorious struggle for political democracy to end the capitalist dictatorship in which democracy finds everywhere its most insidious and relentless foe'. This was the clearest possible statement that capitalism was an undemocratic system and that its antidote, socialism, could be achieved through democratic means, through the ballot box. It was not clear from the rest of 'Labour and the Nation' or indeed from the 1929 Labour Party manifesto precisely how this democratic conversion was to be achieved. Its few clear commitments were drowned in a sea of optimistic rhetoric. But there was one pledge that was inescapable: the pledge that a Labour Government would end the 'scourge' of unemployment.

No phrase came more easily to the eloquent lips of Ramsay MacDonald during the election campaign, and as soon as he got to Downing Street he put together a powerful team to root out the scourge. At its head was the new Lord Privy Seal, Jimmy Thomas, who personified the theory that the way to get things done was through the ballot box. In his scourge-stopping team, MacDonald had George Lansbury, the old champion of municipal defiance, and Sir Oswald Mosley, a dashing young baronet and former Tory who had been elected Labour MP for Smethwick in a by-election in 1926. All three men in their different ways believed that unemployment was, in MacDonald's word, a 'scourge' inflicted upon workers by Tory Governments wedded to the capitalist system, and that a Labour Government committed to full employment could and would do away with it.

This basic view was shared by all sections of the Labour Party, including two young MPs who were first elected in 1929 – Aneurin Bevan, 32, for Ebbw Vale, and Jennie Lee, 25, for North Lanarkshire. Both came from Marxist and syndicalist backgrounds and after the defeat of 1926 turned to the Labour Party and the parliamentary road to socialism. Both had been militant supporters of A. J. Cook and the striking miners, but both were shaken by the defeat of the General Strike and the miners. There were limits to their aspirations in Parliament but they hoped at the very least for an improvement in the conditions of the people who had sent them there.

All the economic forecasts that swept Labour to office in the spring of 1929 were set fair. Throughout that fine and optimistic summer, as the new ministers took their seats in Whitehall and found them comfortable, the men who worked in and relied on stock exchanges on both sides of the Atlantic beamed with confidence. On 22 October, Thomas J. Lamont, senior partner of the leading New York stockbrokers J. P. Morgan, sent a personal memorandum to President Herbert Hoover: 'The future appears brilliant. We have the greatest and soundest prosperity and the best material prospects of any country in the world.'

The following day, panic broke out on the New York Stock Exchange. A week later the Great Crash had, at a stroke, and for reasons no one could identify, turned the brilliant future into a dust bowl. The Great Crash spread to Britain, where, despite the new Labour Government's commitment above all else to removing the scourge of unemployment, it continued remorselessly, up from 1.5 million in January 1930 to 2 million in July to 2.5 million in December to 3 million in the spring of 1931. Whole areas inhabited by Labour's most faithful voters – miners, shipyard workers, engineering workers, electricians, labourers – were turned into wastelands. Jimmy Thomas's solution was to continue his dinners with the rich, and to give voice from time to time to his hope that things could only get better. 'I have no hesitation in saying there is a trade improvement,' he intoned on

4 November 1929. But unemployment went on rising, and the wretched Thomas found he had no means of stopping it. He resorted to vague appeals to faith in 'this old country' and the inevitability of turning tides. By May 1930, his impotence was so obvious, and his state of mind so unpredictable, that MacDonald shipped him off to the Colonies office.

The Labour leaders remained resolute in their determination that nothing could be done. The Chancellor of the Exchequer, Philip Snowden, was determined not to take any measures that might threaten the value of sterling, whatever the cost to the lives of millions of workers. Snowden also bitterly opposed any measure to take more industry into public ownership. The bigger and more devastating the economic crisis of capitalism, the more rigidly he clung to capitalist orthodoxy.

In October 1930, the Prime Minister, Ramsay MacDonald, went to Llandudno to deliver his last speech to a Labour Party conference. After an awful overture, dripping with sentiment, mourning the death in an air crash of his friend the Secretary of State for Air, Lord Thomson, he went on to assert that 'the Government has fulfilled the confidence that you reposed in it at the last election'. Undaunted by this fantastic claim – the unemployment figures had doubled in Labour's first year of office – MacDonald reminded his audience of the essence of his political creed – gradualism, or, to use the word that appealed especially to MacDonald, evolution. The great advantage of evolutionary socialism, he reminded the conference, was that it was always evolving. There were always those, he said, who complained that the socialists had not got to their journey's end, but there was always an answer to them: 'No, we have not, but we are going to get there.'

Turning finally to unemployment, he introduced into Labour politics a new concept: that of the inevitable impotence of all national governments, including the one he led. 'Is there a man or woman here,' he asked, 'who does not know that the unemployment which started last October and November is an unemployment of a totally different nature from that which we faced at the last general election and told you what we should do? It has been caused by events, by forces, and by movements common to the whole world.' Proof of this, he said, was the rate of unemployment in the United States and Germany – even higher than in Britain. Moreover, 'every one of the proposals made by our Tory and Liberal opponents for dealing with unemployment are really in operation in those hard-hit countries'. It was therefore 'a very good rule for us to observe' that 'we should learn by example and experience and not jump in expecting salvation by roads which those more heavily doomed than we ourselves have pursued and into situations in which they have landed themselves'.

The theme of his Government's impotence recurred again and again throughout this extraordinary speech. At each point, it was clear that the Prime Minister had no practical or tangible solution to unemployment, which imposed by far the greatest burden on the people who voted Labour. So far in his speech, he had teetered on the edge of sanity. In his peroration on this subject, however, he careered right over it:

But I cannot finish even this hurried survey without telling you this: as the result of a most careful examination and testing and producing of schemes and ideas we have come to this conclusion, that the great work of every constructive government must be to put its population upon the land. There is something permanent. There is a case of planting. There is a case where you take men – I do not mean their bodies but also their minds and their souls – off the pavements which have no roots and no rootable capacity, and put them in the fields where they till and they grow and they sow and they harvest. [A voice: 'And they starve.'] Yes, that is our problem which can be settled; and after all that does not differentiate them from their fellows in the towns – and where health and strength and mental power and imagination can come back, and where, in the worst of times, if they produce their own food, there is just a little, at any rate, in the meal barrel. It may not be luxurious but it is healthy and I wish there were some more of us sticking to that rough humble fare than there are in these somewhat degenerate days so far as luxuries are concerned.

What was the response of the Labour Party delegates to this proof positive that their leader was going off his rocker? Was it to at least set in motion, as tactfully as possible, machinery to elect a new leader? The answer came in a massive ovation for the wizard of Lossiemouth. Delegates went home reassured that as long as Ramsay Mac could make such glorious speeches, the future of Labour was safe.

But the wizard could do nothing to stop the relentless rise of unemployment that soon after the Llandudno speech topped 3 million. Bankers and speculators throughout the world started to sell sterling. The Government responded by setting up a committee dominated by bankers and speculators. In the early summer of 1931, the committee, under Sir George May, former head of the Prudential Insurance Company, proposed a solution to the problem of unemployment – to cut the already diminutive public spending and to slash unemployment benefit by 20 per cent. The argument of Sir George and his colleagues was that the financial and economic crisis was so severe that the most drastic sacrifices were called for. On 11 August, the Deputy Governor of the Bank of England, Sir Ernest Harvey, and a fellow director gave MacDonald and Snowden the Bank's version of the crisis.

They gave the same version to the Tory and Liberal Treasury spokesmen, Neville Chamberlain and Herbert Samuel. In a letter to his admirer and assistant, Philip Cunliffe-Lister, Chamberlain revealed what the banker had told him: that the country was 'on the edge of the precipice' and that unless something drastic was done it would topple over. There then followed the extraordinary sentence: 'The cause of the trouble was not financial but political, and lay in the complete want of confidence in His Majesty's Government existing among foreigners.' The remedy, the bankers concluded, lay 'in the hands of the Government'. No clearer statement exists in all British history of the determination of a wealthy minority, in this case the bankers, to unseat an elected Labour Government.

The advice had an electric effect on the Prime Minister and Chancellor, who made up their minds immediately to do everything in their power to carry out the recommendations of the May Committee. These proposals, however, managed to revive the supine leaders of the TUC. They made it clear that they could not possibly accept cuts in public spending or in unemployment benefit. MacDonald, Snowden and Thomas realized that the Labour Government could not continue, so they looked around for an alternative. This was provided by no less a person than His Majesty the King, who was very right wing and quickly accepted the arguments of the Liberal leader, Herbert Samuel, that the best way to impose more grief and wretchedness on the unemployed was to get the leaders of the Labour Party to do the dirty work. So it was that MacDonald, on 31 August 1931, found himself in Buckingham Palace being begged by the King to exchange his leadership of a Labour Government for leadership of a Tory one. So it was that the man who had played such a major role in forming the Labour Party as an independent democratic force in British politics agreed to a plan, proposed by royalty, to lead a 'National' Government composed almost entirely of Tories and Liberals.

The Labour Cabinet ministers originally chosen by MacDonald were kept waiting while he went to the palace and peremptorily sacked when he returned. They were asked if they wanted to join MacDonald's new 'National' Government, and most of them declined. Snowden and Thomas accepted with alacrity. Snowden continued as Chancellor and, in September 1931, took Britain off the gold standard that he had previously argued was the cornerstone of modern civilization. Thomas stayed on in ostensible charge of the Colonies. All three men played an entirely undistinguished and servile role in the 'National' Government. MacDonald became an earl and Snowden a viscount. Both died in 1937. Thomas resigned from the Cabinet in 1936 after being caught leaking budget secrets to his friends in the stock exchange, and died, a despised and corrupt drunk, a few years later.

The Labour Party that remained was duly trounced in the general election that October – though 6,649,630 people loyally voted Labour, they returned only 52 MPs. The MacDonald/Snowden/Thomas fiasco dominated all discussion and debate. Almost every assumption that had led to the formation of the Labour Party, its reconstitution in 1918 and its attempted gradual march to socialism had been thrown into reverse by what Ralph Miliband dubbed the 'obscene charade' played out by MacDonald, Snowden and Thomas.

The first casualty was the notion that democratically elected government could proceed gradually to pass laws to improve the conditions of the working people. Those conditions had, in every area of workers' lives, spectacularly deteriorated under a Labour Government. The policies carried out by that Government had been dictated not by Parliament or by any other democratic process but by forces outside the control of government. At the climax of the charade the elected Prime Minister took his orders about the Government he should lead from the unelected (and bitterly reactionary) King George V.

Most of the Labour Party leaders were defeated in the election. The few who survived were mainly from the left. The new leader was George Lansbury. His chief ally in those early years of the National Government was a seasoned barrister and unlikely left-winger called Sir Stafford Cripps (Cripps's father, Lord Parmoor, was a Tory aristocrat). Cripps was 40 when he fought the 1929 election. His interest in politics was only recent. But his reputation at the Bar was enough to persuade MacDonald, and a safe seat was duly found for him at Bristol, which Cripps won handsomely at a by-election in January 1931. His elevation to Solicitor General – and his subsequent knighthood (when the King asked him what on earth a respectable aristocrat like him was doing in the Labour Party) – took place without his spending a day on the back benches or for that matter as a rank-and-file member of the Labour Party. His loyalty to Labour at that time seemed vague. In the days following the MacDonald fiasco of the summer of 1931, he was unsure whether to follow the three apostates into the National Government. He stayed with Labour and by a slender margin managed to win his Bristol seat in the 1931 general election.

The lessons of the 1931 disaster and the continuing economic crisis rapidly converted Cripps to a Marxist position that seemed many miles away from his Christian origins. In opposition, he spent many hours with his new leader, George Lansbury, discussing the future of the Labour

Party. He came quickly to the conclusion that the conventional view about democratic socialism – the idea that socialism could be achieved by 'gradual supersession' of capitalism brought about by elected Labour Governments – had been terminally damaged by the economic crisis of 1931, and that a very different view of politics had to be developed if Labour was ever to achieve any of its aspirations. The fundamental fact about the 1931 crisis that loomed over every other issue, he concluded, was that capitalist forces outside the democratic arena had plainly been more powerful than the democracy itself and that therefore democracy could be made to work on behalf of labour only if elected Labour took drastic steps to curb the inevitable counter-attack from capitalism.

Cripps did not develop these ideas entirely on his own. Lansbury, for instance, supported him, and he could rely on the backing of another radical knight, Sir Charles Trevelyan, who had resigned as Minister of Education in the MacDonald Government in protest against the Government's reactionary drift, and, at the other end of the class divide, the newly elected young South Wales miner Aneurin Bevan. But Cripps's analytical brain, simple writing style, organizational single-mindedness and vast personal wealth combined to set off a debate in the Labour Party which for the first time confronted the obvious fact that the mere election of a Labour Government was not enough to secure the central aims of the Labour Party such as the common ownership of the means of production, distribution and exchange.

The 1931 debacle coincided with the decision of the ILP to leave the Labour Party. This left an organizational gap on the left of the Labour Party which Cripps and fellow socialists moved swiftly to fill. The Socialist League was formed on the eve of the 1932 Labour Party conference with the specific aim of using Labour's democratic machinery to pull the Party to the left. At the 1931 conference at Scarborough, a dismal affair in which no one dared predict the electoral disaster that was about to engulf the Party, Cripps gave notice of his approach: 'The time has come when we can no longer try with one hand to patch up the old building of capitalism and with the other hand to build the new building of socialism.' A strategy was urgently needed to ensure against a similar surrender of a future Labour Government to undemocratic forces. To this strategy the Socialist League, enriched with some of the finest minds and spirits in the Party, immediately addressed itself.

The high point of their achievement was the Labour Party conference of 1932, at which delegates supporting the Socialist League carried all before them. Resolution after resolution was passed demanding that the next

Labour Government use all possible powers, including emergency powers, to establish a socialist society and to usher in the public ownership of the means of production, distribution and exchange. Sir Charles Trevelyan moved that on coming to office the next Labour Government should immediately bring forward socialist legislation 'so that the Party could stand or fall on the principle in which it has faith'. The most prominent supporter of the resolution from the floor was the Postmaster General in the MacDonald Government and former Mayor of Stepney, Clement Attlee:

I think that the events of last year have shown that no further progress can be made in seeking to get crumbs from the rich man's table. We are bound in duty to those whom we represent to tell them quite clearly that they cannot get socialism without tears, that whenever we try to do anything we will be opposed by every vested interest, financial, political and social, and I think we have got to face the fact that, even if we are returned with a majority, we shall have to fight all the way, that we shall have another crisis at once, and that we have got to have a thought-out plan to deal with that crisis; that we have got to put first things first and that we have not got to wait until our mandate has been exhausted and frittered away but we have got to strike while the iron is hot.

This sort of talk was obviously too much for the Party's veteran secretary, Arthur Henderson, who tried to object to the resolution on the grounds that it was 'tying your own hands', but he was so roundly heckled that the chairman was forced to call for a fair hearing for Henderson. In the event the resolution, together with a number of others calling for decisive socialist action from the next Labour Government, was carried unanimously.

The biggest challenge to the executive came in an amendment moved by ILP executive member Frank Wise calling for a Labour Government immediately to nationalize the joint stock banks 'with a view to utilizing available capital and credit resources'. The Party executive decided to make a stand against this amendment. Into the argument burst one of the movement's most impressive and powerful figures, Ernest Bevin, the General Secretary of the Transport and General Workers' Union (T&GWU), which he had helped to create almost single-handed from a variety of separate dockworkers' and transport workers' unions in 1922.

Bevin was born in poverty in Somerset in 1881 and had organized dockers and carters in Bristol in the early years of the century. He had joined the Council of Action and organized British workers' resistance to the Government's attempts to send troops and arms to Russia after the revolution there. He built up the union very much in his own image, independent and strong. His reputation was established soon after his death in 1951 by a huge and comprehensive biography by Oxford professor Alan Bullock. No one can deny the extent and variety of Bevin's achievements, still less his impact on the labour movement in the 1920s and 1930s. Yet even the devoted professor found it hard to defend his hero on the big issues of the first of those decades. Bevin was instrumental, for instance, in the two great trade-union surrenders of the period – of the Triple Alliance in 1921, and of the 1926 General Strike. Until the fall of the second Labour Government, Bevin's socialism, which he declared only occasionally, was vague. He was much more interested in organizing his union and defending working people from the ravages of capitalism than in replacing capitalism. In late 1929, MacDonald appointed him to the Macmillan Committee, chaired by a judge and consisting almost entirely of bankers and financiers, to investigate and recommend on the system of finance. Bevin listened carefully as the country's top bankers and industrialists were interrogated by the Committee's most articulate member, the economist Maynard Keynes. Bevin seemed to accept the theory, quite common on the left, that bankers and financiers, rather than the capitalist system itself, were responsible for the workers' distress. In a minority 'reservation' to the Committee's report, Bevin widened his criticism. 'Private enterprise having proved totally unable to lift this country out of the morass in which it is, there seems no alternative but for the state to grapple with the problem and for large measures of state planning . . . to be adopted.'

When the Labour Government collapsed in 1931, Bevin stood for Parliament for Labour in Gateshead, where a 1929 Labour majority of 16,749 was converted into a National Liberal majority of 12,938. The shock of the MacDonald apostasy and the defeat at Gateshead forced Bevin to take politics much more seriously. For a short time he accepted the chairmanship of the Society for Socialist Information and Propaganda, but soon fell out with the other organizers. Throughout his life Bevin protested that he was nothing more than a plain man from the working class who held little in common with 'intellectuals' on the left, who were, he argued, much less dependable. In fact, as so often when 'plain men' deride intellectuals, the real division for Bevin was much more mundane. Many of the people he denounced as 'intellectuals' – Aneurin Bevan, for instance – had just as solid a trade-union background as he had, while his closest and most consistent supporters in the Labour Party – Hugh Dalton, for instance – were upper-class intellectuals by any definition. The real split over the joint stocks banks motion at the 1932 Labour Party conference, and often afterwards, was not between intellectuals and 'plain men' but between right and left.

Bevin was firmly on the right in that debate, but not always so. In another debate at the same conference he found himself on the opposite side to another leading figure in the labour movement, the former Mayor of Hackney and Minister for Transport in MacDonald's Government, Herbert Morrison. The debate here was about the form of public ownership that should replace the bankrupt private enterprise. Everyone favoured control by publicly appointed boards. Morrison wanted them appointed on merit – the best people for the top jobs. Bevin strongly resisted that view. Instead he proposed that trade unionists should take their place on the board as of right. Bevin had heard top bankers and industrialists at first hand, and found them wanting. Workers should replace them in high positions, and the best place to find workers capable of such jobs was the trade unions. This controversy was not settled at the 1932 conference, but rumbled on for more than 40 years.

In the debate about nationalization of the banks, Bevin complained that the nationalization amendment moved by Frank Wise would be 'tying our hands' and that a Labour Government should not be bound by a string of commitments to 'take over things' without proper argument. The joint stock banks and the acceptance houses in the City, he said, were outdated institutions that should not detain a future Labour Government. Cripps spoke late in the debate, lashing out at what he detected as the 'gradualist approach' of Bevin and other opponents of the amendment. The Wise amendment, he declared, 'raises perhaps the most important issue that is going to come before this conference. The issue is whether we intend, immediately upon coming to power, to seize the power of finance which is now in the hands of capitalists or whether we propose to temporize.' This argument and its relevance to the 1931 debacle persuaded the conference. The amendment was carried by 2,241,000 votes to 984,000. By a convincing margin, and against the executive and the block vote of the T&GWU, the Labour Party committed itself to the nationalization of the joint stock banks. Dalton and Bevin never forgot this defeat or forgave Cripps for his part in it.

Buoyed by this success, Cripps, with the support of the vivacious socialist publisher Victor Gollancz, started commissioning what he called Forum Lectures as well as pamphlets from prominent Socialist League supporters. Most of the pamphlets were reprinted in two books published by Gollancz – *Problems of a Socialist Government* (1933) and *Problems of the Socialist Transition* (1934). *Can Socialism Come by Constitutional Methods?* was the title of Cripps's pamphlet. It demanded a dramatic break with all previous Labour policies and a determination to use the powers bestowed on the British people by their vote to challenge the undemocratic powers that lurked outside its walls and continually threatened its survival:

The Labour Party is not now concerned so much with some particular political orientation of capitalist society as with the change from capitalism to socialism. Continuity of policy – even in fundamentals – can find no place in a socialist programme. It is this complete severance with all traditional theories of government, this determination to seize power from the ruling class and transfer it to the people as a whole that differentiates the present political struggle from all those that have gone before.

This theme persisted throughout the lectures. In *Democracy – Real or Sham?*, Cripps demonstrated how the failures of the old parliaments, before the franchise, had persisted into the new parliaments and how the arguments about capitalist economic crisis had been allowed to dominate the arguments about genuine workers' democracy. One serious problem, in an age when fascism had been victorious in Germany and Italy, was that people confused the arguments for reconstituting democracy in a socialist fashion with the fascist arguments for doing away with democracy altogether. 'The solution of our problem today,' he emphasized, 'does not depend upon our maintaining intact the whole machinery of government as it has been handed down to us. It depends, on the contrary, on an ability to reorganize and rationalize that machinery before the mass of the people are persuaded to discard it in the mistaken belief that it can no longer serve their purpose.' The old system of parliamentary representation provided the perfect cover for capitalists undemocratically to control the economy and therefore assert their power over the people. The situation called for the most drastic measures from the next Labour Government. On the first day after being elected, the Labour Government should bring in an Emergency Powers Bill to give ministers control over finance houses and banks. If the Bill was threatened by the House of Lords, ministers should promptly nominate enough Labour peers to give them control of the Lords which would then, by means of its new majority, dissolve itself.

A consistent theme of almost all the essays was voiced by Harold Clay, a senior official of the Transport & General Workers' Union. He told the Leicester conference in 1932: 'I believe in political democracy, but I don't believe that can become complete until you have industrial democracy.' In his contribution to *Problems of a Socialist Government*, Clay wrote:

Capitalism is inconsistent with the idea of economic democracy. Though under that system political democracy, i.e. Victorian parliamentarianism, has developed, the utilization of land and capital is autocratic and the worker has, apart from the negative control exercised by the trade unions, no effective voice on questions of industrial policy or on the matters relating to workshop administration which vitally affect him.

Of all the post-mortems on the tragedy of 1931, none was so effective as the reflections of R. H. Tawney, the author of *The Acquisitive Society*, which had made such an impact ten years earlier. Tawney had continued quietly teaching for the Workers' Educational Association and at the London School of Economics, and had watched in horror as the first and second Labour Governments drifted to disaster. A series of his lectures were brought together in a single volume, *Equality*, published in 1931, before the fall of the Labour Government in that year. As a philippic against capitalism, *Equality* was every bit as powerful as *The Acquisitive Society*, if not more so. But the question he didn't really answer was: is the democracy of Parliament strong enough to do away with capitalist inequality? The problem, he recognized, was immense:

The democratic formula is not easily applied to cure the evils of inequality, since inequality enfeebles, if it does not destroy the common philosophy required for its application. If sharp class divisions are inimical to democracy, it is not certain that the former are not tougher than the latter. The lever which lifted political and religious boulders will snap when used to move economic mountains, and government by persuasion finds its charms begin to fade when the fate of the persuaded is not temporary eclipse but permanent abdication. As the strain of the conflict increases, the mask will slip, to reveal, behind the decorous manoeuvres of parliamentary duellists, unreconciled classes locked in naked opposition. Either democracy will drop punctilio and show its teeth; or its claws will be clipped by constitutional changes.

Through most of the rest of the 1930s, Tawney mused on the catastrophe of 1931, and when, in 1938, he produced a new, cheaper edition of *Equality*, he scrapped his introductory chapter and its conclusion and wrote a much longer and more persuasive section entitled 'Democracy and Socialism'. The economic crisis of 1931, he argued, had exposed the central weakness of democracy in capitalist society: its instability. What was the reason for that instability?

The source of the dangers confronting it is not difficult to discern. It consists in the conflict between the claims of common men to live their lives on the plane which a century of scientific progress has now made possible and the reluctance of property to surrender its special privileges. The result is a struggle which, while it lasts, produces paralysis and which can be ended only by the overthrow either of economic and social privilege or of political equality. Democracy in short is unstable as a political system as long as it remains a political system and nothing more. The politics of our age are variations of that theme. Liberalism left the conflict to take its course; by its refusal to face the brutal realities of the economic system, it destroyed itself as a party. Fascism silences the conflict by silencing its victims ... Socialism would end the conflict by ending the economic conditions by which it is produced.

And then again, harking back to the Levellers and the English Revolution, he wrote:

That democracy and extreme economic inequality form, when combined, an unstable compound, is no novel doctrine. It was a commonplace of political science four centuries before our era. Nevertheless, though a venerable truism, it remains an important one, which is periodically forgotten and periodically therefore requires to be rediscovered ... In all countries in Europe, a time lag has intervened between the extension of political rights to fresh sections of the population, and the discovery by the latter of the most effective methods of using them ... When democracy is passive, there is no motive for meddling with it. A different situation arises when democracy comes to life and when its pressure on established interests becomes continuous and severe.

The debacle of 1931 was proof of the instability of democracy under capitalism. Because the financial power rested with an unelected minority, and because the elected Government had miserably failed even to challenge let alone replace that power, democracy had proved so unstable as to be worse than useless. It was therefore imperative not to throw out the notion of democracy but to continue to work within it in the ruthless determination that if and when democracy led to any sort of office, even minority office, an elected Labour Government should proceed to 'a decisive break with the whole policy of capitalist governments'; to use the political democracy to forge an economic democracy without which the political democracy could only bring further distress and misery to the workers and the poor.

He summed up this view in an essay, 'The Choice Before the Labour Party', published in the *Political Quarterly* in 1934. After mercilessly pummelling the ministers in MacDonald's Government who 'crawled slowly to their doom', he exposed them in language which still resonates 70 years later:

They threw themselves into the role of the Obsequious Apprentice, or Prudence Rewarded, as though bent on proving that, so far from being different from other governments, His Majesty's Labour Government could rival the most respectable of them in cautious conventionality.

He mocked the former Labour leaders' obsession with 'titles and such toys', and denounced them as 'stalwarts who sit up and beg for social sugar plums' and revel in ridiculous uniforms such as the ones that had fascinated Jimmy Thomas. 'Livery and an independent mind go ill together,' he reminded them, and asked, 'How can followers be Ironsides if leaders are flunkies?' The 'fundamental question', he emphasized, was 'Who is to be the master?' – socialism or capitalism. And in the coming battle to replace the latter with the former, he used perhaps his most famous metaphor: 'Onions can be eaten leaf by leaf, but you cannot skin a tiger paw by paw: vivisection is its trade and it does the skinning first.' In other words, unless the next elected Labour Government confronted capitalism as though it were a tiger to be tamed, its ministers would be gobbled up.

Years later, Tawney was eulogized by right-wing leaders of the Labour Party, most ardently by the Labour leader Hugh Gaitskell and one of his more articulate disciples, Roy Hattersley. As they struggled in opposition and in government to skin the capitalist tiger paw by paw, few of these leaders bothered to recite or even to read the professor's furious attacks on the compromisers, vacillators and honours-grubbers of the second Labour Government, nor his consistent warning, which he went on delivering until he died in 1964, that political democracy without economic democracy was an 'unstable compound', balanced uneasily between the tiger-tamer and the tiger, and capable in the worst instance of devouring future Labour governments more powerfully based than either of Ramsay MacDonald's.

As the National Government showed itself every bit as incapable as its predecessor of dealing with financial crisis and unemployment, so Cripps, Tawney and their allies in the Socialist League, with the support of the Labour leader, George Lansbury, redoubled their efforts to commit the Labour Party to the drastic action which they believed would be necessary for the survival of the next Labour Government. There were already signs, however, that the right-wing leaders of the trade unions, of whom the most articulate was Ernest Bevin, were increasingly irritated by the apparently irresistible advance of the Red Squire, as Cripps became known, and the League. At the 1933 conference in Hastings, Cripps moved the reference back of the executive statement 'Socialism and the Conditions of the People' 'with instructions to specify the means to be adopted by the next Labour Government for a rapid and complete conversion of the capitalist into the socialist system'. The motion proposed, for the next Labour Government, the immediate abolition of the House of Lords, the passing of an Emergency Powers Act, the revision of parliamentary procedure placing much more control at the disposal of Parliament, and an economic plan for industry and trade that would abolish unemployment and poverty. 'I think,' Cripps argued, 'that anybody who looks around this country at the present time must realize that that conviction of the effectiveness of social democracy is one which has got to be rammed home if we are going to keep with us all the keener elements in our movement.' He and his fellow Socialist Leaguers seemed strangely reluctant to push their amendment to a vote. After a short intervention from George Lansbury, the conference agreed, with Cripps's consent, to remit the amendment for further discussion to the executive, and for the latter to produce a statement for full debate at the next year's conference at Southport. The decision to remit irritated many League supporters at the conference, and was probably the result of those long late-night discussions in Parliament between Lansbury and Cripps.

The decision proved disastrous for the League. It gave more time for the right-wing Party leaders, Hugh Dalton, Herbert Morrison and the trade-union leaders, to regroup and organize a counter-attack. In the year between Hastings (1933) and Southport (1934), moreover, Italian and German fascism was strengthened, and another general election loomed. The 1931 fiasco slid into the background, and the arguments about how a new Labour Government should deal with undemocratic forces were overtaken by the more immediate argument about how Labour was going to get into office in the first place.

The pendulum swung from left to right. At Southport in 1934, the League tabled 75 amendments to the executive statement 'For Socialism and Peace'. All 75 were defeated by huge majorities with the big unions voting systematically against. The League survived but the aspirations of its founders, reinvigorated by the recruitment to its executive in 1933 of the former Communist and tireless organizer J. T. Murphy, subsided.

All the efforts on the left were directed to the general election in 1935. Democratic socialists hoped that the 1931 disaster would appear as a blip in history and that, in spite of the National Coalition which was still in place, the onward march of British Labour would proceed to take advantage of universal suffrage. The results cruelly rejected such hopes. Labour, of course, won more votes than in 1931 – 8,325,491 compared to 6,649,630 – but its percentage of the vote was roughly the same as in 1929. Labour had a respectable showing in the House of Commons (154 seats) but faced combined National ranks, now totally dominated by Tories, of 429 MPs. It was small comfort to Labour that the Liberal Party was well and truly destroyed, with only 21 seats. National Labour and National Liberal were now irrelevant. The huge Tory monolith, under its new, bland Prime Minister, Stanley Baldwin, seemed impregnable.

Previous electoral defeats, including the rout of 1931, had inspired the left to new efforts to strengthen Labour's socialist and democratic commitment. The defeat of 1935 had the opposite effect. Official Labour became obsessed with respectability. Opposition in the House of Commons became formal and dry. At the Labour Party conference just after the election, the old trouper George Lansbury and his pacifist views were unceremoniously booted out. The new leader, almost by accident, was the unassuming former leader of Stepney Council, Clement Attlee. One of the myths about the 1930s, propagated many years later by Anthony Crosland, was that the issues for the left during the 1930s were clear-cut. 'Rereading this history of the 1930s,' wrote Crosland in a book review, 'one feels a shameful but pronounced nostalgia. Tragic as the outcome usually was, the fight itself was exhilaratingly clear-cut and righteous; one knew what to do and where the enemy was and what was the order of battle. There were no greys in the picture.'

This nostalgic assessment was wrong in almost every particular. The political picture, especially on the left, was almost uniformly grey. There seemed almost total confusion as to the order of battle. As the grim decade moved to its close, the political scene in Europe was increasingly dominated by fascist governments hostile to any form of democracy, let alone socialism. In Germany, Italy and Japan fascist forces ruled by terrorizing all opposition. Fascism swept to power, usually by entirely undemocratic means, in Austria, Czechoslovakia and Spain. In Britain, the Tory Government under its new leader, Neville Chamberlain, seemed increasingly sympathetic to the new fascist powers and increasingly reluctant to act against blatant fascist aggression in Abyssinia or in Spain. On the left, the Socialist League and others argued for a United Front in the labour movement, and then, as democratic Spain went down to armed fascist rebellion, for a Popular Front of all anti-fascist forces. Both proposals were implacably opposed by the Labour leadership, which won vote after vote at Labour Party conferences against any alliance with Communists or anyone else.

Despite these majorities, there were plenty of signs in the years after 1935 of the strength of left-wing aspirations in the rank and file. In France, after a general strike, a Popular Front government of the left was elected, though it lamentably failed to come to the aid of its beleaguered friends in Spain. In Britain in 1936, the year of the fascist generals' uprising in Spain, the publisher Victor Gollancz started a Left Book Club, hoping for a membership of five or six thousand to revive socialist ideas. He, John Strachey and Harold Laski selected books of the month that were then available free to club members. The club soon outstripped Gollancz's most extravagant hopes. By 1939, membership had climbed to 57,000, ensuring a readership for the books of the month beyond the wildest dreams of any author. Many of the books were based on reportage – from the pits, from prisons, from China, Spain, Italy and Germany. The political line was almost uniformly that of the Communist Party, to which, in the Club's halcyon years, Gollancz, Cripps, Strachey (who was a Party member in all but name) and, to a lesser extent, Laski all adhered. The line demanded slavish support for what was then known as the Soviet Union, but was in fact the Russian Empire. Books such as *I Went to the Soviet Arctic* (1939), *Moscow 1937* (1937) and anything by Pat Sloan preached the most abject subservience to the Moscow line. Anything that smacked of Trotskyism or dissidence was immediately rejected. Scores of books about Spain peddling the Party line were published, while the best piece of reportage from the front line of the Civil War, George Orwell's *Homage to Catalonia* (1938), was not even considered. Nor was *Black Jacobins* (1938), C. L. R. James's glorious account of the Haitian Revolution led by the slave Toussaint L'Ouverture and its connection with the French Revolution, though a much inferior book on the same subject became the Club's book of the month. The only real argument between the selectors was over the draft of a small book by H. N. Brailsford, *Why Capitalism Means War* (1938), which made a few sharp criticisms of the Moscow show trials, and the judicial murder of old Bolsheviks in Russia. Gollancz and Strachey were utterly opposed to such a shocking deviation, and would have turned the book down had not Laski threatened to resign in protest.

It is easy to see how and why so many socialists in those days were influenced by the Communist Party. The Russian economy appeared to be planned. Though the planning was entirely bureaucratic and tyrannical, Russian institutions at least pretended to be controlled by the workers. Russia looked like a socialist beacon in a frothing, tempestuous, capitalist/fascist ocean. The critical faculties of many British visitors to Stalin's Russia appeared to vanish as soon as they got to Moscow. I recall a conversation in 1963 with the veteran Glasgow revolutionary Harry McShane, in which he described his awe on arriving in his hotel in Moscow as head of a delegation from Scottish trade unions in 1931. 'I sat in my hotel room all night, transfixed, listening to the trams in the street,' he said. 'And I thought, these are our trams, the workers' trams.' Doris Lessing, in her novel *The Golden Notebook* (1962), described the fantasies of a well-meaning Communist who visited Russia and imagined that he was to be summoned to Stalin's office for a friendly man-to-man chat about the state of affairs in Britain. Perhaps the most appalling book in the Left Book Club series was entitled *Soviet Communism: A New Civilisation* (1937) by Sidney and Beatrice Webb. The title had originally carried a question mark, which, probably under the influence of Victor Gollancz, was dropped.

More influential than the ideological pull from Moscow was the obvious fact that the Communist Party was seen to be doing something about the conditions of the workers in Britain. The chief reason for the weakness of Labour during the whole decade was the inertia of the employed working class. Cowed by the betrayal of their leaders, terrified by the threat of unemployment, and intimidated by anti-union laws passed by the Tory Government, organized workers during the decade hardly ever stirred themselves to take strike action. In the whole decade, there were only two strikes that cost the employers more than half a million days of lost labour: a cotton workers' strike in Lancashire in 1932 and a London bus workers' strike in 1937. Both were defeated.

What mobilization there was against the Government and the system was organized in the main by the Communist Party. Communists were chiefly responsible for organizing opposition to Sir Oswald Mosley's British Union of Fascists at their big rally at Olympia in 1934 and at Cable Street in 1936, when an enormous crowd stopped a fascist procession. Communists were also active in organizing the British section of the International Brigade that held up Franco's armies for so long outside Madrid. The 'hunger marchers' from Scotland and the North of England, symbols of the stubborn resistance of the unemployed, were organized by the Communist-controlled National Unemployed Workers' Movement. Outstanding campaigners like Wal Hannington in England, Arthur Horner in Wales and Harry McShane in Scotland were widely respected in the working-class movement, and Harry Pollitt, General Secretary of the Communist Party for most of the decade, was an infectious speaker with a savage wit that inspired many an enthusiastic rally.

Though it never achieved the electoral success of its namesakes in France and Italy, the British Communist Party grew steadily through the decade, and its influence outside the ranks of the Party was always strong. Sir Stafford Cripps, for instance, fell increasingly under the influence of Harry Pollitt. When Cripps started a socialist weekly, *Tribune*, in 1937, the original editor was a stalwart of the Socialist League, William Mellor, who had been a founder member of the Communist Party but had left it in disgust at theoretical zigzags and Stalinist hagiography. Before long, however, Cripps agreed to turn the paper into something more amenable to Pollitt and the Communist Party. Mellor was sacked and replaced with a Communist stooge. For a short time, *Tribune* appeared as yet another Communist propaganda sheet.

Seventy years later, it is easy to see the frightful flaws in the Communist position. The first was that the Party, like its equivalents in the rest of Europe, became an arm of Russian foreign policy. This was seen by many Communists as its main attraction, when the horrors of Stalinism were not as obvious as they should have been. Yet one of its many drawbacks was the continual chopping and changing of both policy and principle. In the late 1920s and early 1930s, for instance, Communist policy had insisted that social democrats were as much a threat to peace and progress as were the fascists. To prove this theory, Stalinists invented the venomous (and ridiculous) phrase 'social fascists', which was liberally sprayed over ILP and Labour Party supporters, left and right alike. The theory was adopted wholesale by the German Communist Party whose leader, Ernest Thaelmann, summed up his perspective in the memorable phrase: 'After Hitler, our turn.' After Hitler, Thaelmann and his supporters were at last united with the social democrats – in Nazi concentration camps and torture chambers.

This policy of isolation and denunciation of social fascists had been mercilessly attacked in a series of articles by the exiled Russian revolutionary leader, Leon Trotsky. Trotsky emphasized the importance to labour of democratic forms, even in capitalist society, and the hideous consequences of allowing fascists to gain power by splitting the anti-fascist forces. He called for a United Front of all parties associated with labour to keep the fascists at bay. This policy was ridiculed by Communists and social democrats. They continued relentlessly to savage each other until the worst of Trotsky's predictions came true. Less than ten years later, Communist policy on the United Front lurched violently in the opposite direction. Communists called first for a United Front, and then with increasing hysteria for a Popular Front, until the zigzag was brought shuddering to a halt by a non-aggression pact between Stalin and Hitler, and the sudden discovery by Communists that a war against Hitler was not an anti-fascist war, in which Communists should take sides with the armies fighting against fascism, but an anti-imperialist war, in which Communists should take sides against their government and the capitalist class throughout the world. These zigzags had their roots in the most fundamental flaw to which the Communists were exposed: the contempt for democracy. The democracy of the soviet system ushered in by the Russian Revolution had been completely destroyed by the Stalin regime, which seized complete control of the Russian Communist Party apparatus after 1928 and used it to stamp out every vestige of democracy in the soviets and the state.

The Nazi–Russian pact brought the unity of the left, so studiously built up by Communists during the years of the Left Book Club, to a shuddering halt. All three of the Club's selectors abandoned the Communists. Gollancz commissioned a Left Book entitled *The Betrayal of the Left* (1941), in which he, George Orwell, Arthur Koestler and others roundly denounced the pact and its Communist sympathizers. Strachey, in his new book, *A Programme for Progress* (1940), cut his Communist connections. So did Cripps. So did Laski. The Left Book Club continued to publish outstanding titles without ever again achieving the circulation or enthusiasm of the late 1930s. At *Tribune*, Aneurin Bevan took over the editorship and hauled the paper back from the Stalinist abyss, employing the arch-enemy of Stalinism, George Orwell, as literary editor with a weekly column.

The consistent feature of this period of Communist ideological dominance of the left in the late 1930s was a total lack of interest or concern with the plight of British democracy or its relevance to British socialism. Not one of the 257 editions published by the Left Book Club examined the relationship between the extended franchise and the possibilities it opened up for British socialist advance. As the war approached, the furious arguments about the importance of protecting a future Labour Government from subversion by undemocratic capitalist forces suddenly died down. In a little book called *Democracy Up-to-Date*, published in 1939, Stafford Cripps outlined a series of reforms which he argued would be necessary to update British democracy. Gone was the need for an Emergency Powers Act, for a break with continuity of policy, for the nomination of enough peers to abolish the House of Lords. In their place was a list of mundane proposals for streamlining parliamentary procedure. In this relaxed approach to the future of parliamentary democracy, Cripps found himself at one with his former tormentors in the Labour leadership. They too were unconcerned with any future battle or opposition from capitalism. Instead they fixed their eyes exclusively on the need to prove themselves fit to govern and on the inevitability of gradualness. Ironically, just as Cripps was deserting his former Marxist militancy, he was expelled from the Labour Party for advocating a Popular Front against fascism.

The menace of fascism dominated the end of the decade. One result was a series of shifts in attitudes to rearmament and war. Even after the pacifist Lansbury was removed from the Party leadership in 1935, there were several left-wingers who maintained their opposition to both. Their approach was based not on pacifism – though the horrors of the First World War were more than enough to warn against a second – but on principled opposition to the capitalist enemy at home, represented by the Tory Government, its press and backbenchers in increasingly overt sympathy with the British Union of Fascists, Hitler, Mussolini and Franco. Among those who articulated this approach was Stafford Cripps.

In Ben Pimlott's book *Labour and the Left in the 1930s* (1977), he savages Cripps for making in late 1936 a series of 'outrageous speeches' that appear to show some sympathy for Nazi Germany. The truth, however, is that throughout his life Cripps was stoutly and implacably opposed to the Nazis. The real reason for his 'outrageous' speeches, which were supported by the National Union of Mineworkers, was Cripps's abiding suspicion and contempt for the Tory Government, its Empire and its big business financiers, who would profit from a war. Cripps's attitude to war was spelled out in another book, published by Gollancz in 1936, called *The Struggle for Peace*. Cripps was assisted in this work by Michael Foot, a young journalist not long down from Oxford who had fought Monmouth for Labour in the 1935 general election. Foot had abandoned his Oxford Liberalism and was an irrepressible socialist and anti-imperialist. His notes for Cripps, which made up almost half the book, highlighted the endless build-up of armaments and the arrogance and exploitation of the British Empire. Cripps's book did not advocate rearmament. Instead it argued for a rather vague complicated alliance of undefined socialist countries that could gradually replace the League of Nations and eventually overwhelm the fascist powers.

The same basic line, in slightly different and more accessible language, was taken by Aneurin Bevan. At the Labour Party conference at Bournemouth in 1937, Bevan spoke, to rapturous applause, against Dalton's proposal that the Labour Party should support the Tories' rearmament policies:

We should say to the country we are prepared to make whatever sacrifices are necessary, to give whatever arms are necessary in order to fight fascist powers and in order to consolidate world peace, but we are not going to put a sword in the hands of our enemies that may be used to cut off our own heads.

He argued that by adopting the rearmament policies of Neville Chamberlain and his fellow appeasers in the Cabinet Labour would be consigning its own independence to the foreign policy priorities of a Tory Party whose Cabinet was plainly sympathetic to the fascist powers. Despite the delegates' applause, Bevan's speech did not win the day. Dalton's policy of support for the Government's rearmament policy was carried overwhelmingly, and continued to be carried in the two years up to the declaration of war.

As the defeats of the left mounted, as the Popular Front Government in France collapsed, as the fascist suppression of 'Red' Vienna and Hitler's conquests of Austria and Czechoslovakia in 1938 were not resisted, above all as the heroic supporters of the elected Government in Spain went down in a cascade of blood to the fascists, the line of Cripps, Bevan and the Labour left shifted to increasingly firm support for the only force apparently capable of stopping Hitler: the British Government and its armies.

When Hitler invaded Poland in September 1939, and after even Neville Chamberlain, still vacillating, was forced to declare war on Germany, the future for socialists seemed bleak indeed. More than half of Europe was under fascist rule. The working-class representatives in the fascist-run countries had either signed up or, if they protested, had been imprisoned or executed. There was no government and hardly an independent labour party that could credibly fly the anti-fascist banner. One by one, the former socialist opponents of war conceded that there was no alternative but to support the British military effort against fascism, while striving to maintain support for the organized working class and for the socialist idea. Across the left, the debates between anti-war campaigners and anti-fascist rearmers continued. George Orwell, when he came back from fighting fascists in the Spanish Civil War, was horrified by the prospect. He joined the ILP, the only British party with a consistent anti-war line. Jennie Lee, a stalwart of the ILP, broke with her party on the issue, insisting that the Second World War was not the same as the first. She did not, however, break with her socialism. She wrote to John McNair, general secretary of the ILP:

I passionately share the view of the ILP that it is to an uprising of the workers of the world we must look for a real democratic victory and the winning of permanent peace. But that does not exempt any of us from our share of responsibility in maintaining the military front ... It may be true that workers have never won their rights on a foreign field – but they can lose them there, as millions of poor people in Europe can testify today. How can they be given even the beginnings of hope until the military power of their oppressors has been broken?

It was a question that quickly persuaded almost all socialists to support the British war effort. Aneurin Bevan agreed with Jennie Lee, his wife. Victor Gollancz made his new position clear in *The Betrayal of the Left*. George Orwell wrote patriotic essays in a collection significantly entitled *The Lion and the Unicorn* (1941), and organized patriotic broadcasts for the BBC. John Strachey forsook the Communists and joined the Labour Party. Stafford Cripps, while still an MP, became special envoy to the new Prime Minister, Winston Churchill, in Russia, and as soon as he had had a good look at Soviet Communism, decided he did not like it. The Labour Party teamed up with the Tories in a coalition that turned out to be very different from its predecessor in 1915–18. The price Labour demanded was the removal of the Prime Minister, Neville Chamberlain, who was replaced by Winston Churchill in May 1940. After Hitler's invasion of Russia in 1941, the Communist Party line switched once more. Communists became the most vociferous supporters of the war effort. This universal conversion was on the face of it reminiscent of what had happened in 1914, but its effect on the left and almost everywhere else in society was entirely different. In contrast to the mass chauvinist hysteria of 1914, the mood in 1939 was altogether more sombre, less hysterical. After 1940, support for the war effort went side by side with a surge of socialist and democratic ideas throughout Britain such as had never before been experienced.

1940–51: The Stupendous Convulsion

> *Democracy is unstable as a political system as long as it remains a political system and nothing more, instead of being, as it should be, not only a form of government but a type of society, and a manner of life which is in harmony with that type. To make it a type of society requires an advance along two lines. It involves, in the first place, the resolute elimination of all forms of special privilege which favour some groups and depress others, whether their sources be differences of environment, of education, or of pecuniary income. It involves, in the second place, the conversion of economic power, now often an irresponsible tyrant, into a servant of society, working within clearly defined limits and accountable for its actions to a public authority.*
>
> R. H. Tawney, quoted in *Keeping Left* (1950), by a group of 12 Labour MPs, including Ian Mikardo, Barbara Castle, Richard Crossman, Stephen Swingler and George Wigg

Rhys Davies had been left-wing Labour MP for Westhoughton, Lancashire, for 20 years, and when he went to the rostrum at the Labour Party conference in 1942, he could not believe that the political tumult in the country and in his constituency was hardly recognized by the delegates. There seemed to him to be two quite different moods: on the one hand what Aneurin Bevan called 'a stupendous convulsion' in the minds of the British people, and on the other a placid complacency in the minds of most Labour Party delegates.

The stupendous convulsion was in evidence in hundreds of different manifestations. The reasons for it have been debated endlessly ever since. To start with, the war was going badly, and although people welcomed the eviction in 1940 of the Tory old guard and the appointment of Winston Churchill as Prime Minister, they were worried about the way the war was being run. The prospect of a German invasion had been postponed by the air-force victories at the Battle of Britain, but there had been no victories on land to compensate for the humiliation at Dunkirk. There was fear of a Nazi victory, but at the same time, the war itself, and the Nazi blitzes, created a spirit of defiance that very quickly grew into collective endeavour and socialist aspiration.

Rationing, a burden for the rich minority, brought a measure of economic security to the working masses. Suddenly, there was little or no unemployment. Workers could join trade unions and even go on strike without harassment. Women workers were recruited in huge numbers. Women were often left alone to fend for their homes and children, and were often glad of it. Half a century later, John Boorman's film *Hope and Glory* (1987) told the story of his London wartime childhood and of his mother's surprised enjoyment of her sudden independence. *Out of the Cage* (1987) was the by-no-means exaggerated title of a book by Gail Braybon and Penny Summerfield on women workers in the war.

In the army, the newly formed Bureau of Current Affairs devoted itself to blatant left-wing propaganda, much of it written by Communists and socialists. In or out of uniform, millions of people without wealth awoke from a long and miserable apathy. They read more and more widely. A craving for self-education swept the country and especially the armed forces. Ernest Watkins, editor of the Army Bureau of Current Affairs journal, *War*, wrote in a rather bland account of the post-war Labour Government entitled *The Cautious Revolution* (1951):

On Christmas Eve 1944 I remember coming across a friend of mine, in command of an engineers' unit, sitting in a bitterly cold attic in the shattered town of Nijmegen in Holland, studying, by the light of a small paraffin burner, an officially issued army textbook on the law of town planning. During those six years vast numbers like him read about law and medicine, sociology and bee-keeping, economics and mining engineering, and if you had asked them why their answers would have been some variation of 'I just thought I would try and catch up on things'.

People who previously had never even imagined such things went to concerts, discussed politics, danced and engaged with their fellow human beings. The result was an intense mass radicalization, the exhilarating march to the left referred to by Rhys Davies and a sprouting of all kinds of democratic ideas the like of which had not been sampled in Britain since the Chartists. George Orwell, in *The Lion and the Unicorn* and in his regular dispatches to the left-wing American journal *Partisan Review*, observed this process with his customary frankness. There was a move to economic equality, he reported, which resulted in more and more democratic aspirations. The ancient ties that bound the prostrate multitude to public-school 'blimpocracy' were being cut. Increasingly, the common people were bound together in solidarity and comradeship, and the yearning for a new social order based on both could be heard on every street corner, in every shop, in every workplace. The railings round the gardens in central London were being ripped down. They were needed to feed the insatiable demand for scrap iron in the munitions factories, but their demolition opened up spaces in the city that had previously been reserved for the high and mighty. Indeed, almost everything that was happening was marvellously demeaning to those high and mighty. What Orwell called 'the drowsy years' were over: 'Being a socialist no longer means kicking against a system which in practice you are fairly satisfied with.' He concluded: 'We cannot win this war without introducing socialism, nor establish socialism without winning the war.' He set out a minimal socialist programme – nationalization of land, mines, railways, banks and major industries, and a ruthless tax policy to limit the incomes of the rich.

Orwell noticed that the left-wing spirit in the country seemed to grow hugely as the British war effort failed. The nadir of that effort was in 1942, in Africa, when the British were defeated at Tobruk. The military disasters stoked up political rage against the Government. From 1940, the Government was a coalition. War Cabinet positions were shared between Tories and Labour. The Labour Party had endorsed its leaders' decision to join the coalition, and colluded in an electoral truce whereby neither party would fight by-elections in seats held by the other. In those anxious days in 1942, the truce was challenged not by official Labour but by Independents standing on vaguely radical platforms. In March, Denis Kendall, a manager of a local engineering firm with a liberal reputation, decided to stand, without organization or resources, against Sir Arthur Longmore, a former air-force chief and an unrepentant imperialist, in a by-election in the safe Tory seat of Grantham. The Communist Party, eager to demonstrate its enthusiastic and patriotic support for the war, threw its resources behind Sir Arthur. But Dennis Kendall won the seat with 50.8 per cent of the poll. This triumph for anti-Government forces was repeated the following month (April 1942) in another rock-solid Tory seat, Rugby, by the trade-union leader and former Labour MP W. J. Brown, who came to the constituency at the last moment, stood as an Independent and beat another Tory knight, Sir Claude Holbrook, winning 51.8 per cent of the vote. The same day, an even more remarkable victory over the Tories was notched up in Wallasey,

Merseyside, by George Reakes, a former supporter of Neville Chamberlain. Standing on an anti-Tory platform, Reakes took 60.6 per cent of the vote and reduced the Tory vote by 35 per cent. These three upsets were followed almost at once by the extraordinary triumph of Tom Driberg, a young left-wing journalist on Lord Beaverbrook's *Daily Express*. At Maldon, in darkest Tory Essex, Driberg called himself Independent Labour and fought the campaign on the weaknesses of Churchill's war strategy and on socialist policies which he went on supporting for the rest of his life. In a far bigger turn-out than in the other by-elections (44.4 per cent), Driberg won 61.3 per cent of the total vote to the Tories' 31.3 per cent.

The reaction of the Labour leaders to these results was to try to force Labour supporters in the constituencies not just to stand aside at by-elections in Tory-held seats but also actively to campaign, speak and canvass for the Tory nominee. This was too much for most local Labour parties, who openly flouted their leaders' instructions. At the 1942 Labour Party conference, held just before the Maldon by-election, the executive (by a narrow majority) proposed a motion to oblige Labour Party members to campaign for Tories in Tory-held by-election seats. The motion was carried, but by such a slim majority (1,275,000 to 1,209,000) that the executive effectively backed off. At Maldon, lots of Labour Party members campaigned for Tom Driberg.

The tide against the Government, and their own leaders' complicity in it, remorselessly continued. Sir Richard Acland, a Liberal MP, formed a new organization called Commonwealth and fielded by-election candidates in Tory-held seats. In the single month of February 1943, Commonwealth or Independent Labour candidates won 30 per cent of the votes at Ashford, 48 per cent at Midlothian, 46 per cent at King's Lynn, 40.3 per cent at Portsmouth North, 38 per cent at Bristol Central and 46 per cent at Watford. In April, Commonwealth beat the Tory at Eddisbury, Cheshire, in a high turn-out, and in January 1944 slaughtered the Tories at Skipton, North Yorkshire. The following month, Charlie White, standing as Independent Labour on a socialist platform and with almost unanimous support from local Labour Party members, won a historic victory over the Tories at West Derbyshire, where the turnout was 65.4 per cent. The ILP came within a whisker of taking Tory Bilston, near Wolverhampton, and in April 1945 Commonwealth won Tory Chelmsford.

These victories reflected the widespread hostility to the Coalition Government. Yet in Parliament that hostility came only from a small minority of Labour MPs, led usually by Aneurin Bevan, editor of *Tribune*, who, inside the Commons and outside it in innumerable meetings and *Tribune* editorials, denounced the Government partly for its conduct of the war but mostly for its timidity over issues at home and its nervousness of the increasingly socialist aspirations of the people. In *Partisan Review* in January 1944, George Orwell wrote: 'The Government's whole policy, internal and external, continues to move more and more openly to the right, while public feeling continues to swing leftward as strongly, I should say in a more disillusioned way, as it did in 1940.' Orwell was the first to concede that the same could be said of public opinion and the Government during the First World War, and wondered whether the end of the war would be followed as in 1918 by a Government which would 'chuck it all down the drain as soon as they are back in office'. He thought not. 'The people have grown too wise to be fooled again,' he concluded. The Labour leaders were 'terrified of power', but if they had the guts to go for it, they could well achieve it. Though no one was more sensitive than Orwell to what he called 'the various features of capitalism that make democracy unworkable', he concluded that 'Parliament has justified its existence during the war, and I even think that its prestige has risen slightly in the last two or three years'. This was chiefly because MPs had 'retained their power of criticism' through the protection afforded them by the law of privilege. Though he did not name his editor at *Tribune*, he praised the 'small handful of MPs' who had regularly lambasted the Government over all sorts of issues, including Regulation 1AA, which made it a criminal offence to incite workers to go on unofficial strike. The Regulation was proposed by the Minister of Labour, Ernest Bevin, and was approved by the House of Commons, though most Labour MPs abstained from voting.

The Regulation was Bevin's response to a rash of unofficial strikes in the mines, most of which had been successful. It was agreed and defended by the General Council of the TUC, most of whose members saw unofficial strikes as a threat to their authority. Aneurin Bevan denounced it mercilessly in the House of Commons as a sign of increasing corporatist control by industrialists and trade-union leaders acting in concert to curb the rank and file. He called it 'the enfranchisement of the corporate society and the disenfranchisement of the individual'. For such forthright opposition, he would normally have been expelled from the Parliamentary Labour Party but he survived by a narrow majority – yet another sign of the stupendous convulsion he had identified.

What was the effect of that convulsion on the Labour Party? Party membership, already substantial at the beginning of the war, grew steadily. There were 2,663,000 members in 1939 and 3,039,000 in 1945. Much of this increase was due to the growth of the trade unions at a time of full employment. But individual membership in the constituencies was up too: from 408,844 to 497,047. By the end of the war, the apathy that Rhys Davies attacked in 1942 had vanished. Labour had built a powerful electoral machine that could intervene at any level in British society.

The growth and success of Labour during the Second World War has been subjected to differing interpretations. In 1975, Dr Paul Addison published *The Road to 1945: British Politics and the Second World War*. His basic proposition was that the foundations of Labour's progress were laid down by the Coalition Government, according to 'blueprints from above'. The experience of the Coalition, he argued, changed the approach of Clement Attlee, Labour's leader, from socialist convictions to consensus politics. Similarly trade unionists at the top of the Labour Party, men like Ernest Bevin and George Isaacs, were tempted away from loyalty to their class towards loyalty to their country. During the war, the argument continued, the two major parties converged in ideas and policies. The Tories lost their enthusiasm for capitalism and the Labour leaders lost their enthusiasm for socialism. The result was Butskellism, a combination of the Tory Education Secretary, Rab Butler, and Labour's rising star, Hugh Gaitskell.

This approach was enthusiastically endorsed by the Labour leaders in the Coalition and their supporters at the time and since. It has often been adopted in part by critics on the left, who argued that the Labour Government of 1945 did very little more than the Tories would have done, and that the consensus policies of the Coalition paved the way for and explained the policies of the Labour Government after the war.

Addison's thesis was confronted and effectively demolished in *Labour's War*, a book by Professor Stephen Brooke, published in 1988. Brooke was concerned not so much with Attlee, Bevin, Morrison and other Coalition Government ministers but with rank-and-file Labour Party members. The consensus of the Coalition, he concluded, obscured rather than explained what was happening in the Labour ranks. The ordinary members were working out policies for a Labour Government that were wholly different from the work of ministers, including Labour ministers. The process, he argued, went back not to the start of the Coalition Government but to the reorganization of Labour following the catastrophe of 1931. Unheralded organizations such as the Socialist Medical Association (SMA) and the National Association of Labour Teachers (NALT) took on the long and arduous business of constructing socialist policies in the areas in which they worked. From these discussions, and from resolutions at Labour Party conferences came, for instance, the concept of a national health service, founded on the principle that health care should be available to everyone free of charge, and paid for out of general taxation. From NALT came the notion of a secular comprehensive state education service, again funded by general taxation, which would do away for ever with privileged education such as that provided by the public schools.

These policies were anathema to the Tory and Liberal parties. They were thrashed out and championed not so much by Labour Party leaders as by rank-and-file members who wanted to change the world in which they worked: people like W. G. Cove, a former miner who became a teacher and, in 1929, MP for Ramsay MacDonald's old seat at Aberavon. Cove was often in conflict with the Labour leaders, many of whom had gone to public or grammar school and secretly approved of a tripartite system that separated people early in their lives from high-fliers (sheep) and low-fliers (goats).

Even more influential was the SMA, led by doctors like Somerville Hastings, former Labour MP for Reading, and David Stark-Murray, Labour candidate for Richmond in 1945. Such men and their associations were not at all interested in consensus politics. Nor were they impressed with Rab Butler's Education Act of 1944. The Act, they argued, reinforced the divisive sheep and goats system in British schools. Nor were they impressed by the apology for a health service proposed by the Tory Health Minister, Henry Willink. They wanted a national health service and a comprehensive education system and knew they would get nothing like either from the Coalition or from any consensus arising from the Coalition.

Another example of the drift of Labour thinking during the war was the Beveridge Report on social insurance. Sir William Beveridge was not a socialist – he was a Liberal. Indeed, towards the end of the war he was elected, unopposed by any of the major parties, as Liberal MP for Berwick-upon-Tweed. His report outlining a system of social insurance that covered everyone in the country 'from the cradle to the grave' became one of the most popular documents of the war. The report itself, hardly exciting reading, sold a staggering 600,000 copies. Beveridge, whose considerable qualities did not include humility, described the reaction to his report – in December 1942 – as 'boom and boycott'. 'I became,' he revealed, 'at a blow one of the best-known characters in the country.' A Gallup poll discovered that 19 out of 20 people in the country had heard of the Beveridge Report. Sir William related in his own book how he 'often caught young women surreptitiously sketching me as they sat opposite me in the train between Oxford and Paddington. If I liked the looks of the young woman, as I generally did, I asked to be shown the result and autographed it for her.' He revelled in the adoration, but noticed that his adorers did not include the Government and certainly not Winston Churchill. Most Tories, including Churchill, saw the Report as a dangerous warning of the state interference that would follow the war if the socialists were given free rein. Sir William was boycotted by Government. The Prime Minister was always too busy to see him. Eventually, Labour raised the Report in the House of Commons and some Labour MPs signed a special motion unsuccessfully demanding its implementation. Labour members of the War Cabinet, notably Herbert Morrison, were embarrassed and suggested to Beveridge that he 'damp down unreasonable demands'. But the Report, which Beveridge freely acknowledged had been inspired by the TUC, had already been published as detailed policy by the Labour Party.

So, by 1945, in three major issues of the day at least, Labour had constructed its own policy quite independently of Tories and Liberals, and hostile to both.

Inside the Labour Party there was a sharp shift to the left. In Parliament this shift was represented by Aneurin Bevan; outside Parliament by all sorts of thinkers, headed as always by Professor Tawney. In 1941, while the war still hung in the balance, Tawney wrote a stirring pamphlet entitled *Why Britain Fights*. 'Democracy? It is good, but not enough,' he wrote, picking up and extending his theme of the 1938 edition of *Equality*.

Our political institutions are, on the whole, a source of pride. Our economic institutions and the social system based on them, ought to be the same; in fact they are not . . . Democracy is unstable as a political system as long as it remains a political system and little more, instead of being, as it might be, not only a form of government, but a type of society and a manner of life in harmony with that type.'

In an address to the Fabian Society in 1944, the professor refurbished his old theme, stressing the crucial difference between a democracy limited to periodical voting (political democracy) and a democracy that sought to transform economic hierarchy and autocracy into something that could change the lives of working people. The lecture was entitled 'We Mean Freedom'. It repeated the basic principles set down in *Equality* and enlarged them into something approaching a programme for a Labour Government.

Tawney had stood three times for Parliament since 1918. He lost heavily to the Liberals in Rochdale in that year, and in 1922 and 1924 came much closer to being elected at Tottenham South and Swindon, but had since given up any serious prospect of taking part himself in such a Government.

This abstinence strengthened his insistence on a theoretical framework for any new Labour Government. 'Socialists,' he demanded, 'must state the meaning of freedom in realistic and constructive terms, not as a possession to be defended but as a goal to be achieved. They must make it clear that their policy is to end economic as well as political power responsible to authorities acting for the nation.'

What did this mean in terms of practical politics? It meant 'a genuine and decisive transference of economic sovereignty'. It meant that 'the key points of strategic positions of the economy shall be removed from the sphere of private interests and held by public bodies'. Private economic power, if left to its own devices, would find itself and the citizens over whom it held sway at the mercy of the instability that had ruined so many lives in the 1930s. The 'serious danger' for the post-war period was that 'the conditions of freedom may be too long delayed that failure to achieve it may discredit democracy'. What the cautious Fabians made of this urgent call to action to challenge the economic tyranny of capitalism is not recorded. When Tawney was safely dead (in 1962), Fabians of all kinds worshipped at his grave. Few of them recalled his anxious pleas for action to transform political liberty into economic liberty.

An even more influential thinker in the Labour Party was Harold Laski. The effect of this dapper little academic on the thinking of Labour in the 1920s and 1930s had been immense. During the war, Laski's influence rose still further. Though, like Tawney, he was never an MP – he never stood for Parliament – he was consistently elected to the Party's National Executive at the top of the list of members elected by the constituencies. As the 'stupendous convulsion' and the explosion of democratic ideas during the war gathered pace, Laski was inspired to commemorate both in a new book. Its title, *Reflections on the Revolution of Our Time* (1943), was modelled on Edmund Burke's *Reflections on the Revolution in France*, not because Laski agreed with Burke but because he didn't. Burke's *Reflections*, he explained, had led to reaction. Laski's, by contrast, he insisted, was intended as a beacon of progress.

Laski was a discursive and in many ways a reckless writer. His ideas often collided with each other. His historical sorties into, for instance, the Russian Revolution are almost impossible to follow. George Orwell savaged his prose style as hopelessly obscure. But Laski's indignation with the state of capitalist society and his determination to convey to others the urgency of replacing it were infectious. In the *Reflections* he returned again and again to the same theme that had preoccupied Tawney – the incompatibility of capitalism, a society based on class hierarchy, with a political democracy based on popular elections. How could the democracy of regular elections to Parliament and councils sit side by side with industrial, commercial and financial organizations run on lines entirely contrary to democracy?

A decade earlier, in October 1932, Laski had written:

I started a little book that burned inside me ... It is a philosophic-historic explanation of why capitalism and democracy are incompatible; with a discussion of how the institutions of capitalist democracy, being built on inescapable contradictions, issue inevitably into revolution. I would go to the stake for it, and I think it is the most creative book I have ever written.

The book, *Democracy in Crisis* (1933), was almost uniformly pessimistic in predicting that there could be no compromise between democracy and capitalism and a violent clash between the two was inevitable. In 1933, Laski wrote an introductory essay – 'The Present Position of Representative Democracy' – in a collection entitled *Where Stands Socialism Today?* 'Sooner or later,' he declared, 'Great Britain has to face the issue of whether it will adjust its economic and social constitution to the political democracy upon which its legislative constitution depends.' There was no forecast as to how and when such a time might arise, except the assurance that if British society became even more unequal, 'the disproportion between the political democracy and the economic oligarchy will be even more striking than it is now'. For the rest of the 1930s, Laski was inclined to let this matter drop. The argument was replaced by the debate about the measures a future Labour Government would have to take to deal with the counter-attack from capitalism. As the Communist Party and Russian Government influence on the British Labour left grew in the 1930s, so the issue of democracy became slightly embarrassing and effectively vanished. Interest in the issue was revived by the democratic upheavals during the war. In his *Reflections*, Laski returned to the theme with much greater vigour and conviction.

Borrowing again a title from another celebrated English writer, William Hazlitt, Laski called his introduction 'The Spirit of the Age'.

The history of political democracy in the period since the French Revolution is the history of its acceptance so long as the masses do not seek to extend it to the planes of economic and social life. On those planes, the attempt of democratic principles to make their way has been resisted with the same firmness as the feudal aristocracy showed in its struggle with the rising middle class. On the evidence, the fact is so far inescapable that if those who live by owning have to choose between the continuance of their ownership and the continuance of democracy they will choose the continuance of ownership. They will insist with obvious sincerity that they do so in the interests of the whole community.

Laski went on to argue that western democracies were locked in an impasse between political democracy and economic oligarchy. They could not stand still in the impasse. Either economic oligarchy would impinge upon democracy, or democracy would encroach on economic oligarchy. Socialists should hope and plan for the latter. 'To the masses, as distinct from their rulers, victory means extension of the frontiers of democracy from those political boundaries at which they now so largely halt, to the social and economic fields.'

What did that mean in terms of practical politics? Though from time to time in his life Laski flirted with the idea of violent revolution, he never lost hope in what he called, in his book, 'revolution by consent'. In practical terms this meant revolution brought about by an elected Labour Government. In the past, especially after 1931, any argument based on the election of such a Government had seemed unreal, almost utopian. But in 1944, in the stupendous convulsion, a Labour Government with a majority was suddenly a real prospect. Such a Government would, Laski argued, be confronted at once with the central issue of his book: namely 'we cannot postpone the issue of the purpose of a planned society without jeopardizing the existence of democracy when the war is over'. Public opinion, he concluded, was 'ready for fundamental change' but what should that change be, and how would it extend political democracy to the economic and social sphere?

Here there is a gap in Laski's argument. Discussing the effect of the war on the mind of the masses, he concluded that people will be satisfied with quite limited accomplishments:

They [the mass of the people] will not endure, after victory, the persistence of mass unemployment . . . they will not accept the re-emergence of distressed areas . . . they will not submit at least peacefully to any rebuilding of Britain which enables the ground landlord and the speculative builder to profiteer out of the sufferings of Coventry and Plymouth, East London and Merseyside.

This seemed like a list of quite modest proposals, later identified more specifically as the nationalization of the land, the banks, transport, fuel and power. But Laski's message went deeper. It was an argument urging an elected Labour Government relentlessly to invade the territory of the rich, and occupy it in the interests of the workers and the poor. Laski stressed a difference in principle between the economic oligarchy at the centre of the capitalist system and the economic democracy that had to be ushered in by a socialist Government. The elected Government needed in principle to harass and invade the territory of the rich to the extent that an economic democracy was established by the political democracy. The boundaries of such measures were not defined.

Nevertheless, the impact of such ideas on the British people as they emerged from the horrors of possible defeat by fascism and contemplated a peaceful post-war world was enormous. Laski's work and his influence in the Labour Party, though it horrified the Labour leaders, especially Attlee, enthused the rank and file. At a time when the theoretical contribution of the Communist Party was almost entirely devoted to supporting the most extreme reactionaries in by-elections and to unctuous hero-worship of the Russian dictator, Stalin, Laski's emphasis on democracy went a long way to reconciling socialist and democratic ideas. His views on these matters were shared by Aneurin Bevan. Less than a year after Laski published his *Reflections*, Bevan wrote a sparkling booklet entitled *Why Not Trust the Tories?* (1944). His main aim was to warn his readers against voting Tory in a post-war general election, and to remind them of the disaster that followed the Tory vote after the First World War:

Popular government, universal suffrage, rights of agitation and organization, all those varied activities and institutions which are summed up in the phrase 'modern democracy' are alien to the Tory mentality . . . They [the Tories] never looked on Parliament as a place where they shared power with the masses . . . Democracy is poison to the Tory's whole conception of life.

Universal suffrage had given the ordinary man and woman the right to be consulted. 'He is charged with the responsibility for events but not with the power to shape them. The real power is in the hands of those who have held it all along.' The role for the ordinary voter was clear. 'He either steps back to the shadows of history once more or into the light of full social maturity. Property rules with his permission.'

What needed to be done?

The people must be brought to see that social affairs are in a bad state, because the people themselves have not clothed the bones of political democracy with the flesh of economic power. Until they do, it is nonsense to talk of the people's rule . . . the economic structure of Britain is the domain of private adventure. The prime motivator in industry and finance is the property owner and/or his hirelings. It is he who employs and dismisses. It is he whose wishes direct industrial enterprise and the use of credit . . . Parliament, therefore, legislates in a framework formed for it by the decisions of individuals who consult no one and nothing but their private interests. Parliament is therefore always after the fact, conditioned by what the City or some great captain of industry decides.

The problem for the Tory therefore is 'always the same: how to induce the many to vote the few back into power at each election'.

The booklet ends by telling the story of Thomas Rainsborough at the Putney Debates with which this book begins. 'Rainsborough lost,' Bevan concluded. 'Property was too strong for him.' And so, finally: 'The three elements are now present: democracy, poverty and property. There is no rest between them; rather a ceaseless struggle and ferment.' The British people were now facing a general election in which they could choose not to go back to the dark days of the inter-war years and their terrible dictatorships and wars. 'Watch you are not caught in the same way,' was Bevan's warning.

The following spring, the German High Command surrendered to the Allies in Europe. The war against Japan continued in the Far East but Churchill decided on an early election. Some Labour ministers, including Attlee and Bevin, were reluctant to give up their senior posts and keen to keep the Coalition going at least until the war against Japan was over. All the Labour ministers in the War Cabinet, including Herbert Morrison, the Home Secretary, who did not want to continue in the Coalition, were nervous about Labour's chances. When the 1944 Labour Party conference, against the advice of the executive, passed a composite motion calling for a wide extension of public ownership, Morrison sought out the mover of the motion, a young delegate from Reading, Ian Mikardo. 'He stepped up to me,' Mikardo recorded, 'and laid a friendly hand on my shoulder. "Young man," he said, "you did very well this morning. That was a good speech you made – but you realize, don't you, that you've lost us the general election." ' Despite this pessimism from on high, the conference committed Labour to fight the election as an independent party. The election campaign took place through most of June 1945, drawing enormous crowds and intense discussion and enthusiasm. No one paid much attention to the opinion polls, all of which showed dwindling support for the Tories. Most commentators preferred to believe that 'the country' would rally behind their victorious war leader.

Polling day was 5 July. The results were not declared for three weeks to allow the service vote to be properly counted – the first of many major differences between this post-war election and the last one. I was seven and a half years old that July day, and I shall never forget it. My father had just been appointed to the post of Colonial Secretary (second in command) in the Caribbean island of Jamaica, and was home on leave waiting to start his new job. We stayed with his father, the former Liberal MP Isaac Foot, in his huge house, groaning under the weight of 50,000 books, at Callington in Cornwall. The political situation was explained to me as follows. Grandpa Isaac, who was 65, was standing for the Liberals in Tavistock and had a good chance of winning. Uncle Dingle was Liberal MP for Dundee and had been a member of the Coalition Government. He was a sure-fire certainty to get back into Parliament. My uncle John, a speaker of sparkling wit and persuasive power, was Liberal candidate for his father's old seat at Bodmin, and was also favourite to be elected. The only certain loser was the upstart and renegade Uncle Michael, who had abandoned the Liberal Party for Labour and was fighting, against hopeless odds, a Liberal National minister in Plymouth, Devonport. The minister, Leslie Hore-Belisha, had been elected in 1935 with an impregnable majority of more than 11,000. We stayed up most of the night. The first family result to be declared was sensational: Michael had won Devonport by 2,013 votes. It seemed to me quite obvious, as I staggered off to bed, that the others would now win easily. But the next day was all gloom. One by one, the Liberals went down – first Dingle, then John, then the old man. I remember reflecting that something very extraordinary was going on – though there was no one around to explain it to me, least of all my grandfather who shut himself up in his bedroom for five days leaving strict instructions that none of us grandchildren (whom he adored and who adored him) were allowed anywhere near him.

Something very extraordinary indeed had happened. The people had voted in the most decisive manner imaginable to dispense with the old political order. Labour won 393 seats compared to 154 in 1935, and had a majority of 145 over all other parties, nearly 200 over the Tories. The extent of the damage to the Liberal Party was terminal. They were down to 12 seats. Throughout that long summer night in the towns and cities of Britain the results were greeted with unprecedented enthusiasm by a working class that could at last enjoy the fruits of its enfranchisement. In Cardiff, as in several other cities, all the Tory seats were lost to Labour, and the young naval lieutenant James Callaghan recalled later how he and his two triumphant colleagues were carried from the town hall on the shoulders of jubilant supporters. He was moved to quote from Wordsworth on the French Revolution:

Bliss was it in that dawn to be alive,
But to be young was very heaven.

In Leeds on that same night, one of the new victorious candidates was a young civil servant called Hugh Gaitskell. In the Lancashire market town of Ormskirk, formerly held by a reactionary Independent, another civil servant, Harold Wilson, a former Liberal who had worked for Sir William Beveridge, was elected for Labour with an astonishing majority of more than 7,000. A third of the new Parliamentary Party were sponsored by trade unions. Like their millions of supporters in the country all these men rejoiced in the fact that at last Labour had secured an impregnable parliamentary majority, and could now take part in nothing less than the complete overhaul of the British economy. In his autobiography, written many years later after he had been Prime Minister, James Callaghan recalled that one of the most inspiring thoughts of the time had come directly from the theoretical work of Tawney, Laski and Bevan. 'We would,' he wrote, 'use economics to serve the people's needs.'

The new Prime Minister was Clement Attlee; the new Foreign Secretary (appointed apparently on the strong recommendation of the American Government) was Ernest Bevin. The new Chancellor was Hugh Dalton, the new Lord President in charge of the Government's programme was Herbert Morrison. These appointments straight from the old War Cabinet were predictable. Less predictable was the promotion of two men who only six years earlier had been expelled from the Labour Party for their left-wing 'extremism', Aneurin Bevan and Stafford Cripps. Bevan was shot into the Cabinet as Minister of Housing and Health, and charged with the creation of a national health service. Cripps had been Churchill's ambassador to Russia in the early 1940s. His experiences of bureaucratic state capitalism there had dimmed his pre-war enthusiasm for Marxism. He had returned to Britain in 1942 and served briefly in Churchill's War Cabinet and later as Minister for Aircraft Production. He did not rejoin the Labour Party until early in 1945, and was returned as Labour MP for his old seat, Bristol East, almost tripling his 1935 majority. Attlee named him as the new Government's President of the Board of Trade. Did Cripps even remember those furious pamphlets and books he had written for the Socialist League in the early 1930s? Did he recall all the conditions he had set out then for immediate and drastic action to protect a new Labour Government from the counter-attack of capitalism? The basic conditions he had set down for such action were now fulfilled. Labour had achieved an impregnable parliamentary majority for an openly socialist programme (the Labour manifesto had proclaimed: 'the Labour Party is a socialist party and proud of it'). According to Cripps's own prescription in the 1930s, now, if ever, was the time for immediate emergency legislation to assert the control of the elected Government over the capitalists who controlled the economy. Now was the time to demonstrate the Government's repugnance for 'continuity of policy'. But these pre-war commitments seemed almost totally to have vanished from the mind of Stafford Cripps. As President of the Board of Trade, and later as Chancellor of the Exchequer, he devoted himself to reassuring the people of the Government's acceptability. He associated himself with slightly messianic ideas of self-sacrifice and austerity, and the only book he published during the five years he held high office was a slim volume of Christian sermons.

As for Cripps's former broadsides against continuity of policy, a rather different view was adopted by Herbert Morrison. In a memorandum to the Liberal leader Clement Davies in 1946, Morrison urged: 'We should try to maintain continuity and not set up something new and different from the past.'

For all these doubts and inhibitions, the Labour Government set about what its ministers saw as their main task with admirable speed and dispatch. All the Labour leaders, left and right, saw that their first main job was to rescue the failing industries of the nation from the greed and inefficiency of private enterprise. In the sharpest possible contrast to the prevarication and deception on the issue that followed the First World War, the new Labour ministers in several different departments eagerly set about the complicated and unprecedented business of taking into public hands several great industries. The Minister of Fuel and Power, Emmanuel Shinwell, immediately embarked on a plan to nationalize the coal industry and place it in the hands of a new national coal board. The second reading of the Bill to nationalize coal was in January 1946, just six months after the election. The Tory Opposition was stunned almost into silence by the boldness of the proposals. Even the Mining Association, representing 97 per cent of the coal-owners, could only raise a half-hearted murmur of protest, and settled for some hard bargaining on the terms of compensation. More than a hundred years of uncontrolled exploitation of British miners effectively came to an end on New Year's Day 1947, when ownership was transferred to the National Coal Board. The Board put up posters outside every pit proclaiming that the industry would now be managed 'on behalf of the people'.

The same urgency and sense of purpose ran through every department of state. In rapid succession, electricity, gas, civil aviation, cable and wireless, railways and most road haulage were nationalized. Common to all these moves were plaintive cries of muted dismay from the Tory benches. Side by side with this tremendous transfer of power came legislation to allow the trade and industry departments to redistribute and reorganize industry. The effect of this legislation on former 'distressed areas' was dramatic. The city of Dundee, for instance, was revitalized by the massive transfer of jobs and industrial activity under Labour's distribution-of-industry laws, which explicitly bucked the laws of the market. At the Ministry of National Insurance, James Griffiths led the charge to pass into law what Sir William Beveridge had proposed in 1942. The result was a system of social security and national insurance that lasted unchallenged for the rest of the century, including an Industrial Injuries Act that at last compensated workers who were maimed in the course of their work. Even the Attorney General, Sir Hartley Shawcross, whose Tory sympathies were later immortalized by a political sketch-writer renaming him Sir Shortly Floorcross, did his bit in that dawn of democratic socialism. He dispensed with the hated Trades Disputes Act of 1927, mocking the Tories' arguments that the trade unions' new powers legally to picket in solidarity with other workers in struggle was a threat to freedom.

By far the greatest achievement was that of Aneurin Bevan in facing down the opposition of doctors to his proposals for a national health service. To herald the creation of the National Health Service, the Government's Central Office issued a leaflet for mass distribution in February 1948 whose plain language reflected the spirit of the times every bit as much as those posters outside the nationalized pits:

Your new National Health Service begins on 5 July. What is it? How do you get it? It will provide you with all medical, dental and nursing care. Everyone – rich or poor, man, woman or child – can use it or any part of it. There are no charges, except for a few special items. There are no insurance qualifications. But it is not a 'charity'. You are all paying for it, mainly as taxpayers, and it will relieve your money worries in time of illness.

Thus was born, at a time of almost unrelieved national economic crisis, by far the most popular institution in Britain for the next half century and beyond.

A decade later, in *Parliamentary Socialism*, a seminal book on the history of British Labour, Ralph Miliband summed up the nationalization measures of the Labour Government as follows: 'From the beginning, the nationalization proposals of the Government were designed to achieve the sole purpose of improving the efficiency of the capitalist economy, not as marking the beginning of its wholesale transformation.' That conclusion, made in the heady days of 1960, when Miliband's book was first published, and 1973, when it was reissued, seems a little harsh. The nationalization proposals, including the planned distribution of industry and the formation of a National Health Service and a system of social security based on national insurance, carried out precisely what the Labour manifesto had promised. To this extent the democratic process was vindicated.

What about the democratization of the economic and industrial process so firmly set out by Ralph Miliband's teacher Harold Laski, by R. H. Tawney and by Aneurin Bevan before the war ended? The first answer was that the nationalizations in themselves were a huge democratic advance on the system of private enterprise they replaced. The point was made in the very first debate on coal nationalization by Emmanuel Shinwell, Minister of Fuel and Power. The new National Coal Board, he said, must 'conform to general Government policy'. The Board would be answerable to the Minister, who in turn was answerable to Parliament. This meant a great deal more than a notional responsibility. It meant, for instance, that elected ministers had to answer questions about the policy of the boards from elected MPs. In this crucial sense, it substantially democratized the industry. It brought responsibility for the affairs of a fifth of the entire economy into the arena of an elected assembly. In this crucial sense, too, all the nationalizations and social reforms of the Labour Government in the first flush of the 1945 victory seized economic power from the small groups who had previously run the industries and transferred it into the hands of boards, whose members were nominated and approved by Parliament and whose policies were, at whatever distance, subject to parliamentary scrutiny and censure. The nationalizations and the Health Service meant that the control of vast sections of the nation's industries and services were subject to the control of a democratically elected assembly. To assess this achievement, as Ralph Miliband did, solely in terms of the effects it had on capitalist efficiency seems to miss the point, and to misunderstand the deep resentment the process stirred in the minds of capitalists, old and new – a resentment that was to return with a savage vengeance when the right-wing of the Tory Party revived in strength and confidence under Margaret Thatcher 30 years later.

By the same democratic test, however, the nationalization proposals, and even the National Health Service, fell far short of the democratization that Laski and Bevan had called for in the war. The new boards were bureaucratically conceived and bureaucratically selected. Trade-union leaders featured prominently among the new directors. James Bowman,

Deputy General Secretary of the miners' union, became chairman of the National Coal Board. Lord Citrine, retired General Secretary of the TUC, was put in charge of the new British Electricity Authority. Many members of the new health boards were taken from elected local authorities. But in general the men (almost all men) put in charge of the new industries would not have been out of place on the boards of private industries and services. The thinking (if that is the right word) behind what later became known as 'Morrisonization' was best expressed not by Morrison but by the President of the Board of Trade, Sir Stafford Cripps. In a speech in October 1946, Cripps put a novel interpretation on his insistence in 1933 that a new Labour Government must devote itself to 'a complete break with what has gone before'. 'There is not yet a very large number of workers in Britain,' he lamented, 'capable of taking over large enterprises. Until there are more workers on the managerial side of industry, I think it would be almost impossible to have worker-controlled industry in Britain, even if it were on the whole desirable.'

The last eight words exposed what was really going on in Sir Stafford's mind. The science of management was basically something that could only be understood by people who had some experience of management. On the whole, those people had always been confined to what Sir Stafford in his Marxist days would have called the ruling class. Now he deduced that because there were very few workers who had been managers, it was fruitless for a new Labour Government to usher or even encourage workers into management. Such a course would not work – 'even if it were on the whole desirable'. On this analysis, shared enthusiastically by Morrison and Dalton, the change in the ownership of industry could not result in any real change in the class background of the people who traditionally ran that industry.

The second failure in the nationalization plans was the level of compensation paid out to the former owners of industry. This was accurately described by Kenneth O. Morgan as 'inconceivably generous'. The coal-owners, for instance, responsible for at least a century of exploitation, starvation and eviction in the mining areas, picked up £164 million in Government stock (equivalent in 2002 to more than £2.5 billion). This massive pay-out, repeated in the proposals for electricity, gas, cables and aviation, tipped the balance of class forces in the direction of the rich. More than any other Government measure, the compensation largesse ensured that the rich and the super-rich kept their distance from the poor during the period of the Labour Government. Indeed, some argued that the payment of such huge sums in compensation for clapped-out old stock and vulnerable industries diverted the resources of the rich into more profitable areas than they would otherwise have occupied.

Curiously, there was very little Labour opposition in any of the nationalization debates to the level of compensation shelled out. The few angry noises came mainly from the Communist MP for West Fife, William Gallacher, and supporting fellow travellers. There were other flaws in the nationalization measures that obstructed the democratization of industry. Perhaps the worst of these was the concession to hospital consultants that they could supplement their already generous payments from the NHS with fees from private practice, a concession that hobbled the NHS for all its subsequent history and in the process greatly increased the power and privilege of the rich. But the general picture in the middle of 1947, in spite of the hideous winter with which the year had started and the coal crisis that dominated it, was that the Labour Government had made huge advances into economic territory previously occupied exclusively by the rich.

Much has been made of the failure of the Tory Party to oppose Labour in any of the crucial nationalization and insurance projects of the time. But the truth is that the Conservative Party throughout that early period was a demoralized rump. Bankers, industrialists and Tories were clinging on desperately to their property, and arguing against nationalization, if at all, not on principle but over the details of compensation. The Tories were of course appalled at the prospect of the democratization of the economy, but they preserved their bile and strength for a time when they could command much wider popular support and when Labour's progress threatened the basic economic oligarchy that they represented.

That time came soon enough. Most commentators on the post-war Labour Government agree that the Government's six years in office had two distinct periods. Until the end of 1947, the new ministers were almost entirely absorbed in the nationalization and welfare Acts. When these were on the statute book, the momentum slowed. Ministers seemed to lose their conviction and their unanimity. Left-wing ministers like Bevan and Griffiths demanded more nationalization and more egalitarian measures, while other ministers, led by Morrison of the old school and Gaitskell of the new, called for a pause in the socialist advance and a period of 'consolidation'. These arguments between socialists and consolidators broke out all over the place – in Parliament, where the Tories started to regain their confidence; in the ministries, where the 'consolidators' were cheered on by the civil servants; and in the Labour Party National Executive, where the debates raged about the nationalization of iron and steel, which had been in the Labour Party manifesto, and the nationalization of the insurance companies, which had not. James Griffiths, the Minister for National Insurance, argued persuasively that the private insurance companies controlled economic resources far in excess of what was tolerable in an age when social security for all was a national priority, and that this power could be used to the benefit of all citizens, especially the elderly, if the insurance companies were nationalized. If he had lived through the 1980s and 1990s, he could have added that publicly owned and controlled insurance companies would never have tolerated the staggering corruption of the private-pension misselling scandals of those years. Indeed, if the insurance companies had been nationalized by the first majority Labour Government, the very notion of a private pension, dependent on the rise and fall of the stock exchange, might have been expunged for ever, and the crucial subject of security in old age might have been confined to the provision of a proper and generous state pension.

In those long and furious arguments on the executive through 1948, Griffiths had the constant support of Aneurin Bevan. Recalling one walk back in the dark from the executive meeting in Smith Square to the House of Commons, a new member of the executive, Michael Foot, recalled Bevan's impatience with this apparently perpetual argument. ' "It is a form of torture unknown to the ancients," he would say, "to be compelled on the last Wednesday of every month to convert the leaders of the Labour Party afresh to the most elementary principles of the Party; to be compelled to fight every inch of the way to recapture territory occupied by Beveridge." ' At meeting after meeting, however, Morrison, backed by Hugh Dalton, warned that the nationalization of the insurance companies might lose the votes of thousands of agents paid by the companies who had direct access to workers' homes. More than once, the left won this argument on the executive, and the proposal to nationalize the insurance companies went to the Labour Party conference in 1949, where it was accepted. Yet it was never promoted to Government policy and never formed part of an election manifesto. The proposals were watered down into a compromise that infuriated the insurance companies without taking their huge power for Parliament or the people. The proposal to nationalize iron and steel, a long-standing Labour commitment, was converted into a modest Steel Bill. The date for enacting this Bill was postponed again and again, and was eventually fixed for after the next election, due (at the latest) in July 1950.

The Steel Bill was fought with the most relentless determination by the iron and steel masters. They refused to take part in any of the Government's plans for a gradual takeover of their economic power, boycotting the interim organizations set up by the elected Government, and engaging in a virulent propaganda campaign in the country against what they called the 'confiscation' of a profitable and efficient industry. The same arguments were used, even more ferociously, by the Tory family in charge of Tate & Lyle, the sugar conglomerate threatened by Labour's tentative proposal to nationalize sugar. During this widespread and eventually successful campaign, a heroic 'Mr Cube' supported by the popular, but unelected, broadcaster Richard Dimbleby, threw down his challenge to the elected Government.

A document produced by Labour's National Executive Policy Committee in November 1947, right at the hinge of the Government's turn to consolidation, called for a new round of nationalizations to supplement and strengthen the round so successfully accomplished. The chairman of the committee, Herbert Morrison, was appalled by the proposals. Borrowing arguments directly from the Tory newspapers, he told his colleagues, 'We definitely do not want to nationalize the small man, the shop round the corner . . . we must take care not to muck about with private enterprise merely for the purpose of being spiteful.' The committee's proposals, however, made no reference to the small man or the corner shop. They were not motivated by spite. They argued for democratic control of irresponsible and unaccountable monopolies such as Tate & Lyle, the Prudential and ICI. But Morrison and the trade-union representatives won the argument and from then on Labour proceeded much more cautiously.

The new caution was not inspired simply by a desire among Labour's moderates to 'go easy' on proposals that might unleash controversy at the next general election. There were other extra-parliamentary factors that harked back to the warnings of Sir Stafford Cripps and the Socialist League in the 1930s. In his book on the period, *Labour in Power* (1984), Kenneth O. Morgan dismisses the claim that what he calls 'the supposedly hostile constitutional structure' can in any way be blamed for the failures of the Labour Government. He recalls with some derision the view of Labour theorists in the 1930s 'that the system itself – the monarchy, the House of Lords, the civil service, the City and attendant capitalist institutions, the sources of information and communication – were hopelessly biased against a Labour Government'. He shows that throughout that post-war Government, the monarchy stood aside, the House of Lords was called into effective opposition only once (on the Steel Bill, as a result of which its delaying powers were heavily restricted), and the civil service remained effectively neutral. But what of 'the City and its attendant capitalist institutions'? Paradoxically, Morgan's account gives more than a glimpse of how the extra-parliamentary power of money and wealth played havoc with the Labour Government, especially in the year of the turn, 1947, and in the run-up to the devaluation of sterling in 1949.

An economic crisis was caused in August 1947 by the earlier decision of the Labour Government to make sterling 'convertible' into dollars from that date, in exchange for a hefty loan from the United States. The result was, Morgan reported, 'a tidal wave of selling' and 'a huge outflow of capital'. The Cabinet, according to Morgan, was 'brought to its knees' and 'the strength and virility of the Labour Government fled, never to return'. The same picture was painted in the other outstanding history of the period, *Never Again!* (1992) by Peter Hennessy. After describing a dithering Prime Minister, a drunk Foreign Secretary and a distraught Chancellor, Hennessy concluded: 'The Cabinet had no real idea what to do as the gales of the world economy roared in through the door opened by the restoration of convertibility.'

What had happened? The currency traders, who between them had very few votes, started gambling by exchanging sterling for dollars, as they were entitled to do under an agreement signed by Labour ministers in the months after the war. The result was a drain on sterling reserves unimaginable by the most pessimistic Cabinet minister. The drain went on and on, through all that summer. There was only one way the torrent of sterling out of Britain could be staunched – by the suspension of convertibility. At the last moment, as a desperate Dalton grovelled at its feet, the American Government agreed to suspend the conditions they had imposed. In September, the President of the Board of Trade, Harold Wilson, who, at 31, had only just been appointed as the youngest Cabinet minister to take such office since universal suffrage, sent a note to Dalton outlining another reason for the crisis. Speculators, he observed, had spent the whole crisis feverishly betting against the value of sterling and in the process causing untold damage to the British economy. This was the first inkling Wilson had of the menace of currency speculators, later dubbed the gnomes of Zurich, who wreaked such havoc on the Labour Governments he later led.

The convertibility crisis taught the Labour ministers a grim lesson about the unseen market forces that could, when least expected, change the course of elected politicians. Almost exactly the same thing happened two years later, in 1949, when the same manic selling of sterling forced the Government, against the inclination of Attlee, Cripps and Bevin, to devalue the pound. The devaluation, ardently supported by Hugh Gaitskell and Douglas Jay, economic secretary to the Treasury, seems to have worked as the British economy regained its momentum in late 1949. But the truth, as

Kenneth O. Morgan discerned, was that 'the revival owed a great deal to quite extraneous factors' such as the health of the US economy.

A combination of these 'extraneous factors' and the Labour ministers' own lack of purpose and direction threw the Government into a quite different posture to that adopted by the confident expropriators of 1945 and 1946. One of the sharpest about-turns was performed by Hugh Dalton. Soon after taking office, he had scoffed at those who suggested that extra-parliamentary forces of capitalism could or would deflect him from his socialist aims. 'Make me Chancellor of the Exchequer,' he had demanded, 'and give me a good Labour majority in Parliament and I will undertake the nationalization of the Bank of England over a dinner party.' He was duly made Chancellor of the Exchequer. A dinner party was not necessary. A cup of tea with Lord Catto, the Bank's Governor, was enough to get the Bank of England nationalized in 1945. But in June 1949, in the devaluation crisis, Dalton's diary departed from its normal arrogant tone:

Very serious dollar situation. Gap widening and reserves running down . . . Cripps says that the danger is that within twelve months all our reserves will be gone. This time there is nothing behind them and there might be a complete collapse of sterling. We meet again in the afternoon, without officials. Cripps gets authority to stop all purchases of gold and dollars . . . As we go out, Addison says, '1931 all over again.' I say, 'It reminds me awfully of 1947. Will we ever be free?'

Slowly, but more and more resolutely, the Labour ministers followed the advice constantly offered them by the newspapers to dismantle their own economic controls. On 5 November 1949, to celebrate Guy Fawkes Day, Board of Trade President Harold Wilson lit a 'bonfire of controls' and wiped out a lot of mainly petty wartime restrictions over industry and commerce. No one mourned most of these controls, but the political point of the bonfire seemed to be that all controls were increasingly irrelevant, and that the Government was removing them. The chief effect was to raise the confidence of the rich, who now felt that the worst of Labour was over. Harold Wilson basked in the praise of Tory MPs, and started to believe that his own political aims were not very different from theirs. He prided himself as a champion of both public and private enterprise. Sir William Darling, Tory MP for Edinburgh South, asked him in April 1949: 'Is it the view of the Right Hon. gentleman that the more socialism there is in this country, the more successful private enterprise will be?' Wilson replied: 'On the limited experience of the last few years that is certainly so.'

There were plenty of other examples of the reactionary drift of the Government after the first fine careless rapture of 1945 and 1946. Bruised and perplexed by the two flights of sterling in 1947 and 1949, confused by the split between the majority of ministers who were scared to move further forward and the small but powerful minority who insisted that they must, the Government became increasingly susceptible to the calls to stand still and 'consolidate'.

The Tawneyite slogans were still there of course, to be flourished in policy statements. In April 1949, the Labour Party issued a 'statement on policy' for discussion at that year's party conference. The opening section, entitled 'Our Socialist Faith', set out four 'basic principles'. The first three were 'to abolish extremes of wealth and poverty', 'to place economic power in the hands of the nation' and 'to enlarge the productive power of the nation, to banish mass unemployment and to raise the standard of life of the people'. The section went on: 'Fourth, we believe that only by creating a flourishing and sensible democracy, as virile in industry as in the council chamber and Parliament, can we enhance human dignity and individual freedom.' This fourth basic principle was proof that the theoretical teachings of Tawney, Laski and Bevan were still influential at Labour Party headquarters, though the document itself was singularly silent on the means by which this virile democracy was to be established. It was still an idealistic aspiration, while practical policy was all about consolidation.

Consolidation meant that in many areas where Labour backbenchers and supporters in the constituencies had hoped for reform there was no reform at all. The public schools, a quaint name for schools from which children of the public are resolutely banned, were left untouched, as was the division of state secondary schools into grammar schools for the sheep and secondary modern schools for the goats. As the wartime prophet of a new socialist dawn, J. B. Priestley, remarked, the Government's commitment to civil liberties and criminal justice did not even rise to an attempt to abolish capital punishment. One of the most shocking miscarriages of justice in British history – the conviction in 1950 of the young semi-literate Welshman Timothy Evans for the murder of his wife and child – took place under the Labour Government, and when Evans was sentenced to death by hanging, Labour's Home Secretary Chuter Ede refused to commute the sentence. In foreign affairs, Government policy under Ernest Bevin seldom differed from that of the Tories. With the single and monumental exception of independence for India, ministers followed the path set down by Herbert Morrison when he proclaimed his faith in 'the jolly old empire'. In two important areas in that empire, Labour supervised partitions of old colonies that resulted in the retrenchment of deeply reactionary and privileged minorities. In Palestine, Labour favoured the Zionists, who won affectionate approval especially from the left of the Party.

In Northern Ireland, Labour reinforced the 'Protestant Parliament for a Protestant State' proclaimed by Sir James Craig, later Lord Craigavon, the bigoted Orangeman who became Northern Ireland's first Prime Minister. Labour's Ireland Act (1949) established a separate Protestant state in the gerrymandered six counties of the North in perpetuity, in spite of a mass revolt on the Labour benches and the sacking by Attlee of four parliamentary private secretaries. The vote on Ireland was one of the few revolts organized by Labour's left wing after the consolidation of 1947–8. The brunt of left-wing opposition to Government policy on foreign affairs was carried by the small clutch of fellow travellers who adopted a basic position that any policy pursued by Stalinist Russia had to be defended against any policy pursued by the West – a position so transparently indefensible that it could not be sustained. Among the persistent fellow travellers were three distinguished barristers: D. N. Pritt, Independent Labour MP for Hammersmith North, who beat the Labour candidate in 1945; John Platts-Mills, Labour MP for Finsbury; and Leslie Solley, Labour MP for Thurrock. All three made no secret of their Communist sympathies and were eventually kicked out of the Parliamentary Party. In spite of their steadfast defence of civil liberties in their court cases, their enthusiasm for Stalin's Russia was greater than their enthusiasm for democracy. They represented a curious phenomenon of left-wing politics in the post-war period. The National Council of Civil Liberties, founded in 1934, became increasingly controlled by members of the Communist Party politically devoted to Stalin's Russia, in which there were no civil liberties of any description.

A further sign of the drift to the right caused by the paralysis of consolidation was the reaction of the Government to unofficial strikes, especially in the docks. The Transport and General Workers' Union, still under the influence of Ernest Bevin, was almost wholly absorbed in the politics and priorities of the Government. The problems of sections of workers, who had previously looked to the union in times of trouble, were left almost entirely to a new group of unofficial leaders and militants, many of whom were Communists. In the spring of 1948, and again a year later in 1949, a rash of unofficial strikes paralysed the London docks. The Government responded by invoking the hated Emergency Powers Act rushed through Parliament in the darkest days of the Lloyd George Coalition after the First World War. Prime Minister Attlee broadcast to the nation about the emergency caused by the strikes, and the Government, including left-wing ministers like Aneurin Bevan, went to war on the strikers, denouncing them as Communists and threatening them with prosecution for sedition.

In the previous decade, Sir Stafford Cripps and his colleagues in the Socialist League had urged the next Labour Government to resort to emergency powers legislation to stave off a counter-attack from capitalism. Instead, the Labour Government, spurred on by their new Chancellor of the Exchequer, Sir Stafford Cripps, resorted to the Emergency Powers Act passed (in the teeth of intense Labour protest) by the Lloyd George Coalition Government in 1920. Troops were moved in to break the strikes, and Government-backed strike-breaking continued until the strikes were defeated. The lash of Government propaganda flayed the striking dockers as Communists. Some of them were Communists, but the real problem was the bureaucratic nature of the National Dock Labour Scheme, always remote from the dockers' very real grievances, especially over the absurd amount of overtime they were expected to work. The dockers' rank-and-file organizations may have been led by Communists but, unlike the bureaucrats on the Dock Labour Board or the union leaders, the strike leaders were all elected and responsible to meetings and decisions of the strikers.

The knee-jerk reaction of the entire Labour Government, cheered on by the Tories, to lambast the strikers and to encourage the breaking of the strikes by troops was perhaps the most visible sign of the widening gap between the Government and the rank-and-file workers' democracy that senior ministers like Cripps and Bevan had in the past so staunchly defended. However, the level of industrial disputes was of a quite different dimension from the turbulent years after the First World War. In 1946, 2,158,000 working days were 'lost' in strikes, compared with 34,969,000 in 1919, and for the first five years after the Second World War, 9.7 million days were lost in strikes compared with 178 million in the five years after 1918. In 1950, the last full year of the Labour Government, there were fewer days lost in strikes than in any year after the war. The overall picture was one not of industrial conflict but of industrial peace. This was reflected in the even more remarkable figures for the percentage of workers who were unemployed, never more than 1.7 per cent during the whole period and as low as 1.1 per cent in 1951.

Despite the doubt, drift and uncertainty of the Labour Government during consolidation, the electorate responded to the Government with enduring solidarity. In the entire period from 1945 to 1951, Labour lost only one by-election, and that was a hybrid affair at Glasgow, Camlachie, in January 1948, where the result was confused by an ILP candidate. In almost all the other by-elections, the closer the contest was, the larger the

Labour vote. This good news for the Government was, however, tempered by what was happening to the Opposition vote. The by-elections consistently showed a steep decline in the Liberal vote, and in most cases a consequent increase in support for the Tories.

Sensing that the Government had run out of steam, several ministers pressed for an election in 1949. For reasons never made clear, Attlee ducked the more convenient date of October 1949 and chose instead to dissolve Parliament as soon as MPs returned from their Christmas holidays. This meant that the election was held in the unfavourable month of February 1950, in midwinter. The result for Labour was far from disappointing, and very far from the meltdown in Labour support many MPs had been expecting. Instead, after the highest turn-out in British electoral history – 83.9 per cent, compared to 72. 6 per cent in 1945 – the Labour vote soared, from 11,967,746 to 13,266,176. The Tory vote rose even faster – from 9,972,010 to 12,492,404. The only loser was the Liberal Party. They fielded 475 candidates who managed to get less than half a million votes more (and 3 fewer MPs) than the 306 candidates who stood in 1945. Undoubtedly, the Liberal collapse aided the Tories. But the Tory advance was far bigger than the Liberal decline. Labour had every reason to be satisfied with the results. The working-class vote responded magnificently to the huge advances into territories previously regarded as the exclusive preserve of private enterprise, but the collapse of the centre and the revival of the Tory Party left Labour with only a slender majority in the House of Commons – seventeen over the Tories and only five overall.

Within a few months of the new Government taking office, two of its most senior ministers, Cripps and Bevin, were dead. Nye Bevan was transferred to the Ministry of Labour, later described as the bed of nails. Harold Wilson stayed at the Board of Trade while Hugh Gaitskell, the articulate right-wing Member for Leeds South, took over at the Treasury. At once, Gaitskell and the Government were plunged into another crisis not of their own making – in far-off Korea. Communist-controlled North Korea invaded South Korea, an ally of the capitalist West, and the United States eagerly leaped into the fray. The US looked to their old ally Britain for economic and military aid in the Korean War. Both were readily forthcoming. Gaitskell in particular, then and for the rest of his career, proved a doughty supporter of the United States Government. He drew up a stiff budget to meet the demands of rearmament, asking for £4,700 million – an enormous sum at that time – much of which would have to come out of other Labour plans for public spending. Included in his list of cuts was a proposal to levy charges on false teeth and spectacles, until then provided free by the NHS. The proposals led to furious protests from Aneurin Bevan, and an irreconcilable split between him and Gaitskell. In April 1951, Bevan resigned in protest at the charges, and was joined by Harold Wilson and a junior minister, John Freeman.

The resignations came at a most damaging time for the Labour Government. Though ministers were able to complete the nationalization of iron and steel, they fell back from almost every other possible socialist advance. Their foreign policy, under the new Foreign Secretary, Herbert Morrison, became even more committed to the 'jolly old empire' than it had been under Bevin. Gaitskell's resolute commitment to the £4,700 million for rearmament hamstrung the administration, which stumbled on to what they and everyone else regarded as almost certain defeat in the election, finally designated for October 1951. The only people who seemed reluctant to accept a Labour defeat and a Tory victory were the electors. The most astonishing figure from that 1951 election was the Labour vote – which was up again from 13,266,176 to 13,948,883. This was 48.8 per cent of the total vote, the highest ever achieved by the Labour Party. The Tories also increased their vote, but got a quarter of a million fewer votes than Labour. They were able to form a Government because of an uneven balance of votes, very heavy in the Labour industrial constituencies of the North, not so heavy in the South and Midlands. Now the Tories had a majority of 17 in the House of Commons, but as the new Prime Minister Churchill made clear more than once in his first few months in the House of Commons, the Tories were still shattered by the strength and power of the Labour vote and to some extent continued to be influenced by it all through their 13 years of office.

The continued loyalty to Labour of such a large slice of the electorate from 1945 to 1951 and in all three general elections of the period, taken together with the sustained interest and vigour with which people voted, the growth of Labour Party membership and the effectiveness of Labour's election machine, were all a tribute to the democratic achievements of the Labour Government, chief among which were the nationalizations, including national health and national insurance. Even after all the Government's reactionary policies in foreign affairs are taken into account, no one can deny the huge democratic strides that Labour took in that post-war Government, nor the handsome way in which those advances were defended at the polls by so many millions.

But that is only part of the story, rather a small part. The real picture of Britain under that first majority Labour Government emerges only after applying what may be called the Tawney test. Tawney had emphasized the instability of parliamentary democracy as long as that democracy applied only to the vote at election times and did not extend into the economy. He updated that analysis in later editions of *Equality* and in a chapter entitled 'Social Democracy in Britain' in an American compendium, *The Christian Demand for Social Justice* (1949): 'Democracy is unstable as a political system as it remains a political system and little more, instead of producing, as it should, its own type of society and a manner of life in harmony with that type.' This was, almost word for word, a quotation from the latest rewritten version of his masterpiece, *Equality*. It did not include the passage from *Equality* that followed directly on the above, and explained it:

To make it that type of society requires an advance along two lines. It involves, in the first place, the resolute elimination of all forms of special privilege which favour some groups and depress others, whether their sources be differences of environment, of education, or of pecuniary income. It involves, in the second place, the conversion of economic power, now often an irresponsible tyrant, into a servant of society . . .

The shift in emphasis in the reprinted essay conveniently stripped the principle – economic democracy rather than simply political democracy – of the practical proposals that gave it force. It also made it easier to judge the impact of the Labour Government's measures against the test: did it create an economic democracy?

In general, Tawney himself seemed at least partly satisfied with the effect of those measures. He argued that the nationalizations and social service reforms had provided some stability for the British people. They had for instance stabilized employment, stabilized investment and improved the quality of British democracy. 'Popularly elected chambers began to prescribe minimum standards of life and work.' On the other hand, there was much more work to be done to achieve anything like the socialist commonwealth he aspired to – 'four-fifths of private industry were still in private hands' and the balance of power still favoured the capitalist. In a later essay, 'British Socialism Today', published in *Socialist Commentary* in June 1952, Tawney expressed his general satisfaction with the record of the post-war Labour Government, but concluded: 'If a socialist Government means business – if it intends to create an economic system socialist all through, and not merely at the top – then it must take the initiative, force the pace.' He was pleased but not satisfied. He died before 1964, the year Labour was next elected with a majority.

The Tawney test seemed to have been partially and temporarily passed by the post-war Labour Government. A more detailed analysis of the same test came in a book published in 1955 and written by an American socialist and academic, Arnold Rogow, aided by Peter Shore, later a Labour MP and secretary of state. *The Labour Government and British Industry*, still the best and fairest assessment of the achievements and limitations of that historic post-war Labour Government, exposes the weaknesses that the Government could not overcome and left behind.

To start with, there was never any coherent overall plan for industry. There was a substantial increase in exports, but the direction of those exports was never planned, so they went wherever their capitalist exporters wanted. In spite of all the financial controls, there were no controls of the 'hot money' which left the country in search of less controlled markets abroad. Of the £645 million that left the country in the six years of Labour government, £350 million was 'hot money' that went into areas that were not even known to ministers. At home, Rogow and Shore concluded, 'the shape of the economy, the decisions as to the quantity and kind of industrial output required' was 'left substantially to market forces'.

The atmosphere of planlessness, moreover, was increased by the 'air of surprise and the evidence of unpreparedness with which each successive crisis was greeted'. Though the nationalizations undoubtedly did represent a shift in power, the personnel who took over the new enterprises 'were extensively drawn from the ranks of private industry. Only 9 of the 47 board members of the new nationalized industries came from the trade unions, and all nine were full-time officials. To that extent the democratization of industry by public ownership was weakened by surrendering control of the industries to the same sort of people from whom it had been taken.' In the same way, the authors assess the impact of the Government's efforts to narrow the gap between rich and poor. On the one hand, Labour measures ensured that the gap certainly did not increase. Stern taxes on big incomes (up to 19 shillings and 6 pence in the pound (20 shillings) for even the mildly rich, restricting everyone to an income of not more than £6,000 a year) cut down the ostensible flaunting of great wealth, but on the other hand, these taxes were seriously sabotaged by compensation following nationalization, by all sorts of hidden practices to avoid taxation and the total lack of any capital gains tax. In the same way, Labour's Monopolies Act (1948), designed to stop restrictive practices and price-fixing among industrialists, turned out to be a completely futile measure. Indeed, only two orders were made against employers under the Act, both utterly impotent.

Rogow and Shore appreciated, as did the employers at the time, that the real battle of the post-war Labour Government was about economic control. 'The control of industry gave crucial power over the economy to the

Government' and was therefore bitterly resisted by the employers, by their newspapers and by the Tory Party. This resistance, weak and fumbling in 1945 and 1946, grew in vigour and intensity after 1947: 'There was a determined struggle for power in industry.' The central battlefield for this struggle was selected by the employers in the iron and steel industry, who could not for a moment countenance the nationalization of steel, even after it was declared by the elected Government as their policy. The employers used every conceivable tactic to frustrate the measure. In the face of the massive anti-nationalization campaign by Lord Lyle and his family, the Government, Rogow and Shore observed, were 'silent and powerless'. Even the harmless policy of encouraging development councils representing both sides of industry – a policy initially welcomed by the employers – suddenly became evidence of the Government's determination to 'grab' all private industry. Harold Wilson, who had presided so proudly over the early development councils, was shocked to the core. 'I was more than a little surprised,' he wrote later, 'at the sudden hostility which blew up. A hostility which in some way became infectious covered a number of industries which had previously accepted or supported the idea of development councils, and now turned against it.' He did not realize that what was happening was a surge of confidence in a class of people whose wealth and power no longer seemed as threatened as it did in 1945. In the new atmosphere, what Wilson later called 'ancestral voices' were raised with greater stridency, and any cooperation between Government and industry now had to be opposed as backdoor nationalization and confiscation. In all this, Rogow and Shore noticed, the Government 'hesitated and temporized'. Steel nationalization was put off until after the election, and the Labour manifestos in 1950 and 1951 proposed that less than 3 per cent of the economy should be taken over by the Government. 'The limits of planning,' the authors warned, 'were determined by the power interests of affected groups.' A future Labour Government 'will have to overcome industrial opposition' and 'unless a way is found to vote socialists as well as socialism into office political change in Britain and elsewhere will continue to lose much of its significance'. In general, Rogow and Shore concluded that the Government, in spite of its advances and in spite of its continuing support from the electorate, had failed the Tawney test.

Perhaps the sharpest assessment of the 1945–51 Labour Government came from its most successful secretary of state, Aneurin Bevan. His book, *In Place of Fear*, written with the help of his wife, Jennie Lee, appeared a few months after the 1951 election. It went into several editions in many languages and was as widely read as it was vilified in reactionary newspapers. Its theme was the 'unbridgeable antagonism between private wealth, poverty and political democracy'. The function of political democracy was 'to expose wealth-privilege to the attack of the people. It is a sword pointed at the heart of property-power.' In this endeavour, the greatest enemy of socialist democracy was a failure to understand the ongoing battle between property and democracy: 'Either poverty will use democracy to win the struggle against property, or property, in fear of poverty, will destroy democracy.' Turn aside from that central struggle, Bevan warned, and 'our political vitality is sucked away, and we stumble from one situation to another, without chart, without compass and with the steering wheel lashed to a course we are no longer following'. Without the clear guide to action presented by a clear objective, the Labour Party faced a future dominated by the 'most dangerous of all' predicaments for a progressive party – 'responsibility without power'. A refusal to grapple with the vast power of private property led to 'helplessness in face of economic difficulties', which in turn corroded not just socialist ideas but parliamentary democracy itself. The reason was simple: 'People have no use for an institution which pretends to supreme power but does not use it.' The role of socialist ministers 'is reduced to that of public mourner for private economic crimes'. The conclusion was unequivocal: 'Political freedom must arm itself with economic power.' If Parliament didn't exert its power over the economy, then the private interests that wielded economic power would 'leave Parliament with responsibility and property with power'. So 'to the socialist, parliamentary power is to be used progressively until the mainstreams of economic activity are brought under public direction'.

Those who bought and read *In Place of Fear* might have expected an account of the achievements and failures of the Labour Government. Far more important to Bevan, however, was the reassertion of the fundamental aim of Labour in Parliament, namely to seize for democracy the economic power wielded by a wealthy hierarchy. That objective far outsoared any 'practical proposal' to nationalize this or that industry. Labour, he wrote, 'did not learn' this crucial lesson. The 'economic adventurers have been curbed and controlled', but they still held sway over the huge majority of the country's economic interests. They still made decisions about the disposal of most of the surplus created by British workers, and as a result the British people were 'disfranchised at the very onset'.

Perhaps recalling Tawney's warnings about the instability of parliamentary democracy presiding over an economy dominated by private enterprise, Bevan turned his fire on the Labour leaders. In spite of all the Labour Government's achievements, he concluded:

Judged from any angle, the relations between public and private enterprise have not yet reached a condition where they can be stabilized. That is why it is so foolish for certain Labour men to preach 'consolidation' at this stage. Before we can dream of consolidation, the power relations of public and private property must be drastically altered. The solutions of the problems I have been discussing cannot be approached until it becomes possible to create a purposive and intelligible design for society. This cannot be done until effective social and economic power passes from one order of society to another. At the moment we are between two worlds. We have lost the propulsion of one and we have not yet gained the forward thrust of the other. This is no place in which to halt.

No wonder the 'consolidators', the Gaitskells and the Morrisons and their acolytes among younger and even more ambitious Labour MPs detested Bevan's book and the intellectual influence it wielded on so many Labour supporters. No wonder that they devoted so much of their energies in the Tory years that followed to ensuring that the Labour leaders halted between the two worlds and then made a determined effort to retreat to the one they had once set out to change.

Unstable Compound 1: 1951–70

That democracy and extreme economic inequality form, when combined, an unstable compound, is no novel doctrine. It was a commonplace of political science four centuries before our era. Nevertheless, though a venerable truism, it remains an important one, which is periodically forgotten and periodically therefore requires to be rediscovered . . .

R. H. Tawney, *Equality* (1938 edition)

The Tory Party held office for 13 years after their narrow victory in the 1951 election. Under two new leaders, Anthony Eden and Harold Macmillan, they won the general election of 1955 with an overall majority of 60 and in 1959 with a majority of 100. The Liberal Party won six seats in each election, though the Party doubled its share of the poll in 1959. Though the Labour Party lost both elections, the Labour vote stayed high. There were 12,405,254 Labour voters in 1955 and 12,216,172 in 1959.

Despite their majorities, the Tory ministers never lost sight of the huge Labour vote. Churchill himself constantly expressed dismay at the looming Labour electoral menace. With the single exception of steel, which was privatized in 1954, the Tories did not restore to private enterprise the industries and services nationalized by Labour. Labour's blueprint for the nationalized industries was studiously copied. Indeed, when a vacancy occurred at the head of the National Coal Board in 1960, the Tories persuaded Alf Robens, a prominent Labour frontbencher, to take the chairmanship, and a peerage to match. The National Health Service and the system of national insurance ushered in by Labour were left intact. There were no new NHS prescription charges, for instance, until 1960 – and even then the basic charge was only a shilling (5p).

The Tories' determination not to rock the boat was assisted, if not inspired, by a period of peacetime prosperity never before experienced in

Britain. Never more than 3 per cent of the population were unemployed. One result was that trade unions flourished. A new breed of militant, especially in the burgeoning car industry, grew more confident and more impatient. Strikes proliferated. The workers were neither passive nor content. The divisions in society, the huge gap between the rich on the one hand and the workers, the pensioners and the poor on the other, became more, not less apparent in what became known as the age of the affluent society.

The effect of the electoral defeats on the Labour Party was devastating, but not catastrophic. Labour support remained high, and could be mobilized. In his voluminous diaries for the period, Coventry Labour MP Dick Crossman wrote often of the rank-and-file meetings he attended in the East Midlands, packed with young trade unionists and shop stewards, all of them on the left. In 1956, when British forces were sent in to assist the capture of the Suez Canal from the Egyptian Government, the Tories were forced to retreat, at least in part by the massed ranks of the Labour Party rank and file, who demonstrated under the banner 'Law not War'.

As Crossman's diaries also make clear, in the first period of opposition, the Labour leaders were locked in almost permanent conflict with each other. In the red corner was the towering figure of Aneurin Bevan, who continued to demand that Labour pursue more public ownership. 'Now that we are once again engaged in policy-making,' he wrote in *Tribune* in June 1952, 'it is essential that we should keep clear before us that one of the central principles of socialism is the substitution of public for private ownership.' In the pink corner were most of the other Labour leaders, supported by a majority of Labour's National Executive and Parliamentary Party. They spent most of the 13 years seeking a way round this 'central principle'. They blamed Labour's losses on what they regarded as the 'dogma' of public ownership. They regarded that dogma as a millstone dragging Labour to defeat. It would continue to do so, they moaned, unless Labour learned to live more contentedly with the predominantly private enterprise economy, and shaped their policies to that effect.

The leader of this faction was Hugh Gaitskell, who, as Chancellor of the Exchequer in 1951, had insisted on the reckless rearmament programme to bolster the war in Korea and had imposed charges on the free National Health Service. Gaitskell's 1951 budget had driven Nye Bevan out of the Labour Government and the argument between the two men continued for the best part of the 1950s. Gaitskell was elected Labour leader in 1955, with more than twice as many MPs' votes as Bevan. Eventually the two formally made up their quarrel in time for the 1959 election. But Bevan could see the slow disintegration of Labour's commitment to public owner-ship and economic democracy, the main sign of which was the contempt which Gaitskell and his acolytes showed for democracy within the Labour Party, whether in or out of Parliament. The process of argument and discussion that was so vital to the health of the Labour Party was restricted by rigid parliamentary rules, enforced by the diktat and intrigue of the Party leadership. Thus, for instance, the group calling itself the Bevanites in the Parliamentary Labour Party was, after two years, denounced as 'a party within a party' and banned. The Gaitskell leadership was bitterly opposed by the rank and file in the constituencies and their elected represen-tatives to the National Executive. The Gaitskell faction always triumphed, thanks to the support of the trade-union leaders and their block votes at conference. Yet when some trade-union leaders broke ranks, and helped the constituencies to a historic victory on the issue of unilateral nuclear disarmament in 1960, the Gaitskell faction promptly organized a campaign to reverse the vote – a campaign which was formalized and even named, the Campaign for Democratic Socialism, and which was a more active and relentless party within the party than anything the Bevanites ever attempted.

Aneurin Bevan died of stomach cancer in July 1960, but the diaries kept by the journalist Geoffrey Goodman show Bevan's depression at the course the Party was taking under Gaitskell's leadership. 'I am heartily sickened by the Parliamentary Labour Party,' Goodman records him saying. 'It is rotten through and through, corrupt, full of patronage and seeking after patronage, unprincipled . . . it isn't really a socialist party at all.'

Richard Crossman's diaries throughout the 1950s are obsessed with the battle between the Gaitskellites and the Bevanites. Crossman started the decade as a Bevanite, later became a Gaitskellite and then, as he observed the disaster of Gaitskell's leadership, swung back again. He was a brilliant propagandist. His articles and especially his speeches were laced with an irresistible satirical wit, but his diaries reflect very little ideological commit-ment. The possibility of a clash between representative democracy and economic oligarchy did not seem to interest him at all. The same lack of interest in ideology was a feature of the rest of the Bevanite left. Though *Tribune* continued to be published, there was no major work at the time to spell out the meaning of socialism or to argue about its relevance to the future of democracy.

The ideological field was taken over by two books, both published in 1956 and reprinted many times thereafter. The first was John Strachey's *Contemporary Capitalism*. We left John Strachey back in 1940 as he was rapidly retreating from a decade of hardline Communist propaganda. In opposition after 1951, he flitted from left to right, unable to reconcile his admiration for Bevan with his instinctive support for Gaitskell. The certainty and clarity of his ideas in his Communist youth were replaced by uncertainty and vacillation. All that remained of his former self was his writing style. The course and destination of his ideological journey from left to right was set out in *Contemporary Capitalism*.

In the 1930s, it had seemed to Strachey, capitalism was doomed. Only a revolution could establish a society tolerable to the masses of the people. In the 1950s, capitalism boomed. Fewer and fewer people in Britain could be said to be suffering from it. It followed, he deduced, that capitalism was entering a new stage, which he dubbed the 'last phase', since it seemed certain to him that the next phase would be unrecognizable as capitalism. What had brought about this momentous change in society? The answer, he thought, was plain – parliamentary democracy. It was true, he reflected, that fully fledged universal suffrage had been part of the political scene for only 37 years or so, and even more true (as he forgot to mention) that the desperate capitalist crisis he analysed so brilliantly in the 1930s had taken place against a background of universal suffrage. But still, he argued, in 1955 capitalism had been tamed by democracy. The democratic pressures of the voting system, bolstered by the freedoms of speech, opinion and association, played so vital a role in capitalist society that it 'goes far to determine who shall be rich and who shall be poor'. The institutions of democracy, among which he included fully legalized trade unions, 'if they work effectively, create an all-pervading climate of opinion which has profound economic consequences. It is as if this almost indefinable social category, modern democracy, had leant its soft weight upon the economic system and gradually bent it into a new shape.'

The influence of his Marxist youth, however, was not entirely lost on the mature Strachey. He had seen and learned enough to realize the strength and resilience of capitalism, even in its so-called last stage. He could see the new power and influence of what he called the 'oligopolies', the massive concentrations of economic power forming in the western world. He could detect the growth and corrupting influence of unearned income among the capitalists and their camp followers – a development which disgusted him and which he described as 'moral poison'.

And so he identified the central battle of the time – the battle between the irresponsible greed of capitalism and the collective responsibility of democracy. In a fascinating passage, he concluded:

The main trends in the political and economic fields are running in opposite directions. The extension of the franchise and its increasingly effective use, the consolidation of trade unionism, have diffused political power through the major last-stage capitalisms to a varying but significant degree. But in the same decades economic power has been steadily concentrated into the hands of the major oligopolies. Such contradictory trends can hardly coexist indefinitely. One must overcome and absorb the other.

Strachey warned against what he called 'social democratic complacency'. On all sides he could see 'the attempt on the part of capital, highly organized and integrated in the oligopolies, to manipulate and distort, and if necessary frustrate the workings of contemporary democracy to its own advantage'. As one example he cited the weaknesses of the 1945–51 Labour Government as portrayed in Arnold Rogow's book. As another, he noticed the growth of the banks, once 'a humble handmaid of industrial production', into a 'mighty engine of control capable, if acting in step with the State, of modifying the whole economic climate'.

He likened the tussle between democracy and capitalism to a tug of war, and warned Labour supporters against any complacency that they were bound to win. But then quite surprisingly and without any real argument to back it up, Strachey's book collapses into the very complacency he warned against. 'The democratic method is showing possibilities of being able successfully to undertake the critical task of subsuming capitalism into something that would be quite unrecognizable by the name.' It was as though he had, over 300 pages, asked the right questions without ever answering them.

By exposing the clash between democracy and capitalism, he unleashed a set of other questions to which he did not or could not reply. First, had the crisis of capitalism, whose nature Strachey himself had so powerfully exposed 20 years earlier, been even partially ended or solved by parliamentary democracy? Was there not some economic development within capitalism that more adequately explained the post-war boom, with its strong trade unions and welfare state? Strachey dealt quite briefly with what he called the 'communist' argument that post-war capitalism had been stabilized by heavy arms expenditure. He agreed that military spending was the only form of public expenditure that was 'respectable' to capitalists, and agreed that throughout the Cold War investment in arms in Britain and the United States had been huge. He conceded that this extra arms-spending filled the gap between wages and prices that he himself had exposed as a central flaw in the capitalist system. But he denounced the overall view as a 'caricature'. After unconvincingly dispensing with the argument about the economic consequences of an arms economy, Strachey left his readers with little else but faith and hope that in the critical struggle between capitalism and democracy, democracy would prevail. He made no attempt even to outline the measures that a future Labour Government would have to take to protect democracy from the oligopolies. He quoted approvingly from Nye Bevan, but gave no clue as to whether, in the argument about nationalization, Bevan should be supported against Gaitskell or vice versa. This was surprising, since Strachey had addressed the problem directly in an article in the *New Statesman* in the same year, 1956: 'If socialists lose sight of the central importance of social ownership of the means of production, they will cease in a very real sense to be socialists at all: they will subside into the role of well-intentioned, amiable, rootless, drifting social reformers.'

Though perhaps he did not know it, John Strachey was himself travelling on the road to the land of what we can call the WIARDS (well-intentioned amiable rootless drifting social reformers). In the remaining seven years of his life (he died suddenly in 1963 at the age of 61), he fell increasingly into the clutches of Labour's right wing, whose intellectuals grouped round the prestigious monthly magazine *Encounter*. It was not until the late 1960s that it emerged that the Congress of Cultural Freedom, which published *Encounter*, was funded by the CIA.

Strachey's *Contemporary Capitalism* was widely praised, but it was eclipsed by the other major book published in the same year: *The Future of Socialism* by Tony Crosland. Long before he started his book, Crosland had become a full member of WIARDS. Even the title of his book was unclear. In the opening chapter, he declared that his society was not capitalist. He came to this conclusion by redefining capitalism:

The proper definition of the word capitalism is a society with the essential social economic and ideological characteristics of Great Britain from the 1830s to the 1930s; and this, assuredly, the Britain of 1956 is not. And so to the question 'is this still capitalism?' I would answer 'no'.

There was no need to define capitalism by any of the standard criteria – ownership and/or control of the means of production, unequal distribution of wealth, the power of the rich and the impotence of the poor. If you insist, without any attempt to prove the point, that capitalism requires the characteristics of the century from the 1830s to the 1930s, then assuredly, the Britain of 1956 falls outside the definition. But the real question was this: if British society was not capitalist, why bother at all with socialism or its future? Many years later the tradition set in motion by Crosland's book would lead to the junking by official Labour of the word socialism. But in 1956, there were still far too many people in the Labour Party who considered themselves socialists for any enthusiastic Labour careerist to be able to abandon the word. So Crosland defined socialism in his own terms. What mattered was control, not ownership. If society was to be made more equal, the economy had to be controlled by well-meaning, amiable, rootless, drifting social reformers who would organize taxation and investment policy to ensure fair shares for all.

The central conclusion of the book is that the economic and social questions that once hypnotized the Labour Party were irrelevant. 'We should not,' he warned, 'judge a Labour Government's performance primarily by its record in the economic field. Full employment and at least a tolerable level of stability are likely to be maintained.' Measures should be taken to ensure more equality and welfare, but above all else loomed the LAGIP factor – 'Liberty And Gaiety In Public life'. Crosland waxed eloquent on the sort of society he wanted to see:

We need not only higher exports and old-age pensions. But more open-air cafes, brighter and gayer streets at night, later closing hours for public houses, more local repertory theatres, better and more hospitable hoteliers and restaurateurs, brighter and cleaner eating houses, more riverside cafes, more pleasure gardens on the Battersea model, more murals and pictures in public places, better designs for furniture and pottery and women's clothes, statues in the centre of new housing estates, better-designed street lamps and telephone kiosks, and so ad infinitum.

It was the picture of a paradise for a people whose basic economic problems had been solved.

Totally absent from Crosland's book was even a glimmer of apprehension about any looming struggle for economic power. Where Strachey warned that democracy would have to assert itself over oligopoly, Crosland did not even recognize the concept of hostile oligopolies. Underlying his entire argument was the need for Labour to make peace with the people who held economic and industrial power, and above all to drop its commitment to nationalization or any other form of public ownership. The book drew some angry reactions from the left. In *Tribune*, Will Camp, who had fought Solihull for Labour in 1950, advised Crosland to reread Rogow and Shore on the power of private enterprise over the post-war Labour Government, and reflect on how much more devastating that power might be if a future Labour Government proceeded in the illusion that it could take economic power without resorting to public ownership. But mostly, as Will Camp predicted, Crosland's book was hailed and glorified. When I went to Oxford University in 1958, *The Future of Socialism* was the most widely discussed and the most influential of all political theory. It swung the intellectual pendulum away from traditional Labour remedies and towards the Gaitskell leadership. No book since the war had as powerful an effect on the politics of the Labour Party. A new edition was published specially for the 1959 election, which Labour lost. Dick Crossman, who was very active in organizing Labour's campaign, noticed how enthusiasm and hope on the Labour side rose during the first weeks of the campaign and then suddenly slumped. Crossman argued with some force that the Labour momentum was lost from the moment Gaitskell suddenly, and without consultation, announced that a Labour Government would not increase income tax: a pledge that was immediately denounced by the Tories as ridiculous and, more silently, by the left as reactionary.

The result of the 1959 general election stunned and horrified the Labour Party. The Gaitskell faction, in the ascendancy throughout the election campaign, immediately concluded that the defeat was the fault of the left, which had been almost completely obscured throughout the campaign. Although Crosland's book had been reprinted for the election, Crosland and Co. concluded that the election had been lost because their ideas had not been disseminated widely enough. Accordingly, in the weekend after the election, a Gaitskellite faction, led by Douglas Jay, resolved to try to alter Clause IV of the Party Constitution that committed the Party to secure for the workers the full fruits of their industry on the basis of the common ownership of the means of production. This Clause, argued the right, was irrelevant and out of date and should be replaced by a formula recognizing the mixed economy. The proposal caused a storm at the special Labour Party conference called after the 1959 election. Furious outbursts from the left demanded loyalty to public ownership, and in the end the right withdrew. At the conference the following year, the leadership was defeated on the issue of nuclear weapons – a defeat reversed in 1961. But during those two years the assault on Clause IV was beaten back.

Bevan's death in 1960 robbed the left – and public ownership – of their most powerful advocate. The Party became obsessed with a new issue – Britain's entry into the European Common Market. Through the early 1960s, though the Tory Government was divided and hamstrung, Labour did not seem to progress. Crossman's diaries told of his and his colleagues' frustration with Gaitskell's dour and undemocratic leadership, and Crossman himself contemplated leaving politics altogether. Then, quite suddenly, the whole political scene was shifted. In December 1962, Hugh Gaitskell was admitted to hospital with a minor infection. The infection turned out to be a dangerous viral disease affecting the immune system and in January 1963 Gaitskell died. His faction promptly split. They were unhappy about his natural right-wing successor, a vivacious, articulate but often drunken bully called George Brown. A small minority preferred James Callaghan. Many more abandoned the right wing altogether and voted for the third candidate, Harold Wilson. At that time, only MPs could vote for the Party leader. But the contest was followed with great interest and considerable participation by the Party's rank and file.

I was myself a young socialist delegate to the General Management Committee (GMC) of the Labour Party in Glasgow, Woodside. Woodside was a Tory seat but in 1962 our candidate, Neil Carmichael, won a famous by-election for Labour. One of our GMC delegates was an ardent Roman Catholic called James McKenna Quinn. For years we young socialists taunted Quinn, who responded sometimes with rage but usually with slightly condescending good humour. I still remember the change of mood when the GMC met to discuss the choice by MPs of a new Labour leader. Quinn spoke with sincerity and passion in recommending Harold Wilson. I was struck by the thought that delegates like Quinn not only believed that they mattered, they did matter. Similar meetings with similar outcomes took place all over the country and when the vote was taken in Parliament, Wilson triumphed by 144 votes to Brown's 108.

As Crossman had predicted, Wilson proved a much more acceptable leader than Gaitskell. His association with the Bevanites in the 1950s brought him strong support from the left, his unrivalled ability to master a brief, his grasp of economics, his increasingly caustic speaking style and mischievous wit assured him a relatively easy run in the rest of 1963 and the first nine months of 1964. In election year, he made a series of keynote speeches. The controversy over public ownership was discreetly buried. Wilson borrowed from Bevan the phrase committing the Party to an assault on the 'commanding heights' of the economy. Clause IV stayed in place. Five rebels on defence who had had the whip withdrawn came back into the Party fold. Leading Labour Party figures like Michael Foot and Judith Hart, in the interests of Labour unity, resigned from the executive of the Campaign for Nuclear Disarmament. In Parliament and in the councils, there was a huge revival of Labour unity and hope.

The Party strode, united and confident, into the general election of October 1964, and won it. Labour won 317 seats, the Tories 304 and the Liberals 9. In the general Labour rejoicing, few noticed that the Labour vote was slightly lower than it had been in the terrible defeat of 1959 (down from 12,216,172 to 12,205,808), and that the Labour victory came about because the Tory vote had slumped from 12,985,081 to 11,676,512. Since the turn-out was slightly down, the Labour triumph had been achieved not by a surge of enthusiasm for Labour but by a transfer of Tory votes to the Liberals. Such matters seemed of small consequence as the new Labour Prime Minister, Harold Wilson, and his new Cabinet took office.

The imperialist Lord Cromer was not among those elected as a member of the new Government. As a hereditary peer, indeed, he was not even entitled to vote. He was a Tory, and had been appointed by the Tory Government as Governor of the Bank of England. As such he played as prominent a part in the new Labour Government as did any elected poli-tician. He was worried most of all by the huge deficit in the balance of payments left to the Labour Government by its predecessor. Years later the phrase 'doing a Maudling' became common in British public life. It described what happened in the first nine months of 1964 as the Tory Chancellor of the Exchequer, Reginald Maudling, opened the economic throttle and allowed the boom he had engineered to continue at full speed regardless of the consequences to the balance of payments. The total deficit was estimated at £800 million. Urgent meetings were held by the new Government's leaders to discuss remedies. Harold Wilson, his deputy George Brown (Economic Affairs) and James Callaghan (Chancellor of the Exchequer) decided at once not to devalue or float the pound – a strategy that Wilson believed had led to the defeat of the previous Labour Govern-ment and which anyway would lead to immediate cuts in wages and salaries. The emergency budget introduced by Callaghan on 11 November was designed to 'stop the bleeding'. Many of the promises made by Labour at the election were shelved. The promised rise in old-age pensions was postponed for six months. But some reforms were carried out at once – notably the abolition of National Health Service prescription charges. Otherwise, because of the crisis, the budget was neutral.

Neutrality, however, was nothing like enough for Lord Cromer. He wanted a wage freeze, cuts in public spending and a rise in unemployment: precisely the measures introduced by the Tories in 1961, and mercilessly mocked by Harold Wilson in his election speeches. Less than a week after the budget, Cromer was in Downing Street, arguing for a sharp rise in the bank rate. His demands were accompanied by another wave of selling of sterling and on 23 November the bank rate was raised from 5 to 7 per cent. All Wilson's speeches in the run-up to the election had stressed the need for growth and for an end to what he called the Tory obsession with 'stop–go' economics. Growth depended on a low bank rate. So did a go–go economy. Yet in response to the wave of selling sterling that followed the budget, the Labour Government raised the bank rate. Still, Cromer and the bankers were not satisfied with the extent of the stop. The sale of sterling continued and the reserves were raided. Years later, in his book on the Labour Government, Wilson himself described his argument with Cromer on the evening after the rise in the bank rate (24 November 1964):

Not for the first time, I said that we had now reached the situation where a newly elected Government with a mandate from the people was being told, not so much by the Governor of the Bank of England but by international speculators, that the policies on which we had fought the election could not be implemented; that the Government was to be forced into the adoption of Tory policies to which it was fundamentally opposed. The Governor confirmed that that was in fact the case.

Genuinely shocked, Wilson drew the political conclusions.

I asked him if this meant that it was impossible for any government, whatever its party label, whatever its manifesto or the policies on which it fought an election, to continue, unless it immediately reverted to full-scale Tory policies. He had to admit that that was what his argument meant, because of the sheer compulsion of the economic dictation of those who exercised economic power.

Lord Cromer never denied the thrust of this conversation, the consequences of which were so catastrophic for parliamentary democracy. His argument was that he was driven by the extent of the economic crisis to demand the suspension of the democratic process. Wilson's reply, according to his own account, was bold indeed. He warned the Governor that 'in these circumstances there was nothing left for me to do but to appeal to the democracy I was being asked to repudiate, to go back to the electorate for a mandate giving me full powers to deal with the crisis'. If he did so, he assured the Governor, he would 'have a landslide'. Cromer 'admitted ruefully' that that was probably true, but he clearly felt that the means of achieving such a landslide would be 'bad for Britain and bad for sterling'. After this exchange, Wilson's account goes on, Cromer left Downing Street, went back to the City and managed to raise 3 billion dollars in a loan to Britain from the central bankers, thus ensuring a temporary halt to the sterling crisis.

This account of a historic and open conflict between the City of London and its bankers on the one hand and the elected Government on the other is almost certainly accurate. What is extremely doubtful is the sincerity of

Wilson's threat. A few weeks after achieving parliamentary office, Wilson was hardly in the mood to resign and seek a new mandate, even if he ever imagined such a course. His inference that the Governor of the Bank of England was so scared by the possibility of a Labour landslide that he slunk off to raise a new loan is also a little hard to believe. What is certain is that the threat of a sterling crisis was not dispelled by the November loan but continued to disrupt the Labour Government for the next three years and, more indirectly, for the rest of its time in office.

On 20 December 1964, Dick Crossman ruminated in his diary:

Throughout the week it became clearer and clearer that confidence had not been restored; that the new 3 billion dollar loan was being rapidly eaten away, that the City of London and the bankers of Zurich just weren't prepared to give the Labour Government their confidence.

Crossman was inclined at the time to put some of the blame on the elected Government. 'There was,' he reflected at the start of the new year, 1965, 'our innocence in insisting on the increase in old-age pensions and the abolition of prescription charges, despite the warning of the Treasury.' Crossman had spent almost his entire political life making propaganda for higher old-age pensions. He had strongly supported Aneurin Bevan's resignation from the Labour Government in 1951 on the issue of dental and spectacles charges. Yet now he was a minister, and his Government was racked by an economic crisis, he put some of the blame on his own Government for announcing (and postponing) a rise in old-age pensions and for abolishing prescription charges. Barbara Castle, who was in the Cabinet as Minister for Overseas Development, noted in her diaries in February, from a conversation with the Chancellor of the Exchequer, James Callaghan, that the money from the bankers' loan would run out by May and that he had no doubt at all that the bankers 'would expect us to introduce deflationary measures as the price of their further support'. Callaghan complained that 'every time he announced an increase in public expenditure, he received some letter of protest from the bankers who were our creditors'. Years later, when he wrote his memoirs, Callaghan recalled how he was swept up by forces far beyond his control:

In all the offices I have held I have never experienced anything more frustrating than sitting at the Chancellor's desk watching our currency reserves gurgle down the plughole day after day and knowing that the drain could not be stopped . . . It was like swimming in a heavy sea. As soon as we emerged from the buffeting of one wave, another would hit us before we could catch our breath.

The buffeting, made worse by the fact that Labour's parliamentary majority was further reduced by Foreign Secretary Patrick Gordon Walker's historic achievement – losing two safe seats (Smethwick and Leyton) in three months – went on all through spring and early summer. It developed into further crisis in high summer. The best account of the crisis of the summer of 1965 comes from Clive Ponting, a civil servant who climbed to the top of the Ministry of Defence and who was prosecuted in 1984 for leaking secret documents about the sinking of the Argentinian cruiser *General Belgrano* in the Falklands War. In 1989, he published a book about the 1964–70 Labour Government entitled *Breach of Promise*. He revealed for the first time that behind the backs of the Cabinet, a deal was struck between the British and American Governments. In exchange for the United States helping the pound and staving off British devaluation, the British Government would deflate the economy at home, initiate a statutory incomes policy, back the American war in Vietnam and, most importantly, maintain a substantial military force East of Suez. All these things happened – every one of them in direct breach of Labour Party policy and the Government's intentions. In his Bevanite days, Harold Wilson had eloquently opposed Western imperialism in Indo-China, whether French or American. Labour Party policy was opposed to the American invasion of Vietnam, to deflationary measures and to wasteful defence spending on the old imperial pattern. Yet in secret meetings with their American counterparts and under the constant threat of an economic crisis they did not create, understand or halt, the Labour Government embarked on all these policies.

Ponting suggests that Wilson concurred with these policies in order to buy a valuable breathing space, and, if so, he temporarily achieved his aim. The six months that followed the American rescue of the summer of 1965 were blessed with relative economic stability in which Wilson revelled. 'The economy is strong, employment is strong and the pound is strong,' he told a cheering Labour Party conference in September without disclosing the methods – or the price – by which that stability was secured. Back in the Commons in November, he boasted: 'We are carrying through one of the most massive programmes of social and economic reform in our long parliamentary history.' The pause in the series of crises that had restricted and dominated the first year in government lasted just long enough for the Labour Party to win another election. In January 1966, the Party won a resounding victory at a by-election in Hull, and went on to win a huge victory – by nearly a hundred – in a general election in March.

For the first time since 1945, the Labour vote was up – by nearly a million to 13,096,629, 48.1 per cent of the total electorate, only slightly lower than the record in 1951. If Labour ministers were the 'masters now' in 1945, they were even more the masters in 1966 – and the conditions were far more favourable. There was no war in which British forces were involved, no unemployment to speak of. Nothing now seemed beyond the powers of the new Labour administration. Many Labour supporters assumed that the Party would proceed to carry out its promises and shift the balance of political and industrial forces in Britain inexorably to the left.

The first assault from the new Government, however, came not on sterling speculators, still less on the owners and controllers of capital, but on Labour's own supporters. The National Union of Seamen was affiliated to the Labour Party and for 50 years had paid its subscriptions without a whisper of a demand. Almost immediately after the election, however, the union was involved in a pay dispute with the British shipping industry. The union called a strike, to which the members responded with alacrity. There was no strike pay, but the seamen made it clear that there was to be no breach of solidarity. The strike rolled on until the effect began to be noticed in the City of London. A great clamour was set up in the press for the Labour Government to impose its will on the strikers and force them back to work. At once senior ministers threw all their influence against the seamen. The reason for this was the incomes policy forced on the Government by their deal with the US Government the previous summer. Again and again Wilson and Ray Gunter, his Minister of Labour, explained that the seamen's modest wage demands, designed to lift out of poverty some of the lowest-paid workers in the country, would 'breach the dykes of the incomes policy' on which the Government depended. An independent inquiry, headed inevitably by a judge, suggested a compromise. The union rejected it. On and on went the strike through the early summer until it was finally settled in June on terms not entirely unfavourable to the workers. The Government's insistence on its incomes policy lost it one of its ablest Cabinet ministers, Frank Cousins, who had taken leave of absence from his post as General Secretary of the biggest union in the country, the Transport and General Workers' Union, to be elected to Parliament and to become Secretary of State for Technology in the Wilson Government. His promotion was intended as a sign to the unions that their leaders were personally committed to the trade unions. Cousins's resignation – on the grounds that Labour's incomes policy demonstrated unforgivable solidarity with the employers – showed how the balance had shifted since the days of Bevin. In an irascible speech in the Commons, Wilson alleged that the seamen were being led by a 'tightly knit group of politically motivated men'. The speech infuriated wide sections of the Labour Party. The 400,000-strong London Labour Party unanimously passed a motion in support of the striking seamen. Wilson was later to blame the seamen and their union for the disasters that quickly overcame the Labour Government. But the seamen were not responsible. The real culprits were the same as before.

On 11 July, long after the seamen had returned to work, another wave of sterling sales hit the financial markets. It went on and on, apparently without end. On 20 July, Black Wednesday as it came to be known, Wilson rose in the Commons and effectively reversed all the economic priorities he had so studiously recited in the months before the two elections his party had won. More than £500 million was slashed from Government spending. For the first time since 1931, a total wage freeze was announced as Government policy. It was to last for six months, followed by another six months of severe wage restraint. For all his political life, Wilson had argued for economic growth, freely negotiated wage agreements and social justice. Now he was abandoning all three for economic stagnation and what he once called 'a one-sided pay pause'. The reason for this historic and devastating about-turn was beyond his control. He was carrying out policies at the behest of people who did not vote for him and whom he could not influence. Sadly, he even abandoned the cheeky language with which he had once assaulted the gnomes of Zurich. Now his tone as well as his policy grovelled to the men of money. The run on sterling was not, he told the Commons, a 'machination of some bearded troglodytes deep below ground speculating in private gain'. On the contrary, it was 'precautionary'. Men with money were obliged, after all, to protect it, especially when that wealth was under threat from tightly knit politically motivated men in government whose only claim to power was that they had been elected by a majority of their compatriots.

The July measures were agreed without dissent by the Cabinet and hailed in the right-wing press. But the effect on the Labour movement, and on Labour voters, was catastrophic. In 1967, Labour lost control of the Greater London Council and hundreds of council seats. By-elections came and went, all with enormous and unprecedented slumps in the Labour vote. In September and November, Labour lost marginal Cambridge and then safe seats at Walthamstow, Leicester South West and even Hamilton, near Glasgow, where its vote slumped by nearly 30 per cent. Seats occupied by Labour for the whole century were now being won by Tories or Nationalists. As they deserted their voters, Labour ministers stayed true to the forces that had not elected them, true to the American barbarism in Vietnam, true to the one-sided pay pause, true to the pound sterling. The last of these commitments was constantly threatened until in November 1967 it was jettisoned. After another bout of sterling sales, the Government finally devalued the pound.

The devaluation ushered in another set of unelected masters, this time from the International Monetary Fund. They were brought in to 'advise' on the measures now necessary to 'sustain' the devaluation and they insisted, first, on the restoration of NHS prescription charges and the postponement of the raising of the school leaving age. When Labour ministers argued that both these were the precious heritage of the Labour Party, the IMF insisted all the more firmly for their inclusion in the package. On the day after devaluation, Dick Crossman asked James Callaghan to ensure that the Government raised family allowances for the poor. Callaghan replied, 'Sorry, old boy, the IMF won't allow it.' Crossman ruminated, 'so we're back under the control of the bankers'. Not that they had ever been out of it.

Callaghan was replaced as Chancellor by the former Gaitskellite Roy Jenkins, but the change made no difference to the control of the economy. Through 1968 and 1969, Jenkins floundered in as heavy seas as ever buffeted his predecessor. Again and again he turned down the legitimate demands of the Labour Party and TUC because, he argued, they were unacceptable to the central bankers or the IMF. One by one, what was left of the policy commitments at the election were jettisoned. A favourite pledge of Wilson's – to build 500,000 houses by 1970 – was abandoned. A Cabinet meeting in February 1967 discussed another issue of principle – the universal payment of family allowances. Chancellor Callaghan thought people should be means-tested before such allowances were paid. The very right-wing Minister of Pensions, Peggy Herbison, complained bitterly. Her belief in universality was central, she said, to everything she was doing at the Ministry of Pensions. Describing the argument, Dick Crossman wrote: 'This ... episode was the watershed, the great divide ... What the Chancellor was saying was verbatim what the Tories were saying ... I hadn't come into the Cabinet to do this kind of thing.' The vote that day went against the Chancellor but the policies he pursued did not waver from the Tory position. The dispute ended a few months later in the most significant resignation during the whole Labour Government. Stunned by the Chancellor's insistence on cutting a rise in the old-age pension, the ultra-loyal Peggy Herbison resigned as Pensions Minister. Her place was taken by Judith Hart, a stalwart of the left. A bubble over her photograph in *Private Eye* had her saying: 'Mummy called me Judith because she had a lisp.'

At the beginning of 1968, Dick Crossman concluded: 'Our foreign policy is virtually the same as the Tories'.' This view was dramatically illustrated when a gang of army colonels toppled the democratic Government in Greece and embarked on a long period of fascist rule. Michael Stewart, Labour's Foreign Secretary, argued in Cabinet for appeasing the colonels and continuing to sell them arms.

Other big political stories of the time exposed the reluctance of Labour ministers to interfere with the priorities of big business. Chief among these was the scandal at Bristol Siddeley Engines, whose directors stole £5 million from the Government. Figures for wages paid to workers on overhaul contracts for military aircraft were deliberately fabricated so that the company could claim far more than they were entitled to. Somewhat reluctantly, the Government set up an inquiry under a respected scientist, Sir Roy Wilson. Sir Roy held his hearings in secret and his report named no names. But it revealed the astonishing fact that the company's executive committee had received monthly reports during the four years of the theft, and must have been fully aware of the lies their company were telling the Government in order fraudulently to extract for their benefit huge and regular wads of taxpayers' money. The Government responded by removing from public office two of the company's directors – the chairman, Sir Reginald Verdon-Smith, and the sales director, a former Tory candidate called Brian David-son. A howl of Tory fury protested against these feeble punishments. Meanwhile the managing director of Bristol Siddeley Engines was not touched. In his speech on the case, the Secretary of State for Technology, Anthony Wedgwood Benn, announced that the managing director held no public appointments. This was nonsense. Sir Arnold Hall, the managing director of Bristol Siddeley Engines, was an industry chieftain much prized by the Labour Government. He served on its advisory council on scientific policy – a committee regarded as specially important by the Prime Minister and by Dick Crossman, whose diary described Sir Arnold as a 'civilized man'. The Bristol Siddeley scandal was dramatic proof of the double standards of the Government when it came to deceit and theft of Government money. Poor people who cheated on their benefits were denounced and hounded to jail. But when big business stole millions from the taxpayer, the thieves were slapped gently on the wrist, or not exposed at all.

The same priorities were in evidence when a huge block of council flats built for working-class tenants in East London – Ronan Point – collapsed as a result of a design failure. The Government refused to blame the contractors – who had strong connections to the Tory Party – and awarded them the contract for repairing the blocks threatened by the design faults.

The pattern of a democratically elected Government at the mercy of undemocratic powers in the banks and big business emerged on all sides. No one noticed this process more keenly than Dick Crossman. The over-powering impression that emerges from his diaries during his six years in the Wilson Cabinet is one of despair and disillusionment. He summed up the early period of government (1964–6) when he was Secretary of State for Housing as follows: 'The main trouble is that we haven't delivered the goods.' After the 1966 election, when Crossman became Lord Privy Seal and Leader of the House of Commons (1966–1970), his disillusionment found full expression.

25 Sept 1966: I don't feel I'm part of a Government pledged to fundamental change, with any idea of where it's going . . .

31 Dec 1967: This Government has failed more abysmally than any Government since 1931.

18 Feb 1968: For an ever-increasing number of Labour voters, there is no differ-ence between our Government and a Tory Government.

17 March 1968: I've never felt a greater sense of the Government's impotence than I do now . . . the truth is that we shan't get control of the economy.

12 Sept 1968: In this instance [the merger between GEC and English Electric] the Government was pushed aside in the creation of a vast concentration of power which will enable these industrialists to free themselves from accountability to the public.

1 Dec 1968: By Jove we are in a bad way now, there's no doubt about it.

4 Jan 1969: I must say I am more depressed than ever.

20 March 1969: We are floundering deeper and deeper.

31 Dec 1969: I admit our Labour Government hasn't broken through the problem of the inequality of power or of social inequality. This, the distinctive feature of Labour thinking, binding together left and right of the Party, has not been put into practice.

And finally:

16 April 1970: I have lost the spirit, the dynamic . . . I don't act . . . I am too old, too divided and anyway I don't want Labour to win the election.

Dick Crossman never reflected in any depth on the reasons for the imbalance of power or the impotence of the Government he so graphically described. He was broken by the experience, and did not stand for re-election in 1970. He became a surprisingly ineffectual editor of the *New Statesman*, and died of cancer in 1974.

Crossman's constant friend and ally in the Wilson Cabinet was Barbara

.astle. She was from the outset one of the few successes in the Cabinet. Whether defending the overseas aid budget or as Secretary of State for Transport (1965–9), she proved herself a competent administrator and a doughty campaigner for what she believed. Her Transport Act of 1968 was one of the few genuine attempts since the previous Labour Government to challenge the enormously powerful private transport lobby. She was, in those early years, constantly worried that the Wilson Government would betray the black majority in Rhodesia, a British colony, where a white minority Government under Ian Smith declared unilateral independence from Britain in 1965. On this issue, Government policy was laid down by the chiefs of the armed forces, so there was no military intervention. Harold Wilson did his utmost to do a deal with Ian Smith and legitimize his rule, but Smith was having none of it. Smith's obduracy prevented the sell-out for which Wilson strove – and Barbara Castle was safe. The toppling of the Smith Government was left eventually to the struggle of the black people of Rhodesia.

Castle's diaries for the period show she too was often unhappy in her work. Sitting at the Lord Mayor's banquet in November 1966, she confessed herself 'nauseated by all the lavishness' and she 'suddenly wondered what we were all doing there among our enemies'. In the debate on family allowances and universality a week later she sighed: 'Here we go whoring after Tory remedies again.' Grappling with a speech for the Labour women's conference in May 1967, she found to her horror: 'The trouble is that there isn't a major item of Government policy with which I agree.' In May 1968, the month of the historic revolt of students and workers in Paris, she mused that she was 'fascinated by the almost impossibility of a social democratic Government running capitalism'.

Her peculiar solution to the problem of a social democratic Government running capitalism began to take shape after her promotion. She became First Secretary for Employment and Productivity and applied her mind to the trade unions and their continuing confidence and power, neither of which had been seriously dented by the Labour Government. Strikes, mainly unofficial, proliferated, achieving substantial gains in workers' living standards. Like the seamen's strike in 1966, these strikes continued to annoy Labour ministers. Barbara Castle started by recognizing the unions as partners in carrying out Labour's agenda, but as the strikes grew more effective in the later half of 1968, her irritation grew. In November 1968, she called a high-level conference, at Sunningdale, Berkshire, to settle Government policy on these matters. Central to the discussions was the Donovan Report, the result of a Royal Commission, whose basic recommendations were that the unions should be rationalized and strengthened, but that their fundamental independence from the law and the Government should be maintained. The employers were infuriated by the Commission, but in general the Donovan proposals were accepted by the Government, at least until Barbara Castle became First Secretary of State. At that Sunningdale conference, at which the employers were much more heavily represented than the unions, the role of a Labour Government at a time of increasing industrial militancy was anxiously discussed. 'A consensus emerged,' wrote Barbara Castle, 'that we rejected the concept of collective laissez faire, and were in favour of state intervention in industrial relations.' She went on:

In general we accepted the Donovan analysis, though we thought it had its weaknesses. Like Donovan, we rejected the legal enforcement of collective agreements, and banning of sympathetic strikes and the closed shop. But we were also deeply disturbed by the industrial anarchy which was doing so much harm to the economy and by the fact that so many strikes seemed to be directed more against the community than the employer.

The central problem, she mused, was: 'How could one bring more order into industrial relations without putting unacceptable curbs on what we called the "primitive power" of workers to defend their own interests?' Gradually, ideas for a solution began to emerge. Where workers went on strike in breach of procedural agreements negotiated by their union, they should be obliged by law to observe a 'cooling-off period' during which they and the employers would revert to the status quo before the strike started. This idea appealed, she reported, not just to the employers but also to most of the Labour ministers at the conference. The ideas at the Sunningdale conference were quickly converted into a White Paper, written mainly by Barbara Castle herself and named 'In Place of Strife'. The most contentious proposals in the White Paper dealt with the awkward question of workers' intransigence. What would happen if unofficial strikers ignored the cooling-off period and stayed out on strike? In such circumstances, the White Paper made clear, 'penal clauses' would come into effect. The intransigent workers would be prosecuted and, if they persisted, punished by fines and prison sentences.

The White Paper appalled the trade unions. Even the most reactionary union leaders were troubled by Castle's penal clauses. They left the unions more exposed to the Government and the criminal law than at any time since the war. Moreover, the proposals were more interventionist than anything the Tories had even suggested in 13 years of office.

The arguments from the trade unions against 'In Place of Strife' stemmed more from a primeval fear of attack than from any logic. This may have been because the rational arguments against the proposals forced the discussion back on class lines. However they were presented or put into effect, the proposals would weaken the organized workers and strengthen the employers. The Labour Party had come into existence in order more forcefully and effectively to shelter the trade unions from the law of the land, and in 1969 the unions were still the backbone of the Labour Party. Though most trade unionists would have agreed that the Labour Government had to govern, and should not in any sense be in hock to the unions, they did not regard it in any way part of a Labour Government's agenda to promote laws that would subject the basic business of trade unions, including strikes, to the courts. A further argument, used at the time with considerable force by trade-union militants, was that the Labour Government was singularly weak when seeking to fulfil its social obligations to the poor and to the workers. As we have seen in a whole series of policies, the Government had been consistently 'blown off course' by forces beyond their control. As Barbara Castle herself admitted in May 1968: 'Some of us had got so afraid of the gnomes that we barely dared open our mouths about any of our socialist aims.' The popularity of the Government had plummeted as a result. In sharp contrast to what had happened in 1945–51, by-elections were regularly lost to the Tories, even in relatively safe Labour seats. Council elections were even more catastrophic. Many trade unionists felt that they had lost out on most of the Labour Government's measures, and now the Government was threatening even their ability to defend themselves in the one area they could do so – on the shop floor.

Through the early months of 1969, there was a great wave of workers' protest. So strong was the influence of the unions on Labour that the protest engulfed even the Parliamentary Labour Party. To Barbara Castle's intense disgust, the protest was taken up by members of the Cabinet who had started their lives as trade unionists. Otherwise moderate and right-wing ministers, even James Callaghan, distanced themselves from 'In Place of Strife'. Though Barbara Castle and Harold Wilson were almost entirely isolated in their support for the proposals, they both threatened to carry the dispute through, if necessary, to resignation. The trade unions, however, did not budge. In place of 'In Place of Strife' they offered a tame and effectively meaningless 'solemn and binding' undertaking to supervise and control unofficial strikes. The undertaking, dubbed 'Solomon Binding' by Fleet Street wags, was accepted by the Government and the whole dispute disintegrated in a whimper. Barbara Castle's effort to extend her notion of social democratic Government into the field of trade unionism was an abject failure. Irritated by the Government's impotence under pressure from representatives of the ruling class she had set out to topple, she had tried in the name of rationality and order to use the power and influence of the elected Government to weaken the working class she had set out to defend. Her effort exposed only the Government's impotence. The debacle over 'In Place of Strife' heaped yet more obloquy on the Government, and 1969 ended with Labour in a desperate position.

Perhaps the most curious feature that stands out on looking back at that Labour Government is the difference in the mood and aspirations of ministers on the one hand and of workers, students and socialists outside Parliament on the other. Crossman, in his diaries, reflected on this phenomenon. On New Year's Eve 1969, he dictated:

Some days ago I saw ... an extraordinary interview with John Lennon ... He was the only person who said that it hadn't been a bad decade, that we'd made enormous advances and that a lot of people were happier than before. In their own way, he and the Beatles were saying: 'We disown the whole Establishment not out of utter depression and pessimism but because we are confident of the future and that we can take over and create a world of peace and unity.'

As Crossman recognized, John Lennon was irritated by people in high places who talked and behaved as if the 1960s was a decade of decline and depression. 1968, described by Crossman as 'a terribly depressing year', had been, outside Parliament and the Cabinet, a year of constant tumult from below, constant change and constant hope. The revolutionary events and general strike in France in May, the uprising in Prague in August, the first civil rights marches in Northern Ireland, the mass demonstrations against the Vietnam War all over the world, including the United States, and the burgeoning of the American civil rights movement, were all evidence of new democratic forces flexing their muscles outside the ruling parliaments, congresses and bureaucracies.

In Britain in 1968, there were two huge demonstrations against the Vietnam War. Ministers, Crossman and Castle included, could not appear in public without being picketed and heckled by angry demonstrations. The demonstrators were almost certainly the same kind of people that had flocked to calls from the very same ministers when they had been campaigning before they were elected – Barbara Castle, for instance, had chaired the anti-apartheid movement and had led angry crowds to Trafalgar Square and the South African Embassy. The militancy of the new demonstrations and occupations puzzled and irritated the Labour ministers.

They could not understand or tolerate the mixture of rage, scepticism and mockery that inspired the demonstrations. At the time, it seemed to those of us who were taking part in the agitations that there was an increasingly unbridgeable gulf between Labour politics at Westminster, where the Government was constantly compromising with the American war in Vietnam and the colonels in Greece, and the revolutionary spirit that was emerging among the youth.

I myself left the Labour Party in the spring of 1967, after a grim evening canvassing for Labour in the Greater London Council elections. I was canvassing in exactly the same Kilburn streets that the year before had produced a Labour majority for the first time ever in London's Hampstead constituency. In 1966, people were enthusiastic about the Labour Party and keen to get to the polls. In 1967, their reaction was sour, even hostile. 'Vote Labour? Why should we?' they asked. 'Can you give us a single good reason to do so?' I couldn't, so I left.

There was a brief moment in 1969 when the two contrasting political worlds seemed to coincide. On 17 April, a by-election took place in Mid Ulster, a seat held by the Unionist Party in Northern Ireland. Ever since the partition of Ireland in 1922, politics in the British-occupied North had been dominated by the Ulster Unionist Party, whose sole preoccupation was to retain Protestant ascendancy in the six counties of Northern Ireland. Since at least a third of the population there were Roman Catholics, Unionist policy was directed to suppressing the civil rights, including the voting rights, of the Catholic population. As a result, the voting system in Northern Ireland was a hideous mess, and the ward boundaries in many local authorities, including Northern Ireland's second city, Derry, were grotesquely rigged so that the Protestant minority in those areas could cling to office. In 1968, the fever of revolt that swept Europe East and West penetrated into Northern Ireland. In October, a civil rights demonstration in Derry was brutally beaten up by the Royal Ulster Constabulary, a sectarian force consisting almost entirely of Protestants whose concept of law and order was Protestant law and Protestant order. The October demonstration in Derry was seen by the Orange authorities as an intolerable public challenge to that law and order, and was beaten into submission. The fact that an elected MP, Gerry Fitt, was beaten up in the process alerted the world press, and for the first time for nearly half a century the violent and sectarian rule in Northern Ireland came to the shocked attention of large numbers of people all over the world.

By chance, I was debating at Queen's University Belfast in the week after that demonstration. The huge hall was packed with students, almost all of them outraged at what had happened in Derry. A protest meeting in the same hall was being planned for the following day, but the police needed names of sponsors. There was a hushed silence as the consequences of handing in names to the police were considered. A strong voice rang out: 'I have nothing to lose! I'll volunteer!' and a tiny young woman strode to the front, to loud applause.

Bernadette Devlin was one of the many miracles of the time. She had struggled to the university from a working-class background in Cookstown, Co. Tyrone. Very quickly she established herself as a powerful force in the new movement for civil rights. She took part in the courageous People's Democracy march from Belfast to Derry in January 1969. The march was physically attacked all along the way by thugs openly supported by Unionist politicians. When the Unionist MP for Mid Ulster, which included Cookstown, died, many anticipated a standard sectarian squabble in which republicans and nationalists argued over a candidate to fight the Unionist. In the event, and as a direct result of the events in Derry, the path was cleared for a most unusual Unity candidate – Bernadette Devlin. The turn-out for the by-election was huge – 91 per cent of the electorate voted, and Bernadette Devlin was declared the winner with 53.3 per cent of the vote.

She brought to Westminster a flavour of the revolt that was taking place not just in Northern Ireland but in many other places too. Standing behind the Speaker's chair for her maiden speech, the ageing and increasingly cynical Dick Crossman was spellbound by what he called 'a tremendous performance'. He summed it up like this:

Everything was barred – the English were hopeless, the Orange regime and the O'Neill concessions were hopeless, the Southern Irish Government and the English Government were hopeless. Everything would lead to disaster and everybody was to blame for the situation in Ireland. She spent her time building the barricades for a class war. The left-wing Labour backbenchers cheered, all the Members falling over themselves to congratulate her as actors congratulate one another. I suppose that in a few days' time they will realize the significance of what she has said.

Bernadette Devlin did not give up or betray her principles. She became more and more socialist in her attitudes, and again and again took her fury about British rule in Ireland to the floor of the House of Commons and to the mass demonstrations and agitations outside. When, on May Day 1969, a huge demonstration marched against 'In Place of Strife', Devlin spoke at the rally and marched the whole way. All through her time as an MP, she strove to use her position as a representative to impress on the authorities the full extent of the exploitation and discrimination suffered by the people who elected her. When rampaging police killed a Catholic worker in his home in Derry, her response was to form a one-woman, all-night picket of protest outside 10 Downing Street, an act which once again succeeded in irritating Dick Crossman.

Bernadette Devlin's dramatic entry into parliamentary politics was like a rude noise in church. For a brief moment she combined the strong and emerging revolutionary feelings outside Parliament with the status of an elected MP, and caused something close to consternation among those who were trying to carry on their social democratic business in Parliament. Wherever she went outside Parliament she drew enormous crowds. She was a brilliant public speaker and had the most extraordinary knack of plucking the appropriate words from thin air and, apparently without preparation or strain, forming them into perfect sentences and enriching the result with an invigorating intensity and passion. The crowds came not just to marvel at her talent but also to bask in the appreciation of someone who combined the anger and aspirations of the time with a mandate from her electors.

While she continued on her militant path, Labour ministers continued to cower in terror of the undemocratic financial and industrial forces which had already brought them to their knees. As the prospect of another election loomed and people were once again faced with the stark choice of voting for a discredited Government or the Tory Party, the pendulum of the polls swung back again. In the run-up to the election of June 1970, Labour actually took the lead in the polls and sustained it up to election day. Beaming in the bright sunshine of that early summer, Harold Wilson toured the country full of confidence. When a heckler shouted to him to 'go home', he replied that he was indeed going home – to 10 Downing Street. In general, however, the acerbic cheek and militancy of his electioneering in 1964 and even in 1966 was replaced by a presidential pomposity and complacency. Above all, he told ministers, the boat must not be rocked. When Anthony Wedgwood Benn, already on the way to his historic conversion to Tony Benn, delivered a furious onslaught on the rise of racialism in the Tory Party, Wilson issued the sternest instructions that no such speech should be made again by Benn or any other minister. His instructions were obeyed and he continued his complacent march – to defeat. The results shocked him to the core. The Labour vote was down from 13,096,629 in 1966 to 12,208,758, while the Tory vote went up. In the House of Commons, the Tories under the stiff and unpopular Edward Heath had a majority of 30. The Liberals, squeezed almost to death, were down to six MPs. The trend to the right was universal across the country. In Mid Ulster, however, Bernadette Devlin, with a 90 per cent poll, increased her vote and her majority.

One interesting feature of the shock results was the equanimity with which they were greeted by Labour leaders. I recall a phone call from my father, Hugh Caradon, who had for all the period of the Labour Government been a minister of state at the Foreign Office and UK ambassador at the United Nations. As I started to commiserate with him, he cut me short. 'I feel an overwhelming sense of relief,' he bellowed jubilantly down the phone. When I read later (and wrote) about Labour's plans for further treachery in Rhodesia, and about the close connections of Harold Wilson's retinue to the Government of Israel and its illegal occupations and settlements, I understood what he meant. The same relief seemed to be widespread among Labour ministers. In the country, however, Labour supporters were not at all relieved. As they contemplated five years led by Edward Heath, who with his Shadow Cabinet had outlined a series of crudely right-wing policies at the Selsden Park Hotel near Croydon, many of them continued to deplore the frightful failure of the first Labour Government to be elected in peacetime with a substantial majority. This discontent was by no means confined to the left of the Party. The Fabian Society published 16 essays from centrist and right-wing intellectuals entitled *Labour and Inequality* (1972). Its conclusion, by Peter Townsend, was as follows:

Really big structural reforms eluded the Labour Government. The Government strayed from moral authority over race and withdrew from the obstinate pursuit of socialist objectives. Its social achievements were much smaller than claimed or believed at the time by Labour ministers. Major onslaughts on inequality and poverty were required but not mounted. Although support for the social services was maintained during severe economic difficulties, that support was not exceptional in scale nor was it inspired by one of a number of possible socialist strategies.

This sad and reluctant conclusion was sustained by a volley of statistics in all 16 essays. In their wretchedness, the Party members' only comfort was the fact that the core of the Party, the trade unions, had escaped the grasping fingers of the Labour administration and retained their independence and strength.

Unstable Compound 2: 1970–79

*We face an economic typhoon of unparalleled ferocity, and we
cannot run away from it.*

Michael Foot, Secretary of State for Employment,
in a speech to the Parliamentary Labour Party, 22 July 1975

The Tory administration that took office in the summer of 1970 had not
expected to do so. The shadow ministers who met at the Selsden Park Hotel
had devised a set of policies that conformed to their reactionary prejudices
and could be distinguished from what Labour had already done. The result
was a ragbag of partial privatizations and cautious sell-outs to the racist
minorities of South Africa and Rhodesia. The only big issue uniting the
Tories was the urgent need to control the trade unions and to use the law
to do so.

The problem for them was that their party was committed against a
statutory incomes policy. Almost at once, however, an incomes policy was
cobbled together by the incoming Treasury ministers. It was known as 'n
minus one'. This policy dismissed the idea that pay claims should be dealt
with according to their merits. The only way the Government could control
public-sector pay claims, it seemed to the new ministers, was to insist that
every pay settlement in the public sector was lower than the last one. Such
an arbitrary policy was wholly unacceptable to the trade unions, so the
Government, pretending all the time to 'consult' the unions, embarked on
a policy of confrontation with any section of public-sector workers who
put in a claim.

The first to raise their heads were the local government manual workers.
Their strike in late 1970 caused predictable chaos, and the unions agreed
finally to accept the recommendations of an independent committee of
inquiry. To Heath's horror, the committee reported: 'Given the pace of
inflation in this country as a whole, there is no chance that it can be arrested

by a somewhat smaller increase for local authority employees. All that would achieve would be a deterioration in their position without a significant benefit to the country as a whole.' Considering the council workers' claim on its merits, therefore, the committee recommended increases of £2.50 a week, 75p more than the employers' final offer. Heath was furious. He went on television to denounce the report. For him, any wage increase in the public sector was a menace to the economy. The council workers were the lowest of the low. Thanks to the elected local authorities, their workers' jobs were relatively secure and they were all in trade unions. They were precisely the workers whose pay, according to Selsden Park dogma, should be kept rigidly under control. Professor Hugh Clegg, the unions' nominee on the arbitration committee, was immediately victimized. He lost his job as chairman of the Civil Service Arbitration Committee.

Heath and his wage-controllers cast around for what he later called 'at least one strike in the public sector' that the Government could 'face down'. His chance came quickly enough. Around 125,000 workers in the power stations started to work to rule in support of a substantial pay claim. The workers were represented in the main by the electricians' union, whose leader, Frank Chapple, a former Communist who had turned full circle, hated the very idea of a major strike but could feel the hot breath of his members down his neck. Woodrow Wyatt, who was on the electricians' union payroll, and who was normally bitterly opposed to trade-union militancy, devoted his column in the *Sunday Mirror* to the case for the power workers' claim. For once, the obsequious Wyatt was out on a limb. The rest of the press, left and right, assaulted the normally quiescent power workers. Stunned by the ferocity of media hostility – individual power workers were abused and assaulted – and by the employers' deliberate cuts in electricity supply, the unions quickly agreed to a court of inquiry. The court's proposed settlement was a welcome victory for Heath's ministers.

They then cast around for another public-sector claim that could be dealt with in the same way. Soon, they were engaged in a long battle with the post-office workers, whose union was led by a mild-mannered right-winger called Tom Jackson. The national strike of postal workers, including telecommunications workers, lasted for 47 days – through January, February and the first week of March 1971. The workers responded loyally but passively. The entire postal service was shut down, but the Government urged employers to hold out against the strike in the national interest. They were able to do so partly because the telephone system continued to function and partly because the strikers obeyed their leaders' call to sit the strike out without doing anything to increase its effect.

The settlement of the postal dispute was a triumph for the 'n minus one' formula and Tory ministers were jubilant. With the victory over the power workers and the postal workers under their belt, Ministers felt that they could now proceed with legislation to discipline unofficial strikers where Labour and Barbara Castle had failed. The result was the Industrial Relations Act, a vast measure whose byzantine clauses and conditions boiled down to a simple proposition not dissimilar to Barbara Castle's: legal control over unofficial industrial strikes. Unions were expected to register under the Act. If they did so, they kept some of their immunity for their members who went on strike, though even that immunity depended on the strikes being 'lawful', that is if they were strikes for themselves and not for anyone else. At the core of the new Tory law was the determination to wipe out solidarity action.

What should the unions do? I was fortunate enough to be a delegate from my union to the TUC in Blackpool in 1971, where the argument was fought out at the highest intellectual level. Most delegates when they went to Blackpool were resigned to registration. That way, after all, they could keep their jobs and their unions intact. The case against registration was led by two left-wing union leaders, Jack Jones of the T&GWU and Hugh Scanlon of the Amalgamated Engineering Union (AEU). 'Every scratch can lead to gangrene,' warned Scanlon. If the unions cooperated with the Government by registering under the Act, they would lose their ability to fight for their members and in the end they would lose their independence. Gradually, the argument swung against registration, and the vote – by 3 to 2 – followed the argument. The whole experience was a lesson in a quite different form of democracy from that practised day by day in Parliament. This was a democracy whose roots were sunk in working-class self-interest, and the standard of debate measured up to it.

There were plenty of other reasons in the autumn of 1971 why a genuine working-class democracy was able to assert itself so powerfully. Earlier in the year, the workers in the Scottish shipyards owned by Upper Clyde Shipbuilders had refused to accept the decision of the Tory Government to close the firm down and chuck all the workers on the dole because UCS no longer made a profit. The Industry Secretary, former Confederation of British Industry (CBI) chieftain John Davies, had outlined his philosophy soon after taking up his post by announcing that there would be no more 'lame ducks'. Loss-making firms, he asserted, could no longer look to Government to bale them out. They would be closed, their workers sacked.

This hard line had already been dented when Rolls-Royce went bust and had to be nationalized to save its valuable technology, especially in aero engines. But Davies's hardline policy had in general been pursued with predictable results. Unemployment soared to peaks unheard of since the 1930s. At the end of 1971, with more than a million unemployed, with at least two big unions in the public sector defeated in open class warfare, and with the Industrial Relations Act on the statute book, the Tories could well have expected a series of easy victories over the pestilential trade unions and their even more pestilential unofficial strikers. The successful occupation on the Clyde by the shipyard workers was not part of their plan, but on its own it could probably have been isolated and contained.

Then it was 1972, the most tempestuous year of the post-war period, during which every Tory policy and strategy was reversed, not by parliamentary opposition but by the actions of organized workers. First came the coal miners, whose standard of living and security of employment had been systematically eroded by the Labour Government and who had at the end of 1971 submitted a not very audacious wage claim to bring themselves up to the standard they had enjoyed when their industry was nationalized 23 years earlier. The Government contemptuously dismissed the claim, and the overtime ban that backed it up.

Miners? Who were they and who should take them seriously? Had they not been pulverized in 1921 and 1926? Who had heard a cheep out of them since? Even if they did go on strike, were there not huge reserves of coal at the power stations, enough surely to grind the miners down every bit as effectively as the power and postal workers had been? Woodrow Wyatt in the *Mirror* joyfully discarded the capricious militancy (backed by his retainer from the Electrical Trades Union) with which he had defended the power workers the previous year. The miners, he exulted, 'have more stacked against them than the Light Brigade in their famous charge'.

Someone, however, had blundered. Supported by a majority in a ballot, the miners struck on 9 January 1972. Every pit was closed. From the outset there was no sign of the passivity that had done so much to demoralize the striking power and postal workers a year earlier. Flying pickets laid siege to the power stations, rendering almost useless the huge coal stocks that had so bolstered the Tory ministers. Not only power stations but also coke depots were picketed. A huge coke depot at Saltley Gate, about a mile from the centre of Birmingham, where pickets started on 3 February, turned into a major confrontation. If the miners' pickets had been left on their own, the police would easily have outnumbered them. They would not have been able to stop lorries taking coke from the depot, and over the next few days there would almost certainly have been many arrests and lots of violence. But the miners' pickets, which built up to 3,000 within a week, were not left on their own. On 10 February, they were joined by at least 20,000 Birmingham workers, most of them from car and engineering factories. The police had built up their number to 800, but they could not contain the size of the crowd. The cry went up 'close the gates!' and the gates were closed. The Chief Constable of Birmingham had assured Home Secretary Reginald Maudling that the miners would close the Saltley depot 'over my dead body'. When the depot was shut down, Reginald Maudling was, he wrote later, 'inclined to inquire after the Chief Constable's health'.

The Saltley closure enthused the already confident miners. Not much later the lights started to go out all over Britain and the machinery in the factories to slow down. Tory ministers were suddenly engulfed in panic. The whole country was grinding to a halt in circumstances in which they, the elected Government, could do nothing to get it going again. To save face, a 'court of inquiry' under Lord Wilberforce was set up. It heard evidence for two days and reported two days later! It recommended a 20 per cent basic increase for the miners, and a settlement that should have cost the Government £85 million – compared to the £25 million they had offered the miners the previous October. In arriving at this figure, Wilberforce broke all the Government's rules set down for pay settlements in the public sector. But still his proposals were not enough for the National Union of Mineworkers. The union scented victory, and intended at last to exact revenge for 1921, for 1926 and for all the exploitation, starvation and despair suffered by miners in the past. For four more days of growing February darkness, the miners' executive discussed the offer, at first rejecting it wholesale, and finally, by 16 votes to 9, accepted a package whose cost had grown to £117 million. The entire Government incomes policy was smashed to smithereens.

No wonder Edward Heath was depressed. He knew that the miners' settlement would not be seen as a 'special case' – as he tried to describe it. The settlement lifted the morale and confidence of trade unionists everywhere. They noticed that the miners, for all their astonishing victory, had carried with them not just the entire Labour movement but had also converted that most intangible phenomenon, public opinion. Even the *Sun* newspaper, under its new owner Rupert Murdoch, supported the miners.

The historic miners' victory in the spring of 1972 was not inevitable. At the start of the strike, the Government held all the important cards. There was enough coal at the power stations to stave off the effects of a miners' strike for at least as long as in 1921 and 1926. The union leadership was conservative and unrepresentative. The loyalty of the strikers to their union on its own did not guarantee victory, as had been seen in the postal workers' strike. The element of the dispute that had not been anticipated by the Government and the employers was picketing. Unlike the postal workers, the miners were not prepared to sit at home and leave the battle over their wages and conditions to their union leaders. From the first day of the strike, the rank and file under local initiative and newly elected local leaders resolved to make sure that the stakes in the dispute – so heavily stacked against them – were tipped decisively in their direction. In this bold endeavour they relied on the solidarity of workers in other industries. If the electricity industry was to be prevented from using and enlarging stocks of coal, the miners needed the support of power workers, dockers and railway workers. That required extensive picketing. If the miners' families were to be protected from starvation, they needed the support of working families outside their industry. That meant the invasion of cities and towns all over Britain by bands of strikers, some of them picketing, others collecting money and lobbying for support. So it was that the miners' strike of 1972 transformed British industrial relations not by the actions of the Government, or even the miners' union executive, but by the actions of rank-and-file miners.

All this led to an unparalleled blossoming of democracy. Political discussion and debate, for so long confined to parliamentary chambers, suddenly became part of the daily lives of many thousands of workers. Anyone even remotely involved in those nine dramatic weeks can testify to that. Here was a democratic movement inspired by action from below which gave a previously humiliated and defeated section of the British working class new confidence and a new yearning to play a part in the democratic process.

The rest of 1972 was dominated by the miners' victory. When the railway workers threatened a strike in support of their own wage claim, the Government threw what it regarded as its killer punch. For years, Tory ministers had been deceived by their own propaganda that strikes were the work of unrepresentative militants, usually inspired by sinister left-wing political organizations. Strikes were therefore the work of minorities. Now the Industrial Relations Act gave the Tory Government and its new industrial court the power to place these matters in the hands of a majority of the workers involved by ordering a ballot. All three rail unions therefore were obliged to ballot their members with the question 'are you prepared to take industrial action' in support of their claim. Almost unanimously, the newspapers and industrial correspondents used every trick in their repertoire to explain to railway workers the full horror of a yes vote. The result, announced on 31 May 1972, was as follows: yes, 129,441; no, 23,181 – a 5 to 1 majority on a 90 per cent turn-out. I can remember reading that result on a glorious June morning and reflecting that it provided the most powerful proof of a different and more vibrant democracy than anything the newspapers could claim, however vast their circulation. The vote was a further humiliation for the Government, whose new Employment Minister, Maurice Macmillan, promptly gave the railway workers everything they asked for.

Then came the engineering workers in the Manchester area, who copied the tactic pioneered by so many students over the previous five years of occupying their premises in support of their demands. Then, in the summer, came the extraordinary release, after an application of that rare litigant, the Official Solicitor, of five dockers imprisoned for contempt of court under the Industrial Relations Act. Then came the long and almost unreported struggle and victory of the building workers – so often the Cinderellas of the trade-union movement. Victory after victory swept through the movement. The Government's incomes policy was reduced to ruins. Tony Benn's diaries for the period noted how Industry Secretary of State John Davies reversed his entire policy on lame ducks and then, in quick succession, reversed his entire policy on industrial subsidies and unemployment.

The release of the five dockers exposed the vulnerability of the Industrial Relations Act – a vulnerability from which it never recovered. The mood of working people and their organizations was transformed by these victories. The policies of the elected Government were exposed and reversed. Prime Minister Heath and his Chancellor, Anthony Barber, introduced a new policy for industry. Where previously they had insisted that there should be no Government subsidies for industry, they now announced enormous industrial subsidies.

The mass workers' revolt of 1972 was not confined to industry. It inspired socialists all over Britain. In the small Derbyshire town of Clay Cross, whose people had elected 11 councillors, all working class, all Labour, the council refused to raise the rents as the Tory Government's Housing Finance Act 1972 demanded. The Government and its agents, in the shape of the unelected district auditor (whose equivalent had caused such fury among the elected council and electorate at Poplar half a century earlier), declared war on the council. Invigorated and inspired by the miners' victory, the 11 stood firm. They insisted that they had been elected on a clear programme of refusing to raise rents, and that four of them had been re-elected on the same policy in the very year the Act became law 'with the enthusiastic support of large sections of British Labour'. To a clamour of protest all over the Labour movement, the councillors were disqualified, surcharged and bankrupted. The Labour Party's instant response was to treat the councillors as martyrs, and to seek to reassure them that they would be reinstated and compensated by a future Labour Government. Resolution 191 of the Labour Party conference deplored the vacillation of the Party's National Executive on the issue. The executive speaker in the debate was the Deputy Leader of the Party, Ted Short, who explained that there were legal problems for a new Government seeking retrospectively to lift penalties imposed by law, and this was why the executive had vacillated. But he insisted that Clay Cross was different. 'Clay Cross,' he said, to cheers, 'is something special. It really is. I think everybody in Britain, in the Labour movement and outside, is full of sympathy and admiration for the stand David Skinner and his colleagues have taken.' The critical resolution was carried, on a show of hands, almost without opposition. There was not a person in the hall who did not believe that the Clay Cross councillors, so defiant of Tory laws in the interests of their electorate, and cruelly punished by the Tories, would be properly compensated by the next Labour Government.

The industrial and democratic volcano of 1972 also transformed the Labour Party. Barbara Castle discovered how wrong she had been, and how no future Labour Government could ever again propose anything like 'In Place of Strife'. New discussions were started between the Labour leadership and the TUC. One result was the publication at the 1973 Labour Party conference of 'Labour's Programme'. A decade later, the Tory leaders and their press jeered at the Labour Party manifesto, describing it as 'the longest suicide note in history'. By the same measure, the 1973 'Programme' would have wiped out the possibility of Labour ever again being elected. It was far to the left not just of the 1983 manifesto but of similar programmes in 1945, 1950 and 1951. It opened with a triumphant declaration of faith: 'We are a democratic socialist party, and proud of it.' It went on to identify the main problem of British society as the power and irresponsibility of the rich.

The 'main socialist aims' of the Party were then listed. First came FISP, 'a fundamental and irreversible shift in the balance of power and wealth in favour of working people and their families'. Then came the aspiration 'to make power fully accountable to the community, to workers and to the consumer'. In a purple passage, the 'Programme' trumpeted:

The cornerstone of democratic socialism is a constant awareness of the need to improve democracy, by making power in all its forms more accountable. It is not enough to vote each year for local councils and twice a decade for Parliament. We must have government by consent, with democratic institutions, in the workplace.

Or again:

The central question is who wields economic power in Britain? Shall an elected Government take powers for the community, or shall we try for ever to run a system where Savundra, John Bloom and Bernie Cornfield [three prominent capitalist crooks of the time] are regarded as wizards until their empires collapse, leaving the public to pick up the pieces?

The conclusion for even the most casual reader was obvious. The next Labour Government must establish rigid control of the economy, and take over the reins of economic power from people like Savundra, Bloom and Cornfield. Labour was committed to a fundamental and irreversible shift of power. There could be no hope of FISP as long as the rich remained so rich. FISP could only be accomplished by a strenuous attack on the rich. Denis Healey, who was Shadow Chancellor of the Exchequer, was attributed as saying that he intended to 'squeeze the rich until the pips squeaked', words he always denied using. At the 1973 Labour Party conference, however, he did say that his proposals for redistribution of income in Britain would be met by 'howls of anguish from the rich'. Finally, 'Labour's Programme' repeated the Party's commitment widely to extend public ownership by nationalizing aircraft, shipbuilding and North Sea oil and by taking control of substantial shareholdings in a wide range of privately owned industries.

The industrial disputes continued, at a more relaxed pace, through 1973. The Tory Government seemed helpless in face of the organized workers' victories. Some Tory leaders were prepared for abject surrender and even defeat. At Christmas 1973, Industry Secretary of State John Davies recorded, he called his family together and warned them that they would be unlikely ever again to meet in similar circumstances of confidence and prosperity. Other ministers were less pessimistic, but all of them realized that they were being defeated on the industrial battlefield, and that they must somehow devise a counter-attack. Margaret Thatcher, Secretary of State for Education, later recorded her deep dissatisfaction with what she regarded as the conciliatory policies of her Government. She took part in the capitulation to the miners, but at least she realized that it was a capitulation. She wrote in the second volume of her autobiography, *The Path to Power* (1995):

For me, what happened at Saltley took on no less significance than it did for the Left. I understood, as they did, that the struggle to bring trade unions properly within the rule of law would be decided not in the debating chamber of the House of Commons, or even on the hustings, but in and around the pits and factories where intimidation had been allowed to prevail.

In the key struggle, in other words, her side had lost at Saltley, and if ever they got into government again, they must take the battle into the very class battlefield where it had been so decisively lost.

For the moment, however, there seemed to be no stopping the onward march of the organized workers. In November 1973, the miners voted again for action in support of another big wage claim. A ballot for a strike showed a huge increase in support for militant action. Even in the Nottingham area of the National Union of Mineworkers, traditionally the most 'moderate', miners voted overwhelmingly for another strike. As a strike approached, the Tory leaders decided to stand and fight. On 7 February 1974, three days before a full miners' strike began, Edward Heath dissolved Parliament and called a general election on the issue of 'who runs the country?' – the elected Government or the NUM.

The Labour Party manifesto proclaimed its new 'social contract' with the trade unions, and indicated that it would settle the miners' claim in line with that contract. On other issues, Labour's manifesto was quite different from its predecessors in 1970 or 1966. The basic points of the 1973 programme were restated. 'The points set out in this manifesto,' it boasted, 'are socialist aims and we are proud of the word ... it is indeed our intention to bring about a fundamental and irreversible shift in the balance of power in favour of working people and their families', to eliminate poverty, to 'make power in industry genuinely accountable to the workers and the community at large' and 'to achieve far greater economic equality, in income, wealth and living standards'.

Looking back on that election, which I spent in the editorial offices of *Socialist Worker*, I can remember very clearly the strong feeling of disbelief that the Tories were winning hands down. Almost every poll gave the Tories a clear lead. The polls seemed to be suggesting a complete divergence between the huge increase in working-class confidence since 1970 and the way people would vote. This all seemed most unlikely, and so it proved. The result of the election was a stalemate. The Tory vote was substantially down on 1970 – from 13,145,123 to 11,862,250. The Labour vote was down too, from 12,208,758 to 11,645,616. The real shock was the rise in the Liberal vote from just over 2 million to over 6 million – and a rise in the number of Liberal MPs from 6 to 14. Another quirk of the electoral system gave Labour MPs, with fewer votes, a slight edge over Tory MPs – 301 seats to 297. So who was to run the country? After a short, rather pathetic, bid to patch together a coalition with the Liberals, Heath resigned as Prime Minister and was replaced by Harold Wilson.

The Labour Government that took office in March 1974 was in one crucial respect substantially different from its predecessor ten years previously. Wilson, Callaghan, Castle, Healey, Jenkins, Crosland were still in the main offices of state. Tony Benn was still there too, but the years in opposition had completely transformed him. He had shed the collaborationist and technocratic image he had nurtured in his previous periods of office and was utterly committed to FISP and the various interventionist means whereby FISP would be achieved. He had become an idol of the left of the Party and his appointment as Secretary of State for Industry was a clear sign of the dramatic change in the Labour Party caused by the industrial convulsions of the early 1970s.

To prove the point, Benn's new minister of state was Eric Heffer, a working-class MP from Liverpool with a Marxist past he was reluctant to deny. An even more significant and dramatic appointment was that of Michael Foot as Secretary of State for Employment. One of the few survivors of the 1945 Labour intake, Foot was probably the most respected and able speaker in the House of Commons and the author of a majestic two-volume biography of Aneurin Bevan. The significance of his appointment was the new pact, thrashed out throughout the period of the Tory Government, between the Labour Party and the trade unions. Never again, it was agreed, would any Labour Government allow itself to be pushed into statutory wage control. From now on a Labour Government would act in partnership with the trade unions, whose leaders would, in effect, be consulted at every stage in the political process. The firmest supporters of this policy in the trade unions were Jack Jones, General Secretary of the T&GWU, and Hugh Scanlon, President of the AEU. This pact with the unions, the central theme of the entire period of Labour Government from 1974 to 1979, was the result of a tacit understanding that the democracy of an elected Labour Government had to coincide with the democracy of the trade-union movement. Somehow, the two democracies had to be reconciled.

The immediate impact of the election and the appointments of Foot, Benn and Heffer were astonishingly decisive. The Government had not got a majority, or anything approaching one. Yet the new administration quickly set about clearing up the mess left by the Tories. Almost at once, a settlement was reached with the miners (without conceding the whole of their claim) and industrial peace in the coalfields was restored. Michael Foot proposed a new trade union and labour relations Act that repealed the Industrial Relations Act. This move was not even opposed by the Tories in Parliament, who hovered and whined in deep disarray. The hated Housing Finance Act with its automatic increases in council-house rents was swiftly repealed. Denis Healey's first budget was fair to the poor and relatively tough on the rich. Considering its lack of a parliamentary majority, the speed with which the new administration dispensed with the Tory residue was remarkable. It was as though the great surge of militancy from below in 1972 to 1974 propelled the Government through the spring and summer of 1974 into an almost feverish determination to carry out its commitments.

In spite of the euphoria, however, there were, even in those first six months, plenty of signs of the extra-parliamentary obstacles that had held up the Labour Government in the 1960s. The CBI, representing British industrialists, had launched a sustained campaign against Tony Benn. This campaign was conducted almost entirely behind the scenes, and orchestrated through the columns of the overwhelmingly Tory press. Benn's efforts to save jobs in workplaces taken over by workers' cooperatives were ridiculed to the point of sabotage. The original draft of his Industry Bill, drawn up in line with Labour's manifesto, which gave huge powers to the National Enterprise Board and the Government, was called in by the Prime Minister's office, rewritten and watered down. The White Paper that had spelled out the interventionist policies of the manifesto became a Green Paper, merely up for discussion. CBI leaders Michael Clapham and Campbell Adamson went to see Wilson as early as May to tell him they could not work with Benn.

Benn's spirited resistance to this campaign infuriated the Prime Minister, who yearned for the earnest young man who had served him so faithfully in the 1960s. In June 1974, a radio broadcast by Benn in which he repeated the manifesto commitments about intervention in private industry so angered Wilson that he summoned the naughty minister to his office and asked him testily: 'Why don't you work harder instead of making all these speeches? Why don't you behave more as you did when you were at the Ministry of Technology?' Benn replied (according to his account) that he worked extremely hard, and that he felt obliged to carry out the manifesto. Wilson fumed, and made it clear that he would not tolerate any more of it.

One issue that drove Tony Benn and Michael Foot into outright opposition to the Government was the demand by James Callaghan, Foreign Secretary, that warships built in British yards for the Chilean Navy should be handed over to the Chilean Government. Less than a year earlier, in September 1973, a fascist coup, organized and financed by the United States, overthrew Chile's elected social democratic Government, murdered its elected president, Salvador Allende, and established a brutal military regime under Augusto Pinochet which killed and tortured thousands of the equivalent of Labour Party supporters in Chile. The provision of military ships to Pinochet's Government was naturally regarded by Labour supporters as monstrous, but despite the opposition in the Cabinet the Government proceeded with the sale of at least one of the ships, and a promise of another. The military-industrial complex and its supporters in the civil service had won a partial, if not conclusive victory over the Party and its more ardent supporters.

There were plenty of other signs that even in those first few heady months, rich and powerful people outside Parliament were preparing for a fight with the elected Government. In an intriguing diary entry for 16 July 1974, Tony Benn described a dinner he attended at the invitation of the directors of the big Midlands steel and engineering company GKN. The GKN chairman, Sir Ray Brookes, 'declared that if I didn't remove GKN from the list of top companies for nationalization within a month, they would cancel all their investment plans for next year'. Not believing what he heard, Benn asked Brookes to repeat his threat. He did so at once, and Benn replied that there was no such list of companies. 'However,' he conceded, 'GKN was among the names of the top 20 companies in the country given to me by the Department, and I had asked the Department to check how much public money they had had.' Benn mused in his diary: 'It was clear that we are facing a strike of capital.' The consequences of such a strike were very clearly recognized by the Chancellor of the Exchequer, Denis Healey, who told Benn some months later that 'the whole of our future depends upon the confidence of businessmen', and that Benn's speeches and the publicity they had attracted 'undermine confidence all the time'. Healey was, like his predecessor in the 1960s, almost exclusively obsessed with the vulnerability of sterling. He produced three budgets in 1974. Each one took the Government further away from Labour's manifesto commitments than the last. On each occasion, and with mounting panic, Healey referred to the balance of payments crisis and the urgent need to stem the sale of sterling.

The drift seems clearer in hindsight than at the time, and in general in those few months of minority government, ministers and their supporters in the country had little or no inkling of the storm that was being prepared for them by unrepresentative minorities. Yet even in those early days, sinister and undemocratic forces were at work. Their aim was to subvert, sabotage and even to overthrow the elected Government.

Colin Wallace was a young information officer employed by the British Army at Lisburn, Northern Ireland. He started work in 1968 as a press officer, but as the conflict between the majority Protestant and minority Catholic communities intensified, he was singled out for promotion and for a different job description in what later became known as 'psychological operations'. He was trained in the techniques of 'black propaganda', the aim of which initially was to spread propaganda against IRA terrorists. As the Tory Government in the early 1970s showed less and less enthusiasm for the conflict in Northern Ireland and for the Protestant ascendancy there, opinion in the officers' messes swung to the view that the ruling Tories, and any Labour Government that might get elected, were soft on terrorism and were therefore traitors to Britain. This ludicrous view was especially influential in the intelligence community of Northern Ireland, control of which was switched in 1973 from MI6 to MI5.

When Labour took office in March 1974, all the worst fears of the intelligence spooks were confirmed. Here, they concluded, was a Government soft on communism and soft on terrorism taking over control of the armed forces in Northern Ireland. During the months between the two Labour Governments, Colin Wallace was preoccupied with a project, code-named Clockwork Orange, whose object was to smear the allegedly treacherous Tory leaders of the past and, more sharply, the new Labour Government. Wallace set to work to construct a number of documents based on entirely false information supplied to him by MI5 officers. Their object was to expose the financial, sexual and political flaws of individual political leaders. One forgery, for instance, was a leaflet calling for mass protest against the army's killing of 13 unarmed demonstrators in Derry in January 1972, on what became known as Bloody Sunday. The leaflet had been issued by a number of civil rights supporters, but Wallace inserted into the list of sponsors the names of Merlyn Rees, Northern Ireland Secretary in Wilson's Government, Tony Benn and two other junior ministers in the Labour Government, Stan Orme and David Owen. Wallace would then show the forged document to visiting journalists, especially American ones. The journalists could look at the document, absorb its message (that Rees and Co. were pro-IRA agitators) and then hand it back. There were several forgeries of the same kind, equally damaging.

The Clockwork Orange documents themselves went further. They listed a number of Labour and Tory leaders and marked their names with a cross if they were suspected of financial skulduggery, personal problems (marital infidelities or homosexuality) or suspect political (Communist) tendencies. The only name on the list marked with crosses under all three headings was the Prime Minister, Harold Wilson. The notes Wallace wrote to back up these documents and suspicions were founded entirely on fallacies and rumours. They gave credence to the most grotesque smears against the people who had been elected to take charge of the armed forces and MI5. The loyalty of the latter was put to the test many years later, when Peter Wright published his memoirs in a book entitled *Spycatcher* (1987). Wright confirmed that he and many other half-crazed MI5 officers had been convinced that Wilson was working for the Russians and that MI5 officers had 'bugged and burgled' their way across London' to seek to prove the point.

The Tory Government's frenzied attempts to ban *Spycatcher* ensured it a massive circulation, but the book itself turned out to be almost unreadable, full of quaint and boring anecdotes, puffed up with prejudice. At the end, however, Wright suddenly disclosed the deep hatred and suspicion of MI5 officers for their Prime Minister. In the 1960s, he revealed, MI5 had worked closely with their agent, Cecil King, chairman of the *Daily Mirror*, in his futile and risible attempt to replace the elected Labour Government with a National Government under Lord Mountbatten. In the first period of Wilson government, ruthless and reckless activity by MI5 officers had driven one Labour minister, Bernard Floud, to commit suicide and another, Niall MacDermot, to resign his office. Wright's book claimed that in 1974 the attack on Wilson from his own intelligence officers was far more virulent than anything that had taken place in the 1960s:

The approach in 1974 was altogether more serious. The plan was simple. In the run-up to the election which, given the level of instability in Parliament, must be due within a matter of months, MI5 would arrange for selective details of the intelligence about leading Labour Party figures but especially Wilson to be leaked to sympathetic pressmen. Using our contacts in the press, and among union officials, word of the material contained in MI5 files and the fact that Wilson was a security risk would be passed around.

The authorities found it relatively easy to pass Wright off as an isolated raving extremist. But his allegations should be read in tandem with those of Colin Wallace, who started trying to publicize his own subversive role when he was summarily sacked from the army in 1975, and continued to do so even after he was convicted in 1981 of killing his best friend (a monstrous conviction that was eventually quashed by the Court of Appeal). Wallace was finally compensated by the state for the gross injustice done to him, but inside prison and out of it he was smeared, sidelined and patronized.

In those volatile months of 1974, senior intelligence officers were working overtime to subvert, disorientate and even overthrow those who were elected to take charge of them. And this was the period when almost every week new, extra-parliamentary organizations, many of them stridently chauvinistic and right wing, were setting themselves up with the ambitious aim to take control of the country if and when the elected Government collapsed. In late 1973, for instance, the Unison Committee for Action was founded by G. K. Young, an extreme right-wing activist who had been deputy head of MI6. In 1974, Colonel David Stirling, a founder of the Special Air Service, set up GB 75, whose declared intention was to prepare for a patriotic seizure of power in the event of the collapse of democratic government.

One result – in Northern Ireland – was catastrophic for the prestige of the new Labour Government. On 13 May 1974, Harold Wilson made a dramatic announcement in the House of Commons. The IRA, he revealed, had concocted what became known as a Doomsday Plot to reduce whole areas of Belfast to rubble and to transport large sections of its Catholic population to the South. The revelation of this secret plot was reminiscent of Wilson's equally dramatic public 'outing' in 1966 of a Communist plot to further the seamen's strike. As he revealed on both occasions, the plots had been unveiled by the security services – in 1966 by the time-honoured practice of tapping the phones of industrial militants, in 1974 by the release of secret IRA documents uncovered by the hard-working patriots in MI5.

Wilson's 'Doomsday Plot' speech caused a sensation. It was wildly applauded by the Conservatives. But it was based entirely on documents recovered by the security services some two years previously that had caused only a ripple of interest at the time. The 'scorched earth policy' was put forward by the IRA solely as a defensive measure in the event of a decisive offensive by Protestant paramilitaries. If, and only if, the Protestants launched an offensive to drive Catholics out of their homes, would the IRA launch a counter-offensive that would lay waste to whole areas of the city and evacuate its threatened minority.

The date of Wilson's announcement had another significance. On that day a band of Protestant sectarians and extremists came together in Belfast, named themselves the Ulster Workers' Council and called a general strike across Northern Ireland. Their demand had nothing to do with workers' wages or conditions. Its aim was entirely political – the removal of the power-sharing executive set up by the Conservative Government the previous year in which for the first time elected representatives of the Catholic or nationalist minority shared the offices of state in Northern Ireland with the Unionists.

This sharing of power was regarded by many Unionists – and by their supporters in the army and in intelligence – as monstrous proof of the treachery of the more liberal Tories and especially of the Labour Government. The purpose of the strike was to put a stop to power-sharing in Northern Ireland. The strike, in short, was a direct and open challenge to elected government in Westminster. It started on the same day – 13 May – that Prime Minister Harold Wilson exposed the Doomsday Plot that never was. The result was that public attention was fixed not on subversive behaviour of the Protestant UWC, but on the old IRA plans that were never carried out.

The UWC strike raced through industry and paralysed even the power stations. Almost at once the authorities threw in the towel. The single demand of the UWC was conceded unconditionally. Power-sharing in Northern Ireland was ended. Direct rule from Westminster was restored, and continued for a quarter of a century. *The Point of No Return* (1975), a book by the *Times* correspondent in Northern Ireland Robert Fisk, describes in detail the degree of cooperation between the British troops and the Protestant subversives. Again and again, Fisk revealed, the army pleaded their impotence to handle the situation, when the evidence suggested the opposite. A Government determined to smash the strike, for instance, could easily have kept the power stations running with English and Scottish technicians and engineers. It was true that the strike had strong support from some Protestants in Northern Ireland. But at least a third of the population were strongly opposed to the strikers, and a vote in the Protestant workforce in the Harland and Wolf shipyard revealed a majority against a strike. The British TUC, to which many workers in Northern Ireland were affiliated, was strongly opposed to the strike and organized a march against it. But the TUC and the Catholic minority had scant support from the British Government. The text of Harold Wilson's broadcast on 16 May, which originally denounced the strike as a 'rebellion against the Crown', was altered at the last moment to remove any reference to rebellion and instead castigated the entire population of Northern Ireland as 'spongers', thus infuriating Protestants and Catholics alike. The message of Fisk's book is quite clear. The British Labour Government capitulated to the demands of a handful of the most extreme reactionaries among their citizens, and in so doing sacrificed its own chosen path to reform.

Their capitulation harked back 60 years – to 1914, when the Liberal

Government, under similar pressure from the military forces they were meant to command, gave way to Ulster Unionists and effectively withdrew from its commitment to Home Rule for all Ireland. In 1914, however, the pressure from the military was backed by an enormous display of British solidarity with Ulster Unionism. Millions of people responded to Tory cries for defiance of the elected majority. In 1974, there were no such demonstrations, no sign at all that the sectarian hysteria of the UWC and its supporters in the army and intelligence had any public support in Britain. Yet the Labour Government's collapse was every bit as abject as that of its Liberal predecessor.

Northern Ireland was not the only area in which the security services harried the Government. Again and again they interfered with Government appointments. They succeeded for at least two years in denying Hugh Scanlon, the engineering union President, any public office on the grounds of his allegedly friendly relations with Communists. Jack Jones, General Secretary of the T&GWU, had never been a Communist, nor had his wife, but both were subjected to an entirely fanciful MI5 account of their days as young Communists. These suspicions, most of them entirely unfounded, prevented Jones's appointment as chairman of the National Enterprise Board. Nor were ministers themselves immune to the consistent and hysterical whispering campaigns led by the security services. At one point Tony Benn became so suspicious about his telephone that he wrote to his colleague in the Cabinet Merlyn Rees, Home Secretary, asking if his phone was tapped. There was a long delay, and Benn had to repeat his question several times. Eventually, Rees wrote back to declare that he could not say yes or no. The matter was cleared up in the end by Prime Minister James Callaghan, who assured Benn that his phone was not tapped – though whether Callaghan's assurance came after he had himself found out that Benn's phone was tapped, and put a stop to it, is still not clear.

Perhaps the most direct attack on a serving Cabinet minister was the MI5 approach to Wilson about his Minister for Overseas Development, Judith Hart. Wilson had to tell her she was being 'positively vetted' by the security services. She demanded to know why, but got no answer beyond the surprising information that she was suspected of having links with the Communist Party. Much later the source of the false rumour emerged. MI5 officers had made inquiries following a tapped telephone conversation Mrs Hart had had with British Communist Party headquarters. She made the call to check information about the imprisonment in Chile of British Communist Party members. MI5 then checked her file and found a photograph of a Mrs Hart at a Communist Conference in Eastern Europe in 1950. The picture was complete! Judith Hart was a closet Communist! Only later did it emerge that the woman who attended this conference was someone quite different, Mrs Tudor Hart, a well-known Communist.

The security services knew perfectly well that the photograph was not of Judith Hart. In 1950, when she was a young Labour candidate in Bournemouth, they had shown the photograph to her election agent, who declared immediately and emphatically that the woman in the photo was not Judith Hart. So although they knew the smear was false, the mendacious fanatics in MI5 persisted in raising it with the Prime Minister. Not much later, Judith Hart was sacked from the Cabinet.

Considering the extent and ferocity of these extra-parliamentary assaults – and the fact that Labour ministers were governing without a parliamentary majority – the survival of the administration through those awkward months of 1974 was remarkable. It was as though the confidence instilled in them by the rank-and-file agitation, crowned by another miners' victory, helped them keep on course.

That confidence lasted through the year. In September, only six months after the election, Wilson dissolved Parliament and sought a new mandate on the basis of roughly the same manifesto – and the Government's performance. Polling day was 10 October. The exit polls predicted a big majority for Labour, the result so dreaded by MI5 and the military extremists, and the results gave them a substantial majority of 42 over the demoralized and divided Tories. But when the minor parties were counted in, including a surprisingly resurgent Scottish Nationalist Party (up from 7 seats to 11) the overall majority was only 4. Harold Wilson, with almost exactly the same team, including Benn at Industry and Foot at Employment, took office with a majority and every hope of survival for a full term, with far less interference from outside bodies.

The first eight months of the new majority Government were absorbed, however, in an awkward if familiar issue – Europe. The terms signed by Edward Heath in 1973 for Britain's entry into the Common Market had been overwhelmingly opposed by the Labour Party, and Harold Wilson and his Foreign Secretary, James Callaghan, were sent back to Europe to negotiate better terms. The vast majority of British big business supported entry on the existing terms. Many business chieftains were distressed at the commitment, forced on Labour through an initiative from Tony Benn, that any new terms should be subjected to a referendum whose result would be binding on the Government. The prospect that such a referendum might come out against entry into the Common Market filled bankers and industrialists with panic and gloom. They took comfort from the number of convinced pro-Europeans in the Cabinet, led by Home Secretary Roy Jenkins and Prices Secretary Shirley Williams.

More was required, however, to ensure that the British people understood the needs of their economic and industrial leaders, and voted accordingly. A new organization, Britain in Europe, was set up, with unlimited funds, to argue for continued membership of the Market. When Callaghan returned from Europe with what, he argued, were the best new terms he could get, the Labour Party was not impressed. A dangerous and almost unprecedented split opened in Labour ranks. The Party's executive and the majority of the rank and file were against the new terms, and voted accordingly at a special conference. The central argument that persuaded them was the damage the Market would do to parliamentary democracy. The new terms did nothing to alter the plain fact that membership of the European Community meant a transfer of power from elected parliaments to the unelected European Commission. On the other hand, however, most Labour MPs and a large majority in the Cabinet approved the terms. Wilson himself was in favour of staying in, but he was sensitive to the intense danger of opposition from his own party. In a sense, he was saved by the referendum. He proposed a solution to the split in Labour ranks by allowing ministers and MPs to take sides in the debate on the referendum, even if that meant that they could openly criticize each other's views. This solution was acceptable to ministers on both sides of the argument, and, as the set period for the debate approached, Cabinet ministers divided. Seven of them, Benn, Foot, Castle, Peter Shore, chief whip John Silkin, Scottish Secretary Willie Ross and Energy Secretary Eric Varley were against the terms. The rest were in favour.

The open rifts in Labour ranks ensured a delicate and difficult time for the Government, and all other political and industrial battles seemed to hang fire. There was political calm before the storm, as the vote was anxiously awaited on both sides. The seven Cabinet members' arguments for a No vote were to some extent discredited by their willingness to stand on the same platform as opponents from the right and even the extreme right. Such people were not in the least bit interested in the perils to democracy in the Market, and opposed entry for blatantly nationalistic and racist reasons. But in truth, with the leaders of all three major parties in uncompromising support of a Yes vote, and the most extravagant spending from Britain in Europe, the No campaign never really stood a chance. The pro-Marketeers spent £1,365,583 against the antis' £133,629. The entire national and provincial press supported entry. The referendum, held on 5 June, produced an overwhelming victory for the Party leaders and the press: 17,378,571 votes for Yes, 8,470,073 for No.

At once Wilson moved to carry out a promise he had made to the CBI. On the Monday after the referendum result, he sacked Tony Benn as Secretary of State for Industry and offered him the same position at the Department of Energy. Benn knew he was under threat (Wilson himself had leaked a story to the *Daily Telegraph* that Benn was likely to go), and knew he was being demoted. After a day and a night's miserable rumination, he accepted Energy and was replaced at Industry by the much more pliable Eric Varley. Both inside and outside the Cabinet, Tony Benn symbolized the socialist and democratic advances of the early 1970s. His removal from the key position of Industry was greeted with undisguised jubilation by the captains of industry and the press barons. He was sidelined – and the Government's commitment to state intervention was sidelined with him. That month of June 1975, which had started with the overwhelming decision on Europe followed closely by the toppling of Tony Benn (Eric Heffer, his socialist deputy, had been sacked several weeks earlier for making an anti-Market speech in the Commons), switched the balance in the Government from left to right. Until June, the industrial and political momentum to the left had been maintained. After June, it slowed and then stopped.

Almost at once, the most familiar of all the extra-parliamentary obstacles to dog the advance of British Labour – the weakness of sterling – arose again like a ghastly ghost to push the ministers from their stools. In his last volume of memoirs, Harold Wilson described the unfolding crisis of the summer in uncharacteristically vivid language. The problem that had faced the Cabinet ever since they took office the previous year was inflation. Part of it was caused by the meteoric rise in oil prices since the Arab–Israeli War in 1973, part of it by the rise in wages brought about by trade-union militancy. The index for wages in all industries and services had risen between March 1974 and March 1975 by 32.9 per cent. Prices had gone up much less sharply, partly due to controlled rents and food subsidies – but they rose over the same period by 21 per cent. The Government, according to Wilson, knew they had to act. But what could they do? Above all they were committed against the remedy their predecessors had introduced at a similar period of panic in 1966 and the Tories had followed from 1972 – statutory wage control. Some other remedy had to be found. For Wilson, the key event that summer was the National Union of Mineworkers' conference. The more militant areas of the NUM were demanding a basic minimum of £100 a week for face workers. If that were conceded, Wilson argued, wage inflation would have roared through the rest of industry, paralysing the Government. Wilson had agreed to speak at the miners' conference and was preparing a dramatic intervention to stem the tide. He described what happened next:

In advance of that [the NUM conference] we were living on borrowed time. But what of the bailiffs, in the shape of the international financial community, from cautious treasurers of international corporations, multi-nationals, to currency operators and money speculators? Would they give us time to win the support of the miners and take all necessary corrective action? The answer came on 30 June. I was in Stoneleigh to open the Royal Agricultural Show . . . My speech, carefully prepared and checked with the Treasury the previous Friday was on the theme of 'no panic'. It was just as I was leaving to fly to London that grim messages reached me from the Treasury via Number 10 that the foreign exchange markets were in turmoil.

So much sterling was sold that the value of the pound against other currencies fell more than on any other day in anyone's memory. Wilson's call for 'no panic' had been answered by a show of panic from the people who owned sterling all over the world. The pound was on the slide, and, as so often in the 1960s, the Labour Government was on the slide as well. In a series of panic meetings with the trade unions, a new policy emerged. It was still wage restraint, but it was 'voluntary'. The trade-union leaders agreed to restrict their pay demands inside the new limit of £6 a week, well below the rate of inflation. The policy was enshrined in a White Paper and in a new Bill that swept through Parliament by the end of July. These dramatic measures had been caused, as Wilson himself conceded, not by ministers making decisions in Cabinet, but by 'bailiffs' selling sterling all over the world.

The panic measures to deal with the July crisis of 1975 (so similar in tone and content to the July crisis of 1966) were accepted by left-wing trade-union leaders and by left-wing Labour MPs largely on the grounds that they were mainly concerned with wage restraint, and that the precious parts of the Labour heritage, notably the National Health Service and social services in general, were not affected. Barbara Castle, the Secretary of State for Social Services, did not agree. In a furious debate in the Cabinet, she pointed out that the measures implied deep cuts in precisely the most sacrosanct Labour areas. She showed the impact of the Chancellor's plans. In 1974–5, spending under the heading of 'health and personal social services' increased by 4.2 per cent. This would be converted by 1978–9 into a drop of minus 1.2 per cent. 'For the first time since its inception,' she concluded, 'expenditure on the NHS would show an actual decline.' At the Cabinet meeting on 14 July, she saw the argument drifting away from her. 'Harold Lever tossed me a note adjuring me not to look so miserable. I tossed him one back. "I see no reason for a Labour Government. We have adopted the Tory mores. The only difference is that we carry out Tory policies more efficiently than they do."'

The job of defending the new Government policy of wage freeze fell to the Employment Secretary, Michael Foot. In a speech on 22 July he told MPs, 'We face an economic typhoon of unparalleled ferocity, and we cannot run away from it.' This theme persisted into his speech to the Labour Party conference in September. 'We face an economic typhoon of unparalleled ferocity, the worst the world has seen since the 1930s. Joseph Conrad wrote a book called *Typhoon*, and at the end he told people how to do it. He said: "always facing it, Captain MacWhirr, that's the way to get through."' Appealing to his audience to face up to the economic typhoon, he called for 'socialist imagination' and 'the red flame of socialist courage'. He got a standing ovation, and conference supported the new policy, just as Parliament had done. In his biography of Michael Foot, Mervyn Jones has a playful dig at the references to Conrad's *Typhoon*. In the novel, he points out, Captain MacWhirr shows no imagination at all, let alone any socialist courage. On the contrary, he was obtuse to the point of bigotry, especially when confronted with books about navigation. But the real significance of the 'typhoon' approach was not its literary accuracy. It was the suggestion that the economic crisis, the recession, could be likened to a shift in the weather, a sudden storm, whose origins, even if they could be identified, had nothing whatever to do with the remedies necessary to deal with them. Why was the world in recession? Why, after 30 years of relative growth, full employment and expanding public services, was it suddenly necessary for a Labour Government and its trade-union allies to throw all three into reverse? Encouraging Labour Party delegates to 'face it' provided no explanation as to why 'it' had happened or why the way to deal with it was to throw into reverse the very policies that had brought Labour to office in the first place.

Did wage restraint, as many on the left argued, dispose of the need for cuts in the public services Labour held most precious? The answer came the following year, 1976, during which more and more strenuous attempts were made by forces far beyond the control of the Labour Government to cut its commitments to public spending. A revealing account of these harrowing developments comes from the man at the centre of them, Denis

Healey, Chancellor of the Exchequer from 1974 to 1979, in his memoirs. Marx and Adam Smith, he wrote, had 'failed to allow for the ways in which political democracy would enable people to create institutions to protect themselves from the operation of market economics'. The way forward, Healey argued, was for politicians to use the powers granted them by political democracy to control events, and most of all to control labour. But almost the whole of his account of those times testifies to his own impotence. For instance: 'Wrestling with such problems, which were generated by foreigners over whom I could have no control, consumed an increasing share of my time at the Treasury'; 'It had become impossible to discover with any accuracy how much additional demand the Government should inject into the economy so as to produce full employment'; 'I soon discovered that most important numbers were nearly always wrong'.

His first budget was based on a figure for public spending that was £4,000 million too low, while 'two years later the budget estimate of the PSBR was £2,000 million too high'.

Politically, by far the most difficult part of my ordeal was the continual reduction of public spending: almost all of the spending cuts ran against the Labour Party's principles, and many also ran against our campaign promises . . . here again my task was complicated by the Treasury's inability to know exactly what was happening or to control it.

The year turned out to be one of consistent horror for the Labour Government, a horror from which it seemed ministers could never recover. The Government borrowed money from the International Monetary Fund to stem the adverse flow of sterling. The first tranche of IMF money came in December 1975, and the flow continued all through 1976. Naturally the IMF wanted security for its loan, and the security it wanted was cuts in public spending on hospitals, roads, schools and even in the money the Government gave to industry to help it invest. All these were imposed by the Labour Cabinet, with only the occasional gesture of revolt from the back benches. In March, a substantial number of left-wing backbenchers voted with the Tories against the Government, but the consequent Government defeat was reversed by a vote of confidence. On and on, through the spring and summer, went the drain on sterling and the demand for more cuts in public spending. The week of the Labour Party conference in September was an especially dreadful one for Denis Healey. He broke off his meetings with IMF officials (who were staying under false names at Brown's Hotel in London) to fly to the conference in Blackpool and announce to the jeering delegates that he had come 'from the battlefront'. This was true in a sense, but it was a battle against unelected bankers that he always lost. The effect of his cuts on the British people was a 2 per cent drop in disposable income. The spending cuts as always hit the poorest sections of the country (the people who voted Labour) far worse than the rich, and the proud pledge to shift the balance of power from the wealthy to the workers had been ignominiously abandoned.

The Government's one major 'success' in those first four years was in relation to the trade unions. Ministers could not control the market, the sale of sterling or the pressure from the IMF, but they could do all in their power to restrain their own side, and to quench the fires of industrial militancy that had so terrified the ruling class in the early 1970s. The General Council of the Trades Union Congress, including the 'terrible twins' Jack Jones and Hugh Scanlon, had agreed the wage restraint of 1975, and policed it efficiently through the turbulent years of 1976 and 1977. The number of days of strike action were cut drastically from the high peak of 23,909,000 in 1972 to 6,012,000 in 1975 and 3,284,000 in 1976. Industrial militancy, so much a feature of the early 1970s, became much less fashionable. In late 1976, a small dispute at a photographic processing plant in North London called Grunwick became a symbol of that decline. Many of the workers at Grunwick were Asian immigrants from East Africa. Unhappy with their conditions and the bullying management, a few of them tried to organize a trade union and were promptly sacked. No one noticed the dispute at first, but it gradually became a trial of strength on the issue of trade-union recognition. The employers, who refused to contemplate recognizing a trade union, had the support of the Conservative Party and a new well-endowed organization with cloudy right-wing origins called the National Association for Freedom. The workers' union, a small conventional and right-wing organization called APEX, was able early on to call on the support of three prominent right-wing Labour MPs, who were sponsored by the union – Shirley Williams, Fred Mulley and Denis Howell. These three very senior MPs paraded dutifully on the picket line in support of the elementary principle of the right of workers to join a trade union.

Curiously, this right had not been enshrined in the Labour Government's trade-union laws of 1974 and 1975. This body of employment law was, Michael Foot later claimed to me, with justification, 'the most powerful pro-trade union legislation ever put on the statute book'. It introduced for the first time a comprehensive and formidable body of law enforcing safety at work. There was however a fatal flaw in it. There was no legal right to join a trade union, or any legal restriction on employers sacking workers who went on strike, even if they went on strike for the right to join a trade union. The Tories and the employers seized on these gaps in the law, proclaimed the 'inalienable right' of employers not to recognize trade unions and dug in for a long fight.

Before long, the small Grunwick factory became the centre of a national dispute of historic importance. The TUC supported the strikers. Vast demonstrations were called to support the pickets, and attracted support from some of the trade-union heroes of the early 1970s, notably Arthur Scargill, who led a big delegation of Yorkshire miners and was arrested on the Grunwick picket line. As the Government dithered on the sidelines (and the three picketing ministers slid into the background), two other forces intervened to pump new confidence into the employers and their Conservative allies. The Metropolitan police mobilized vast forces, quite out of proportion to the significance of the dispute, to 'defend' the beleaguered company and the few workers who crossed the picket lines. Everyone on those picket lines was amazed and shocked by the brutality of the police, especially the special squads of police that had been trained to keep the pickets at bay. In his novel *The Rotters' Club* (2001), published more than 20 years later, Jonathan Coe graphically described the effect of the police intervention and its demoralizing influence on workers from the Midlands who went to Grunwick.

In 1977, when the post-office workers' union 'blacked' all mail to Grunwick, the National Association for Freedom took its expensive lawyers to the High Court, where a judge declared the blacking illegal and threatened the union with sequestration of its assets if it did not lift the blacking immediately. So while the police protected the employers at the factory gate, the judiciary protected them in the High Court. The elected Government, ostensibly in support of the impoverished workers at Grunwick and their right to join a trade union, were, once again, impotent. The employers and their Tory allies won the battle.

The dispute at Grunwick was, in effect, the beginning of the success of the counter-attack against the victorious trade-union armies of the early 1970s. Even though the issue was elementary – trade-union recognition – even though the workers at Grunwick were supported by the TUC and the entire trade-union movement, they were still beaten in open conflict. The forces of the right, led by the new Tory leader, Margaret Thatcher, who had defeated Edward Heath in 1975, sensed for the first time that there was a road back from what they regarded as the unmitigated disasters of 1972.

At the time, it was hard to believe that the long victorious march of organized British labour was coming to an end. I myself had left a comfortable and enjoyable journalistic job in 1972 to become a full-time reporter on *Socialist Worker*, a weekly revolutionary socialist paper financed and controlled by a tiny organization called the International Socialists. My reason for joining the paper was a firm conviction that the capitalist world was on the verge of a revolution, and that the organized workers of Britain would be in the forefront of that revolution. The evidence for that conviction was the relentless march of the trade unions that seemed to me to promise a more vigorous and healthy democracy than anything that came out of Parliament. In 1976, for instance, when I was heavily engaged in reporting the Grunwick dispute, the impotence of the elected Labour Government was clear enough. That part of the formula, as it were, was proved. Despite the shameful outcome of the Grunwick dispute, it seemed that the industrial successes of the past were irreversible. In the 1960s, after all, when I first became politically aware, the workers and their organizations had easily survived the disasters of the Wilson Government, Vietnam, Rhodesia, 'In Place of Strife' and all the rest. Surely they would survive again.

The problem was a servile Government which needed to be replaced by a new, non-Communist revolutionary party. This was the confident theory that led early in 1977 to the replacement of the International Socialists by a party, the Socialist Workers Party, for which I wrote the founding pamphlet, based on John Strachey's pioneering work in the 1930s, *Why You Should be a Socialist*. The same confident thinking inspired the new SWP to stand candidates in elections. In March 1977, I was persuaded to stand for the SWP in Stetchford, Birmingham. Despite an army of enthusiastic socialists who came to help me, canvassing in Birmingham proved pretty fruitless. One incident sticks in my mind. Early on we came across a Leyland shop steward who was very keen on my candidature and promised his support. On polling day we went to see him again. There was no reply at the door, and we went round the back of the house to his garden where he was quite plainly hiding. 'Have you voted?' I called cheerily over the fence. Yes, he said, he had, and then admitted, grudgingly, that he had voted for the National Front. I pondered this for some months afterwards. How could this man have made such a gigantic swing from left to right? I concluded that he was like many others disgruntled with the Government, but preferred a right-wing solution to a left-wing one. Well, I barely polled 1 per cent, and the fascists did much better, beating the Liberals with 8.2 per cent. Two rock-solid Labour seats in the Midlands – Walsall and Stetchford – had been lost to the Tories, and the fascists had notched up huge votes.

What was happening? Exactly the opposite of what we had so fervently hoped and believed. The politics of the working class had moved not to the left, as we assumed, but to the right. Hope had been transformed into scepticism. The first real inroads into living standards had led to profound disillusionment with the Government. Somehow Labour (Austin Mitchell) managed to cling on in Grimsby, but in Ashfield the Labour candidate managed to lose a 20,000 majority.

The combined effect of these by-elections meant that Labour lost its majority in Parliament and in early 1977 cobbled together a deal with the Liberals. The minority Labour Government seemed to be stumbling to defeat. But then, as the economy improved and oil from the North Sea came on stream, there were clear signs of recovery. In May 1978, there was a by-election in Hamilton in the West of Scotland, the scene of a humiliating by-election defeat by the Scottish National Party 11 years earlier. On a high turn-out (72.1 per cent), Labour increased its share of the poll to 51 per cent and slaughtered the Nationalists. This extraordinary result marked a recovery in Labour's electoral fortunes and held out every chance of a Labour Government being re-elected. How to interpret this result? It was a sign perhaps of a growing fear of the deeply reactionary crew that had taken over the Tory Party, but proof also that the Labour Government was not as doomed as many of us believed.

It was unquestionably true that the Labour Government of 1974–9 was a dreadful disappointment to Labour supporters. It was demonstrably true that it failed by a huge margin to shift the balance of power in Britain towards working people and their families. But it was also true that by the autumn of 1978 the Government had survived the economic typhoon they did not understand or explain and, despite their tiny majority, had managed to carry out several measures that did make Britain a more democratic place than when they started. Chief among these measures was the advance towards comprehensive education, perhaps the boldest of all the experiments of the Wilson Government. The promise by Tony Crosland, Wilson's first Education Secretary back in the 1960s, that he was going to 'destroy every fucking grammar school in the country' was not achieved and in one case, in Tameside in Greater Manchester, was obstructed by the judiciary. But under Education Secretary Shirley Williams, many grammar schools were changed into comprehensives, often against the will of their head teachers and with universally democratic results.

Ailing industries, such as British Leyland, Chrysler and all aircraft and shipbuilding were nationalized and prised out of the control of private boardrooms and into the rather reluctant hands of accountable ministers.

Tied cottages and the subservience they forced on farm labourers were brought to an end. Five measures, all promised in the manifesto, went through the House of Commons by slender majorities and a procedural 'guillotine'. In view of what happened later, it is worth recalling that the 1974–9 Labour Government made a sustained and in some respects courageous effort to stay on track and carry out its democratic responsibilities. The undoubted fact that it strayed from its path, and never really recovered it, should not detract from that. It owed a lot to the constant sniping in the Cabinet of Tony Benn and the presence throughout the period of Michael Foot, whose faith in the trade unions as effective partners never dwindled. Yet the failure of the Government as a force not just for socialism but also for democracy is what emerges from any final account of it.

The nationalizations, for instance, though preferable to the old private monopolies, were all in industries that had failed under their private owners. The bold policy of imposing planning agreements on the private monopolies was not even attempted. In five years of Labour government there were only two planning agreements signed, both with industries that were already publicly owned. Perhaps the most depressing example of all the Government initiatives was the attempt to democratize industry by ensuring that the workers played some part in the management. Partly out of deference to the former T&GWU leader and Foreign Secretary Ernest Bevin, the Government consigned their policy on this issue to a Royal Commission under Alan Bullock, the Oxford professor and author of a vast biography of Bevin. When the Bullock Report was finally published in 1977, its majority favoured the TUC proposal for controlling boards in industry, half of whom would be nominated by the trade unions. The minority proposed much less. The very suggestion that workers should have any power in private industry filled the employers with a fury that they sustained for many months. In February 1977, Lord Watkinson, President of the CBI and a former Tory MP, told the National Economic Development Council:

If the Government decides to press ahead with legislation based on the Bullock majority report, it will not only be introducing highly divisive legislation: it will also be showing complete disregard for the efficient management of our major companies on which the economic future of our country depends.

CBI opposition continued unabated. It had a strong supporter in the Cabinet in the shape of Edmund Dell, Financial Secretary to the Treasury, a former Communist who, soon afterwards, walked out of the Government into a much more comfortable and agreeable job in the City. The Liberals too, by now cooperating with the Government, could not tolerate the Bullock majority report and the whole exercise collapsed.

The faint cheers raised for the Labour Government of the 1960s for what might be called the liberal reforms it allowed through Parliament – the abolition of capital punishment, the relaxing of barbaric persecution of homosexuality and the reform of abortion laws – could find no echo in the late 1970s. Denis Healey, for instance, records the deep hostility of Prime Minister Callaghan to any reform of the Official Secrets Act, which secured enormous and draconian powers for the state and the civil service. Despite some feeble efforts, there were no reforms of the House of Lords, whose vast Tory and hereditary majority continued unchanged. The deportation in 1977 of Philip Agee, former and reformed agent of the CIA, and a friendly journalist Mark Hosenball was a clear sign that the reactionary tradition of the Home Office and its intelligence advisers was entirely safe with Labour. As Tony Benn mused about this measure (and new laws instituting an offence of criminal trespass) in his diary: 'We are a most illiberal Government.' Indeed, the whole of Benn's diaries for the period are proof of his impression that power had effectively been surrendered to the people who had always had it. His family were constantly harassed by an ugly combination of the intelligence services and the *Daily Mail*. His influence as Energy Secretary over the oil companies did not even extend to safety (he could see the 1988 Piper Alpha disaster ten years in advance of it happening, but nothing was done to prevent it). When 600 people were sacked by Spillers in his constituency, his impotence to do anything to save them appalled him. 'A Labour Government, Labour legislation and the monopoly situation have all conspired to increase the power of capital and decrease the power of labour,' he wrote. And some months later, still in his constituency, when a board mill was closed by Imperial Tobacco, sacking 650 workers, he recalled that the company had had a £750,000 grant from the Labour Government, which was absolutely powerless to stop the sackings.

Similarly desperate conclusions were drawn by Barbara Castle in her diaries from 1974 to 1976. These were dominated by her long struggle to carry out the manifesto commitment to abolish pay beds in National Health hospitals. Even this clear pledge, utterly justified by the very nature of the NHS and by elementary notions of democracy, set in motion the most hysterical and savage opposition from the consultants. The richer and greedier they were, the more they hated the left-wing secretary of state, and were eventually rescued from the full extent of the Labour manifesto by Harold Wilson's friend Lord Goodman, who, for a suitable fee, was always ready to represent the most reactionary and plutocratic influences in the land.

The awesome consequences of the Government's drift became very clear almost as soon as Callaghan decided not to call an election in the autumn of 1978. He and those advising him were hypnotized by their own success in persuading the unions to moderate their demands. They began to think that the success of their social contract, so remarkable after three and a half years, would continue at least through one more winter and their position would inevitably improve as the North Sea oil revenues came on stream. No prediction could have been more disastrous. The signs were all there. The Government's chief ally in the unions, Jack Jones, lost his call for more restraint at the T&GWU conference in the summer of 1978. He retired. His successor, Moss Evans, was less inclined to bail the Government out. The TUC that year called for unfettered wage bargaining. The social contract was finished.

Years of the frustration of wage restraint and public-spending cuts burst out in what became known as the 'winter of discontent'. Local government workers went on indefinite strike. So, much more seriously, did lorry drivers. Strike after strike pulverized the country. Indeed the number of days spent on strike in 1979 was greater even than in 1972. Many of these strikes unleashed much of the same democratic spirit as their predecessors in 1972 and 1974. I still recall a sense of wonder and admiration at the way in which the transport drivers of Hull took control of their industry and ran it safely and properly in the best interests of the community. The ability – and the yearning – for democratic control was there in abundance. But the reaction in the labour movement and in the country was quite different. I remember reporting the TUC conference of 1976 for *Socialist Worker*, and being astonished when a delegate from the miners' union was openly jeered. What had only two years previously been a spirit of solidarity with the miners had changed into a spirit of hostility. The miners were suddenly envied for what they had achieved. The feeling that all workers were in the same boat, and that the strongest should break their employers on behalf of the weakest – all that had gone as early as 1976. The constant emphasis not just on restraint and sacrifice but also on leaving the problems of the day to leaders – to union leaders, chancellors, ministers – all this turned most of the strikes in late 1978 and 1979 into bloody-minded expressions of revenge and self-interest. And for that decisive shift of mood, the Labour Government of the time was primarily responsible.

The most striking feature of the 1964–70 Labour Government – the sense that in spite of the constant backsliding by the Government the movement outside went on growing in confidence and strength – was missing under its successor ten years later. It was as though the great strikes and occupations of the early 1970s had brought the movement to the brink, and the initiative had passed to the Labour Government. The Government strove with all its might to hold back the heavy locomotive set off by the strikes, and in the end it succeeded. The strikes slowed, and so did the spirit of confidence in the movement. The 'winter of discontent' was indeed a huge spurt of industrial activity but it was an effort from which the confidence of the earlier period had vanished. There was a sullen pessimism about the activity, which left the movement even more vulnerable than usual to the hysterical shrieking of the media.

The winter dragged on to what seemed like its inevitable conclusion. A no-confidence motion in the Government was eventually passed in Parliament – by one vote – and a general election held on 3 May 1979. The Tories won with an overall majority of 41 and Margaret Thatcher became Prime Minister.

New Labour = Old Tory:
The Tory Counter-attack and the Labour Surrender

The Tories used their years in opposition to work out a counter-attack on all the assaults on their hierarchical society since Labour was elected in 1964. Their first task was to end the consensus politics that had dominated the Party since the war. Early in 1975, the man the extreme right regarded as the chief traitor to the true Tory cause, Edward Heath, was challenged and beaten for the leadership of the Party by Margaret Thatcher. Thatcher's allies in the Tory Party were far further to the right than any of Edward Heath's. Her guru was the slightly batty right-wing ideologue Sir Keith Joseph. Her adviser on Northern Ireland was the hard-right Unionist Airey Neave. And one of her most devoted new allies was a man who had been thrown out of Heath's Government in 1972 for being too right wing – Nicholas Ridley, second son of a coal-owning viscount in Northumberland.

All these men and many others had been influenced by a 'new philosophy', the aim of which was to embark on a militant programme for their class. Their super-guru was the Austrian professor Friedrich Hayek. His view, described by Thatcher as 'supreme', was that capitalism was a system founded on liberty, and that any organization, such as a trade union, that threatened the equilibrium of the capitalist system was a menace to that liberty. He conceded, rather reluctantly, that some form of democratically elected assembly was necessary, so long as it did not interfere with the symmetry of the free market.

Hayek's basic view was that trade unions should be so hobbled by law as to render them as ineffective as the old friendly societies. This was the philosophy that inspired the Tory Employment Acts of the 1980s, carried on and reinforced in the early1990s. Much of the damage was done in the first Act, introduced almost as soon as the Tories were returned in 1979, and presided over by the bumbling James (later Lord) Prior, who hardly seemed to realize what he was doing. He was followed by Norman (later Lord) Tebbit and David (later Lord) Young, who certainly did realize what they were doing. In successive Acts throughout the decade, the Tory

Government re-established the unions' liabilities in tort that had been abolished in 1906. They removed the right of workers to take any strike or other industrial action in solidarity with other workers (a practice known as 'secondary picketing'), prescribed draconian rules for the election and behaviour of officials, and even set up a special commissioner's office to protect what they called the 'paramount' rights of the non-unionist. The combined impact of these laws reduced almost to nothing the legal power and influence of the trade unions and left individual trade-union officers in terror of legal actions which could impose not only massive fines but also entitled the courts to 'sequester' (steal) the assets of the unions which most union leaders regarded as their life blood. Professor Lord Bill Wedderburn observed that the purpose of 'this step-by-step salami slicing of the workforce was to designate permissible limits of the collective – a logical development of the new philosophy'.

The job of righting and avenging the defeats of the early 1970s, however, could not be accomplished simply by changing the law. Thatcher believed that the unions had to be beaten in open conflict. To work out an effective strategy, she turned to her friend and confidant Nicholas Ridley. In the late 1970s, in the run-up to the election, Ridley chaired the Party's policy group on nationalized industries. In May 1978, a copy of his group's final report was mysteriously leaked to the *Economist*.

Much of the document set out new targets for the nationalized industries, but its theme was simple: how to defeat the unions. Section five was reported like this:

In choosing which strikes not to fight, the team has classified industries into three categories of vulnerability with a) sewerage, water, electricity, gas and the health service in the most vulnerable sector, b) railways, docks, coal and dustmen in an intermediate group, and c) other public transport, education, ports and telephones and steel in the least vulnerable group.

In an annexe to the report, Ridley and Co. set out their thoughts on the coming struggle in the coal industry. It emphasized the need not to pick a fight in the least vulnerable or even the intermediate group but to concentrate on the weakest, least organized groups, and to plan for an 'eventual battle on ground chosen by the Tories'. Assuming that this eventual battleground turned out to be the pits, the plan recommended a Thatcher Government to build up coal stocks and to reorganize the police into a 'large, mobile' national force capable of facing down a national strike.

The first sign of the Tory counter-attack against the unions was at British Leyland, the huge car company based in Birmingham. In 1977, the Labour

Government approved the appointment of a tough class warrior as BL's deputy chairman. He was Ian MacGregor, who had won his spurs in the United States as chairman of a company, Amax, and had defeated the miners' union there in a long and bitter struggle. As soon as the Tories were elected, MacGregor sprang into action. It was largely his influence that prompted the chairman of British Leyland, Michael Edwardes, to sack Derek 'Red Robbo' Robinson, the Communist convenor at the Longbridge plant in Birmingham.

With Leyland tamed, the Tories turned their attention to the British steel industry, headed by a nationalized corporation chaired by the patrician Sir Charles Villiers. Villiers was no match for the gung-ho chief executive of the Corporation, Sir Robert 'Black Bob' Scholey, who was given the green light to fight the steel unions for however long it took to break them. Before 1979 was out, the steel workers were told there was no money to meet their wage claim, and that the Government was aiming at 10,000 job losses in quick time. The strike that followed in the early months of 1980 was much more spirited than the Government and the employers had imagined. But in the end, the compromise that was reached, though claimed as a victory by the main union's general secretary, Bill Sirs, was nowhere near the original claim and left the union far too weak to withstand the tremendous onslaught on jobs that followed. Part One of the Ridley Plan had been accomplished, and soon after Sir Keith Joseph, Secretary of State for Trade and Industry, announced the appointment of Ian MacGregor as chairman of the British Steel Corporation. MacGregor promptly set about mopping up steel workers' jobs.

The Thatcher Government was plunged almost immediately into a deep recession, with mounting unemployment and a steep slide in their ratings in the opinion polls. In 1981, moreover, the Ridley Plan suffered a sharp setback. David Howell, the Energy Minister, a mild-mannered gentleman who represented Guildford, announced the closure of 50 loss-making pits. The response came at once not so much from militant leaders – Arthur Scargill was elected President of the NUM in 1981 but did not take office until 1982 – as from rank-and-file miners all over the country. A series of unofficial strikes spread through the coalfields before anyone could stop them. None of the precautions against a miners' strike so carefully set out in the Ridley Plan had been put in place. The Government was not ready for the strikes, and immediately surrendered to them. The wretched Howell had to throw in the towel, and announce that in fact no pits were due to close. He was shifted from the hot seat at Energy and, a decade later, promoted to the House of Lords.

The shock of what Nigel Lawson, who became Energy Secretary later that year, called a 'humiliating episode' reminded the Tory ministers of the lurking menace of the miners' union and sharpened their dedication to the Ridley Plan. In 1982, the railways were next in line for frontal assault, and a messy dispute followed about shift patterns and what became known as 'flexible rostering'. The result of that dispute was a draw, but the preparations for the really big battle – with the miners – continued apace.

The Thatcher Government was lifted out of the doldrums of the most severe recession since the war by the defection from Labour of a 'gang' of four right-wingers, Roy Jenkins, Shirley Williams, Bill Rodgers and David Owen. Their defection and the formation of their new Social Democratic Party caused havoc in the Labour Party. As we have seen, the Party had been formed by an alliance of socialists and trade unionists, and had rapidly replaced the Liberal Party as the natural political representative for working people. Many instinctive Liberals joined the Labour Party. After 1945, as Labour proved its ability to win a majority in the House of Commons, more Liberals, anxious to achieve office, lined up with Labour. My uncle Dingle Foot, for instance, who had been a Liberal MP in the war, and had been successively defeated as a Liberal in post-war elections, joined the Labour Party in 1957 and was instantly selected to fight and win a by-election at Ipswich – a seat which he held until 1970, when he lost by 13 votes. I can vouch for the fact that my uncle's politics never deviated an inch from his Liberal origins, even when he became a member of the Labour Government. Many Liberals like him, in Parliament and outside it, went the same way. They did not especially like trade unions and were deeply suspicious of public ownership, but they tolerated their differences quite comfortably in exchange for office.

This coalition had survived without too much fuss since the 1920s. It was shaken to its roots by the advance of the left in the Labour Party in the years following the 1979 defeat. The Party careered to the left without apparently noticing that the British people in general were moving to the right. The first casualties were the former Liberals in the Party, including the 'Gang of Four'. The formation of the SDP was, as soon became clear, no more than an assertion by several former Labour Party supporters that they were, in truth and in fact, Liberals. Before long the SDP vanished into oblivion, and its leaders vanished into the Liberal Party, renamed the Liberal Democrats. But before the SDP collapsed, it did terrible electoral damage to the Labour Party, helping to lose it two general elections by large margins in 1983 and 1987. The percentage of the vote won by the Tories did not move significantly from 1979, but the Labour vote was split. Indeed, in

1983 the Alliance of SDP and Liberals came within an ace of achieving a bigger percentage of the poll than Labour – 25.4 per cent to Labour's 27.6 per cent.

Back in office with a huge majority, Tory ministers turned all their attention to the fulfilment of the Ridley plan and what Nigel Lawson called 'squaring up to Scargill'. In this endeavour, they were greatly assisted by incentive deals imposed on the miners against their will as expressed in a ballot in 1977. These deals ensured big increases in the pay of miners at profitable pits without conceding increases across the board. The chief effect of this was to split the miners between those on high-productivity incentive pay and those in less profitable pits. In turn, this led to a decline in the cohesion of the early 1970s. Three times after he became NUM President in 1982, Arthur Scargill and his supporters tried to persuade miners to strike nationally in protest against pit closures, and three times, by substantial majorities, the miners voted him down. The lesson had some bearing on the way in which the more active trade unionists among the miners saw the ballot. It was now clear that the splits engineered by the incentive pay deals left it open to some miners to vote to take no action against attacks on others. The democracy of the strike ballot began to lose its impact as more and more miners voted to take no action in defence of the jobs of others.

At the same time, the other recommendations of the Ridley Plan were carefully put into effect. Stocks of coal at the power stations were increased, and only marginally depleted by an overtime ban called in the autumn of 1983. New oil-fired power stations were opened and kept in readiness. Most importantly, the police force was quietly but systematically reorganized, and a national anti-strike police force set up and prepared for combat. The reorganized police had an excellent opportunity to try out new tactics against strikers and supporters in a dispute over union recognition at a newspaper plant at Warrington. Even so, the Government and its Coal Board were astonished by the reaction to the closure of Cortonwood colliery in March 1984. A national strike developed almost from nowhere. Within a few weeks, some 150,000 miners were on strike and taking part in a battle with the Government neither side could afford to lose.

At the very beginning of the strike, Arthur Scargill and his union were involved in another dispute that had huge implications for the future of democracy in Britain. The Mineworkers' Pension Scheme had grown into one of the richest and most powerful funds in the country. Years and years of deducting pension contributions from a quarter of a million miners had built up the fund into billions of pounds. Who controlled this vast hoard of money? In the post-war years of consensus the trustees of the pension fund were divided 50–50 between five trustees from the National Union of Mineworkers and five from the National Coal Board. There was no provision in law for what happened if the trustees were evenly split. Soon after taking office as elected President of the union, Arthur Scargill proposed that the fund should be invested, at least in part, in British industries and services whose products were used by or relevant to British miners. He proposed among other things that the fund should buy the *Daily Mirror*, a newspaper read by 80 per cent of miners, and Theakston brewery, whose product was widely favoured by miners. There was plenty of money in the fund to buy both, and a lot more besides. And both the *Mirror* and Theakston were making good profits. Accountants commissioned by the union could prove quite easily that these purchases would be good investments for the fund. The Scargill proposals were supported by the five NUM delegates and opposed by the five from the NCB. The deadlock came to the High Court and the legal arguments were heard by the Vice Chancellor, Sir Robert Megarry. Unfortunately, since the miners' strike started almost simultaneously, neither Scargill nor any of his senior officials could give much time to the case, but it posed delicate problems for British democracy.

For many years, supporters of capitalism had argued that the undemocratic hierarchical nature of the system had been changed. Most of British industry, it was argued, was now owned in effect by workers' pension funds and insurance companies to which workers contributed. The dispute over the Mineworkers' Pension Scheme tested that argument to the full. At stake was the inviolability of the rule of the City of London, its investment bankers and accountants. If the workers could decide how their contributions could be spent, then the essence of capitalist control – the alleged expertise of capitalist controllers to assess what would or would not be in the people's interests – would be threatened. There was a further threat in the Scargill proposals to what was laughably called the freedom of the press – the name given to the freedom of newspaper proprietors and editors to publish what they please. The influential *Daily Mirror*, which, with the enthusiastic support of Margaret Thatcher, was sold during the miners' strike to a celebrated crook called Robert Maxwell, was 'in peril' of falling into the hands of the National Union of Mineworkers and its elected leaders. The employers' trustees, supported by terrified accountants and anxious City slickers of every variety, testified that their own investment portfolio, based on buying and renting property in the United States, would provide a better return for the fund. This view was upheld by Vice Chancellor Megarry. After the strike was defeated, control of the pension fund was swiftly shifted away from the NUM and split up among smaller unions, including management organizations. The awful shadow of democratic control of one of the largest pension funds in the country disappeared. The *Daily Mirror* remained in the safe hands of Robert Maxwell, who to the enormous relief of his employees died in 1991, and whose replacement, a year later, David Montgomery, launched a ferocious and victorious attack on organized trade unions employed by the *Daily Mirror*. No one noticed, however, that the pension fund investments favoured by the National Union of Mineworkers turned out to be substantially more profitable than those maintained by the employers.

The miners' strike, the greatest act of sustained defiance in the history of British labour, lasted longer even than its predecessors in 1921 and 1926. In March 1985, just over a year after the strike had started, the miners, through their elected organizations, decided to return to work and did so, still showing unity and defiance. Anyone who took the miners' side and was associated with those long months of struggle will remember how much of the argument revolved around the issue of democracy. Again and again well-meaning people who supported the miners could be heard repeating, 'I wish Scargill had held a ballot.' The fact that the strike took place for a full year without the miners being balloted was used to castigate the strike as undemocratic. The enormous power and significance of a year-long strike by 150,000 workers was, through this argument, dwarfed by the failure to secure a vote for it. The strike was therefore denounced as 'illegitimate'.

There were, however, counter-arguments based on a rather different way of looking at the world. As we have seen, Scargill had failed to win three strike ballots because of the divisions among miners caused by the incentive agreements that had been pushed through by the employers in spite of a ballot vote against them. The ballot results left the NUM leadership with the agonizing prospect that pits could be closed piecemeal, one by one, or two by two, and that the union would be prevented by hostile ballot results from responding. This was the background to the confrontation that was started by the closure, without consultation, and in defiance of all agreements, of Cortonwood colliery in Yorkshire. Encouraged by the executive, and by a wave of flying pickets from the threatened pits, strike after strike led very quickly to a massive national confrontation, in which pretty well all the pits in Yorkshire, Scotland, Wales and most of the Midlands were on strike, leaving only the traditionally less militant areas, Nottinghamshire and Leicestershire, at work.

To those who bleated, 'I wish Scargill had had a ballot', there was a prompt reply: 'Suppose he had had a ballot and lost it – what then?' Were the miners' leaders expected to stand aside while the Government and its newly appointed National Coal Board laid waste to the British coal industry? The truth was that actions spoke louder than ballots. The sheer size and breathtaking solidarity of the mass strike was the fact, and the suggestion that the action should have been put at risk by a ballot was an argument that could be sustained only by enemies of the miners' union. Very soon, moreover, the democratic potential of the miners' strike was every bit as obvious as it had been in 1921 and 1926, if not more so. Anyone who visited any of the areas affected by the strike was struck by the extraordinary changes that took place in the strikers and their supporters. The traditional insularity of the pit villages was shattered by the need to seek support, including financial support, across the country. Miners and their families travelled far more widely than in the strikes of the 1970s – both inside Britain and outside. Even more than in the conflicts of the past, the women in the miners' areas were emancipated almost overnight. Technically, they had been emancipated in 1918 and 1928 by the granting of the suffrage. But the emancipation of the women in the mining areas in 1984 and 1985 far outstripped the emancipation of the suffrage. Ideas of women's liberation, about male chauvinism and the role of women in the household flourished in the mining areas that spring and summer of 1984 as never before.

The arguments spilled over into all sorts of other issues. On my way to speak to miners at Easington colliery in September, I was met by a miner at Durham station. On our drive, he apologized for being a racist. I contested his assessment of himself, and he admitted his own surprise at the amount of money and food collected for his union by the impoverished Asian communities in Leeds and Newcastle. He was, he agreed, confused on the issue, and what confused him was the constant clash between bigoted ideas about the 'pollution' of his race by immigrants from abroad and the demolition of those ideas in the reality of his struggle. Old prejudices that had been allowed to fester in the isolated treadmill of everyday work and life were being challenged and reversed. In the huge mass meetings addressed by Scargill and two other leading NUM members, Mick McGahey and Peter Heathfield, there was, among the younger miners in particular, a yearning for understanding not just of the immediate issues of the strike but also of other matters outside the areas and outside the country. The strike produced a convulsion of thought and democratic ideas that far exceeded anything unleashed by the processes of electoral democracy.

Essential to the preservation and advance of these ideas was industrial activity. No one understood this better than Government ministers, and the Prime Minister in particular. As Nigel Lawson, who was Energy Minister before becoming Chancellor of the Exchequer in the years of the strike, explained in his interminable autobiography, the whole thrust of Government policies (and public spending) in those months was applied to smashing the miners. The encouragement given to the breakaway union in Nottinghamshire, combined with the movement of coal to and from the power stations, the opening of new and very expensive oil-fired power stations, the new dependence on nuclear power and above all the transformation of the police into a violent occupying force in the mining areas – all these brought victory to the Government. That victory, however, was neither inevitable nor necessary. It was assisted at least in part by the consistent failure of NUM leaders to use the one power at their disposal – the involvement of mass pickets. In area after area, even in Yorkshire, the management of the strike was left to the leadership. Again and again, too, there were opportunities for other unions, notably in the docks and railways, to invigorate the strike by solidarity action. That these opportunities were not taken was largely due to the passive reaction of the TUC, whose officers, like the Labour Party leaders, intervened again and again to discourage such action.

The resulting defeat of the miners was a terrible blow to the labour and working-class movement. Sensing their victory, and revelling in it, the Tories proceeded to mop up in areas where trade unions were still strong. In January 1986, the newspaper proprietor Rupert Murdoch moved his papers – the *Times*, the *Sunday Times*, the *Sun* and the *News of the World* – out of their offices in and around Fleet Street, where the trade unions were highly organized, to a fortress at Wapping where the print unions were banned. The resulting strike and mass picket at Wapping were eventually broken by using non-union and pliant 'scab' union labour in the fortress and non-union lorry firms to distribute the papers. Murdoch and his henchmen were assisted not only by the Government but also by the police who attacked the pickets with all the savagery their colleagues had so successfully refined in the mining areas. Indeed, the effect of the miners' strike on police behaviour spread far outside industry. In 1985, Wiltshire police attacked a convoy of lorries carrying people to a solstice celebration at Stonehenge. In that attack the police – the so-called 'rural bobbies' – behaved in a manner more appropriate to savages.

The final round of what may be called the Thatcher/Ridley offensive against the organized working class came in 1989 with a successful assault on one of the last bastions of union power: the docks. The Dock Labour

Scheme, introduced more than 40 years previously by Ernest Bevin in a bid to stop the hiring of casual labour, was wound up. The docks were privatized and hundreds of trade unionists sacked. Much later, industrial tribunals held that almost all these workers had been sacked unfairly. They were compensated with cash payments, but they were not reinstated. The final round had been won by the employers – as all the other rounds had been.

After winning all these early battles – and re-establishing undemocratic hierarchy – in open class warfare, the Tory Government turned to the even more important business of destroying any vestige of democracy in industry. The process was called privatization. It started gingerly at first in a few marginal establishments that had got into public ownership more by accident than by design. But the process rapidly gathered pace as the victories against the trade unions were notched up. Telephones and telecommunications were privatized in three instalments in 1984 to 1986; Cable and Wireless in 1985; British Gas in three instalments from 1986 to 1988, with a heavily promoted advertisement campaign featuring a mythical con man called Sid who knew how to make money by buying the new shares; the huge publicly owned bus industry in 1986; British Airways and the British Airports Authority in 1987; British Steel in 1988; the water companies in England and Wales in 1988 to 1990; and electricity in 1991.

By the end of the decade, when Thatcher was finally pushed out after an unstoppable public campaign against what she regarded as her 'flagship', the poll tax, pretty well all the industries so painfully and carefully brought into public ownership by post-war Labour Governments were back in the hands of shareholders, bankers and speculators. To their intense relief, Tory ministers were no longer accountable or answerable to Parliament or any other democratic body for any of the activities of this huge swathe of British industry. For good measure, the elected Greater London Council was abolished. The reason, as the Tory chairman, Norman Tebbit, crudely blurted out, was that the elected GLC was not only Labour but dangerously socialist. Two years later, after a reckless combined parliamentary intervention from Tebbit and the former Tory Defence Secretary Michael Heseltine, the Inner London Education Authority, which had succeeded in no small measure in redistributing educational resources in the capital from the rich to the poor, was also abolished leaving the poorer boroughs to try to educate their children without any assistance from their wealthy neighbours.

The Thatcher Government also rid itself of the old elected metropolitan boroughs that controlled the big urban areas of the country. The Labour councillors who controlled these boroughs could draw on a huge rating base, and could therefore divert at least some of the proceeds from the rich to the workers and the poor. An example of this was cheap bus fares in places like South Yorkshire, made possible by the structure and rating base of the South Yorkshire Metropolitan Council. Once the metropolitan councils were abolished, the remaining councils found it much more difficult to maintain cheap services.

The relentless destruction of democracy went on after 1987, when Mrs Thatcher won a third general election, and after 1992 when the Tories, under Thatcher's nominee John Major, won a fourth term. In 1989, Thatcher's favourite minister, Cecil Parkinson, delighted the Tory Party conference with an exciting new plan to privatize one of the last bastions of public ownership, the railways. This long-drawn-out and deeply corrupt process continued until it was completed in the Tories' last full year of office, 1996. In 1992, Industry Secretary Michael Heseltine announced the effective closure of most of the rest of the coal industry, and the remainder was promptly flogged off to a family of commodity speculators.

During all this period systematic attempts were made by the Government to introduce the 'market' into the National Health Service and to bring back selection into state schools. The Tories set up a special front organization, funded by public money, whose purpose was to encourage the conversion of comprehensive schools into so-called 'grant-maintained schools', whose chief characteristic was selection by ability. The common feature of all these policies was that the running of the country could best be left to a wealthy privileged minority, that 'private' or 'free' enterprise was preferable to public enterprise and that the democratic process should be strictly confined to electing a government either in Parliament or council that could not even supervise the monopolies and bureaucracies controlling the affairs of the country.

What was the effect on the Labour Opposition of this Tory rampage? Initially, the anti-union laws and the privatizations were strenuously opposed in Parliament. But as the laws were passed, and the workers were defeated in open struggle, the Opposition began to founder. After the 1983 defeat, the new Labour leader, Neil Kinnock, appointed two of his promising young backbenchers, Gordon Brown and Tony Blair, to the Commons committee dealing with the latest of the anti-union laws. Both young men opposed the Bill chiefly on grounds of democracy. 'The Bill,' said Tony Blair, 'has nothing to do with democracy – it has everything to do with the rights of British trade unionists to organize freely in the association of their choice.' The young MP was swimming in familiar waters.

He was a barrister specializing in trade-union law, and in the early 1980s had written articles attacking the earlier Tory proposals for trade union 'reform'. He argued these were not reforms at all, but a strengthening of the employers and the rich against the ability of trade unions to organize against them.

The defeats of the trade unions in the 1980s changed the attitude of the Labour leaders to all these matters. They began to equivocate on all the Tory proposals, and, quite quickly, to come round full circle to support them. Right up to the 1992 election, when he could not coherently answer a question from Jonathan Dimbleby on secondary picketing (he was not in favour of it, but then again he was not against it), Neil Kinnock backed down from his opposition to the anti-union laws. The same impression – that in the new political mood set by Thatcher, Labour was ditching its earlier commitments to trade unions – emerged from Labour's attitude to almost everything else. Kinnock himself made clear that he was no longer committed to unilateral nuclear disarmament or to opposing the European Common Market. The same was true of privatization. In the House of Commons and in the country, Labour opposed every one of the major Tory privatizations. In every single instance, their spokespeople pledged a new Labour Government to take the privatized industry or service back into public ownership.

A good example was the privatization of electricity. On 12 December 1988, for instance, Tony Blair, by then a new member of the Shadow Cabinet, rose in Parliament to put the Labour view. 'We are proud,' he said, 'that we took the industry into public ownership. When we come to power, it will be reinstated as a public service for the people of this country and will not be run for private profit.' By the Labour Party conference, Blair had developed a nice line in conference rhetoric:

At the outset we said that privatization would mean higher prices, and it has done. We warned that the Government would introduce a special nuclear tax for private nuclear power and it has. We said that the Government would be forced to admit there was no choice for the consumer, and now they have. Born out of dogma, reared on deceit, this privatization is now exposed for what it is and always has been, private prejudice masquerading as public policy. Let us send this message to the Government. We do not want it postponed, we do not want it delayed, we do not want it put off – we want it abandoned here now and for ever.

The delegates rose for the solemn ritual of the standing ovation. There were some perhaps old enough to remember the sleepless nights put in by a former leader of their party when he was Minister of Fuel and Power,

Hugh Gaitskell, as he steered the nationalization of electricity (and gas) past an outraged Tory Party. In 1989, and the surrounding years, Labour MPs were moved to similar cheers as their leaders denounced the privatization of steel, aircraft, shipbuilding, gas, coal, water and, most shocking of all, the railways. In each case, Labour's reaction to privatization threatened the very future of the newly privatized industry. If Labour was indeed going to take the industry back into public ownership, the security of the new stock was threatened. What was the use of buying shares in a privatized industry if a new Government that might be elected at any time was going to renationalize it? So Labour's reaction to the privatizations was closely studied by the new monopolies and their armies of banks and investment advisers. They were all greatly relieved as the commitments made so hotly at the time of the privatizations were hastily abandoned. Even as early as the 1992 election, the Labour Party manifesto had dropped the commitments to bring electricity, water and the others back into public ownership. Tony Blair's proud boast, for instance, to reinstate electricity as a public service was replaced by a vague commitment to extend public control of the industry. In each case, by the 1992 election, the new private monopolies born out of dogma and reared on deceit could relax in the knowledge that the dogma and the deceit – and the profit – would be continued under a future Labour Government.

After 1992, the chief difficulty for the privatizers, so boosted by John Major's unexpected spring victory over Neil Kinnock, was the threat to their new proposal to privatize the railways. This proposal was immediately and profoundly unpopular, and was supported throughout by no more than 11 per cent of the population. It could have been brought abruptly to a halt by a firm and unequivocal commitment by Labour to renationalize the industry on taking office. The very threat of a democratic purpose that would stop the undemocratic process of privatization would have kept the greedy speculators at bay. At the outset, the Labour leaders responsible for the industry realized how important their commitment was, and gave voice to it. At the Labour Party conference in 1993, Labour's spokesman on transport, John Prescott, could not have been more forthright. 'Let me make it crystal clear,' he said, 'that any privatization of the railway system that does take place will, on the arrival of a Labour Government, be quickly and effectively dealt with.' The industry, he promised, 'will be returned to public ownership'. The following year (1994), Labour's transport spokesman, Frank Dobson, told the conference: 'Let me give this pledge not just to this conference but to the people of Britain. The next Labour Government will bring the railway system back into public ownership.' The next year

(1995), Labour's transport spokesman, Michael Meacher, warned any speculators hovering about the railways to keep their distance. 'The railways,' he said, 'depend on public subsidies to the tune of £1.8 billion a year. There is no guarantee that the subsidies will continue.'

Then, suddenly, all these pledges and threats were cut off. There were new Labour spokespeople on transport – Clare Short and Andrew Smith – yet neither of them would commit a future Labour Government to public ownership of the railways. Avoiding dogma and deceit, Tony Blair, the new Labour leader, appeared to commit the Party to a publicly owned and publicly accountable railway, but even that vague pledge did not appear in the Labour manifesto for the 1997 election. Thus it was that all the Tory attacks on the labour movement, all the anti-union laws, all the privatizations, were not even threatened by the 1997 Labour election manifesto. There were no proposals to reconstitute the GLC or ILEA or the metropolitan borough councils. The huge swathes cut by successive Tory Governments into the flesh and blood of British social democracy were not even threatened with reversal, whatever happened at the polls.

What had happened? The relentless advances of the Tories in their long period of office had transformed the Labour Party. Cowed and humiliated by successive election defeats, the Party had, for the first time in its history, cut itself off from its roots and abandoned its historic mission to democratize British society. The process lunged forward after an accident of death. In May 1994, John Smith, the natural heir to Neil Kinnock, died from a heart attack. Smith had always been on the right of the Party, but he was not a liberal. He hailed from the social democratic right and indeed in his short period as leader distanced himself from the more ludicrous manifestations of Kinnock's 'modernization'. Out went Peter Mandelson, an ambitious TV producer, who had joined the Communist Party at school but ever since had moved to the right. Mandelson had been Kinnock's 'director of communications', and had impressed the Welshman with his alleged 'wizardry' over the media. He had developed methods of singling out and either seducing or bullying individual journalists into more amenable coverage of Labour and its leader. Mandelson was unpopular in Labour circles, and there was much rejoicing when he was sent packing by Smith.

Smith also made sure that in Britain and in Europe, he kept faith with the socialist left, repeating again and again his commitment to public ownership and full employment. His death, widely and genuinely mourned throughout the Labour movement, ushered in the hard right of the party. At once, the media unanimously proclaimed that the obvious successor was the young barrister MP for Sedgefield, Tony Blair. Blair was easily elected over his two rivals, Margaret Beckett and John Prescott, and at once, with tremendous energy, set about establishing 'New Labour', a party based on the mass Labour vote and the politics of the Social Democratic Party. Peter Mandelson, who, like Blair, had picked up a plum safe seat in the North-East, was back in charge of communications.

There was only one frontbencher in the new Labour team who could have run Blair close for the leadership. He was Gordon Brown, who had been elected to Parliament (for the impoverished Scottish town of Dunfermline) in the same year as Blair and had served with Blair on the committees for one of the early anti-union laws. Unlike Blair, Brown could boast a socialist background. In the 1970s, his politics were set out in what he called the 'Red Papers for Scotland' and were extremely left wing. He called for the nationalization of all the basic industries, and for democratic control of those industries. His socialist inspiration lasted into the 1980s. He wrote a rather dull biography of Jimmy Maxton, the furious socialist orator of the ILP, and in 1988 published a frontal assault on Thatcherism entitled (in a parody of Margaret Thatcher's ludicrous quotation from St Francis of Assisi) 'Where There is Greed'. At the centre of Brown's attack in that book was his assault on privatization and the greed that inspired it and gained from it. Some time in the years after the book was published – probably after Labour's election defeat in 1992 – Brown must have taken stock of his position and decided to tolerate and indeed proclaim the retreat from socialist and democratic politics. At any rate, before the 1994 leadership election, allegedly at a posh restaurant in Islington, he sat down with Blair and agreed to give him a free run for the leadership in exchange for a commitment that he, Brown, could be Chancellor of the Exchequer for as long as he liked.

At his first Labour Party conference in 1994, Blair indicated his intention of ridding the Party of Clause IV of the Constitution, and effectively ruling out all further commitments to public ownership. In an energetic tour of the constituencies and unions, Blair pleaded his case with Party members, and eventually secured a huge majority for the ditching of Clause IV. The Clause was replaced with a series of semi-literate clichés that no one remembers.

Blair's pitch was very simple. Labour could not win without the changes he was advocating. Long years of defeat had cowed what was left of the Labour Party membership. Most of the dedicated left had been expelled. Most of the remaining members would do anything for victory. Blair had a pleasing tone and a nice young family. He delighted the Party conference in the three years he addressed them as Leader of the Opposition. There were many delegates who did not like the path the Party was treading, but no one dared to rock the boat.

What was the intellectual basis of this sudden and decisive conversion? In 1996, the former Social Democrat Roger Liddle and Peter Mandelson published a book with the arresting title *The Blair Revolution: Can New Labour Deliver?* The strategy of New Labour, the book revealed on its first page, 'is to move forward from where Margaret Thatcher left off rather than dismantle every single thing she did'. And, 'we have to be clear where the Conservatives got things right'. A close study of the following 274 pages (a grim struggle through dreadful prose and endless clichés) leaves the reader unclear what exactly the Tories got wrong, still less whether there was a single Tory policy that should be dismantled. The anti-union laws were praised. Privatization had 'brought about improvements' and some increased productivity. Some of the privatized companies like British Telecom and British Gas 'can now claim to be world class'. There should be no mass renationalization – indeed nothing should be brought back into public ownership. Indeed Labour should be determined to 'change from the municipal socialism and centralized nationalization of the past'.

Did this mean a shift towards non-municipal socialism or decentralized nationalization? Not at all. It meant no nationalization and certainly no socialism. Not just the concept but the word itself was anathema to the authors. They believed utterly in the 'rigour of competitive markets' and were concerned for Labour to find ways 'the market economy can be helped to prosper'.

They heralded an idea that was to become the cornerstone of New Labour economic policy: partnership between private and public enterprise. They argued that the job of Government was not to intervene in the economy, not even to buy a stake in the economy, but to hold the ring in such a way as to ensure that private enterprise flourished. Their utopian aim was to preside over a society where efficiency and social justice improved side by side. There were no specific proposals on tax, but it seemed to follow from lost elections in the past that there should be no increases in tax. The emphasis was on the magic word 'stability'. The authors were self-confessedly scared of a suspicious City and jittery financial markets. Nothing could be done unless the economy was stable.

Side by side with this enthusiastic commitment to do nothing to upset the rich and powerful, the authors developed an authoritarian and disciplinarian tone toward those who they felt were failing the nation. Labour in the past, they claimed, had been soft on crime, and that had to stop. There should be more imprisonment, more punishment. The middle class were fleeing state schools and the National Health Service and this was not the fault of the Tory attacks on both but mainly the fault of the 'educational egalitarians' who cared too much about the structure of schools (were they selective or comprehensive?) rather than their standards. There should be more discipline for 'inadequate parents' and a ban on benefits for those who refuse to participate or who drop out.

Anyone with the stomach to finish the book must have been astonished at the extent of the revolution proposed. Nearly a hundred years of Labour theory was being turned on its head. The role of an elected Labour Government was no longer to intervene in the economy in the interests of the people who voted for it. Instead, its role was to stand aside from disciplining the rich and powerful, and reserve its indignation and discipline for people at the bottom of the pile. The effect on the democratic process was devastating. There might indeed be a change of Government at the polls, but any Labour Government elected on the basis of the Mandelson/Liddle philosophy would promise, in effect, no change.

The real meaning of New Labour shines quite clearly from the book. New Labour meant Old Tory or at best Old Liberal. Two veteran socialists, Ken Coates and Michael Barratt Brown, did their best to alert the movement to what was going to happen. Their book, *The Blair Revelation* (1996), stripped Mandelson and Liddle of their spin and gloss, and denounced the backsliding even from the days of John Smith. But the apprehension of a few socialists was quickly overwhelmed by the prospect of electoral victory. As the polls stayed obstinately in Labour's favour, that victory seemed more and more certain. All sorts of unlikely corporate creatures clambered on to the bandwagon. On 12 May 1994, the day John Smith died, Patricia Hewitt, former press secretary to Neil Kinnock and deputy chairman of Labour's new think tank, the IPPR, got a new job as director of research at a leading industrial and financial consultancy called Andersen Consulting, a sister organization to the huge American-based accountants Arthur Andersen. Arthur Andersen had been banned from all Government work since the huge financial scandal involving John deLorean in Northern Ireland in the 1980s. But the ban did not stretch to Andersen Consulting – one of the first City institutions to realize the likelihood of a Labour victory and to take the necessary precautions. In the summer of 1996, Andersen Consulting organized a trip to an Oxford college for about a hundred Labour shadow ministers, who were lectured by City experts on how to be business friendly. More and more wealthy firms clamoured for a place at the £500-a-plate dinners organized by the Labour Party. Victory fever swept through every corner of the Labour movement. Control over the manifesto, once so ardently contested by the rank and file, was surrendered entirely to Blair, Mandelson, Liddle and their circle. Anyone who read it in 1997, and had read its predecessors when Labour was last in office, must have been astonished at the huge ideological ground conceded to the Tories. A party that in 1979 declared itself proud to be socialist now announced, in effect, that it was proud not to be socialist.

One message emerged to dwarf all the others. New Labour was not really Labour at all. It was, above all, new. The word appeared over and over again – once it popped up three times in the same short sentence. Out went the old ideology. Out went public ownership – in its place the 'private finance initiative', which had already been denounced as Tory trickery by several backbenchers and even Harriet Harman from Labour's front bench. Out went increases in tax. Income-tax rises, including rises in the top rate of tax, affecting little more than 1 per cent of the population, were specifically ruled out. Labour pledged its Government to stick for two years to the rigid limits on public spending set by the Tories. Comprehensive schools needed to be modernized too, and many of them turned into 'faith schools'. But there would be no new pro-union laws, just the old anti-union stuff promulgated by the Tories. No one could complain that the deeply reactionary and undemocratic nature of New Labour was not set out in the manifesto. On the contrary. Again and again, the manifesto gave the impression of being written specifically for the rich businessmen and bankers who flocked to those Blairite dinners.

The few socialists left in the Party held their breath hoping that the ideological shift to the right was a trick to make it easier to win the election, and that once the election was won, Labour would return to its old commitments to public enterprise, to the poor and the dispossessed. It was no doubt this lingering hope that helped Labour to their triumphant and emphatic victory in 1997. Some 13,517,911 people voted Labour, an increase of nearly 2 million on 1992. Labour polled 43.2 per cent of the total vote. The Tory and Liberal Democrat vote fell. The 'swing' to Labour from the Tories was double that of the swing to the Liberals. Labour's overall majority in the new Parliament was a fantastic 179 over all other parties. The Tories were out, humiliated. The new Labour Government seemed omnipotent.

Curiously, however, some of the immediate beneficiaries in the new administration in 10 Downing Street were not Labour people at all. They were former Social Democrats. Roger Liddle, Peter Mandelson's co-author, became the Prime Minister's adviser on defence and Europe, and Derek Scott on economics. Scott had stood for the SDP in Swindon in 1983 and

1987, in both cases splitting the Labour vote and letting a Tory in. In 1998, these former opponents of Labour were joined in Downing Street by a new education adviser, Andrew Adonis, who had been a candidate for the Liberal Democrats. Liddle's devotion to an open democratic society was revealed during the 'cash for access' scandal that emerged in 1998. Masquerading as an American businessman who wanted to do business with top people, *Observer* journalist Gregory Palast recorded Liddle boasting about his influence and power. Referring to a young researcher, Derek Draper, employed by Peter Mandelson, Liddle was quoted as saying: 'There is a circle and Derek is part of that circle. Anyone who says he isn't is an enemy. Just tell me who you want to meet and Derek and I will make the call for you.' Draper himself expanded on this theme: 'There are 17 people in this country who count, and to say that I am intimate with every one of them is the understatement of the century.'

Among the 17 people who counted was Bernie Ecclestone, the Formula One motor racing billionaire. Before the election, Ecclestone, who had in the past supported the Tories, slipped the Labour Party a million pounds. Soon after the election, New Labour ratted on its firmest manifesto promise: to ban tobacco advertising. Any ban, it was announced, would not apply to the biggest tobacco advertisers: motor racing. When the media naturally connected this unexpected decision with the million-pound donation, a harassed Blair appeared on television to assure his audience that he was a 'straight guy' – and the million pounds was returned to the billionaire. At a stroke, within a few months of the election, Blair and his office secured a reputation for the 'sleaze' for which they had denounced the Tories. The reputation stuck with them. The master of communications Peter Mandelson had to resign twice from the Labour Cabinet – once when it emerged that he had, without telling anyone, borrowed £370,000 from a Cabinet colleague, Geoffrey Robinson, to buy a mansion, and the second time for intervening to inquire about a British passport for one of the billionaire Hinduja brothers, who were wanted in India for the most monstrous corruption involving an arms company. Such unfortunate episodes were almost inevitable considering the way in which New Labour ministers flung themselves at the feet of their benefactors in the City and elsewhere. But previous Labour administrations had had their slices of sleaze, and cynics could well accept New Labour sleaze with a patient shrug. What was much more shocking was the systematic way in which the Blair Government set about dismantling the democratic traditions of their Party and their predecessors.

Up to and including the general election campaign, Blair had mocked the

Tory 'quangos', quasi-non-Government (and non-elected) organizations, taking control of the country's industries and services. Gordon Brown, in his last Labour Party conference speech before the election, attacked what he called 'the quango state that threatens democracy'. Within months of the election of his Government, however, a huge rash of non-elected 'task forces' had been established to supervise pretty well every industry and service in the country. These task forces were quangos in all but name. They provided positions of power and influence for all those businessmen who had guzzled at Labour's tables. A survey of the first 3,000 people appointed to the task forces was carried out and published by Democratic Audit (an organization that had effectively exposed and denounced the Tory quangos) in 2000. Only 73 (2 per cent) of the task force members were trade unionists. More than a third (1,107) were from businesses, banks and trade associations, and most of the rest were spin doctors, consultants, bankers and special advisers.

A common bond between the new ministers and their new band of advisers was the same distrust of public enterprise that had inspired Margaret Thatcher. The new Labour administration brought nothing new into public ownership. Ministers seemed determined to transfer any democratic responsibility to private enterprise. It was as though all the careful arguments of Laski, Tawney, Bevan and more recent Labour leaders like Tony Benn and Michael Foot were either forgotten or cast aside. On the railways, where the mess left by the Tory privatizations quickly grew out of control, the same Tory gang were left in charge. As each set of new bosses and regulators failed, so more bosses and regulators of exactly the same ilk were appointed to prolong the disaster. Despite an assurance from the Labour spokesman for transport in 1996 that 'our air is not for sale', Britain's air-traffic-control system was flogged off to a consortium of privately run airlines. Railtrack, the company chosen by the Tories to run the railway, became a symbol of incompetence and decay, and eventually collapsed into receivership. Its shareholders, after setting up a terrific howl of protest, were duly compensated at the expense of the taxpayer. The train-operating companies, including Virgin and Stagecoach, made hefty profits while the subsidies paid to them by the taxpayer grew even bigger than under the Tories. In a typical move, an executive of Virgin, whose father was an executive at Stagecoach, was appointed chairman of the Strategic Rail Authority. Again and again in different industries and enterprises the regulators and others responsible for supervising industries and services were chosen from the boardrooms of the most successful and powerful companies.

In his seminal book, *Captive State* (2000), journalist George Monbiot published a 'Fat Cats' Directory', in which he listed the wealthy businessmen who were appointed to positions of power and influence by New Labour. Naturally, in this new order, the privatized industries and utilities stayed under private control. The companies that took over electricity and gas were reconstituted into one big private monopoly (Transco National Grid) responsible for distributing heat and light into every British home. The monopoly turned its attention to speculation: to buying companies in other countries, many of which purchases turned out to be disastrous.

One way forward for the new utility monopolies was to buy and sell each other. Water companies were the most frequent victims of these market place adventures. Wessex Water, for instance, was sold to a subsidiary of the American energy giant Enron, which went bankrupt after a prolonged exercise in the most revolting corruption. Enron's accountants, very much at the centre of these allegations, were Arthur Andersen, sister company of the former New Labour favourites Andersen Consulting, and employers of Patricia Hewitt, who, after leaving Andersen, was elected a Labour MP for Leicester in 1997 and climbed the ministerial ladder rapidly, ending up in the Cabinet as Secretary of State for Trade and Industry. New Labour, incidentally, quickly cleared up the long-running Government dispute with Arthur Andersen and started to choose senior executives and regulators from the company. The deputy chairman of the new supreme regulator, the Financial Services Authority, came straight from Arthur Andersen.

In previous Labour Governments, ministers had seen it as their job to extend their influence over private industry and increase parliamentary responsibility for industrial and commercial matters. New Labour ministers adopted the opposite policy. They bent over backwards to increase the powers of private entrepreneurs, businessmen, bankers and accountants and to devolve public responsibility from elected office. The supreme example, the very first act of New Labour in government, was to surrender the crucial power of setting the bank rate – the rate of interest charged by British banks – to a quango of 'experts' – all of them wealthy and powerful people – coordinated by the Bank of England. This decision by the new Chancellor, Gordon Brown, was widely acclaimed as 'responsible', whereas in terms of the control over the economy by the elected Parliament, it was exactly the opposite. It was Gordon Brown, moreover, who masterminded the central policy of the New Labour Government in the public services – the Private Finance Initiative. This initiative set out to seduce private money into Government initiatives on the security of the Government property involved. For instance, private investors were urged to spend money on hospitals and schools in exchange for regular annual repayments by the taxpayer, with the ownership of the property eventually reverting to the company. This initiative was started by the Tories, and variously denounced by Labour MPs and even shadow ministers. Yet when New Labour took office, ministers encouraged and even provoked a massive switch to private enterprise. By the end of the century almost every public-spending project had been engulfed by PFI.

The most extravagant example was in the health service. A huge wave of new hospital building was set in motion under PFI. Labour MPs argued that they would not have got the new hospitals without PFI. The counter-argument was that all the hospitals could have been much cheaper in the long run, and without surrendering control of them, under the old system of public finance. Another argument, even more powerful, was that the concessions demanded by the private consortia that built the hospitals led to fewer hospital beds and many more sackings of staff. A survey of the first 14 PFI proposals for new hospitals by Professor Allyson Pollock and her team at the School of Public Policy at University College London showed a 30 per cent reduction in the number of beds compared with the hospitals they replaced, and a 25–30 per cent reduction in staff. The new University College Hospital in London, for instance, would have cost £140 million under the old scheme of public finance. Under PFI, by the time the new scheme was signed in 2000, the eventual cost had escalated to more than a billion pounds.

There was little sign either that people supported the new PFI schemes or, as ministers constantly alleged, that they did not understand them. One of Professor Pollock's most influential research projects was at Worcester, where she demonstrated how the new PFI scheme for a hospital meant the closure of acute-hospital facilities at Kidderminster. The scheme led to an explosion of popular protest and the formation of a new party, Health Concern, committed to the principles of the National Health Service, against the cuts and against PFI. The new Party rapidly took control of the local councils, and in the 2001 general election its representative, retired hospital consultant Richard Taylor, easily defeated the sitting New Labour MP.

Professor Pollock continued her work into other areas where PFI was demolishing former Labour commitments to public ownership. Her team tracked the continued New Labour enthusiasm for PFI, for instance in the state schools in the London Borough of Haringey and in the area of long-term personal care. In all these instances, the researchers noted that the private companies were constantly being baled out with Government subsidies and that information vital to any rounded criticism of the project was systematically withheld, both by ministries and by local authorities. The excuse ('commercial in confidence'), so often mocked by social democrats in the past, became standard by-words for New Labour ministers who wanted to keep the public uninformed.

Professor Pollock identified another threat to public enterprise – from the World Trade Organization and its treaty that set up the General Agreement on Trade in Services (GATS). Their argument was that the treaty provided the WTO with new powers to promote 'pro-competitive domestic policies'. Such powers were reflected in New Labour's Competition Act 2000, which restricted the ability of public bodies such as the National Health Service to refuse contracts to private companies because for some reason they were found distasteful. A glorious example of the effect of this policy came in 2001 when Treasury ministers agreed to the sale under PFI of almost every tax and customs office in the land. The lucky buyers were a company of international speculators presided over by George Soros, whose judicious sale of sterling in 1992 forced the Tory Government to scuttle out of the European Exchange Rate Mechanism. Soros's company buying the buildings was registered in Bermuda, a tax haven. When some MPs (usually Liberal Democrat) dared to ask why and how tax inspectors chasing down tax avoidance all over Britain were now working from offices that had been sold to a company blatantly avoiding tax, the Inland Revenue and their PFI-crazy ministers whined that they had no alternative. WTO and EU rules, they argued, insisted that they could not ignore a bid from a company even when that company was flouting the central purpose of the organization whose buildings were up for sale! Another excuse, even more revealing, was that the Inland Revenue Board knew perfectly well that their buildings were being sold into a tax haven, but did not even tell Treasury ministers. For this blatant breach of elementary democratic responsibility, there was no public reproach, no sacking, no disciplinary action.

The drive against democracy proceeded in all sorts of directions. Though ministers and both 1997 and 2001 manifestos proclaimed Labour's commitment to the principle of a free state education service for all, and despite David Blunkett's 'read my lips' conference pledge not to introduce selection by exam or interview into the state school system, selection was widespread by the time he left office after four years as Education Secretary. The Blair Government's commitment to 'faith schools' further weakened the Party's previous loyalty to secular comprehensive schools, open to all. In case anyone didn't understand what the Government was doing, the Prime

Minister's official spokesman referred out loud to 'bog standard comprehensives'. Here was proof that the pained elitist tone about the decline of
schools in deprived areas in *The Blair Revolution* by Mandelson and Liddle
was being crudely translated into Government policy.

The New Labour (Old Tory) Government launched a furious and sustained assault on a policy right at the centre of the democratic socialist
tradition. Often in the past, Neil Kinnock had warmed his audiences with
reminders that he was the first member of his family to go to university,
and that this had been made possible by Labour education policies and the
provision of free university education for all who could pass the exams.
Such free access was a cornerstone of British social democracy. But almost at
once New Labour destroyed it. Tuition fees were introduced for university
students. Perhaps to reassure the increasing number of their supporters
who were disgusted by these fees, New Labour actually inserted a direct
pledge into their 2001 election manifesto – that a New Labour Government
would not introduce 'top-up' fees for the top universities. Months after
they were re-elected, deeply impressed by the whining of top people in top
universities, the Prime Minister and his entourage (including the former
Liberal Democrat Andrew Adonis) started arguing for top-up fees, and
later (though only with a slender parliamentary majority) introduced them
into law.

The very language of the new ministries emphasized their deep suspicion
of democratic thought. A fashion arose for appointing 'czars' to take control
of different areas of public policy. There was a 'drugs czar' and even a
'czar' (or czarina) to make sure that impoverished people were cleared away
from the city streets. None of the politicians or broadcasters who cheerfully
recycled the name 'czar' seemed even aware that they were borrowing the
concept from arguably the most totalitarian regime in history.

Perhaps the most democratic achievement of elected Labour over the
whole century was the building of council houses to let at rents the workers
could afford. Labour (and Tory) councils, encouraged by Labour Governments, built more than 14 million council houses. The endeavour was the
essence of social democracy. It was socialist because it favoured the workers
and the poor. It was democratic because the landlord was the elected
authority, responsible to the tenants. Much of the pride of the Labour Party
was based in its stock of council houses. For all three post-war Labour
Governments under Attlee, Wilson and Callaghan, council housing was a
firm priority and all three encouraged and assisted councils to build more.

The Blair administration took exactly the opposite view. Council-house
building was effectively stopped. Instead, the Government encouraged and

bribed councils to flog their housing stock to housing associations and others, who became 'registered social landlords'. Such bodies, often idealistic at first, were inclined to degenerate quite quickly as their managers and directors, many of them filched from the local authorities, discovered the advantages of their undemocratic status, chiefly their ability to evict troublesome tenants, to raise rents, to sell empty homes – and to increase their remuneration. Tenants were offered a vote as to whether they wanted to change landlords from the elected councils to the new associations. These contests were heavily tilted in favour of the associations by various bribes – chiefly better borrowing facilities for the new registered landlords. Even so, tenants in some of the bigger authorities, notably Birmingham, voted to stay with their elected landlord, and were punished accordingly. The whole process was supervised not by a Secretary of State for Housing but by a junior minister, somewhere at the backside of the Department for Local Government.

Memories of the disasters that overtook the Labour Governments of the 1960s and 1970s are always tinged with regard for the reforms made in those years to ancient laws and customs that gravely affected human rights and civil liberties. Under a Labour Government (though not necessarily by Government Bills) measures were taken to wipe out capital punishment and ancient prohibitions on homosexuals, and to allow women to have safe abortions. No such claim can be made for New Labour. Home Secretaries Jack Straw and David Blunkett have proved as reactionary as any of their Tory predecessors, including even the crusted Tory ideologue Michael Howard. The Terrorism Act, which came into force in March 2001, classifies 21 groups as terrorist and deprives their members of basic civil liberties. The statements by Blunkett and Straw on immigration, on asylum seekers and on crime would be applauded wildly at any Tory conference. Every year of the first New Labour Government, the number of people in prison rose – to an all-time (and intolerable) record.

Two more matters arise before we get a complete picture of the impact the two Blair Governments had on the British social democratic tradition. The first is financial stability. Again and again, Liddle and Mandelson in their 'mould-breaking' book, and Blair himself in the two Labour manifestos, nominated the guiding principle of their policies as 'stability'. Gordon Brown's 'prudence' (was the word borrowed, even by accident, from Professor Tawney's mockery of the Ramsay MacDonald Governments as 'prudence rewarded'?) led, he argued, to security not just from the booms and busts of the past but from the erratic intervention in the smooth process of democratic government by irresponsible capital. Their regime, New

Labour claim, has been smoother, less unstable than its predecessors because the Government has proved so determined not to raise taxes for the rich or to intervene in the movements of the markets. They go on to claim that the 'unstable compounds', outlined above, of 1964–1970 and 1974–9 have not been repeated under new Labour precisely because the trade unions have been kept right out of the government process, because nothing has been nationalized and because so much policy-making has been handed over to the representatives of rich corporations.

The argument seems to have been sustained by the relative financial stability of the late 1990s. Every year under Blair and Brown there has been reasonably regular economic growth. But both men know perfectly well that they do not control the shifts in the economy and the swings in the state of the market. What they seem unable to countenance is that the more they relax their already marginal control over the economy, the more certainly they consign their Governments to forces beyond their control. An ominous sign of this was the concession by Brown at the end of 2002 that his forecasts for the economy were all wrong. He made what he called necessary adjustments (chiefly by borrowing much more than he intended), but he could give no credible guarantee that the stability he believes he has achieved can be sustained, or that the capitalist economy he has guarded so prudently won't rebound on him and lurch into precisely the cycle of boom and bust that he so often derided. We have seen how the democratic controls wielded – or threatened – over industry and finance by past Labour Governments led to some sort of confidence and a half-hearted (if largely unconvincing) assurance that the elected Government remained in charge of the economy. No such confidence or assurance exudes from the Blair/ Brown Government. They have abrogated not just their ability but even their desire to control the market economy. They admire it so much that they no longer want to control it. So they don't.

The second point is convergence. Social and political scientists could not help noticing during the years of New Labour Government that its policies converged with those of its Tory predecessors. In his 1999 book *The Political Economy of New Labour*, the Birmingham University academic Colin Hay carefully traced this process. In industrial policy, training, education, pensions, crime, he found an almost complete convergence between New Labour and Tory policies. Of course, the Tory Party cannot properly oppose increasing privatization or PFI – they started both. They can't demand an extension of public ownership and control – they are ideologically opposed to both. Of course they cannot propose more council houses – they started the move to sell them off. Of course they can't propose freeing the trade unions from Tory anti-union laws. Of course they cannot dare support more liberal policies on crime or immigration or civil liberties. They cannot do anything about any of these major issues and the more New Labour endorses and carries out Tory policies, the more hopelessly shackled the Tory Party becomes. Whether their leader is able (like William Hague) or hopeless (like Iain Duncan Smith) makes not the slightest difference.

Convergence is disastrous for everyone in a democratic society but especially disastrous for the Opposition. Though both parties and their spokespeople made every effort during the general election of 2001 to concentrate on their differences, convergence kept creeping back on to the agenda. The electorate got the point at once. Labour won the election by another massive majority. But their vote (10.7 million) was dramatically lower not just on 1997. It was three-quarters of a million down on 1992, when Labour lost the election. The Tory vote was down too, and so was the Liberal Democrat vote. Indeed, the most striking feature of the voting figures in 2001 was the huge number of voters who did not vote. With the single exception of 1918, when the vote had just been granted and the people were recovering from a ghastly and pointless world war, there never was a time when fewer people used their right to vote than in 2001. The percentages of the electorate voting were as follows: 1922, 73.0; 1923, 71.1; 1924, 77.0; 1929, 76.3; 1931, 76.4; 1935, 71.1; 1945, 72.8; 1950, 83.9; 1951, 82.6; 1955, 76.8; 1959, 78.7; 1964, 77.1; 1966, 75.8; 1970, 72.0; February 1974, 78.8; October 1974, 72.8; 1979, 76.0; 1983, 72.7; 1987, 75.3; 1992, 77.7; 1997, 71.5; 2001, 59.1.

All sorts of pundits and commentators declared themselves 'shocked' at the 2001 abstention. Why so suddenly had such a huge proportion of British voters not bothered to vote? Predictably, the experts preferred to blame the electors themselves. A common view was that the electors must be stupid or lazy. Hasty and ill-thought-out proposals were rushed forward to introduce new ways of voting, voting on the internet, voting by post. Some arrogant experts proposed, preposterously, that voting should be made compulsory by law. None of these measures or threats made much difference. In elections in Scotland and Wales, in local elections, in new elections for mayors, the majority of the electorate stubbornly insisted on not voting. As the pattern settled down, the cries of anguish from the commentators settled down. So what, they asked themselves, if so many people don't vote? Aren't most of those people poor or black or disabled or otherwise a menace to the comfortable lives of professional politicians and their great army of advisers and commentators? Were not the voting patterns settling down into something reassuringly similar to that which exists in the United States, where elections are held between two parties with policies long since converged, none of which for a moment threaten the established order? And is not this situation much more amenable to the politicians and their commentators? Can they not then relax and play their games about politics even more comfortably than previously?

Politics and commentary on politics become a professional game, quite free of any genuine controversy and certainly quite free of any danger from the dispossessed who have understood the situation and absented themselves from the voting process. That way, no one blames the politicians or political parties or the corporations for the collapse of the democratic process. A mere glance, however, at the voting figures since 1922 shows the peaks of social democratic strength, when social democratic government could do something or at least try to do something for the workers and the poor, and what happened when, after almost exactly a hundred years, British Labour first abandoned socialism and then, as a direct consequence, abandoned democracy as well.

As long ago as 1938, Professor Tawney argued that there was an essential contradiction between capitalism and democracy and that unless elected Labour Governments challenged capitalism, and took control of it, capitalism would counter-attack and the chief casualty would be democracy. While modern Labour politicians still pretend to revere the Professor, they don't seem to notice that his most persuasive and appalling prophecy has come true in the most alarming fashion. The capitalist tiger has quite easily devoured its social democratic tamer and its supporters look forward to a period of uninterrupted exploitation without the slightest concern about elections.

Conclusion:
Their Democracy and Ours

But never mind. 'God save the king' and kings!
 For if he don't, I doubt if men will longer.
I think I hear a little bird, who sings
 The people by and by will be the stronger.
The veriest jade will wince whose harness wrings
 So much into the raw as quite to wrong her
Beyond the rules of posting; and the mob
At last fall sick of imitating Job.

At first it grumbles, then it swears, and then,
 Like David, flings smooth pebbles 'gainst a giant.
At last it takes to weapons such as men
 Snatch when despair makes human hearts less pliant.
Then comes the tug of war; 'twill come again
 I rather doubt and I would fain say 'fie on't',
If I had not perceived that revolution
Alone can save the earth from hell's pollution.

Lord Byron, Don Juan (1823)

The first theme of this book is that the notion that society should be run by a representative democracy originally horrified the propertied minority because democracy threatened their property. Their opposition was out-right and violent through the whole of the seventeenth and eighteenth centuries. It grew to fever pitch when it was threatened with a revolution under the Chartists, a movement that explicitly merged the demand for the vote with an equally insistent demand for a share of the property. After the Chartists' agitation died down, the wealthy minority adjusted their reaction to the case for some meaningful popular stake in the political process. They conceded the vote rather reluctantly to urban skilled workers in 1867 and, less reluctantly, to skilled and semi-skilled agricultural labourers and miners in 1884. Their opposition to further extensions of the franchise, to women and the very poor, returned during the Great Unrest from 1911 to 1914. It subsided, as the agitation subsided, during the early months of the First World War, but the vote was finally granted to almost everyone in 1918.

The second half of the book covers the remorseless tussle between the unelected forces of property and elected Labour Governments that dared to challenge them. It discusses the effect of universal suffrage on British Labour, its main beneficiary. It traces the history of the Labour Governments of the twentieth century and how they proceeded towards and retreated from their stated aim to transform British capitalism into British socialism. The conclusion, which takes us up to the beginning of the twenty-first century, is that this grand aim has been surrendered and abandoned. At the end of this process, the right-wing leaders of the Labour Party argue that the reason for the change in Labour's policies is the change in British society. The modern and relevant priority, they claim, is for fair and decent government that holds the ring between the rich and poor and is no longer interested in redistributing wealth or power.

In contrast to their predecessors, both Governments under Blair have positively basked in the admiration and gratitude of the rich. In the distribution of wealth and power, in access to education and health care, in the construction of decent homes, in security in old age, Britain remains a profoundly divided society. Millions of its people are still without property, dignity or hope and are still denied access to the fruits of their labour. These divisions are replicated even more horrifically all over the world. Two-fifths of the world population don't get enough to eat and even more have no access to clean drinking water. These hungry and thirsty masses live side by side with, and completely in thrall to, a small, increasingly obstinate and increasingly rich minority who use their wealth, their media and their armies to protect their property, their privileges and their power.

The extent of these divisions is almost beyond belief, and the gap is constantly growing. Many enlightened modern commentators concentrate their attention on the gap between rich and poor countries. This gap is indeed shocking, but much more shocking, and much more relevant, is the gap between rich and poor within each country. The richest nation in the world – the United States of America – is grotesquely deformed. A contemporary survey for the Federal Reserve in 2003 found that the 'net worth' of the richest 10 per cent in the US was, from 1992 to 1998, 13 times the net worth of the poorest 20 per cent. In the three years after 1998, that gap grew so that the richest 10 per cent had 22 times more than the poorest 20 per cent. On the other hand, another survey at about the same time showed that the continent with the most millionaires is Asia, most of whose people are desperately poor.

The division of the world along these lines is not merely unfair, indefensible and intolerable. It forges the rich minority into an economic oligarchy, a ruling class far more powerful than any elected Government. Elected Governments are no match for this class, whose supporters are and always have been thoroughly disgusted by and contemptuous of democracy in any shape or form. The rich have learned to live with parliamentary democracy because they have so easily been able to undermine the slightest tendency of parliaments to represent the interests of the masses. If anyone could have taken General Ireton to one side in 1647 and explained to him how the organized power of the rich could easily patronize or suppress even a sign of the economic egalitarianism he feared, perhaps he would have been less distressed at the notion of universal suffrage.

The system of society favoured by the rich across the world, capitalism, is in its essence and in its daily dealings with human beings wholly hostile to democracy. In all its manifestations it is hierarchical and bureaucratic. It responds not to the needs of the majority but to the vagaries of the market, the so-called 'laws' of profit and loss. The theory of the democracy of the market starts from the principle that people will buy what they want, and that therefore the market will ensure that goods will be produced, distributed and exchanged in proportion to how much they are needed. Thus, it is argued, markets will ensure a democracy in production and distribution. People will make the things that people need and distribute them accordingly. It only takes a moment to realize the fundamental flaw in this argument. 'Market democracy' can only begin to work in an egalitarian society – where people have roughly the same wealth. In those circumstances, if they buy what they need and want, the market will provide some semblance of economic democracy. But by the same token the whole equilibrium of market democracy is thrown into chaos by the sort of inequality that prevails throughout the modern world. Indeed, the more unequal the society, the more hopeless and unfair is the working of market democracy, and the more the wrong things are produced and distributed.

The inequality of capitalist society, in other words, is the chief destroyer of its pride and joy, its market democracy. Its disciplines are enforced not democratically, but arbitrarily. Its rewards are handed out according to mysterious assessments of ability or by the blind chance of heredity. None of these disciplines or rewards is subject to reason or even to debate. Despite the flamboyant riches it showers on the privileged few, the system leads necessarily to the most monstrous deprivation and wretchedness for the mass of the human race. A peculiarly contemptible notion introduced by the rich in an attempt to explain or excuse their wealth is that of 'trickling down'. Minority wealth is good, so runs the theory, because it provides the only way for wealth to grow and because it eventually will trickle down to the poor. All the evidence points to the reverse. When wealth increases, it stays obstinately with the wealthy. Rather than trickle down, it gushes up.

The antidote to capitalism, socialism, rests on three pillars, dependent on each other: a planned economy, equality and democracy. Production and its accompanying services must be planned. Distribution of what is produced must be guided by the principle that all human beings have an equal right to live and enjoy the produce of their cooperative labour. But the central principle, the one that must govern the planning and the distribution if either is to work, is democracy, control from below.

Capitalism is in permanent conflict with all three ideas, but particularly with democracy. Capitalism and democracy are always in conflict, and the history of all capitalist states that have conceded universal suffrage has been, in part at least, a history of that conflict. What has happened in all those countries, including Britain, is that the forces of capitalism have conquered democracy, subdued it, suppressed its impact and left it to wither in irrelevance.

The case against capitalism, and for a democratic socialist society to replace it, seems every bit as strong in 2003 as it was when the vote was first granted to most people some 85 years ago. Yet the sad fact is that in those years Labour Governments, including particularly the majority Labour Government that came to office at the end of the twentieth century, have done little or nothing to achieve the Party's founding aim – namely to use the power given them by the franchise to represent the organized workers and to close the gap between the rich and the workers in this country or in any other. In the past Labour ministers used to apologize for this failure. Now they boast about it.

Oh well, comes the sceptics' reply, it's all the fault of democracy. Under a democracy, the argument continues, we get the Governments we deserve, and all the Labour Governments were elected. This response ignores the main message of this narrative: that the electoral process, whenever it favours labour and the poor, has been constantly thwarted by undemocratic forces it does not control.

Chief among these is the power of wealth. Again and again through the twentieth century, Labour Governments with good parliamentary majorities have been humbled and cut down by financial 'crises'. Even in the

1940s, when they were strongest, Labour ministers were constantly looking over their shoulders at the City of London for fear of a bankers' coup like the one that destroyed their Government in 1931. By a mixture of determination, ideological commitment and good fortune, that post-war Government and its socialist reputation survived, but the Wilson Government that came to office in the mid 1960s had its promises, its thrust and its purpose thrown into reverse by developments beyond its control, orchestrated by the representatives of the rich who were not elected by anyone. Similarly, Labour ministers in the 1970s were plagued throughout by financial crises, sudden lurches in the value of the pound, which demanded – and achieved – quite different policies from the ones they themselves had proclaimed. More than once, their policies on quite crucial issues were overturned by the courts or the police.

All Labour administrations have been harassed and libelled by corrupt media, especially corrupt newspaper proprietors, recklessly dodging taxes and wielding their power without responsibility, famously dubbed the prerogative of the harlot. So effective was the harassment from the most powerful of these proprietors, Rupert Murdoch, that Blair, before the 1997 election, made peace with Murdoch and, in exchange for Murdoch's papers' support at election times, faithfully followed the proprietor's agenda for Government media policy.

The impotence of elected government in the face of these undemocratic forces has a long and miserable history. Even the Tory administrations that ruled from 1979 to 1997 had no answer to financial crises such as the exchange rate crisis of 1992 in which, according to the then Chancellor of the Exchequer, Kenneth Clarke, the elected Government was 'completely out of control'. Those Tory ministers, however, assumed complete control when they were cutting down the organizations of labour, the trade unions, and reforming local authorities. They cut such a deadly swathe through what was left of Labour's social democratic achievements that the Labour Party, in a desperate struggle to keep their craft afloat, threw overboard their aspirations and policies and finally settled down with a conservative leader and an entourage of advisers and consultants ideologically indistinguishable from their Tory predecessors. A new politics has emerged, founded on the American model, and entirely divorced from the ideological disputes between capitalism and socialism that characterized the past. The new politics, agreed by all the contestants, effectively rules out of the political process at least 15 per cent of the people at the bottom of the pile. As a consequence, those people don't vote, and the process continues. So, in an age where socialist priorities are more relevant and vital than ever before, the conventional route to socialist progress through electing Labour Governments has been comprehensively blocked.

This is not the fault of the technical workings of the electoral system. In *Where is Britain Going?*, his magnificent philippic against Ramsay Mac-Donald and MacDonaldism, written in 1926, Leon Trotsky insisted, rightly, that the democratic electoral system in Britain was flawed because it did not give a vote to all adult British citizens. Women under 30 and young people under 21 still couldn't vote. Those gaps have since been closed – in 1928 and in 1969. Now the Government is flirting with new laws to bestow the vote on young people between the ages of 16 and 18. Everyone can vote. Nor is there a deficiency in access to the vote by region. The Blair Government set up devolved parliaments in Scotland and in Wales, and is apparently committed to regional assemblies with some tax-gathering powers in the English regions. The result has not been a flowering of democracy. Turn-outs at the elections for the devolved assemblies in Scotland and in Wales, and for the new mayors arbitrarily established in some cities, have been even lower than in general elections. Moreover, the new assemblies have shown almost exactly the same tendencies to legislative impotence and personal corruption as at Westminster. Even the desperate attempts to make voting easier – by post or via the internet – have made only marginal difference to the voting figures.

The failure of the search for a convenient or easy solution to the problem of voters' apathy suggests that the real reason for the low turn-outs and the convergence of the attitudes of political parties lies much deeper – in the very structure of society. The distinctive characteristic of our society is that it is split into classes. This is not merely an empirical fact, proved by the glaring differences between the rich and the rest. The concept of class runs deeper than the mere facts of inequality. The rich are not simply a small group of people who have struck lucky. Nor are they distinguished by the remarkable fact that they can pass on their riches to their children, whose inherited wealth has no connection whatever to their achievement. Pretty well all the wealth of the rich can be attributed in one way or another to exploitation of other people – either through rents or interest or dividends, wealth that accrues simply because it is there in the first place, or profit, which is the surplus value of an industrial or commercial enterprise. The rich know they are rich mainly through inheritance, exploitation, luck or trickery. They know they have no 'right' whatsoever to their wealth. They therefore cling together in a spirit of class solidarity and invent and legislate the 'rights' of property. They show intellectual and political solidarity with each other. The point of such solidarity is to keep rich, and the best way of keeping rich is to make sure that the barbarians at the gate, those who are not rich at all, are kept preferably out of sight, maybe at a distance but certainly under control.

No one in all history has attracted more ignominy and scholarly abuse than Karl Marx. Each generation of intellectuals buries him, and then exhumes him in order to bury him again. At his funeral, in London's Highgate in 1883, attended by 11 people, his friend and collaborator Frederick Engels explained that Marx attracted all this antagonism because he had discovered and proclaimed 'the simple fact, hitherto concealed by an overgrowth of ideology, that mankind must first of all eat and drink, have shelter and clothing, before it can pursue politics, science, religion and art; and that therefore the production of the immediate material means of life and consequently the degree of economic development . . . form the foundation upon which the forms of government, the legal conceptions, the art and even the religious ideas of the people concerned have been evolved . . . instead of vice versa as has hitherto been the case'.

In the same speech, Engels likened Marx's great discovery to that of Charles Darwin's discovery of evolution. But Marx was different from Darwin in one crucial respect. Darwin was embarrassed by his revolutionary discovery, and terrified of the use that might be made of it by agitators and subversives. He therefore kept it quiet until the Chartist agitation was over. Marx, on the other hand, Engels went on, 'was before all else a revolutionary. His real mission in life was to contribute in one way or another to the overthrow of capitalist society and of the forms of government which it had brought into being.' Those who owned most of the wealth and controlled the forms of government, the legal conceptions, the enforcement and publication of those conceptions by armies and by police, media, art and religion formed themselves into a ruling class and used the powers at their command to ensure their predominance.

Marx and Engels lumped all these agents of capitalism under the heading of 'the state', a notion substantially developed by the Marxists who led the Bolshevik Revolution of October 1917. In his book *Imperialism and World Economy*, published in 1915, Nikolai Bukharin, perhaps the most sensitive and articulate of the Bolshevik theorists, predicted that the ruling class was continually merging its previously feuding components into a single power, 'the state'. The state, he argued, was beginning to behave more and more like 'the executive committee of the ruling class'. The various components of the state – the police, the armed forces, the civil service, media, judiciary and so on – were not, as they pretended, 'neutral' between rich and poor. On the contrary, they were organizing themselves increasingly into 'one solid reactionary mass', less and less tolerant of 'democratic and liberal arguments'. In this new situation, Bukharin predicted, parliaments would lose the purpose they used to have when different sections of the ruling class resolved their differences in parliamentary chambers: 'Parliament at present serves as a decorative institution; it passes on decisions prepared beforehand in the businessmen's organizations and gives only formal sanction to the collective will of the consolidated bourgeoisie as a whole.'

Bukharin's view was expanded in Lenin's *State and Revolution*, written in the year of the October Revolution, 1917. Much of what both men wrote about the state was coloured by the centralization and draconian decrees forced on the European, Russian and American ruling classes in wartime. But the basic point survived through the whole of the twentieth century and beyond. The continual strengthening of the state under finance capital led to a withering away of the democratic processes of parliaments. In Britain, as the century wound its way to its Blairite anti-climax, the 'neutral' state became less and less neutral and the democratic processes more and more neutered. Big business had never been subject to democratic decision-making and by the end of the century even the formal democracy of shareholders' meetings had degenerated from deference into farce. Parliamentary responsibility for nationalized industries was consistently weakened by privatization and part-privatization. Questions in Parliament, especially if they touched on the hallowed ground of the 'security' or 'intelligence' services, were consistently ignored. Freedom of information legislation was consistently watered down and postponed. Local government, often with its own consent and by its own hand, was effectively deprived of meaningful democratic control. Council housing, at least formally controlled by an elected body, was systematically flogged off to associations and 'arm's-length managements', none of them elected. So was education, financed by ratepayers but increasingly run by firms and experts way out of the reach of ratepayers. The 1984–5 miners' strike encouraged the Tory Government of the time to streamline the police force and bring the local forces further under the control of the centralized state.

In almost every area of local life, the 'executive committee of the ruling class' strove, usually successfully, to remove the influence of elected councils and parliaments and replace it with consultants and experts answerable only to their shadowy executives. Trade unions, which had some form of democratic structure, were consistently cut out of public life and even out of the media. The unions themselves became less and less democratic. The merger between the engineers' and electricians' unions in the 1990s, for instance, dispensed with the vibrant democratic constitution of the old

AEU and replaced it with a system of largely unelected officials presided over by a general secretary, elected only occasionally. Discussion and debate, the hallmark of the early trade unions, were discouraged and even ridiculed. Many of the new trade-union bosses, once elected, assumed they were in power for ever. In 2001, when he didn't like the result of elections for a new general secretary to the country's largest civil service union, the PCS, the sitting general secretary blithely continued in office and tried to sack the elected general secretary – until he was prevented from doing so by the High Court. In other unions, attempts were made, sometimes successfully, to do away with annual elections and annual conferences. Plunged almost constantly into verbal disputes that made up in puny rhetoric what they lacked in popular significance, the House of Commons increasingly lost respect even for its 'decorative' quality. While Parliament lost any power or prestige it may have had, the organs of real power, big business and banks, increasingly backed by police, civil servants and media, and endless hosts of consultants and lobbyists, became increasingly unaffected by the popular vote, yet increased their influence over every aspect of national life.

Internationally, the process was even more dramatic. The bureaucrats who put together the Treaty of Rome in 1956 as the foundation of a European Union were at best uninterested and at worst downright hostile to extending democracy. The affairs of the new Union were blithely put in the charge of an appointed Commission, with a huge supporting bureaucracy far out of the reach of any electorate. When a European Parliament was grudgingly conceded much later, the powers of its elected Members were crudely subordinated to those of the unelected Commission. The MEPs' power and authority went down almost as fast as their salaries and expenses went up. The European Parliament is still, in effect, subservient to the unelected Commission. One result of this undemocratic structure was an almost continual Euro-corruption on a scale far more revolting even than anything that took place in the member states. Similarly, the international bodies that determine the standards and texture of life all over the world are all deeply undemocratic. The United Nations is controlled not by the nations of the world but by a cabal of Governments of rich and powerful nations called the Security Council. The World Bank and the International Monetary Fund, which lay down the economic laws by which many hundreds of millions of poor people starve to death, are elected by, and democratically responsible to, no one. The World Trade Organization seeks all the time to interfere with and dictate to elected Governments, instructing them, for instance, to uphold the sacred principle of competition, even where that competition leads directly to greater exploitation, greater sickness and greater poverty. Everywhere the grim predictions of Bukharin and Lenin are being vindicated. Popular democracy is out. Capitalist bureaucracy is in.

Originally, the spokesmen for the ruling class, as the Putney Debates so graphically revealed, were hostile to the franchise because the vote was a threat to their property. Unable to resist the rising demand for some representation in the control of society, the ruling class developed ways to influence, bend, twist and if necessary smash any forces of democratic resistance that emerged from elections. They soon discovered that the power and will of the elected Governments were as nothing compared to their own power and will. As Labour ministers experienced to their horror, a mere flick of the financial tiller was enough to reverse the combined will of a Labour Cabinet, even when that will was backed by majorities of votes. The blatant assaults on elected Government by a whole host of state representatives – notably by the common law made over centuries by judges who clung relentlessly to the values of their class, or by the media, which throughout the process was almost universally owned and directed by peculiarly corrupt members of the same class, by generals and police chiefs whose class loyalties have never been in doubt, and by a civil service whose mandarins, despite the screens of neutrality behind which they hide, have been uniformly loyal to their class. The unimaginable power wielded by this combination of industrial and financial chieftains, their toadying press, their police chiefs, their generals and admirals and their judges is incomparably greater than the formal powers wielded by elected Governments. The elected so-called 'secretaries of state' are in reality prisoners of state.

Parliamentary democracy is no match for this unelected oligarchy. The history of the twentieth century in Britain has shown that whenever a Labour Government in parliamentary office has found itself in conflict with the class wielding economic and industrial power, the Government has been resisted, humiliated or defeated, usually all three. On all sides, the elected Government is at a disadvantage. Its members are elected by geographic constituency and are constrained by the necessity to represent all their constituents whatever class they come from or support. Elected Governments move at a snail's pace, from Bill to Bill, formality to formality. Their ministries are cluttered with the most ridiculous pomp and tradition. They are obliged to submit their proposed laws to the Crown and to the House of Lords, which is dominated by the 'great and good' (not elected). They are permanently subject to laws made by judges (not elected), enforced by police and army chiefs (not elected), and drawn up and supervised by civil servants (not elected). The ruling-class chieftains have at their disposal whole armies of their own advisers and intellectuals, none of them elected. They take daily decisions affecting hundreds of thousands of people, sacking them, disciplining them, cutting their wages, sending them off to war, without any real threat of obstruction from the elected Parliament.

British representative democracy is founded on the notion of one person, one vote. An industrial magnate has one vote, and so does each worker he can sack or impoverish. A millionaire landlord has one vote, and so does every person he evicts. A banker has one vote, so does every person impoverished by a rise in the bank rate or a financial takeover. A newspaper proprietor has one vote, so does each of the readers he deceives or seduces every day of the week. Are all these people really equally represented? Or does not the mighty, unrepresentative economic power of the wealthy minority consistently and completely overwhelm the representative power of Parliament?

Corruption in all its forms has always been a consistent companion of class rule. One of the promises of the early social democrats was that they would put a stop to corruption. In fact, corruption has prospered mightily in the age of social democracy. Again and again, social democratic representatives have found themselves at the mercy of the capitalist bribe. The ministerial career of Jimmy Thomas, the trade-union leader who played so heroic a role in the betrayal of the general strike, ended with a whimper when he was caught leaking budget secrets to his wealthy golfing mates who speedily converted the information into a ripe profit on the stock exchange. The notorious Poulson scandal of the 1960s engulfed whole Labour councils who were bewitched by the Methodist architect and his Methodist largesse. T. Dan Smith, a Labour hero of the early 1960s, felt it was time he turned his considerable talent into making money for himself and ended up in prison with Poulson. New Labour in the mid 1990s made a lot of political capital out of 'sleaze', a new word coined to describe the rather minor Tory Party corruption of that period. Yet when Labour ministers took office in 1997, and flung themselves headlong at the feet of the rich, they felt, like Dan Smith, that their time had come. Very soon their dependence on consultants and lobbyists from industry and finance landed the new Government in further heaps of sleaze, as we have seen. Another example was when the great sleaze slagheap of Enron finally collapsed in bankruptcy in 2000. Labour ministers scurried to cover the tracks of Enron consultants at Labour Party dinners and the close contacts the Labour leaders had established with Enron's corrupt accountants. Corruption is a natural ally of capitalism, and British Labour, as it made peace with capitalism, increasingly fell victim to corruption.

All this sad history could lead to nothing but despair. If there is no hope of using our representative democracy to curb the monopolists and their corruption, what aspirations are left? What alternative can there be but to fall into line with the politicians who have transferred their allegiance to the rich, and cooperate with them in the hope that we can dislodge a few crumbs from the rich man's table and prise them into the mouths of the hungry millions?

The first point I would like to make in answer to these questions is that scepticism about the parliamentary road does not mean that we can cheerfully abandon it to its totalitarian enemies. Louis MacNeice may have been technically wrong in 1938 when he wrote in his *Autumn Journal* that our 'top-heavy, tedious parliamentary system / Is our only ready weapon to defeat / The legions' eagles and the lictors' axes'. But nothing excuses surrender to those legions and those axes. Whatever its chronic weaknesses and paralyses, the parliamentary system and the thin gruel of democracy it offers us are indispensable to any agitation for progress. The mere fact, for instance, that this book can be published and these views circulated is evidence of the value of the 'bourgeois freedoms' many socialists deride. Indeed, derision of such 'bourgeois freedoms' was one of the reasons for the collapse of so many socialists over such a long period into the awful mire of Stalinism, in which, in the name of socialism, the leaders and inspirers of the Russian Revolution, including Nikolai Bukharin, Leon Trotsky and countless of their supporters all over the world, were slaughtered. The Stalinist illusion hypnotized socialists everywhere for much of the twentieth century with incalculably disastrous results for the people and the organizations of the labour movement not just in Russia, China and Eastern Europe but everywhere. So every invasion of those freedoms, every backsliding from parliamentary democracy into bureaucracy, every banned article, false imprisonment, phoney arrest or prosecution, every clause of furtively delegated legislation, every new attempt by bodies such as the European Union or the World Trade Organization to impose rules restricting the democratic process calls for the most forthright opposition in the name of democracy.

But the argument cannot stop there. Defending parliamentary freedoms is wholly defensive. It offers nothing but an endless, wearisome and probably hopeless fight against the odds. And as parliamentary democracy grows weaker, as it loses its own impetus and fewer and fewer people even bother to vote, so it becomes harder to defend. The weakness of representative parliamentary democracy lies in the fact that it is nothing like representative or democratic enough. And as it subsides under more and more public disregard, it provides less and less opportunity to its citizens to defend it against its enemies. So, to return to a question asked by Lenin a hundred years ago, what is to be done?

One answer can be found in the body of Labour theory traced in this book, that parliamentary democracy can be used to usher in an economic democracy. This was the view of Tawney, Laski and Bevan, all of whom argued, with varying degrees of passion, that unless elected Labour Governments democratized industry and the economy they would be overcome and swallowed by undemocratic capitalism. That prediction has been most solemnly vindicated in recent history, but can the course of history be changed? Is there any hope for a new initiative to use parliamentary democracy and the Labour Party to make a further spirited attempt to replace capitalism with social democracy? Such an effort would be well worth supporting, but what are its chances of success? The grim truth is that long years of convergence between the labour and capitalist parties, long years of parliamentary corruption and cretinism, have taken their toll on the public perception. The very language of Parliament has become stale. Though there are some signs that people will vote for single and usually local issues, there are larger signs of enduring popular fatigue with politicians' promises. The impotence of elected politicians has infected the electorate, who are less and less inclined to respond. Any attempt to revive the flagging system with even more radical and bolder initiatives seems condemned to the same apathy.

There is another theme in this narrative that runs side by side with and complements the theme of parliamentary impotence. This is the theme of resistance from below.

Despite their control of Parliament and the state, the ruling class have not had it all their own way. Nor have they been able to confine resistance to Parliament. They have had to contain long periods of working-class resistance much more difficult to control than opposition in Parliament. Before the vote was won, the resistance in Britain included the Levellers, the furious revolutionaries of 1831, the Chartists and the Marxists who followed in their footsteps, the heroic strikers of the 1880s and 1890s, and the Great Unrest of 1911 to 1914. After the vote was won, there was the outburst of strikes in 1921, the General Strike of 1926, the almost continual trade-union victories of the 1960s, the glorious summer of 1972. All these were much more difficult for the ruling class to predict or contain than anything that happened in Parliament.

Often in these periods, the rich had to make real concessions, greater concessions than they had to make in Parliament. The strikes provided the workers with a battering ram that proved far more capable of breaking through the organized ranks of the ruling class than measured opposition from Parliament.

What were the features of these strikes that made them so dangerous to the rulers? First was the spirit of sacrifice – 'unless you concede our demands, we will refuse to work for you, and in the process we will not accept your wages'. The spirit of sacrifice leads to a spirit of solidarity. The strikers seek and welcome support from other workers not necessarily affected by the same complaint. This is the solidarity that led, for instance, to the miners' victory at Saltley in 1972, and eventually to the miners' victory in that year that so comprehensively changed the political (and parliamentary) landscape. Of all the notions that terrify the rich and powerful, none frightens them more than acts of industrial solidarity. The very formation of the Triple Alliance during the First World War was enough to stiffen the determination of the rulers that, above all, the Alliance had to be crushed. And even 60 years later when the Tory Government swept to office in 1979, the new ministers applied themselves ruthlessly to new laws whose central objective was to stamp out solidarity action that had come to be known as secondary picketing.

The ruling-class fear of strikes goes even deeper than the fear that they might lose an isolated conflict or two. Anyone who has ever been involved at any level in strike action can testify to the enormous changes it inspires in the workers involved. More often than not, the workers who in the normal course of events are the most conservative and docile become in times of strikes the most radical. Far more than any law or any promise of a law, such action leads people to ask questions about power in society. Why are we doing the work we are told to do? Why are our employers – men and women like the rest of us – honoured, feted and paid such ridiculous 'remuneration'? Who decides these things and why do they decide them? All the ludicrous prejudices of capitalist societies, racism, sexism and the rest, are suddenly subject to question. The industrial and service chieftains and their bankers understand this threat every bit as clearly as the strikers. They bend every power at their disposal in the media and the courts, if necessary in the police and army, to stamping out that threat. Even 30 years after their last notable successes, the influence of strikes is still fundamental. Though of course there have been other manifestations of popular protest – the poll-tax demonstrations of 1990 and the huge anti-war protests of 2002 and 2003 are obvious examples – the transforming power of strikes and trade-union action remains supreme.

Common to all this resistance has been a yearning for a new democracy.

Often this yearning showed itself in a more practical form: a form based on the notion of electing representatives at the place of work. Inside the outer shell of the trade-union movements, for instance, in which officials, though sometimes elected, are mostly appointed and, as a result, much less responsive, there are hundreds of elections of shop stewards who are not paid extra for their work and who owe their positions to their constant accessibility to the people who elect them. This concept of elected officials representing workers has a long history that bursts into life in times of revolution. The distinguishing feature of the Russian Revolutions of 1905 and 1917 was the formation of soviets, workers' councils, voted in and answerable to groups of workers according to their numbers. The central characteristic of the period between the two Russian Revolutions of 1917 was the growth of soviets alongside the growth of parliamentary parties. There was a struggle for supremacy between the two, a struggle that developed with breathtaking speed into a struggle for state power. Without that struggle in the soviets, and the victory in them of the revolutionary party (Bolsheviks) against the parliamentary parties, the second Russian Revolution of 1917 would never have taken place.

The survival of that Revolution depended on the democracy thrown up by the soviets, and when most of the workers in the industrial soviets were effectively destroyed in the civil war and counter-revolution that followed, the Russian Revolution perished. After the German Revolution of 1918, a host of workers' and soldiers' councils took charge of the economy and the society. The dignity, humility and efficiency of these organizations have been set out in a host of invigorating histories of the period, in Sebastian Haffner's *Failure of a Revolution* (1969) or in Richard Watt's magnificent account of the Versailles Treaty and its aftermath, *The Kings Depart* (1968), or in Evelyn Anderson's Left Book Club history of the Revolution, *Hammer or Anvil* (1945), in which she eloquently traced a direct line from the suppression of the workers' and soldiers' councils by the post-war social democratic government of Fritz Ebert, Philip Scheidemann and Gustav Noske to Hitler. Haffner's account of the formation of the councils, the straightforward uncomplicated manner with which they assumed and maintained control of ravaged post-war German society, is especially impressive since its author was a confirmed 'moderate' social democrat.

These quintessentially democratic organizations, responsive and sensitive to the people they represented, able and willing to plan the complex economies that were suddenly so surprisingly at their disposal, came out of revolutions. The idea of revolution is constantly mocked as an irrelevance. But even in recent times, a series of revolutionary movements have threatened capitalist or state capitalist society. The Hungarian Revolution of 1956, the General Strike and the students' revolt in France in 1968, the mass uprising that followed the toppling of the fascist dictator of Portugal in 1974, the overthrow of the Shah of Persia in 1979, the Solidarity workers' movement in Poland in 1981 and the toppling of the dictators of Eastern Europe which followed throughout the 1980s, even the overthrow of Slobodan Milosevic in Yugoslavia at the beginning of the twenty-first century – all of these were the result of mass action by millions of people. Many of these movements demanded the replacement of dictatorship with parliamentary democracy. But where parliamentary democracy was already established – in France for instance – the movements threw up demands for a different form of workers' democracy, for workers' councils led by elected officials who could be recalled by vote of the people who elected them and were knitted together across a whole country.

Anyone lucky enough to walk the streets of Lisbon at any time between the spring of 1974 and the autumn of 1975 could not fail to be overcome by the democratic spirit that engulfed the whole city – indeed the whole country. The most backward place in Europe became overnight the most advanced, the most argumentative, the most constructive, the most intellectual. Top of the bestseller list in Portugal for weeks on end in 1975 was Lenin's *State and Revolution*, a work written in the months between the two Russian Revolutions of 1917, and devoted to the argument that a new workers' state must be founded on institutions much more democratic than Parliament could ever be.

Every one of these movements was smashed or sidelined. In France, only months after 1968, the electorate voted for a right-wing Government. Portugal slithered back into an uneasy and generally reactionary parliamentary democracy. In Eastern Europe, elected parliaments replaced the former dictatorships. Iran became engulfed in a religious autocracy. In every one of these places, the new Governments have sided unequivocally with the rich. More and more people in all of them are beginning to recognize the limitations of the parliamentary democracy, or the religious autocracy, for which they settled.

The history of the British democratic movement as set out here has another theme. This is that each successive defeat of rank-and-file resistance has been followed by a retreat into parliamentary democracy. The great strikes of agricultural workers in the 1870s were followed, on their defeat, by a switch to Parliament. The deterioration of Joseph Arch from militant leader to pliable MP followed quite naturally. The defeat of the great Manningham strike in Bradford in the 1890s led to the formation of the

ILP. The extinguishing of the Great Unrest of 1911 to 1914 led to the Representation of the People Act; the defeat of the agitations of 1921 to renewed interest in the Labour Party and the first Labour Government of 1924; the defeat of the General Strike to the second Labour Government; the mass agitation of 1972 to the 1974 Labour Governments. The defeat of the miners in 1985 drove Labour right back into its parliamentary shell. Only twice in this history, in 1945 and, more arguably, in 1964, does Labour's parliamentary success not follow industrial defeat. In every other case, the success represented a falling back from aspirations for a genuine, living and vibrant democracy into a much weaker and less representative one. The comprehensive rejection of socialist ideas by the Labour Governments under Tony Blair after 1997 took place in an atmosphere of almost universal industrial peace in which the unions remained shackled by Thatcher's laws and the workers became increasingly passive and demoralized by their passivity. On the back of this passivity, the Labour ministers, many of them socialist and libertarian firebrands in their youth, basked in the enjoyment of their new importance and abandoned their youthful aspirations.

There is an exception to this sad left-to-right ritual dance that represents some sort of a guide for the future. Anthony Wedgwood Benn was born with a political golden spoon in his mouth. His father was a Liberal who joined the Labour Party and became a member of two Labour Governments – and a Viscount. When he was only 25, young Tony 'inherited' Sir Stafford Cripps's safe seat at Bristol. After campaigning successfully to reject his inherited title, he became, on his own admission, a compliant and even right-wing secretary of state in the 1964–70 Labour Government, and a senior figure in the 1974–9 Government. During the early 1970s, no one knows quite when, he moved sharply to the left, developed a rich, mocking sense of humour and started making overt socialist propaganda. None of this was strong enough to pull him out of the Wilson or Callaghan Governments, but in the early 1980s he resumed his socialist pilgrimage and in 1981 was only very narrowly defeated for the deputy leadership of the Labour Party. During all this time he kept a daily diary – perhaps the most formidable document of a century of Labour Party history. His political development can be traced in his forewords to the seven volumes as they came out. The diaries for 1963–7, for instance, unquestionably the most right-wing period of his long parliamentary career, were published in 1987, the year he launched, in his Chesterfield constituency, a socialist conference to unite and inspire the rank and file outside Parliament. The foreword to that volume set out his most explicit concerns about the value of parliamentary democracy. He emphasized four lessons he had learned from his long parliamentary experience. The first two were the 'feudal structure' of Crown and Lords and the power of patronage wielded by the leader of the Labour Party. He went on:

Third, as a minister, I experienced the power of industrialists and bankers to get their way by the use of the crudest form of economic pressure, even blackmail, against a Labour Government. Compared to this, the pressure brought to bear in industrial disputes by the unions is minuscule. This power was revealed even more clearly in 1976 when the IMF secured cuts in our public expenditure.

The fourth lesson related to the power of the media, which 'like the power of the medieval church ensures that the events of the day are always presented from the point of view of those who enjoy economic privilege'. Tony Benn's conclusion was as follows:

These lessons led me on to the conclusion that Britain is only superficially governed by MPs and the voters who elect them. Parliamentary democracy is, in truth, little more than a means for securing a periodical change in the management team, which is then allowed to preside over a system that remains in essence intact. If the British people were ever to ask themselves what power they truly enjoyed under our present political system they would be amazed to discover how little it is, and some new Chartist agitation might be born and might quickly gather momentum.

Tony Benn kept up his diary through the rest of the 1980s and for all of the 1990s too. He watched in bemused dismay while a new leader of the Labour Party was elected from a quite different tradition from the one he grew up in. He observed how speedily New Labour ditched what was left of its social democratic heritage – Clause IV, public ownership, the welfare state, comprehensive education. He was naturally not even considered for office in Tony Blair's administration after 1997, and seethed on the back benches as his party in government stumbled from reaction to reaction until it became indistinguishable from the Tories. In all this time he made himself available to any organization outside that was resisting this slide. Any workers fighting redundancy, any school standing up for the comprehensive system, any persecuted foreigner seeking asylum could rely on his active support. Again and again, he deliberately abandoned his base in Parliament and worked among those who, he hoped and believed, would one day trigger a new Chartist agitation, and a revolution from below.

In 1999, after two years of the Blair Government, he made a historic announcement: he would not be standing for Parliament in the 2001 general election. He would be leaving Parliament 'in order to devote more time to politics'. His own enormous experience in the highest places in the land drove him to the conclusion that the place to fight was in the lowest: that any future for an egalitarian socialist society rested not on what happened in Parliament but on the resistance and determination of the workers and the poor. Some pointed out rather churlishly that this decision came at a time when his parliamentary career might have been over anyway. He was 74, and in any case his constituency, Chesterfield, was lost in the 2001 election to the Liberals. But his resolve never wavered. Despite his age and the cruel death from cancer of his wife, he continued resolutely down the path he had set himself: to argue and agitate for change from below. During all this time he remained a member of the Labour Party, and refused to call on Labour Party members to leave and transfer their allegiance to any other socialist organization. Indeed, whenever the matter arose, he would specifically resist any such conclusion, declaring on at least one occasion that he did not approve of socialists outside the Labour Party coming together in a separate organization.

Considering his long political career and his enormous service to Labour, it is easy to see the reasons for that conclusion. But it is also equally easy to see the contradiction in it. The central feature of socialism is the principle of cooperation, of the pooling of individual human resources in the interests of everyone. It follows that it is difficult, if not impossible, to be an effective socialist on your own. Socialists have to combine with other socialists in order even to start to achieve their aim. This seems so fundamental, so elementary, that it is almost embarrassing to repeat it. It is the basic inspiration of every trade union, let alone socialist organization. The first aim of every socialist must surely be to find others who agree, and with whom to combine. How else is there the slightest chance of confronting the enormous power of the state? Combination brings with it the ability to compete with that power: to produce and to distribute socialist propaganda in newspapers and other media, to coordinate solidarity between workers in different employments and in different countries, to link the struggles and the lessons of the past with the struggles of the present. All these tasks would be quite impossible for single individuals, unless they are obscenely rich and if they are socialists they are unlikely to be rich at all.

There is another even more crucial reason for such combination. I have argued that history shows that real advances for the workers and the poor came from strikes. Yet each wave of strikes recorded here subsided, and the political advances that accompanied them subsided with them. The syndicalist revolutionaries that argued that the strike-power of the workers was enough on its own to smash the power of the state and replace it, were thrown off course by those defeats. It became plain that direct workers' action on its own was not enough to change the nature of society. The defeats had to be analysed and explained. The temptation to rebound from those defeats into Parliament or local councils had to be resisted. Once again, such resistance was impossible without socialist organization that could be sustained through the peaks and troughs of the direct action. That action was indispensable, but not on its own enough to complete the revolution.

There is one further reason, even more powerful, for socialist organization. As we have seen, pretty well every revolution or attempted revolution in recent times has been overthrown, dissipated or corrupted into something unrecognizable from the aspirations of its founders. One reason for this is that as each revolution reached its peak, the people who made it were faced with a power vacuum. On such occasions, there were plenty of siren voices – come, let us elect a new Parliament, come, let us set up a new Parliament, come, let us unite behind God or Allah and seek his guidance – but very little organization for pushing forward to create out of the revolutionary ferment a new democracy tougher and more durable than the tragically weak and impotent democracies of the past. Building a socialist party has as its eventual objective the aim, in the event of huge spontaneous explosions of revolt, of providing an alternative to the various formulas of hierarchical society – of setting out a credible road to a much more representative and durable democracy than has ever been seen before. This is not a matter, as with the Guild Socialists at the beginning of the century, of setting out neat and precise formulae as to how a socialist democracy would be constituted. But it does require a resolute belief that a socialist democracy works according to the extent to which it reaches downwards, organizes and offers a real voice and a real vote to the humblest and poorest people, cuts down hierarchical power and roots itself in elective institutions based on the places where people work.

Cooperative working, mass production, is the most effective base for a socialist democracy. But workers' councils elected there are not the only form such a democracy can take. As fewer and fewer people work together in big workplaces, so the basic unit of a new democracy may change. Lone workers, old-age pensioners, child carers, single parents and countless others may not find easy access to workers' councils. So any modern revolution would have to fashion new, more relevant groupings to form the democratic base of society. Their distinguishing characteristics would be that they are elected, that they are responsive to the people who elect them and, above all, that they are immune from the cloying and wholly undemocratic patronage of the rich and privileged. A vibrant socialist party that relates to the struggles of the workers and the dispossessed in every area of life, that seeks to draw from past struggles the lessons that can help the present ones, seems to me not a luxury but a priority.

In the period of the degeneration and collapse of Stalinism, many people on the left have shrunk from such a party. They have shrunk particularly from what they call 'vanguardism' – the notion that the party sets itself above the class and imagines that it can on its own do the democratic job that only the masses can achieve. Such people shrink from the concept of 'leadership'. They denounce as fundamentally undemocratic the very idea that any set of people can aspire to lead the masses. But in a sense every expression of opinion, the very essence of democracy, is an expression of leadership. 'I think we should do this, march here, strike here, mobilize somewhere else' – all these are expressions of leadership, of pointing in a direction and urging people to follow. This is the real meaning of democratic leadership. In a world where so many people are demoralized, depressed or sensitive to outright right-wing, militaristic or even fascist solutions to their problems, the failure to organize in order to persuade and lead in a socialist and democratic direction is irresponsible.

All my adult life has been spent as an active member of a revolutionary socialist party, the International Socialists, later the Socialist Workers Party. I have experienced as widely as anyone else in the last 40 years the many obstacles against which such a party has constantly to struggle. The menace of sectarianism – the biblical assertion that our sect is right and all the others wrong – haunts anyone who has ever taken part in such activity. With it goes dogmatism, doctrinaire assertiveness, stale and meaningless language, constant repetition of allegedly incontrovertible texts, all of which leads not to leadership of the masses but to isolation from them. I have had my fill of all these horrors, but none of them is half as destructive as abstinence or apathy. The socialist who joins nothing and links with nobody is the most useless of all.

Another related problem is that of fanaticism. Many young people when they first join a revolutionary socialist organization are astonished at popular indifference to their enthusiasms. In their new excitement in the struggle, it is hard to credit that many people, if not most of them, do not want to devote their lives to politics. Even if they are basically sympathetic to socialist aims, most people prefer to do something else, to devote their precious spare time to activities that have nothing to do with politics. Patience is not a quality normally associated with revolutionary socialists, whose impatience and frantic determination to do in hours and weeks what may take many years, is often their worst enemy. Yet that (usually youthful) impatience is an absolutely essential ingredient of any socialist organization. It is the theme of Shelley's 'Ode to the West Wind' (1820). He wrote it in a mood of despair after reading a vicious review of his longest poem. He was worried that he was getting old – he was 27! – and that no one was listening to his revolutionary views. As he contemplates what seemed like his hopeless failure, he takes courage from the strength of the wind, the herald of the revolution. What mattered above all, he concluded, was to remain a threat to the rulers of society, to remain fierce and to remain impetuous. 'Be thou, Spirit fierce, / My spirit! Be thou me, impetuous one!' Impatience and urgency are the watchwords of successful agitation, and to abandon either is to abandon the ideas that gave rise to them in the first place.

Another feature of this narrative might help. Again and again as I grappled with this history, I was struck by the dramatic and sometimes very sudden changes in the political landscape. Sudden brightness can emerge from what seem like endless years of gloom. Encrusted reaction can turn almost overnight into great radical movements that can change the world. The changes are, I have argued, almost always associated with people's actions from below. That action, especially strikes, transforms not only popular moods but individuals as well. Standard biographies often assume that their subjects are consistent and can be analysed as though their characters were fixed and permanent. In reality, their only permanent feature is their susceptibility to change. How to equate Ben Tillett, the fiery revolutionary strike-leader on the London docks in 1889, with the frightful TUC compromiser of 1927? How to explain the rampant revolutionary George Julian Harney with the nationalistic 'Citizen Hip Hip Hurrah' mocked by Marx? Is Joseph Arch, the courageous strike-leader of 1874, really the same person as the drivelling Liberal MP a quarter of a century later? What about George Eliot, the young enthusiast for the Paris Revolution of 1848 and the stern critic of the extension of the franchise in 1867? Nor is the drift always from left to right, from enthusiasm to despair. How can the deeply reactionary young Peter Porcupine turn into the angry old radical William Cobbett, so admired by Marx? And what exactly did happen to Tony Benn to change him from the keen young technocrat into the eloquent reformer of his old age?

Most of these changes reflect more general changes in the political landscape, almost all of which have been brought about by sudden and sporadic movements from below. All these movements, the revolutionary outburst of 1646 and 1647, the Paineite revolt of the 1790s, the massive wave of violence in 1831, the Chartists, the London dock strike of 1889, the Great Unrest from 1911 to 1914, the agitations of 1919 and early 1920, the General Strike, the 'stupendous convulsion' during the Second World War, the glorious summer of 1972, all these arose unpredictably, suddenly, out of the blue. This is the tug of war which will certainly, as Byron predicted, 'come again', and is well worth organizing for.

What hope is there, then, that a new democracy will emerge from the ashes of the failed social democracy of the last century? As we have discovered often enough in this narrative, the European Labour movement was for most of the twentieth century hypnotized by a fascination with Stalinist Russia. The destruction of the Russian soviets in the 1930s did nothing to dissuade socialists from referring obstinately to a 'soviet union' – without soviets! When Stalinist state capitalism collapsed – as it was bound to do – the immediate effect was to damage the very idea of socialism, even when it was proclaimed by socialists who had opposed Stalinism. The early 1990s were a rotten time for socialists. It seemed as though the capitalists and their apologists in the boardrooms and universities were to have it all their own way. Then, at the end of the decade, a new movement suddenly and spontaneously sprang to life. It called itself, apparently without prompting, anti-capitalism. It grew at tremendous pace. It reached world headlines with a vast demonstration in the heart of United States capitalism, Seattle. Its target was the World Trade Organization, a symbol of world capitalism and its relentless desire to snuff out what is left of public ownership and public responsibility. In the WTO's sights were organizations like the British National Health Service, always a threat to the vast and sprawling chaos of private health insurance. The object of the WTO and the myriad international organizations around, the G7, G8, OECD etc., etc., was to step behind the democratic process in advanced capitalist countries and establish an independent source of rules and regulations that would eventually paralyse the functions of the NHS and any other organization that dared to buck the market.

The Seattle demonstration of November 1999 took complacent Western Governments and business by surprise. It was followed in rapid succession through the next three years by huge demonstrations protesting at other bodies representing international capital – in Nice, Genoa, Florence, Barcelona, Prague, Gothenberg, Millau, Quebec, Washington. The demonstrations linked organized labour with environmentalists and young people infuriated by the headlong rush to what Byron called 'hell's pollution'. In 2002 and 2003, these demonstrations were matched by even bigger protests against the rush by the right-wing US Government to a wholly unjustified war in Iraq, a war that, as I write this, looks as though it may engulf the Middle East and eventually the whole world.

This vast new movement is split into many different sections and views. Despite its umbrella names – anti-capitalism or Globalize Resistance – this movement is not uniformly socialist. But a theme common to them all is a yearning for a new democracy, a different social order that will replace hierarchical capitalism and what is left of its throttled democracy. Indeed, one of the most exciting aspects of the new movement is the variety and enthusiasm of its literature and ideology. A spate of books, articles and essays seeking new democratic forms poured on to the World Wide Web. Naomi Klein's *No Logo* (2000), George Monbiot's *Captive State*, the effervescent Michael Moore's *Stupid White Men* (2001) all became best-sellers. Popular film-makers like Michael Mann, thriller-writers like John Le Carré turned their formidable skills to exposing the throttling of human health and independence by the multinational tobacco and pharmaceutical industries. Most of the authors accept that if the world is to be saved from environmental disaster, its international economies need to be planned democratically. This must mean that new elective institutions involving workers, consumers and pensioners will have to be set to work to wrest control of industry and services from the greedy and irresponsible minority now in charge.

Do the links between the different productive and service organizations in society have to be either market-based or hierarchical? No, says Pat Devine in his 1988 study, *Democracy and Economic Planning*. They can be democratic, based on elections and negotiation. Much of the trilogy by York University Politics professor Alex Callinicos, *Equality* (1999), *Against the Third Way* (2001) and *An Anti-Capitalist Manifesto* (2003), explores in detail the 'demand for a democratization of the economy' and, taking up the argument from the other author of another book called *Equality*, R. H. Tawney, the 'problem of how democracy can be extended to the economy'.

In *Market-Driven Politics*, a powerful and too-little-noticed book that came out in 2000, Colin Leys exhaustively demonstrated the corrosive and hierarchical capitalist influence that has eaten away at two of Britain's most popular publicly owned institutions, the National Health Service and the BBC. Leys summed it up like this: 'The one potential general source of dynamism that does not mimic market incentives and the distortions they produce in public services is a thoroughgoing democratization, something that has rarely been seriously explored.'

Some of the books mentioned above (notably George Monbiot's sequel to *Captive State*, *The Age of Consent* (2003), in which he set out in idealistic fashion how the United Nations and other international organizations could be more democratically organized) propose utopian democratic solutions whose perfections and imperfections dodge the vital question, how is the 'thoroughgoing democratization' to be achieved or, to go back to Lenin, what is to be done? This book has explored the seductive possibility that a new egalitarian and democratic world society can be created bit by bit through institutions established and tolerated by the society it seeks to replace. The abject failure of that project in the country where it was first advanced, Britain, is now plain for all to see. Revolution from above is nonsense. Revolution from below remains an enticing possibility and is worth fighting for. The seeds of the new society can only be sown in the struggle against the old one.

Such a struggle is not one cataclysmic heave. It shows itself in a million different forms, from great outbursts of revolt to tiny gestures of resistance. The job of socialists and democrats, instead of seeking to cure those problems from above, is to identify with and take part in the struggles from below and link them together. This does not mean that Parliament and elections to it can be ignored. It does mean, however, that the main job of socialists is to relegate Parliament to the sidelines it has chosen for itself and to concentrate on politics where it matters, among and on behalf of the dispossessed. Above all, this requires, more than ever before, the coordination of socialists and revolutionaries in an organization dedicated and resolved enough to confront the organized capitalist state with the only force capable of defeating it, the organized working-class movement, and of forging the huge disparate mass of opposition into a combined revolutionary unit.

For most of the 1970s, I worked on a small paper called *Socialist Worker*. It was, and is, sold as widely as possible by a handful of agitators. The few full-time journalists on the paper were all my friends, all exceptionally able and engaging people. The gentlest and most dedicated of them was a professional sub-editor called Geoff Ellen. He came from Chelmsford in Essex and was among other things an absurdly devoted West Ham supporter. He spent pretty well all his spare time organizing for socialism. There was not a trade unionist in Essex he had not tried to push or pull into some form of revolt. On Tuesday nights we were kept late at work by the printing of the last few pages, and indulged ourselves in takeaway kebabs and long heart-searching conversations.

As the great industrial climax of the early 1970s, to our astonishment, fell back, I began privately to worry that the entire revolutionary project, and the ideas that gave rise to it, were misconceived. One evening, as we waited for the proofs, I blurted out my apprehensions to Geoff. I had joined the staff of *Socialist Worker* in the autumn of 1972, at a time of huge convulsions and great hope for the future. If anyone had asked me, I would have said at once that I was hoping for, and confidently expecting, a revolution. By late 1975, however, I complained to Geoff, that change had not come. It was obviously not going to come from Harold Wilson or Denis Healey, but we had always known that. In the decline of the movement, the issue seemed to have changed. Was the revolution going to come at all? And if not, what was to become of us if our grand aim in life was to be frustrated and even ridiculed? To my enormous relief, Geoff cheered me up with his speciality: a huge all-enveloping grin. 'If the revolution doesn't come,' he said, 'there is nothing much we can do about that. Whether it comes or not, there is nothing for us to do but what we are doing now, fight for it, fight for the workers and the poor.' Some years later, Geoff Ellen, still a young man, went to bed one night with a headache and died from a brain haemorrhage. He had left *Socialist Worker* to work for the *Guardian*, and had done exceptionally well there. All his adult life, he stuck firmly by his advice to me that dark winter evening in 1975, and so, I hope, have I.

Bibliography

Notes to Crows and Eagles at Putney*

I have made good use of the following books:

1. On the background to the Civil War and the English Revolution, the grandest book is still Samuel Gardiner's four-volume *History of the Civil War, 1642–1649* (London: Longman, 1888), especially his long passage in the first volume on the influence of the Puritans. Other outstanding historians of this period who have helped me are Christopher Hill, *God's Englishman* (London: Weidenfeld & Nicolson, 1970) and *The World Turned Upside Down: Radical Ideas during the English Revolution* (London: Penguin, 1975); and Brian Manning, *The English People and the English Revolution* (London: Heinemann, 1976) and *1649: The Crisis of the English Revolution* (London: Bookmarks, 1992). *The History of the English Revolution*, by F. Guizot (London: George Bell, 1884), was lucky enough to be reviewed by Karl Marx – the review is better than the book. Yet another expert account is *The Great Rebellion 1641–1660*, by Ivan Roots (London: Batsford, 1966).

2. On the Leveller movement in general, the outstanding work for me was *The Levellers and the English Revolution*, by H. N. Brailsford (London: Cresset Press, 1961), which was not quite finished when the author died and had to be completed by Christopher Hill. Others I have plundered are *The Leveller Movement*, by Theodore Pease (Washington, DC: The American Historical Association/London: Oxford University Press, 1916); *English Democratic Ideas in the Seventeenth Century*, by G. P. Gooch (Cambridge: Cambridge University Press, 1927); and *The Levellers: A History of the Writings of Three Seventeenth-Century Social Democrats: John Lilburne, Richard Overton, William Walwyn*, by Joseph Frank (Cambridge, Mass.: Harvard University Press, 1955).

On individual Levellers, I have enjoyed *The Writing of Walwyn*, edited by Jack R. McMichael and Barbara Taft (Athens, Ga.: University of Georgia Press, 1989); *Freeborn John: A Biography of John Lilburne*, by Pauline Gregg (London: Dent, 1986); *John Wildman, Plotter and Postmaster: A Study of the English Republican*

---

* These are the last notes left by the author.

Movement in the Seventeenth Century, by Maurice Ashley (London: Jonathan Cape, 1947); *A Revolutionary Rogue: Henry Marten and the English Republic*, by Sarah Barber (Stroud: Sutton, 2000).

3. The Putney Debates have come down to us by a mixture of journalistic tenacity and luck. They and the later Whitehall Debates were attended by the army secretary, William Clarke, who had developed his own form of shorthand. He took the debates down verbatim, and went on his enterprising journalistic way, somehow getting himself on to the scaffold of Charles I in time to report the King's beheading. Clarke, a Fellow of All Souls College, Oxford, left his carefully sorted papers to his son George. George, a solid Restoration Tory, was anxious to keep the papers secret, but mercifully did not destroy them. He quarrelled with the authorities at All Souls and skulked off to Worcester College, to which he bequeathed his vast library. There the priceless scribbled record of these historic debates rested all through the eighteenth century and for much of the nineteenth. In 1888, a young Oxford history don and specialist in the English Revolution, Charles Firth, called on H. A. Porter, librarian at Worcester, who remarked in passing that he had some papers Firth might be interested in. He handed over the bound copies of Clarke's notes of the Putney Debates. Firth passed them to his mentor, Samuel Gardiner, who included them in his *History*. Much later, in 1938, another Oxford don, A. S. P. Woodhouse, produced a complete and skilfully edited version of the debates under the title *Puritanism and Liberty: Being the Army Debates (1647–9) from the Clarke Manuscripts*. All the quotes from the debates in this chapter are taken from the Dent edition of that book (1986). Another entertaining and helpful account of the debates is *Soldiers and Statesmen: The General Council of the Army and Its Debates, 1647–48*, by Austin Woolrych (Oxford: Clarendon Press, 1987). Mr Woolrych doesn't like the agitators very much and, I imagine, doesn't really think that people like that should be playing an important part in politics. He paints Thomas Rainsborough as a rather loony sectarian, but his account is fascinating none the less. An even more recent account of the debates can be found in *The New Model Army in England, Ireland and Scotland*, by the Canadian historian Ian Gentles (Oxford: Blackwell, 1992).

4. Most of the Leveller pamphlets and proclamations are available in the original (in the British library) and in a number of collections. A paperback *Freedom in Arms: A Selection of Leveller Writings*, edited by A. L. Morton, was published by Lawrence & Wishart in 1975. Seventeen pamphlets (a tiny fraction of the total) are set out in full, including *The Agreement of the People*. Another extremely useful book, which includes the text of the Heads of the Proposals and *The Case of the Army*, is *The Good Old Cause: The English Revolution of 1640–1660* (London: Cass, 1969), a narrative sustained by speeches and quotations of the time. This was edited by Christopher Hill and a young communist disciple of his, Edmund Dell, who went on to become a secretary of state in a Labour Government – and ended up as a company chairman in the City of London. The Digger Movement was explored by another of Hill's students, David Petegorsky, in a

little book widely distributed through Victor Gollancz's Left Book Club in 1940: *Left-Wing Democracy in the English Civil War* (London: Sandpiper, 1999). There are many published selections of the writings of Gerrard Winstanley, and an excellent novel about the eviction of the Diggers by General Fairfax: *Comrade Jacob*, by David Caute (London: André Deutsch, 1973).

The following concise (and necessarily incomplete) bibliography has been compiled (by John Foot and Clare Fermont) with reference to the text and the author's notebooks and library. Where possible we have cited the edition used by the author.

Other Texts from Crows and Eagles at Putney

Thomas Carlyle, *Oliver Cromwell's Letters and Speeches* (London: Chapman & Hall, 1973).

I. Deane Jones, *The English Revolution: An Introduction to English History, 1603–1714* (London: Heinemann, 1931).

John Milton, *Areopagitica and Other Prose Works* (London: Dent, 1955).

The Not-So-Great Reform Act

A. J. Ayer, *Thomas Paine* (London: Secker & Warburg, 1988).

John Belchem, *Orator Hunt: Henry Hunt and English Working-Class Radicalism* (Oxford: Clarendon Press, 1985).

Edmund Burke, *Reflections on the Revolution in France* (London: J. Dodsley, 1790).

George Gordon, Lord Byron, *Don Juan*, in *Works of Lord Byron*, Vol. XV (London: John Murray, 1833).

John Cannon, *Parliamentary Reform, 1640–1832* (Cambridge: Cambridge University Press, 1973).

William Carpenter, *Political Letters and Pamphlets* (Carpenter, 1830–31).

William Cobbett, *Cobbett's Two-penny Trash, or, Politics for the Poor* (London: printed by the author, 1831–2).

G. D. H. Cole, *The Life of William Cobbett* (Glasgow: Collins & Sons, 1924).

Moncure Daniel Conway, *The Life of Thomas Paine* (London: Watts & Co., 1909).

R. R. Fennessy, *Burke, Paine and the Rights of Man* (La Haye: Martinus Nijhoff, 1963).

Eric Foner, *Tom Paine and Revolutionary America* (Oxford: Oxford University Press, 1976).

Paul Foot, *Red Shelley* (London: Sidgwick & Jackson, 1980).

R. F. Foster, *Modern Ireland, 1600–1972* (London: Allen Lane, 1988).

William Godwin, *Enquiries concerning Political Justice and Its Influence on Morals and Happiness* (London: Robinson, 1796).

Daniel Green, *Great Cobbett: The Noblest Agitator* (London: Hodder & Stoughton, 1983).

Richard Holmes, *Shelley the Pursuit* (Weidenfeld & Nicolson, 1974).

Stanley Jones, *William Hazlitt: A Life* (Oxford: Oxford University Press, 1989).

John Keane, *Tom Paine: A Political Life* (London: Bloomsbury, 1995).

John Mitchel, *The History of Ireland: From the Treaty of Limerick to the Present Time* (Glasgow: Cameron & Ferguson, 1869).

Tom Paine, *Common Sense* (London: J. S. Jordan, 1791).

——, *The Rights of Man: Being an Answer to Mr. Burke's Attack on the French Revolution* (London: J. S. Jordan, 1791).

——, *The Rights of Man: Part the Second* (London: J. S. Jordan, 1792).

——, *The Writings of Tom Paine*, ed. Moncure Daniel Conway, 4 vols. (New York: The Knickerbocker Press, 1894–6).

——, *The Tom Paine Reader* (London: Penguin, 1987).

Tom Paulin, *The Day-Star of Liberty: William Hazlitt's Radical Style* (London: Faber & Faber, 1998).

Edward Pearce, *Reform! The Fight for the 1832 Reform Act* (London: Jonathan Cape, 2003).

Poor Man's Guardian, Vols. 1–4 (London: Merlin Press, 1969).

Percy Bysshe Shelley, *The Complete Poetical Works* (Oxford: Oxford University Press, 1956).

——, *Shelley's Revolutionary Year*, with an introduction by Paul Foot (London: Redwords, 1990).

E. A. Smith, *Reform or Revolution? A Diary of Reform in England, 1830–32* (Stroud: Sutton, 1992).

Thomas Spence, *Pig's Meat: Selected Writings of Thomas Spence, Radical and Pioneer Land Reformer* (Nottingham: Spokesman, 1982).

E. P. Thompson, *The Making of the English Working Class* (London: Penguin, 1968).

E. P. Thompson and George Rude, *Captain Swing* (London: Pimlico, 1993).

Gwyn Williams, *The Merthyr Rising* (London: Croom Helm, 1978).

Audrey Williamson, *Thomas Paine: His Life and Works* (London: Allen & Unwin, 1973).

Llewellyn Woodward, *The Age of Reform 1815–1870* (Oxford: Clarendon Press, 1962).

Revolt of the Chartists

Asa Briggs, *Chartist Studies* (London: Macmillan, 1959).

John Charlton, *The Chartists: The First National Workers' Movement* (London: Pluto, 1997).

Arthur Hugh Clough, *The Poems of Arthur Hugh Clough* (Oxford: Oxford University Press, 1968).

G. D. H. Cole, *Chartist Portraits* (London: Macmillan, 1941).

T. A. Devyr, *The Odd Book of the Nineteenth Century* (New York: Greenpoint, 1882).

Benjamin Disraeli, *Sybil; or, The Two Nations* (London: Henry Colburn, 1845).

Frederick Engels, *The Condition of the Working Class in England*, ed. Victor Kiernan (London: Penguin, 1987).

Robert G. Gammage, *The History of the Chartist Movement, 1837–1854* (London: Merlin Press, 1969).

Eva Haraszti, *Chartism*, tr. Sandor Simon (Budapest: Akademiai Kiado, 1978).

Mick Jenkins, *The General Strike of 1842* (London: Lawrence & Wishart, 1980).

London Working Men's Association, *The Rotten House of Commons* (London, 1837).

William Lovett, *Life and Struggles of William Lovett* (London: MacGibbon & Kee, 1967).

Mark O'Brien, *Perish the Privileged Orders: A Socialist History of the Chartist Movement* (London: Redwords, 1995).

Alfred Plummer, *Bronterre: A Political Biography of Bronterre O'Brien* (London: Allen & Unwin, 1971).

Poor Man's Guardian, Vols. 1–4 (London: Merlin Press, 1969).

John Saville, *Ernest Jones: Chartist* (London: Lawrence & Wishart, 1952).

——, *1848: The British State and the Chartist Movement* (Cambridge: Cambridge University Press, 1990).

A. R. Schoyen, *The Chartist Challenge* (London: Heinemann, 1958).

Percy Bysshe Shelley, *Hellas: A Lyrical Drama* (New York: Garland, 1985).

E. A. Smith, *Reform or Revolution? A Diary of Reform in England, 1830–32* (Stroud: Sutton, 1992).

Dorothy Thompson, *The Chartists: Popular Politics in the Industrial Revolution* (Aldershot: Wildwood House, 1986).

The Leap in the Dark

George Eliot, *Felix Holt, the Radical* (London: Penguin, 1972).

F. W. S. Craig, *British Parliamentary Election Results 1832–1885* (London: Macmillan, 1977).

——, *Chronology of British Parliamentary By-Elections 1833–1987* (Chichester: Parliamentary Research Services, 1987).

Charles Dickens, *Bleak House* (London: Penguin, 1996).

Royden Harrison, *Before the Socialists: Studies in Labour and Politics 1861–1881* (London: Routledge & Kegan Paul, 1965).

Karl Marx, *Inaugural Address to the International Working Men's Association* (Glasgow: Socialist Labour Party of Great Britain, 1920).

——, *Capital: A Critique of Political Economy*, tr. Samuel Moore and Edward Aveling (London: Allen & Unwin, 1938).

——, 'Address to the General Council of the International Working Men's Association on the Civil War in France, *1871*', in Eugene Schulkind (ed.), *The Paris Commune of 1871: The Views from the Left* (London: Jonathan Cape, 1972).

John Stuart Mill, *Considerations on Representative Government*, People's Edition (London: Longman Green, 1865).

Charles Seymour, *Electoral Reform in England and Wales: The Development and Operation of the Parliamentary Franchise, 1832–1885* (New Haven, Conn.: Yale Historical Publications, 1915).

Women

George Barnes, *From Workshop to War Cabinet* (London: Herbert Jenkins, 1924).

Logie Barrow and Ian Bullock, *Democratic Ideas and the British Labour Movement, 1880–1914* (Cambridge: Cambridge University Press, 1996).

(Ernest) Belfort Bax, *Essays in Socialism, New and Old* (1907).

Annie Besant, *Annie Besant: An Autobiography* (London: Fisher Unwin, 1893).

Sarah Boston, *Women Workers and the Trade Union Movement* (London: Davis-Poynter, 1980).

A. Briggs and J. Saville, *Essays in Labour History, 1886–1923* (London: Macmillan, 1967).

John Charlton, *It Just Went Like Thunder: The Mass Movement and New Unionism in Britain, 1889* (London: Redwords, 1999).

George Dangerfield, *The Strange Death of Liberal England* (London: Constable & Co., 1936).

Barbara Drake, *Women in Trade Unions* (London: Labour Research Dept and Allen & Unwin, 1921).

Frederick Engels, *The Origin of the Family, Private Property and the State* (Chicago: Charles H. Kerr, 1902).

Millicent Garrett Fawcett, *Women's Suffrage: A Short History of a Great Movement* (Edinburgh: T. C. & E. Jack, 1912).

Brian Harrison, *Separate Spheres: The Opposition to Women's Suffrage in Britain* (London: Croom Helm, 1978).

George Haw, *The Life Story of Will Crooks MP: From Workhouse to Westminster* (London: Cassell & Co., 1917).

John Hodge, *Workman's Cottage to Windsor Castle* (London: Sampson Low, n.d.).

Bob Holton, *British Syndicalism: 1900–1914* (London: Pluto, 1976).

Cheryl R. Jorgensen-Earp (ed.), *Speeches and Trials of the Militant Suffragettes: The Women's Social and Political Union, 1903–1918* (London: Associated University Presses, 1999).

F. M. Leventhal, *The Last Dissenter: H. N. Brailsford and His World* (Oxford: Clarendon Press, 1985).

J. Liddington, *The Life and Times of a Respectable Rebel: Selina Cooper, 1864–1946* (London: Virago, 1984).

J. Liddington and J. Norris, *One Hand Tied Behind Us: The Rise of the Women's Suffrage Movement* (London: Virago, 1978).

Andro Linklater, *An Unhusbanded Life: Charlotte Despard, Suffragette, Socialist and Sinn Feiner* (London: Hutchinson, 1980).

Tom Mann, *Tom Mann's Memoirs* (London: MacGibbon & Kee, 1967).

Jane Marcus (ed.), *Suffrage and the Pankhursts* (London: Routledge, 1987).

Hannah Mitchell, *The Hard Way Up: The Autobiography of Hannah Mitchell, Suffragette and Rebel*, ed. G. Mitchell (London: Faber & Faber, 1968).

Molly Murphy, *Molly Murphy: Suffragette and Socialist* (Salford: Institute of Social Research, University of Salford, 1998).

John Stuart Mill, *The Subjection of Women* (London: Longman Green, 1869).

Harriet Taylor Mill, *The Enfranchisement of Women* (London: Virago, 1983).

Christabel Pankhurst, *Unshackled! The Story of How We Won the Vote* (London: Hutchinson, 1959).

Sylvia Pankhurst, *The Suffragette: The History of the Women's Suffrage Movement 1905–1910* (London: Gay & Hancock Ltd, 1911).

——, *The Suffrage Movement: An Intimate Account of Persons and Ideals* (London: Longmans Green, 1931).

Jane Purvis, *Emmeline Pankhurst: A Biography* (London: Routledge, 2002).

Marion Ramelson, *Petticoat Rebellion: A Century of Struggles for Women's Rights* (London: Lawrence & Wishart, 1967).

Constance Rover, *Women's Suffrage and Party Politics in Britain 1866–1914* (London: Routledge, 1967).

Jonathan Schnear, *Ben Tillett: Portrait of a Labour Leader* (London: Croom Helm, 1982).

Percy Bysshe Shelley, *Revolt of Islam: A Poem in Twelve Cantos* (London: Ollier, 1818).

Norbert Soldon, *Women in British Trade Unions, 1874–1976* (Dublin: Gill & Macmillan, 1978).

South Wales Miners' Federation, Unofficial Reform Committee, *The Miners' Next Step: Being a Suggested Scheme for the Reorganisation of the Federation* (London: Tonypandy, 1912; repr. London: Pluto, 1973).

Ann Stafford, *A Match to Fire the Thames* (London: Hodder & Stoughton, 1961).

Ray Strachey, *The Cause: A Short History of the Women's Movement in Great Britain* (London: G. Bell & Sons, 1928).

——, *Millicent Garrett Fawcett* (London: John Murray, 1931).

Margaret Thomas, *This was My World* (London: Macmillan, 1933).

Will Thorne, *My Life's Battles* (London: George Newnes, n.d.).

Ben Tillett, *A History of the London Transport Workers' Strike, 1911* (London: National Transport Workers' Federation, 1912).

Dona Torr, *Tom Mann and His Times*, Vol. 1 (London: Lawrence & Wishart, 1956).

Chushici Tsuzuki, *Tom Mann, 1856–1941* (Oxford: Oxford University Press, 1991).

Sidney and Beatrice Webb, *The History of Trade Unionism, 1666–1920* (printed by the authors for the Trade Unionists of the United Kingdom, 1919).

H. G. Wells, *The Labour Unrest* (reprinted from *The Daily Mail*; London: Associated Newspapers Ltd, 1912).

Mond's Manacles

Caroline Benn, *Keir Hardie* (London: Hutchinson, 1992).

Eduard Bernstein, *Evolutionary Socialism*, tr. Edith C. Harvey (London: Independent Labour Party/Socialist Library, 1909).

Aneurin Bevan, *In Place of Fear* (London: Heinemann, 1952).

Noreen Branson, *Poplarism 1919–1925: George Lansbury and the Councillors' Revolt* (London: Lawrence & Wishart, 1979).

David Butler and Gareth Butler, *British Political Facts 1900–1994* (London: Macmillan, 1994).

G. D. H. Cole, *Chaos and Order in Industry* (London: Methuen, 1920).

G. D. H. Cole and William Mellor, *The Meaning of Industrial Freedom* (London: Allen & Unwin, 1918).

A. J. Cook, *The Mond Moonshine: My Case Against the 'Peace' Surrender* (London: Workers' Publications, n.d.).

——, *The Nine Days: The Story of the General Strike, Told by the Miners' Secretary* (London: printed by the Cooperative Printing Society, 1926).

A. J. Cook and J. Maxton, *Our Case for a Socialist Revival* (London: Workers' Publications, n.d.).

F. W. S. Craig, *British Parliamentary Results 1918–1949* (Glasgow: Political Reference Publications, 1969).

W. J. Davis, *The British Trades Union Congress: History and Reflections* (London: Trades Union Congress Parliamentary Committee, 1910).

T. S. Eliot, *Collected Poems 1909–1962* (London: Faber & Faber, 1963).

Christopher Farman, *The General Strike, May 1926: Britain's Aborted Revolution* (London: Panther, 1974).

George Lansbury, *My England* (London: Selwyn & Blount, 1934).

V. I. Lenin, *Left-Wing Communism, an Infantile Disorder* (London: Lawrence & Wishart, 1934).

——, State *and Revolution* (London: Lawrence & Wishart, 1942).

David Lloyd George, *War Memoirs*, 6 vols. (London: Nicolson & Watson, 1933–6).

Richard Lyman, *The First Labour Government 1924* (London: Chapman & Hall, 1957).

Rosa Luxemburg, *The Mass Strike* (London: Merlin Press, 1906).

James Ramsay MacDonald, *Socialism and Society,* 2nd edn (London: Independent Labour Party/Socialist Library, 1905).

——, *Socialism and Government,* 2 vols. (London: Independent Labour Party/Socialist Library, 1909).

——, *The Socialist Movement* (London: Williams & Norgate, 1911).

——, *Parliament and Revolution* (Manchester: The National Labour Press Ltd, 1919).

——, *Socialism: Critical and Constructive,* 2nd edn (London: Cassell & Co., 1924).

David Marquand, *Ramsay MacDonald* (London: Jonathan Cape, 1977).

William Mellor, *Direct Action* (London: Leonard Parsons, 1920).

Kenneth O. Morgan, *Consensus and Disunity: The Lloyd George Coalition Government 1918–1922* (Oxford, Clarendon Press, 1979).

Raymond Postgate, *The Life of George Lansbury* (London: Longmans, 1951).

Arthur Ransome, *Six Weeks in Russia, 1919* (London: Redwords, 1992).

Jonathan Schneer, *George Lansbury* (Manchester: Manchester University Press, 1990).

John Shepherd, *George Lansbury: At the Heart of Old Labour* (Oxford: Oxford University Press, 2002).

Robert Smillie, *My Life for Labour* (London: Mills & Boon Ltd, 1924).

R. H. Tawney, *The Acquisitive Society* (London: Gollancz, 1937).

Jimmy Thomas, *When Labour Rules* (London: Collins, 1920).

——, *My Story* (London: Hutchinson, 1937).

The Grey Decade

C. Addison *Problems of a Socialist Government* (London: Gollancz, 1933).

H. N. Brailsford, *Why Capitalism Means War* (London: Gollancz, 1938).

Richard Stafford Cripps, *The Struggle for Peace*, with notes by Michael Foot (London: Gollancz, 1936).

——, *Democracy Up-to-Date* (London: Allen & Unwin, 1939).

Ruth Dudley Edwards, *Victor Gollancz* (London: Gollancz, 1987).

The Fabian Society, *Where Stands Socialism Today?* (London: Rich & Cowan, 1933).

L. Anderson Fenn et al., *Problems of the Socialist Transition* (London: Gollancz, 1934).

Lion Feuchtwanger, *Moscow 1937* (London: Gollancz, 1937).

Victor Gollancz et al., *The Betrayal of the Left: An Examination and Refutation of Communist Policy from October 1939 to January 1941* (London: Gollancz, 1941).

Ruth Gruber, *I Went to the Soviet Arctic* (London: Gollancz, 1939).

C. L. R. James, *The Black Jacobins* (London: Allison & Busby, 1989).

Paul Laity (ed.), *Left Book Club Anthology* (London: Gollancz, 2001).

Doris Lessing, *The Golden Notebook* (London: Michael Joseph, 1964).

John Lewis, *The Left Book Club* (London: Gollancz, 1970).

George Orwell, *Homage to Catalonia* (London: Secker & Warburg, 1938).

——, *The Lion and the Unicorn: Socialism and the English Genius* (London: Secker & Warburg, 1941).

Ben Pimlott, *Labour and the Left in the 1930s* (London: Allen & Unwin, 1977).

John Strachey, *A Programme for Progress* (London: Gollancz, 1940).

R. H. Tawney, *The Choice Before the Labour Party* (London: Socialist League, 1933).

——, *Equality*, 3rd edn ('substantially revised') (London: Allen & Unwin, 1938).

Sidney and Beatrice Webb, *Soviet Communism: A New Civilisation* (London: Gollancz, 1937).

The Stupendous Convulsion

'A Group of Members of Parliament', *Keeping Left: Labour's First Five Years and the Problems Ahead* (London: New Statesman and Nation, 1950).

Paul Addison, *The Road to 1945: British Politics and the Second World War* (London: Jonathan Cape, 1975).

Geoffrey Bell, *Ulster's Protestants* (London: Pluto, 1982).

Aneurin Bevan (Celticus), *Why Not Trust the Tories?* (London: Gollancz, 1944).

——, *In Place of Fear* (London: Heinemann, 1952).

William Beveridge, *Social Insurance and Allied Services* (London: HMSO, 1942).

Gail Braybon and Penny Summerfield, *Out of the Cage: Women's Experiences in Two World Wars* (London: Pandora Press, 1987).

Stephen Brooke, *Labour's War: The Labour Party during the Second World War* (Oxford: Clarendon Press, 1992).

Alan Bullock, *Ernest Bevin: A Biography* (London: Politico's, 2002).

Simon Burgess, *Stafford Cripps* (London: Gollancz, 1999).

James Callaghan, *Time and Change* (London: Collins, 1987).

Hugh Dalton, *Memoirs: Call Back Yesterday* (London: Frederick Muller, 1953).

——, *The Second World War Diary of Hugh Dalton*, ed. Ben Pimlott (London: Jonathan Cape, 1986).

Bernard Donoughue and G. W. Jones, *Herbert Morrison: Portrait of a Politician* (London: Weidenfeld & Nicolson, 1973).

Peter Hennessy, *Never Again: Britain, 1945–1951* (London: Jonathan Cape, 1992).

Mark Jenkins, *Bevanism: Labour's High Tide* (London: Spokesman, 1975).

Isaac Kramnick and Barry Sherman, *Harold Laski: A Life on the Left* (London: Hamish Hamilton, 1993).

H. Laski, *Democracy in Crisis* (London: Allen & Unwin, 1933).

——, 'The Present Position of Representative Democracy', in The Fabian Society, *Where Stands Socialism Today?* (London: Rich & Cowan, 1933).

——, *The State in Theory and Practice* (London: Allen & Unwin, 1935).

——, *Marx and Today*, Fabian Publications Research Series, no. 73 (London: Gollancz, 1943).

——, *Reflections on the Revolution of Our Time* (New York: Viking, 1943).

'Licinius', *Vote Labour? Why?* (London: Gollancz, 1945).

Ian Mikardo, *Back-bencher* (London: Weidenfeld & Nicolson, 1988).

Ralph Miliband, *Parliamentary Socialism: A Study in the Politics of Labour* (London: Merlin Press, 1973).

Kenneth O. Morgan, *Labour in Power* (Oxford: Clarendon, 1984).

Ben Pimlott, *Hugh Dalton* (London: Jonathan Cape, 1985).

Alistair Reid, *United We Stand: A History of Britain's Trade Unions* (London: Penguin, 2004).

Arnold Rogow and Peter Shore, *The Labour Government and British Industry, 1945–1951* (Oxford: Blackwell, 1955).

R. H. Tawney, *Why Britain Fights* (London: Macmillan, 1941).

——, 'Social Democracy in Britain', in William Scarlett (ed.), *The Christian Demand for Social Justice* (New York: New American Library, 1949).

——, 'British Socialism Today', *Socialist Commentary*, June 1952.

Ernest Watkins, *On the Work of the Labour Government* (London: Secker & Warburg, 1951).

Unstable Compound 1

Barbara Castle, *The Castle Diaries, 1964–70* (London: Weidenfeld & Nicolson, 1984).

——, *The Castle Diaries, 1974–76* (London: Weidenfeld & Nicolson, 1990).

C. A. R. Crosland, *The Future of Socialism* (London: Jonathan Cape, 1956).

Richard Crossman, *The Diaries of a Cabinet Minister: Minister of Housing, 1964–66*, Vol. 1 (London: Hamish Hamilton, 1975).

——, *The Diaries of a Cabinet Minister: Lord President of the Council and Leader of the House of Commons, 1966–68*, Vol. 2 (London: Hamish Hamilton, 1976).

——, *The Diaries of a Cabinet Minister: Secretary of State for Social Services, 1968–70*, Vol. 3 (London: Hamish Hamilton, 1977).

——, *The Backbench Diaries of Richard Crossman*, ed. Janet Morgan (London: Hamish Hamilton, 1981).

Department of Employment and Productivity, 'In Place of Strife: A Policy for Industrial Relations' (London: HMSO, 1969).

Bernadette Devlin, *The Price of My Soul* (London: Pan, 1969).

Paul Foot, *The Politics of Harold Wilson* (London: Penguin, 1968).

Anthony Howard, *Crossman: The Pursuit of Power* (London: Jonathan Cape, 1990).

Eamonn McCann, *War and an Irish Town* (London: Penguin, 1974).

Anne Perkins, *Red Queen: The Authorized Biography of Barbara Castle* (London: Macmillan, 2003).

Ben Pimlott, *Harold Wilson* (London: HarperCollins, 1992).

Clive Ponting, *Breach of Promise: Labour in Power 1964–1970* (London: Hamish Hamilton, 1989).

Thomas Dan Smith, *An Autobiography* (Newcastle: Oriel Press, 1970).

John Strachey, *The Nature of Capitalist Crisis* (London: Gollancz, 1935).

——, *Contemporary Capitalism* (London: Gollancz, 1956).

Sunday Times Insight Team, *Ulster* (London: Penguin, 1972).

G. W. Target, *Bernadette: The Story of Bernadette Devlin* (London: Hodder & Stoughton, 1975).

Hugh Thomas, *John Strachey* (London: Methuen, 1973).

Peter Townsend and Nicholas Bosanquet (eds.), *Labour and Inequality* (London: Fabian Society, 1972).

Harold Wilson, *The Labour Government, 1964–1970: A Personal Record* (London: Weidenfeld & Nicolson, 1971).

——, *Memoirs, 1916–1964: The Making of a Prime Minister* (London: Weidenfeld & Nicolson, 1986).

Unstable Compound 2

Tony Benn, *Diaries, 1940–2001: Out of the Wilderness, 1963–67*, Vol. 2, ed. Ruth Winstone (London: Hutchinson, 1987).

——, *Diaries, 1940–2001: Office without Power, 1968–72*, Vol. 3 (London: Hutchinson, 1988).

——, *Diaries, 1940–2001: Against the Tide, 1973–76*, Vol. 4, ed. Ruth Winstone (London: Hutchinson, 1989).

——, *Diaries, 1940–2001: Conflicts of Interest, 1977–80*, Vol. 5, ed. Ruth Winstone (London: Hutchinson, 1990).

——, *Diaries, 1940–2001: The End of an Era, 1980–90*, Vol. 6, ed. Ruth Winstone (London: Hutchinson, 1992).

——, *Diaries, 1940–2001: Years of Hope, 1940–62*, Vol. 1, ed. Ruth Winstone (London: Hutchinson, London, 1994).

——, *Free at Last! Diaries 1991–2001*, ed. Ruth Winstone (London: Hutchinson, 2002).

Lord Bullock, *Report of the Committee of Inquiry on Industrial Democracy* (London: HMSO, 1977).

Jonathan Coe, *The Rotters' Club* (London: Viking, 2001).

Robert Fisk, *The Point of No Return: The Strike which Broke the British in Ulster* (London: André Deutsch, 1975).

Michael Foot, *Aneurin Bevan, 1897–1945*, Vol. 1 (London: MacGibbon & Kee, 1962).

——, *Aneurin Bevan, 1945–1960*, Vol. 2 (London: MacGibbon & Kee, 1973).

Paul Foot, *Why You Should be a Socialist* (London: Socialist Workers Party, 1977).

——, *Who Framed Colin Wallace?* (London: Macmillan, 1989).

Denis Healey, *The Time of My Life* (London: Michael Joseph, 1989).

Labour Party National Executive Committee, 'Labour's Programme for Britain: Annual Conference 1973' (London: The Labour Party, 1973).

Mervyn Jones, *Michael Foot* (London: Gollancz, 1994).

David Leigh, *The Wilson Plot* (London: Heinemann, 1988).

David Skinner and Julia Langdon, *The Story of Clay Cross* (London: Spokesman, 1974).

John Strachey, *Why You Should be a Socialist* (London: Gollancz, 1938).

Margaret Thatcher, *The Path to Power* (London: HarperCollins, 1995).

Harold Wilson, *Final Term* (London: Weidenfeld & Nicolson, 1979).

Peter Wright, *Spycatcher: The Candid Autobiography of a Senior Intelligence Officer* (London: Viking, 1987).

New Labour = Old Tory

Ken Coates and Michael Barratt Brown, *The Blair Revelation: Deliverance for Whom?* (London: Spokesman, 1996).

Paul Foot, *P. F. Eye: An Idiot's Guide to the Private Finance Initiative*, *Private Eye* supplement, March 2004.

Colin Hay, *The Political Economy of New Labour* (Manchester: Manchester University Press, 1999).

Nigel Lawson, *The View from No. 11* (London: Bantam, 1992).

Roger Liddle and Peter Mandelson, *The Blair Revolution: Can New Labour Deliver?* (London: Faber & Faber, 1996).

George Monbiot, *The Captive State: The Corporate Takeover of Britain* (London: Macmillan, 2000).

Allyson Pollock, *Public Services and the Private Sector: A Response to IPPR* (London: Catalyst Trust, 2001).

Paul Routledge, *Gordon Brown: The Biography* (London: Simon & Schuster, 1998).

Their Democracy and Ours

Evelyn Anderson, *Hammer or Anvil: The Story of the German Working-Class Movement* (New York: Oriole, 1973).

Tony Benn, *Diaries* (see under Unstable Compound 2).

Nickolai Bukharin, *Imperialism and the World Economy* (London: The Merlin Press, 1972).

Alex Callinicos, *Equality* (Cambridge: Polity, 2000).

——, *Against The Third Way* (Cambridge: Polity, 2001).

——, *An Anti-Capitalist Manifesto* (Cambridge: Polity, 2003).

Pat Devine, *Democracy and Economic Planning: The Political Economy of a Self-Governing Society* (Oxford: Blackwell, 1988).

Frederick Engels, *The Fourteenth of March 1883: Frederick Engels on the Death of Karl Marx* (London: Martin Lawrence Ltd, 1933).

Sebastian Haffner, *Failure of a Revolution: Germany 1918–19* (London: André Deutsch, 1973).

Naomi Klein, *No Logo* (London: HarperCollins, 2000).

John Le Carré, *The Constant Gardener* (London: Hodder, 2001).

V. I. Lenin, *State and Revolution* (London: Lawrence & Wishart, 1942).

Colin Leys, *Market-Driven Politics: Neoliberal Democracy and the Public Interest* (London: Verso, 2000).

Louis MacNeice, *Autumn Journal: A Poem* (London: Faber & Faber, 1939).

George Monbiot, *The Age of Consent: A Manifesto for a New World Order* (London: HarperCollins, 2003).

Michael Moore, *Stupid White Men, and Other Sorry Excuses for the State of the Nation* (London: Penguin, 2002).

Leon Trotsky, *Where is Britain Going?* (London: Communist Party of Great Britain, 1926).

Robert Watt, *The Kings Depart: The German Revolution and the Treaty of Versailles, 1918–19* (London: Penguin, 1973).

Index

our left foot

On 10 October 2004, a capacity audience filled London's Hackney Empire to celebrate Paul Foot's life and work. Presented by Michael Rosen, the evening included contributions from Michael Foot, Tony Benn, John Pilger, Rory Bremner, Dave Spart, Mark Steel, John Rees and many others associated with Paul's journalism, campaigning and politics. OUR LEFT FOOT is an edited version of the evening's highlights. It includes archive footage of Paul's appearances on BBC's *Question Time*, some of his speeches and some of his television investigations.

This is what they said about the night:

"Moving and funny, but serious and stimulating… not a dud speaker among the 20 or so who paid tribute."
Marcel Berlins, Columnist, *Guardian*

"I went to the Hackney Empire and I was very affected by that. If you have [Paul's] pure energy and justice and curiosity and prolific output you can't fail but to have an effect on the world."
Saffron Burrows, Actress

The DVD can be bought online at www.fulcrumtv.com or by ringing FulcrumTV on 020 7939 3160.